CANON LAW, CAREERS AND CONQUEST

A study of the politics of episcopal elections in twelfth- and thirteenth-century Normandy and Greater Anjou. This was a crucial period in the development of canon law and Jörg Peltzer offers the first analysis to bring together legal theory and practice, local custom and politics. He explores the development of electoral theories and examines each election in context, offering insights into the varying balance of royal, papal, and regional baronial power and the various career paths leading to an episcopal see. He shows how different systems of patronage worked, to what extent they were vehicles of social mobility, and how aristocratic families were structured. By comparing electoral practices in Normandy and Greater Anjou before and after the Capetian conquest the book significantly enhances our understanding of the theory and practice of canon law, local politics in Normandy and Anjou, and the high politics at the Capetian and Angevin courts.

JÖRG PELTZER is Lecturer in Late Medieval History at the University of Heidelberg.

Cambridge Studies in Medieval Life and Thought
Fourth Series

General Editor:
ROSAMOND McKITTERICK
Professor of Medieval History, University of Cambridge, and Fellow of Sidney Sussex College

Advisory Editors:
CHRISTINE CARPENTER
Professor of Medieval English History, University of Cambridge, and Fellow of New Hall

JONATHAN SHEPARD

The series Cambridge Studies in Medieval Life and Thought was inaugurated by G.G. Coulton in 1921; Professor Rosamond McKitterick now acts as General Editor of the Fourth Series, with Professor Christine Carpenter and Dr Jonathan Shepard as Advisory Editors. The series brings together outstanding work by medieval scholars over a wide range of human endeavour extending from political economy to the history of ideas.

For a list of titles in the series, see end of book.

CANON LAW, CAREERS AND CONQUEST

Episcopal Elections in Normandy and Greater Anjou,
c. 1140–c. 1230

JÖRG PELTZER

CAMBRIDGE
UNIVERSITY PRESS

CAMBRIDGE UNIVERSITY PRESS
Cambridge, New York, Melbourne, Madrid, Cape Town, Singapore, São Paulo, Delhi

Cambridge University Press
The Edinburgh Building, Cambridge CB2 8RU, UK

Published in the United States of America by Cambridge University Press, New York

www.cambridge.org
Information on this title: www.cambridge.org/9780521880626

First published 2008

Printed in the United Kingdom at the University Press, Cambridge

A catalogue record for this publication is available from the British Library

ISBN 978 0 521 88062 6 hardback

In Erinnerung unseres Großvaters

CONTENTS

MAPS

NB: The boundaries are approximate. Exclaves have not been included. The maps are intended to show the geographical situation and the extent of each diocese. Monasteries, important castles, and towns whose names are mentioned in the text are generally included, but completeness is not aimed at.

TABLES

PREFACE

In 1883, Albert Hauck wrote in the preface to his study on the elections under Merovingian kings that there was hardly a need to explain the general interest of this work. He referred to the contemporary struggle between state and church in Germany.[1] Fifty years later, in 1933, Geoffrey Barraclough's statement on medieval ecclesiastical elections also bears the mark of his time. He declared that 'it is striking enough that the Church had the wisdom to reject the democratic fallacy of counting heads, and to attempt an estimate of the intelligence and enlightened good faith of the voters'.[2] In focusing on law, the work of pressure groups, and a change of regime, this study, too, represents dominant features of its time. Yet it is hoped that the following pages do some justice to the episcopal elections in Normandy and Greater Anjou between *c.* 1140 and *c.* 1230 and contribute to a better understanding of the issues discussed.

Work on this project started as a D.Phil. thesis at Oxford University in 1999 and ever since I have enjoyed the support of a great number of people and institutions. I owe the greatest debt to my supervisor, Dr Jean Dunbabin. Always supportive and resourceful in advice, she also undertook the laborious and occasionally painful work to rescue the language of this book from too much German input. I am also very grateful to Prof. Nicholas Vincent, Norwich, who not only shared with me his unrivalled knowledge of the collections of the French and English archives, but also gave permission to consult the forthcoming edition of Henry II's charters. I am also greatly indebted to my examiners, Prof. Maria João Branco, Lisbon, and Prof. Daniel Power, Swansea, for fruitful discussions and helpful suggestions. I would also like to thank Dr Martin Brett, Cambridge, Dr Ludwig Falkenstein, Aachen, Prof. Bernd

---

[1] A. Hauck, *Die Bischofswahlen unter den Merovingern* (Erlangen, 1883), Vorrede.
[2] G. Barraclough, 'The Making of a Bishop in the Middle Ages', *Catholic Historical Review*, 19 (1933), 275–319, 277.

Preface

Schneidmüller, Heidelberg, and Prof. Klaus van Eickels, Bamberg, for their comments on parts of the thesis. For further generous advice on individual points I am very grateful to the late Prof. Rees Davies, Dr Clarence Gallagher, Prof. Henry Mayr-Harting, Prof. Richard Sharpe, the late Patrick Wormald, all Oxford, Dr Judith Everard, Cambridge, Dr Peter Clarke, Southampton, Dr Martin Bertram, Rome, Dr Joachim Dahlhaus, Heidelberg, Prof. Gero Dolezalek, Aberdeen, and Prof. Kenneth Pennington, Washington. I also owe many thanks to those who supported my research in France: Annie Dufour and Monique Peyrafort-Huin, both IRHT, the staff of the German Historical Institute, Paris, in particular Prof. Rolf Grosse, Jean-Loup Lemaître, the staff of the Archives Départementales and Bibliothèques Municipales in Normandy, Anjou, Maine, and Touraine, and the collaborators of the *Fasti ecclesiae Gallicanae* project, notably Hélène Millet and Annick Gosse-Kischinewski. I would also like to express my gratitude to Dr Jörg Müller, PD Gisela Drossbach, and Prof. Andreas Thier, now Zurich, who have made my visit to the Stephan Kuttner Institute of Medieval Canon Law, Munich, such a pleasant and fruitful experience.

Family and friends have made this work much easier. They provided support, inspiration, occasionally shelter, and had to cope with large amounts of proof-reading. I owe my greatest debt to my wife, Silvia Galbusera, and to our families, the Peltzers, Hecks, Galbuseras, and Marianis. Further thanks are due to Stephen Bell, Hugh Doherty, Dr Bernard Gowers, Dr Klaus Oschema, Allan Pengelly, Dr Justin Pniower, and Dr Nicolas Victoir.

This study was facilitated by a generous two-year scholarship of the German Academic Exchange Service (DAAD), a three-year studentship of the Arts and Humanities Research Board (AHRB), a one-year Lothian studentship of the Faculty of Modern History, Oxford, and minor contributions by Christ Church, Oxford. The German Historical Institute, Paris, and the Master and Fellows of Peterhouse, Cambridge, gave me the opportunity to finish the project in the most comfortable and inspirational of working and living conditions. I am very grateful to all of these institutions for their support. I also wish to thank the editorial board of the Cambridge Studies in Medieval Life and Thought series, Prof. Christine Carpenter, Prof. Rosamond McKitterick, and Dr Jonathan Shepard, for having accepted the manuscript for publication. Finally, my thanks are due to the staff at Cambridge University Press for their careful editing of the text. The manuscript was completed in December 2005. Works published after that date could not be systematically taken into account. This is regrettable, but, in return for a properly produced book, I hope the reader will forgive this shortcoming.

EDITORIAL NOTE

References to papal letters (except for those letters incorporated in Gratian's *Decretum* and earlier decretal collections) generally include in square brackets the letters' numbers in Jaffé and in Walther Holtzmann's alphabetically arranged calendar *Regesta decretalium saeculi XII* (*WH*) for the period up to 1198 and to Potthast for the period after that date. Papal letters that made their way into the *Quinque compilations antiquae* (1/2/3/4/5 *Comp.*) and/or the *Liber extra* (*X*) include (a) the reference to their full editions if they are edited in *Die Register Innocenz' III.*, *Honorii III Romani pontificis opera omnia,*[1] or *Les registres de Grégoire IX,*[2] (b) their place in one of the *Quinque compilations antiquae*, (c) their place in the *Liber extra*, and (d) their number in Jaffé, Holtzmann's *Regesta decretalium*, or Potthast.

According to the quoting style used in this book the volume numbers of the *Collection Housseau*, also known as *Collection de Touraine et Anjou*, are given in roman numerals. Philippe Lauer attributed arabic numerals to all volumes of the collection, but also roman numerals to the first eleven volumes. Since volume roman two and three are counted as arabic 2, 1 and 2, 2 the volume numbers thereafter do not coincide.[3] It should be noted, therefore, that the roman numerals used in this book refer to Philippe Lauer's arabic numerals, not the roman ones.

---

[1] *Honorii III Romani pontificis opera omnia*, ed. C. Horoy (Medii aevi bibliotheca patristica seu ejusdem temporis patrologia ab anno MCCXVI usque ad concilii Tridentini tempora IV) (4 vols., Paris, 1879–80).

[2] *Les registres de Grégoire IX. Recueil des bulles de ce pape*, ed. L. Auvray (Bibliothèques des écoles françaises d'Athènes et de Rome, 2nd sér., IX) (4 vols., Paris, 1890–1955).

[3] P. Lauer, *Collections manuscrites sur l'histoire des provinces de France. Inventaire* (2 vols., Paris, 1905–11), II, p. 352.

ABBREVIATIONS

AD	Archives Départementales
Bambergensis	W. Deeters, *Die Bambergensisgruppe der Dekretalensammlungen des 12. Jhdts.* (Bonn, 1956)
BAV	Biblioteca Apostolica Vaticana
BM	Bibliothèque Municipale
BNF	Bibliothèque Nationale de France
1/2/3/4/5 Comp.	*Quinque compilationes antiquae nec non collectio canonum Lipsiensis*, ed. E. Friedberg (Leipzig, 1882)
Decretum Gratiani	*Corpus iuris canonici*, ed. E. Friedberg (2 vols., Leipzig,1879/81), I
Diceto	*The Historical Works of Master Ralph de Diceto, Dean of London*, ed. W. Stubbs (Rolls Series LXVIII) (2 vols., London, 1876)
EHR	*English Historical Review*
Fr.	*Collectio Francofortana*
GC	*Gallia christiana* (16 vols., Paris, 1744–1887)
Gesta regis	*Gesta regis Henrici secundi Benedicti abbatis: The Chronicle of the Reigns of Henry I and Richard I, A.D. 1169–1192, Known Commonly under the Name of Benedict of Peterborough*, ed. W. Stubbs (Rolls Series IL) (2 vols., London, 1867)
Gilb.	*Collectio Gilberti*
Housseau	Paris, BNF Collection Housseau
Howden	*Chronica Rogeri de Hovedene*, ed. W. Stubbs (Rolls Series LI) (4 vols., London, 1868–71)
Jaffé	*Regesta pontificum Romanorum ab condita ecclesia ad annum post Christum natum MCXCVIII*, ed. P. Jaffé, revised W. Wattenbach et al. (2 vols., Leipzig 1885–8)
MGH/MGH	Monumenta Germaniae historica
MIC	Monumenta iuris canonici

Abbreviations

MTB	*The Materials of the History of Thomas Becket*, ed. J.C. Robertson and J.B. Sheppard (Rolls Series LXVII) (7 vols., London 1875–85)
N.S./*N.S.*	New Series
PL	*Patrologiae cursus completus. Series latina*, ed. J.P. Migne (221 vols., Paris, 1844–65)
Potthast	*Regesta pontificum Romanorum inde ab anno post Christum natum MCXCVIII ad annum MCCCIV*, ed. A. Potthast (2 vols., Berlin, 1874–5)
PR [regnal year], [ruler]	*The Great Roll of the Pipe*
Register Innocenz' III.	*Die Register Innocenz' III.*, ed. O. Hageneder et al. (Publikationen der Abteilung für historische Studien des österreichischen Kulturinstituts in Rom I–IV; Publikationen des historischen Instituts beim österreichischen Kulturinstitut in Rom V–) (9 vols., Rome, 1968–)
RHF	*Recueil des historiens des Gaules et de la France*, ed. L. Delisle et al. (24 vols., Paris, 1869–1904)
1/2/3 Rot.	*Rotomagensis prima/secunda/tertia*: C. Cheney and M. Cheney, *Studies in the Collections of Twelfth-Century Decretals. From the Papers of the Late Walther Holtzmann* (Monumenta iuris canonici series B: corpus collectionum III) (Vatican City, 1979) [*1/2 Rot.*]; C. Cheney, 'Decretals of Innocent III in Paris, B.N. MS LAT. 3922A', in C. Cheney, *The Papacy and England. 12th–14th centuries* (London, 1982), no. IV, pp.149–63 [*3 Rot.*]
Rot. chart.	*Rotuli chartarum in turri Londonensi asservati*, ed. T.D. Hardy (London, 1837)
Rot. pat.	*Rotuli litterarum patentium in turri Londonensi asservati*, ed. T.D. Hardy (London, 1835)
Savigny KA	*Zeitschrift der Savigny-Stiftung für Rechtsgeschichte. Kanonistische Abteilung*
Torigny	'Chronica Roberti de Torigneio, abbatis monasterii Sancti Michaelis in Periculo Maris', in *Chronicles of the Reigns of Stephen, Henry II and Richard I*, ed. R. Howlett (Rolls Series LXXXII) (4 vols., London, 1884–9), IV
WH	Walther-Holtzmann-Kartei: *Regesta decretalium saeculi XII*, http://www.kuttner-institute.jura.uni-muenchen.de (last visit: 17 Aug. 2004)
X	*Corpus iuris canonici*, ed. E. Friedberg (2 vols., Leipzig, 1879–81), II

Chapter 1

INTRODUCTION

The bishop occupied a central place in medieval society.[1] He was the
spiritual leader of the people and the clergy and exercised the supreme
jurisdictional authority over ecclesiastical matters in his diocese. The
bishop was also a secular lord. His significance varied according to the
extent and wealth of his temporal possessions, but he could count among
the most powerful political players in the region, possibly exercising
influence well beyond his diocesan borders. Thus combining spiritual
and secular powers the bishop was a focal point for the flock, the local
ecclesiastics and the pope, the aristocracy and the ruler; his election was of
great interest to many people.

A considerable number of studies have been devoted to the episcopal
election. They have analysed its 'political' side, that is the nature and
extent of the influence of different groups interested in its outcome, and
they have examined its 'normative' side, that is the development of the
regulations for electoral procedure aimed at guaranteeing the selection of a
suitable candidate.[2] In a recent survey Franz-Reiner Erkens has emphasised

---

[1] A useful introduction to the role of the bishop in the middle ages is J. Gaudemet, *Le gouvernement de
l'église a l'époque classique. II. Le gouvernement local* (Histoire du droit et des institutions de l'église en
occident VIII, II) (Paris, 1979), pp. 7–215.

[2] The formation of the legal theory of episcopal elections from its beginnings to 1140 has recently
been examined by A. Thier, 'Hierarchie und Autonomie. Regelungstraditionen der
Bischofsbestellung in der Geschichte des kirchlichen Wahlrechts bis 1140' (Ludwig-Maximilians-
Universität, Munich, Habilitationsschrift, 2001). What follows is a selection of studies dealing with
elections up to 1100. The geographical area is limited to France. For the late antiquity and the
Merovingian empire, see F. X. Funk, 'Die Bischofswahl im christlichen Altertum und im Anfang
des Mittelalters', in F. X. Funk, *Kirchengeschichtliche Abhandlungen und Untersuchungen* (Paderborn,
1897), pp. 23–39; Hauck, *Die Bischofswahlen unter den Merovingern*; E. Vacandard, 'Les élections
épiscopales sous les Mérovingiens', in E. Vacandard, *Etudes de critique et d'histoire religieuse* (3 vols.,
Paris, 1905–12), I, pp. 123–87; P. Cloché, 'Les élections épiscopales sous les Mérovingiens', *Moyen
Age*, 25 (1925), 203–54; D. Claude, 'Die Bestellung der Bischöfe im merowingischen Reiche',

the significance of the period from the late eleventh to the mid-thirteenth century in the development of episcopal elections. In this period, the framework in which elections took place changed. Until the late eleventh century the papacy played only a minor role; elections were decided on the local level, that is between the ruler, the local aristocracy, and the local clergy. Local custom set the norms for the procedure. By the mid-thirteenth century, however, the papacy had become a very important force in elections, and canon law usually set the norms.[3] This period of change can be divided into two phases. In a first phase, starting at the end of the eleventh century, the papacy fought against the investiture of bishops by the ruler in its attempt to restore the liberty of the church. In the course of this battle, the papacy promoted the idea of an election by the clergy without secular interference.[4] This first phase, characterised by high-profile clashes between popes and rulers, ended in the early twelfth century when the investiture of bishops was settled by a compromise: the ruler renounced the investiture of the bishop with crosier and ring. The pope in turn accepted that the bishops swore fealty to the ruler for their temporal possessions. In England the bishops were allowed to do homage to the king. The question of elections was of secondary importance in this compromise; the ruler preserved much of his influence,[5] and the electoral

Savigny KA, 49 (1963), 1–75; F. Lotter, 'Designation und angebliches Kooperationsrecht bei Bischofserhebungen. Zu Ausbildung und Anwendung des Prinzips der kanonischen Wahl bis zu den Anfängen der fränkischen Zeit', *Savigny KA*, 59 (1973), 112–50; R. Gryson, 'Les élections ecclésiastiques au IIIe siècle', *Revue d'histoire ecclésiastique*, 68 (1973), 353–404; R. Gryson, 'Les élections épiscopales en occident au IVe siècle', ibid., 75 (1980), 257–83; G. Scheibelreiter, *Der Bischof in merowingischer Zeit* (Veröffentlichungen des Instituts für österreichische Geschichtsforschung XXVII) (Vienna, 1983), pp. 128–71; U. Nonn, 'Zwischen König, Hausmeier und Aristokratie – Die Bischofserhebung im spätmerowingisch-frühkarolingischen Frankenreich', in F.-R. Erkens (ed.), *Die früh- und hochmittelalterliche Bischofserhebung im europäischen Vergleich* (Beihefte zum Archiv für Kulturgeschichte XLVIII) (Cologne, 1998), pp. 33–58. For the period from the Frankish empire to the late eleventh century, see P. Imbart de la Tour, *Les élections dans l'église de France du IXe au XIIe siècle. Etude sur la décadence du principe électif (814–1150)* (Paris, 1890); G. Weise, *Königtum und Bischofswahl im fränkischen und deutschen Reich vor dem Investiturstreit* (Berlin, 1912); R. Schieffer, 'Bischofserhebungen im westfränkisch-französischen Bereich im späten 9. und im 10. Jahrhundert', in Erkens (ed.), *Bischofserhebung*, pp. 59–82; J. Englberger, 'Gregor VII. und die Bischofserhebungen in Frankreich. Zur Entstehung des ersten römischen Investiturdekrets vom Herbst 1078', in ibid., pp. 193–258; A. Becker, *Studien zum Investiturproblem in Frankreich. Papsttum, Königtum und Episkopat im Zeitalter der gregorianischen Kirchenreform 1049–1119* (Schriften der Universität des Saarlandes) (Saarbrücken, 1955).
[3] F.-R. Erkens, 'Die Bischofswahl im Spannungsfeld zwischen weltlicher und geistlicher Gewalt. Ein tour d'horizon', in Erkens (ed.), *Bischofserhebung*, pp. 1–32, p. 21; cf. Barraclough, 'The Making of a Bishop in the Middle Ages', 275–319; K. Ganzer, *Papsttum und Bistumsbesetzungen in der Zeit von Gregor IX. bis Bonifaz VIII. Ein Beitrag zur Geschichte der päpstlichen Reservationen* (Forschungen zur kirchlichen Rechtsgeschichte und zum Kirchenrecht IX) (Cologne, 1968).
[4] Infra, pp. 20–2.
[5] P. Classen, 'Das Wormser Konkordat in der deutschen Verfassungsgeschichte', in J. Fleckenstein (ed.), *Investiturstreit und Reichsverfassung* (Vorträge und Forschungen XVII) (Sigmaringen, 1973), pp. 411–60.

procedure remained hardly defined. The decisive development of episcopal elections took place in the second phase which can roughly be dated between 1140 and 1230. In this period the papal court became commonly accepted as the highest authority in ecclesiastical matters and a routine of dispensation of justice and interpretation of law emerged. At the court, in legal practice, as well as in the originating schools, in theory, canon law was intensively examined and greatly developed.[6] These developments greatly affected episcopal elections and it is for that reason that this study focuses on the period between *c.* 1140 and *c.* 1230.

Despite the general awareness of the importance of the period for the history of episcopal elections a statement made by Bernhard Schimmelpfennig in 1990 still holds true today: there are no studies of episcopal elections of the twelfth and thirteenth centuries that equally consider the existing law and individual rights, contemporary legal theory, the local conditions, and the political background.[7] The studies examining elections in this period focus on particular aspects. They analyse the role of the ruler, or of the cathedral chapter, or of the pope.[8] But this limitation involves neglecting the enormous complexity of episcopal elections during this period. They were not just a matter of kings or popes, not just a matter of legal theory or local custom. Elections were very dynamic processes subjected to the influence of multiple factors. King, pope, local aristocracy, clergy, and the rising urban elites: all had potential interest in the election of a bishop. The king may have seen the chance to promote a man of his entourage to a position of great influence, or to satisfy the ambitions of an important ally. In any case he was interested in securing a bishop loyal to him. The pope hoped for men acting as conduits of his policy and authority. The local aristocracy and the urban

---

[6] P. Landau, 'Die Durchsetzung neuen Rechts im Zeitalter des klassischen kanonischen Rechts', in G. Melville (ed.), *Institutionen und Geschichte. Theoretische Aspekte und mittelalterliche Befunde* (Norm und Struktur. Studien zum sozialen Wandel in Mittelalter und früher Neuzeit I) (Cologne, 1992), pp. 137–55, pp. 137–43.

[7] B. Schimmelpfennig, 'Papst- und Bischofswahlen seit dem 12. Jahrhundert', in R. Schneider and H. Zimmermann (eds.), *Wahlen und Wählen im Mittelalter* (Vorträge und Forschungen XXXVII) (Sigmaringen, 1990), pp. 174–95, p. 174.

[8] For example, M. Pacaut, *Louis VII et les élections épiscopales* (Bibliothèque de la société d'histoire ecclésiastique de la France) (Paris, 1957); H. Müller, *Der Anteil der Laien an der Bischofswahl. Ein Beitrag zur Geschichte der Kanonistik von Gratian bis Gregor IX.* (Kanonistische Studien und Texte XXIX) (Amsterdam, 1977); R. Helmholz, *The Spirit of Classical Canon Law* (The Spirit of the Laws) (Athens, Ga., 1996), pp. 33–60; G. von Below, *Die Entstehung des ausschließlichen Wahlrechts der Domkapitel. Mit besonderer Rücksicht auf Deutschland* (Leipzig, 1883); E. Roland, *Les chanoines et les élections épiscopales du XIe au XIVe siècle (Etude sur la restauration, l'évolution, la décadence du pouvoir capitulaire) 1080–1350* (Aurillac, 1909); K. Ganzer, 'Zur Beschränkung der Bischofswahl auf die Domkapitel in Theorie und Praxis des 12. und 13. Jahrhunderts', *Savigny KA*, 57 (1971), 22–82, 58 (1972), 166–97; C. Cheney, *Pope Innocent III and England* (Päpste und Papsttum IX) (Stuttgart, 1976), pp. 121–78; R. Foreville, *Le pape Innocent III et la France* (Päpste und Papsttum XXVI) (Stuttgart, 1992), pp. 138–48; Ganzer, *Papsttum*.

elites considered the control of a bishopric as a means to extend their local influence and to gain access to a great source of patronage for younger members of their families. The clergy had different interests again. The need for a man well suited for the spiritual tasks of his office, and political motives of some sort directed the decision of the members of the cathedral chapter and the heads of the local religious houses. The extent to which one group was able to promote its influence depended very strongly on the behaviour of the others. The king, for example, might intervene vigorously in an election to a very important bishopric but not in one to a less significant see. The pope would only become active in this period if the election was brought to his court. He was not a regular, but an optional, participant. The activities of other electors often led to a clash of legal theory with local custom. This continually reshaped the legal framework of elections. Given this field of tension between groups with different interests, legal theory, and custom, episcopal elections in this period can only properly be analysed if all these factors are taken into account.

The questions arising from such an approach form two groups. One group deals with the 'normative' side to elections focusing on legal practice and theory. First, the very basic question on what canon law and its commentators had to say on episcopal elections needs considering. This will also allow us to address the problem of what role local custom played in the long-term development of canon law. Turning to the application of canon law in the locality the following questions emerge. How strongly was canon law modified by local customs, or, phrased perhaps more appropriately, what were the particularities of the local interpretation of canon law? To what extent had local churchmen access to developments in canon law taking place elsewhere, notably in the schools or at the papal court? If so, did they also contribute to it, and did they make use of their knowledge in practice? If this was the case, when and why did they apply their knowledge? The answers to these questions provide some insight into the making of canon law and contribute to a better understanding of the complex process that led to the application of a relatively unified and harmonised canon law across western Europe in the mid-thirteenth century.

The second group of questions examines the 'political' side of elections. The principal question here concerns the factors leading to the election of a particular bishop. What were the circumstances of his election? Then, turning from the particular to the general, the questions arise which groups were generally most successful in promoting their candidates, whether the pattern of groups involved changed over time, and what were the structures of patronage, that is what were the most promising routes to a bishopric?

Two considerations were decisive for the choice of Normandy and Greater Anjou as the geographical area for this study of episcopal elections between 1140 and 1230: first, the need to analyse in detail local power structures makes it hardly feasible to examine larger geographical areas, such as the French kingdom or the Empire. On the other hand, if the results of the analysis are to have some bearing on the general understanding of episcopal elections, the scope cannot be limited to a very small number of dioceses. Normandy and Greater Anjou provide an almost ideal solution to this problem. Small enough to enable an investigation of local power structures, the two regions also permit the drawing of conclusions of a more general character. Not only do ten dioceses constitute a fairly broad foundation, but more importantly the regions are suited for comparison. Normandy's history had been distinct from that of Greater Anjou before the Angevin counts added the duchy to their dominions in 1144.[9] Thus, by examining and comparing the elections in both areas, it will be possible to identify local particularities.

Second, the political history of Normandy and Greater Anjou between *c.* 1140 and *c.* 1230 offers the opportunity to examine elections in periods of crisis and stability, and, more specifically, it allows a comparison between Angevin and Capetian attitudes. In 1135 Henry I, king of England and duke of Normandy, died, leaving his daughter Empress Matilda as heiress. Then, in a coup his nephew, Stephen of Blois, seized the throne. In the subsequent years Matilda and her husband Geoffrey Plantagenet, count of Anjou, Maine, and Touraine, engaged in a bitter fight with Stephen for her inheritance, which eventually they won. In 1144 Geoffrey completed the conquest of Normandy and in 1153 Stephen and Matilda agreed that after Stephen's death Matilda's son, Henry, would succeed to the English throne. By that time Henry had already succeeded his father in Greater Anjou and Normandy and had acquired the duchy of Aquitaine by virtue of his marriage to Eleanor of Aquitaine in 1152. Thus, when Henry acceded to the English throne in 1154 he began to reign over what is known as the 'Angevin empire', stretching from the Scottish Border in the north, to the Pyrenees in the south. Normandy and Greater Anjou were important dominions in their own right, but their geographical situation linking Henry II's dominions

---

[9] J. Given, *State and Society in Medieval Europe. Gwynedd and Languedoc under Outside Rule* (Ithaca, 1990), pp. 11–15, discusses methodological questions arising from comparing two regions. For the history of Normandy and Greater Anjou prior to the mid-twelfth century, see O. Guillot, *Le comte d'Anjou et son entourage au XIe siècle* (2 vols., Paris, 1972); J. Chartrou, *L'Anjou de 1109 à 1151. Foulques de Jérusalem et Geoffroi Plantagenêt* (Paris, 1928); B. Lemesle, *La société aristocratique dans le Haut-Maine (XIe–XIIe siècles)* (Rennes, 1999); D. Bates, *Normandy before 1066* (London, 1982); D. Bates, 'Normandy and England after 1066', *EHR*, 104 (1989), 851–80; D. Bates, 'The Rise and Fall of Normandy, c. 911–1204', in D. Bates and A. Curry (eds.), *Normandy and England in the Middle Ages* (London, 1994), pp. 19–35; D. Douglas, *William the Conqueror*, 2nd edn (Yale, 1999); J. Le Patourel, *The Norman Empire* (Oxford, 1976).

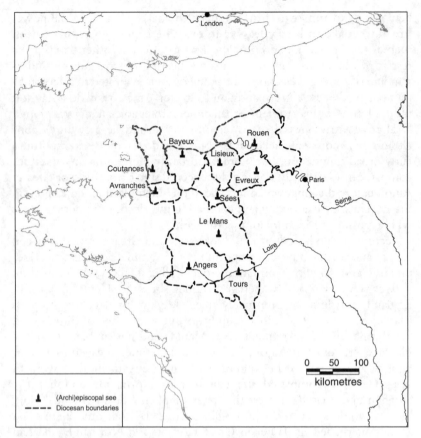

Map 1 The dioceses of Normandy and Greater Anjou

enhanced their significance even further. Henry and his sons Richard and John governed Normandy and Greater Anjou for sixty years until 1204/6 when Philip II Augustus, king of France, conquered them. In 1214 Philip successfully defended his conquest against King John and when in 1230 King Henry III failed to regain Normandy and Greater Anjou, the fate of these regions was decided. They were to stay with the Capetians.[10]

---

[10] R.H.C. Davis, *King Stephen, 1135–1154* (London, 1967); E. King (ed.), *The Anarchy of King Stephen's Reign* (Oxford, 1994); D. Crouch, *The Reign of King Stephen, 1135–1154* (Harlow, 2000); W. L. Warren, *Henry II*, 4th edn (Yale, 2000); M. Pacaut, *Louis VII et son royaume* (Bibliothèque générale de l'école des hautes études; vi^e section) (Paris, 1964); J. Boussard, *Le comté d'Anjou sous*

Introduction

There are only a few cursory studies of episcopal elections in Normandy and Greater Anjou for this period, and because they focus entirely on the ruler, they hardly take into account the role of the aristocracy.[11] This, however, misses an opportunity to gain insight into the development of local power structures during this period. The elections can indicate rivalries between the local aristocrats, the degree of royal authority in the region, and, in this particular case, the impact of the Capetian conquest on local power structures. An understanding of these structures is also a very important factor in the assessment of royal intervention in elections. Historians have depicted the Angevins as firmly, occasionally brutally, pursuing their own interests.[12] Some scholars, notably Marcel Pacaut and John W. Baldwin, have contrasted the apparently

---

Henri Plantagenêt et ses fils (1151–1204) (Bibliothèque de l'école des hautes études; IVᵉ section, sciences historiques et philologiques CCLXXI) (Paris, 1938); J. Boussard, *Le gouvernement d'Henri II Plantagenêt* (Paris, 1956); J. Gillingham, *Richard I* (Yale, 1999); M. Aurell, *L'empire des Plantagenêt 1154–1224* (Paris, 2003); J. Gillingham, *The Angevin Empire*, 2nd edn (London, 2001); R.-H. Bautier, 'Conclusions. « Empire Plantagenêt » ou « espace Plantagenêt ». Y eut-il une civilisation du monde Plantagenêt?', *Cahiers de civilisation médiévale*, 29 (1986), 139–47; M. Powicke, *The Loss of Normandy 1189–1204. Studies in the History of the Angevin Empire*, 3rd edn (Manchester, 1999); R. Turner, *King John* (London, 1994); N. Vincent, *Peter des Roches: An Alien in English Politics, 1205–1238* (Cambridge Studies in Medieval Life and Thought) (Cambridge, 1996); D. Carpenter, *The Minority of Henry III* (London, 1990); R. Stacey, *Politics, Policy, and Finance under Henry III, 1216–1245* (Oxford, 1987); J.W. Baldwin, *The Government of Philip Augustus: Foundations of French Royal Power in the Middle Ages* (Berkeley, 1986); C. Petit-Dutaillis, *Etude sur la vie et le règne de Louis VIII (1187–1226)* (Bibliothèque de l'école des hautes études; IVᵉ section, sciences historiques et philologiques CI) (Paris, 1894); E. Berger, *Histoire de Blanche de Castille, reine de France* (Bibliothèque des écoles françaises d'Athènes et de Rome LXX) (Paris, 1895).

[11] I. Shaw, 'The Ecclesiastical Policy of Henry II on the Continent', *Church Quarterly Review*, 151 (1951), 137–55, 147–53; R. Foreville, 'L'église anglo-normande au temps du bienheureux Achard de Saint-Victor, évêque d'Avranches (1161–1171)', in R. Foreville, *Thomas Becket dans la tradition historique et hagiographique* (London, 1981), no. I, pp. 163–76, pp. 164–5; M. Pacaut, *Elections*, pp. 79–81; D. Walker, 'Crown and Episcopacy under the Normans and the Angevins', in R. Brown (ed.), *Anglo-Norman Studies V. Proceedings of the Battle Conference 1982* (Woodbridge, 1983), pp. 220–33, pp. 222–5; R. Turner, 'Richard Lionheart and the Episcopate in his French Domains', *French Historical Studies*, 21 (1998), 517–42, 523–8; Turner, *King John*, pp. 153-4; S. Packard, 'King John and the Norman Church', *Harvard Theological Review*, 15 (1922), 15–40, 16–24; O. Pontal, 'Les évêques dans le monde Plantagenêt', *Cahiers de civilisation médiévale*, 29 (1986), 129–37, 130, 132, 137; D. Power, *The Norman Frontier in the Twelfth and Early Thirteenth Centuries* (Cambridge Studies in Medieval Life and Thought) (Cambridge, 2004), pp. 134–9; Cheney, *Innocent III*, pp. 121–78; J. W. Baldwin, 'Philip Augustus and the Norman Church', *French Historical Studies*, 6 (1969), 1–30, 4–9; Baldwin, *Philip*, pp. 179–81, 305–9, 437–41. For studies focusing on England, see S. Mooers Christelow, 'Chancellors and Curial Bishops', in C. Harper-Bill (ed.), *Anglo-Norman Studies XXII. Proceedings of the Battle Conference 1999* (Woodbridge, 2000), pp. 49–69; S. Marrit, 'King Stephen and the Bishops', in J. Gillingham (ed.), *Anglo-Norman Studies XXIV. Proceedings of the Battle Conference 2001* (Woodbridge, 2002), pp. 129–44, pp. 138–9; R. Foreville, *L'église et la royauté en Angleterre sous Henri II Plantagenêt (1154–1189)* (Paris, 1943), pp. 96–106, 373–88, 476–88; R. Turner, 'Richard Lionheart and English Episcopal Elections', *Albion*, 29 (1997), 1–15; M. Gibbs and J. Lang, *Bishops and Reform, 1215–1272, with Special Reference to the Lateran Council of 1215* (Oxford, 1934), pp. 53–93.

[12] Shaw, 'Ecclesiastical Policy', 152; Walker, 'Crown and Episcopacy', p. 224; for Richard, see Turner, 'Richard and the Episcopate', 523, 527–8; Sidney Packard stresses King John's brutal

authoritarian and wilful approach of the Angevins with the seemingly more lenient and modest attitude of the Capetians.[13] John W. Baldwin suggested that during his struggle with King John Philip II lured the Norman episcopacy with the promise of free canonical elections. According to Baldwin, Philip kept his promise after the conquest.[14] A detailed examination of the individual elections will make it possible to identify more precisely to what extent, when, where, and why the Angevins and Capetians were active in episcopal elections. The resulting patterns allow a more comprehensive assessment of Angevin and Capetian policy and contribute to a better understanding of the impact of the conquest on Normandy and Greater Anjou.[15] A clearer view on the process of the transition from Angevin to Capetian rule, in turn, will also shed some light on the general problem of how royal lordship functioned in the central middle ages.

METHODOLOGY
Electoral theory

Around 1179, the canonist Bernard of Pavia wrote in his *Summa de electione* that three aspects should be considered in an election: the power to vote, the suitability of the elect, and the electoral procedure.[16] Taking Bernard's statement as a guideline, I have selected four themes to analyse the 'normative' side to elections:

behaviour taking the election of Sées in 1201–3 as an example, 'King John and the Norman Church', esp. 20–4; Odette Pontal depicts John as a tyrant, 'Les évêques dans le monde Plantagenêt', 137. Recently, however, Daniel Power advanced a more balanced view of the Angevin treatment of the Norman church, 'Angevin Normandy', in C. Harper-Bill and E. van Houts (eds.), *Companion to the Anglo-Norman World* (Woodbridge, 2003), pp. 63–85, pp. 78–81; D. Power, 'The Norman Church and the Angevin and Capetian Kings', *Journal of Ecclesiastical History*, 56 (2005), 205–34.
[13] Pacaut, *Elections*, p. 78; Baldwin, 'Philip Augustus and the Norman Church', 4–9; Baldwin, *Philip*, pp. 180–1, 306–9; B. Guillemain, 'Philippe Auguste et l'épiscopat', in R.-H. Bautier (ed.), *La France de Philippe Auguste. Le temps de mutation. Actes du colloque international organisé par le C.N.R.S. (Paris, 29.9.–4.10.1980)* (Colloques internationaux du centre national de la recherche scientifique DCII) (Paris, 1982), pp. 365–84, p. 380; Pontal, 'Les évêques dans le monde Plantagenêt', 135; R. Foreville, 'Innocent III et les élections épiscopales dans l'espace Plantagenêt de 1198 à 1205', in *Recueil d'études en hommage à Lucien Musset* (Cahier des annales de Normandie XXIII) (Caen, 1990), pp. 293–9, p. 293; Turner, *King John*, p. 153.
[14] Baldwin, 'Philip Augustus and the Norman Church', 4, 30; Baldwin, *Philip*, p. 307.
[15] On the impact of the conquest, see Baldwin, *Philip*, pp. 191–328; J. Strayer, 'Normandy and Languedoc', *Speculum*, 44 (1969), 1–12; L. Musset, 'Quelques problèmes posés par l'annexion de la Normandie au domaine royal français', in Bautier (ed.), *La France de Philippe Auguste*, pp. 291–309; Power, *The Norman Frontier*, esp. pp. 413–66; L. Grant, *Architecture and Society in Normandy 1120–1270* (New Haven, 2005), pp. 147, 202, 231–4.
[16] 'Bernardi Summa de electione', in *Bernardi Papiensis (Faventini episcopi) Summa decretalium*, ed. E. Laspeyres (Regensburg, 1860), pp. 307–23, p. 308.

(A) The composition of the electoral body with a particular emphasis on the role of the prince, the cathedral chapter, and the question of absent canons. A great number of elections in Normandy and Greater Anjou (e. g. Rouen (1184, 1235–7), Lisieux (1141–3, 1200–1), Sées (1144–7, 1201–3), Tours (1174, 1228), Angers (1153–6, 1200–2)) will show that the definition of who constituted the electoral body was one of the great controversial issues of the time.

(B) The different types of vote used: unanimous vote, scrutiny, and compromise. The increasingly sophisticated use of electoral procedures is particularly well illustrated by elections at Rouen (1235–7) and Evreux (1220, 1236).

(C) *Sanior et maior pars*, i.e. the question of which party triumphed in a split election, if the candidates were suitable and the electoral procedure not flawed. This problem arose, for example, at Bayeux (1205–6, 1231), Tours (1208), and Rouen (1221–2).

(D) The suitability of the candidate. Elections at Rouen (1221-2, 1230-1, 1235–7), Sées (1144–7), or Avranches (1198–1200) will demonstrate what criteria of suitability were applied and in which circumstances they were emphasised as a necessary condition for eligibility.

To these should be added:

(E) Episcopal translation.

When Bernard wrote his *Summa de electione* episcopal translations were not a central concern of canon lawyers or the pope. Twenty years later, however, Pope Innocent III made the regulation of episcopal translation a major theme of his pontificate, and the translation of William de Chemillé from Avranches to Angers in 1197–9 became one of his test cases.[17] This theme, therefore, is of particular interest for the present study.

The proper assessment of the impact of canon law on electoral practice in Normandy and Greater Anjou requires two preliminary investigations. First, an examination of the development of canon law and its interpretation by the legal experts, the canonists, during the period from *c.* 1140 to *c.* 1230. Second, an analysis of the spread of canon law and canonistic thought in Normandy and Greater Anjou in this period.

The body of canon law consisted of patristic texts, of canons laid down by ecclesiastical councils, and of decretals issued by popes. Canon law was principally preserved through collections of selected texts. It was, therefore, both conservative and innovative. Conservative, because in principle canons and decretals were perennially valid. Innovative, because the ancient texts could receive a new meaning through mutilation and/or

---

[17] Infra, pp. 156–64.

through the context in which the compiler of a collection placed them. Innovative also, because a council or a pope could steer the content and contemporary interpretation of canon law by issuing new legislation.[18] Thus the direction of canon law could vary substantially over time.

Arguably the most important collection of canon law between *c.* 1140 and *c.* 1230 was the *Concordia discordantium canonum*, commonly known as *Decretum Gratiani*. Anders Winroth has recently shown that the *Decretum* originated in two recensions written between 1139 and 1158 at the latest. He has also suggested that at least two authors were responsible for the recensions, identifying the author of the first as Gratian.[19] In his work Gratian attempted to harmonise a great number of apparently contradictory canons relating to all kinds of ecclesiastical matters including episcopal elections. Although the earlier collections of canon law like Burchard's *Decretum* or the works attributed to Ivo of Chartres continued to be in use for some time after Gratian's work had emerged,[20] the *Decretum* quickly became the basis of the scientific examination of canon law.

To keep abreast of the latest conciliar legislation and the increasing number of papal decretals sent to every corner of the Latin world canonists continued to compile collections, and by the end of the twelfth century a great variety of them existed across Europe. Among these local collections Bernard of Pavia's *Compilatio prima* (1188–92) was the most successful; in the two decades following its compilation *Compilatio prima* became the universally recognised decretal collection. Subsequently the papacy played an active role in the compilation of the decretal collections. In 1209/10 Innocent III promulgated *Compilatio tertia*, soon to be followed by the composition of the private collection *Compilatio secunda* (1210–15), of Johannes Teutonicus' *Compilatio quarta*

---

[18] Thier, 'Hierarchie und Autonomie', pp. 262–322; for patristic texts in canon law, see C. Munier, *Les sources patristiques du droit de l'église du VIIIᵉ au XIIIᵉ siècle* (Mulhouse, 1957).

[19] A. Winroth, *The Making of Gratian's Decretum* (Cambridge Studies in Medieval Life and Thought) (Cambridge, 2000), pp. 136–45, 175–92; cf. T. Lenherr, 'Die vier Fassungen von C.3 q.1 d. p. c. im Decretum Gratiani. Zugleich ein Einblick in die neueste Diskussion um das Werden von Gratian's Dekret', *Archiv für katholisches Kirchenrecht*, 169 (2000), 353–81. These results are currently debated among scholars. For a dissenting opinion, see C. Larrainzar, 'La ricerca attuale sul "Decretum Gratiani"', in E. de León and N. Álvarez de las Asturias (eds.), *La cultura giuridico-canonica medioevale. Premesse per un dialogo ecumenico* (Pontificia università della Santa Croce. Monografie giuridiche xxii) (Rome, 2003), pp. 45–88.

[20] Cf. M. Brett, 'Canon Law and Litigation: The Century before Gratian', in M. Franklin and C. Harper-Bill (eds.), *Medieval Ecclesiastical Studies in Honour of Dorothy M. Owen* (Studies in the History of Medieval Religion vii) (Woodbridge, 1995), pp. 21–40, p. 23; P. Landau, 'Vorgratianische Kanonessammlungen bei den Dekretisten und in den frühen Dekretalensammlungen', in S. Chodorow (ed.), *Proceedings of the Eighth International Congress of Medieval Canon Law. San Diego, University of California at La Jolla, 21–27 August 1988* (MIC series C: subsidia ix) (Vatican City, 1992), pp. 93–116.

(*c.* 1217), and of Pope Honorius' III *Compilatio quinta* which was pro-mulgated in May 1226.[21] While *Compilationes quarta* and *quinta* struggled for recognition, the other collections were widely accepted. In addition, local decretal collections continued to be used. This led to confusion in the courts, since one collection could contain material that contradicted what was found in another. Intent on improving this state of affairs, Gregory IX ordered a new compilation. On his command Raymond de Peñafort compiled the *Liber extra*, which appeared in 1234 and, highly successful, replaced the older works in the schools as well as in the courts.[22]

Gratian's *Decretum* and the decretal collections stimulated an extensive examination of canon law in principal centres of learning of the time. In Bologna the so-called Bolognese school of canonistic thought emerged, in Paris the French school, and in England, most notably in Oxford, the Anglo-Norman school. At these centres, masters commented upon Gratian's *Decretum* and the decretal collections, discussed legal problems, taught their pupils how to analyse canon law, and presented their own interpretations or at least those they judged most appropriate.[23] This structure of working and learning could lead to different traditions of thought in the schools, but they were by no means isolated from each other. There was a continuous exchange between them, as teachers and students moved from one centre to the other. Stephen of Tournai, for example, studied canon law at Bologna and his *Summa* on the *Decretum* counts among the works of the Bolognese school. Yet when he returned

---

[21] S. Kuttner, *Repertorium der Kanonistik (1140–1234). Prodromus corporis glossarum* (Studi e testi LXXI) (Vatican City, 1937), pp. 322–3, 345, 355, 372–3, 382–3; J. Sayers, *Papal Government and England during the Pontificate of Honorius III (1216–1227)* (Cambridge, 1984), pp. 133–52; O. Hageneder, 'Die Register Innozenz III.', in T. Frenz (ed.), *Papst Innozenz III. Weichensteller der Geschichte Europas* (Stuttgart, 2000), pp. 91–101, p. 100.

[22] M. Bertram, 'Die Dekretalen Gregors IX.: Kompilation oder Kodifikation?', in C. Longo (ed.), *Magister Raimundus. Atti del convegno per il IV centenario della canonizzazione di San Raimondo de Penyafort (1901–2001)* (Institutum historicum Fratrum Praedicatorum. Dissertationes historicae XXVIII) (Rome, 2002), pp. 61–86; Kuttner, *Repertorium*, pp. 373–85, 447–8; J. Hanenburg, 'Decretals and Decretal Collections in the Second Half of the Twelfth Century', *Tijdschrift voor Rechtsgeschiedenis*, 34 (1966), 552–99, 588. For collections compiled after 1234, see M. Bertram, 'Die Konstitutionen Alexanders IV. (1255/56) und Clemens' IV. (1265/1267). Eine neue Form päpstlicher Gesetzgebung', *Savigny KA*, 88 (2002), 70–109; M. Bertram, 'Vorbonifazische Extravagantensammlungen', ibid., 89 (2003), 285–322.

[23] Cf. G. Le Bras et al., *L'âge classique 1140–1378. Sources et théorie du droit* (Histoire du droit et des institutions de l'église en occident VII) (Paris, 1965), pp. 266–90. In this work, Charles Lefèbvre distinguished the writings of the French from the works of the short-lived Rhenanian school. He emphasised, however, their close relationship, pp. 282–6. Today, the works of the Rhenanian school are subsumed under the works of the French school, R. Weigand, Art. 'Kanonistik', in W. Kasper et al. (eds.), *Lexikon für Theologie und Kirche*, 3rd edn (11 vols., Freiburg, 1993–2001), V, cols. 1188–97.

to France he was probably a stimulating influence on the first works of the French school.[24] The Englishman Richard de Mores is another illuminating case. In general the Bolognese school greatly influenced the writings of the Anglo-Norman canonists at the end of the twelfth century.[25] But Richard's career demonstrates that influence could go in the opposite direction. At the age of twenty-five he wrote at Paris his *Summa quaestionum* that counted among the works of the Anglo-Norman school. He then moved on to Bologna and his later writings are considered as works of the Bolognese school influenced by the Anglo-Norman tradition.[26]

This mobility between the schools needs to be taken into account when considering which canonistic theories were known in Normandy and Greater Anjou at the time. Clearly, it cannot be assumed that the clergy in Normandy and Greater Anjou were more familiar with the Anglo-Norman school than with the French or Bolognese schools. Thus the analysis has to consider texts from all canonistic schools. My selection of texts is based on their importance for the formation of the mainstream(s) of canonistic thought. Such an approach evidently runs the risk of missing precisely the minor work X that the Norman canon Y picked up at Z while travelling and which subsequently influenced his thought on episcopal elections. In order to minimise that risk – due to the hazards of manuscript preservation even the analysis of all known canonistic writings would be subjected to it – I have selected a broad range of works. There are the obvious choices from the Bolognese school: Rufinus, Stephen of Tournai, Johannes Faventinus as representatives of what can be named the first generation of Bolognese canonists working between *c.* 1145 and *c.* 1175.[27] I have chosen Bernard of Pavia's *Summa de electione* and Huguccio of Pisa's *Summa decretorum* from the second generation (*c.* 1175 – *c.* 1192), and Bernard of Pavia's *Summa decretalium* and Alanus Anglicus' two recensions of the *Apparatus Ius naturale* from the third (*c.* 1192 – *c.* 1210). The fourth generation (*c.* 1210 – *c.* 1225) is represented by Laurentius Hispanus, Johannes Teutonicus, Tancred, Damasus, Vincentius Hispanus, and Raymund de Peñafort. The works

[24] S. Kuttner, 'Les débuts de l'école canoniste française', in S. Kuttner, *Gratian and the Schools of Law 1140–1234* (London, 1983), no. VI, pp. 193–204, pp. 195–6. *Die Summa des Stephanus Tornacensis über das Decretum Gratiani*, ed. J. F. von Schulte (Giessen, 1891); H. Kalb, *Studien zur Summa Stephans von Tournai* (Innsbruck, 1983).

[25] R. Weigand, 'Die anglo-normannische Kanonistik in den letzten Jahrzehnten des 12. Jahrhunderts', in P. Linehan (ed.), *Proceedings of the Seventh International Congress of Medieval Canon Law, Cambridge, 23–27 July 1984* (MIC series C: subsidia VIII) (Vatican City, 1988), pp. 249–63.

[26] Müller, *Anteil*, p. 133 and n. 72; Zwettl, Stiftsbibliothek 162, fos. 145r–173r.

[27] The division into generations follows the system adopted by Müller, *Anteil*.

of the French school can be divided into two generations. My analysis of the first generation (1165–90) is mainly based on the *Summa Parisiensis,* the *Summa Coloniensis,* and Peter of Blois' *Speculum iuris canonici.* Two *Apparatus* have been chosen to represent the second generation (1200– 10): *Ecce vicit leo* and *Animal est substantia.* The most short-lived of the three schools, the Anglo-Norman school, produced works between *c.* 1175 and *c.* 1210. For it, I have largely relied on Master Honorius' *Summa decretalium quaestionum* and *Summa De iure canonico tractaturus,* the closely related *Summa Omnis qui iuste iudicat,* Richard de Mores' *Distinctiones decretorum,* and the glosses on the *Decretum* found in MS 283/676, Gonville and Caius College, Cambridge (John of Tynemouth).[28]

---

[28] For bio-bibliographical information on medieval canonists, their writings, and on anonymous works, see http://faculty.cua.edu/pennington/biobibl.htm (last visit: 12 Mar. 2003); for the early glosses on Gratian's *Decretum,* see R. Weigand, *Die Glossen zum Dekret Gratians. Studien zu den frühen Glossen und Glossenkompositionen* (Studia Gratiana xxv–xxvi) (Rome, 1991). In addition to the works already quoted the editions and manuscripts used are: *Die Summa decretorum des Magister Rufinus,* ed. H. Singer (Paderborn, 1902); Oxford, Bodleian Library, Canonici Miscellanea 429 (Johannes Faventinus); Paris, BNF Lat. 3892 (Huguccio); *Bernardi Papiensis (Faventini episcopi) Summa decretalium,* ed. E. Laspeyres (Regensburg, 1860), pp. 1–283; Paris, BNF Lat. 3909 (Alanus Anglicus 1st rec.); Paris, Bibliothèque Mazarine 1318 (Alanus Anglicus 2nd rec.); B. McManus, 'The Ecclesiology of Laurentius Hispanus (c. 1180–1248) and his Contribution to the Romanization of Canon Law Jurisprudence, with an Edition of Laurentius' Apparatus glossarum in Compilationem tertiam' (2 vols., Syracuse Univ., Ph. D. thesis, 1991); Vatican City, BAV Vat. Reg. Lat. 977, fos. 1r–296r (Laurentius Hispanus, *Glossa Palatina*); 'Joannis Teutonici Apparatus in concilium quartum Lateranense', in *Constitutiones concilii quarti Lateranensis una cum commentariis glossatorum,* ed. A. García y García (MIC series A: corpus glossatorum II) (Vatican City, 1981), pp. 175–272; *Johannis Teutonici Apparatus glossarum in Compilationem tertiam,* ed. K. Pennington (MIC series A: corpus glossatorum III) (Vatican City, 1981); 'Apparatus glossarum in Compilationem quartam', in *Antiquae collectiones decretalium,* ed. A. Agustin (Paris, 1609), pp. 797–843 (Johannes Teutonicus); Bamberg, Staatsbibliothek Can.13 (Johannes Teutonicus, *Glossa ordinaria*); Vatican City, BAV Vat. Lat. 1377, fos. 2r–98v (Tancred, *Glossa ordinaria* on *Compilatio I*); fos. 101r–145v (Tancred, *Glossa ordinaria* on *Compilatio II*), fos. 148r– 279r (Tancred, *Glossa ordinaria* on *Compilatio III*); 'Damasi Apparatus in concilium quartum Lateranense', in *Constitutiones concilii quarti Lateranensis,* ed. García y García, pp. 388–460; Karlsruhe, Badische Landesbibliothek Aug. per. 40 (formerly Aug. XL), fos. 231r–290v (Vincentius Hispanus, *Apparatus* to *Compilatio III*); 'Vincentii Hispani Apparatus in concilium quartum Lateranense', in *Constitutiones concilii quarti Lateranensis,* ed. García y García, pp. 271–383; *San Raimundo de Penyafort. Summa iuris,* ed. J. Rius Serra (Barcelona, 1945); *S. Raimundus de Pennaforte: Summa de iure canonico,* ed. X. Ochoa and A. Diez (Universa bibliotheca iuris I) (Rome, 1975); *The Summa Parisiensis on the Decretum Gratiani,* ed. T. McLaughlin (Toronto, 1952); *Summa 'Elegantius in iure divino' seu Coloniensis,* ed. G. Fransen and S. Kuttner (MIC series A: corpus glossatorum I) (4 vols., New York, 1969–90); *Petri Blesensis opusculum de distinctionibus in canonum interpretatione adhibendis, sive ut auctor voluit Speculum iuris canonici,* ed. T. Reimarus (Berlin, 1837); Paris, BNF N. A. Lat. 1576 (*Apparatus Ecce vicit leo*); Bamberg, Staatsbibliothek Can.42 (*Apparatus Animal est substantia*); *Magistri Honorii Summa 'De iure canonico tractaturus'. I,* ed. R. Weigand et al. (MIC series A: corpus glossatorum V/1) (Vatican City, 2004); Zwettl, Stiftsbibliothek 162, fos. 179r–213r (Honorius, *Summa decretalium quaestionum*); Rouen, BM 743, fos. 1r–142r (*Summa Omnis qui iuste iudicat*); G. Silano, 'The Distinctiones Decretorum of Ricardus Anglicus: An Edition' (Toronto Univ., Ph.D. thesis, 1981).

The second preliminary enquiry focuses on the spread of canon law and canonistic thought in Normandy and Greater Anjou. Charles Duggan has shown that English churchmen were not only aware of the developments in canon law after 1140, but also significantly contributed to it.[29] In order to make any comparable statement about the situation in Normandy and Greater Anjou it is necessary to investigate the local contemporary library holdings and the education and eventual canonistic activities of local churchmen. For that purpose I have examined library catalogues, local decretal collections, and the careers of canons. The outcome of this research is bound to represent only a fraction of the actual knowledge of canon law. Only a few library catalogues for the period exist, and research has shown that they are unlikely to represent the total of books actually held by the libraries.[30] Palaeographical studies have demonstrated that some *scriptoria* in Normandy and Greater Anjou copied works of canon law in the eleventh and twelfth centuries.[31] Future research will undoubtedly increase our knowledge of this matter. Members of cathedral chapters bore in increasing numbers the title of *Magister*, but the field of their studies can be identified only in a few cases.[32] Finally, it can be supposed that there was a continuous informal exchange of information between individuals and institutions.[33]

---

[29] C. Duggan, 'The Reception of Canon Law in England in the Later-Twelfth Century', in S. Kuttner and J. J. Ryan (eds.), *Proceedings of the Second International Congress of Medieval Canon Law, Boston College, 12–16 August 1963* (MIC series C: subsidia I) (Vatican City, 1965), pp. 359–90; cf. similar studies by Winfried Stelzer for Austria and Peter Landau and Johannes Fried for the German part of the Empire, W. Stelzer, *Gelehrtes Recht in Österreich. Von den Anfängen bis zum frühen 14. Jahrhundert* (Mitteilungen des Instituts für österreichische Geschichtsforschung. Ergänzungsband XXVI) (Vienna, 1982); P. Landau, 'Die Anfänge der Verbreitung des klassischen kanonischen Rechts in Deutschland im 12. Jahrhundert und im ersten Drittel des 13. Jahrhunderts', in *Chiesa diritto e ordinamento della 'societas christiana' nei secoli XI e XII* (Miscellanea del centro di studi medioevali XI) (Milan, 1986), pp. 272–97; J. Fried, 'Die Rezeption Bologneser Wissenschaft in Deutschland während des 12. Jahrhunderts', *Viator*, 21 (1990), 103–45.

[30] B. Munk Olsen, 'Les bibliothèques bénédictines et les bibliothèques de cathédrales: les mutations des XIᵉ et XIIᵉ siècles', in A. Vernet (ed.), *Histoire des bibliothèques françaises* (3 vols., Paris, 1989), I, pp. 31–44, p. 31.

[31] For a study focusing on one particular city, see J. Vezin, *Les Scriptoria d'Angers au XIᵉ siècle* (Bibliothèque des hautes études; IVᵉ section, sciences historiques et philologiques CCCXXII) (Paris, 1974). For a study looking at a group of manuscripts, see S. Williams, *Codices Pseudo-Isidoriani. A Palaeographical-Historical Study* (MIC series C: subsidia III) (New York, 1971).

[32] In general, see J. W. Baldwin, 'Studium et Regnum: The Penetration of University Personnel into French and English Administration at the Turn of the Twelfth and Thirteenth Centuries', *Revue des études islamiques*, 44 (1976), 199–215; J. Barrow, 'Education and the Recruitment of Cathedral Canons in England and Germany 1100–1225', *Viator*, 20 (1989), 117–38. For the Norman cathedrals and the church of Angers, see the lists provided by David Spear, Vincent Tabbagh, Jean-Michel Matz, and François Comte, infra, p. 16 n. 36.

[33] Cf. M. Peyrafort-Huin, *La bibliothèque médiévale de l'abbaye de Pontigny (XIIᵉ –XIXᵉ siècles). Histoire, inventaires anciens, manuscrits* (Documents, études et répertoires LX) (Paris, 2001), pp. 101–14.

Introduction

Electoral practice

The election of a bishop meant that a decision-making process had come to a close. Every process was unique. These are trivial truths. Yet they are well worth repeating, because they point to the risks inherent in a selective analysis of elections: the generalisation of features that in fact were particular to the case studied. This risk is enhanced by the rarity of documentation on elections during this period. For many elections the electoral procedure is not recorded. Information on procedures usually arises from disputed elections which caught the attention of a chronicler and/ or were brought to the papal court. A dispute, however – although it might yield information on the use of canon law – is only of limited value when the aim is to investigate the 'normal'. This study, therefore, will consider all the elections that took place between c. 1140 and c. 1230. To ensure proper assessment of regional particularities and continuities the elections will be studied diocese by diocese.

Decision-making processes are informal. The regulations assigned the day, the time, and the location for the official discussion of the candidates, but whether preliminary talks were held, which people participated if they were, and what was actually discussed, was generally not recorded.[34] The groups supporting a particular candidate and their motives for so doing can only be indirectly identified. The most promising way to achieve an indirect identification is the prosopographical approach.[35] The bishop was elected because his electors knew him, because they thought he would be the right man to fulfil their ambitions. Thus the greater the historian's knowledge about the individual bishop, the greater his chance of identifying the groups and interests involved in his election. The bishop's origin, his family connections, and his career, therefore, have to be scrutinised in detail.

Prosopographical research into a group of people of the twelfth and early thirteenth centuries – even a group as prominent as candidates for

---

[34] Concerning monastic elections such information does occasionally survive, e. g. *Cronica Jocelini de Brakelonda de rebus gestis Samsonis abbatis monasterii Sancti Edmundi*, ed. H.E. Butler (London, 1949), pp. 16–24; *The Chronicle of the Election of Hugh Abbot of Bury St. Edmunds and Later Bishop of Ely*, ed. R.M. Thomson (Oxford Medieval Texts) (Oxford, 1974).

[35] Cf. N. Bulst, 'Zum Gegenstand und zur Methode von Prosopographie', in N. Bulst and J.-P. Genet (eds.), *Medieval Lives and the Historian: Studies in Medieval Prosopography. Proceedings of the First International Interdisciplinary Conference on Medieval Prosopography, University of Bielefeld 3–5 December 1982* (Medieval Institute Publications, Western Michigan University) (Kalamazoo, 1986), pp. 1–16; S. Weinfurter, '"Series episcoporum" – Probleme und Möglichkeiten einer Prosopographie des früh- und hochmittelalterlichen Episkopats', in ibid., pp. 97–112. For two examples demonstrating the usefulness of the prosopographical approach for the analysis of episcopal elections, see H. Zielinski, 'Zu den Hintergründen der Bischofswahl Pibos von Toul 1069', in ibid., pp. 91–6, and C.B. Bouchard, 'The Geographical, Social and Ecclesiastical Origins of the Bishops of Auxerre and Sens in the Central Middle Ages', *Church History*, 46 (1977), 277–95.

bishoprics – faces considerable problems. The sources are far richer for Normandy and Greater Anjou than, for instance, Aquitaine, but they are still so scarce that sometimes hardly more than the name of the candidate can be identified with certainty. This difficulty increases when looking at the composition of the cathedral chapters. It is hardly possible to establish the composition of an entire chapter at any given time during this period. The main sources for identification in the twelfth century are the witness lists of episcopal charters. With the disappearance of these witness lists around 1200, the identification of canons becomes considerably more difficult and an already incomplete picture of the composition of the cathedral chapters becomes even more defective. Despite these difficulties scholars have devoted much energy in recent years to identifying cathedral canons on both sides of the Channel, and their work,[36] complemented by further extensive search through published and unpublished charters and cartularies of Normandy and Greater Anjou,[37] permits at least occasional conclusions on the composition of a cathedral chapter at a certain time.

Many of the canons are only known by their Christian names and often no further information about them is available. Statements about the identity of interest groups within a chapter, therefore, remain in many cases hypothetical. There are some means, however, to increase the plausibility of a hypothesis. First, it is possible to identify some canons whom the sources described as related to each other and/or to the elect. The impact of relatives on ecclesiastical institutions was substantial.

---

[36] For England, see the volumes of *John Le Neve: Fasti ecclesiae Anglicanae, 1066–1300*, published under the auspices of the Institute of Historical Research, London. For an analysis of such lists, see J. Barrow, 'Origins and Careers of Cathedral Canons in Twelfth-Century England', in *Medieval Prosopography*, 21 (2000), 23–40. Currently, Hélène Millet is heading the research project *Fasti ecclesiae Gallicanae* that aims at establishing lists of the members of the French cathedral chapters for the period between 1200 and 1500, cf. P. Desportes and H. Millet, *Diocèse d'Amiens* (Fasti ecclesiae Gallicanae I) (Turnhout, 1996), pp. xix–xx. Concerning the dioceses of Normandy and Greater Anjou, three volumes have been published so far, V. Tabbagh, *Diocèse de Rouen* (Fasti ecclesiae Gallicanae II) (Turnhout, 1998); J.-M. Matz and F. Comte, *Diocèse d'Angers* (Fasti ecclesiae Gallicanae VII) (Turnhout, 2003); P. Desportes et al., *Diocèse de Sées* (Fasti ecclesiae Gallicanae IX) (Turnout, 2005). David Spear has compiled lists on the canons of the Norman cathedral chapters up to 1204, *The Personnel of the Norman Cathedrals during the Ducal Period, 911–1204* (Fasti ecclesiae Anglicanae) (London, 2006); D. Spear, 'Power, Patronage and Personality in the Norman Cathedral Chapters, 911–1204', in C. Harper-Bill (ed.), *Anglo-Norman Studies XX. Proceedings of the Battle Conference 1997* (Woodbridge, 1998), pp. 205–22.

[37] I have based the list of cartularies on D. Spear, *Research Facilities in Normandy and Paris. A Guide for Students of Medieval Norman History. Including a Checklist of Norman Cartularies* (Greenville, 1993), pp. 28–53; C. Bourlet et al., *Répertoire des microfilms de cartulaires français consultables à l'I.R.H.T.* (Orleans, 1999). For a recent survey on editions of episcopal cartularies in France, see M. Parisse, 'La recherche française sur les actes des évêques. Les travaux d'un groupe de recherche', in C. Haidacher and W. Köfler (eds.), *Die Diplomatik der Bischofsurkunde vor 1250. La diplomatique épiscopale avant 1250. Referate zum VIII. Internationalen Kongreß für Diplomatik, Innsbruck, 27. September–3. Oktober 1993* (Innsbruck, 1995), pp. 203–7.

Throughout the middle ages complaints were made that precisely in places where relationships should not matter, that is in ecclesiastical communities, they played a very important role.[38]

A second means which may lead to the identification of an interest group is the identification of a common patron, i.e. a group of canons who owed their entry to the chapter to the same person. This examination is based on the careers of the canons. A group of canons may have entered the chapter under a certain bishop and may have advanced their careers during his episcopate. In this case, the bishop was the likely patron. In other cases some canons may have been very close to the king or the pope before their entry into a chapter. In this case, royal or papal influence may have caused their promotion.

Then there is the analysis of witness lists of episcopal charters. Many of the warnings David Bates and Alheydis Plassmann have issued on the subject of royal charters also hold true for episcopal charters. Witnesses may be inscribed because the business of the charter directly concerned them, or because their position demanded the presence of their name, or because accidentally they were present at the recording.[39] Such appearances reveal very little about the relationship among the witnesses and between the witness and the issuer. This approach, therefore, may be of little value in itself. However, witness lists can be of help where a group of people repeatedly appearing as witnesses also shared bonds of kinship and/or patronage.

The methodological approach adopted requires the examination of a great variety of sources. Charters, letters, inquests, chronicles, poems, obituaries: all can provide useful information. The flow of information, however, is not equal across time and space. On the one hand there are the hazards of the survival of sources from medieval to modern times. For example, the Archives Départementales of St Lô and the Bibliothèque Municipale of Tours were destroyed during World War II and as a consequence a great number of charters illuminating the history of these regions vanished. On the other hand there are changes that occurred in the twelfth and thirteenth centuries which affected the value of sources for the present study. One such change, the disappearance of witness lists of episcopal charters around 1200 and its implications for the analysis of

---

[38] K. Schreiner, 'Versippung als soziale Kategorie mittelalterlicher Kirchen- und Klostergeschichte', in Bulst and Genet (eds.), *Medieval Lives*, pp. 163–80.

[39] D. Bates, 'The Prosopographical Study of Anglo-Norman Royal Charters', in K.S.B. Keats-Rohan (ed.), *Family Trees and the Roots of Politics. The Prosopography of Britain and France from the Tenth to the Twelfth Century* (Woodbridge, 1997), pp. 89–102; A. Plassmann, *Die Struktur des Hofes unter Friedrich Barbarossa nach den deutschen Zeugen seiner Urkunden* (MGH, Studien und Texte xx) (Hanover, 1998), pp. 1–18.

cathedral chapters, has already been discussed. Others concern the sources from which 'direct information' on electoral practice can be gathered; that is any kind of account explicitly dealing with the circumstances and procedure of an election. They are mainly found in records of the papal and royal administration, whose number increased significantly from around 1200. From that time onwards registers of documents issued by the papal, the English, and the French chancery exist, and the French and English royal archives collected incoming material, such as charters and letters addressed to the king, inventories, financial accounts, and returns from inquests.[40] The growth in the amount of extant documentation means an increasing likelihood of finding material relating to elections. This must be considered when the role of the ruler and of the pope in elections before and after 1200 is assessed.

'Direct information' on elections can also be found in chronicles and here, too, the extent of information varies over time. Chronicles are often the only source recording the election of a bishop and while in many cases they simply mention the date of the election and the name of the elect, they occasionally offer more detailed accounts. The information given by local chronicles is increased in the last quarter of the twelfth century by what Antonia Gransden has labelled the 'golden age of historiography'.[41] English chroniclers like Ralph de Diceto or Roger of Howden took a great interest in politics and government.[42] Dealing not only with England but also with the continental dominions of the Angevin kings, they add to our knowledge of episcopal elections on both sides of the Channel. This additional information ceases in the thirteenth century. After the conquest English chroniclers were less interested in the daily matters of the continent and the gap they left was only unsatisfactorily

---

[40] For a comparative analysis, see N. Vincent, 'Why 1199? Bureaucracy and Enrolment under John and his Contemporaries', in A. Jobson (ed.), *English Government in the Thirteenth Century* (Woodbridge, 2004), pp. 17–48; for England, see M. Clanchy, *From Memory to Written Record, England 1066–1307*, 2nd edn (Oxford, 1993), pp. 68–73; *The Memoranda Roll for the Michaelmas Term of the First Year of the Reign of King John (1199–1200)*, ed. H. G. Richardson (Pipe Roll Society N.S. XXI) (London, 1943), pp. xi–xcviii; for France, see Baldwin, *Philip*, pp. 401–23; R.-H. Bautier, 'Cartulaires de chancellerie et recueils d'actes des autorités laïques et ecclésiastiques', in O. Guyotjeannin et al. (eds.), *Les cartulaires. Actes de la table ronde organisée par l'école nationale des chartes et le G.D.R. 121 du C.N.R.S. (Paris, 5–7 décembre 1991)* (Mémoires et documents de l'école des chartes XXXIX) (Paris, 1993) pp. 363–77, pp. 363–6; M. Nortier, 'Les actes de Philippe Auguste: notes critiques sur les sources diplomatiques du règne', in Bautier (ed.), *La France de Philippe Auguste*, pp. 429–51; for the papal registers, see Hageneder, 'Die Register Innozenz III.', pp. 91–101; L. Boyle, *A Survey of the Vatican Archive and its Medieval Holdings* (Pontifical Institute of Medieval Studies. Subsidia mediaevalia I) (Toronto, 1972), p. 7.

[41] A. Gransden, *Historical Writing in England* (2 vols., London, 1974–82), I, p. 219.

[42] *Diceto*; *Howden*; *Gesta regis*. On the identification of Roger of Howden with the author of the *Gesta regis*, see D. Corner, 'The Gesta Regis Henrici Secundi and Chronica of Roger, Parson of Howden', *Bulletin of the Institute of Historical Research*, 56 (1983), 126–44.

filled by chroniclers of the Capetian kingdom. There was no contemporary French equivalent to the English 'golden age of historiography'. Local chronicles occasionally provide valuable information,[43] but when they fail the historian has to be content with the considerably less informative *Gesta Philippi Augusti* started by Rigord in the 1180s, and completed by the royal cleric William Le Breton, and the *Philippidos*, a work on the reign of Philip Augustus also compiled by William Le Breton.[44] As a consequence the picture of elections, in particular of the extent of royal activity, is bound to differ between Angevin and Capetian chronicles, and this difference must be borne in mind when comparing Angevin and Capetian attitudes towards elections.

---

[43] E.g. the chronicles of Rouen and Tours, 'E chronico Rotomagensi', in *RHF*, XVIII, pp. 357–62, XXIII, pp. 331–43; *Recueil de chroniques de Touraine*, ed. A. Salmon (Collection de documents sur l'histoire de Touraine I) (Tours, 1854).

[44] *Œuvres de Rigord et de Guillaume le Breton*, ed. H.F. Delaborde (Société de l'histoire de France) (2 vols., Paris, 1882–5); Baldwin, *Philip*, pp. 396–401.

Chapter 2

ELECTORAL THEORY

THE CANON LAW OF EPISCOPAL ELECTIONS UP TO 1140

Canon law prescribed that a bishop had to be elected. Recently Andreas Thier has scrutinised the development of episcopal elections in canon law up to 1140. According to him, in late antiquity election by *clerus* and *populus* meant their examination of an already nominated candidate rather than their free choice. In the fifth century, the legislation of Pope Celestine I and Pope Leo I changed the meaning of election: the electors were given free choice. However, in the period between the seventh and the eleventh centuries, when the selection of the bishop was dominated by the ruler, the election was little more than a formality conveying consent to the ruler's will.[1]

The orientation of canon law changed in the course of the eleventh century when the papacy started to spearhead the Gregorian reform movement. Intent on realising the claim of papal supremacy and releasing the church from local dependencies, the reformers battled against simony, clerical marriage, and, towards the end of the eleventh century, increasingly also against lay investiture.[2] They used the conservative and innovative nature of canon law both as their base and as a weapon to achieve their aims. Canon law provided a considerable number of the texts that inspired and justified their ideas. Reformers organised these texts in collections which became powerful promoters of their cause. In addition,

---

[1] Thier, 'Hierarchie und Autonomie', pp. 319–20.
[2] A. Fliche, *La réforme grégorienne* (Spicilegium sacrum Lovaniense; études et documents VI, IX, XVI) (3 vols., Louvain, 1924–37); S. Beulertz, *Das Verbot der Laieninvestitur im Investiturstreit* (MGH, Studien und Texte II) (Hanover, 1991); W. Hartmann, *Der Investiturstreit* (Enzyklopädie deutscher Geschichte XXI) (Munich, 1993), pp. 9–64, 78–82; G. Tellenbach, *Libertas. Kirche und Weltordnung im Zeitalter des Investiturstreits* (Forschungen zur Kirchen- und Geistesgeschichte VII) (Stuttgart, 1936), pp. 109–62; G. Tellenbach, '"Gregorianische Reform". Kritische Besinnungen', in K. Schmid (ed.), *Reich und Kirche vor dem Investiturstreit. Vorträge beim wissenschaftlichen Kolloquium aus Anlaß des achtzigsten Geburtstags von Gerd Tellenbach* (Sigmaringen, 1985), pp. 99–113.

the popes used their capacity to convoke councils to make canon law that suited the interests of the reformers.[3]

Episcopal elections were not at the centre of the reform. But simony and lay investiture frequently occurred when a candidate acceded to a bishopric, because rulers invested bishops with the temporal and spiritual powers of their new office. Thus rulers could also sell a see to the highest bidder. This state of affairs ran diametrically contrary to the reformers' aims, and as a sub-plot of their fight for the *libertas ecclesiae* the reformers stressed that lay princes should not nominate bishops. Instead they emphasised the ancient canonical principle of the election by *clerus* and *populus*. However, the reformers gave a new meaning to this formula. They interpreted it as the clergy making the decision and the people applauding the clergy's choice without actually having an active electoral right.[4] Pope Gregory VII also tried to add a hierarchical principle to the electoral process. According to him, the metropolitan and/or the pope had to approve the clergy's choice.[5] Urban II further specified the requirements a candidate had to fulfil in order to be eligible. At the council of Benevento in 1091, it was decreed that those elected should already be priests or deacons. In rare cases, and with permission by the archbishop or pope, subdeacons could also be elected.[6] This decision was reiterated in similar terms at the council of Clermont four years later.[7]

The reformers did little more to regulate episcopal elections. Yet, their emphasis on free, canonical election by the clergy, the suitability of the candidate, and the monitoring capacity of the archbishop or the pope were crucial to the development of canon law. Although later popes were less radical in their approach, these three points remained at least in theory principles of episcopal elections. Furthermore, the papal attempt to implement free election by the clergy opened the way to more precise regulation of the electoral procedure. As long as the election was only a formality to confirm the ruler's choice, electoral procedure was of little significance. In contrast, a free election raised not only the question of who among the

---

[3] Thier, 'Hierarchie und Autonomie', pp. 218–58. For the collections, see P. Fournier and G. Le Bras, *Histoire des collections canonique en occident depuis les fausses décrétales jusqu'au décret de Gratien* (Bibliothèque d'histoire du droit) (2 vols., Paris, 1931–2), II, pp. 3–313; L. Kéry, *Canonical Collections of the Early Middle Ages (ca. 400–1140). A Bibliographical Guide to the Manuscripts and Literature* (History of Medieval Canon Law) (Washington, 1999), pp. 203–94.

[4] Thier, 'Hierarchie und Autonomie', pp. 215–39. [5] Ibid., pp. 239–58.

[6] R. Somerville, *Pope Urban II, the Collectio Britannica, and the Council of Melfi (1089)* (Oxford, 1996), pp. 302–3, c. 1.

[7] R. Somerville, *The Councils of Urban II. Decreta Claromontensia* (Annuarium historiae conciliorum supplementum I) (Amsterdam, 1972), p. 73, c. 4, where only the pope is referred to as the authority to decide over the eligibility of a subdeacon.

clergy should be voting, but also how they should vote and how the votes should be weighed up.

At the time, these questions arose most prominently in disputed papal elections. In urgent need to legitimise their election candidates were looking hard for arguments in their favour. This stimulated thought in particular on the composition of the electoral body and the counting of votes. In 1059, for example, Pope Nicholas II decreed that in order to elect a pope, the cardinal bishops should first consider potential candidates and then consult the cardinal priests on this matter; finally, the other clergy and the people of Rome should give their consent. This decree served the double purpose of justifying Nicholas' own disputed election of late 1058 and of providing clearer rules for subsequent elections.[8] In the split elections of 1130 and 1159 the discussion mainly focused on the issue of majority; in each case the contending parties claimed to constitute the *sanior pars* and thus to represent the decisive majority.[9] This eventually led to the decision of the Third Lateran Council in 1179, which decreed that, if unanimity could not be achieved, the candidate elected by two-thirds of the cardinals would become pope.[10] The shaping of the papal electoral procedure also had its effect on episcopal elections. While its rules were not automatically applied to episcopal elections, they served as important signposts in the development of the electoral procedure in the twelfth and thirteenth centuries.

THE RECEPTION OF THE GREGORIAN REFORM IN NORMANDY AND GREATER ANJOU

The Norman clergy came into contact with reform ideas during William the Conqueror's reign (1035–87). In subsequent decades the leading Norman churchmen showed an interest in the developments of papal policy and canon law alike.[11] The bishops of Bayeux, Evreux, and Sées

---

[8] R. Schieffer, *Die Entstehung des päpstlichen Investiturverbots für den deutschen König* (MGH, Schriften XXVIII) (Stuttgart, 1981), pp. 48–9; D. Jasper, *Das Papstwahldekret von 1059. Überlieferung und Textgestalt* (Beiträge zur Geschichte und Quellenkunde des Mittelalters XII) (Sigmaringen, 1986), pp. 101–2.

[9] For the election of 1130, see F.-J. Schmale, *Studien zum Schisma des Jahres 1130* (Forschungen zur kirchlichen Rechtsgeschichte und zum Kirchenrecht III) (Cologne, 1961), pp. 145–61; for the election of 1159, see *Councils and Synods with Other Documents relating to the English Church. I. A.D. 871–1204*, ed. D. Whitelock et al. (2 vols., Oxford, 1981), II, pp. 835–41 (with references to earlier English literature); M. Pacaut, *Alexandre III. Etude sur la conception du pouvoir pontifical dans sa pensée et dans son œuvre* (L'église et l'état au moyen âge IX) (Paris, 1956), pp. 102–5; W. Madertoner, *Die zwiespältige Papstwahl von 1159* (Dissertationen der Universität Wien CXXXVI) (Vienna, 1978).

[10] *Conciliorum oecumenicorum decreta*, ed. G. Alberigo et al., 3rd edn (Bologna, 1973), p. 190, c. 1.

[11] H. Böhmer, *Kirche und Staat in der Normandie im XI. und XII. Jahrhundert. Eine historische Studie* (Leipzig, 1899), pp. 270–83.

attended Urban II's council at Clermont in 1095,[12] when the canon on the suitability of a bishop already cited was promulgated. The council also prohibited lay investiture, explicitly stating that kings and other princes should not confer ecclesiastical honours.[13] Twenty-six years later, in 1119, the Norman bishops attended the general council of Rheims, at which Pope Calixtus II forbade simony and lay investiture of bishoprics and abbeys.[14] Another major transmitter of the reform ideas was Ivo, bishop of Chartres. Not only did he fight personally for canonical elections and suitable candidates in Normandy,[15] but more importantly the collections of canon law attributed to him, the *Decretum* and the *Panormia*, started to circulate there shortly after 1100. Another collection, the closely related *Tripartita*, also spread across the duchy in the first half of the twelfth century. At Fécamp the scribe William *Peccator* produced a copy and the copy held at St Evroul may have been there since before 1150.[16] These works contained canons stressing that bishoprics should not be acquired through simony, and that laymen should not take part in episcopal elections.[17]

---

[12] The other bishops sent representatives, *The Ecclesiastical History of Orderic Vitalis*, ed. M. Chibnall (Oxford Medieval Texts) (6 vols., Oxford, 1969–80), V, book IX, pp. 18–9.

[13] Somerville, *Decreta Claromontensia*, p. 77, c. 19.

[14] *Orderic*, ed. Chibnall, VI, book XII, pp. 252–77; cf. R. Somerville, 'The Councils of Pope Calixtus II: Reims 1119', in S. Kuttner and K. Pennington (eds.), *Proceedings of the Fifth International Congress of Medieval Canon Law, Salamanca, 21–25 September 1976* (MIC series C: subsidia VI) (Vatican City, 1980), pp. 35–50.

[15] Cf. his engagement in the affair of Lisieux. In 1105, Ivo wrote letters to the Norman bishops asking them to take a firm stand against Ranulf Flambard, who had bought the see to install one of his sons as bishop. Ivo admonished them to elect a bishop according to the *mos ecclesiastica*. He asked Pope Paschal II to intervene, when Flambard, who had abandoned the idea of making one of his sons bishop, acquired the see for one of his clerics, 'Epistolae Ivonis Carnotensis episcopi', in *RHF*, XV, pp. 69–177, p. 134, no. 99; cf. C.W. David, *Robert Curthose, Duke of Normandy* (Harvard Historical Studies XXV) (Cambridge, Mass., 1920), pp. 151–3.

[16] For the spread of these collections in Normandy, see L. Barker, 'Ivo of Chartres and the Anglo-Norman Cultural Tradition', in M. Chibnall (ed.), *Anglo-Norman Studies XIII. Proceedings of the Battle Conference 1990* (Woodbridge, 1991), pp. 15–33, esp. pp. 24ff. The *Tripartita* was probably not compiled under Ivo at Chartres, M. Brett, 'Urban II and the Collections Attributed to Ivo of Chartres', in Chodorow (ed.), *Proceedings of the Eighth International Congress of Medieval Canon Law*, pp. 27–46. For the copy of the *Tripartita* made at Fécamp, now preserved at Paris, BNF Lat. 3858B, see B. Branch, 'Willermus Peccator et les manuscrits de Fécamp 1100–1150, *Cahiers de civilisation médiévale*, 26 (1983), 195–207, 203; Brett, 'Canon Law and Litigation', p. 37 n. 58. The St Evroul copy of the *Tripartita*, now preserved at Alençon, BM 135 (not consulted), was written in the first half of the twelfth century. Both copies contain *Tripartita A* and *Tripartita B*, which is a typical feature of *Tripartita* manuscripts, cf. Brett, 'Urban II and the Collections Attributed to Ivo of Chartres, pp. 29–32. I would like to thank Dr Martin Brett for his help with the *Tripartita* and its copies, cf. also following note.

[17] 'Panormia', in *PL*, CLXI, cols. 1045–343, 3.8, 3.9; 'Decretum', in *PL*, CLXI, cols. 47–1022, 5.75, 5.119–23. The *Tripartita* also contains *Decretum*, 5.120–3 (*Tripartita A*: 5.120–2; *Tripartita B*: 5.123). A provisional version of the new edition of the *Panormia* by Bruce Brasington and Martin Brett is available at http://wtfaculty.wtamu.edu/~bbrasington/panormia.html (last visit: 12 Mar. 2003).

Yet despite this exposure to the reform ideas, the Norman clergy was reluctant to adopt the reformers' attitude towards the ruler's intervention in episcopal elections. The Norman dukes traditionally played a leading role in ecclesiastical matters and the reform movement did little to alter this.[18] It was deeply entrenched in the consciousness of the Norman clergy that the duke disposed of bishoprics at his will. For example, when the Norman bishops returned from the council of Clermont, they published a significantly modified version of the decrees. If Orderic Vitalis' account is accurate, the Norman bishops only decreed that no layman should place a priest in a church or deprive him of it without the bishop's consent. The prohibition of investiture of bishops and abbots by the ruler was not mentioned. The canon on the suitability of the bishops was totally omitted.[19] When a short while later the controversy between Henry I and Anselm, archbishop of Canterbury, over the election and investiture of bishops broke out, the so-called *Norman Anonymous* was compiled in defence of the ruler. The author, who shows a great familiarity with current works of canon law and theology, believed in the nearly theocratic position of the Norman dukes and assigned the leadership of the church to the ruler.[20]

---

[18] Bates, *Normandy before 1066*, pp. 1–43, 226–35; Douglas, *William the Conqueror*, pp. 105–32, 317–45. Orderic commented that the duke failed to implement the canons published by the Norman bishops after the council of Clermont (1095), *Orderic*, ed. Chibnall, v, book ix, p. 25. This indicates that the Norman clergy expected the duke to play a leading part in ecclesiastical affairs.

[19] *Orderic*, ed. Chibnall, v, book ix, pp. 18–25. The modification of the decrees may already have begun at Clermont. The copy at Orderic's disposal featured two interesting variants from the canons decreed there. It repeated that bishops and abbots should not receive any ecclesiastical dignity from the hands of rulers or any other lay persons. But it lacked the canon forbidding bishops and priests to swear fealty to the king or any other lay person. It also contained a slightly different version of the canon concerning episcopal elections: those elected should already be priests, deacons, or subdeacons, and of legitimate birth, except in cases of great need or when papal permission had been granted, *Orderic*, ed. Chibnall, v, book ix, pp. 10–15, 18–21; Somerville, *Decreta Claromontensia*, p. 78, c. 20, pp. 83–98. These variants might be due to the hazards of manuscript transmission, but could also indicate the predilections of the note-taker at the council.

[20] The *Anonymous* was perhaps composed at Rouen. On this text, which has been much debated among scholars, see G. Williams, *The Norman Anonymous of 1100 A.D.* (Harvard Theological Studies xviii) (Cambridge, Mass., 1951); N. Cantor, *Church, Kingship, and Lay Investiture in England 1089–1135* (Princeton Studies in History x) (Princeton, 1958), pp. 174–97; R. Nineham, 'The So-called Anonymous of York', *Journal of Ecclesiastical History*, 14 (1963), 31–45; *Die Texte des Normannischen Anonymus*, ed. K. Pellens (Veröffentlichungen des Instituts für europäische Geschichte Mainz xlii. Abteilung für abendländische Religionsgeschichte) (Wiesbaden, 1966); K. Pellens, *Das Kirchendenken des Normannischen Anonymus* (Veröffentlichungen des Instituts für europäische Geschichte Mainz lxix. Abteilung für abendländische Religionsgeschichte) (Wiesbaden, 1973); W. Hartmann, 'Beziehungen des Normannischen Anonymus zu frühscholastischen Bildungszentren', *Deutsches Archiv für Erforschung des Mittelalters*, 31 (1975), 108–43; E. Kantorowicz, *The King's Two Bodies. A Study in Medieval Political Theology*, 7th edn (Princeton, 1997), pp. 42–61 (first published in 1957); Y. Sassier, *Royauté et idéologie au Moyen Age. Bas-Empire, monde franc, France (IVᵉ–XIIᵉ siècle)* (Paris, 2002), pp. 272–4.

In Normandy, therefore, the reformers' concept of an episcopal election had modified existing ideas only to a certain degree by 1140. The reform sharpened the awareness that episcopal sees were not for sale, and that a candidate should meet at least some standards, but in general it could not eradicate the belief that the duke had the right to participate in the election.

In Greater Anjou the impact of the Gregorian reform was much more direct than in Normandy. The difference between the two regions is nicely demonstrated by the way the canons of the council of Clermont were published. Whereas in Normandy the bishops published a modified and, for the duke, advantageous version, in Greater Anjou Pope Urban II himself held a synod at Tours in 1096, at which he repeated the statutes of the council.[21]

Canon law and the issues of the reform were increasingly discussed in the region in the second half of the eleventh century, and ecclesiastics participated actively in its spread. At Angers, pupils of Fulbert of Chartres had played an important part in the creation of the cathedral school, which counted among its scholars Geoffrey, later abbot of Ste Trinité of Vendôme and a radical supporter of the reform.[22] Local *scriptoria* responded to the demand for useful material on canon law. Three, probably four, copies of the Pseudo-Isidorian decretals originated in the region in the eleventh century.[23] A further copy, written in the tenth century at St Aubin, Angers, is perhaps identical with the copy mentioned in the mid-twelfth-century library catalogue of the same monastery.[24] Probably around 1100, St Aubin also owned copies of the letters of Fulbert and Ivo of Chartres, Burchard of Worms' *Decretum*, the canons of Gregory VII's synod of November 1078, and parts of the so-called Collection in Four Books, an anonymous canonical collection compiled in the second half of the eleventh century. Some of these copies were probably made at St Aubin itself.[25] At Le Mans, Bishop Hildebert de Lavardin (1096–1125), a supporter of the reform

---

[21] *Orderic*, ed. Chibnall, V, book IX, pp. 28–9. For the impact of the reform on the archdiocese of Tours, see also J.-M. Bienvenu, 'La réforme grégorienne dans l'archidiocèse de Tours', in G.-M. Oury (ed.), *Histoire religieuse de la Touraine* (Tours, 1975), pp. 75–91.

[22] Vezin, *Scriptoria d'Angers*, pp. 9–16.

[23] Williams, *Codices Pseudo-Isidoriani*, pp. 33–4, 41, 54–5, 69–70, 125–32; Vezin, *Scriptoria d'Angers*, p. 143 n. 1; on the making of the Pseudo-Isidorian decretals, see now K. Zechiel-Eckes, 'Ein Blick in Pseudoisidors Werkstatt. Studien zum Entstehungsprozess der Falschen Dekretalen', *Francia*, 28/1 (2001), 37–90.

[24] Williams, *Codices Pseudo-Isidoriani*, pp. 4–5; L.W. Jones, 'The Library of St Aubin's at Angers in the Twelfth Century', in L. W. Jones (ed.), *Classical and Mediaeval Studies in Honor of Edward Kennard Rand* (New York, 1938), pp. 143–61, p. 153.

[25] These works were in possession of St Aubin by the mid-twelfth century. However, since all of these copies appear to have been made or completed in the eleventh century, they may have been available at St Aubin by 1100. For the works attributed to St Aubin, see Vezin, *Scriptoria d'Angers*, pp. 32–4, 57–8, 263–5, 274–5, amending earlier research by S. Kuttner and R. Somerville, 'The

movement, promised the bishop of St David's, Wales, to send him the decretal collection he was compiling as soon as he had finished working on it.[26]

Like their Norman counterparts, then, the clergy in Greater Anjou was exposed to and interested in the reform ideas and the latest collections of canon law. However, they dealt differently with the reformers' concept of an episcopal election. In contrast to the Norman clergy, who refrained from questioning the duke's traditional role in the electoral process, influential sections of the Angevin clergy appear to have embraced, at least in theory, the idea of an election without the secular ruler.

THE CANON LAW OF EPISCOPAL ELECTIONS BETWEEN C. 1140 AND C. 1230

The formation of the cathedral chapter as electoral body

The exclusion of the *religiosi viri*

At the Second Lateran Council in 1139 Innocent II decreed that the canons of a cathedral church should not exclude *religiosi viri* from episcopal elections. Any election performed without their counsel and consent was invalid and the electors should be excommunicated.[27] Gratian and Stephen of Tournai took this decree into account.[28] Stephen commented that Innocent II had created new law, since before 1139 the right to elect had lain with the cathedral chapter. Stephen possibly had in mind Gratian's reference to the canons of two unidentified councils, one of which was allegedly held at Nicea, which stated that election by the clergy of the

---

So-called Canons of Nîmes', *Tijdschrift voor Rechtsgeschiedenis*, 38 (1970), 175–89, 187–8; Jones, 'The Library of St Aubin's at Angers in the Twelfth Century', pp. 151–3; J. Rambaud-Buhot, 'Un corpus inédit de droit canonique de la réforme carolingienne à la réforme grégorienne', in *Humanisme actif. Mélanges d'art et de littérature offerts à Julien Cain* (2 vols., Paris 1968), II, pp. 271–81, pp. 272, 279; for the parts copied from the Collection in Four Books, see *Diversorum patrum sententie sive collectio in LXXIV titulos digesta*, ed. J. Gilchrist (MIC series B: corpus collectionum I) (Vatican City, 1973), pp. xvii, lxi–lxii; for this collection in general, see Fournier and Le Bras, *Collections*, II, pp. 19–20, 235–40; J. Gilchrist, 'The Manuscripts of the Canonical Collection in Four Books', *Savigny KA*, 69 (1983), 64–120.

[26] 'Ven. Hildeberti epistolae', in *PL*, CLXXI, cols. 141–312, lib. II, no. 27. It is unknown whether Hildebert ever achieved the completion of his collection. The claim that Hildebert had at his disposal Ivo's *Decretum* and the *Panormia* has not yet been subjected to modern scrutiny, F. X. Barth, *Hildebert von Lavardin (1056–1133) und das kirchliche Stellenbesetzungsrecht* (Kirchenrechtliche Abhandlungen XXXIV–XXXVI) (Stuttgart, 1906), pp. 5–19.

[27] *Decreta*, ed. Alberigo et al., p. 203, c. 28.

[28] *Decretum Gratiani* D. 63 c. 34; *Summa des Stephanus*, ed. von Schulte, p. 89; Ganzer, 'Beschränkung', 36–7, 41; Müller, *Anteil*, pp. 31–2, 47. Rufinus and Johannes Faventinus believed that they should be consulted, *Rufinus*, ed. Singer, pp. 153, 155; Oxford, Bodleian Library, Canonici Miscellanea 429, fo. 37ra–b (Johannes Faventinus); Ganzer, 'Beschränkung', 40–1; Müller, *Anteil*, pp. 44–6, 49.

cathedral church was sufficient.[29] Stephen was only partially correct. Innocent's canon was certainly new in the sense that it was the first papal legislation to stipulate participation by the *religiosi viri*. But the pope did not intend to introduce a new practice. In France in the eleventh and early twelfth centuries *religiosi viri* participated in elections. At Angers in 1101, for instance, the cathedral chapter invited the bishops of the neighbouring dioceses, abbots, and other *religiosi viri* to take part in the election of a new bishop.[30] Towards the middle of the twelfth century, however, the role of the *religiosi* had become increasingly limited.[31] With his decree Innocent II intended to stop this development.

But his attempt was in vain. The formation of the cathedral chapter as the exclusive electoral body was irreversible and this was accepted by papal legislation and canonistic theory in the course of the second half of the twelfth century. The author of the *Summa Coloniensis* (*c.* 1169) still used Innocent's decree to show that the *religiosi* of the diocese should take part in the election,[32] but the contemporary *Summa Parisiensis* stated that an election was valid even if the *religiosi* had not been invited. Innocent's decree granted them no more than the possibility of protest against the election of an unsuitable candidate.[33] Even less significance was attributed to the decree in two other *Summae* of the French school, *Tractaturus magister* and *Et est sciendum*, both written in the 1180s. According to *Tractaturus magister* the participation of the *religiosi* had been abolished because of contrary contemporary custom.[34] *Et est sciendum* declared that the contemporary custom of cathedral chapters electing the bishop without the *religiosi* contradicted Innocent's decree, but that the decree itself was invalid, because the much older and therefore more weighty canon of the council of Nicea had constituted the cathedral chapter as the electoral body.[35]

---

[29] *Decretum Gratiani* D. 63 p.c. 34. Gratian based his argument on a canon listed in the *Brevatio canonum* compiled by Ferrandus between 523 and 546. Referring to this text Gratian named the councils as 'septimo concilio Nicensi et Macerensi'. As a result decretists referred to the canon of the council of Nicea in support of the argument that the vote of the cathedral chapter was sufficient. However, according to Ferrandus' latest editor, Charles Munier, the passage of this canon reads 'Concilio Septimunicensi. Concilio Macrianensi', *Conciliae Africae A.345–A.525*, ed. C. Munier (Corpus christianorum Series latina CCLIX) (Turnhout, 1974), p. 288, c. 11. In any case, the councils referred to are unknown, cf. Müller, *Anteil*, p. 32 n. 45.

[30] *Cartulaire de l'abbaye de la Trinité de Vendôme*, ed. C. Métais (5 vols., Paris 1893–1904), II, no. 401.

[31] Roland, *Chanoines*, pp. 36–43.

[32] *Summa Coloniensis*, ed. Fransen and Kuttner, I, pp. 130–1, c. 36. Klaus Ganzer probably overlooked this particular canon and thus comes to the misleading conclusion that the *Summa Coloniensis* considered the cathedral chapter as the exclusive electoral body, 'Beschränkung', 62.

[33] *Summa Parisiensis*, ed. McLaughlin, p. 56; Ganzer, 'Beschränkung', 61; Müller, *Anteil*, p. 52.

[34] Ganzer, 'Beschränkung', 64; Müller, *Anteil*, p. 72.

[35] Ganzer, 'Beschränkung', 64–5; Müller, *Anteil*, pp. 72–3.

The contemporary works of the canonists belonging to the Anglo-Norman school followed the same course, but attributed greater authority to Innocent's decree. The author of the *Summa Omnis qui iuste iudicat* (*c.* 1186) was undecided whether the decree was valid or not. He explained that some believed it was null, as the canon of Nicea was older. Others disagreed, because with the authority of a general synod the pope could override an earlier decision, especially when it had not dealt with a question of faith. The author himself believed that the *religiosi*, whose number should be limited to those of the episcopal city and its immediate vicinity, should take part in the election; their consent, however, was not necessary. In his discussion of whether members of exempt houses should take part in the election, he argued that they ought not to, because the principle *Quod omnes tangit, ab omnibus debet expediri* did not apply to them.[36] As to archiepiscopal elections, he declared that suffragans had no right to participate, unless the canons were divided or elected an unsuitable candidate.[37] Honorius, in his *Summa decretalium quaestionum* (1186–8) stated that the election of the cathedral chapter was valid without the consent of the *religiosi*, who, however, should not be excluded on purpose.[38] John of Tynemouth saw no difficulty in accepting Innocent's decree: *religiosi*, which included the parochial clergy, should take part in the election.[39]

Representatives of the Bolognese school of the late twelfth century still believed in the validity of Innocent's decision, even though they, too, started to adjust their position to electoral practice. Huguccio dealt in some detail with the composition of the electoral body. He distinguished

[36] Here, the author referred to an old legal principle which was revived in canon law in the third quarter of the twelfth century. For *Quod omnes tangit*, see Y. Congar, 'Quod omnes tangit ab omnibus tractari et approbari debet', *Revue historique du droit français et étranger*, 37 (1958), 210–51; G. Post, 'A romano-canonical maxim – quod omnes tangit – in Bracton', *Traditio*, 4 (1946), 197–251. Bernard of Pavia already referred to this principle in his *Summa de electione* (*c.* 1179). Avoiding the question of whether Innocent's decree prevailed over the canon of Nicea, he argued that all clergy who were accountable to the bishop, i.e. the clergy of the cathedral church, the abbots, and heads of other churches as well as the chaplains of the episcopal city, should participate in the election, since the leader should be elected by all those led by him. Bernard considered the cathedral chapters to be the principal voters. He states that if there was dissent between the canons and the other ecclesiastics, the chapter's decision prevailed, 'Summa de electione', in *Bernardi Papiensis*, ed. Laspeyres, pp. 309–10; Ganzer, 'Beschränkung', 72. Another work of the Bolognese school, the *Apparatus Ordinaturus magister*, also alludes to this principle in its discussion of the electoral body, when stating that 'omnibus preficiendum ab omnibus debere probari', Müller, *Anteil*, p. 99.

[37] Rouen, BM 743 (E 74), fos. 32vb, 33va; Ganzer, 'Beschränkung', 69–71. When commenting on the rights of the suffragan bishops, the author probably had in mind the dispute between the cathedral chapter of Canterbury and the suffragan bishops concerning their respective electoral rights during the election of 1184. For this election, see Foreville, *L'église et la royauté*, pp. 479–80.

[38] Zwettl, Stiftsbibliothek 162, fo. 197rb; Müller, *Anteil*, pp. 130–1; similar *Magistri Honorii Summa 'De iure canonico tractaturus'. I*, ed. Weigand et al., pp. 201–2.

[39] Cambridge, Gonville and Caius College 283/676, fos. 40vb, 42va; Müller, *Anteil*, pp. 132–3.

between the clergy of the episcopal city, who should take part in the discussion about a suitable candidate, but not in the election itself, and the *clerici religiosi*, i.e. the leading secular and regular clergy of the diocese, who should participate in the election. Huguccio was aware that elections often went ahead without the *clerici religiosi*. According to him, this remained unpunished because the papacy had silently accepted this custom.[40] Only a few years later, around 1192, in the first version of his *Apparatus Ius naturale*, Alanus Anglicus watered down the role of the *religiosi*, who according to him consisted of abbots, priors, and experienced chaplains. They had to be consulted in the process, but had no right to participate in the actual choice. If canons and *religiosi* differed in their opinion, the canons' decision prevailed. Only if the *religiosi* were excluded on purpose should the election be quashed.[41]

The Third Lateran Council did not explicitly deal with the question of the electoral body, but the canon stating that the opinion of the greater and wiser part of the chapter should prevail in all decisions made in churches[42] strongly suggests that the chapter was accepted as the exclusive electoral body. The 'silent acceptance' by the papacy of an election held without the participation of *religiosi viri* was ended by Innocent III in 1200 with the decretal *Dilecti filii clerici* (= *Cum ecclesia Sutrina*). The chapter of Sutri had elected a new bishop, but the ecclesiastics of the other collegiate churches of the city appealed against the election. They asserted that the canons had performed the election without them, even though they had the right to participate. The canons denied this, but an enquiry showed that the ecclesiastics had participated in the previous three elections. Innocent declared the election void and granted the ecclesiastics participation in a new election. However, he stated that on the grounds of *canonica statuta* – possibly Gratian's reference to the councils of Nicea and *Macarensi*[43] – the right to elect the bishop lay generally with the cathedral chapter, unless local custom assigned an electoral right to a third party. This was not the case at Sutri, because the participation in three previous elections was not sufficient to create such a custom. Therefore, while the ecclesiastics should participate in the present election, they had no such right in any future election at Sutri.[44] Thus Innocent III turned on its head the argument of a considerable number of canonists. In so doing he solved the problem that had troubled them: that overwhelmingly electoral practice was not in conformity with Innocent II's decree and that popes did not enforce this decree.

---

[40] Paris, BNF Lat. 3892, fos. 75ra, 76ra, 79ra; Ganzer, 'Beschränkung', 50–2.
[41] Paris, BNF Lat. 3909, fos. 12vb, 13rb; Ganzer, 'Beschränkung', 55–6; Müller, *Anteil*, pp. 139–41.
[42] *Decreta*, ed. Alberigo et al., pp. 212–13, c. 3.   [43] See supra, pp. 26–7.
[44] *Register Innocenz' III.*, II, no. 271 (283) [= Potthast, I, no. 947].

Innocent III's decretal had an immediate impact on canonistic thought. It was quickly incorporated into decretal collections, among which was the collection at Rouen,[45] and canonists made it an integral part of their discussion of the electoral body. An exception was the French *Apparatus Ecce vicit leo* (1202–10). It took notice of Innocent III's decretal, but when it explained that an election could be valid without the participation of the *religiosi* it still referred to the council of Nicea, custom, and the silent approval of the popes. According to *Ecce vicit leo* the consent of the *religiosi* was required, and if they asked to participate in the election, they ought not to be excluded.[46] In contrast, the nearly contemporary and closely related *Apparatus Animal est substantia* (1206–10) was greatly influenced by Innocent III's decretal, stating that according to the *ius commune* the cathedral chapter elected the bishop.[47] Another French *Apparatus, Set dic quod in omnibus* (1202–10), stated the same: the cathedral chapter elected the bishop; the regulations of the Second Lateran Council were superseded by Innocent III's decretal.[48]

The Bolognese school was also influenced by Innocent III's decretal. In his second recension of *Ius naturale* (after 1204) Alanus modified his earlier statement on the electoral body. Referring to the decretal, he explained that while, according to the *ius regulare*, the cathedral chapter performed the election, this could be disregarded if local custom determined a different electoral body.[49] Laurentius Hispanus and Johannes Teutonicus tried to create a theory accommodating both ideas, declaring that the chapter was the electoral body, but the *religiosi* should be asked for their counsel, even though their dissent did not invalidate the election.[50] Laurentius' and Johannes' attempts to secure at least some official influence for *religiosi* were fruitless. The Fourth Lateran Council referred to the cathedral chapter as the sole electoral body[51] and later canonists considered the participation of *religiosi* as exceptional. Raymond de Peñafort, for instance, believed that *religiosi* who happened to be present at the location at which an election was due should be invited to participate. However,

---

[45] *3 Comp.* 2.5.1 = *X* 2.12.3 = *2 Rot.* 1.4.4 (2b), Paris, BNF Lat. 3922A, fo. 210va; for its appearance in other collections, see *Register Innocenz' III.*, II, no. 271 (283). For the decretal collection at Rouen, see infra, pp. 61–2.

[46] Paris, BNF N. A. Lat. 1576, fo. 106rb; Ganzer, 'Beschränkung', 66–7; Müller, *Anteil*, pp. 160–1.

[47] Bamberg, Staatsbibliothek Can.42, fo. 44va; Ganzer, 'Beschränkung', 69; Müller, *Anteil*, p. 163.

[48] Müller, *Anteil*, p. 169.

[49] Paris, Bibliothèque Mazarine 1318, fo. 70va; Müller, *Anteil*, p. 143.

[50] Vatican City, BAV Vat. Reg. Lat. 977, fos. 46va, 47va, 49rb (Laurentius, *Glossa Palatina*); Bamberg, Staatsbibliothek Can.13, fos. 40ra, 41vab (Johannes, *Glossa ordinaria*); Ganzer, 'Beschränkung', 56–60; Müller, *Anteil*, pp. 173–4, 185–6.

[51] 'Concilii quarti Lateranensis constitutiones', in *Constitutiones concilii quarti Lateranensis*, ed. García y García, pp. 1–118, pp. 70–1, c. 24.

the chapter's opinion always prevailed, as the *religiosi* were not part of the electoral body.[52]

The exclusion of the prince

In D. 63 of the *Decretum* Gratian assembled the numerous texts dealing with the participation of the ruler in episcopal elections. Having contrasted the canons prohibiting their participation with those allowing it, Gratian came to the conclusion that the election had to be made by the clergy alone. The people and the princes had no right to participate in the election, but their consent was required after the election had been completed.[53]

Canonists of the early Bolognese school (*c.* 1145 – *c.* 1175) were slightly more precise than Gratian in defining the prince's role: Stephen of Tournai accepted that laymen could participate in an election in order to prevent any machinations.[54] Together with Rufinus and Johannes Faventinus, he believed the *arbitrium* and the *consilium* of the *honorabiles* were necessary.[55] Most notably, Johannes Faventinus attributed electoral right also to founders and benefactors of collegiate churches, including cathedral churches. For that reason princes, who in principle had no electoral rights, might often take part in elections.[56]

Similar opinions can still be found among the second generation of canonists belonging to the Bolognese school (*c.* 1175 – *c.* 1192). On principle they refused princes an electoral right,[57] but their most prominent representative Huguccio did not exclude them. He believed that patrons had an electoral right and since cathedral churches could have patrons, they could participate in episcopal elections. Furthermore he repeated Rufinus' argument that the *maiores* had to be consulted in the

---

[52] *Summa iuris*, ed. Rius Serra, pp. 120–1; *S. Raimundus de Pennaforte: Summa de iure canonico*, ed. Ochoa and Diez, col. 176. For the opinion of other canonists of the thirteenth century, see Ganzer, 'Beschränkung', 78–82.

[53] *Decretum Gratiani* D. 63; Müller, *Anteil*, pp. 25–34. The papal electoral decree of 1059 is not among these canons. Evidently, Gratian, who incorporated this decree in the section on the hierarchy of the ecclesiastical offices (D. 23 c. 1), did not attach great significance to its clause on the ruler's role in papal elections. Later canonists occasionally included the papal electoral decree in their discussion of (episcopal) elections, but overall the decree did not play a central role in their arguments concerning the participation of the ruler, Müller, *Anteil*, passim; for the papal electoral decree of 1059 and the almost endless debate on the significance of the so-called *Königsparagraph*, see Jasper, *Das Papstwahldekret von 1059*, pp. 3–9.

[54] *Summa des Stephanus*, ed. von Schulte, pp. 89–90; Müller, *Anteil*, pp. 47, 51.

[55] *Summa des Stephanus*, ed. von Schulte, p. 89; *Rufinus*, ed. Singer, p. 155; Oxford, Bodleian Library Canonici Miscellanea 429, fo. 37rb (Johannes Faventinus); Müller, *Anteil*, pp. 45, 49, 51.

[56] Oxford, Bodleian Library Canonici Miscellanea 429, fo. 37rb; Müller, *Anteil*, pp. 49, 51.

[57] Müller, *Anteil*, pp. 78–119. Cardinal Laborans, however, believed that princes should not be excluded from the electoral process. Yet they should not influence the clergy's decision, ibid., pp. 92, 119.

31

electoral process; electoral right could also be conferred on laymen by the electoral body.[58]

At least four papal decretals significantly contributed to reshaping the thought of the Bolognese school in the early thirteenth century. The decretal *Nobis fuit* issued by Clement III in 1190 determined that in a church belonging to a religious community (*conventualis ecclesia*) patrons had no active electoral right unless through their jurisdiction,[59] that is through publicly known rights valid for a particular territory.[60] Instead, the patron should be asked for his consent after the election had taken place.[61] Thus Clement's decretal allowed all those patrons, who through long-established custom or a specifically acquired privilege held an electoral right, to continue their participation in elections. *Nobis fuit* concerned the *ius patronatus*, not episcopal elections, but canonists, familiar with Huguccio's doctrine that cathedral churches could also have patrons, considered the decretal to present a model that should analogously apply to episcopal elections. This was the line taken by Alanus Anglicus in his second recension of his *Apparatus Ius naturale*. On the grounds of *Nobis fuit*, Alanus refuted Huguccio's opinion. He stated that patrons now had the right to participate in an election only through custom or if they had acquired a special privilege.[62] Alanus' pupil, William of Gascony, followed this opinion, whilst admitting that some canonists attributed electoral right to those who had founded and enriched churches.[63] But the mainstream of the Bolognese school had by then completely accepted the new doctrine. Laurentius Hispanus' *Glossa Palatina*, written between 1210 and 1214, explicitly refuted Huguccio's interpretation and argued that patrons could have an electoral right only on grounds of jurisdiction and custom.[64] Johannes Teutonicus hardly differed from his colleagues in arguing that only custom, not donation, could assign an electoral right to the patron. From his point of view, all patrons were equal, regardless of how much they donated to a church.[65] Both Laurentius and Johannes, however, believed that laymen could specifically be invited to participate in an election.[66]

---

[58] Paris, BNF Lat. 3892, fos. 74vb–75ra, 78ra; Müller, *Anteil*, pp. 112–13, 115.

[59] *2 Comp.* 3.24.2 = X 3.38.25 [= Jaffé, II, no. 16466; *WH* 663abc].

[60] J. Avril, 'Sur l'emploi de jurisdictio au moyen âge (XIIe–XIII^e^s.)', *Savigny KA*, 83 (1997), 272–82.

[61] *2 Comp.* 3.24.2 = X 3.38.25 [= Jaffé, II, no. 16466; *WH* 663abc].

[62] Paris, Bibliothèque Mazarine 1318, fo. 70rb; Müller, *Anteil*, pp. 143–5.

[63] Müller, *Anteil*, pp. 152–3.

[64] Vatican City, BAV Vat. Reg. Lat. 977, fo. 46vb; Müller, *Anteil*, pp. 173–5.

[65] Bamberg, Staatsbibliothek Can.13, fo. 39rb; Müller, *Anteil*, pp. 184–5.

[66] Vatican City, BAV Vat. Reg. Lat. 977, fo. 47ra (Laurentius, *Glossa Palatina*); Bamberg, Staatsbibliothek Can.13, fo. 39va (Johannes, *Glossa ordinaria*); Müller, *Anteil*, pp. 175, 185.

Two other decretals were of significance in reducing the prince's influence in episcopal elections. *Cum terra*, issued by Celestine III in 1191/2, and *Quod sicut*, issued by Innocent III in 1202, both tackled the timing of princely intervention. According to them the prince should not be asked for his consent after the nomination of the candidate(s), but after the election had taken place.[67] Thus here, as in *Nobis fuit*, the aim was not to exclude the prince from the electoral process altogether, but to redefine his position. He should not any longer be actively involved in the selection of the candidate.

The validity of *Nobis fuit*, *Cum terra*, and *Quod sicut*, however, was limited by exceptions. *Nobis fuit* itself provided one of them in the patron's jurisdiction: that is, a long-established custom or a specifically acquired privilege permitted the patron to take part in the election of a particular church. A second exception was provided by the decretal *Quia requisistis* issued by Alexander III and widely spread as part of *Compilatio secunda*. In this decretal Alexander gave permission to a chapter which feared to hold the election without King Henry II's consent (*assensus*), to approach the king and choose a suitable person together with him.[68] Despite the fact that this was precisely the order of procedure that the two subsequent decretals *Cum terra* and *Quod sicut* forbade – the latter even dealt with an election in the Angevin realm – canonists like Johannes Teutonicus recognised *Quia requisistis* as an exception to the rule, which could be accepted if there was little chance of holding the election otherwise.[69]

Bolognese views on the electoral rights of a patron or prince were to a certain extent summarised by Raymond de Peñafort's *Summa iuris* (1216– 22). Canon twenty-five of the Fourth Lateran Council had made clear that any ecclesiastical election conducted by the secular power was invalid.[70]

---

[67] *2 Comp.* 1.3.6 = *X* 1.6.14 [= Jaffé, II, no. 17656; *WH* 319]; *Register Innocenz' III.*, v, no. 82 (83) = *3 Comp.* 1.6.13 = *X* 1.6.28 [= Potthast, I, no. 1735].

[68] *2 Comp.* 1.3.2 [= Jaffé, II, no. 13728; *WH* 810]. It also appears in Antonio Agustin's edition of *Compilatio prima*, *1 Comp.* 1.4.5, 'Antiquarum collectionum decretalium. Liber primus. Brevarium extra Bernardi praepositi Papiensis', in *Antiquae collectiones*, ed. Agustin, pp. 1–149, p. 4. The canon did not appear in the manuscripts of *Compilatio prima* consulted by Emil Friedberg. According to Friedberg, Agustin found this canon only in a Barcelonese manuscript, *1 Comp.* 1.4.5 and note. The decretal was, however, part of the collection *Francofortana*, Fr. 10.4, Paris, BNF Lat. 3922A, fo. 178va, cf. infra, p. 81; I would like to thank PD Gisela Drossbach for her information that the decretal appears also in the other copies of the *Francofortana*. I have been unable to identify the election concerned.

[69] Müller, *Anteil*, p. 185; the reference to *Quia requisistis* is omitted in Bamberg, Staatsbibliothek Can.13, fo. 40rb. An opinion similar to Johannes' is found in an anonymous *Apparatus* preserved in Madrid; Müller, *Anteil*, pp. 176–81, esp. p. 179. Another canonist, Paulus Ungarus, also tolerated *Quia requisistis* under specific circumstances, but made clear that any custom that violated the liberty of the church was invalid, ibid., p. 196.

[70] 'Concilii quarti Lateranensis constitutiones', in *Constitutiones concilii quarti Lateranensis*, ed. García y García, p. 71.

This was also the basic principle in Raymond's work. However he allowed for four exceptions: (A) if there was fear that the election might cause a great scandal; (B) if the patron had acquired a special privilege; (C) if the patron had the customary right; (D) if he had acquired the electoral right because he had founded the church. Raymond admitted that other canonists believed the last two exceptions to be invalid. Once the election was completed, the consent of the patron, the prince, and the people should be requested. Yet, even without the people's consent, the election was valid.[71]

The first generation of canonists belonging to the French school (*c.* 1165 – *c.* 1190) allowed patrons the right to participate in elections, but denied that this affected episcopal elections, since cathedral churches did not have patrons, because they belonged to the community or, as the *Summa Permissio quedam* argued, because cathedral churches presided over other churches and patrons were only allowed to take part in elections at subordinate churches.[72] As to the participation of princes, however, opinions diverged. The *Summa Coloniensis* (*c.* 1169) stated that the emperor should not take part in an election proper. Although it stipulated that his consent should be asked for before the bishop's consecration, it attached little weight to disapproval.[73] Sighard of Cremona, writing between 1179 and 1181, came to no conclusion on lay participation,[74] and Peter of Blois, writing between 1175 and 1190, believed that laymen needed to be specially invited.[75] Other works were more favourable towards princes. The *Summa Parisiensis* (*c.* 1165–70) emphasised that the prince's consent, the *voluntas principis*, had to be received. The emperor enjoyed this right particularly in churches where he held the *regalia*.[76] The consent of the prince was also demanded by the *Summa Antiquitate et tempore* (after 1170).[77] The author of another French *Summa, Tractaturus magister* (1182–5), believed that in some churches which had been founded by a prince, the prince retained some electoral rights. The author abstained, however, from defining these rights.[78]

The works of the second generation of the French school (*c.* 1200 – *c.* 1215) are more consistent in minimising the participation of laymen in elections. The *Apparatus Ecce vicit leo* (1202–10) allowed it if the patron had

---

[71] *Summa iuris*, ed. Rius Serra, pp. 119–20; *S. Raimundus de Pennaforte: Summa de iure canonico*, ed. Ochoa and Diez, cols. 174–6; Müller, *Anteil*, pp. 198–9.

[72] Müller, *Anteil*, pp. 52–77; for the *Summa Permissio quedam*, see ibid., p. 75.

[73] *Summa Coloniensis*, ed. Fransen and Kuttner, I, pp. 121–4; Müller, *Anteil*, pp. 54–8.

[74] Müller, *Anteil*, pp. 66–9.

[75] *Speculum*, ed. Reimarus, p. 94, c. 51; Müller, *Anteil*, pp. 64–5. For the date, see R.W. Southern, 'The Necessity of Two Peter of Blois', in L. Smith and B. Ward (eds.), *Intellectual Life in the Middle Ages. Essays Presented to Margaret Gibson* (London, 1992), pp. 103–18, p. 110 n. 12.

[76] *Summa Parisiensis*, ed. McLaughlin pp. 54–6; Müller, *Anteil*, pp. 52–3.

[77] Müller, *Anteil*, pp. 58–61. [78] Ibid., pp. 71–2.

received a special privilege.[79] *Apparatus Animal est substantia* (1206–10) repeated this, adding that princes could be invited to guarantee a proper and peaceful electoral procedure.[80]

The prince's position is particularly strong in the works of Anglo-Norman canonists. The *Summa Omnis qui iuste iudicat* (c. 1186) used the already familiar concept that the founder and benefactor of a cathedral church was to be admitted among the electors.[81] Honorius declared in his *Summa decretalium quaestionum* (1186–8) that the custom of some cathedral churches gave the prince the right to participate in the election.[82] Within the next decade John of Tynemouth, although opposed to the idea that patrons and benefactors of episcopal churches had the right to participate in the election, declared that the custom in some parts of England required the prince's consent.[83] Other works were more hesitant in counting the ruler among the electors: Honorius qualified his view in his *Summa De iure canonico tractaturus* (1188–90) arguing that the prince's consent should be given to an election, even though it was not necessary.[84] Richard de Mores' position was similar. In his work *Summa quaestionum* (1186–7) he specified that laymen ought to be invited to the election to give their consent, but that the election was still valid, even if they did not participate.[85] In his *Apparatus* to *Compilatio prima* he made clear that the shallow voices of the people (*vane voces populi*) should not be heard in the selection process. Ten years later, in his *Distinctiones*, he differentiated between the different layers of lay society and declared that the *maiores* among the laymen should be invited to give their consent to the decision taken by the electoral body.[86] By the beginning of the thirteenth century the new definition of the ruler's role in episcopal elections had reached the Anglo-Norman school. The *Summa Prima primi uxor Ade* (1200–10) declared that princes might have had the right to take part in elections in past times, but more recent laws had annulled that right. The author allowed the participation of laymen, and hence princes, only if they had been invited to attend to give advice or

[79] Paris, BNF N. A. Lat. 1576, fos. 101ra–b, 103va, 104vb; Müller, *Anteil*, pp. 157–60.
[80] Bamberg, Staatsbibliothek Can.42, fos. 42vb–43ra, 43va, 44ra; Müller, *Anteil*, pp. 162–7.
[81] Rouen, BM 743 (E 74), fo. 32rb; Müller, *Anteil*, p. 123.
[82] Zwettl, Stiftsbibliothek 162, fo. 197rb; Müller, *Anteil*, p. 130.
[83] Cambridge, Gonville and Caius College 283/676, fos. 40rb, 41ra; Müller, *Anteil*, pp. 131–2.
[84] *Magistri Honorii Summa 'De iure canonico tractaturus'*. I, ed. Weigand et al. , pp. 195–6; Müller, *Anteil*, pp. 125–6.
[85] Zwettl, Stiftsbibliothek 162, fo. 148rb; Müller, *Anteil*, p. 133.
[86] Avranches, BM 149 (*Apparatus to Compilatio prima*), fo. 8ra; Müller, *Anteil*, p. 134; Silano, 'The Distinctiones Decretorum of Ricardus Anglicus: An Edition', p. 197; Müller, *Anteil*, p. 134. Both works are counted among the writings of the Bolognese school, Müller, *Anteil*, p. 133 n. 73.

to fight off heretics. Referring to *Nobis fuit* he believed that the patron should give his consent only after an election had been completed.[87]

Three significant conclusions can be drawn from the foregoing analysis. First, it is notable that up to the last quarter of the twelfth century representatives from all schools admitted the prince among the electors. His participation was justified by long-established custom, by the prince's role as patron of cathedral churches, or by his capacity to guarantee a fair and peaceful election. Second, the particularly strong position of the prince in Anglo-Norman works is apparent. Third, in all traditions, from the 1190s onwards, princely consent was delayed until after the election had taken place. Papal legislation, which itself may well have been influenced by, for example, the *Summa Coloniensis*, decreed that the prince's consent was not required after the nomination, that is during the process of the selection of candidates. If it was deemed necessary, he could be asked for his consent after the election had taken place. This became the consensus among canonists from all schools, even though the Bolognese school in the early thirteenth century still accepted some exceptions allowing the prince to participate in an election. The prince no longer counted among the electors. This development reached its logical conclusion during the pontificate of Gregory IX. In the decretal *Massana ecclesia* he declared that laymen must not take part in episcopal elections. Any election where they did take part would be invalid, and any contrary custom was corrupt.[88]

Absent canons

Each canon of a cathedral chapter had the right to vote and each vote carried the same weight. Innocent III stressed this principle in the famous decretal *Venerabilem* issued in 1202. The disregard of one elector was a greater obstacle to a correct electoral procedure than the opposition of many.[89] This, however, caused a major practical problem, since for a variety of reasons (studies, papal or royal service, chapter business, etc.) an increasing number of canons were absent from the cathedral church. In his *Summa decretalium*, written in the 1190s, Bernard of Pavia considered the proposition that there was a distinction between those who were absent on church business – who should be summoned and waited for – and those who were absent for their own business – who should not be

---

[87] Müller, *Anteil*, p. 136.

[88] *Les registres de Grégoire IX*, ed. Auvray, I, no. 695 = X 1.5.56 [= Potthast, I, no. 9545].

[89] *3 Comp.* 1.6.19 = X 1.6.34 [= Potthast, I, no. 1653]; cf. the use of this argument by Raymond de Peñafort to reason that all those who had the right to elect and could comfortably be reached should be called together for the election, *Summa iuris*, ed. Rius Serra, p. 121; *S. Raimundus de Pennaforte: Summa de iure canonico*, ed. Ochoa and Diez, cols. 178–9.

waited for. Although not opposed to this proposition, Bernard considered another solution more appropriate: the canons who were absent with the licence of the chapter should be summoned and waited for, unless they were so far away that they could not be recalled without endangering the church in the meantime. Those who were absent without such a licence had forfeited their right to take part in election.[90]

A number of papal decisions assisted later canonists in discussing the problem. According to Gregory I's decretal *Quanto*, which was collected in Gratian's *Decretum*, the distance between Milan and Genoa was within the limits requiring the recall of a canon.[91] Innocent III's decretal *Cum inter* (1199) pointed out that local custom played an important role in defining the prescribed distance. In the case of the church of Capua, Palermo was outside the limits allowed for by local custom. Innocent reasoned that too long a delay of an election was dangerous and should therefore be avoided.[92] In his interpretation of this decretal, Johannes Teutonicus pointed out that custom could define not only what was too far, but also what was a tolerable distance.[93] In another decretal, *Coram*, Innocent III declared that all those from within the province should be called to the election, but it is unclear whether he meant the diocese or the ecclesiastical province.[94] The pope was particularly concerned that those who could attend the election without facing great obstacles should do so. This was expressed in his decretal *Quod sicut* issued in 1202[95] and reiterated in the otherwise vague statement of canon twenty-four of the Fourth Lateran Council, *Quia propter*.[96] In their discussion of this matter leading canonists such as Johannes Teutonicus came to the conclusion that *Coram* constituted the new law.[97] But *Coram* was not the final decision. In 1231, Gregory IX issued the decretal *In Genesi legitur* ending the electoral dispute at Bayeux. One of the parties had argued that a canon living near Lyons

---

[90] 'Summa de electione', in *Bernardi Papiensis*, ed. Laspeyres, pp. 314–15.

[91] *Decretum Gratiani* D. 63 c. 10.

[92] *Register Innocenz' III.*, II, no. 181 (190) = *3 Comp.* 1.6.3 = *X* 1.6.18 [= Potthast, I, no. 852].

[93] 'Joannis Teutonici Apparatus in concilium quartum Lateranense', in *Constitutiones concilii quarti Lateranensis*, ed. García y García, p. 212.

[94] *4 Comp.* 1.3.1 = *X* 1.6.35 [= Potthast, I, no. 5027].

[95] *Register Innocenz' III.*, V, no. 82 (83) = *3 Comp.* 1.6.13 = *X* 1.6.28 [= Potthast, I, no. 1735].

[96] 'Concilii quarti Lateranensis constitutiones', in *Constitutiones concilii quarti Lateranensis*, ed. García y García, pp. 70–1.

[97] *Johannis Teutonici*, ed. Pennington, pp. 46–7; 'Apparatus glossarum in Compilationem quartam', in *Antiquae collectiones*, ed. Agustin, p. 799. Tancred followed his opinion in his commentary on *3 Comp.* 1.6.3, Vatican City, BAV Vat. Lat. 1377, fo. 159va. In his commentary on *3 Comp.* 1.6.3 Vincentius Hispanus possibly also referred to *Coram* when stating 'crederem autem eos vocandos si sunt in provintia eadem [manuscript reads provintiam eandem] et ita video scribere dominum Innocentium in causa Reginorum canonicorum', Karlsruhe, Badische Landesbibliothek Aug. per. 40 (formerly Aug. XL), fo. 237vb.

had to be summoned to the election at Bayeux, because according to the custom of the Gallican church canons must be summoned *de toto regno Francie*.[98] Gregory IX accepted this argument, and Raymond de Peñafort incorporated the decretal in the *Liber extra*;[99] thus the custom of the Gallican church became canon law.

Canons aware of the necessity to assemble the entire chapter could use this as a weapon to prevent the election of an unwelcome candidate by walking out of the electoral assembly. Innocent III's decretal *Cum olim nobis* issued in 1200 dealt with this problem. It stated that if members of the chapter had left the electoral assembly and refused to return, even though they had been recalled, the electoral right lay with the remaining party.[100] In his comment on *Cum olim nobis*, Johannes Teutonicus refined Innocent's argument. Referring to D. 63 c. 11 he stated that canons had to be recalled not once, but several times.[101]

Voting procedures

In high medieval thought the rightful choice of a leader came through divine inspiration, for the authority to rule was given by God. Such inspiration showed in a unanimous election.[102] Far into the twelfth century unanimity was considered to be an essential part of episcopal selections. But unanimity was often impossible to achieve. Several expedients were applied to overcome this problem. To achieve a unanimous result, dissenting voices were either integrated, that is they changed their minds and joined the majority, or they were excluded, that is they were asked to depart from the place of the election thereby ceasing to be electors, or they were regarded as insignificant.[103]

---

[98] *Les registres de Grégoire IX*, ed. Auvray, I, no. 741.   [99] X 1.6.55 [= Potthast, I, no. 9544].
[100] *Register Innocenz' III.*, II, no. 265 (277) = *3 Comp.* 1.6.4 = X 1.6.19 = *2 Rot.* 1.4.3 (2a), Paris, BNF Lat. 3922A, fo. 210va [= Potthast, I, no. 949].
[101] *Johannis Teutonici*, ed. Pennington, p. 50.
[102] A. Esmein, 'L'unanimité et la majorité', in *Mélanges Fitting* (2 vols., Montpellier, 1907–8), I, pp. 357–82, pp. 359–63; P. Grossi, 'Unanimitas. Alle origine del concetto di persona giuridica nel diritto canonico', *Annali di storia del diritto*, 2 (1958), pp. 229–331, pp. 256–314; J. Gaudemet, 'Unanimité et majorité (observations sur quelques études récents)', in *Etudes historiques à la mémoire de Noël Didier* (Paris, 1960), pp. 149–62, pp. 152–6; W. Maleczek, 'Abstimmungsarten. Wie kommt man zu einem vernünftigen Wahlergebnis?', in Schneider and Zimmermann (eds.), *Wahlen und Wählen*, pp. 79–134, pp. 81–2; Thier, 'Hierarchie und Autonomie', pp. 133–42.
[103] Maleczek, 'Abstimmungsarten', pp. 95–6; K. Ganzer, 'Das Mehrheitsprinzip bei den kirchlichen Wahlen des Mittelalters', *Theologische Quartalschrift*, 147 (1967), 60–87, 64–7. Klaus Ganzer summarises this article in his *Unanimitas, maioritas, pars sanior. Zur repräsentativen Willensbildung von Gemeinschaften in der kirchlichen Rechtsgeschichte* (Akademie der Wissenschaften und der Literatur. Abhandlungen der geistes- und sozialwissenschaftlichen Klasse, Jahrgang 2000, IX) (Stuttgart, 2000), pp. 1–13. The *Summa Coloniensis* (c. 1169) still emphasised that 'modus autem episcopalis electionis is esse debet ut unanimiter et sollempniter fiat', *Summa Coloniensis*, ed. Fransen and Kuttner, p. 123, c. 39.

In the course of the twelfth century the ancient concepts of *sanioritas et maioritas* were increasingly accepted as sufficient criteria to decide episcopal elections.[104] This moderated the significance of unanimity in the selection process from the imperative to the optional. Canon sixteen of the Third Lateran Council in 1179 was a landmark in this development, stating that all decisions in the churches had to be taken according to the will of the *plures et se[a]niores fratres*.[105] The decision of *sanior et maior pars* replaced unanimity as the normative way to select a candidate. Thirty-six years later, canon twenty-four of Lateran IV officially declared election by divine inspiration as an exceptional case which was available in addition to the usual forms, scrutiny and compromise.[106] The replacement of unanimity by the will of the *sanior et maior pars* was part of the process which slowly shaped a clear nominal distinction between selection and election. In the thirteenth century, this process culminated in the so-called *electio communis*, i.e. the election of the bishops in two steps: the first step, the *nominatio*, served to select the elect. The second step, the *electio*, was the constitutional act. In the name of the electoral body one of its members performed the candidate's solemn election to which all the others consented.[107] In this last act the principle of unanimity was clearly recognisable; however, its role in the selection of the candidate had ceased. For this, two other methods were used: scrutiny and compromise.

According to *Quia propter* a scrutiny was performed in the following way: the chapter nominated three of its members to ascertain individually and secretly the vote of each elector, to write the votes down, and to publish them. They then had to compare the votes and to nominate the candidate who had received either all or those of the greater and wiser part of the chapter.[108] The scrutiny was first recorded at papal elections in the middle of the twelfth century, but seems to have been in use some time before that.[109]

---

[104] Infra, pp. 41–8.
[105] *Decreta*, ed. Alberigo et al., pp. 219–20. The manuscript tradition offers both *seniores* and *saniores*. Before and after 1179 *sanior* was the term usually employed in the context of determining the majority in an election, cf. infra, pp. 41–8. It is therefore likely that in this particular case *senior* meant the same as *sanior*.
[106] 'Concilii quarti Lateranensis constitutiones', in *Constitutiones concilii quarti Lateranensis*, ed. García y García, pp. 70–1, c. 24. However, it should be noted that the idea of convincing other members of the electoral body to adhere to the opinion of the majority was still applied in elections in the late thirteenth century, Maleczek, 'Abstimmungsarten', pp. 95–6.
[107] A. von Wretschko, 'Die Electio communis bei den kirchlichen Wahlen im Mittelalter', *Zeitschrift für Kirchenrecht*, 11 (1901), 321–92.
[108] 'Concilii quarti Lateranensis constitutiones', in *Constitutiones concilii quarti Lateranensis*, ed. García y García, pp. 70–1, c.24.
[109] Maleczek, 'Abstimmungsarten', pp. 114–15.

An election through compromise meant that the chapter commissioned a small, variable number of suitable men, often members of the chapter, to elect the bishop in its place. Instances of the use of compromise occasionally appeared in the early middle ages, but it became frequent only from the beginning of the twelfth century.[110]

The increasing appearance of scrutiny and compromise was noticed by canonists. In his *Summa de electione* (c. 1179) Bernard of Pavia also talked of a method that could be characterised as a mixture of scrutiny and compromise. The electoral body selected men who counted the votes of the electors. These men then examined the suitability of the candidate who had been chosen by all or at least by the majority. If he was suitable they elected him.[111] This 'hybrid' indicates that there was not a single universally recognised set of rules regulating voting procedures. On the theoretical side of the problem, Bernhard's *Summa de electione* can be interpreted as the first attempt to provide such rules. Their lack was a source of great inconvenience. Johannes Teutonicus stated that some canons would elect their candidate and then immediately appeal to the papal court to prevent any other election.[112] It was to eradicate these uncertainties and abuses of canon law that the canon *Quia propter* was promulgated at the Fourth Lateran Council. An election should be held only by scrutiny, by compromise, or by divine inspiration.[113] With this canon, commented Johannes Teutonicus, the door to discord and hairsplitting had been closed.[114]

But his view was too optimistic. Canon twenty-four determined the three admissible voting procedures, but these were not yet fully developed and thus could be variously interpreted. In 1208, for example, Robert d'Ablèges, bishop of Bayeux, confronted Innocent III with the following problem: a chapter had chosen seven *compromissarii* to elect their dean. One of the *compromissarii* had received three votes. Was he to become the new dean? Innocent III responded that, if he was a suitable person and consented to his election, he should be. The pope's

---

[110] Ibid., pp. 108–12.
[111] 'Summa de electione', in *Bernardi Papiensis*, ed. Laspeyres, pp. 317–18. This method was still recognised by Pope Boniface VIII, Schimmelpfennig, 'Papst- und Bischofswahlen seit dem 12. Jahrhundert', p. 193.
[112] 'Joannis Teutonici Apparatus in concilium quartum Lateranense', in *Constitutiones concilii quarti Lateranensis*, ed. García y García, p. 212. Johannes had in mind the case which had been decided by Alexander III through the decretal *Consideravimus*. An incident like this happened at Bayeux in 1205, see infra, pp. 138–9.
[113] 'Concilii quarti Lateranensis constitutiones', in *Constitutiones concilii quarti Lateranensis*, ed. García y García, pp. 70–1, c. 24.
[114] 'Joannis Teutonici Apparatus in concilium quartum Lateranense', in *Constitutiones concilii quarti Lateranensis*, ed. García y García, p. 212.

solution, which made its way into *Compilatio tertia* and subsequently into the *Liber extra*,[115] was considered highly significant by the canonists of the early thirteenth century. According to them it implied that in the circumstances at Bayeux the vote of the elected could decide his election. This meant an important modification of the canonistic principle that no one could receive an office through his own action.[116] The analysis of the elections taking place in Normandy after 1215 will show that there were further problems hampering the smooth and peaceful course of an election. However, despite its shortcomings in elaborating and precisely defining the individual voting procedures, *Quia propter* was an enormous step forward. Episcopal elections became increasingly institutionalised.

Sanior et maior pars

The previous section has shown the importance of the concept of unanimity for episcopal elections in general and its influence on voting procedures into the twelfth century. Yet, concepts of majority and minority already existed along with unanimity. In fact expedients for dealing with dissenting voices in elections had been developed very early. Canon six of the council of Nicea (325), for instance, decreed that the decision of the numerical majority (*plurimorum*) should stand, while the opposition of two or three could be ignored.[117]

Sanioritas, i.e. moral superiority, as a means to decide split elections was also recognised a long time before the twelfth century. It was applied both to the candidate and to the electoral body. Gratian included in his work the famous decretal of Pope Leo the Great who had decided that if the election was split the candidate should be chosen 'qui maioribus iuvatur studiis et meritis'.[118] As to the electoral body, Benedict of Nursia's regulation of abbatial elections was of great influence. He had decreed that an abbot should be elected either by the unanimous vote of the community or by the part of the community – however small it might

---

[115] *3 Comp.* 1.6.18 = X 1.6.33 [= Potthast, I, no. 3538]; cf. infra, p. 65.
[116] This interpretation, however, was later refuted by Bernard of Parma and Innocent IV, H. Dondorp, 'Die Zweidrittelmehrheit als Konstitutivum der Papstwahl in der Lehre der Kanonisten des dreizehnten Jahrhunderts', *Archiv für katholisches Kirchenrecht*, 161 (1992), 396–425, 417–25.
[117] *Decreta*, ed. Alberigo et al., pp. 8–9; L. Moulin, 'Sanior et maior pars. Note sur l'évolution des techniques électorales dans les ordres religieux du VIᶜ au XIIIᶜ siècle', *Revue historique de droit français et étranger 4ᵗʰ sér.*, 36 (1958), 368–97 and 491–529, 375–6; Thier, 'Hierarchie und Autonomie', pp. 130–3.
[118] *Decretum Gratiani* D. 63 c. 36; Ganzer, 'Mehrheitsprinzip', 67.

be – which had the sounder judgement (*sanior consilium*).[119] It is not clear whether Benedict attributed such sounder judgement to a defined group of people; recently Andreas Thier has proposed that this group might have consisted of the senior members of the monastic community,[120] among whom were presumably the office holders.

In episcopal elections the principle of the *sanior pars* was occasionally mentioned throughout the early middle ages. It referred to politically influential secular and ecclesiastical groups. Yet, during this period the concepts of *sanioritas* and numerical majority were not further elaborated. One reason was the all-important principle that elections should be unanimous. Another was the tight control of elections by secular rulers. Either they installed the bishop at the beginning of the electoral process or they decided after the election whether to accept the candidate. In case of a split election they determined who constituted the *sanior pars*.[121] Thus the ruler's will was the decisive criterion. The principles of *sanioritas* and majority, however, were revived during the Gregorian reform movement. In particular the popes saw the opportunity to influence episcopal elections by deciding who constituted the *sanior pars*.[122] In this they did not succeed immediately, but their efforts stimulated thought on the weighing up of votes. An additional impetus was given by the disputed papal elections of 1130 and 1159,[123] revealing the need for a clear regulation of what constituted majority.

In the canonistic interpretation of this question three elements regularly appear: (A) the number of the voters; (B) their authority/dignity/merits; (C) their intentions (*zelus*). Rufinus presented two sets of possibilities. (1) A numerical majority: if there is a numerical majority and both sides are of equal authority and have been guided by good intentions, the election should be decided in favour of the numerical majority. If the numerical majority was not guided by good intentions, but simony was not involved and their candidate was suitable, they should nonetheless win the election, especially, if the greater authority was with them. If the minority had the

---

[119] *Benedicti regula*, ed. R. Hanslik (Corpus scriptorum ecclesiasticorum latinorum LXXV) (Vienna, 1970), c. 64; Moulin, 'Sanior et maior pars', 376–8; Thier, 'Hierarchie und Autonomie', pp. 142–50.

[120] Thier, 'Hierarchie und Autonomie', pp. 146–8, who sums up the earlier debate; Ganzer, 'Mehrheitsprinzip', 69, quotes some earlier incidents when the *sanior pars* played a role in an episcopal election, but stresses that they were neither the source of Benedict's thought, nor did they explicitly bring forward the concept that a numerically smaller part would win the election if it represented the *sanior pars*.

[121] Ganzer, 'Mehrheitsprinzip', 72–3.

[122] Ibid., 75–8; Thier, 'Autonomie und Hierarchie', pp. 257–8; A. Carboni, '"Sanior pars" ed elezioni episcopali fino alla lotta per le investiture', *Archivio giuridico 'Filippo Serafini' 6th ser.*, 27 (1960), 76–127, 117–23.

[123] See supra p. 22.

greater authority and was guided by good intentions, the numerical majority by bad intentions, the numerical minority should win. If the numerical minority had the greater authority, but both parts were guided by good intentions, the archbishop or the pope should decide which of the candidates was worthier. If both candidates were equal, then a third party should be elected. (2) An equally or nearly equally divided number of votes: if both sides had the same authority and were guided by good intentions, the archbishop or the pope should decide the election. If one side was guided by good intentions, it won the election. If both sides were guided by bad intentions, then the decision devolved again to the archbishop or pope. The same should happen if the party having the greater authority had been inspired by worldly desires or if there was animosity between the parties. If the party with the greater authority was guided by good intentions, the lesser party by worldly desires, the former should win.[124]

Stephen of Tournai offered a more precise definition of what constituted the dignity of an electing party that could convey greater authority in a split election. It was defined not only by the offices (*honores*), but also by the merits, virtues, and knowledge (*scientia*) of the voters. In his discussion of the question of majority Stephen modified Rufinus' doctrine very little. If the numbers were equal and both sides were guided by good intentions, the party with the greater authority should win. He specified that if the numerical majority was also of greater dignity and the numerical minority was guided by bad intentions, it did not matter whether the majority was guided by good or bad intentions. If, however, the numerical majority was guided by bad intentions, and the minority had dignity and good intentions, the latter party prevailed. If both sides were guided by good intentions, dignity neutralised the numerical majority and the decision devolved to the archbishop or pope.[125] The Bolognese school very quickly summarised these explanations by stating that the party which possessed two of the three elements, dignity/authority, number, and good intentions, won the election.[126]

In general the thought of the French school hardly differed from that of the Bolognese. Like Stephen of Tournai, the anonymous author of *Summa Coloniensis* argued that dignity consisted not only of offices, but also of merits and virtues. If number and dignity were equally divided and both parties elected with good intentions, the pope or the archbishop

---

[124] *Rufinus*, ed. Singer, pp. 50–2. Johannes Faventinus follows Rufinus, Oxford, Bodleian Library Canonici Miscellanea 429, fos. 12vb–13rb.

[125] *Summa des Stephanus*, ed. von Schulte, pp. 33–4.

[126] 'Summa de electione', in *Bernardi Papiensis*, ed. Laspeyres, pp. 315–16; P. Aimone-Braida, 'Il principio maggioritario nel pensiero di glossatori e decretisti', *Apollinaris*, 58 (1985), 209–85, 258, 262–3.

decided the election. If the numbers were equally divided, but one side had greater dignity and good intentions, the candidate of the latter party prevailed. If both sides elected with bad intentions their candidates were to be rejected regardless of the number and dignity of their parties. If both parties had good intentions and were equal in terms of dignity, but one candidate had received a greater number of votes, the numerical majority decided the election. If, however, the numerical minority had greater dignity, it neutralised the greater number and the outcome of the election was even. So far the anonymous author was very much in line with the Bolognese school. But he added a new significant element to the discussion. He argued that if the numerical majority was two-thirds, the election was valid in any case.[127]

Ten years later this principle was adapted in the regulations of the Third Lateran Council, which marked an important step in the formation of a more precise definition of majority. Canon one decreed that the pope had to be elected by a majority of two-thirds, otherwise his election was invalid. The canon explains that such a large majority was necessary, because the principle of *maior et se[a]nior pars* could not be applied to papal elections, since the pope had no superior who in case of a split election could decide which party was *maior et se[a]nior*.[128] The two-thirds majority, however, was not to be applied to other ecclesiastical elections. These were regulated by canon sixteen. This decreed that all decisions in churches had to be taken 'quod pluribus et se[a]nioribus fratribus visum fuerit'.[129] The canon put an official end to the idea that these decisions had to be unanimous. It did not, however, specify the relationship between the *plures* and *se[a]niores*. The preference for the numerical majority in papal elections created a precedent which influenced episcopal elections in the long run. In the short term, however, canonists used familiar concepts to define majority.

The commentaries of Peter of Blois, written between 1175 and 1190, and Huguccio, written in the 1180s, show that the French and Bolognese schools continued to think along the same lines.[130] Both agreed that the

---

[127] *Summa Coloniensis*, ed. Fransen and Kuttner, I, pp. 134–7, c. 44–8. The anonymous author did not fully repeat Stephen's discussion of the point on what happened if one side had the greater number and the other the greater dignity. He only repeated that if both parties were guided by good intentions, greater dignity could neutralise greater number. *Summa Gallicana-Bambergensis* is another example of a *Summa* of the French school arguing along the lines set out by the Bolognese school, Aimone-Braida, 'Principio maggioritario', 270–1.

[128] *Decreta*, ed. Alberigo et al., p. 190.   [129] Ibid., p. 193.

[130] For Peter of Blois, see *Speculum*, ed. Reimarus, pp. 92–3, c. 50. For Huguccio, see Paris, BNF Lat. 3892, fo. 79rab; cf. Brendan McManus' edition of this commentary on the basis of Paris, BNF Lat. 15396, fo. 73rab, 'The Ecclesiology of Laurentius Hispanus (c.1180–1248)', I, pp. 60–1, p. 60 n. 104.

right to vote lay with the party that obtained two out of three elements; *auctoritas* residing in those who held the major offices in a church (arch-deacons, provosts, deans, archpriests); *numerus*, referring to the numerical majority; and *bonus zelus*, referring to those who elected not out of worldly desires but on the merits of the candidate and his utility for the community.[131] If both sides were guided by good intentions, but one side had the greater number and the other the greater authority, both elections carried the same weight. The same was the case if both had the same number, dignity, and good intentions. In these cases the archbishop had to decide the election. The thought of the Anglo-Norman school did not differ: *Omnis qui iuste iudicat* propagated the principle that two elements prevailed over the third.[132]

In the 1180s a copy of the collection *Francofortana* came to the cathedral chapter of Rouen.[133] It was supplied with an *Apparatus* which included a commentary on canon one of the Third Lateran Council. This laid down the three usual elements to be considered while weighing up the votes: *numerus*, *zelus*, and *meritus*. Having defined them in the terms common to contemporary scholastic tradition,[134] it then explained that according to canon sixteen of the Third Lateran Council the party which had all three elements should win the election. A numerical minority could win an election, if it had authority and good intentions. But if it had only authority while good intentions lay with the greater number, both elections should be quashed. This then led the author of the *Apparatus* to consider the status of a candidate whose election had been declared void. Could he stand again? If the electoral procedure had been faulty, he could. However, if the election had been quashed because of him, he could not stand again. Then, combining questions of majority and the candidate's suitability the author stated that if an unsuitable candidate had been chosen unanimously, the election still had to be quashed. However, if the electors had been guided by bad intentions, but had chosen a suitable candidate, the election could still be valid unless it had been gained through promises. Finally, the *Apparatus*

---

[131] This is Huguccio's definition. Cf. the definition of the author of *Summa Tractaturus magister*, belonging to the French school and written only a very short time before Huguccio's commentary: 'numerus in multitudine et paucitate, dignitas in honoribus et moribus, zelus in ratione et contentione', Aimone-Braida, 'Principio maggioritario', 273.

[132] *Summa Omnis qui iuste iudicat*, Rouen, BM 743 (E 74), fos. 8vb–9ra; cf. Aimone-Braida, 'Principio maggioritario', 276–7; *Magistri Honorii Summa 'De iure canonico tractaturus'. I*, ed. Weigand et al., pp. 72–3, takes the same view.

[133] Infra, pp. 61–2.

[134] *Decreta*, ed. Alberigo et al., p. 211, c. 1 = Fr. 10.1, Paris, BNF Lat. 3922A, fo. 178r, lower margin: 'Ubi scissura fit in electione distingui debet: [A] numerus eligentium: [1] maior; [2] par; [3] minor; [B] meritum: [1] dignitatis; [2] scientie; [3] sanctitatis; [C] zelus: [1] bonus; [2] malus.'

asked what would happen if two parties of equal number, merit, and good intentions each nominated a suitable candidate. In his answer to this question the author, who up to this point was very much arguing along the main lines of contemporary thought, deviated from current opinion: he doubted that both candidates should be rejected.[135]

Compilatio tertia promulgated in 1209/10 incorporated the decretal *Dudum* which had a major impact on the weighing up of votes. In 1203, Innocent III had ordered papal judges delegate to decide a specific disputed election in the following way: if the candidate was suitable they should confirm his election, because nearly two-thirds of the electors, all with good intentions, had voted for him, even though the electors of his opponent had the greater authority and apparently their good intentions had not been doubted.[136] Perhaps influenced by the regulation of the papal election, Innocent III here broke with the principle of equality between number, authority, and intentions that had thus far dominated the weighing up of votes.

His decision attributed greater weight to the numerical majority and canonists noticed this immediately. In the second recension of his *Apparatus Ius naturale*, Alanus Anglicus referred to this decretal when he stated that number prevailed over authority in split elections.[137] Laurentius Hispanus understood the decretal similarly: number prevailed over authority; the latter should only be considered if the former was evenly divided.[138] Johannes Teutonicus argued along the same lines. Referring to Innocent

---

[135] Paris, BNF Lat. 3922A, fo. 178r, lower margin: 'Pars maior numero merito zelo semper obtinet ut in Later. concil. Cum in cunctis [Lat. III c. 16] et D.lxv c.i [D. 65 c. 1]. Pars minor numero sed maior merito et zelo vincit ut in extrav. In prepositi electione [Jaffé –; *WH* –; X-]. Quid si pars minor vincit merito sed vincitur zelo? Uterque electus cassatur ut di.lxxi c.ii Si duo [D. 71 c. 2]. Eo notato quod si quis cassatur vitio eligentium non suo ibi vel alibi eligi non prohibetur ut in extra. [et] vii q.i Presentium [C. 7 q. 1 c. 3]. Sed si qua electi culpa ibi potest deprehendi alibi ordinetur et numquam ibi ut ii q.i In primis [C. 2 q. 1 c. 2]. Si igitur omnes consentiant sed in malum cassatur ut in extrav. In prepositi Ar. xviii q.ii Si quis abbas [C. 18 q. 2. c. 15]. Quid si malo zelo consentiant sed in bonum? Forte stabitur neque favore ecclesie etc Ar. xxviii d. De Siracusane [D. 28 c. 13] et i q.i Quibusdam [C. 1 q. 1 c. 117].' Continued in right-hand margin at lines 25 and 32: 'Quid si fuerint ibi due partes equales numero merito zelo et utraque nominat bonum? Numquam uterque punietur D.lxxviii Si duo for[te] [D. 79 c. 8] infra extra. In prepositi.' Dealing with the specific problem of the two-thirds majority at a papal election, the *Apparatus* asks: 'What if this total [i.e. the two-thirds majority] should be short of one man? What if that man ['cum aliis' adds the version of the *Apparatus* in another copy of the *Francofortana*, London, British Library Egerton 2901, fo. 19ra] is guided by good intentions and the other two-thirds are guided by bad intentions? What if the two-thirds and the remaining third are guided by bad intentions?: [at line 34] "Quid si unus de hoc numero desit? Quid si ille bono ducitur zelo? Due partes malo? Quid si tam due partes quam tercia malo ducitur [Egerton 2901, fo. 19ra: ducuntur] zelo?"'

[136] *Register Innocenz' III.*, VI, no. 36 = *3 Comp.* 1.6.7 = *X* 1.6.22 [= Potthast, I, no. 1877].

[137] Aimone-Braida, 'Principio maggioritario', 265. This particular passage is not in Paris, Bibliothèque Mazarine 1318, fo. 74va–b.

[138] McManus, 'The Ecclesiology of Laurentius Hispanus (c.1180–1248)', I, p. 266.

III's decretal he refuted Huguccio's doctrine that two elements always prevailed over the third. Instead he argued that, if there was a great numerical majority, there was no need to evaluate authority and intentions. Only if the difference in numbers was very small or none should authority and intentions be considered.[139] Master Tancred followed the opinion of Laurentius and Johannes. Explicitly referring to Johannes, he believed that if there was a difference in number, the numerical majority always prevailed.[140] Vincentius Hispanus, however, saw the matter differently. He stated that number and good intentions prevailed over authority, that authority and good intentions prevailed over number, but that authority and number did not prevail over good intentions. If, however, authority was on the one side, number on the other, and good intentions on both, one had to distinguish between several cases. (A) If the difference in numbers exceeded by far the difference in authority, then the numerical majority prevailed. (B) If the difference in authority exceeded by far the difference in number, authority prevailed. Authority also prevailed if the numerical advantage was only small in comparison to the difference in authority.[141]

Raymond de Peñafort summed up the differing canonistic views on how to weigh up votes. First he explained the school of thought represented most prominently by Huguccio, that two elements prevailed over the third. Stating that some *doctores* did not agree with this, he mentioned the doctrines of Vincentius, Johannes, and others who, according to Raymond, believed that if the numbers were equally divided, but one party had the greater authority, the latter prevailed. If, however, one side had the greater number and the other the greater authority three results were possible. (A) If the difference in numbers exceeded by far the difference in authority, then the numerical majority prevailed. (B) If the difference in authority exceeded by far the difference in number, authority prevailed. (C) If there was little difference between the two, both were equal. Finally Raymond gave his own hesitant judgement. Referring to *Dudum* and its implication that number prevailed over authority, he

---

[139] For the *Glossa ordinaria*, see Bamberg, Staatsbibliothek Can.13, fo. 41va; Aimone-Braida, 'Principio maggioritario', 268–9; for *Compilatio tertia* and *Compilatio quarta*, see *Johannis Teutonici*, ed. Pennington, p. 59; 'Apparatus glossarum in Compilationem quartam', in *Antiquae collectiones*, ed. Agustin, p. 800. Concerning the case that both parties were equal in number, authority, and intentions, and that both candidates had the same merits, Johannes quoted the standard solution of quashing both elections. He added other opinions favouring the election of the more experienced churchman, or the decision of the archbishop, or a judge having the authority to force the contending parties to come to a solution. It was also possible that the lot decided such an election, Bamberg, Staatsbibliothek Can.13, fo. 41va; Aimone-Braida, 'Principio maggioritario', 268–9.

[140] Vatican City, Vat. Lat. 1377, fo. 162rb; Aimone-Braida, 'Principio maggioritario', 282.

[141] Karlsruhe, Badische Landesbibliothek Aug. per. 40 (formerly Aug. XL), fo. 239rb.

47

asserted that for this to work there had to be a great numerical majority. But Raymond did not state precisely what the difference was between a small and great numerical majority or between small and great authority. According to him this decision had to be left to judges of individual cases. As to the good intentions, however, Raymond had a firm opinion: like Vincentius he claimed that good intentions were always necessary to make an election valid.[142]

When a few years later Raymond compiled the *Liber extra* he included in the section on elections the decretal *Ecclesia vestra destituta* of Honorius III, which thus far had only been preserved in the little regarded *Compilatio quinta*.[143] In this decretal Honorius III dealt with the split election at Rouen in 1221–2. He ordered a new election, accepting the argument that although one candidate had received more votes than the other candidates, he had not received the absolute majority.[144] The decretal was a significant contribution to procedural thinking, since it offered the opportunity of determining what constituted a sufficient numerical majority.

Despite the increasing importance of the numerical majority the concept of seniority, and thus of *dignitas* and *zelus*, had not disappeared. Throughout the thirteenth century it continued to play a significant role in the discussion of the canonists and in papal judgements. For instance, Gregory IX's decretal *Ecclesia vestra* insisted that *maior et sanior pars* was not always identical with numerical majority.[145] However, at the council of Lyons in 1274 a further step towards the dominance of the numerical majority was taken. The party that obtained two-thirds of the votes in a split election was automatically judged to be the *sanior pars*.[146]

Suitability

A bishop had to meet certain criteria as spiritual leader of his flock and as foremost representative of the church and its ideals in his diocese. In his long list of desiderata, Gratian named intelligence, aptness in learning, a

---

[142] *Summa iuris*, ed. Rius Serra, pp. 121–3; *S. Raimundus de Pennaforte: Summa de iure canonico*, ed. Ochoa and Diez, cols. 178–80.

[143] *Honorii III Romani pontificis opera omnia*, ed. Horoy, IV, epistolae lib. VI, no. 38 = 5 *Comp.* 1.5.6 = X 1.6.48 [= Potthast, I, no. 6832].

[144] 'invenimus, quod illi, . . ., licet maiorem partem facerent partium comparatione minorem, non tamen ad maiorem partem pervenerunt'.

[145] X 1.6.57 [= Potthast, I, no. 9546].

[146] Ganzer, 'Mehrheitsprinzip', 80–5; Maleczek, 'Abstimmungsarten', pp. 122–4; K. Pennington, 'Bishops and their Dioceses', in P. Erdö and P. Szabó (eds.), *Territorialità e personalità nel diritto canonico ed ecclesiastico: Il diritto canonico di fronte al terzo millennio: Atti dell' XI congresso internazionale di diritto canonico e del XV congresso internazionale della società per il diritto delle chiese orientali* (Budapest, 2002), pp. 123–35; online: http://faculty.cua.edu/pennington/BishopsDioceses.htm (last visit: 12 Mar. 2003).

moderate temper, a chaste and abstemious life, a sense of responsibility for his affairs, kindness, compassion, profound learning, knowledge of canon law, an awareness of the meaning of the Scriptures, training in ecclesiastical doctrines, and above all the catholic faith.[147] Gratian also repeated Urban II's decree of the council of Benevento (1091) that the elect had to be in higher orders; subdeacons could only be elected if there was a need and permission was granted by either the archbishop or the pope.[148] Finally Gratian quoted decretals stating that the bishop ought to be found among the clergy of the diocese.[149]

Rufinus summarised Gratian, stating that a candidate had to be worthy and experienced. According to him, the requirement of a 'sense of responsibility for his affairs' meant that the prelate had to be shrewd and experienced in secular matters in order to administer his diocese properly. Rufinus also commented that subdeacons could be elected with papal permission.[150] Stephen of Tournai declared in his later glosses that the criteria were an honest life, expertise in administrative matters, and learning in the Scriptures. He specified, however, that if only two of these conditions were met, provided that *honestas vitae* was among them, the elect could be accepted.[151] The *Summa Coloniensis* also stipulated learning but equally stressed the necessity for high standing, unimpeachable birth, and a flawless body.[152]

Shortly before the Third Lateran Council Bernard of Pavia distinguished three main criteria: *vita, scientia et integritas*. *Vita* meant to have a good reputation and a clean conscience; *scientia* comprised expertise in administrative matters and Scriptures, the latter to such a degree that the candidate was not only capable of understanding their content, but also of teaching them; *integritas* consisted of literacy and proper birth, i.e. not born of a widow nor of a bigamous or corrupted marriage nor of servile condition. Furthermore the candidate should not be a neophyte, nor physically handicapped, nor struck down by ill fortune.[153] Huguccio

---

[147] *Decretum Gratiani* D. 23 c. 2.   [148] Ibid. D. 60 c. 4; see supra, p. 21.   [149] Ibid. D. 61 c. 13, 16.

[150] *Rufinus*, ed. Singer, pp. 50–2. Rufinus enlarged on the fact that a subdeacon *could* become bishop while it was necessary to be in the rank of deacon to ascend to the offices of archpriest or archdeacon. He then went on to explain the difference between the offices at great length, *Rufinus*, ed. Singer, p. 52. Johannes Faventinus followed Rufinus in these matters, Oxford, Bodleian Library Canonici Miscellanea 429, fos. 13rb, 36rb.

[151] *Summa des Stephanus*, ed. von Schulte, pp. 33–4, 86; R. Weigand, 'Studien zum kanonistischen Werk Stephans von Tournai', *Savigny KA*, 72 (1986), 349–61, 355.

[152] *Summa Coloniensis*, ed. Fransen and Kuttner, pp. 132–3, c. 40. *Vitae* from the tenth to the twelfth centuries attribute in particular these latter qualities to the ideal courtier bishop, C. S. Jaeger, 'The Courtier Bishop in *Vitae* from the Tenth to the Twelfth Century', *Speculum*, 58 (1983), 292–325, esp. 297–307.

[153] 'Summa de electione', in *Bernardi Papiensis*, ed. Laspeyres, pp. 316–17.

finally emphasised the importance of a profound knowledge of canon law and at least some experience in secular law.[154]

In the second half of the twelfth century the papacy was seriously concerned about the suitability of bishops for their office. Led by Alexander III, the Third Lateran Council in canon three stressed that a candidate ought to be in higher orders and be at least thirty years of age. In addition he ought to be born of a legitimate marriage and recommended by his *vita* and *scientia*.[155]

At the time of the Third Lateran Council the condition of belonging to a higher clerical order was no longer an impediment for subdeacons to become bishop. Having belonged to the lower orders and therefore having been ineligible for a bishopric, the subdeacon's status began to change as a result of the Gregorian reform movement in the second half of the eleventh century. Subdeacons started to be seen as belonging to the higher orders. Yet, in terms of their eligibility to bishoprics their status remained ambiguous. As mentioned above Urban II decreed at the council of Benevento that subdeacons could only be elected with the permission of the archbishop or the pope. At Clermont in 1095 he re-emphasised that subdeacons could only be elected with papal permission.[156] Widely diffused through pre-Gratian decretal collections and then Gratian's *Decretum* itself, the decree of the council of Benevento defined until the end of the twelfth century the official doctrine on the eligibility of subdeacons. In practice, however, subdeacons were increasingly regarded as belonging to the higher orders and by the fourth quarter of the twelfth century electors and canonists were in no doubt about the eligibility of subdeacons.[157] Honorius, for example, who wrote only a few years after the Third Lateran Council, counted subdeacons among those who were in higher orders.[158] Alanus Anglicus, writing around 1192, was more explicit. He stated that subdeacons were in higher orders and could be elected without dispensation.[159] This was not yet the official papal doctrine, but elections of subdeacons to bishoprics happened so frequently that by the 1190s Celestine III considered such promotions no longer

---

[154] Paris, BNF Lat. 3892, fo. 24ra. Similarly the *Apparatus Ecce vicit leo*, Paris, BNF N. A. Lat. 1576, fo. 46ra.
[155] *Decreta*, ed. Alberigo et al., pp. 212–13.   [156] See supra, p. 21.
[157] The transition of the subdeacon from the lower to the higher orders is analysed by R. Reynolds, 'The Subdiaconate as Sacred and Superior Order', in R. Reynolds, *Clerics in the Early Middle Ages. Hierarchy and Image* (Aldershot, 1999), no. IV, pp. 1–39.
[158] Zwettl, Stiftsbibliothek 162, fo. 192ra; *Magistri Honorii Summa 'De iure canonico tractaturus'*. I, ed. Weigand et al., p. 190; similarly the *Summa Omnis qui iuste iudicat*, Rouen, BM 743 (E 74), fo. 31va.
[159] Paris, BNF Lat. 3909, fo. 12ra.

problematic.[160] In 1207, finally, Innocent III paid tribute to these developments when he adopted current thought and practice as the new official papal doctrine. Stating that subdeacons counted by now among the higher orders and therefore could be elected to bishoprics, he decided the matter conclusively.[161] Unsurprisingly, then, his decision very quickly became part of the *ius commune*.[162]

In his other decretals touching upon the problem of suitability Innocent III followed the line set out by his predecessors.[163] In canon twenty-six of the fourth Lateran Council, he emphasised that those who confirmed elections must scrutinise whether the elect had sufficient *scientia*, impeccable *mores*, and was at least thirty years of age.[164] However, doubts about the candidate's age could be waived if the other two criteria were met, and necessity and utility required his election. This is evident in Innocent's letter *Cum olim nobis* to the chapter of Capua.[165] In the letter *Innotuit nobis* to the archbishop of Canterbury in 1200, the pope explained the procedure if a chapter wished to have a bishop who they knew did not fulfil all the conditions. The chapter of Worcester had elected the archdeacon of Evreux, Mauger. When Innocent heard that Mauger was of illegitimate birth he declared his election void. He explained that only the pope had the right to dispense. In these circumstances the chapter had to ask the pope for permission to elect the candidate.[166] Alexander's and Innocent's decisions finally found their way into the *Liber extra*, where they formed the core of the decretals regulating suitability.

There they were complemented by Gregory IX's decision of the disputed election at Rouen in 1231. In *Dudum ecclesia Rothomagensi* the pope had judged the elect, Thomas de Fréauville, unsuitable, because at the time of his election he had held without papal dispensation more than

---

[160] W. Holtzmann, 'Kanonistische Ergänzungen zur Italia pontificia', *Quellen und Forschungen aus italienischen Archiven und Bibliotheken*, 37 (1957), 55–102, 38 (1958), 67–175, II, 72–3, no. 62 = *1 Rot.* 3.3, Paris, BNF Lat.3922A, fo. 152vb [= Jaffé –; *WH* 419]

[161] *3 Comp.* 1.9.6 = *X* 1.14.9 [= Potthast, I, no. 3233].

[162] Cf. the commentary of canonist Albertus on c. 2 of *Compilatio secunda* (before 1215), Karlsruhe, Badische Landesbibliothek Aug. per. 40 (formerly Aug. XL), fo. 84ra. In the 1220s Raymond de Peñafort referred to this decretal commenting that at the time of his writing subdeacons could be elected *de iure communi*, even though this had once been opposed, *Summa iuris*, ed. Rius Serra, p. 128; S. *Raimundus de Pennaforte: Summa de iure canonico*, ed. Ochoa and Diez, col. 191.

[163] *Register Innocenz' III.*, II, no. 176 = *3 Comp.* 1.6.2 = *X* 1.6.17 [= Potthast, I, no. 836]; *Register Innozenz' III.*, II, no. 265 (277) = *3 Comp.* 1.6.4 = *X* 1.6.19 [= Potthast, I, no. 949]; *Register Innocenz' III.*, VI, no. 36 = *3 Comp.* 1.6.7 = *X* 1.6.22 [= Potthast, I, no. 1877].

[164] 'Concilii quarti Lateranensis constitutiones', in *Constitutiones concilii quarti Lateranensis*, ed. García y García, pp. 71–2.

[165] *Register Innozenz' III.*, II, no. 265 (277) = *3 Comp.* 1.6.4 = *X* 1.6.19 [= Potthast, I, no. 949].

[166] *3 Comp.* 1.5.6 = *X* 1.6.20 [= Potthast, I, no. 953]; cf. Cheney, *Innocent III*, pp. 63, 142–3.

one benefice to which the cure of souls was attached.[167] The papacy had been battling hard against pluralism. At the Third Lateran Council, Alexander III in canons thirteen and fourteen, prohibited the accumulation of wrongful acquisitions. Clerics found guilty were to be deprived of their benefices.[168] At the Fourth Lateran Council, Innocent III emphasised in canon twenty-nine that no cleric should hold two benefices with cure of souls. Within a church no one should have more than one dignity or one benefice even if cure of souls was not attached. Exceptions for famous and learned clerics could only be made by the pope.[169] However, the papacy's success in eradicating pluralism was limited.

One of the reasons for the difficulties in implementing the canons was canon law itself. Besides the exception created by canon twenty-nine of the Fourth Lateran Council, several older canons permitted simultaneous possession of more than one church. In its commentary on canon fourteen of the Third Lateran Council, the *Apparatus* to the collection *Francofortana* preserved at Rouen quoted several circumstances in which more than one church could be held: (A) if the churches were poor; (B) if the cleric held a second church in commendation; (C) if a special privilege was granted; (D) if the churches served to repay costs the incumbent had incurred through a benefice or office.[170] Laurentius Hispanus and Johannes Teutonicus went a step further and stated that for just and necessary reasons a bishop or

---

[167] *Les registres de Grégoire IX*, ed. Auvray, I, no. 655 = X 1.6.54 [= Potthast, I, no. 8306].

[168] *Decreta*, ed. Alberigo et al., pp. 218–19.

[169] 'Concilii quarti Lateranensis constitutiones', in *Constitutiones concilii quarti Lateranensis*, ed. García y García, pp. 73–4.

[170] Gloss on *Fr.* 16.3, Paris, BNF Lat. 3922A, fo. 182rb: 'C.i q.i Quam pio [C. 1 q. 2 c. 2]; Quam [?C. 23 q. 4 c. 10]; xvi q.vii Decimas nemini [C. 16 q. 7 c. 7]. C.xxi q.ii Sicut [C. 21 q. 2 c. 4]; vii q.i Sicut alterius [C. 7 q. 1 c. 39]. Ar. contra xii, q.ii Volterane [!] [C. 12 q. 2 c. 25]; Concesso [C. 12 q. 2 c. 26]; De redditibus [C. 12 q. 2 c. 28]; C.lxxiii Consuluit [D. 79 c. 9]; D.lxx Sanctorum [D. 70 c. 2]; non enim si plures sed pauperes contra canones facit ut x q.ii Unio [C. 10 q. 3 c. 3]; nec si unam habet titulatam et aliam commendatam, ut xxi q.i Qui duas [C. 21 q. 1 c. 3]. Licet si duas ex speciali privilegio ut xxi q.i Relatio [C. 21 q. 1 c. 5] et xvi q.i Et temporis qualitas [C. 16 q. 1 c. 48]. Ceterum in pluribus [cancelled: quas et] potest pro impenso beneficio vel officio beneficiari, ut xii q.ii Quicumque suffragio [C. 12 q. 2 c. 66]. Redditus autem sufficientiam xx marcas interpretamur ut infra extrav. Constitutus [Jaffé –; *WH* 179; *X* –]'; similar arguments were put forward by the *Magistri Honorii Summa 'De iure canonico tractaturus'*. I, ed. Weigand et al., pp. 209–10. Having quoted the canons supporting the simultaneous tenure of more than one church Honorius commented, p. 110: 'In casibus autem premissis sine omni dispensatione ecclesie possint due assignari ab eo ad quem collatio pertinet. Nam id olim fuisse indultum sufficit ut ad ius commune tractum uideatur.' In May 1198, Innocent III sent a letter to the chapter of Bayeux which probably added to the confusion over this issue. The canons explained that according to the approved custom of the church of Bayeux some of their prebends were connected with parish churches to which the cure of souls was attached. In light of the prohibition of pluralism by Lateran III the canons were uncertain whether canons who received a dignity in the church of Bayeux to which the cure of souls was attached could simultaneously hold such prebends. Innocent answered that even though papal dispensation should not be required in such a case, he, in order to calm their conscience, nevertheless allowed them to

anybody else could hold more than one benefice, even without consultation with the pope. One of these reasons, Johannes argued, could be the poverty of the diocese.[171] Johannes' influential colleague Tancred brought forward six cases in which the simultaneous possession of at least two churches was acceptable: (A) by dispensation of the ecclesiastical superior; (B) if the revenues of one church were insufficient to maintain the cleric; (C) for lack of clerics; (D) by papal concession; (E) if the cleric held the second church in commendation; (F) if the benefices were dependent on one another.[172] He also stated that a cleric could receive in addition to his first benefice a prebend without cure of souls in another diocese, if such grants were customary and if the pope tolerated this custom.[173] Commenting on canon twenty-nine of Lateran IV, Vincentius Hispanus allowed the holding of several *prebendae* on condition that they had been received from the same bishop.[174] These opinions were not unanimously accepted among canonists. Damasus, for instance, stated that, with very few exceptions, not more than one benefice could be held.[175]

The question of cure of souls created further problems: a clear definition of what constituted cure of souls had not yet been achieved, and hence the status of individual benefices could be ambiguous.[176] Thus the academic discussion among canonists produced a sizeable number of grounds for defending simultaneous possession of several churches. Gregory IX's decretal *Dudum ecclesia Rothomagensi* did not solve these ambiguities. Yet, for the first time a papal decree declared explicitly that a candidate guilty of unlicensed pluralism was unsuitable to be elected to an episcopal see.

---

hold simultaneously dignity and prebend, 'rigore non obstante concilii', *Antiquus cartularius ecclesiae Baiocensis, livre noir*, ed. V. Bourrienne (Société de l'histoire de Normandie) (2 vols., Rouen 1902–3), II, no. 326 [= Potthast -].

[171] McManus, 'The Ecclesiology of Laurentius Hispanus (c.1180–1248)', I, p. 469; for Johannes, see K. Pennington, 'The Canonists and Pluralism in the Thirteenth Century', *Speculum*, 51 (1976), 35–48, 42 and n. 27.

[172] For Tancred's final version of his commentary, finished around 1220, see Vatican City, BAV Vat. Lat. 1377, fo. 120va. Tancred mainly referred to Gratian's *Decretum*. In support of (A) he quoted D. 70 c. 2; of (B) C. 10 q. 3 c. 3 and D. 70 c. 2; of (C) C. 21 q. 1 c. 1; of (D) C. 21 q. 1 c. 5; of (E) C. 21 q. 1 c. 3; of (F) *1 Comp.* 1.8.5 = *Bambergensis* 20.4; Tancred merely repeated what he had stated in his earlier version, written between 1210 and 1215; cf. Pennington, 'Canonists and Pluralism', 37–8 and n. 16 (edition). One of Innocent III's decretals could also be interpreted to the effect that even though excessive accumulation of benefices was to be reprimanded, simultaneous possession of a small number of churches was permitted, *Register Innocenz' III.*, I, no. 414 = *3 Comp.* 3.5.4 = *3 Rot.* 16, Paris, BNF Lat. 3922A, fo. 119va–b [= Potthast, I, no. 420].

[173] Vatican City, BAV Vat. Lat. 1377, fo. 222rb; cf. Pennington, 'Canonists and Pluralism', 43.

[174] 'Vincentii Hispani Apparatus in concilium quartum Lateranense', in *Constitutiones concilii quarti Lateranensis*, ed. García y García, pp. 324–5.

[175] 'Damasi Apparatus in concilium quartum Lateranense', *Constitutiones concilii quarti Lateranensis*, ed. García y García, pp. 432–3. For other canonists critical of Johannes' point of view, Pennington, 'Canonists and Pluralism', 42–4.

[176] Cf. 'Vincentii Hispani Apparatus in concilium quartum Lateranense', in *Constitutiones concilii quarti Lateranensis*, ed. García y García, p. 324.

Episcopal translation

The early church was in principle opposed to episcopal translations. It accepted, however, that if there was urgent necessity and great utility, local synods could authorise them.[177] In most places, synods continued to perform this function throughout the early middle ages, although in Italy the papacy emerged very early as the authority over episcopal translations.[178] It was only during the Gregorian reform movement that the popes claimed exclusive control. But despite the reformers' efforts,[179] local customs and the authority of the provincial synod continued to affect events.

Gratian did not treat this question in detail. In *Causa 7 quaestio 1*, he contrasted the texts in favour of papal authority with those backing local synods, but refrained from giving a final judgement between them.[180] In the following decades, canonists from the Bolognese and Anglo-Norman schools stated that only the pope could translate.[181] But the right of the synod was not forgotten. Towards the end of the century an anonymous glossator of Bernard of Pavia's *Compilatio prima* commented on the conciliar canon *Non liceat*[182] that an episcopal translation had to be authorised by the synod.[183] This diversity of opinions was mainly due to the fact that episcopal translations were not a major issue of papal politics in the second half of the twelfth century;[184] only limited efforts were made to support papal authority and to eliminate contrary local customs.[185]

This, however, would change with the pontificate of Innocent III. From the beginning, he was concerned to have it universally accepted that only the pope could translate bishops. He solved the problem of inconsistent canon law by introducing a new claim. According to him

---

[177] S. Scholz, *Transmigration und Translation. Studien zum Bistumswechsel der Bischöfe von der Spätantike bis zum Hohen Mittelalter* (Kölner historische Abhandlungen XXXVII) (Cologne, 1992), pp. 1–101; Cheney, *Innocent III*, p. 71.

[178] Scholz, *Transmigration*, pp. 89–105.

[179] Cheney, *Innocent III*, pp. 71–2; K. Pennington, *Pope and Bishops: The Papal Monarchy in the Twelfth and Thirteenth Centuries* (Philadelphia, 1984), p. 86; Scholz, *Transmigration*, pp. 190–8.

[180] *Decretum Gratiani* C.7 q. 1, cc. 19–42, esp. cc. 34–9.

[181] For the Bolognese school, see Paucapalea, Rufinus and Huguccio, *Die Summa des Paucapalea über das Decretum Gratiani*, ed. J. F. von Schulte (Giessen, 1890), p. 73; Singer, *Rufinus*, ed. Singer, pp. 291; Pennington, *Pope and Bishops*, pp. 88–90; for the Anglo-Norman school, see *Summa Omnis qui iuste uidicat*, Rouen, BM 743 (E 74), fo. 64va.

[182] This canon issued at the council of Sardica (343) forbade bishops moving from one church to another, *1 Comp.* 3.4.1; Pennington, *Pope and Bishops*, pp. 76, 90.

[183] Pennington, *Pope and Bishops*, p. 90.

[184] This is also suggested by the organisation and content of *Compilatio prima*. It contains no rubric on episcopal translation. *Non liceat* is not quoted in the rubric dealing with episcopal elections, but is quoted in the rubric dealing with non resident clerics, *1 Comp.* 3.4.1.

[185] Pennington, *Pope and Bishops*, pp. 90–5.

the pope's rights to translate rested not on the precedents of Peter or any other pope, but were of divine origin. Thus the pope judged the desirability of episcopal translations through God's authority. Innocent also defined the procedure: the bishop's translation had to be postulated at the papal court before he could be elected by his new chapter.[186] Within ten years of its publication Innocent III's theory was accepted by canonists.[187] In his decretal collection completed in 1201, Rainier of Pomposa included a section on episcopal translations quoting two of Innocent III's decretals, *Inter corporalia* (1199) and *Ne si universis universa* (1198). The latter included the pope's earlier letters on the matter, *Cum ex illo generali* (1198) and *Cum ex illo* (1198).[188] The author of the *Apparatus Animal est substantia* quoted *Inter corporalia* when stating that only the pope could translate bishops.[189] The section 'de translatione episcopi et electi' of Petrus Beneventanus' *Compilatio tertia* consisted entirely of decretals issued by Innocent in his first two years in office: *Cum ex illo generali, Inter corporalia, Quanto personam* (1198), and *Licet in tantum* (1200).[190] Raymond de Peñafort after having stated in his *Summa iuris* that only the pope could authorise episcopal translations,[191] simply repeated the section 'de translatione' of *Compilatio tertia* in the *Liber extra*.[192]

Conclusion

Canon law regulating episcopal elections developed considerably between *c.* 1140 and *c.* 1230. Local custom played an important role in this development. It became part of canon law by two routes. There was the direct route through the papal court, i.e. a litigant party used local custom to defend its position and the pope accepted it. There was also the indirect route through the canonists. They took local custom into account when discussing individual problems. Their teachings influenced lawyers who undertook litigation at the papal court and

[186] Ibid., pp. 15–17, 89–90, 95–7; Cheney, *Innocent III*, pp. 72–3; Scholz, *Transmigration*, p. 207.
[187] Cf. Pennington, *Pope and Bishops*, pp. 15–42.
[188] 'Prima collectio decretalium Innocentii III', in *PL*, CCXVI, cols. 1173–272, cols. 1197–1201, 5.1 = *Register Innocenz' III.*, I, no. 530 (532) [= Potthast, I, no. 575]; 5.2 = *Register Innocenz' III.*, I, no. 117 [= Potthast, I, no. 108] (*Cum ex illo generali* = *Register Innocenz' III.*, I no. 50 [= Potthast, I, no. 52]; *Cum ex illo* = *Register Innocenz' III.*, I, no. 51 [= Potthast, I, no. 53]).
[189] Bamberg, Staatsbibliothek Can.42, fo. 69vb.
[190] *3 Comp.* 1.5.1; *3 Comp.* 1.5.2; *3 Comp.* 1.5.3 = *Register Innocenz' III.*, I, no. 335 [= Potthast, I, no. 352]; *3 Comp.* 1.5.4 = *Register Innocenz' III.*, II, no. 266 (278) [= Potthast, I, no. 942].
[191] *Summa iuris*, ed. Rius Serra, p. 135; *S. Raimundus de Pennaforte: Summa de iure canonico*, ed. Ochoa and Diez, col. 204.
[192] X 1.7.1–4.

occasionally even became popes themselves.[193] Canon law, therefore, was not the product of secluded theoretical discussions in Rome, Bologna, or elsewhere. It was the result of continuous exchange between electoral custom, papal decisions, and canonistic discussion. This exchange transformed the canon law of episcopal elections from a rather ill-defined and ambiguous series of precedents into an almost coherent body that provided precise – though by no means exhaustive – regulations. Over time, canon law became more unified, as did cano-nistic thought. In the course of the first half of the thirteenth century the interpretation of canon law was increasingly dominated by the thought of the Bolognese school, relegating other traditions to secondary local influence.[194]

THE SPREAD OF CANON LAW IN NORMANDY AND GREATER ANJOU BETWEEN C. 1140 AND C. 1230

Normandy

Library catalogues demonstrate the commonness of pre-Gratian collec-tions in Normandy in the second half of the twelfth century. The list of the books Philip de Harcourt, bishop of Bayeux, donated in 1163 to the monastery of Bec shows that besides works on Roman law he owned copies of Burchard of Worms' and Ivo of Chartres' *Decretum* as well as Ivo's letters. Bec also owned copies of the letters of Hildebert, bishop of Le Mans, and a rich collection of patristic texts and anonymous collections of canon law.[195] Bec's collection served as a source for neighbouring abbeys. The abbey of Lyre enriched its library by making its own copy of a substantial part of the works preserved at Bec. The scribes copied, for example, Gratian and the letters of Ivo and Hildebert. In addition Lyre

---

[193] Cf. James Brundage's analysis of such careers for the period from *c.* 1230 onwards, J. Brundage, 'From Classroom to Courtroom: Parisian Canonists and their Careers', *Savigny KA*, 83 (1997), 342–61.

[194] In general the French school continued to play an important role in the first decades of the thirteenth century, but appears to have markedly suffered from Pope Honorius III's ban of civil law teaching in Paris, which was issued in 1219. In practice, this ban also reduced the teaching of canon law; for the activities of the French school in the early decades of the thirteenth century, see K. Pennington, 'The French Recension of Compilatio tertia', *Bulletin of Medieval Canon Law New Series*, 5 (1975), 53–71; P. D. Clarke, 'The Collection of Gilbertus and the French Glosses in Brussels. Bibliothèque royale, MS 1407–09, and an Early Recension of Compilatio secunda', *Savigny KA*, 86 (2000), 132–84; for Honorius III's ban, see J.W. Baldwin, *Masters, Princes and Merchants. The Social Views of Peter the Chanter and his Circle* (2 vols., Princeton, 1970), I, pp. 86–7 and infra, p. 70.

[195] H. Omont, *Catalogue général des manuscrits des bibliothèques publiques de France* (64 vols., Paris, 1886–1989), II, pp. 385–99.

owned a copy of the *Panormia* attributed to Ivo.[196] Further copies of the *Panormia* were held at Mont-St-Michel and at St Evroul.[197] St Evroul also housed a copy of Ivo's letters; at the monastery of Fécamp, Burchard's and Ivo's *Decretum* were available among other anonymous collections of canon law.[198] Finally, palaeographical evidence points to Normandy as the place of origin for twelfth-century copies of the Pseudo-Isidorian decretals and Ivo's *Decretum*.[199]

Gratian's *Decretum* itself reached Normandy very shortly after its compilation. Philip de Harcourt acquired it before 1163,[200] and the monastery of St Evroul got hold of a copy between 1150 and 1200.[201] Its impact was so great that in the second half of the twelfth century a scribe erased other matters from a manuscript of Robert de Torigny's chronicle in order to mention the compilation of the *Decretum* among the events of the year 1130. The scribe added that the *Decretum* was useful for the cases heard at the papal and other ecclesiastical courts. He also knew that, shortly after its completion, Omnebene, bishop of Verona, a pupil of Gratian, had compiled an abbreviated version.[202]

The contemporary Norman library catalogues are of little help in identifying the holdings of post-Gratian works on canon law. The names of famous and influential canonists of the second half of the twelfth century like Stephen of Tournai and Huguccio of Pisa do not appear in these lists.[203] The extent to which members of the Norman clergy up to

---

[196] G. Nortier, *Les bibliothèques médiévales des abbayes bénédictines de Normandie. Fécamp, Le Bec, Le Mont Saint-Michel, Saint-Evroul, Lyre, Jumièges, Fécamp, Saint-Wandrille, Saint-Ouen* (Caen, 1966), pp. [123]–[42]; Omont, *Catalogue*, II, pp. 379–83.

[197] M. Brett, 'Creeping up on the Panormia', in R. Helmholz et al. (eds.), *Grundlagen des Rechts. Festschrift für Peter Landau zum 65. Geburtstag* (Rechts- und staatswissenschaftliche Veröffentlichungen der Görres-Gesellschaft N.F. XCI) (Munich, 2000), pp. 205–70, pp. 262, 267; Omont, *Catalogue*, I, p. 189, II, p. 261.

[198] Nortier, *Bibliothèques*, pp. [6]–[30], [108], [119]–[23]. Burchard's influence can be traced in post-Gratian decretal collections. The collections of the Ivonian circle seem to have influenced in particular post-Gratian canonists of the French school, Landau, 'Vorgratianische Kanonessammlungen bei den Dekretisten und in den frühen Dekretalensammlungen', pp. 93–116.

[199] A copy of the Pseudo-Isidorian decretals may have arrived at Mont-St-Michel in the twelfth century, Williams, *Codices Pseudo-Isidoriani*, pp. 6–7, 20–1, 29–30, 42, 125–32. Dr Martin Brett generously provided the information on the copy 'D' of Ivo's *Decretum* (= Vatican City, BAV Vat. Pal. Lat. 587, fos. 1r–105r).

[200] Omont, *Catalogue*, II, p. 396.

[201] For St Evroul, see Nortier, *Bibliothèques*, p. [108]; Omont, *Catalogue*, II, pp. 468–9.

[202] *Torigny*, pp. xxxix–xli, 118 and n. 2. Omnebene worked on his abbreviation of the *Decretum* around 1156. He became bishop of Verona in 1157, R. Weigand, 'Frühe Kanonisten und ihre Karrieren in der Kirche', *Savigny KA*, 76 (1990), 135–55, 137–8.

[203] Items are labelled similarly to the *Corpus canonum imperfectum* or the *Liber canonum* held in the cathedral library of Rouen. For holdings of the cathedral library of Rouen in the twelfth century, see P. Langlois, *Recherches sur les bibliothèques des archevêques et du chapitre de Rouen* (Rouen, 1853), pp. 4–15, 61–4; Omont, *Catalogue*, I, pp. x–xii.

c. 1180 became acquainted with the works of Gratian and later canonists at centres of studies like Paris, Bologna, and Oxford can only be guessed.[204] Arnulf of Lisieux perhaps studied pre-Gratian material in Italy and Paris in the 1130s.[205] The Italian Roland, dean of Avranches from the early 1160s until his election to the see of Dol in 1177,[206] may have gained some experience in legal matters before his arrival at Avranches.[207] Peter of Blois, the letter-writer, who was in the service of Rotrou, archbishop of Rouen (1164/5–1183), in the mid-1160s and again in the early 1170s, had studied *inter alia* the letters of Hildebert, bishop of Le Mans, at Tours in the 1140s and Roman law at Bologna between *c.* 1150 and 1155.[208] Gerald de Barri reported the famous story of Master Roger the Norman, canon at Rouen from *c.* 1165 and dean of the chapter there between 1199 and 1200,[209] listening to the lectures he [Gerald] gave on law, in particular on Gratian's *Decretum*, at Paris between 1176 and 1179. According to Gerald the 'famous doctor' Roger had studied law in Bologna, and had taught the arts in Paris.[210] Further evidence for the contact between the schools at Paris and the Norman clergy is provided by Master John de Hauteville's poem *Architrenius* written in the 1180s and dedicated to Walter, archbishop of Rouen (1184/5–1207). John, canon at Rouen in 1199,[211] vividly described the harsh life of the Paris students and the pretentious

---

[204] H. Müller, *Päpstliche Delegationsgerichtbarkeit in der Normandie (12. und frühes 13. Jahrhundert)* (Studien und Dokumente zur Gallia pontificia IV, I–II) (2 vols., Bonn, 1997), I, pp. 204–10, has shown that the study of law was no prerequisite for being appointed as papal judge delegate. They were chosen because of their status or practical jurisdictional expertise.

[205] *The Letters of Arnulf of Lisieux*, ed. F. Barlow (Camden Society 3rd ser. LXI) (London, 1939), pp. xiii–xix; cf. Somerville, *Pope Urban II*, p. 68; J. Peltzer, 'Conflits électoraux et droit canonique. Le problème de la valeur des votes lors des élections épiscopales en Normandie au Moyen Age central', *Tabularia « Etudes »*, 6 (2006), 91–107, 99–100 (31 Oct. 2006: http://unicaen.fr/mrsh/crahm/revue/tabularia/peltzer.pdf).

[206] Flers, BM 22 (formerly F 9) (cartulary, abbey of Savigny), fos. 26r–27r, no. 19; *Torigny*, pp. 275–6.

[207] After his election to the see of Dol in 1177 he spent years at Rome litigating for the promotion of Dol to an archbishopric, *infra*, pp. 178–9.

[208] R.W. Southern, 'Blois, Peter of (1125x30–1212)', in *Oxford Dictionary of National Biography*, http://www.oxforddnb.com/view/article22012 (last visit: 23 Mar. 2005); R.W. Southern, *Scholastic Humanism and the Unification of Europe. II. The Heroic Age* (Oxford, 2001), pp. 178–206; Southern, 'The Necessity of Two Peter of Blois', pp. 103–18.

[209] Spear, *The Personnel*, pp. 204, 261.

[210] *Giraldi Cambrensis opera*, ed. J. Brewer et al. (Rolls Series XXI) (8 vols., London, 1861–91), I, pp. 45–8; for the date, R. Bartlett, *Gerald of Wales 1146–1223* (Oxford, 1982), p. 133. Gerald recorded that Norman had studied at Bologna 'in legibus', which probably refers to civil law rather than to canon law, since Gerald appears to have distinguished between the *leges* that referred to civil law and the *canones* that referred to canon law, *Giraldi Cambrensis*, ed. Brewer et al., VII, pp. 57–8; cf. S. Kuttner and E. Rathbone, 'Anglo-Norman Canonists of the Twelfth Century', *Traditio*, 7 (1949–51), 279–358, 295.

[211] Rouen, BM 1193 (Y 044) (cartulary, cathedral chapter of Rouen), fos. 62v–63v, no. 69.

attitudes of the professors.[212] In light of this, there is reason to suppose that Dean Norman's career was not unique among the Norman clergy. Like their English colleagues,[213] Norman ecclesiastics studied canon law in the second half of the twelfth century.

The interest in canon law among Norman churchmen was certainly raised by a number of high-profile events in the second half of the twelfth century. The split papal election of 1159, for example, stimulated thought on electoral procedure throughout the church. Arnulf of Lisieux, who championed the cause of Roland Bandinelli (Alexander III), emphasised Roland's suitability and the canonically proper procedure of his election. Roland's opponent Octavian (Victor IV), by contrast, was unsuitable and had been elected by a minority of three, who themselves were unworthy electors.[214] It is most likely that these issues were discussed when in 1160 the Norman bishops and barons met at Neufmarché to deal with the split election.[215] Similarly, the Becket dispute must have stimulated interest in canon law among Norman churchmen. Precise information is lacking, but it can be fairly assumed that leading Norman prelates like Rotrou, archbishop of Rouen, and Arnulf of Lisieux, who both played a prominent role in the dispute, made themselves familiar with the canonistic thought on the legal issues of the conflict.[216] Norman prelates were also familiar with the legislation of the great ecclesiastical councils of the time. In 1163, Alexander III convened a council at Tours, which all Norman

---

[212] *The Anglo-Latin Satirical Poets and Epigrammatists of the Twelfth Century*, ed. T. Wright (Rolls Series LIX a–b) (2 vols., London, 1872), I, pp. xxv–xxx, 275–91, 308–25.

[213] Kuttner and Rathbone, 'Anglo-Norman Canonists', pp. 284–9.

[214] *Arnulf*, ed. Barlow, nos. 28, 29. It should be noted that Arnulf had used the same arguments to discredit the election of Gerald at Sées in 1144–7, cf. infra, pp. 117–18. In the course of the disputed papal election of 1130 Arnulf had supported Innocent II's election also claiming that he was of greater suitability and that he had been elected by the *pars potior*, 'Arnulfi Sagiensis archidiaconi postea episcopi Lexoviensis invectiva in Girardum Engolismensem episcopum', ed. J. Dieterich, in *Libelli de lite imperatorum et pontificum saeculis XI. et XII. conscripti*, ed. E. Dümmler (Monumenta Germaniae historica) (3 vols., Hanover, 1887–91), III, pp. 81–108, p. 101.

[215] *Torigny*, p. 207; F. Barlow, 'The English, Norman and French Councils Called to Deal with the Papal Schism of 1159, *EHR*, 51 (1936), 264–8.

[216] For the Norman bishops and the Becket conflict, see J. Peltzer, 'Henry II and the Norman Bishops', *EHR*, 119 (2004), 1202–29, 1213–17; cf. Kuttner and Rathbone, 'Anglo-Norman Canonists', 288–9; B. Smalley, *The Becket Conflict and the Schools. A Study of Intellectuals in Politics* (Oxford, 1973), pp. 160–7. Debating with Peter the Chanter in the schools of theology Master Roger the Norman argued that Becket was not a martyr, J.W. Baldwin, 'A Debate at Paris over Thomas Becket between Master Roger and Master Peter the Chanter', *Studia Gratiana*, 11 (1967), 119–32; Smalley, *The Becket Conflict and the Schools*, pp. 201–2. Whether Roger, an expert in civil law, used canon law to support his argument is unknown. In any case, the debate may have further stimulated his interest in canon law, cf. supra, p. 58; for contemporary canonistic thought on the matter of criminous clerics, see C. Duggan, 'The Becket Dispute and the Criminous Clerks', *Bulletin of the Institute of Historical Research*, 35 (1962), 1–28.

prelates except the bishop of Bayeux attended.[217] Sixteen years later, in 1179, the presence of the Norman bishops at the Third Lateran Council was less impressive. Despite the summons by Alexander III to all Norman clergy,[218] the Norman bishops abstained except for the ageing Giles du Perche, bishop of Evreux, and Henry, bishop of Bayeux, who is known to have at least departed for the eternal city.[219] Nonetheless the council's decrees made their way into Normandy. Robert de Torigny owned a copy[220] and decretal collections available in Normandy after *c.* 1180 contained them.[221] Significantly, churchmen referred to them in their letters and charters. Bishop Henry of Bayeux, for example, justified his conferral of the church of Asnelles (cant. Ryes, Calvados) to Gregory, archdeacon of Bayeux, with canon eight of the Third Lateran Council. The abbot of St Julien of Tours, who held the right to provide for the church of Asnelles, had failed to present a candidate for more than six months and thus the right of provision devolved to the bishop.[222] The canons at Bayeux were also well aware of the decisions of the Third Lateran Council relating to pluralism. In 1198, they wondered whether canons of their church violated the *statuta concilii generalis* (probably canons thirteen and fourteen), if they simultaneously held a dignity and a benefice that both demanded the cure of souls.[223]

Summarising these findings it can be said that at least some Norman churchmen were familiar with Gratian and the developments in canon law before *c.* 1180. On occasion they intensively discussed legal issues and thus sharpened the general awareness of canon law in the region; Normandy was certainly not 'out-of-the-loop' concerning the knowledge of the latest canon law. Yet, overall it appears that up to *c.* 1180 reception of rather than a contribution to the general development of canon law was characteristic for Norman ecclesiastics. The reverse, however, applies for the following period between *c.* 1180 and *c.* 1230, when Norman canonists actively contributed to the spread and interpretation of canon law.

[217] R. Somerville, *Pope Alexander III and the Council of Tours* (Center for Medieval and Renaissance Studies) (Berkeley, 1977), p. 28. Philip de Harcourt, bishop of Bayeux, died in February 1163, see infra, p. 137.

[218] *Torigny*, pp. 278–8.

[219] For Giles, see R. Foreville, *Latran I, II, III et Latran IV* (Histoire de conciles œcuméniques VI) (Paris, 1965), p. 389. For Henry, see a charter of William, dean of Bayeux, issued on 31 December 1178: 'quod cum dominus vir Henricus Bajocensis episcopus ad concilium Romae profecturus vices suas in episcopatu Bajocensi nobis comisisset', Alençon, AD Orne H 1956 (charters concerning the abbey of Troarn).

[220] *Torigny*, pp. 284–5.   [221] See infra, pp. 61–3.

[222] *Chartes de Saint-Julien de Tours (1002–1300)*, ed. L.-J. Denis (Archives historiques du Maine XII, I–II) (Le Mans, 1912–13), no. 119; *Decreta*, ed. Alberigo et al., p. 215, c. 8.

[223] See supra, n. 170.

In the course of the second half of the twelfth century ecclesiastics across Europe compiled decretal collections to keep abreast of the latest conciliar legislation and papal decisions. In Normandy churchmen started to do so perhaps around 1180. Two unsystematic, so-called primitive collections, the collection *Cantabrigensis*, compiled between 1177 and 1179, and the collection *Parisiensis prima*, which contained the decrees of the Third Lateran Council and was completed by 1181, originated in France.[224] It has recently been argued that they may have been compiled in Normandy.[225] While this claim requires further critical examination, there is no doubt about the significant contribution of Norman churchmen to the compilation of systematic collections after 1185. Here they were at the forefront of European canonistic activity until the beginning of the thirteenth century.

Arguably the most impressive evidence for increasing examination of canon law after 1185 is the large manuscript preserved in the Bibliothèque Nationale de France in Paris, Lat. 3922A. The volume was almost certainly compiled at Rouen between *c.* 1185 and *c.* 1215. It comprises an abbreviation of Gratian, material on civil law, several decretal collections, and individual decretals.[226] The volume was not the random result of materials purposelessly thrown together, as becomes very clear from the organisation of the decretal collections. Each one is a collection in its own right. Yet they were compiled to complement each other; hardly any decretal is quoted more than once. Thus they formed a large comprehensive collection, the core of which was a copy of the *Francofortana* (Sens?, *c.* 1183),[227] which had reached Rouen soon after 1185. This was enhanced by a second collection probably compiled at Rouen, which Walther Holtzmann named *Rotomagensis prima*. *Rotomagensis prima* itself was made up from several collections. Its skeleton was the *Appendix Concilii Lateranensis* (England?, 1181–5) as well as material from Italian collections, the *Wigorniensis* group (Exeter/Worcester, *c.* 1181), extracts from the papal registers, originals found in Norman archives, and other unknown

---

[224] C. Duggan, *Twelfth-Century Decretal Collections and their Importance in English History* (University of London Historical Studies XII) (London, 1963), pp. 47–8, 128–30, 135; E. Friedberg, *Die Canones-Sammlungen zwischen Gratian und Bernhard von Pavia* (Leipzig, 1897), pp. 5–21, 45–63.

[225] P. Landau, 'Collections françaises du XIIe siècle', paper delivered at 'La Curie romaine et la France. 3ème rencontre de la Gallia Pontificia', German Historical Institute, Paris, 10 Sept. 2003. I would like to thank Prof. Landau and PD Gisela Drossbach for having sent me a transcript of this paper.

[226] For this and much of what follows, C. Cheney and M. Cheney, *Studies in the Collections of Twelfth-Century Decretals. From the Papers of the Late Walther Holtzmann* (MIC series B: corpus collectionum III) (Vatican City, 1979), pp. 135–207; C. Cheney, 'Decretals of Innocent III in Paris, B.N. MS LAT. 3922A', in C. Cheney, *The Papacy and England. 12th–14th centuries* (London, 1982), no. IV, pp. 149–63.

[227] P. Landau, 'Die Entstehung der systematischen Dekretalensammlungen in der europäischen Kanonistik des 12.Jahrhunderts', *Savigny KA*, 65 (1979), 120–48, 137–43.

sources.[228] The later insertions to *Rotomagensis prima* were drawn from a lost archetype of the *Appendix Concilii Lateranensis*, the works of Gilbert (1202–4) and Rainier of Pomposa (after 1201), and from an extract from the papal registers.[229] Besides *Rotomagensis prima* two further collections engrossed the *Francofortana*: *Rotomagensis secunda* and *Rotomagensis tertia*. *Rotomagensis secunda* was based on a version of Bernard of Pavia's *Compilatio prima* (Bologna, 1188–90) and nearly fifty decretals drawn from other sources among which were again the collections of Gilbert and Rainier.[230] *Rotomagensis tertia*, of which the latest item dates from 25 May 1207, consisted of excerpts from the papal registers.[231] The manuscript also lists decretals from Gilbert and Rainier of Pomposa which had not yet been quoted. This abbreviated collection of Gilbert contains some material which cannot be found in other collections of Gilbert.[232] Rainier of Pomposa's collection has an appendix of eleven decretals. This appendix includes the latest decretal of the entire manuscript: Innocent's letter *Per tuas nobis litteras intimasti* dating from 8 August 1213.[233]

This short description of the contents of Paris, BNF Lat. 3922A immediately shows that its author was an expert in canon law, who brought with him and/or received the latest decretal collections. Probably starting his work at Rouen shortly after 1185, he provided the local clergy with a comprehensive collection of current canon law.

During the same period two other decretal collections were compiled in Normandy, the collection *Sangermanensis* and the collection *Abrincensis prima*.[234] The former, compiled around 1198, was based on *Compilatio prima*, the collection *Brugensis* (Rheims, 1187), and the collection *Tanner*

---

[228] Cheney and Cheney, *Studies*, pp. 138, 147, 164–5; Kuttner, *Repertorium*, pp. 290–1; Landau, 'Die Entstehung der systematischen Dekretalensammlungen', 125; Duggan, *Twelfth-Century Decretal Collections*, pp. 51–7.

[229] Cheney and Cheney, *Studies*, pp. 165–8, 213; Kuttner, *Repertorium*, pp. 310–13.

[230] Cheney and Cheney, *Studies*, pp. 138–9, 166; Landau, 'Die Entstehung der systematischen Dekretalensammlungen', 125.

[231] Cheney, 'Decretals of Innocent III in Paris, B.N. MS LAT. 3922A', pp. 149–63; Cheney and Cheney, *Studies*, pp. 136–7.

[232] Cheney and Cheney, *Studies*, pp. 139–40, 166; Kuttner, *Repertorium*, pp. 310–13.

[233] Potthast, I, no. 4789. On this appendix, see Cheney and Cheney, *Studies*, pp. 140–1, 166; S. Chodorow, 'An Appendix to Rainier de Pomposa's Collection', *Bulletin of Medieval Canon Law New Series*, 3 (1973), 55–61.

[234] For these collections, see H. Singer, *Neue Beiträge über die Dekretalensammlungen vor und nach Bernhard von Pavia* (Sitzungsberichte der kaiserlichen Akademie der Wissenschaften in Wien. Philosophisch-historische Klasse CLXXI, 1) (Vienna, 1913); W. Holtzmann, 'Die Dekretalensammlungen des 12. Jahrhunderts. I. Die Sammlung Tanner', in *Festschrift zur Feier des zweihundertjährigen Bestehens der Akademie der Wissenschaften in Göttingen. II. Philologisch-historische Klasse* (Berlin, 1951), pp. 83–145; C. Cheney, 'Three Decretal Collections before Compilatio IV: Pragensis, Palatina I, and Abrincensis II', in Cheney, *The Papacy and England. 12th-14th centuries*, no. V, pp. 464–83.

(England, 1187–91).[235] *Sangermanensis* served as a source for *Abrincensis prima*, which was compiled shortly afterwards.[236] Unlike *Sangermanensis*, which was a reference book of canon law in its own right, *Abrincensis prima* was compiled as a supplement to *Compilatio prima*. Only those decretals which were not listed in *Compilatio prima* were excerpted from *Sangermanensis*.[237] *Abrincensis prima* is preserved as an early thirteenth-century copy in a manuscript formerly owned by the monastic library of Mont-Saint-Michel.[238] The history of this manuscript remains to be written, but it may well have been copied at Mont-Saint-Michel in the first half of the thirteenth century. Its material dates from before 1234 and contains matters relating to Normandy, particularly to Mont-Saint-Michel and to the Avranchin. Besides *Abrincensis prima*, the manuscript contains other works of canon law. There are the *Generalia* of Richard de Mores and his *Apparatus* to *Compilatio prima*, both originally composed in the 1190s; a heavily abbreviated Gratian and a further decretal collection, which Christopher Cheney named *Abrincensis secunda*. This collection is independent of *Abrincensis prima* and was probably copied in the first half of the thirteenth century from a manuscript brought to Normandy. The core of the original of *Abrincensis secunda* was perhaps compiled at the papal court from the registers and drafts of bulls between 1209 and 1214, and was possibly intended to serve as a supplement to *Compilatio tertia*.[239]

The compilations of Paris, BNF Lat. 3922A, *Sangermanensis* and *Abrincensis prima*, show that towards the end of the twelfth century some ecclesiastics in Normandy saw the need for reference books of current canon law. In compiling them, they or the canonists they commissioned deployed considerable skills and expertise. These compilations raise the question of who was behind their making. The answer remains tentative. Paris, BNF Lat. 3922A was probably compiled at Rouen. It may be more

---

[235] The collection *Sangermanensis* is now held at Paris, BNF Lat. 12459; Singer, *Neue Beiträge*, pp. 80–116; Singer's findings concerning the sources of *Sangermanensis* have been superseded by Holtzmann, 'Sammlung Tanner', pp. 83–145. However, Holtzmann's argument that *Tanner* was a Norman and not an English collection as proposed by Singer no longer stands. New findings show that *Tanner* was indeed compiled in England, Landau, 'Die Entstehung der systematischen Dekretalensammlungen', 144–6; for the collection *Brugensis*, see L. Falkenstein, 'Zu Entstehungsort und Redaktor der Collectio Brugensis', in Chodorow (ed.), *Proceedings of the Eighth International Congress of Medieval Canon Law*, pp. 117–60.

[236] Singer, *Neue Beiträge*, p. 77.

[237] Ibid., pp. 80–116; Landau, 'Die Entstehung der systematischen Dekretalensammlungen', 146.

[238] The manuscript is now held at Avranches, BM 149.

[239] Fos. 7r–77v (*Apparatus*), 79r–109r (*Abrincensis prima*), 136r–138v (Gratian), 139r–147v (*Generalia*), 119r–126v (*Abrincensis secunda*), Cheney, 'Three Decretal Collections', pp. 466–72; Kuttner, *Repertorium*, pp. 222–6, 264, 323, 417–18; Landau, 'Die Entstehung der systematischen Dekretalensammlungen', 125; Omont, *Catalogue*, x, pp. 68–73. Where the later additions to *Abrincensis secunda* (up to 1216) were made is unknown.

than mere coincidence that the compilation of this work started at about the time that Walter de Coutances became archbishop of Rouen.[240] Walter was an experienced administrator and perhaps a well-trained canonist.[241] When appointed to the bishopric of Lincoln in 1183, he showed considerable interest in matters of canon law and may have been looking out for material helpful in administering the diocese.[242] He or members of his household could have acquired the latest continental and English collections and brought them to Rouen.[243] In the years after his move to Rouen Walter and his men continued to interest themselves in the latest developments of canon law. Possible transmitters of such knowledge were men like Master Robert Balbus, canon at Rouen from *c.* 1200.[244] Robert can probably be identified with the Master Robert Balbus who, together with the canonist John of Tynemouth, served in Rome as proctor for Hubert Walter, archbishop of Canterbury in the early years of the thirteenth century.[245] Even if Robert was not a canonist himself, he must have had a keen interest in the latest papal decisions and their interpretations, and, equally important, he would have had easy access to such information. In such an environment it is little surprise to find that the systematic collection of decretals continued at Rouen after Walter de Coutances' death. Yet who supervised the work which continued until at least 1213 remains unfortunately obscure.[246]

The identification of the men behind *Sangermanensis* and *Abrincensis prima* is even more difficult. Given the fact that the Rouen collections and *Sangermanensis* are independent of each other, they appear to have been

---

[240] Cf. Landau, 'Die Entstehung der systematischen Dekretalensammlungen', 132, 142.

[241] The case of Walter as a well-trained canonist has recently been argued by P. Landau, 'Walter von Coutances und die Anfänge der anglo-normannischen Rechtswissenschaft', in O. Condorelli (ed.), *'Panta rei'. Studi dedicate a Manlio Bellomo* (5 vols., Rome 2004), III, pp. 183–204.

[242] Walter's keen interest in the administration of a diocese is indicated by his questions to the pope as bishop-elect of Lincoln and during the early years of his pontificate at Rouen, *Papal Decretals relating to the Diocese of Lincoln in the Twelfth Century*, ed. W. Holtzmann and E. Kemp (Lincoln Record Society XLVII) (Hereford, 1954), no. 21 [= Jaffé, II, no. 14965; *WH* 61ab; Jaffé, II, no. 14966; *WH* 61c]; for Normandy, see for example *Papsturkunden in Frankreich. Neue Folge. II. Normandie*, ed. J. Ramackers (Abhandlungen der Gesellschaft der Wissenschaften zu Göttingen; philologisch-historische Klasse; 3. Folge XXI) (Göttingen, 1937), no. 252 [= Jaffé, II, no. 15282; *WH* 254abc]; Jaffé, II, nos. 15185 [= *WH* 792abc], 16594 [= *WH* 376], 17019 [= *WH* 754abcdef]; *Register Innocenz' III.*, I, nos. 259 [= Potthast, I, no. 268], 264 [= Potthast, I, no. 275].

[243] Walter's *nepos*, Master John of Coutances, for example, studied at Oxford before becoming dean of the cathedral chapter of Rouen in 1188, A.B. Emden, *A Biographical Register of the University of Oxford to A.D. 1500*, 2nd edn (3 vols., Oxford, 1989), I, pp. 504–5; D. Greenway, *John Le Neve: Fasti ecclesiae Anglicanae, 1066–1300. III. Lincoln* (London, 1977), p. 36.

[244] Spear, *The Personnel*, pp. 257–8; Archbishop Walter referred to 'plures jurisperitos' whom he had asked for advice concerning the reading of a letter of Innocent III, 'Supplementum ad Regesta Innocentii III Romani pontificis', in *PL*, CCXXVII, cols. 9–282, 276–7, no. 239 [Potthast, I, no. 2359].

[245] C. Cheney, *Hubert Walter* (London, 1967), pp. 166–7.   [246] See supra, p. 62.

compiled at different places. It is tempting to link the origin of the *Sangermanensis* with the arrival of Master Nicholas de Laigle as master of the schools at Avranches in 1198. Nicholas, whose involvement in the electoral dispute at Avranches shows him to have been an expert in canon law,[247] can almost certainly be identified with the canonist Nicholas de Laigle active at Oxford in the early 1190s and bishop-elect of Chichester in 1209.[248] If this identification is correct, his move to Avranches would provide a convenient explanation for the rapid spread of the collection *Tanner* from England to Normandy. But until further research into the collection is undertaken, any such statement is speculative. As to *Abrincensis prima*, the fact that it is preserved in a manuscript held and possibly made at Mont-Saint-Michel[249] does not mean it was compiled there. The collection could well have come to the monastery from elsewhere.

The compilation of the Norman decretal collections and the career of Nicholas de Laigle show that expertise in canon law was available in Normandy at the turn of the twelfth century. In the first decades of the thirteenth century there is some continuing evidence of this. In 1208, Pope Innocent III wondered why Bishop Robert of Bayeux and his entourage, men of great legal expertise, put a problem to him which he considered to be trivial.[250] Innocent's remark may not have been based on actual knowledge of Robert's proficiency in canon law. In the arengas to his letters Innocent regularly referred to bishops learned in canon law.[251] But perhaps there was a kernel of truth in Innocent's characterisation of the legal skills of Bishop Robert and his men. One of the canons at Bayeux, William de Tancarville, candidate for the see in 1231, owned a book defining the jurisdiction of the bishop and the other dignitaries at Bayeux.[252] In 1225, at the council of Bourges, at which the sees from Normandy and Greater

---

[247] See infra, p. 161.

[248] For Nicholas de Laigle's English activities and connections, see D. Greenway, *John Le Neve: Fasti ecclesiae Anglicanae 1066–1300. V. Chichester* (London, 1996), pp. 4, 8–9, 41; Kuttner and Rathbone, 'Anglo-Norman Canonists', 317–21; J. Brundage, 'The Crusade of Richard I: Two Canonical Quaestiones', *Speculum*, 38 (1963), 443–52, esp. 447–8.

[249] See supra, p. 63.

[250] 'Innocentii Romani pontificis regestorum sive epistolarum', in *PL*, CCXIV–CCXVI [–col. 992], CCXV, cols. 1489–90, no. 176 [= Potthast, I, no. 3538]. Innocent III did not do justice to the bishop. Contrary to what his comment might suggest, contemporaries were not sure how to solve the problems raised by Robert. They considered the pope's solutions to be precedent-setting, as is indicated by the inclusion of Innocent's III answers into *X* 1.6.33, 1.29.31; cf. supra, pp. 40–1. This has also been pointed out by K. Pennington, 'Review of Wilhelm Imkamp, *Das Kirchenbild Innocenz' III. (1198–1216)* (Päpste und Papsttum XXII) (Stuttgart, 1983)', *Savigny KA*, 72 (1986), 417–28, 419 n. 7.

[251] Pennington, 'Review of Wilhelm Imkamp, *Das Kirchenbild Innocenz' III. (1198–1216)* (Päpste und Papsttum XXII) (Stuttgart, 1983)', 419.

[252] *Ordinaire et Coutumier de l'église cathédrale de Bayeux (XIIIᵉ siècle)*, ed. U. Chevalier (Bibliothèque liturgique VIII) (Paris, 1902), p. 340.

Anjou were well represented, the proctors of the cathedral chapters showed themselves to be well informed on canon law and its regulations concerning episcopal elections.[253] At Rouen, canon Master G. de *Salomonisvilla* took out a loan to finance his studies in Lombardy,[254] and at Sées, Bishop Gervase counted among his friends Peter of Northampton, a regent master of canon law at Paris.[255] In addition to experts of local origin, papal nominees occupying canonries in cathedral chapters[256] may have had useful legal expertise. As the cases of the disputed episcopal elections will show, cathedral chapters had come to appreciate the value of skilled lawyers for their business. Such lawyers were available in increasing numbers, but so were badly trained men. Trying to guarantee certain standards in practising canon law, Archbishop Maurice convened a provincial synod at Rouen in 1231 to establish that canonists should swear an oath that they would abide by certain basic rules of professional ethics when admitted to practice.[257]

Provincial synods were revived in Normandy during the period between *c.* 1190 and *c.* 1231.[258] Aiming at the implementation of canonical principles, the archbishops attempted to bring the Norman church into line with the regulations set by Rome. In 1190, Archbishop Walter convened a provincial synod at Rouen, at which he published some of

---

[253] R. Kay, *The Council of Bourges, 1225. A Documentary History* (Church, Faith and Culture in the Medieval West) (Aldershot, 2002), pp. 83–95, and Document 1, pp. 270–89.

[254] *Registres de Grégoire IX*, ed. Auvray, I, no. 543 [= Potthast -]; he is perhaps to be identified with Master William de *Salomonisvilla*, Tabbagh, *Diocèse de Rouen*, pp. 175, 209.

[255] C. Cheney, 'Gervase, Abbot of Prémontré, a Medieval Writer', *Bulletin of the John Rylands Library*, 33 (1950), 25–56, 40.

[256] Papal provisions began as requests in return for favours in the twelfth century. Direct papal provisions became common from the early thirteenth century onwards, Kay, *The Council of Bourges, 1225*, pp. 181–5. At Bayeux, the papal subdeacon Saxo held a canonry at the beginning of the thirteenth century, infra, p. 139. For provisions made by Honorius III, see H. Beier, *Päpstliche Provisionen für niedere Pfründen bis zum Jahre 1304* (Vorreformationsgeschichtliche Forschungen VII) (Münster, 1911), pp. 227–8. Pascal Montaubin's forthcoming *thèse* will provide detailed information on canonries held by papal appointees in Normandy and Greater Anjou in the first decades of the thirteenth century. So far, see his article on the see of Chartres, P. Montaubin, 'Les collations pontificales dans le chapitre cathédral de Chartres au XIIIᵉ siècle', in J.-R. Armogathe (ed.), *Monde médiéval et société chartraine. Actes du colloques international organisé par la ville et le diocèse de Chartres à l'occasion du 8ᵉ centenaire de la cathédrale de Chartres 8–10 septembre 1994* (Paris, 1997), pp. 285–99.

[257] J. Brundage, 'The Rise of Professional Canonists and Development of the Ius Commune', *Savigny KA*, 81 (1995), 26–63, 41.

[258] There had been a number of provincial synods in Normandy in the eleventh and early twelfth centuries. But only two took place in the reign of Henry II. Both were held by papal legates at Avranches in 1172 on the occasion of Henry II's reconciliation with the church after Becket's murder; thus they were convened under extraordinary circumstances, R. Foreville, 'The Synod of the Province of Rouen in the Eleventh and Twelfth Centuries', in C.N.L. Brooke et al. (eds.), *Church and Government in the Middle Ages* (Cambridge, 1976), pp. 19–39, pp. 21–32. It should be noted, however, that this picture may partly be due to the relative paucity of Norman chronicle evidence for the second half of the twelfth century.

the decrees of the Third Lateran Council held in 1179. At a synod at Sées in April 1209, the papal legate Guala confirmed statutes issued by Odo, bishop of Paris, between 1197 and 1208 enforcing ecclesiastical discipline. In February 1214, the papal legate Robert de Courson held a synod at Rouen to prepare the Norman clergy for the Fourth Lateran Council.[259] Four Norman bishops, led by Archbishop Robert Poulain, attended the meeting in 1215.[260] Nine years later, in 1224, Archbishop Theobald of Rouen published a shortened version of the canons decreed at the provincial synod of the same year,[261] and in 1231 Archbishop Maurice held a synod at Rouen mentioned above.

Thus between *c.* 1180 and *c.* 1230 canon law was not only received, but also worked upon in Normandy. Some of the Norman clergy had access to the latest developments in canon law – whether they occurred in England, France, or Italy. Decretal collections in particular seem to have attracted their attention. These met a need arising from the everyday problems of administering a diocese at the turn of the thirteenth century. As the ever-increasing number of papal appeals indicates,[262] churchmen had become well aware of the usefulness of canon law to defend or promote their interests. To maintain his diocesan authority, a bishop needed either a profound personal knowledge of canon law or at least men skilled in canon law in his entourage. The making of decretal collections stopped in Normandy in the second decade of the thirteenth century. The compilation of *Abrincensis prima* as a supplement to Bernard of Pavia's *Compilatio prima* shows that Bernard's collection then started to prevail as the reference book of canon law in Normandy.[263]

Greater Anjou

Building on a strong tradition of examining canon law, ecclesiastics in Greater Anjou continued to inform themselves about its development

---

[259] In general, see *Les statuts synodaux français du XIIIe siècle V. Les statuts synodaux des anciennes provinces de Bordeaux, Auch, Sens et Rouen (fin XIIIe siècle)*, ed. J. Avril (Collection de documents inédits sur l'histoire de France XXVIII) (Paris, 2001), pp. 184–5; R. Foreville, 'La réception des conciles généraux dans l'église et la province de Rouen au XIIIe siècle', in *Droit privé et institutions régionales: études historiques offertes à Jean Yver* (Paris, 1976), pp. 243–53, p. 244. For the synod at Sées, see *The Letters and Charters of Cardinal Guala Bicchieri, Papal Legate in England, 1216–1218*, ed. N. Vincent (The Canterbury and York Society LXXXVIII) (Woodbridge, 1996), no. 185.

[260] Foreville, *Latran I*, p. 392.

[261] *Les statuts synodaux français du XIIIe siècle V. Les statuts synodaux des anciennes provinces de Bordeaux, Auch, Sens et Rouen (fin XIIIe siècle)*, ed. Avril, p. 185; Foreville, 'La réception des conciles généraux', p. 245.

[262] Müller, *Delegationsgerichtbarkeit*, I, pp. 9–47.

[263] For England, see Kuttner and Rathbone, 'Anglo-Norman Canonists', 327.

after 1140.[264] They studied canon law, acquired legal texts, and compiled decretal collections. William de Passavant, bishop of Le Mans (1145–87), bequeathed a copy of Gratian's *Decretum* to his chapter.[265] Stephen de Montsoreau, archdeacon of Angers, may have come into contact with canon law during his studies at the schools of Paris at some time between 1149 and 1153.[266] Gerald de Barri's teacher in canon law at Paris in the late 1170s was Master Matthew d'Angers.[267] Matthew's surname may refer only to his place of origin, but might alternatively mean that he had been educated at Angers or even that he had himself taught there. Alexander III's council held at Tours in 1163 helped to promote the latest trends in canon law among the clergy of Greater Anjou.[268] One of the bishops present was Roger, recently elected to the see of Worcester. During the Becket conflict, in late 1167/early 1168, he went into exile and apparently made Tours his principal home. There, he seems to have deepened his knowledge of canon law and it is possible that he also discussed the legal issues of the dispute with local clerics.[269] The churchmen of Greater Anjou also took notice of the Third Lateran Council (1179). Ralph de Beaumont, bishop of Angers, for example, attended it and Bartholomew, archbishop of Tours, was on his way, when illness forced him to return to Tours.[270] Between 1187 and 1191, Clement III reminded Bishop Ralph of canon sixteen when stating that decisions within the church had principally to be taken according to the opinion of the *maior et sanior pars*.[271] Ralph's colleague William de Passavant appears not to have needed such reminders. At around the same time, in 1186/7 he may

---

[264] If the entry of Ivo of Chartres in the catalogue of St Aubin, Angers, dating at the earliest from the thirteenth century, refers to the *Decretum* or the *Panormia*, and if this work was acquired at some time after the mid-twelfth century, i.e. if its absence in the earlier catalogue of St Aubin's was not deliberate, it could be taken as evidence for interest in pre-Gratian material at Angers after 1140, Vezin, *Scriptoria d'Angers*, pp. 215–21; L. Delisle, *Le cabinet des manuscrits de la Bibliothèque Nationale* (3 vols., Paris, 1868–81), II, pp. 485–7; Jones, 'The Library of St Aubin's at Angers in the Twelfth Century', pp. 143–61. At Le Mans, too, there might have been an active interest in pre-Gratian material after 1140. A copy of the *Tripartita* (second half of the twelfth century) is said to be from Le Mans, manuscript 'C'= Paris, BNF Lat. 3858B. Dr Martin Brett kindly provided this information.

[265] *Nécrologe-obituaire de la cathédrale du Mans*, ed. G. Busson and A. Ledru (Archives historiques du Maine VII) (Le Mans, 1906), p. 22.

[266] Angers, AD Maine-et-Loire G 785 (charters), no. 10.   [267] See supra, p. 58.

[268] Cf. Somerville, *Council of Tours*, pp. 1–32, 39–62.

[269] M. Cheney, *Roger, Bishop of Worcester, 1164–1179* (Oxford, 1980), pp. 14–15, 39–40.

[270] For Ralph, see Foreville, *Latran I*, p. 389. Stephen of Tournai wrote to Pope Alexander III that Bartholomew, who had reached Paris, was too sick to continue his journey, 'Epistolae Alexandri III papae', in *RHF*, XV, pp. 744–977, p. 970, no. 412; 'Epistolae Stephani Tornacensis episcopi', in *RHF*, XIX, pp. 282–306, pp. 287–8, no. 12. Bartholomew's illness may have been made up. Pope Alexander had summoned him to the council to answer the case of the Breton bishopric Dol, which hoped to gain the status of an independent archbishopric for Brittany. Bartholomew, who feared a decision against the church of Tours, was trying to delay the case, see infra, pp. 178–9.

[271] *2 Comp.* 3.9.1 [= Jaffé, II, no. 16554; *WH* 523abc].

well have had in mind canon eight of this council when he referred to a decree of Alexander III to justify his appointment of a cleric to a church that had been vacant for over six months, because of a dispute concerning its advowson.[272] The decrees of the council reached Greater Anjou not only through the participants or through individual papal letters, but also through the decretal collection *Appendix Concilii Lateranensis*. Together with several older unidentified canonical collections the *Appendix* served as a source for the original version of the systematic decretal collection named *Bambergensis*, which was compiled within Greater Anjou, perhaps at the cathedral school of Tours, around 1185.[273] The *Bambergensis* quickly reached the schools of Bologna, which points to pre-existing contact between its place of origin and the centre for canon law study in Europe.[274] A collection of a different kind seems to provide further evidence for the familiarity with canon law in Greater Anjou, in particular at Tours. The dictamenal formulary of Bernard de Meung, composed around 1190, contains a number of references to canons of the council of Tours and the Third Lateran Council.[275] A considerable amount or even an early version of the formulary was perhaps compiled at Tours.[276]

Sporadic information indicates that canon law continued to be studied in Greater Anjou in the following years. In 1209 the papal legate Guala confirmed constitutions issued by Geoffrey, archbishop of Tours, Hamelin, bishop of Le Mans, and the chapter of Le Mans, concerning the conferral of churches in the diocese of Le Mans. One regulation tackled the issue of pluralism prohibiting anyone holding an adequate church to receive a second church.[277] In 1215, John, archbishop of Tours, attended the Fourth Lateran Council, and published some of its decrees at a provincial synod held at Tours in 1216/17.[278] Perhaps more significant is the close

---

[272] *Liber controversarium Sancti Vincentii Cenomannensis ou second cartulaire de l'abbaye de St-Vincent du Mans*, ed. A. Chédeville (Paris, 1969), no. 66; *Decreta*, ed. Alberigo et al., p. 215, c. 8.

[273] *Bambergensisgruppe*, p. 33.

[274] Walter Deeters advanced Angers or Tours as place of its origin, *Bambergensisgruppe*, pp. 33–4; Peter Landau argued in favour of Tours and established that the *Appendix* was a source for the original version of the *Bambergensis*, Landau, 'Die Entstehung der systematischen Dekretalensammlungen', 133–7. For further information on this collection, see Holtzmann, 'Sammlung Tanner', pp. 89–90.

[275] C. Vulliez, 'L'évêque au miroir de l'*ars dictaminis*. L'exemple de la *maior compilatio* de Bernard de Meung', *Revue d'histoire de l'église de France*, 70 (1984), 278–304, 288–9, 302–3.

[276] M. Camargo, 'The English Manuscripts of Bernard of Meung's "Flores Dictaminum"', *Viator*, 12 (1981), 197–219, 200–3.

[277] *The Letters and Charters of Cardinal Guala Bicchieri*, ed. Vincent, p. lxxvii, no. 183.

[278] Foreville, *Latran I*, p. 392; *Les statuts synodaux français du XIIIe siècle. I. Les statuts de Paris et le synodal de l'Ouest (XIIIe siècle)*, ed. O. Pontal (Collection de documents inédits sur l'histoire de France IX) (Paris, 1971), pp. 166–8; *Les conciles de la province de Tours (XIIIe–XVe siècles)*, ed. J. Avril (Paris, 1987), pp. 115–25; for the little that is known about previous councils at Tours (1201), Laval (*c.* 1207), and Rennes (*c.* 1210), see ibid., pp. 103–14.

contact between members of the cathedral clergy and centres of canon law. In 1208/9 the cathedral chapter of Le Mans regulated the residential duties of those canons representing either the cathedral church or themselves at Rome and those studying at Paris, Orléans, Bologna, Salerno, and Montpellier.[279] One of the students devoting their time to canon law may have been canon Master William de Rennes, who later gained fame for a gloss on Raymond de Peñafort's *Summa De poenitencia et matrimonio*.[280] Another was possibly Robert de Domfront, canon of Le Mans and later dean of the chapter, who studied in Paris and Lombardy in the 1220s.[281] In 1230 Maurice, bishop of Le Mans, had experts in law advising him on the re-organisation of the administrative structure of the diocese.[282] A letter of Honorius III confirms the presence of legal experts in the archdiocese of Tours.[283] And if the local experts were not able to provide the necessary expertise on a particular matter, the churchmen in Greater Anjou knew where to turn to obtain good counsel. In 1223, Geoffrey de Loudun, then canon of Angers and later chanter and bishop of Le Mans, put a question concerning a disputed tithe to the 'magistri regentes Parisius in decretis'.[284]

Despite being outclassed by Paris in the second half of the twelfth century, Angers appears to have retained a respectable reputation as a centre of law. Hastings Rashdall suggested that in 1219, when the teaching of civil law was prohibited at Paris, some teachers in civil law transferred to Angers.[285] Ten years later, a good number of both students and teachers settled at Angers on the occasion of the dissolution of the university of Paris.[286] The study of civil law was closely connected with the study of canon law. As one medieval proverb states: 'legista sine canonibus parum valet, canonista sine legibus nihil'.[287] Civil law provided 'many fundamental analytical categories – obligation, contract, delict, fraud, surety, prescription , and the like – as well as numerous procedural practices, rules of law and technical vocabulary'.[288] Civil law supplemented canon law in ecclesiastical courts. It also played an important role in the theoretical

---

[279] *The Letters and Charters of Cardinal Guala Bicchieri*, ed. Vincent, no. 188; *Chartularium insignis ecclesiae Cenomanensis quod dicitur Liber albus capituli*, ed. R.-J.-F. Lottin (Institut des provinces de France 2ᵉ sér. II) (Le Mans, 1869), nos. 207–8.

[280] *Enquête de 1245 relative aux droits du chapitre Saint Julien du Mans*, ed. J. Chapée et al. (Société des archives historiques du Conger) (Paris, 1922), p. 40 and n. 3.

[281] Ibid. p. 15.   [282] *Liber albus*, ed. Lottin, no. 232.

[283] *Honorii III Romani pontificis opera omnia*, ed. Horoy, IV, epistolae lib. VI, no. 141 [= Potthast -].

[284] Paris, BNF Collection Housseau, VI, no. 2567.

[285] H. Rashdall, *The Universities of Europe in the Middle Ages*, revised by M. Powicke and A.B. Emden (3 vols., London, 1936), II, p. 153.

[286] Ibid.

[287] F. Merzbacher, 'Die Parömie "legista sine canonibus parum valet, canonista sine legibus nihil"', *Studia Gratiana*, 13 (1967), 273–82.

[288] Brundage, 'The Rise of Professional Canonists and Development of the Ius Commune', 34.

canonistic discussion.[289] A canon lawyer, therefore, needed at least a basic training in civil law. Legists in turn started to recognise the importance of canon law for their profession at the beginning of the thirteenth century. They paid particular attention to the canonistic explanations of procedural law.[290] Thus it is probable that when the legists moved to Angers they provoked the study of canon law there.

As in Normandy, in Anjou papal nominees appear as canons of cathedral chapters.[291] Perhaps they provided some legal expertise in the curia. Finally, in 1231, Juhel, archbishop of Tours, held a provincial synod at Château-Gontier, where the clergy of Greater Anjou issued a canon regulating the admission of lawyers in terms identical to the canon decreed at the synod of Rouen held in the same year.[292]

Thus between *c.* 1140 and *c.* 1230 the clergy in Greater Anjou continued to be well informed about the latest developments in canon law. The compilation of *Bambergensis* and the continuous flow of appeals to the papal court[293] indicate that the readiness they had showed in the late eleventh and early twelfth century to implement canon law in practice continued towards the turn of the thirteenth century. If bishops could not find answers to their problems in the existing law books, they put their questions directly to the pope.[294]

---

[289] S. Kuttner, 'Papst Honorius III. und das Studium des Zivilrechts', in Kuttner, *Gratian and the Schools of Law*, no. X, pp. 79–101, pp. 89–90; C. Munier, 'Droit canonique et droit romain d'après Gratien et les décrétistes', in *Etudes d'histoire du droit canonique dédiées à Gabriel Le Bras* (2 vols., Paris, 1965), II, pp. 943–54.

[290] I. Baumgärtner, 'Was muss ein Legist vom Kirchenrecht wissen? Roffredus Beneventanus und seine Libelli de iure canonico', in Linehan (ed.), *Proceedings of the Seventh International Congress of Medieval Canon Law*, pp. 223–45, pp. 224–6.

[291] See supra, p. 66 and n. 256.

[292] See supra, p. 66 and n. 257. The legislation of these two provincial synods was closely interrelated. Maurice, who was translated from the see of Le Mans to the see of Rouen in 1231, played a significant role in the transmission from Angevin synodal statutes to Normandy, *Les statuts synodaux français du XIII*ᵉ *siècle. II. Les statuts de 1230 à 1260*, ed. O. Pontal (Collection de documents inédits sur l'histoire de France XV) (Paris, 1983), p. 110; O. Pontal, 'Les plus anciens statuts synodaux d'Angers et leur expansion dans les diocèses de l'ouest de la France', *Revue d'histoire de l'église de France*, 46 (1960), 54–67; *Les conciles de la province de Tours (XIII*ᵉ*–XV*ᵉ *siècles)*, ed. Avril, pp. 137–55; J. Avril, 'Naissance et évolution des législation synodales dans les diocèses du nord et de l'ouest de la France (1200–1250)', *Savigny KA*, 72 (1986), 152–249, 178–9, 210.

[293] For Greater Anjou the papal judges delegate have not yet been analysed. For an indication of the abundant number of cases, see *Papsturkunden in Frankreich. Neue Folge. V. Touraine, Anjou, Maine und Bretagne*, ed. J. Ramackers (Abhandlungen der Gesellschaft der Wissenschaften zu Göttingen; philologisch-historische Klasse; 3. Folge, XXVII, (Göttingen, 1956) for the period up to 1198, and Potthast, I, for the period up to 1230.

[294] For example: William, bishop of Le Mans, Jaffé, II, no. 13842 [= *WH* 1036abcde], Bartholomew, archbishop of Tours, *Register Innocenz' III.*, II, no. 74 (77) [= Potthast, I, no. 703], and William de Beaumont, bishop of Angers, Potthast, I, no. 1357.

Conclusion

The analysis of the spread of canon law in Normandy and Greater Anjou between *c.* 1140 and *c.* 1230 has shown that an increasing number of ecclesiastics in both regions were aware of the developments in canon law. They knew of the conciliar decisions and of the latest decretal collections. Members of the higher clergy studied canon law at the schools and some of them used their knowledge to compile new decretal collections. In order to assess the impact this expertise of canon law had on electoral practice it is now necessary to turn to the elections in Normandy and Greater Anjou.

Chapter 3

ELECTORAL PRACTICE: NORMANDY

The geographical limits of the duchy of Normandy coincided almost exactly with those of the ecclesiastical province of Rouen. The dioceses of Rouen and Sées extended beyond the Norman frontier, but the other five dioceses of Evreux, Bayeux, Lisieux, Coutances, and Avranches were situated within the borders of the duchy. The duke was by far the most important lord in the duchy and his control over the Norman church, including episcopal elections, was undisputed by the time of Henry I's death in 1135. The election of Richard, a natural son of Robert, earl of Gloucester, and thus a grandson of Henry I, to the see of Bayeux in 1133–5 illustrates this very clearly. Possibly on Robert's initiative, Henry I brought about Richard's election, but Hugh, archbishop of Rouen, refused to consecrate the candidate, probably on the grounds of Richard's illegitimacy. Henry I then turned to Pope Innocent II, pressing him to order Hugh to comply with his will. Unwilling to risk a breach with Henry over this question, Innocent complied and Hugh consecrated Richard.[1] In the course of the dispute neither Hugh nor the pope questioned Henry's role in the electoral process. After Henry I's death, however, the struggle for succession between King Stephen and the Empress Matilda shook the political landscape in Normandy. While ducal authority weakened, other political forces, notably the aristocracy, increased their power.[2] Robert of Gloucester, for instance, now manipulated his family's control over the see of Bayeux to seize a substantial portion of the Bayeux episcopal estate.[3] This also affected the framework of episcopal elections. Cathedral chapters, leading churchmen, and the

---

[1] *Orderic*, ed. Chibnall, VI, book XIII, p. 442.
[2] M. Chibnall, 'Normandy', in King (ed.), *The Anarchy of King Stephen's Reign*, pp. 93–115; Warren, *Henry II*, pp. 30–1.
[3] *Earldom of Gloucester Charters. The Charters and Scribes of the Earls and Countesses of Gloucester to A.D. 1217*, ed. R. B. Patterson (Oxford, 1973), no. 6.

Map 2 The archdiocese of Rouen

local aristocracy now had a greater opportunity to influence the outcome of elections.

ROUEN

In the history of the duchy, Rouen had long been a major centre before it became something like the 'capital' of Normandy under the Angevins.[4] Its

---

[4] M. de Bouard, 'Le duché de Normandie', in F. Lot and R. Fawtier (eds.), *Institutions seigneuriales (Les droits exercés par les grands vassaux)* (Histoire des institutions françaises au moyen âge 1) (Paris, 1957), pp. 1–33, p. 31; D. Bates, 'Rouen from 900 to 1204: From Scandinavian Settlement to Angevin

archbishop, who invested the dukes with Normandy,[5] was the most powerful prelate in the duchy. Rouen was by far the largest of the Norman
dioceses. It covered the area stretching from approximately the rivers Bresle,
Epte, and Oise in the east to the rivers Risle and Seine in the west, and from
the Channel in the north to the Seine in the south. With the Seine as an
important shipping route, and with Rouen, Eu, and Dieppe as flourishing
towns and harbours, the archdiocese was a prosperous region, from which
the church of Rouen profited much.[6] The archdiocese's long eastern border
was practically identical with the border between the duchy of Normandy
and the Capetian kingdom of France. In the south, the archdiocese even
included substantial territory usually controlled by the Capetians, the French
Vexin.[7] It was therefore only natural that the dukes of Normandy should pay
particular attention to the election of Rouen's archbishops.

The first election with which we are concerned here took place after
the death of Archbishop Hugh d'Amiens in 1164. The only surviving
evidence concerning this comes from an inquest conducted by Philip
Augustus in 1207/8. The jurors stated that it was due to Henry II that
Rotrou de Beaumont had been elected.[8] Rotrou was a member of the
Beaumont family which had been prominent at the ducal/royal court
since the late eleventh century.[9] In 1139, Rotrou's cousins, the twins

"Capital'", in J. Stratford, *Medieval Art, Architecture and Archaeology at Rouen* (The British
Archaeological Association Conference. Transactions for the Year 1986, XII) (Leeds, 1993),
pp. 1–11; B. Gauthiez, 'Paris, un Rouen capétien? (Développement comparées de Rouen et Paris
sous les règnes de Henri II et Philippe-Auguste)', in M. Chibnall (ed.), *Anglo-Norman Studies XVI.
Proceedings of the Battle Conference 1993* (Woodbridge, 1994), pp. 117–36, pp. 117–27; M. Chibnall,
The Empress Matilda: Queen Consort, Queen Mother and Lady of the English (Oxford, 1991), pp. 151–3.
5 Boussard, *Henri II*, p. 373.
6 There is no account of the extent of the temporalities enjoyed by the archbishop and the chapter of
Rouen in the twelfth and early thirteenth centuries. An impression of the church's wealth is given by
the account for the manor of Les Andelys, which the archbishop exchanged with Richard I in 1197 for
other property, *The Itinerary of King Richard I*, ed. L. Landon (Pipe Roll Society N.S. XIII) (London,
1935), p. 132, no. 482. In 1198, the king's officers accounted for 440 li. 16 s., *Magni rotuli scaccarii
Normanniae sub regibus Angliae*, ed. T. Stapleton (2 vols., London, 1840–4), II, p. 449. In the same year the
archbishop was granted over '580 *livres angevins* worth of wine in compensation for damage done to his
lands', V. Moss, 'The Defence of Normandy 1193–8', in Gillingham (ed.), *Anglo-Norman Studies XXIV.
Proceedings of the Battle Conference 2001*, pp. 145–61, p. 156. For other possessions enjoyed by the church
of Rouen, cf. T. Waldman, 'Hugh "of Amiens", Archbishop of Rouen (1130–64)' (Oxford Univ. D.
Phil. thesis, 1970), pp. 28, 37, 105; D. Lohrmann, *Kirchengut im nördlichen Frankreich. Besitz, Verfassung
und Wirtschaft im Spiegel der Papstprivilegien des 11.–12. Jahrhunderts* (Pariser historische Studien XX) (Bonn,
1983), pp. 118–21; Tabbagh, *Diocèse de Rouen*, pp. 3–7.
7 For the Norman and the French Vexin, see Warren, *Henry II*, p. 71.
8 *Les registres de Philippe Auguste, I. texte*, ed. J. W. Baldwin (Recueil des historiens de la France.
Documents financiers et administratifs VII) (Paris, 1992), inquisitiones, no. 18.
9 S. Vaughn, *Anselm of Bec and Robert of Meulan. The Innocence of the Dove and the Wisdom of the Serpent*
(Berkeley, 1987); J. Le Patourel, 'Norman Barons', in J. Le Patourel, *Feudal Empires. Norman and
Plantagenêt* (History Series XVIII) (London, 1984), no. VI, pp. 3–32; D. Crouch, *The Beaumont Twins:
The Roots and Branches of Power in the Twelfth Century* (Cambridge Studies in Medieval Life and
Thought) (Cambridge, 1986).

Waleran count of Meulan and Robert earl of Leicester, became King Stephen's most trusted advisors.[10] Shortly before that, around 1137/8, Rotrou's elder brother, Robert du Neubourg, had changed his attitude towards Waleran, opting to work with his powerful cousin and neighbour instead of against him.[11] Whether Rotrou had a hand in bringing about this *rapprochement* is unknown; in any case the unification of his family's forces in Normandy and at the king's court had an immediate impact on his own career. In 1139, he became bishop of Evreux – the diocese in which the heartlands of the Beaumonts were situated. In these and the following years Normandy suffered in the conflict for the English throne between King Stephen and the Empress Matilda. In 1141 Count Waleran, and in 1153 Earl Robert, changed sides and joined the Angevin court. Robert played an important role in the establishment of Angevin rule in England after 1153. As one of Henry II's chief baronial advisors he became justiciar of England around 1155.[12] In 1154, Robert du Neubourg became seneschal of Normandy.[13] From around the same time Rotrou was involved in diplomatic missions for Henry II.[14] Following Robert du Neubourg's death in 1159, Rotrou acted as seneschal and justiciar of the duchy. He ceased to fulfil these duties only after his election to the see of Rouen in 1164/5.[15]

In early 1164, Rotrou joined Henry II in England and took part in the negotiations between the king and Thomas Becket after the council of Clarendon. The negotiations failed and, when Becket fled the country shortly after the council of Northampton in October 1164,[16] Henry II knew he needed reliable churchmen more than ever. Thus when he received the news of the vacancy of the most important see in his continental dominions, in late 1164, he must have looked for a successor among the men in his closest entourage. At the same time, the Beaumont family was eager to see one of its members ruling the church of Rouen. Throughout the years the Beaumonts had maintained a close contact with the archiepiscopal see. From at latest 1138, Rotrou himself had been one of the archdeacons at Rouen only resigning in 1139 to take up his new

---

[10] Crouch, *Beaumont*, pp. 38–51; cf. Table 1, p. 77.
[11] Robert du Neubourg and Waleran concluded a *conventio* in 1141/2, D. Crouch, 'A Norman "conventio" and Bonds of Lordship in the Middle Ages', in G. Garnett and J. Hudson (eds.), *Law and Government in Medieval England and Normandy. Essays in Honour of Sir James Holt* (Cambridge, 1994), pp. 299–324, pp. 299–306.
[12] Crouch, *Beaumont*, pp. 51–98; F. West, *The Justiciarship in England* (Cambridge, 1966), pp. 35–45.
[13] Boussard, *Henri II*, p. 364 and n. 4.
[14] *Epistolae pontificum Romanorum ineditae*, ed. S. Loewenfeld (Leipzig, 1885), no. 228 [= Jaffé, II, no. 10174; *WH* -]; *The Correspondence of Thomas Becket, Archbishop of Canterbury, 1162–70*, ed. A. Duggan (Oxford Medieval Texts) (2 vols., Oxford, 2001), I, no. 34; 'Epistolarum regis Ludovici VII et variorum ad eum volumen', in *RHF*, XVI, pp. 1–170, p. 111, nos. 340, 341; *PR* 10, H.II, p. 28.
[15] Boussard, *Henri II*, p. 365.   [16] F. Barlow, *Thomas Becket*, 3rd edn (London, 1997), pp. 105–16.

Table 1 *The Beaumont–Neubourg family*

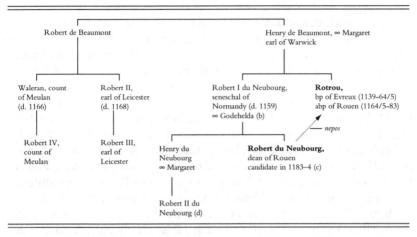

(a) In general, see Crouch, *Beaumont*, p. 16; D. Power, 'L'aristocratie Plantagenêt face aux conflits capétiens-angevins: l'exemple du traité de Louviers', in M. Aurell (ed.), *Noblesses de l'espace Plantagenêt (1154–1224)*. *Table ronde tenue à Poitiers le 13 mai 2000* (Civilisation médiévale XI) (Poitiers, 2001), pp. 121–37, p. 137.

(b) Paris, BNF Lat. 13905 (cartulary of the abbey of Bec), fo. 27r–v. This charter of Robert du Neubourg mentions Robert's mother Margaret, his wife Godehelda, and his sons Henry and Ralph.

(c) *Cartulaire de l'abbaye de Notre-Dame de La Trappe*, ed. M. Le Comte de Charency (Société historique et archéologique de l'Orne) (Alençon, 1889), pp. 445–6, nos. 6, 7; infra, p. 84 n. 60.

(d) Paris, BNF Lat. 13905 (cartulary of the abbey of Bec), fo. 27v: this charter of Henry du Neubourg mentions Henry's mother Godehelda, his wife Margaret, and his son Robert.

role as bishop of Evreux. A relative of his, Giles du Perche, had also been and still was archdeacon there. Through Giles, who named Archbishop Hugh his *patruus*,[17] Rotrou had distant links of kinship to his predecessor in the see of Rouen.[18] The Beaumonts knew that having one of their members as archbishop would not only be useful in promoting their local political interests, but also in providing benefices for family members. It

---

[17] "Epistolae Alexandri III papae', in *RHF*, xv, pp. 744–977, pp. 961–2, no. 398; William fitz Stephen called Giles Hugh's *nepos*, 'Vita sancti Thomae Cantuariensis archiepiscopi et martyris, auctore Willelmo Filio Stephani', in *MTB*, III, pp. 1–154, p. 27. On the *avunculus/patruus–nepos* relationship and the possibility that these terms did not necessarily convey a blood relationship between uncle and nephew in the modern understanding, see infra, pp. 219–29.

[18] *GC*, XI, col. 578; Waldman, 'Hugh "of Amiens"', pp. 4–5. Spear, *The Personnel*, p. 135 n. 4, doubts their kinship.

seems therefore that Rotrou's promotion to the archbishopric in late 1164/early 1165[19] was due both to his closeness to the king and to the considerable influence of his family on both sides of the Channel.

As archbishop Rotrou disappointed neither the king's nor his family's hopes. He continued to be a close advisor of Henry II[20] and acted as a patron for members of his family. Just as he had promoted to the chapter of Evreux relatives or members of families bound to the Beaumonts by feudal ties, so he filled the chapter of Rouen with men who were part of the Beaumont orbit.[21] By the time of his death in 1183 the Beaumont faction dominated the chapter. As his successor the canons wished to elect one of the late archbishop's *nepotes*, Robert du Neubourg, their dean. Robert's career demonstrates Rotrou's role as patron. While Rotrou was bishop of Evreux, Robert had been appointed dean of the chapter there. When Rotrou was promoted to Rouen, Robert followed him, becoming archdeacon and finally dean.[22] In electing Robert, the Beaumont faction hoped to continue profiting from the rich benefices of the church of Rouen. However, the chapter was not the only party involved in the election of 1184. This was apparently the last time that *religiosi viri*, that is bishops, abbots, and possibly priors and other ecclesiastics,[23] participated actively in the negotiations preceding an election. More importantly Henry II showed a lively interest. While the chapter had been meeting in the chapter-house, the king, the suffragans, and many other *religiosae personae* came together, maybe at the royal manor of Quevilly, just outside Rouen. The king apparently would not accept Robert du Neubourg as a suitable candidate and after long and tedious negotiations both parties agreed to decide the election by compromise. The *compromissarii* chose Walter de Coutances, bishop-elect of Lincoln. Ralph de Diceto's contemporary account suggests that compromise was still a relatively rare means to decide an election in the Anglo-Norman world. He stated that in ordering it both parties deviated from the *ius commune*.[24]

Besides Ralph de Diceto there is a second source on the election of 1184. After Archbishop Walter's death in 1207, Philip II ordered an inquest into the royal rights enjoyed in archiepiscopal elections. He took evidence from

---

[19] GC, XI, col. 48, argues for late 1164. *Torigny*, p. 225, places Rotrou's election in 1165. Perhaps Rotrou was elected in late 1164 and consecrated in 1165.

[20] For instance, he was a leading figure in the peace talks with Louis VII in 1166, *MTB*, V, no. 156, and in 1168, *The Letters of John of Salisbury II. The Later Letters (1163–1180)*, ed. C. N. L. Brooke and W. J. Millor (Oxford Medieval Texts) (Oxford, 1974), no. 272. For his constant support to Henry II during the Becket conflict, see ibid., nos. 176, 179, 231, 236; *Correspondence*, ed. Duggan, I, nos. 50, 66, 81, 94, 113, 150, II, nos. 188, 227, 238, 243; *MTB*, V, nos. 101, 106 [= Jaffé, II, no. 11237; *WH* -], 156, 182 [= Jaffé, II, no. 11279; *WH* -]; *MTB*, VI, no. 340, VII, nos. 563–4, 567, 623–6 [= Jaffé, II, nos. 11710–13; *WH* -], 628–31 [= Jaffé, II, nos. 11728, 11721–2, 11729; *WH* -], 732, 742.

[21] Spear, 'Power, Patronage and Personality', pp. 214–16.

[22] Ibid., pp. 214–15.   [23] See supra, pp. 26–31.   [24] *Diceto*, II, p. 21.

a variety of groups: knights, churchmen, citizens of Rouen, the mayor and inhabitants of Les Andelys, and other men. The report on the election of 1184 came from a group of fourteen knights. Their account differs from Diceto's. Whereas he described Walter's election as the result of a true compromise, that is that the *compromissarii* chose Walter without being forced to do so, the jurors assigned it to Henry II's intervention.[25]

At first glance, Diceto's account seems to be accurate. Walter de Coutances had been a canon of Rouen since the late 1160s and is said to have worked for Giles du Perche, archdeacon of Rouen and, since 1170, bishop of Evreux. In 1177, Walter succeeded Ralph de Warneville as treasurer of Rouen.[26] Thus Walter was familiar with the cathedral church of Rouen. However other, more conclusive evidence lends strong support to the account of 1207 that Henry played the decisive role in Walter's election. First, Diceto's account of the event may not be as accurate as it seems. His writings are biased in favour of Henry II and more importantly, Diceto and Walter were close friends, the latter being an important informant of the former for news from across the Channel.[27] If Walter was his source on the electoral procedure at Rouen, Diceto may well have been under the impression that the king did not go beyond his customary role in participating in the discussion of a suitable candidate; a role which Diceto generally appears to have accepted.[28] Moreover, even if Diceto

---

[25] The jurors did not explicitly refer to a compromise. They stated that the king proposed three men, wishing Walter de Coutances to be elected and that the chapter proposed three men, wishing Robert de Neubourg to be elected. It is possible that these men formed the panel of *compromissarii*, each side having received clear instructions about the man they ought to elect, *Registres de Philippe Auguste*, ed. Baldwin, inquisitiones, no. 18.

[26] E. Türk, *Nugae curialium. Le règne d'Henri II Plantagenêt (1145–89) et l'éthique politique* (Centre des recherches d'histoire et de philologie de la IVᵉ section de l'école pratique des hautes études; v, hautes études médiévales et modernes XXVIII) (Geneva, 1977), p. 41; Spear, 'Power, Patronage and Personality', p. 219. Master Odo de Coutances, possibly a relative of Walter, was canon at Rouen by 1188. On the grounds that a Master Odo witnessed a charter of Archbishop Rotrou (*c.* 1169), *Antiquus cartularius*, ed. Bourrienne, I, no. 64. Spear, *The Personnel*, p. 250, suggests that Odo de Coutances had already received his canonry under Rotrou. Odo was active in the royal chancery, and like Walter he may have received a canonry at Rouen at that time, but the evidence is inconclusive; for Odo as a chancery clerk, see P. Poggioli, 'From Politician to Prelate: The Career of Walter of Coutances, Archbishop of Rouen, 1184–1207' (Johns Hopkins Univ., Baltimore, Ph.D. thesis, 1984), p. 351; Rouen, BM 1193 (Y 044) (cartulary, cathedral chapter of Rouen), fo. 68v, no. 84 (charter of Ralph, chancellor of Henry II, William de Malpalu, royal justiciar, and Bartholomew, mayor of Rouen, concerning the acquisition of a house by Walter de Coutances at Rouen; Master Odo de Coutances appears among the witnesses).

[27] *Diceto*, I, p. lxxii; J. Gillingham, 'Royal Newsletters, Forgeries and English Historians: Some Links between Court and History in the Reign of Richard I', in M. Aurell (ed.), *La cour Plantagenêt (1154–1204). Actes du colloque tenu à Thouars du 30 avril au 2 mai 1999* (Civilisation médiévale VIII) (Poitiers, 2000), pp. 171–86, pp. 178–9.

[28] Cf. his accounts of other elections, *Diceto*, I, pp. 306–7, 367–8, ii, pp. 4, 14, 69–70, 105, 107–9, 116, 128, 139.

had information about Henry's activities which went against his understanding of proper electoral procedure, he may not have wished to
compromise Henry or Walter by publishing it.[29] Second, Walter's career
places him much closer to the king than to the cathedral chapter.[30] Despite
being a member of the chapter of Rouen, Walter hardly ever figured
among the witnesses of Archbishop Rotrou's charters.[31] Nor is this
surprising. Walter was a *curialis* par excellence and by the late 1170s the
king's right-hand man.[32] In 1173, he had been made vice-chancellor and
entrusted with the royal seal.[33] In 1175/6, he had received a further income
with the archdeaconry of Oxford.[34] In the following years he had been a
member of royal embassies as messenger for the king[35] and had acted as
royal custodian for the honour of Arundel and the abbeys of Ramsey and
Wilton.[36] Finally, in 1183, he had received the bishopric of Lincoln probably
on royal request.[37]

When, only a short time later, the most important see of Henry II's
continental dominions fell vacant, the king wanted someone who was
familiar with royal politics on both sides of the Channel and ideally
someone who was not a complete stranger to the archdiocese of
Rouen. Walter de Coutances fitted this description extremely well. His
opponent in the election, Robert du Neubourg, dean of the chapter, did
not. Robert appears to have been on friendly terms with Henry. He had
supported the king's cause during the Becket conflict[38] and, when the
people of Le Mans tried to bury Henry the Younger in their cathedral in
1183, Robert's lobbying played a significant part in Henry II's decision to

---

[29] On Diceto's attitude towards canon law, see C. Duggan and A. Duggan, 'Ralph de Diceto, Henry II
and Becket, with an Appendix on Decretal Letters', in B. Tierney and P. Linehan (eds.), *Authority
and Power: Studies on Medieval Law and Government in Honour of Walter Ullmann* (Cambridge, 1980),
pp. 59–81.

[30] In general, see Poggioli, 'Walter of Coutances'; *English Episcopal Acta I. Lincoln 1087–1185*, ed.
D. Smith (London, 1980), pp. xxxviii–xxxix; Tabbagh, *Diocèse de Rouen*, pp. 77–9.

[31] He witnessed a charter of Archbishop Rotrou concerning the abbey of St Georges-de-
Boscherville, Rouen, BM 1227 (Y 52) (cartulary, abbey of St Georges-de-Boscherville),
fos. 47v–48r.

[32] Cf. *Arnulf*, ed. Barlow, no. 126.   [33] *Diceto*, I, p. 367, II, p. 4.

[34] *PR* 22, H.II, p. 47. Walter held also the church of Woolpit and the chapel of Blyth, *Feudal Documents
from the Abbey of Bury St. Edmunds*, ed. D. Douglas (Records of the Social and Economic History of
England and Wales VIII) (London, 1932), no. 97; *Recueil des actes de Henri II, roi d'Angleterre et duc de
Normandie, concernant les provinces françaises et les affaires de France*, ed. L. Delisle et E. Berger (Chartes et
diplômes relatifs à l'histoire de France) (3 vols., Paris, 1916–27), II, no. 462.

[35] *Gesta regis*, I, pp. 168, 334–5; *Diceto*, II, p. 4.

[36] For Arundel see *PR* 25, H.II, p. 38; *PR* 26, H.II, pp. 32–3; *PR* 27, H.II, pp. 145–6; *PR* 28, H.II,
pp. 90–1; *PR* 29, H.II, p. 107; *PR* 30, H.II, pp. 127–8; *PR* 32, H.II, pp. 184–5; *PR* 33, H.II,
pp. 109–11. Walter finally discharged debts resulting from this custodianship in 1188/9, *PR* 1, R.I,
pp. 12–14. For Ramsey and Wilton see *PR* 26, H.II, pp. 26, 122.

[37] *Diceto*, II, p. 14; *English Episcopal Acta I. Lincoln 1067–1185*, ed. Smith, pp. xxxvii, xxxix.

[38] *MTB*, VII, nos. 740, 750–1, 756, 768 [= Jaffé, II, no. 11890; *WH* -].

order the transport of his son's body to Rouen.[39] But Robert was not a member of Henry II's entourage and with Rotrou's death the Beaumont family had lost the direct access to the king that they had enjoyed for three decades. Also the rebellion of 1173–4 may have contributed to Henry II's refusal of Robert's election. Although Robert's brother Henry du Neubourg had fought for him, their kinsmen, Robert, count of Meulan, and Robert, earl of Leicester, son and heir of justiciar Robert, had been strong supporters of the rebels.[40] The young king's rebellion of 1183 may have revived Henry II's memories of these events. Perhaps Henry did not want to take any risks by having Robert elected to the crucial see of Rouen.

According to the jurors' later account of the events in 1184, the chapter approached the king because they saw him disturbed after their refusal to elect Walter de Coutances. They asked Henry whether he would like them to elect Walter by virtue of royal prerogative or by request. The king answered: 'volo et precor ut ita fiat'. The chapter gave in and elected Walter.[41] Whether this was actually the way in which Henry II pushed through Walter's promotion remains obscure. Since the inquest was drawn up for Philip II, the key question in his mind was whether he as ruler of Normandy had any prerogative rights in archiepiscopal elections. At the time of Walter's promotion a considerable number of canonists accepted the king's participation in elections. They thought it necessary that his *voluntas* was considered and that his *consensus* was looked for. Some of the canonists even believed that it was necessary to obtain the ruler's consent.[42] In 1184, therefore, the chapter of Rouen may not have welcomed Henry's actions, but at least a majority of the canons appear to have considered them acceptable. No appeal was launched after Walter's election. Pope Lucius III confirmed his election in November 1184, and in early 1185 Walter was received as new archbishop at Rouen.[43] In 1207, however, canonists no longer thought that the king's will played a necessary part in a valid election. The terms *voluntas/consensus/assensus* no longer conveyed any electoral right pertaining to the ruler. Now they referred to the consent that the ruler could give to a completed election, if the canons asked him to do so.[44] This development in canonistic theory was known at Rouen. The decretal collection *Francofortana* contained *Quia requisistis*,[45] but it also contained *Qua fronte*, which Alexander III

---

[39] *Torigny*, p. 306; *Diceto*, II, p. 20; 'E chronico Rotomagensi', in *RHF*, XVIII, pp. 357–8.
[40] Warren, *Henry II*, pp. 125–39; Boussard, *Henri II*, p. 477 n. 5.
[41] *Registres de Philippe Auguste*, ed. Baldwin, inquisitiones, no. 18.   [42] Supra, pp. 31–6.
[43] 'Lucii III papae epistolae et privilegia', in *PL*, CCI, cols. 1071–376, cols. 1300–1, no. 173 [= Jaffé, II, no. 15117; *WH* -]; *Diceto*, II, p. 33.
[44] Supra, pp. 31–6.   [45] *Fr.* 10.4, Paris, BNF Lat. 3922A, fo. 178va; supra, p. 33.

had sent to Richard, archbishop of Canterbury, condemning elections held in the presence of the king.[46] These two contradictory decretals did not have equal weight in the eyes of a reader at Rouen. The *Apparatus* of the *Francofortana* attributed only very limited validity to *Quia requisistis*, commenting that this decretal might perhaps refer to churches in which the king was the patron or to churches that had not yet been consecrated, before referring to decretals that forbade the participation of the ruler in the electoral process.[47] The question was finally settled by *Rotomagensis prima*. It listed in its section on elections the decretal *Cum terra* which forbade any custom that required the king's consent in the selection process.[48]

At the same time, that is between *c.* 1180 and *c.* 1210, the perception of royal *voluntas* changed significantly. John Jolliffe and Sir James Holt have shown that royal *voluntas* was an essential part of Angevin government. The term *voluntas* represented kingship acting beyond established custom and without the consent of *curia* or *concilium*. Resistance to the royal will usually brought extremely harsh consequences. Already under Henry II there were voices complaining about the royal will as an arbitrary and unjust means of government. During John's reign complaint became a commonplace; the operation of the royal will was no longer considered tolerable.[49] Because Jolliffe and Holt have demonstrated this on the grounds of English sources only, a straightforward application of their results to the situation on the continent cannot be made. But the intensive exchange between Normandy and England makes it at least probable that the Normans were aware of the developments on the other side of the Channel. If so, they, too, no longer accepted royal *voluntas* as a normal part of royal government.

Thus to men familiar with contemporary canon law and/or with the current perception of royal *voluntas* in England, the jurors' answer to the question of the existence of a royal prerogative in archiepiscopal elections at Rouen conveyed a clear 'no'. Philip Augustus may have had access to such expertise, but whether he interpreted the jurors' reply in such a way remains an open question. He may well have considered *voluntas* as a perfectly acceptable means of royal government. Yet, whatever he made

---

[46] *1 Comp.* 2.20.41 = *X* 2.28.25 = *Fr.* 10.5, Paris, BNF Lat. 3922A, fo. 178va [= Jaffé, II, no. 14312; *WH* 755abc].

[47] Paris, BNF Lat. 3922A, fo. 178va: 'Forte loquitur de ecclesia in qua rex habet ius patronatus ut xviii q.ii. Abbatem [C. 18 q. 2 c. 4]. Maxime si non est consecrata ut in extrav. et di.l [gap] et di.lxiii Omnis [D. 63 c. 7] et xvi q.ult. Si quis [C. 16 q. 7 c. 12] et c. aliis.'

[48] *2 Comp.* 1.3.6 = *X* 1.6.14 = *1 Rot.* 3.1, Paris, BNF Lat. 3922A, fo. 152va [= Jaffé, II, no. 17656; *WH* 319].

[49] J.E.A. Jolliffe, *Angevin Kingship*, 2nd edn (London, 1963), pp. 50–109, esp. p. 55; J.C. Holt, *Magna Carta*, 2nd edn (Cambridge, 1992), pp. 75–122.

of the jurors' report, he did not claim an electoral right in any of the following elections at Rouen.

It is not clear whether the jurors frankly stated what they thought had happened, or whether they referred to the king's *voluntas* with the intention of showing that the king had no prerogatives. The group of the fourteen knights that reported the events of the election of 1184 strongly resembled a traditional Norman jury.[50] The knights were based in the region. Some of them had occupied prominent places in the government of the duchy under King John. John de Préaux had been frequently charged with royal missions. Robert de Fréquiennes had also been involved in the administration of the duchy and had acted as representative for John de Préaux's brother, Peter des Préaux,[51] a key administrator of King John.[52] Another juror, Richard de Villequier, had been John's escheator for Normandy in 1203[53] and William *Pantol* may have been related to Robert Pantolf, a former *bailli* of the Lieuvin.[54] Asking men heavily involved in local affairs was certainly the way to find out accurately about the events in earlier years, but it also gave room for the expression of local interests. When the bishop of Coutances, Vivian, wrote to Philip in 1207/8, that the *regalia* of Rouen had never belonged to the dukes of Normandy,[55] the bishop may have intended to save the temporalities of his church from depredation. But the former protégé of King John may also have hoped to limit Philip's influence in Normandy. Whether a similar motivation played a role in the jurors' behaviour cannot be definitely ascertained.

The election of Walter de Coutances' successor, Robert Poulain, came as a surprise to contemporaries.[56] By the time of Walter's death in 1207, the chapter of Rouen was dominated by men close to the late archbishop.[57] The favourites as his successor were certainly among these men. Yet according to a chronicle quoted in the *Gallia christiana* the chapter was not able to agree upon a candidate and the pope delegated judges to supervise the election.[58] Thus controlled, the chapter elected Robert Poulain in 1208. Robert did not figure among the chapter's prominent members. Indeed, the chronicle reporting the dispute described him as the poorest among the canons, but a good and simple man.[59] So Robert cannot have steered his

---

[50] Boussard, *Henri II*, pp. 290–4; Powicke, *Loss*, pp. 63–4.
[51] *Magni rotuli*, ed. Stapleton, II, pp. 501, 512–14.   [52] Powicke, *Loss*, p. 350.   [53] Ibid., p. 77.
[54] *Magni rotuli*, ed. Stapleton, II, pp. lii–iv.
[55] *Le cartulaire de Louviers. Documents historique originaux du Xe au XVIIIe siècle*, ed. T. Bonnin (5 vols., Evreux, 1870–85), I, no. 118.
[56] 'Continuatio altera appendices Roberti de Monte ad Sigebertum', in *RHF*, XVIII, pp. 345–8, p. 347.
[57] Spear, 'Power, Patronage and Personality', pp. 219–20; Poggioli, 'Walter of Coutances', pp. 238–52, 350–8.
[58] *GC*, XI, col. 59.   [59] Ibid.

election from a powerful platform within the chapter. His lack of connections with Walter de Coutances or with any powerful family[60] may have
inspired the papal delegates to see in him a suitable compromise candidate.

Robert's election stands at the beginning of a series of disputed elections
at Rouen that involved recourse to papal authority and canon law, a move
which received a major impetus from the Fourth Lateran Council.[61]

After Robert Poulain's death in 1221, the chapter of Rouen split into
several parties. According to our only source, a papal decretal, one party
promoted Canon Thomas, another the chancellor, William de *Canapello*,
and smaller groups favoured other candidates.[62] The identity of Thomas is
rather unclear. If his name really was Thomas he might be Thomas de
Fréauville, canon of Rouen. But John W. Baldwin suggests that the
original letter referred to Theobald d'Amiens, canon of Rouen since
1199, treasurer there since 1211, and the eventual victor of the dispute.[63]
There is much to be said in favour of this. Thomas de Fréauville was a
candidate in the following election that led to a lengthy process at the
papal court. If Thomas had already been rejected in 1221, this would
certainly have been mentioned in the dispute of 1230. In fact, the insertion
of Thomas in the decretal might have been due to a confusion between
the two disputes. Baldwin's hypothesis, therefore, has been accepted for
the following analysis.

In the election of 1221 Theobald received the majority of the votes. But
after the result had been made public, the chancellor's party appealed to
the papal court, apparently on the grounds that, while Theobald had
received more votes than any other candidate, he had not been supported
by an absolute majority of the chapter. At the time canonists increasingly
linked the *sanior et maior pars* with the majority of votes, but a clear
definition of what constituted a numerical majority was lacking.[64]

---

[60] Robert's *nepos* was not Henry du Neubourg, as is indicated in *Cartulaire de l'abbaye de Notre-Dame de La Trappe*, ed. M. Le Comte de Charency (Société historique et archéologique de l'Orne) (Alençon, 1889), p. 446, no. 7. R., archbishop of Rouen, confirmed in this charter a donation made by his nephew Henry du Neubourg to the abbey of La Trappe. The charter of Henry's donation was issued in 1170 and precedes the archbishop's charter in the systematic cartulary of La Trappe, ibid., pp. 445–6, no. 6. The editor extends 'R. Dei gratia Rothomagensis archiepiscopus' to 'R[obertus] Dei gratia' assuming that the archbishop in question was Robert Poulain. However, Henry du Neubourg's charter shows that Henry was the brother of Robert du Neubourg, dean of Rouen, and therefore a nephew of Archbishop Rotrou. As a consequence R., must be extended to R[otrodus]; cf. Table 1, p. 77.

[61] Cf. supra, p. 67.

[62] *Honorii III Romani pontificis opera omnia*, ed. Horoy, IV, epistolae lib. VI, no. 38 = X 1.6.48 [= Potthast, I, no. 6848].

[63] John W. Baldwin based this suggestion on the assumption that the original letter did not give the name of the candidate in full, but only an abbreviated Th., 'Philip Augustus and the Norman Church', 9 n. 46. For Theobald's benefices at Rouen, see Tabbagh, *Diocèse de Rouen*, pp. 80–1.

[64] See supra, pp. 46–8.

William de *Canapello*'s view that only an absolute majority of the chapter constituted a proper numerical majority was innovative and provided a convenient solution for a complicated problem. Honorius III, therefore, accepted the chancellor's argument and fourteen years later, during another electoral dispute at Rouen, an absolute majority of voters was referred to as a prerequisite for a legitimate election by scrutiny.[65]

Honorius III found another reason to reject Theobald's election, which he saw as procedurally flawed. He argued that Theobald's opponents had appealed to the pope during the electoral process and that therefore Theobald's party should not have completed the election,[66] which he therefore declared void. Yet he also refused to accept the chancellor William de *Canapello* as new archbishop.[67] Instead Honorius III ordered the chapter of Rouen to hold a new election.

This time the chapter chose three *compromissarii*, Ralph de *Castrehan* archdeacon of Caux, John de Roye archdeacon of the Norman Vexin, and the theologian Master Walter de Petit-Pont, to undertake the task. They agreed again on Theobald d'Amiens. They then wrote to the king asking for the return of the *regalia*,[68] and to the pope asking for Theobald's confirmation. But the opposing party had not yet given up. They now turned to another means provided by canon law to prevent Theobald's election. They questioned his suitability by spreading the rumour at the papal court that he was a leper. Thus alerted, Honorius III refused to confirm the election, referring to canon twenty-six of the Fourth Lateran Council, which stated that the election and the elect should be examined before being confirmed. Since none of the participants had appeared before him he would – in order to save them expenses and labours – send papal judges delegate, Gervase, bishop of Sées, Hugh, archdeacon of Rheims and John d'Abbeville, dean of Amiens, to conduct the enquiry.[69] In a second letter the pope asked the delegates to examine with the help of experienced doctors

---

[65] See infra, p. 93.

[66] Honorius III probably had in mind canon twenty-four of Lateran IV, that allowed for a legitimate appeal during the electoral process, 'Concilii quarti Lateranensis constitutiones', in *Constitutiones concilii quarti Lateranensis*, ed. García y García, pp. 70–1.

[67] *Honorii III Romani pontificis opera omnia*, ed. Horoy, IV, epistolae lib. VI, no. 38 = X 1.6.48 [= Potthast, I, no. 6848].

[68] *Layettes du trésor des chartes*, ed. A. Teulet et al. (5 vols., Paris, 1863–1910), I, no. 1513; *Recueil des actes de Philippe Auguste, roi de France*, ed. H.F. Delaborde et al. (Chartes et diplômes relatifs à l'histoire de France) (6 vols., Paris, 1916–), V, chapitre II, no. 12.

[69] Rouen, AD Seine-Maritime G 856 (papal letters concerning the archbishopric of Rouen): letter of the three judges delegate containing Honorius' mandate. The mandate is edited in *Honorii III Romani pontificis opera omnia*, ed. Horoy, IV, epistolae lib. VI, no. 176 [= Potthast, I, no. 6832]; 'Concilii quarti Lateranensis constitutiones', in *Constitutiones concilii quarti Lateranensis*, ed. García y García, pp. 71–2.

whether Theobald was a leper.[70] This proved not to be the case,[71] and Theobald was consecrated archbishop of Rouen on 4 September 1222.[72]

It is certain that neither Theobald d'Amiens nor William de *Canapello* enjoyed particularly close relations with the king or the pope, but it is extremely difficult to identify the men in the chapter who backed the respective candidates. Little is known about the social background of the chancellor Master William. He had been a canon of Rouen since the 1190s and then chanter before he became chancellor.[73] Slightly more information is available on Theobald's background. Born at Amiens, he had close connections with the cathedral church there, since he was cousin to Bishop Arnulf de La Pierre (1236–47).[74] Having entered the chapter shortly before the end of the twelfth century, Theobald may have owed his canonry at Rouen to Archbishop Walter de Coutances. It is notable that, during his time as archbishop, Theobald complained to the pope that Archbishop Robert Poulain had wasted the patrimony of his church.[75] He also refused to provide a former notary of Archbishop Robert, Luke, with a sufficient benefice, which brought him a rebuke from Honorius III.[76] But suggestive as this evidence is, it is not sufficient to conclude that in the electoral dispute of 1221–2 Theobald represented a group owing their careers to Walter de Coutances, opposed by a group close to Archbishop Robert.

---

[70] *Honorii III Romani pontificis opera omnia*, ed. Horoy, IV, epistolae lib. VI, no. 177.

[71] Müller, *Delegationsgerichtsbarkeit*, I, pp. 194–7, has shown that the plaintiff and defendant were involved in choosing the delegates. Ideally, both parties nominated one candidate each, and the pope nominated the third one. In this particular case it is unknown who proposed whom. Of the three delegates enquiring into Theobald's election and health, two may have known Theobald personally. The bishop of Sées, Gervase, had no apparent connections, but the archdeacon of Rheims, Hugh of Burgundy, may have been Hugo *Borgundiensis*, canon of Amiens around 1204. The third delegate, John d'Abbéville, was the dean of Amiens, P. Desportes, *Diocèse de Reims* (Fasti ecclesiae Gallicanae III) (Turnhout, 1998), p. 327; Desportes and Millet, *Diocèse d'Amiens*, pp. 127, 137. Whether John and Hugh were biased towards Theobald remains obscure, but it is remarkable that a brother of John d'Abbéville, Jacob, became archdeacon of Rouen in the 1220s, a post at the disposal of the archbishop, Tabbagh, *Diocèse de Rouen*, p. 224. In this context it is interesting that one of the arbiters, Walter de Petit-Pont, became chancellor at Rouen shortly after Theobald's election, Tabbagh, *Diocèse de Rouen*, p. 60. This may be evidence that Theobald made some concessions to the papal judges delegate in order to assure his election.

[72] Tabbagh, *Diocèse de Rouen*, p. 81.

[73] D. Spear, 'Les dignitaires de la cathédrale de Rouen pendant la période ducale', *Annales de Normandie*, 37 (1987), 121–47, 133.

[74] F. Pico, 'The Bishops of France in the Reign of Louis IX (1226–70)' (Johns Hopkins Univ., Baltimore, Ph.D. thesis, 1970), p. 88 n. 13.

[75] Rouen, AD Seine-Maritime G 1121 (letters of Honorius III concerning the archbishopric of Rouen) (Honorius orders judges delegate to enquire into these allegations).

[76] Rouen, AD Seine-Maritime G 1121 (letters of Honorius III concerning the archbishopric of Rouen); 55 HP 15 (cartulary, St Amand of Rouen), fo. 21r, no. 77 (Notary Luke witnesses a charter of Archbishop Robert).

When Archbishop Theobald died in 1229, the political situation had changed. Philip Augustus had died in 1223, and the premature death of his son Louis VIII in 1226 left the twelve-year-old Louis IX to inherit the crown of France. The government was taken over by Louis VIII's wife Blanche and a circle of advisors who had always been close to Philip Augustus. Some of the magnates of the French realm saw this as a chance to win back part of the power they had lost to Philip Augustus and rebelled. King Henry III supported their movement and started to prepare an expedition to retake possession of the continental dominions lost in 1204/6.[77] Thus at the time of Theobald's death, the climate at the royal court was much more stressful than under Philip Augustus and Louis VIII. The regents did not possess the political strength to enforce their aims but, precisely because of this, they must have been very concerned about events in the regions threatened by the rebellious barons or Henry III. Yet they could count on one very important support throughout Louis IX's minority: the papacy.[78] Its help probably showed in the disputed elections of 1230–1 and 1235–7.

In 1230, the majority of the chapter of Rouen elected their dean, Master Thomas de Fréauville, but a small party led by Archdeacon Master Arnulf appealed to the papal court against his election pleading that he was not a *persona idonea*. Arnulf accused Thomas of cupidity and avarice, because he had accumulated too many benefices with cure of souls. He specified that Thomas held three independent parish churches, together first with the archdeaconry of Amiens and then with the deanery of Rouen, without papal dispensation. Thomas had therefore violated the regulations laid down in canon twenty-nine of the Fourth Lateran Council. Referring to the prohibition of accumulation of benefices made at the Third Lateran Council, this canon declared that no one could simultaneously hold two churches with cure of souls. Only the pope could make exceptions by granting a dispensation.[79] While canon twenty-nine was the cornerstone of Arnulf's charge, he may well have drawn further inspiration from the decretals available at Rouen.[80] *Francofortana* contained canons thirteen and fourteen of the Third Lateran Council that prohibited the accumulation of benefices.[81] *Rotomagensis tertia* contained Innocent III's

---

[77] Berger, *Histoire de Blanche de Castille*, pp. 128–9, 161–86.

[78] Ibid., pp. 47–253. The pope was particularly supportive in 1229–30, ibid., p. 157.

[79] 'Concilii quarti Lateranensis constitutiones', in *Constitutiones concilii quarti Lateranensis*, ed. García y García, pp. 73–4.

[80] It is not clear whether he was already at Rouen at the time of Robert de Courson's council of 1214. Canons twenty-one and twenty-two of this council forbade pluralism, *Concilia Rotomagensis provinciae*, ed. G. Bessin (two parts in one, Rouen, 1717), I, p. 114.

[81] Fr. 16.2/3, Paris, BNF Lat. 3922A, fo. 182rb.

decretal *Cum iam dudum*; in this decretal the pope declared void the election of a provost because he held several offices and benefices simultaneously.[82]

Thomas's party, led by Walter, archdeacon of the French Vexin, did not deny these charges, but excused Thomas by presenting a *concessio*, probably a licence to hold benefices in plurality, from a former archbishop of Rouen, which at least according to the canonist Tancred would have been sufficient to excuse Thomas from the charge of unlicensed pluralism.[83] The pope, however, saw this differently. Probably having in mind canon twenty-nine of the Fourth Lateran Council, he did not accept Walter's argument and, since Thomas was not represented by a proper proxy, he ordered judges delegate to enquire into the case. If they found that the accusations against Thomas were true, they should declare his election void and provide Rouen with a *persona idonea*. If the accusations were false, then they should install him as archbishop.[84] The three papal judges delegate, Adam de Chambly, bishop of Senlis, John de Montmirail, archdeacon of Paris, and the subchanter of Paris, came to the conclusion that the accusations were true, and installed the bishop of Le Mans, Maurice, as archbishop of Rouen.

Now Thomas went to the papal court and appealed against this decision on the grounds that the delegates had not conducted their enquiry according to canon law. Having examined the case, Gregory IX accepted this charge and annulled the decision of the papal judges delegate. But far from giving up, Archdeacon Arnulf, who had also made the journey to the papal court, reiterated his accusations against Thomas. Consequently the case was again heard in the papal court. Confronted with Arnulf's charges, Thomas answered that while it was true that he had held these benefices, this did not violate the regulations of the Fourth Lateran Council. He had received the three parish churches canonically before the Fourth Lateran Council, and since laws were made for the future and – if not explicitly stated – not for the past, he could not be judged guilty. It is not quite clear why Thomas thought that this argument would help his cause. He had been personally present at the Fourth Lateran Council and therefore knew very well that the canon's content was based on the decrees of the Third Lateran Council. Thus there were already laws in place that forbade the simultaneous possession of churches. Master Arnulf spotted this immediately and refuted Thomas' argument. Thomas then deployed another stratagem. He tried to take advantage of the various exceptions canon law provided to allow the simultaneous possession of benefices, some

---

[82] *X* 3.5.18 = *3 Rot.* 31, Paris, BNF Lat. 3922A, fo. 121vb [= Potthast, I, no. 1186].

[83] See supra, p. 53.

[84] *Registres de Grégoire IX*, ed. Auvray, I, no. 455; 'Concilii quarti Lateranensis constitutiones', in *Constitutiones concilii quarti Lateranensis*, ed. García y García, pp. 73–4.

of which were formulated in the local copy of the *Francofortana*.[85] Thomas also attempted to exploit the lack of a precise definition of cure of souls.[86] Thus he claimed to have received a papal dispensation which, however, he had accidentally lost, but whose existence could be testified to by Master Pandulph, subdeacon and papal notary, Master Peter of Burgundy, sub-deacon, and by other men of great authority. He also claimed that the income of his deanery was not sufficient and that therefore he had needed additional benefices. Finally he pleaded that he had not realised that the archdeaconry of Amiens had cure of souls.

But Arnulf was well informed on the canonistic discussion on pluralism and the procedures in the papal chancery, and countered each of Thomas' arguments. He refused to believe in the existence of a papal dispensation. He cast doubt on Thomas' witnesses, explaining that the notary's testi-mony might be unreliable because papal mandates were often altered or nullified after they had been drafted, and Master Peter's declaration could not be accepted because he did not testify it under oath. He also added that, even if such a dispensation did turn up, Thomas should not benefit by it, since he had twice made false statements and three times had not told the whole truth. Furthermore Arnulf declared that Thomas could not hold three churches canonically, since, according to the canons, a cleric could only possess more than one church if two were held as one living or if another church was commended to him. Arnulf also denied Thomas' financial needs, referring to Thomas' s own statement that the deanery had an income of more than 300 *livres tournois*, which was more than sufficient. He further complained that Thomas had not specified the total number of his benefices nor made precise statements about the tenure of the three parish churches together with the archdeaconry of Amiens and the dean-ery of Rouen, nor had he mentioned the papal dispensation when the case had been heard before the papal delegates. Finally Arnulf stated that the tasks of an archdeacon of Amiens as described by Thomas himself were obviously concerned with the cure of souls. When Arnulf's party had finished, Thomas knew that his chances had gone. Consequently he withdrew his case even before Gregory IX pronounced verdict. The pope translated Maurice from the see of Le Mans to Rouen.[87]

Thomas learnt his lesson quickly. Shortly after the process, he wrote to Gregory IX stating that he had resigned the three churches. He asked the pope how he viewed his reputation under these new circumstances. Gregory IX assured him that his reputation was no longer harmed.

---

[85] See supra, pp. 51–3.   [86] See supra, p. 53.
[87] *Registres de Grégoire IX*, ed. Auvray, I, no. 655 = X 1.6.54 [= Potthast, I, no. 8306].

Having thus confirmed his suitability Thomas became eligible and within the next nine months he was successfully elected bishop of Bayeux.[88]

Gregory's decision to annul an election on the grounds of pluralism had ramifications far beyond the Rouen dispute. It set a precedent widely noticed by contemporaries. In 1233, the opponents of the archbishop-elect of Canterbury, John Blund, accused him of pluralism. In opting for this charge they may well have been inspired by Arnulf's success two years earlier. In the event they too were successful for Gregory annulled John's election.[89] The significance of Gregory's decision was also recognised by Raymond de Peñafort. When compiling his *Liber extra* he included the decretal (*Dudum ecclesia Rothomagensi*) in the section dealing with episcopal elections and thus ensured its wide distribution.

The political motives behind the electoral dispute at Rouen in 1230–1 are rather obscure. Thomas de Fréauville belonged to a family from the lesser Norman aristocracy. Their possessions were centred in the north-east of the archdiocese.[90] This, and the fact that during Theobald's time in office Thomas received the archdeaconry of Amiens and became dean of the chapter of Rouen, may be taken as evidence that he had good connections.[91] He also had good connections with the church of Bayeux. In 1221, he appeared as archdeacon there and ten years later he was elected bishop.[92]

The reasons for Arnulf's resistance are not known. A student of canon law and apparently a specialist in cases concerning pluralism,[93] he may have had sincere concerns about the suitability of the candidate, but he

---

[88] The bull recording the process between Thomas and Arnulf dates from 15 May 1231, *Registres de Grégoire IX*, ed. Auvray, I, no. 655. Gregory IX's letter to Thomas dates from 16 June 1231, ibid., I, no. 663. Thomas was elected bishop of Bayeux shortly before 17 March 1232, *Layettes*, ed. Teulet et al., II, no. 2176.

[89] Vincent, *Peter des Roches*, pp. 367–70.

[90] *Registres de Philippe Auguste*, ed. Baldwin, feoda C, p. 287; *Cartulaire de l'abbaye de Saint-Michel du Tréport (Ordre de saint Benoît)*, ed. P. Laffleur de Kermaingant (Paris, 1880), nos. 20, 35, 56, 76, 105, 110; Rouen, BM 1224 (Y 013) (cartulary, abbey of Foucarmont), fo. 128r (Thomas' mother Berta de Fréauville donates an annual rent from her lands in the *vicomté* of Criel to the abbey [1199]); for concessions of Thomas' brother Robert to the abbey in 1208 and 1218, see ibid., fos. 148r–149r. In these charters Robert's wife is named Maria. He also owned property in Eu, if he was identical with the Robert de Fréauville, who in 1225/6 was married to a certain Elizabeth and sold this property to the priory of St Martin-du-Bosc, Rouen, AD Seine-Maritime D 20 (cartulary, priory of St Martin-du-Bosc), fos. 41v–42r.

[91] Tabbagh, *Diocèse de Rouen*, p. 377. He had received the archdeaconry probably in 1222/3, cf. Desportes and Millet, *Diocèse d'Amiens*, p. 43.

[92] Rouen, AD Seine-Maritime G 3835 (charters concerning the cathedral chapter of Rouen) (Master Thomas de Fréauville, archdeacon of Bayeux, is named, together with Gilbert de Marleiz, canon of Rouen, as arbiters by the chapter of Rouen in a dispute with the knight Baudry de Longchamp).

[93] During the electoral dispute at Rouen in 1235 he belonged to the party which challenged William of Durham's suitability on the grounds of pluralism, see infra, pp. 92–5. In November 1235, he reported to the papal court a case of pluralism concerning Drogo de Trubleville, canon of Rouen,

may also have been concerned about the candidate's suitability in a secular context. The Capetian court was still cautious about the allegiance of the Norman clergy. In 1227, Thomas and two canons of the chapter had been prevailed upon to assure the regents that they would not act against king or kingdom before they received permission to cross the Channel to look after the affairs of their church.[94] These worries were not entirely unjustified. After Philip's death in 1223 and again after Louis VIII's death in 1226, agents of the English crown had tried to lure Norman nobles into taking actions against the Capetians.[95] Three years later, in 1229, Henry III, preparing his attack on Normandy, offered John de Fréauville, a brother of Thomas, the lands John previously had held from the countess of Eu in England.[96] Archdeacon Arnulf, who in the course of the disputed election of 1235 was again among the men opposed to a candidate with English connections,[97] was perhaps conscious of this and aimed at excluding those regarded as potentially disloyal by men loyal to the regency, if not by the regents themselves.[98]

Equally obscure are the motives behind the election of Maurice, bishop of Le Mans. It can be speculated that the papal judges delegate chose Maurice because of his reputation as an energetic leader of his church at Le Mans; qualities badly needed to reunite the chapter at Rouen. In addition the judges may have considered that Maurice's appointment gave Queen Blanche and her supporters little reason to worry. Adam de Chambly, bishop of Senlis and one of the three judges, had been in early 1230 among the bishops asked by Gregory IX to defend Queen Blanche against rebellious barons.[99] Adam knew Maurice personally. In late 1229 they, together with the archdeacon of Châlons-sur-Marne, had been charged by Gregory IX to restore peace between the regency and the university of

---

Registres de Grégoire IX, ed. Auvray, II, no. 2826. Perhaps Arnulf had gained his profound knowledge of canon law at Paris. In 1228, he was said to be 'staying in Paris', when he, together with two other judges, settled a dispute concerning the Norman priory of Bourg-Achard, Paris, BNF Lat. 9212 (cartulary, priory of Bourg-Achard), fo. 2r–v, nos. 13–14; cf. L. Passy, 'Notice sur le cartulaire du prieuré de Bourg-Achard', *Bibliothèque de l'Ecole des Chartes*, 22 (1861), 324–67, 23 (1862), 514–36, 22, 361–2. An entry in the obituary of St Victor, Paris, probably provides a further link between Arnulf and the city on the Seine. He may well have been identical with the Master Arnulf, archdeacon of Rouen, who retired to St Victor and is commemorated there on 31 March, *Obituaires de la province de Sens. T. I (Diocèses de Sens et de Paris)*, ed. A. Molinier (Recueil des historiens de la France. Obituaires I), (2 vols., Paris 1902), I, p. 550. No other archdeacon of Rouen named Arnulf is known, Spear, *The Personnel*, pp. 205–18; Tabbagh, *Diocèse de Rouen*, p. 55.

[94] Rouen, AD Seine-Maritime G 4493 (charter concerning the archbishopric of Rouen).
[95] Powicke, *Loss*, p. 269; D. Carpenter, *The Minority of Henry III* (London, 1990), pp. 309–11.
[96] *Close Rolls of the Reign of Henry III* (14 vols., London, 1902–38), I (1227–31), p. 145.
[97] See infra, pp. 92–5.
[98] The regents were well informed about the situation at Rouen, cf. *Cartulaire de Louviers*, ed. Bonnin, I, no. 152.
[99] Berger, *Histoire de Blanche de Castille*, p. 157.

Paris.[100] In spring 1230, Maurice had been busy working against Peter Mauclerc, duke of Brittany, and Queen Blanche's most dangerous domestic opponent.[101] Perhaps mindful of Gregory IX's mandate, Adam considered Maurice a candidate useful both to the church of Rouen and to the queen.

After Maurice's death in 1235, there was again a disputed election which came before the papal court. The majority of the chapter led by the treasurer, Walter de Richepas, wanted to elect the archdeacon of Caux, William of Durham. Their opponents, although the minority, comprised four heavy-weights of the chapter: the dean Stephen de Châteaudun, and three archdeacons. When the treasurer's party elected William despite their resistance, the dean's party appealed to the papal court. There, both parties were asked to give their respective versions of the election. The complexity of the opposing narratives, which, together with Pope Gregory's decision, fill six columns in Lucien Auvray's edition,[102] and the detail with which it shows hair to have been split all argue a considerable degree of canonical learning and an awareness of the loopholes in the canon law on episcopal electoral procedure, which had been sharpened by the chapter's experiences in previous elections.

According to William's party the chapter had come together to elect a new archbishop. The following day, three of its members had conducted a scrutiny, but since no one had received the majority vote, no election had been held. When the next date for election was being discussed, Archdeacon Arnulf and his brother had intervened, threatening an appeal to the pope if the election was not held before 31 March. In order to satisfy their demands, the election had been assigned to 31 March and sealed letters had been sent out to convene the canons for this date. On the election day, forty-one canons had been present, and two canons, Presbyter R. and Master Jocius, who had been prevented from coming by sickness, had nominated proxies. Then one of the dean's party had argued that the election should not be conducted by scrutiny, despite the majority of the chapter having voted for scrutiny. The dean's party had then left the chapter-house in disappointment. Allowing sufficient time between the requests, the remaining majority had asked them three times to return. But the dean's party had not done so. The remaining canons had then nominated three *scrutatores*, and again the dean and his followers had been asked to return to the chapter-house.

---

[100] *Registres de Grégoire IX*, ed. Auvray, I, nos. 374, 375 [= Potthast, I, no. 8466], 381 [= Potthast, I, no. 8467].

[101] Berger, *Histoire de Blanche de Castille*, pp. 171–2.

[102] *Registres de Grégoire IX*, ed. Auvray, II, no. 2796.

But the response had been negative once more. Then canon Gerald de *Saloel* had argued that the election could not proceed either by scrutiny or by compromise, since both ways had already been tried. In order to prevent an election, he had appealed to the pope. The treasurer's party, however, expecting that this appeal would not be taken seriously and fearing that they would not complete the election in time, had elected the *scrutatores* whom they had already nominated. In the subsequent scrutiny, William of Durham had received twenty-four out of the remaining twenty-eight votes. The treasurer's party, therefore, asked the pope to confirm William's election.

According to the opposing account of the dean's party, a compromise had been attempted when the chapter had come together for the first time. Since this compromise had brought no result, a scrutiny had been ordered the next day. During it there had been another attempt at compromise. But the compromise had failed again and the scrutiny had been completed. However, the scrutiny, too, brought no decision, since no candidate had received the majority vote of the chapter. When the canons had been discussing a date for a second election, John de Serqueux, archdeacon of Eu, and Master Gerald de *Saloel* had declared that they would not participate in the election because the chapter had already used all possible ways to elect and thus had fulfilled its task. In these circum-stances, the right of provision passed to the ecclesiastical superior, the pope. Besides, the chapter had not acted canonically in using two methods of election at the same time. Master Gerald had also appealed to the papal court, that neither the electoral day should be fixed nor the letters of convocation sent out unless the condition was inserted that the election was to be held *de jure*. But Gerald's appeal had not been taken seriously. The chapter had then fixed, without proper discussion, 31 March as the day of election. A refusal to revise this decision and to insert 'on the condition of a procedure *de jure*' had caused Master Gerald to renew his appeal.

On the election day, the dean and his party had been urged by others who had wanted to elect William of Durham to take part in the scrutiny. They had answered, however, that compromise was preferable to scru-tiny, since it led to peace not to discord or grief. This argument had not convinced William's supporters, and the dean, three archdeacons, and their followers had left the chapter-house in protest. They had been requested three times to return to the chapter-house. The first time, the dean's party had answered that they would not re-enter unless procedure was first discussed. They had added that, having received advice, they had had serious doubts about the legitimacy of an election considering all the irregularities that had already been committed during the first election. Concerning the second and the third appeal to return to the chapter-house, they answered that they had been given too little time in between these requests to discuss properly the offer of the treasurer's party. When, after a very short delay, the treasurer's party had come for the fourth time to ask them to return to the chapter-house, they had added that they had already nominated three *scrutatores*, the masters Michael de *Barceio*, John de St Lô, and R. de *Tonevilla*. Returning to the chapter-house, the dean's party had said that they were unhappy with the choice of the *scrutatores*, because two, J. de St Lô and R. de *Tonevilla*, had already given their votes to William in the previous scrutiny. The dean's party had also alleged that first there had been no need to conduct the scrutiny, since they had had enough time to hold the election properly; secondly, everybody's vote had been known through previous publication; and thirdly a new scrutiny could not alter the fact that the chapter had violated the regulation of the Fourth Lateran Council by holding the scrutiny and the compromise at the same time. But since the treasurer's party had not been swayed by these points, the dean's party had asked for arbiters to sort out all these matters. When this had been refused, the dean and his followers had appealed to the papal court. Then, despite the appeal and without collecting the votes from the two sick canons, the *scrutatores* had proceeded with the scrutiny, which resulted in William winning the election. To all these complaints about the procedure of the election, the dean's party added in the papal court that William of Durham was guilty of accumulation of benefices. They claimed that he held the benefice of *Leseia*, to which cure of souls was attached, together with his archdeaconry without papal dispensation. In consideration of all these irregularities, the dean and his party asked the pope to declare William's election void.

The treasurer's party denied all these charges. During the first election, they claimed, neither the compromise nor the scrutiny had been conducted in the way the dean's party alleged. Both compromise and scrutiny were accepted ways of electing a bishop and since the Fourth Lateran Council did not inflict punishment on electors as long as the rules set out were not violated, the procedure of the first election did not impede a second election. William's election, they therefore argued, should not be nullified. As to the second election the treasurer's party argued that, taking into account Archdeacon Arnulf's protests, they had correctly handled the fixing of the election day. Concerning Master Gerard's appeal demanding the insertion of the condition in the convocation letters that the election was to be held *de jure*, they claimed that it had been so inserted. The treasurer's party also pointed out that their decision to go ahead with the scrutiny had been correct. They had not harmed the rights of the dean's party either by admonishing them at too short intervals to return to the chapter-house or by the election of the *scrutatores*. They had left enough time in between their visits and they had been ready to accept other *scrutatores* at the dean's party's wish, if the dean's party had been willing to join them in the election. But this offer had been rejected. The treasurer's party added that the majority had wanted the normal way of holding the election, i. e. the scrutiny. Therefore the minority, i.e. the dean's party, could not force the majority to undertake the extraordinary or the voluntary, that is the compromise. Furthermore they had assumed that the minority had tacitly withdrawn its concerns about the scrutiny by assenting to the date of the election. The treasurer's party also asserted that the scrutiny itself had been conducted properly. The *scrutatores* had not visited the two sick canons in order to prevent any fraudulent activities in their absence. As to the charge of pluralism, the treasurer's party believed that William did not hold another benefice with cure of souls apart from his archdeaconry.

On the report of these two parties, the pope commissioned three men staying at Paris at the time – the abbot of Froidmont, Master Peter de Collemezzo papal chaplain and provost of St Omer, and Master Vernatius canon of Treviso. They were to ask William whether he accepted his elevation. If he did not, the chapter was to have the right of election with conditions laid down to protect the dean and his party. If William did accept, the judges were to enquire into the conduct of the scrutiny. They were also to enquire into the nature of William's benefices. They should then resubmit the case to the pope.[103] William, probably realising that being archbishop in the teeth of the opposition of the dean and three archdeacons would become a very difficult task, refused his election and thus the chapter had to re-elect. This time they commissioned six arbiters, who elected one of the papal judges delegate, Peter de Collemezzo. Following the election, the chapter, the king, and a number of bishops wrote to the pope asking him to confirm this decision.[104] Gregory IX did so, and when at first Peter refused, he urged him to accept the see. Peter finally obeyed the papal order and was consecrated on 9 August 1237.[105]

As in the previous electoral dispute, the great expertise of both parties in canon law is evident. The interpretation of canon twenty-four of the Fourth Lateran Council on electoral procedure was the basis of their arguments, which were enriched by a knowledge of current canonistic thought. This is particularly noticeable in their discussion over absent canons. The dean's party had in mind Innocent III's repeated demand

---

[103] Ibid.   [104] Ibid., no. 3281.   [105] Tabbagh, *Diocèse de Rouen*, p. 84.

that all votes should be collected, when they charged the treasurer's party with having ignored the votes of the two sick canons. In their response that this would have endangered the outcome of the election, the treasurer's party probably referred to Innocent III's decretal *Cum inter*. The dispute as to whether the dean's party had been recalled properly to the chapter-house revolved around Johannes Teutonicus' interpretation of Innocent III's decretal *Cum olim nobis*. According to his commentary on this decretal, several recalls were required.[106]

Besides the impact of the general council, papal decretals, and the principal canonists, a local element is recognisable. The previous electoral disputes at Rouen had a considerable influence on the arguments used in 1235. The outcome of the dispute of 1221–2 is reflected in the statement that the scrutiny brought no result, because no candidate had received the absolute majority of the votes. The use of the charge of pluralism, which had been at the centre of the dispute in 1230–1, serves particularly well to illustrate how local knowledge could be exploited. During the negotiations at Rouen, the *idoneitas* of William had never been questioned. None of the appeals threatened or executed had concerned William's character, and even the dean's party, although clearly against William, had not attacked his personal suitability for election. That the dean's party developed this argument only a short time before the process at the papal court is also indicated by the surprise with which it hit William's party. They did not know whether William was a pluralist. If this had been an issue before, they clearly would have had ready a more precise answer to this charge. Going into the process at the papal court the dean's party was apparently not too sure of the strength of their arguments concerning electoral procedure. Searching for a more powerful weapon, they may have been advised by a member of their group, Archdeacon Master Arnulf, to look to the electoral dispute of 1230–1. Then the charge of pluralism had proved to be very efficient and now Arnulf could provide them with his great expertise.[107]

While William's election nicely demonstrates to the modern reader the spread of canon law, Peter's election, albeit stripped of its context, served contemporaries to improve its use. In his handbook of procedural practices in canon law, Roffredus de Epiphanio (*c.* 1170 – *c.* 1243), better known as Roffredus Beneventanus, used Peter's name and his election at

---

[106] See supra, pp. 36–8. The decretal *Cum inter* was available at Rouen in the collection *Rotomagensis secunda*, 2 *Rot.* 1.4.3 (2a), Paris, BNF Lat. 3922A, fo. 210va.

[107] An additional argument for the dean's party to use again this charge may have been Gregory's annulment of John Blund's election to the see of Canterbury in 1233 on the grounds of pluralism, see supra, p. 90.

Rouen to demonstrate some of the procedures of episcopal elections.[108]
He had probably picked up Peter's name and the story of his election to
the see of Rouen at the papal court while working on his handbook.
Aiming at showing the different variants of electoral procedure, Roffredus
did not reproduce the documents actually relating to Peter's election.

It is again extremely difficult to identify the reasons for the dispute
surrounding William of Durham's election. Gerard de *Saloel* and John
de Serqueux were friends[109] who probably had sincere concerns about
canonical procedure, but carried little political weight within the chapter.
Much more powerful were the dean and his party. But there is no precise
information as to why they opposed Archdeacon William. Perhaps the
incident was merely a prolongation of a purely internal power struggle.
There was a disputed election to the deanery in 1233. Dean Stephen de
Châteaudun owed his office to a compromise arranged by Archbishop
Maurice.[110] Although Maurice apparently played a significant role in
arranging this compromise, his firm government of the archdiocese did
little to appease the rivalries within the chapter. After his death, several
groups tried to prevent the executors of his will from carrying it out. One
of the executors was William of Durham,[111] and perhaps his closeness to
Maurice was unacceptable to some members of the chapter. But, as in
1230–1, it is possible that reasons of a wider political impact prevented
William's election to the archbishopric. At the time of his election,
Maurice had been on neutral if not good terms with Queen Blanche.
But this had changed during his time in office. Maurice became involved
in a bitter struggle with the queen over the extent of royal jurisdiction, in
the course of which Blanche confiscated his temporal possessions and
Maurice laid an interdict on royal chapels and the royal *baillis*. Only
when the pope intervened was peace restored between archbishop and
the queen.[112] Perhaps she and her son Louis IX, who by 1235 played a
very active role in royal government,[113] were unhappy with a candidate
who had close connections with the late archbishop. Also there were

---

[108] For Roffredus' career, see G. Ferretti, 'Roffredo Epifanio da Benevento', *Studi Medievali*, 3 (1908–11), 230–87. For his handbook, see *Roffredi Beneventani libelli iuris civilis, libelli iuris canonici, quaestiones sabbatinae* (Corpus glossatorum juris civilis VI) (Turin, 1968, reprint of Avignon, 1500), pp. 339–40.
[109] They made provisions for each other's obituary, Rouen, AD Seine-Maritime G 2094 (obituary, cathedral chapter of Rouen), p. 93: 8 March.
[110] 'E chronico Rotomagensi', in *RHF*, XXIII, p. 334.
[111] *Registres de Grégoire IX*, ed. Auvray, II, no. 2817.
[112] Berger, *Histoire de Blanche de Castille*, pp. 278–80.
[113] J. Richard, *Saint Louis. Crusader King of France* (Cambridge, 1992), pp. 1–62.

other features of William's life that may not have appealed to them. William was a well-known doctor of theology teaching in Paris up to 1229.[114] On the occasion of the dispute between the university and the regents of France, Henry III tried to lure the teachers of Paris to come to England to pursue their studies.[115] William was among those who accepted and possibly went to Oxford. He returned to Paris in 1231, holding the wealthy church of Wearmouth, Durham, from at least 1232. After he renounced his election he received further privileges in England. Thus his familiarity with Maurice, his English connections, or perhaps even his activities in Paris up to 1229 may have made him a problematic candidate. Instead the man chosen by the arbiters, Peter de Collemezzo, was certainly welcomed by Louis IX and Queen Blanche. Peter, an Italian by origin, had been active as clerk to the legate Pandulph in England between 1218 and 1220. Probably during that period, Alice, countess of Eu, presented him to the canonry of Howe, in the church of St Mary, Hastings.[116] In the following years he intensified his French connections. From 1220 onwards he was based in Paris, receiving canonries at Amiens, Thérouanne, probably Chartres, and in 1229 the office of provost at St Omer.[117] During the years of the regency, he worked for the papal legate Romano Frangipani, cardinal-deacon of S. Angelo, who was so close to Queen Blanche that rumours spread that they maintained more than just a business relationship.[118] Peter de Collemezzo had made a name for himself at the royal court particularly through his successful efforts to negotiate a peace in the south of France.[119] In 1227, perhaps in light of Henry III's increasingly aggressive attitude towards the regency, he cut his (institutional) ties with England, resigning his canonry at Howe.[120] Peter was very popular with cathedral chapters across the French realm. He refused election to the see of Châlons-sur-Marne in 1226, allegedly to the see of Tours (1228/9?), and to the see of

[114] For biographical information on William, see Emden, *A Biographical Register of the University of Oxford to A.D. 1500*, I, pp. 612–13.

[115] *Chartularium universitatis Parisiensis*, ed. H. Denifle and E. Chatelain (4 vols., Paris, 1889–97), I, no. 64.

[116] *Acta Stephani Langton Cantuariensis archiepiscopi A.D. 1207–1228*, ed. K. Major (The Canterbury and York Society l) (Oxford, 1950), no. 105.

[117] For his career, see A. Paravicini Bagliani, *Cardinali di curia e 'familiae' cardinalizie dal 1227 al 1254* (Italia sacra. Studi e documenti di storia ecclesiastica XVIII/XIX) (2 vols., Padua, 1972), I, pp. 168–85; Pico, 'Bishops', pp. 158–63. For the canonry at Chartres, see Montaubin, 'Les collations pontificales', p. 298.

[118] Berger, *Histoire de Blanche de Castille*, pp. 104–43, esp. pp. 134–5.

[119] Pico, 'Bishops', pp. 160–1. [120] *Acta Stephani Langton*, ed. Major, no. 105.

Thérouanne in 1229.[121] In light of Peter's high standing with church-men and the king, and considering his connections with northern France, it is possible that the letters sent to Gregory IX pleading with him to accept and confirm Peter's election were not just a mere form-ality, but reflect the fact that the initiative for Peter's election originated among the *compromissarii* at Rouen, possibly influenced by royal interests from Paris, rather than the prompting of the papal court. Those promot-ing his name trusted Peter to reconcile a riven chapter, to be supportive to the royal government, and to be an excellent link with the pope. If this interpretation is correct, it sheds some interesting light on the growing authority of the papacy. Gregory did not nominate the archbishop, perhaps he did not even suggest a suitable candidate, and, yet, the *compromissarii* chose a man who could very well have been a papal nominee. The papal service, apparently, was becoming such a prominent and respected platform that able clerics like Peter could gain a widespread fame for their skills and as a consequence started to be considered as candidates for French bishoprics.

The analysis of the archiepiscopal elections at Rouen between 1164 and 1236 shows a significant change from Angevin to Capetian rule. Henry II was heavily involved, and, if necessary, even overruled the chapter's decision. In contrast, there was no direct royal influence under the Capetians. This shift resulted in a change among the men elected to the see of Rouen between 1164 and 1236. Under Henry II, closeness to the king was a prerequisite for the archbishop. Yet there was a neat difference between Rotrou de Beaumont and Walter de Coutances. Rotrou's career was built on the support from his family and from the king, whereas Walter owed his advancement to the king alone. By the time of Walter's election in 1184, Henry II was at the height of his power and Robert du Neubourg's failure to succeed Rotrou shows clearly that family networks in Normandy under Henry II could flourish only with the king's favour. The elections after 1200 were different and provide an almost perfect example of the dynamics of the growth of papal influence on episcopal elections in the first decades of the thirteenth century. The chapter held the elections and royal influence was informal, if it

---

[121] 'Willelmo chronica Andrensis', in *MGH, scriptores*, XXIV, ed. G. Waitz et al. (Hanover, 1879), pp. 684–773, p. 768; for Châlon-sur-Marne, see 'Chronica Albrici monachi Trium Fontium', in *MGH, scriptores*, XXIII, ed. G. H. Pertz (Hanover, 1874), pp. 631–950, p. 917, and cf. *Registres de Grégoire IX*, ed. Auvray, I, no. 192 [= Potthast, I, no. 8156]; Paravicini Bagliani, *Cardinali di curia*, p. 176. William, abbot of Andres, mentioned Peter's election to the archiepiscopal see of Tours without, however, providing its date. The only opportunity would have been the election of 1228. There is, however, no corroborating evidence for Peter's election at Tours, see infra, p. 185.

was present at all. The disappearance of tight royal control created the opportunity for groups within the chapter to promote their own interests. At Rouen the chapter was so heavily riven by rivalries that each election between 1207–8 and 1235–7 led to an appeal to the papal court. It becomes obvious that, due to the repeated appeals, the chapter started to lose its control over the nominations. It was still a step away from direct papal provision, but the probability of the election of candidates who had closer connections with the pope than with the chapter was rising. Whereas in 1208 and 1222 men from the chapter were elected under the supervision of papal judges delegate, the following two disputes led each to the election of men from outside the archdiocese, strange to the chapter but familiar to the pope.

EVREUX

Situated in the south-west of the archdiocese of Rouen, the diocese of Evreux covered some of the main routes from the Ile-de-France to Normandy.[122] Thus it occupied a territory of extremely high strategic importance during the Angevin–Capetian conflict.

When the see of Evreux fell vacant in 1139, the most influential family in the diocese was the Beaumonts, represented by the twins Waleran count of Meulan and Robert earl of Leicester. The family controlled most of the western part of the diocese. By 1139, Waleran had also extended his influence to the centre, most importantly to Evreux itself. In 1137, Amaury I count of Evreux died, leaving his land to minors. King Stephen took immediate advantage of this situation to reward his followers. He granted Waleran the castle of Evreux, which had been in royal hands since 1135, together with the viscounty of Evreux, which had been held by Count Amaury. Having thus gained control over Evreux, Waleran started to take an active interest in the affairs of the cathedral church there. He confirmed houses in the city to the chapter, and rewarded two of his household clerics with benefices.[123] Thus when the bishop of Evreux, Ouen, died in 1139, Waleran was by far the most important political figure in the diocese and was certainly responsible for the election as bishop of his cousin Rotrou, archdeacon of Rouen.[124] In the following years Rotrou and Waleran tightened the grip of the Beaumonts on the cathedral church of Evreux. Numerous family members and men

---

[122] F. Neveux, 'Les diocèses normands aux XIe et XIIe siècles', in P. Bouet and F. Neveux (eds.), *Les évêques normands du XIe siècle. Colloque de Cerisy-la-Salle (30 septembre – 3 octobre 1993)* (Caen, 1995), pp. 13–18, p. 14.
[123] Crouch, *Beaumont*, pp. 34, 72–3.   [124] *GC*, XI, col. 576.

Map 3 The diocese of Evreux

belonging to their entourages entered the chapter,[125] and by the time of Rotrou's promotion to the archbishopric of Rouen in late 1164/early 1165, their faction dominated there. Yet it took about five years before Rotrou's successor, Giles du Perche, was installed. Other than the income generated for the duke, the Becket conflict may have played a role in keeping the see vacant, but the evidence is not conclusive on this, by Norman standards, extraordinarily long vacancy. Giles du Perche's first patron had been his *patruus*[126] Hugh, archbishop of Rouen, who made him archdeacon of Rouen. After Hugh's death, Giles became the closest

---

[125] Spear, 'Power, Patronage and Personality', pp. 214–15; Crouch, *Beaumont*, pp. 34, 154.
[126] On the meaning of this, see *infra*, pp. 219–29.

collaborator of the new archbishop, his kinsman Rotrou.[127] Giles was also known to Henry II.[128] In 1160, Archbishop Hugh had recognised Alexander III as legitimate pope before Henry had given his authorisation. The king was furious and would have deprived Archdeacon Giles of his possessions, if Chancellor Becket had not interfered.[129] A couple of years later, and under completely different circumstances, Becket again played a principal role in the relations between Henry and Giles. Rotrou's endeavours for Henry during the conflict probably brought Giles closer to the king, who gained confidence in the archdeacon. In late 1169, the king sent Giles together with John, archdeacon of Sées, and John of Oxford to Pope Alexander III to discuss matters concerning his reconciliation with Becket.[130] The king's trust was the final piece necessary to assure Giles' election at Evreux in 1170, which had almost certainly been prepared by Rotrou's strong influence on the chapter. Giles governed the diocese until his death in 1179.[131]

Again the see lay vacant for two years until John fitz Luke was elected in 1181.[132] John probably belonged to a family of citizens of Rouen and had been a canon of the cathedral church there from the mid 1150s.[133] At some point in his career, he had entered royal service where he became a close collaborator of Walter de Coutances. Being at the centre of the royal court, John received the necessary support to become bishop of Evreux.[134]

---

[127] For their family relationship see Waldman, 'Hugh "of Amiens"', pp. 4–5. For their partnership, see Peltzer, 'Henry II and the Norman Bishops', 1213–14, 1218–19.

[128] Giles represented the chapter of Rouen at the donation of half the manor of Kilham by Henry II, *English Episcopal Acta XI. Exeter 1046–1184*, ed. F. Barlow (Oxford, 1996), no. 55. As archdeacon, Giles attested the following royal charters, *Recueil des actes de Henri II*, ed. Delisle and Berger, I, nos. 168, 394.

[129] 'Vita sancti Thomae Cantuariensis archiepiscopi et martyris, auctore Willelmo Filio Stephani', in *MTB*, III, p. 27.

[130] *The Letters of John of Salisbury II. The Later Letters*, ed. Brooke and Millor, no. 298. For Rotrou's activities during the conflict, see Peltzer, 'Henry II and the Norman Bishops', 1213–17.

[131] L. Delisle, *Recueil des actes de Henri II, roi d'Angleterre et duc de Normandie, concernant les provinces françaises et les affaires de France. Introduction* (Chartes et diplômes relatifs à l'histoire de France) (Paris, 1909), p. 363.

[132] The dates given by the chroniclers vary between 1181, *Gesta regis*, I, p. 278, and 1182, ibid., pp. 290–1, *Torigny*, p. 295. John was elected after 16 November 1180 and before March 1182, *Recueil des actes de Henri II*, ed. Delisle and Berger, II, nos. 564, 590. The *Gesta regis*, I, p. 278, therefore, seem to be correct when stating that Henry II gave John the bishopric shortly before his departure from Normandy to England. This crossing took place in July 1181, cf. R.W. Eyton, *Court, Household, and Itinerary of Henry II* (London, 1878), p. 240.

[133] Delisle, *Introduction*, pp. 363, 395–6; Spear, *The Personnel*, p. 248. According to *GC*, XI, col. 579, John was a *nobilis*. Bishop John is not to be mistaken for John fitz Luke, son of Luke, butler of the king's household, who may have been identical with the John fitz Luke who held, at least since 1178, custody of the castle of Montfort-sur-Risle and, from 1180, custody of Bouquelon, Tourneville, and Toutainville, *Magni rotuli*, ed. Stapleton, I, pp. 77, 105.

[134] *Torigny*, p. 295; *Gesta regis*, I, pp. 278, 290. As cleric, John witnessed the following royal charters, *Monasticon Anglicanum: A History of the Abbeys and Other Monasteries, Hospitals, Frieries, and Cathedral and Collegiate Churches with their Dependencies in England and Wales*, ed. W. Dugdale, revised by

John accompanied King Richard to the Holy Land where he died, leaving behind him his relative Luke as his deputy at Evreux.[135] In 1193, the church of Evreux elected Guarin de Cierrey as new bishop. Guarin's family took its name from a small village just outside Evreux. In the second half of the twelfth century, the family moved in the orbit of the two predominant families of the region, the Beaumonts and the counts of Evreux.[136] They also had a major interest in the chapter of Evreux, where Guarin's father or brother, Adam de Cierrey, had founded a prebend.[137] Thus Guarin could count on substantial local support when the see of Evreux fell vacant. Shortly after his election, he joined King Richard in Germany, perhaps to ask for the king's *placet* for his promotion.[138] In fact, he maintained excellent connections with Richard, who employed him several times as a messenger.[139]

J. Caley et al. (6 vols., London, 1817–30), VII, part 1, p. 374; *The Cartae antiquae Rolls 11–20*, ed. J.C. Davies (Pipe Roll Society N.S. XXXIII) (London, 1960), no. 417; *Recueil des actes de Henri II*, ed. Delisle and Berger, I, nos. 421, 440, II, nos. 515, 524, 562, 638, suppl. no. 35. Ibid., II, no. 638, has to be dated 20 January 1174 instead of 20 January 1183, *Calendar of Documents Preserved in France, Illustrative of the History of Great Britain and Ireland*, ed. J. Round (London, 1899), no. 432. Shortly before John's election, Henry II confirmed some acquisitions he had made in Rouen, *Recueil des actes de Henri II*, ed. Delisle and Berger, II, no. 564. Shortly after his election, a Channel crossing of John was paid for by the king, *PR* 28, H.II, p. 155. For his collaboration with Walter de Coutances, see *Gesta regis*, I, p. 291; Peltzer, 'Henry II and the Norman Bishops', 1220.

[135] Müller, *Delegationsgerichtsbarkeit*, II, no. 153; *GC*, XI, col. 582.

[136] Evreux, AD Eure G 122 (cartulary, cathedral chapter of Evreux), fo. 18r–v, nos. 69 (*c.* 1183: Adam de Cierrey witnesses a donation by Amaury III, count of Evreux, to the cathedral church for the celebration of the anniversary of Amaury's father, Simon), 70 (*c.* 1183: Adam de Cierrey witnesses a donation made by Robert, count of Meulan, to the cathedral church for the celebration of Simon's anniversary); fo. 24r, no. 99 (1170–9: Adam de Cierrey witnesses a donation by Amaury de Lacy, another knight from the entourage of Count Robert, to the cathedral church); ibid., H 438 (charters concerning the abbey of Lyre), no. 14 (Adam de Cierrey witnesses a charter of Robert III (?), earl of Leicester); *Cartulaire de l'église de la Sainte-Trinité de Beaumont-le-Roger*, ed. E. Deville (Paris, 1912), no. 37; Crouch, *Beaumont*, pp. 142, 175.

[137] Evreux, AD Eure G 122 (cartulary, cathedral chapter of Evreux), fo. 24v, nos. 101 (Adam's donation), 102 (confirmation of this donation by Adam's son, William de Cierrey; Bishop Guarin, who is named William's brother, appears among the witnesses). Conflicting evidence raises the possibility that Guarin was Adam's brother, not his son, Evreux, AD Eure H 490 (charters concerning the abbey of Lyre): Adam de Cierrey made a donation to the abbey 'in presentia G. Ebroicensis episcopi, assensu et voluntate T. heredis mei, et G. Ebroicensis archidiaconi, et R. filiorum meorum'. Theobald de Cierrey confirmed this grant 'made by his father Adam' 'in presentia venerabilis patris et avunculi mei G. Ebroicensis episcopi', Paris, Archives Nationales AB XIX 3128 (Collection Lenoir), pp. 473–5, no. 57; see also 'Ex obituario ecclesiae Ebroicensis', in *RHF*, XXIII, pp. 460–5, p. 465 n. 3. I am grateful to Prof. Daniel Power for having discussed the pedigree of the Cierrey family with me.

[138] *Registres de Philippe Auguste*, ed. Baldwin, inquisitiones, no. 22.

[139] *Itinerary*, ed. Landon, nos. 440, 457, 481, 482, 488, 500; Diceto, II, pp. 138–9; Howden, IV, pp. 14, 37. Howden, IV, p. 37, listing the participants of Richard's embassy to Otto IV's coronation in 1198 identified Guarin as bishop-elect. There is, however, no indication that Guarin's election had not been confirmed by then, cf. ibid., n. 5, and *Itinerary*, ed. L. Landon, no. 440.

When Guarin died in 1201,[140] the political situation in Evreux had changed. In the treaty of Le Goulet concluded on 22 May 1200, John had surrendered the city of Evreux and most of the county to Philip Augustus.[141] Thus the French king had become the bishop's overlord for the core lands of the bishopric. Philip Augustus immediately took the initiative in the Evrecin, and ordered an inquest into the rights that Henry II and Richard I had enjoyed in episcopal elections at Evreux. The identity of the jurors is unknown, but judging from the other inquests conducted by Philip in Normandy it seems probable that local men, seculars and clergy, were employed. They replied that Henry and Richard had enjoyed no rights. As at Rouen in 1207/8, it is not clear whether the jurors honestly stated what they thought to be the truth or whether they purposely denied the existence of ducal rights in order to limit Philip's influence in the region. In either case, however, their answer is significant for the understanding of the ducal role in the electoral procedure at Evreux in 1200. Either they were convinced that the ducal consent in elections was not required, or at least they thought it likely that Philip would believe such a statement.

Philip made the best of the inquest and used it for propaganda purposes to portray himself to the Norman clergy as a king respectful of the church. Probably in June 1200, he issued a charter to the chapter of Evreux granting them the right 'to elect their bishop freely just as the other canons of French churches have the power to choose their bishops'.[142] The charter was very important. The electoral procedure was put into writing and the ruler was not explicitly mentioned as participating in the election. The clause 'just as the other canons of the French churches have the power to choose their bishops' still left considerable room for interpretation, but in principle the charter took the electoral procedure out of the ill-defined sphere of unwritten custom, which was very much subjected to the ruler's will. The chapter of Evreux clearly felt that this was a significant step forward. The canons asked the pope to confirm the charter. Interestingly the pope's confirmation, dating from 30 April 1201, does not contain the clause referring to the custom of the other French churches. It only states that Philip had renounced any rights in the episcopal elections at Evreux, as was written in his charter.[143] Possibly the chapter aimed at the complete exclusion of royal influence in the electoral process and, with Innocent's

---

[140] *GC*, IX, col. 581. One obituary at Evreux celebrates his anniversary on 16 August, 'Ex obituario ecclesiae Ebroicensis', in *RHF*, XXIII, p. 463. Other obituaries offer 14 August, ibid., n. 10; Paris, BNF N. A. Lat. 1774 (obituary, abbey of Lyre), fo. 23v.

[141] *Recueil des actes de Philippe Auguste*, ed. Delaborde et al., II, no. 623.   [142] Ibid., no. 637.

[143] Evreux, AD Eure G 122 (cartulary, cathedral chapter of Evreux), fo. 3r, no. 6 [= Potthast, I, no. 1363].

confirmation, the canons had now a document that could be referred to in defence of their electoral freedom.

If this was the canons' aim, it proved unsuccessful. In the spirit of the phrase 'just as the other canons of the French churches', the chapter of Evreux had to consider Philip's wish when they elected Robert de Roye, probably in late 1201. Robert was a *nepos* of Bartholomew de Roye, the king's foremost advisor. Bartholomew himself had considerable interests in the Evrecin, as he was married to Petronilla de Montfort, daughter of Simon IV de Montfort and Amicia, daughter of Robert III earl of Leicester.[144] In assuring Robert's election, Philip Augustus clearly intended to strengthen Capetian influence in the Evrecin and to satisfy the wishes of his most trusted aide.

However, Robert's episcopate lasted only a short period of time and, when he died in 1202/3,[145] Philip was at war with King John. Perhaps not wishing to jeopardise any gains in the Evrecin, he did not impose his choice on the chapter of Evreux.[146] The chapter turned to its dean, Luke. Luke's career had been fostered by his relative, the former Bishop John. Canon and archdeacon of Evreux, Luke had acted as John's deputy when John went on crusade; he then became dean of the chapter in the mid-1190s.[147] When he was elected bishop in 1203, he was very much a local choice. It is true that his patron, Bishop John, had had close contacts with the Plantagenet court. But Luke had never joined the royal entourage. Shortly after his election, he found himself in a fierce dispute with parts of the chapter led by the dean, Ralph de Cierrey. Immediately after Luke's election, Ralph set out to the pope to gain privileges for the chapter and to accuse Luke of violating its rights. As most of the accusations referred to Luke's actions as bishop[148] it is possible that Ralph's hostility towards Luke originated only after the election. An alternative explanation would be that Ralph had been a candidate for the bishopric in 1203. During Guarin's episcopate, the Cierreys had maintained their influence in the

[144] Baldwin, *Philip*, pp. 110–14, 308, 439, 512 n. 25. The date of this marriage is unknown, but Bartholomew was active in the area at least since 1200, when he witnessed a charter of William de Marcilly-(sur-Eure) for the hospital of St Nicolas of Evreux concerning an exchange of lands situated at the southern border of the diocese of Evreux, Evreux, AD Eure H-dépôt Evreux G 0007 (cartulary, hospital of St Nicolas of Evreux), p. 11, no. 23. Bartholomew is commemorated in the obituary of Evreux on 10 January, 'Ex obituario ecclesiae Ebroicensis', in *RHF*, XXIII, p. 460.

[145] Spear, *The Personnel*, p. 136.   [146] Powicke, *Loss*, pp. 161–9.

[147] Müller, *Delegationsgerichtsbarkeit*, II, no. 153 (canon and dean); for his archdeaconry, see, for example, Evreux, AD Eure G 122 (cartulary, cathedral chapter of Evreux), fo. 13r–v, no. 48 (*c.* 1183: he witnesses a charter as archdeacon). Spear, *The Personnel*, p. 139, raises the possibility that he resigned his deanship in 1201.

[148] Müller, *Delegationsgerichtsbarkeit*, II, no. 153. One charge, however, referred to the period, when he acted as Bishop John's deputy.

chapter of Evreux. Guarin's *nepos* or brother, Giles, became archdeacon, and Ralph himself, perhaps another *nepos* of Guarin, joined the chapter.[149] At the time of the election, Ralph commanded substantial support within the chapter, for upon Luke's election the canons elected Ralph as their dean. Thus Ralph may well have hoped to succeed Robert de Roye as bishop of Evreux, and, frustrated by his failure, he may have considered the deanery not as a consolation, but as a suitable platform from which to launch attacks against Luke.[150]

Dean Ralph's day came, however, when Bishop Luke died after a long illness in 1220.[151] The canons were well informed about the procedural rules. First, they went to Philip Augustus to seek licence to hold an election. Then, having elected Ralph, they asked Philip to confirm the election and to return the *regalia*. In a letter resembling the standard letters recommended by Roffredus Beneventanus about fifteen years later,[152] they informed the king that they had conducted the election according to the regulations laid down by the Fourth Lateran Council and that they had elected Ralph, a very suitable candidate, unanimously by divine inspiration. The king complied.[153] But Ralph died only three years later. The chapter turned again to one of its members, yet one of a special kind, the abbot of Bec, Richard de St Léger. On 17 July 1223 the canons elected him as their new bishop.[154] The abbot of Bec had only recently become a member of the chapter of Evreux, Bishop Luke and the chapter

---

[149] See supra, p. 103, and n. 137. In a charter for the hospital of St Nicolas of Evreux, issued before Luke's election, Giles, archdeacon, Ralph Louvel, canon, and Ralph de Cierrey, priest, appear among the witnesses. Ralph is not yet named among the canons of the cathedral church, Evreux, AD Eure H-dépôt G 0007 (cartulary, hospital of St Nicolas of Evreux), pp. 17–18, no. 35. Ralph Louvel was a further relative of Guarin, who joined the chapter probably during his episcopate. By 1203 he held the post of an archdeacon, Power, *Norman Frontier*, p. 138 and n. 137.

[150] There is too little evidence to judge whether the conflict between Guarin and Luke was due to personal motives or to a longstanding rivalry between two groups within the chapter. It is noteworthy, however, that having been Bishop John's deputy Luke may already have been a contender for the bishopric in 1193. During the process of 1204–5, Luke received backing from Archbishop Walter, former patron of the late Bishop John, Müller, *Delegationsgerichtsbarkeit*, II, no. 153. Walter's election at Rouen, in turn, had strongly limited the access of the Beaumont clan to the benefices of the archdiocese. Was the conflict Luke–Ralph de Cierrey part of a struggle for patronage between the Beaumonts and Archbishop Walter?

[151] Evreux, AD Eure G 122 (cartulary, cathedral chapter of Evreux), fo. 86v, no. 303: vidimus of a letter of Bishop Ralph de Cierrey dating from October 1220, stating that Ralph had concluded certain business which had originated under his predecessor Luke, but which, due to Luke's long illness and subsequent death, had been left unfinished; *GC*, XI, col. 582.

[152] See supra, p. 96–7.

[153] *Layettes*, ed. Teulet et al., I, no. 1414; *Recueil des actes de Philippe Auguste*, ed. Delaborde et al., V, chapitre II, no. 8.

[154] He was consecrated on 27 August 1223, 'E chronico monasterii Beccensis', in *RHF*, XXIII, pp. 453–60, p. 454; Paris, BNF Lat. 12884 (*Chronicon Beccensi* and charters concerning the abbey of Bec), fos. 308v–309r.

having assigned him a perpetual canonry with all rights and duties.[155] Why the canons chose the abbot is unclear, but in consideration of the abbot's prebend, his election must be understood in the context of local politics rather than as a sudden turn towards regular clergy by the secular chapter of Evreux. After Richard's death, the canons chose again a local man, again from within the chapter and from a family that had already provided two bishops of Evreux: Archdeacon Ralph de Cierrey. The charter in which they announced Ralph's election again displays close familiarity with the standards required by canon law. It informs the chapter of Rouen that having agreed on an election day (2 June 1236), all the canons had been summoned to attend the election. On the appointed day, the canons and the procurators of those canons who could not be present convened and opted for scrutiny as the electoral procedure. Then they counted the votes and examined the merits of the electors and of the elect 'or more appropriately the-to-be elected' – the author of the letter finely distinguished between the nomination and the election of the candidate, thus indicating the emergence of the principle of the *electio communis* in Normandy. The canons found that the *maior et sanior pars* of the chapter had voted for Ralph. Then Canon John de Caen, named procurator by the dean with the consent of the chapter, performed Ralph's official election.[156] After that, the chapter of Rouen examined and approved the elect and the election, because the archbishopric was vacant at the time. Finally Ralph was consecrated by Thomas de Fréauville, bishop of Bayeux, on 21 September 1236.[157]

The elections at Evreux show significant royal involvement up to 1201. This can be explained by the diocese's important strategic position on the Angevin–Capetian border. With the Capetian conquest, this strategic importance disappeared. The royal involvement in elections at Evreux ceased until 1244, when Louis IX caused the elevation of his *curialis*, John de La Cour.[158]

The continuous influence of local families on the elections is evident. In 1139 and 1170, the Beaumonts used their local power and their influence with the king to swing the elections in favour of their relatives. Towards the end of the century, another family, the Cierreys, became the dominant force in the chapter. Being of rather limited political significance and therefore not receiving too much attention from the rulers, they

---

[155] Evreux, AD Eure G 122 (cartulary, cathedral chapter of Evreux), fos. 14v, 16r, no. 55.

[156] Rouen, AD Seine-Maritime G 4494 (charter concerning the election of Ralph II de Cierrey as bishop of Evreux): 'collatione habita meritorum eligentium et electi vel verius eligendi'.

[157] 'Ex chronico monasterii Sancti Taurini Ebroicensis', in *RHF*, XXIII, pp. 465–7, p. 466; 'E chronico Rotomagensi', in *RHF*, XXIII, p. 336; Paris, BNF Lat. 12884 (*Chronicon Beccensi* and charters concerning the abbey of Bec), fo. 331v.

[158] Pico, 'Bishops', pp. 188–9, 194.

managed – possibly in the shadow of the Beaumonts – to intrude them-selves so firmly into the chapter of Evreux that they were able to provide three bishops over a period of forty years stretching from Angevin to Capetian rule. The Cierreys demonstrate very neatly how the secular branch of a family could be outclassed in importance and influence by its ecclesiastical branch. For members of the Cierrey family, it may well have been far more lucrative to join the bishop's entourage – his 'family' – than to attach themselves to the household of the family's secular head.

LISIEUX

John, bishop of Lisieux, died in 1141. Very active on behalf of King Henry I, John had also been a busy and successful patron. One of his *nepotes*, John, became bishop of Sées, and another, Arnulf, was to follow him in the see of Lisieux.[159] Arnulf's election, however, caused considerable trouble. Only a short time before his death, Bishop John had surrendered the bishopric to Geoffrey Plantagenet, whose conquest of Normandy was proceeding steadily. When John died, Geoffrey expected the chapter to approach him in order to receive the licence to elect. This apparently did not happen; instead, the 'clergy and the people' of the diocese of Lisieux elected Arnulf.[160] Outraged, the count did not invest Arnulf with the *regalia*, prevented the elect from taking up his office, and appealed to Innocent II to have Arnulf's election quashed. Clearly, Geoffrey and his advisors considered their claim to be consistent with current canon law. From his point of view, Geoffrey had good reason to be upset. First, the chapter's negligence in seeking the licence to elect was a severe blow to his efforts to establish his authority in the recently conquered territory.[161] More importantly, Geoffrey was angry about the chapter's choice. Two years earlier, Arnulf, then archdeacon of Sées, had been King Stephen's advocate in the papal court against Geoffrey's wife Matilda in the matter of Henry I's succession. Arnulf's counterpart in the papal court was the bishop of Angers, Ulger. According to John of Salisbury, Ulger had on that occasion addressed Arnulf in the following way:

I marvel, Arnulf, at your presumption in attacking now he [Henry I] is dead the man whom you and your fathers and brothers and whole family worshipped as long as he was alive; the man who raised you and all your kindred from the dust. I would

---

[159] *Arnulf*, ed. Barlow, pp. xii–xiii.

[160] *Torigny*, p. 142; *The Letters of Peter the Venerable*, ed. G. Constable (2 vols., Cambridge, Mass., 1967), I, no. 101.

[161] *Sancti Bernardi opera*, ed. J. Leclercq and H. Rochais (8 vols., Rome, 1957–77), VIII, no. 348. For Geoffrey's conquest of Normandy, see Chibnall, 'Normandy', pp. 101–2.

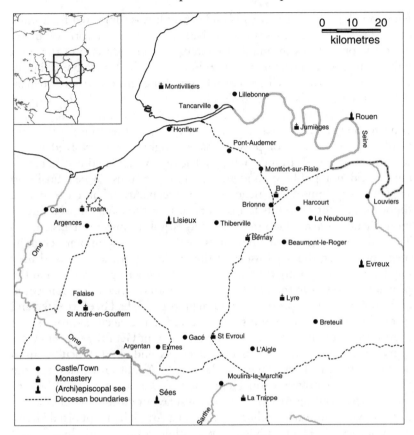

Map 4 The diocese of Lisieux

marvel at the shamelessness of your lies were it not that your whole race is garrulous and deserves to be held up as an example of sinful life and skill and effrontery in lying. In these arts you are conspicuous even among the Normans.[162]

If Ulger's words contained a kernel of truth, then Geoffrey Plantagenet had good reason to be discontent with Arnulf's election at a moment so critical for his campaign in Normandy. But Arnulf fought back. He appealed to the concept of a canonical election free from secular influence, that had been stressed so intensively by the supporters of the Gregorian reform movement. Nearly forty years later, he wrote that he had been elected canonically without the ruler's designation.[163] In his attempt to

[162] *The Historia pontificalis of John of Salisbury*, ed. M. Chibnall (Oxford, 1986), p. 84.
[163] *Arnulf*, ed. Barlow, nos. 124, 132, 137.

109

win over Pope Innocent II to his side, Arnulf was supported by leading ecclesiastics. During his studies he had built up a network of useful personal connections throughout western Europe, and two of the most influential regular churchmen of the time, Peter the Venerable, abbot of Cluny, and Bernard of Clairvaux, wrote to Innocent on Arnulf's behalf. Whereas Peter stressed Arnulf's close connection with the papacy, Bernard emphasised the regularity of Arnulf's election. He urged the pope to defend the *libertas ecclesiae* and to reject the appeal of Count Geoffrey who could not possibly have a right to be involved in the selection process.[164] Innocent firmly backed Arnulf in the struggle,[165] but he did not publicly condemn Geoffrey's claims. When finally in 1143 a compromise was negotiated between Arnulf and the count, Innocent did not object its terms: in return for the payment of a fine of more than 900 *livres*, Geoffrey accepted Arnulf as bishop of Lisieux.[166] These terms conveyed an ambiguous message to contemporary churchmen concerning the legal issues of the conflict. On the one hand they implied that an election was valid without the ruler's participation in the selection process. On the other hand, the enormous size of the fine could be considered as tacit proof that a ducal prerogative had been violated and that in future the duke ought to be involved in the electoral process.

Arnulf's election serves as an example of Count Geoffrey's eagerness to gain control over Norman episcopal elections, and of his difficulties in so doing. Forty years later, the events leading to Arnulf's resignation of the see show that Geoffrey's son Henry now had a far more solid base to operate from. Bishop Arnulf fell from royal favour during the rebellion of 1173–4, when rumours reached the king that Arnulf had supported Henry the Younger.[167] Henry refused any further contact with him[168] and started to put him under pressure. In 1177, the king gave the chapelry of Bosham, which had been in Arnulf's possession since 1155, to Bartholomew, bishop of Exeter.[169] When the papal legate, Peter of Pavia, arrived in France in 1177 to settle the question of the marriage between Duke Richard and Alice, daughter of Louis VII, Arnulf saw a chance for reconciliation. At a meeting the various parties decided that, if Henry paid the bishop's debts, Arnulf would resign his see, so that he could enter a religious house with a clear conscience. But this did not

---

[164] *The Letters of Peter the Venerable*, ed. Constable, I, no. 101; *Sancti Bernardi opera*, ed. Leclercq and Rochais, VIII, no. 348.

[165] *Arnulf*, ed. Barlow, nos. 124, 132.   [166] Ibid., no. 137.

[167] *Gesta regis*, I, p. 51 n. 4, p. 278; *Arnulf*, ed. Barlow, no. 76; G. Teske, 'Ein unerkanntes Zeugnis zum Sturz des Bischofs Arnulf von Lisieux. Ein Vorschlag zur Diskussion (mit Edition)', *Francia*, 16/1 (1989), 185–206.

[168] *Arnulf*, ed. Barlow, nos. 106–8, 110.   [169] Ibid., pp. liii–liv, no. 111.

happen. Henry and Walter de Coutances withheld the money, demanding that Arnulf first secure the election of Walter as his successor.
Increasing the pressure, the king sent Rotrou de Beaumont, Henry,
bishop of Bayeux, Chancellor Ralph de Warneville, and Walter de
Coutances to Arnulf to persuade him to agree to these terms.[170] Arnulf,
however, refused and the struggle entered a more aggressive phase.
According to Arnulf, Walter de Coutances not only used the royal seal
without the king's authorisation to drive him out of his see, but also
offered cash if Arnulf would secure his election with the most important
people and a large part of the chapter.[171] The full strength and severity of
the royal administrative machinery hit Arnulf when a dispute arose concerning the behaviour of one of Arnulf's *nepotes*, a knight. Arnulf was
required to produce him in court and, when he failed to do so, the
seneschal of Normandy, William fitz Ralph, seized the temporalities of
the bishopric.[172] At the same time, Walter de Coutances was busy securing the support of part of the chapter of Lisieux, and when he left for
England in the course of the year 1178, Canon Hubert represented his
interests. Finding allies within the chapter was not very difficult. Arnulf's
ambitious building programme had strained the chapter's revenues heavily. In addition Arnulf's *nepos*, Sylvester, treasurer of Lisieux, harboured a
longstanding grudge against Arnulf and was only too ready to lead a
campaign against him.[173] Yet, although Arnulf asked the pope for permission to resign his see, he resisted Henry's demands to do so under the
conditions set.[174] Finally the pope granted him permission[175] and Arnulf
also came to terms with Henry. In a meeting at Gisors in July 1181, they
agreed that Arnulf should resign his bishopric and that in return Henry
should pay him 200 *livres angevins* for his chattels and an annual rent of the
same amount.[176] Retiring to St Victor, Arnulf died probably within the
next twelve months.[177]

His successor, however, was not to be Walter de Coutances. It seems
that Arnulf's resistance and accusations made Walter an impossible candidate for the see of Lisieux. It may even have been part of the settlement
preceding his resignation that Walter would not become the next bishop.
Instead, Henry II's former chancellor, Ralph de Warneville, followed

---

[170] Ibid., p. liv–lv, nos. 119, 121, 124–6.   [171] Ibid., nos. 125, 137.
[172] Ibid., p. lv, nos. 124–7, 131.   [173] Ibid., pp. lvi–lvii, nos. 33, 89, 119, 126, 132, 137.
[174] Ibid., no. 128.   [175] Ibid., no. 137.   [176] Ibid., p. lix, no. 140; *Gesta regis*, I, p. 278.
[177] *Arnulf*, ed. Barlow, p. lx. C.P. Schriber, *The Dilemma of Arnulf of Lisieux. New Ideas versus Old Ideals*
(Indianapolis, 1990), p. 138, proposes 1184 as the year of Arnulf's death; cf. Spear, *The Personnel*,
p. 171. Her source is *Obituaires de la province de Sens. T. I (Diocèses de Sens et de Paris)*, ed. Molinier, I,
pp. 580–1. Molinier, however, inserted the year of 1184 without further explanation.

Arnulf.[178] There can be no doubt that Henry II was responsible for Ralph's election. Ralph was closely connected with the Angevins. In 1146, Ralph had been treasurer at Rouen[179] and it may have been there that he came into contact with the Empress Matilda's entourage. Probably after John aux Bellesmains' promotion to the see of Poitiers in 1162, Ralph received the office of treasurer at York.[180] By 1170, he also held the office of archdeacon at Rouen.[181] Finally, in 1173, he was made royal chancellor. Since Ralph is said to have disliked life at the royal court, he immediately appointed Walter de Coutances as vice-chancellor to take care of the office.[182] Yet Ralph remained heavily involved in the administration of the ducal demesne in Normandy, where he rendered account *inter alia* for the bailliwick of Vaudreuil.[183] In 1180, he gave back his office of chancellor to the king, who handed it over to his illegitimate son Geoffrey Plantagenet. In return Ralph received considerable amounts of land and perhaps the promise of a bishopric.[184] In any case he became bishop of Lisieux, probably after March 1182.[185]

Unlike Arnulf, Ralph remained in his office until his death in 1191/2.[186] The precise circumstances of the election of his successor, William de Rupierre, are unknown, but since the election occurred while Richard I was on crusade, there was little chance of external interference. William was certainly a local candidate. A member of the Rupierre family whose lands were mainly situated in the Bessin,[187] he had been archdeacon of Lisieux before his election.[188] His career was perhaps supported by Bishop

---

[178] *Howden*, II, p. 260. It should be noted that John de Coutances, a *nepos* of Walter, succeeded Sylvester as treasurer at Lisieux probably shortly after Ralph's accession, Spear, *The Personnel*, pp. 180, 203. Using his close relationship with Ralph Walter thus gained at least something from Lisieux.

[179] Spear, *The Personnel*, p. 219.

[180] C.T. Clay, 'The Early Treasurers of York', *Yorkshire Archaeological Journal*, 35 (1943), 7–34, 20–4.

[181] Spear, *The Personnel*, p. 214.   [182] *Diceto*, I, p. 367.

[183] For Vaudreuil and other responsibilities, *Magni rotuli*, ed. Stapleton, I, pp. 92–4, 98, 122.

[184] *Torigny*, p. 294.

[185] D. Greenway, *John Le Neve: Fasti ecclesiae Anglicanae, 1066–1300. VI. York* (London, 1999), p. 23, argues for 1181 referring to *Howden*, II, p. 260, and *Torigny*, p. 299. The chroniclers' evidence is inconclusive. Henry II's will, however, suggests a date in 1182. The bishops of Lisieux and Coutances were the only Norman bishops who were not mentioned in Henry II's will recorded in March 1182, *Recueil des actes de Henri II*, ed. Delisle and Berger, II, no. 612. Since the bishopric of Coutances was vacant at that time, the bishopric of Lisieux may also have been vacant in March 1182, cf. infra, p. 147.

[186] *GC*, XI, cols. 779–80.

[187] His father was Roger de Rupierre, Paris, BNF N. A. Lat. 1778 (obituary, cathedral chapter of Lisieux), fo. 89v. For the possessions of his family, see, for example, *Register Innocenz' III.*, I, no. 210 [= Potthast, I, no. 224]; *Rot. pat.*, p. 32b; *Rotuli Normanniae in turri Londonensi asservati, Johanne et Henrico quinto, Angliae regibus*, ed. T. D. Hardy (London, 1835), p. 100.

[188] Paris, BNF Lat. 10086 (cartulary, abbey of Troarn), fos. 170v–171r (Archdeacon William witnesses a charter of Bishop Ralph).

Ralph and his *avunculus* John, who was dean of the chapter of Lisieux by the time of William's election.[189] It is possible that not everybody in the chapter and diocese of Lisieux was happy with William's elevation in 1191/2.[190] In 1193, William received permission from Pope Celestine III to redistribute the benefices of any members of the chapter and of any clergy of the diocese who disobeyed his orders.[191] Apparently the bishop had had great difficulty in imposing his authority, but the reason for this is obscure.

After William's death in 1200, the chapter apparently intended to elect a bishop without consulting King John. John, who was possibly aware of the charter of free elections issued by Philip Augustus to the chapter of Evreux in the same year, was alerted. In November 1200 he sent a letter to the dean and the chapter of Lisieux reminding them of his right. John stressed that they knew very well the right (*ius*) and dignity (*dignitas*) he and his ancestors enjoyed in appointing to vacant cathedral churches within their dominions. The appointment to the church of Lisieux depended on old custom (*consuetudo*) and for many reasons on his wish (*voluntas*) and consent (*assensus*). Furthermore, he informed the chapter that he had already appealed to the pope to have his rights protected and that he was renewing this appeal. He ended the letter by prohibiting the chapter from electing anyone without his *voluntas* and *assensus*, adding the unconcealed threat that he expected them to respect his rights as they would want him to respect theirs.[192] The chapter complied, and the dean joined the king in England in January 1201 to reach an agreement about a suitable candidate.[193] Thus King John's firm assertion of his right still prevailed in this case. He had his letter to the chapter inserted in the charter rolls, which at this early stage of their development still included various types of documents issued by the royal chancery. It is possible that this served another purpose than simple preservation. John may have intended to transform his customary right from an orally preserved tradition, which constantly had to be re-enforced, into a customary right, written down, *ius scriptum*, which, preserved among copies of royal charters, acquired the solemn and perennial authority inherent in royal charters. Such *ius scriptum* could provide a powerful basis for the defence of

---

[189] William referred to his *avunculus* John, dean of the chapter, when protecting John's rights in a church given to the priory of Ste Barbe-en-Auge, Caen, AD Calvados 2 D 51 (charters concerning the priory of Ste Barbe-en-Auge). John held the position of the dean already under Bishop Ralph, Paris, BNF Lat. 17137 (cartulary, abbey of St Sauveur-le-Vicomte), fos. 115v–117r, no. 130 (Bishop Ralph, Dean John, and the chapter of Lisieux confirm an agreement concluded in 1147 between Bishop Arnulf and the abbey of St Sauveur-le-Vicomte concerning two churches).

[190] For the date, see Spear, *The Personnel*, p. 171; *GC*, IX, col. 780, proposes 1191, 1192, or 1193.

[191] *Papsturkunden in Frankreich. Neue Folge. II. Normandie*, ed. Ramackers, no. 320 [= Jaffé, II, no. 17028; *WH* -], cf. ibid., nos. 319 [Jaffé -; *WH* -], 321 [= Jaffé, II, no. 17030; *WH* -].

[192] *Rot. chart.*, p. 99a; cf. Cheney, *Innocent III*, p. 127.   [193] *Rotuli Normanniae*, ed. Hardy, pp. 34–5.

royal *voluntas* in episcopal elections against the current developments in canon law.

The king and the dean agreed on the election of Jordan du Hommet. He was archdeacon of Lisieux,[194] and a member of the powerful du Hommet family, hereditary constables of the king in Normandy. His father, Constable William du Hommet, was a major ally of the Plantagenet,[195] and probably pushed Jordan's candidature.[196]

Only a short time after Jordan's election, the pope admonished the bishop for his conduct towards a *nepos* of the late bishop, Archdeacon Hugh de Rupierre. He instructed Jordan that he and Canon O. should refrain from their activities against Hugh. Innocent III took the matter so seriously that he even charged papal judges delegate to impose ecclesiastical censures on Jordan, if the bishop would not obey his orders.[197] Hugh de Rupierre had received the archdeaconry during William's time in office, and it is conceivable that William intended to groom him as his successor. He may therefore have been an alternative candidate in the 1200 election.

In the long run, Bishop Jordan proved to be a bad choice for King John. Despite the king's efforts to ensure the bishop's loyalty,[198] Jordan followed his father's change of allegiance to Philip Augustus in 1204.[199] When Jordan died on the fifth crusade in 1218,[200] neither king nor pope seemed to be interested in the next election. The canons chose a Norman, the theologian William de Pont de L'Arche, who held the see until his death in 1250. In the past, Master William had acted as a proctor for the chapter;[201] and the canons probably wished to be represented by a bishop who was able and willing to defend their rights and interests.[202]

---

[194] *Magni rotuli*, ed. Stapleton, I, pp. lxvi, 363; Caen, AD Calvados H 1217 (charters concerning the abbey of Aunay) (Jordan du Hommet, archdeacon of Lisieux, witnesses a charter of Sylvester de Villiers-le-Sec (dép. Calvados, cant. Ryes) in favour of the abbey of Aunay).

[195] *Rot. pat.*, p. 22a; Powicke, *Loss*, pp. 74, 76, 343, 348; Moss, 'The Defence of Normandy', p. 148. For Jordan's parents, see *Antiquus cartularius*, ed. Bourrienne, I, no. 121; Paris, BNF Lat. 17137 (cartulary, abbey of St Sauveur-le-Vicomte), fos. 262v–263r, no. 387; 'Fragments d'un cartulaire de Saint-Pierre-de-Lisieux', ed. R.N. Sauvage, *Etudes Lexoviennes*, 3 (1928), 325–57, no. 22.

[196] In 1206/7 Jordan stood as principal pledge for his nephew William, who by then had succeeded Jordan's father William du Hommet, to guarantee the constable's fidelity towards Philip Augustus, *Registres de Philippe Auguste*, ed. Baldwin, securitates, no. 3.

[197] *Register Innocenz' III.*, V, no. 142 (143) [= Potthast, I, no. 1809].

[198] *Rotuli Normanniae*, ed. Hardy, p. 117.

[199] Powicke, *Loss*, pp. 330, 343. Jordan joined the Capetian court also outside Normandy, *Recueil des actes de Philippe Auguste*, ed. Delaborde et al., III, no. 1157, IV, no. 1436.

[200] 'Continuatio altera appendices Roberti de Monte ad Sigebertum', in *RHF*, XVIII, p. 348.

[201] Müller, *Delegationsgerichtsbarkeit*, II, nos. 199–200.

[202] In 1224, William counted among the three Norman bishops who retreated from Louis VIII's army claiming that they did not owe personal military service to the king, 'Scripta de feodis ad regem spectantibus et de militibus ad exercitum vocandis, e Philippi Augusti regestis excerpta', in *RHF*, XXIII, pp. 605–723, p. 637, and Petit-Dutaillis, *Louis VIII*, p. 409; cf. infra, p. 165.

Lisieux offers a nice window on to the different phases of ducal/royal control over episcopal elections in Normandy. Geoffrey Plantagenet's struggle with Arnulf indicates that in 1141 he had not yet established his authority in the duchy. Forty years later, however, Henry II's power was so great that he was able to force Arnulf to resign his see and to influence the election of his successor. King Richard's absence gave local networks the opportunity to flourish. King John chose to defend aggressively his customary electoral right against contrary developments in canon law. After the conquest, Philip Augustus observed from a distance the outcome of the election at Lisieux, which by then was controlled by the cathedral chapter.

SÉES

The geopolitical situation of the bishopric of Sées is of particular significance for any analysis of episcopal elections there before 1204/6. Sées was a frontier bishopric, connecting Normandy with Greater Anjou and the Chartrain. Situated between the dioceses of Chartres, Le Mans, Bayeux, Lisieux, and Evreux, its territory covered major routes running from Normandy to Greater Anjou. In the south, the diocese also covered the western Perche territory, which was beyond the Norman frontier.[203] A loyal bishop was therefore of great importance to the efficiency of Angevin rule.

In 1131, John, bishop of Sées, a *nepos* of Bishop John of Lisieux and an elder brother of Arnulf of Lisieux, had transformed the chapter of Sées from secular to regular observance by attracting regular canons, mostly from St Victor, Paris. According to Arnulf, John enriched the cathedral church so much that in the place of thirteen secular canons, thirty-six regular canons were fully provided for.[204] John's reform modified the framework of episcopal elections at Sées. It changed the number and composition of the cathedral chapter and, most importantly, it caused a transfer of electoral custom from St Victor to Sées. At St Victor, after the death of the abbot, the prior would convene the chapter which would charge a group of men to decide who should be the next abbot. He should be chosen from among the canons or, if this proved impossible, from other communities of regular

---

[203] F. Neveux, 'La ville de Sées du haut moyen âge à l'époque ducale', in C. Harper-Bill (ed.), *Anglo-Norman Studies XVII. Proceedings of the Battle Conference 1994* (Woodbridge, 1995), pp. 145–63, p. 147; D. Power, 'What Did the Frontier of Angevin Normandy Comprise?', in ibid., pp. 181–202, p. 191; for the strategic situation of the county of the Perche, see K. Thompson, *Power and Border Lordship in Medieval France. The County of the Perche, 1000–1226* (Royal Historical Society, Studies in History, N.S.) (Woodbridge, 2002), pp. 17–18.
[204] *Arnulf*, ed. Barlow, p. xii–xiii, xxxiv, no. 34.

●	Castle/Town
♠	Monastery
♦	(Archi)episcopal see
- - - - -	Diocesan boundaries
ııııııııı	Border zone of the Angevin empire

Map 5 The diocese of Sées

canons.[205] This custom was, however, not immediately implemented as
the general electoral rule at Sées. Bishop John had not forced the existing
secular canons to become canons regular,[206] and it is possible that this
co-existence and the resulting rivalries were at the root of the electoral
dispute following the bishop's death in 1144. Hugh, archbishop of
Rouen, informed the papal legate, Alberic, cardinal-bishop of Ostia,
that after John's death the prior of the chapter had asked him to call the
bishops of Evreux and Lisieux to be present at the election of John's

[205] *Liber ordinis Sancti Victoris Parisiensis*, ed. L. Jocqué and L. Milis (Corpus Christianorum. Continuatio medievalis LXI) (Turnhout, 1984), c. 1, pp. 15–18; J. Ehlers, *Hugo von St Viktor. Studien zum Geschichtsdenken und zur Geschichtsschreibung des 12. Jahrhunderts* (Frankfurter historische Abhandlungen VII) (Frankfurt, 1973), pp. 9–10.

[206] Arnulf, for example, who had become archdeacon of the church probably in 1124, remained in office until his election to the see of Lisieux in 1141, ibid., p. xiii.

successor, to guide the proceedings through their advice and counsel. Hugh had agreed to call the bishops and had confirmed the prior's threat to excommunicate any canon who nominated or elected someone before the assigned day of election. Then he had heard that, despite the threat, a party of the chapter had elected Gerald, a secular canon of the cathedral chapter,[207] before the assigned day and before the arrival of the *venerabiles personae* of the diocese, the two bishops and the senior archdeacons (*maiores archidiaconi*) of the church of Sées. Therefore, he had sent Arnulf of Lisieux and Archdeacon Lawrence to enquire into the election of Gerald. They had learnt that some members of the chapter had opposed it from the beginning, others had consented to the election through ignorance and simplicity, but that the majority had listened to the advice of Archdeacon William. Asked about his role in the election, William had denied any involvement and had assured the archbishop that he had not pushed for anyone. Claiming that his age and feebleness did not allow him to be active in such matters, he said he would obey whoever became the new bishop.[208] The hint about William's role, however, may not have been entirely misleading. In 1145, thus before the settlement of the dispute, William had witnessed a series of Gerald's charters in favour of the abbey of St Martin of Marmoutier. Another witness was Archdeacon Roger, Gerald's brother and, according to Arnulf, a key supporter of Gerald's candidacy.[209] The two other archdeacons, Henry and Amaury, had at least accepted Gerald's election, since they too gave their counsel and consent. The prior, however, excluded from Gerald's election, is absent from these charters.[210] In this case, therefore, witness lists perhaps reflect political groupings.

In his letter to Pope Eugenius, Arnulf took a very clear stand against Gerald's election and attempted to defame Gerald's supporters. Apart from Gerald's brother, an adolescent, the nucleus of Gerald's supporters consisted of a neophyte from his household, an unnamed relative, and a youth said to be thirsting only for the secular world.[211] Gerald's election was null because, driven by great ambition, he had canvassed his electors, who themselves had been striving for worldly things. Interestingly, Arnulf based his accusation on the bad intentions of Gerald and his supporters,

---

[207] *Torigny*, p. 149.

[208] 'Epistolae Hugonis Rothomagensis archiepiscopi', in *RHF*, XV, pp. 693–703, pp. 696–7, no. 7.

[209] *Arnulf*, ed. Barlow, no. 3. For the identification of Archdeacon Roger with Gerald's brother, see Sées, Bibliothèque de l'Evêché 'Livre blanc' (cartulary, abbey of St Martin of Sées), fo. 142r (Archdeacon Roger, *frater episcopi*, witnesses an agreement concluded by Bishop Gerald between Henry, canon of Sées, and the abbey of St Martin of Sées).

[210] *Cartulaire de Marmoutier pour le Perche. N.-D. du Vieux-Château, Collégiale de Saint-Léonard de Bellême, Prieuré de St-Martin-du-Vieux-Bellême*, ed. R. Barret (Documents sur la province du Perche 3ᵉ sér., II) (Mortagne, 1905), nos. 27–30.

[211] *Arnulf*, ed. Barlow, no. 3.

thus casting doubt on the validity of their vote and on Gerald's suitability. Unlike Archbishop Hugh, he did not emphasise the disregard of himself, Rotrou, and the other *religiosi viri* during the electoral process.[212] This suggests that Pope Innocent II's decree from 1139 prohibiting the exclusion of the *religiosi viri* had only limited impact in Normandy. Arnulf understood the invitation to ecclesiastics from outside the chapter to be optional, not imperative.[213]

In his attempt to persuade Eugenius III to annul Gerald's election, Arnulf also instigated Bernard of Clairvaux to write to the pope.[214] Arnulf was full of admiration for his brother's achievements at Sées, and his concerns about the election of a secular to a regular community were doubtless sincere.[215] But this resentment was probably not the only reason for his anger. There are hints that Gerald's success had thwarted Arnulf's desire to preserve the influence of his family over the see of Sées.

The actions of the prior of Sées after Bishop John's death suggest that he was aware of a powerful faction within the chapter, possibly centred around the remaining secular canons, and that he tried to counter their intentions with the help of the bishops Arnulf and Rotrou. Rotrou may have been invited because of his blood ties to the counts of the Perche, who were the most powerful family in the south of the diocese.[216] But the prior's invitation to Arnulf was surely more significant. Given Arnulf's close connection to Sées, it is conceivable that the prior, Bishop John, and Arnulf had already discussed the matter of the succession before John's death. Arnulf was well aware of the advantages the control of a bishopric involved. His own career had been made possible through his family's control over bishoprics.[217] As much as he wanted the continuation of his brother's reforms, Arnulf probably also intended to keep the bishopric of Sées within his family. But he succeeded only to a limited extent. The pope demanded that Gerald become a regular and swear to uphold the regular chapter of Sées if he wished his election to be confirmed.[218]

---

[212] Arnulf did mention that the election was rushed, but his other statements make clear that his strategy rested on the accusation of bad intentions and unsuitability. Gerald's election ought not to be defended on the ground that it was freely held, because the freedom of election should not serve to do injury to the church. Arnulf claimed that the correct form of election was not sufficient to justify the acceptance of the elect, but that the elect and the usefulness of his election should also be scrutinised, ibid.

[213] This is also indicated by his letter to William, bishop of Le Mans, who, after the election at Tours in 1173–4, had written to him complaining that the chapter of Tours had not invited the suffragan bishops to participate at the election. Arnulf deplored this, but excused the chapter's behaviour by the political circumstances. He recommended William to accept the election, see infra, p. 177.

[214] *Sancti Bernardi opera*, ed. Leclercq and Rochais, VIII, no. 248.   [215] *Arnulf*, ed. Barlow, nos. 34–5.

[216] Waldman, 'Hugh "of Amiens"', pp. 4–5, Thompson, *Perche*, pp. 54–85.

[217] See supra, pp. 108.   [218] *Arnulf*, ed. Barlow, no. 34.

The pope's willingness to accept Gerald may suggest that Gerald had the support of the majority of the chapter. The probably decisive reason not to annul Gerald's election was the intervention by the count of Anjou, Geoffrey Plantagenet.

Shortly after Geoffrey had received the news that the chapter had elected Gerald he sent men to Sées to prevent the elect from taking up his office, on the grounds that the chapter had neglected to seek his licence to elect.[219] Geoffrey had a good political reason to assert his authority in this sensitive border region. In January 1144, he had conquered Rouen and obtained recognition as duke from Louis VII in the summer of that year.[220] In the same year, the count of the Perche, Rotrou, died, and his wife Hawisa married the third-born son of Louis VI, Robert count of Dreux. Since Rotrou's son, also named Rotrou, was still a minor, the couple remained in control of the county of the Perche.[221] Kathleen Thompson has suggested that this marriage might have been part of the 'rapprochement between King Louis, Theobald IV of Blois, and Count Geoffrey which was finalised in the autumn of 1144'.[222] Geoffrey was to be duke of Normandy, while Robert's installation in the Perche served at once as a check on Geoffrey in Normandy and as protection for Theobald.[223] Whether there actually was such an agreement remains a matter of conjecture. In any case Robert's control of the strategically important county of the Perche was as much welcomed by Louis and Theobald as it was a bitter pill for Geoffrey. He held the ducal right to garrison the castle of Bellême,[224] but otherwise had no influence in the area that lay between Normandy, Greater Anjou, and Blois. Anxious to increase his influence in the region and to consolidate his position in Normandy, he could not afford to ignore the disregard of the ducal authority by the cathedral chapter. To what extent the choice of Gerald contributed to Geoffrey's hostility can only be guessed. The sources do not provide evidence that Gerald was supported by Count Robert. It is remarkable, however, that in 1145 Gerald included the king of France and Count Robert in the formula used to date his charters while ignoring Geoffrey Plantagenet's rule in Normandy.[225] This was certainly due to Geoffrey's opposition to his election, but may also point to Gerald's good connections with Count Robert before Geoffrey's intervention.

---

[219] 'Vita sancti Thomae Cantuariensis archiepiscopi et martyris, auctore Willelmo Filio Stephani', in *MTB*, III, p. 65.
[220] Le Patourel, *Norman Empire*, p. 95.   [221] Thompson, *Perche*, pp. 86–8.   [222] Ibid., pp. 87–8.
[223] Ibid., p. 88.   [224] Ibid.
[225] *Cartulaire de Marmoutier pour Le Perche*, ed. Barret, no. 28, and cf. no. 29. I would like to thank Dr Kathleen Thompson for having discussed this point with me. She arrives at a similar conclusion, Thompson, *Perche*, p. 88.

Geoffrey's officers used extreme violence against Gerald and his electors. According to William fitz Stephen, writing shortly after Becket's murder, and Gerald de Barri, writing between 1190 and 1217, they castrated the bishop-elect and several of the canons. Given their distance in time and the fact that both authors quoted this event in passages aiming to demonstrate the evil behaviour of the Angevins towards the church, both accounts have to be treated with caution.[226] Yet Arnulf's letter to the pope confirms that Geoffrey's men acted with great brutality.[227] Geoffrey realised that the measures taken by his men were counterproductive to his aims. According to Arnulf, he withdrew his officers and handed them over to the ecclesiastical courts for punishment. To ensure that no one believed he was working against the *libertas ecclesiae*, he left the entire administration of the church with the archbishop and bishops.[228] Here, Arnulf signalled to the pope that Geoffrey had resigned any part in the electoral dispute.

But Pope Eugenius III was not swayed by this. He could neither accept Geoffrey's claim to be asked for his consent nor the cruel treatment of the elect and the canons. If he had ordered a new election on the grounds of the faulty electoral procedure indicated by Archbishop Hugh and/or on the grounds of an unsuitable candidate propagated by Arnulf, his decision could be interpreted as giving way to the count's argument and thus creating a precedent potentially destructive of his efforts to exclude lay influence from ecclesiastical matters. Therefore, he decided to ignore the arguments brought forward against Gerald's election and accepted Gerald as the new bishop of Sées. Finally he reconciled Gerald with Geoffrey at Paris, at Easter 1147.[229]

The next election at Sées was again disputed. It featured a conflict between the two parties disappointed in the election of 1144, the regular

---

[226] 'Vita sancti Thomae Cantuariensis archiepiscopi et martyris, auctore Willelmo Filio Stephani', in *MTB*, III, p. 65; *Giraldi Cambrensis opera*, ed. Brewer et al., VIII, pp. 160, 301, 309.

[227] *Arnulf*, ed. Barlow, no. 3. Castration was a traditional method the Norman dukes used to punish traitors, K. van Eickels, 'Domestizierte Maskulinität. Die Integration der Normannen in das westfränkische Reich in der Sicht des Dudos von St-Quentin', in I. Bennewitz and I. Kasten (eds.), *Genderdiskurse und Körperbilder im Mittelalter. Eine Bilanzierung nach Butler und Laqueur* (Bamberger Studien zum Mittelalter I) (Münster, 2002), pp. 97–134. If Geoffrey's officers did actually execute the castration, this would shed light on the severity they attributed to the offence of disregarding the duke's right to grant the *licentia eligendi*.

[228] *Arnulf*, ed. Barlow, no. 3.

[229] Eugenius III visited Paris at Easter 1147, not Easter 1146 as indicated by *Diceto*, I, p. 256, Jaffé, II, p. 40. Frank Barlow, who followed Diceto's date of Easter 1146, offers a different sequence of events. According to him Arnulf and Bernard of Clairvaux wrote to Eugenius after the reconciliation, *Arnulf*, ed. Barlow, p. xxxiv. However, not only the later date of Eugenius' visit, but also internal evidence from the letters, suggests that both letters were written before the reconciliation took place. Arnulf informed the pope that Geoffrey had withdrawn from interfering in ecclesiastical affairs and that it was now in the pope's hands to decide the case, ibid., no. 3. There can be no doubt that Eugenius had decided the case by the time of the reconciliation, which was a public

canons on the one side and the Angevins on the other. Bishop Gerald died in 1157, and this time the regular canons reacted quickly. Following their electoral traditions, they chose another regular canon, Master Achard, abbot of St Victor, Paris. Considering the close links between Sées and St Victor their choice was very natural. Yet Henry II was not content with the chapter's procedure, because the canons had not consulted him. He intervened and forced the chapter to elect his almoner Froger, despite the fact that Achard's election had already been confirmed by the pope.[230] The king had little personal opposition to the Englishman Achard. The Empress Matilda had maintained good relations with St Victor and, a couple of years later, Henry recompensed him with the bishopric of Avranches.[231] Yet the abbot was not the man Henry wanted and needed as head of a vital border diocese. The political situation in the south had changed little since 1144. Even though Louis VII's brother, Robert count of Dreux, had left the Perche in 1152, when he married Agnes, heiress of Braine in Champagne, the comital family of the Perche continued to move outside the Angevin orbit. Rotrou III, son of Hawisa, had married Matilda, daughter of Count Theobald IV of Champagne, between the late 1140s and early 1150s, and throughout the 1150s and 1160s the Perche family stayed in close contact with the counts of Champagne and Blois, Matilda's brothers, Henry and Theobald.[232] Theobald, however, was Henry II's fiercest rival in the Touraine in the 1150s. In 1153, Henry refused Theobald homage for the county of Touraine, claiming that Theobald unjustly held the fief of Fréteval which was dependent upon the counts of Anjou. In the subsequent fighting, Henry and his allies were heavily defeated by Theobald. Henry's accession to the English throne in 1154 did not solve his problems in Greater Anjou and the Perche, because Louis VII, who viewed Henry's gains with uneasiness, started to improve his relationship with the counts of Champagne and Blois.[233] Thus Henry faced a Perche–Blois alliance supported by Louis VII that posed a constant threat to Angevin rule in south-west Normandy and eastern Greater Anjou. Henry knew that if he wanted to maintain and to extend his position in the region, the service of a loyal bishop experienced in royal politics would be extremely useful. Archdeacon Froger fitted this requirement much better than Abbot Achard. Froger had been a member of Bishop Arnulf's household. Probably through his master's contacts with

---

display of his confirmation of Gerald's election. For the same reason Bernard's letter, in which he warned Eugenius not to be fooled by Gerald's attempt to obtain papal confirmation, should be dated before Easter 1147, *Sancti Bernardi opera*, ed. Leclercq and Rochais, VIII, no. 248.

[230] *Correspondence*, ed. Duggan, I, no. 170.   [231] See infra, pp. 153–4.

[232] Thompson, *Perche*, pp. 91–6.

[233] Boussard, *Le comté d'Anjou*, pp. 70–5; Pacaut, *Louis VII*, pp. 181–2.

the Angevins he received the archdeaconry of Derby at some time around 1151.[234] After Henry's coronation he was heavily involved in royal affairs. Henry made him his almoner and gave him responsibilities in the administration of lands in Derbyshire and Northamptonshire.[235] When the king chose him to become bishop of Sées, he was sure that Froger would be a reliable representative.

The regular canons at Sées were naturally reluctant to accept the king's intervention and the vacancy of two years' duration was certainly marked by recurring negotiations between king and chapter. Yet, unlike in 1144, there was no bloodshed and no defeat for the Angevin position. In 1159, the chapter acquiesced with Henry's demands and elected Froger.[236] This outcome of the dispute was probably due to several factors. First, Henry's political situation in the region had rapidly improved. In December 1158, he had made an agreement with Count Theobald V as a result of which Theobald gave up the castles of Amboise and Fréteval. A deal concerning Count Rotrou probably was also part of the agreement. Rotrou surrendered the castles of Bonsmoulins and Moulins. In return, Henry recognised Rotrou's lordship of Bellême.[237] Second, the men voting for Achard were not the same as those who had voted for Gerald, and there were good relations between the Empress Matilda and Achard. Unlike Gerald, Achard may not have wanted to resist the Angevins. Whatever the principal reason for which Achard and the chapter gave way to Henry, their decision certainly strengthened the duke's claim to be involved in the selection process of bishops.

Shortly after his election, Froger tried to create the position of a secular archdeacon. Arnulf of Lisieux explained Froger's attempt as the fruit of his affection for his family members. When Froger received permission from

---

[234] Arnulf claimed that he had provided his former *domesticus* Froger with many benefices, *Arnulf*, ed. Barlow, no. 34. For his archdeaconry, see *English Episcopal Acta XIV. Coventry and Lichfield 1072–1159*, ed. M.J. Franklin (Oxford, 1997), p. 129. After his consecration in 1149, the bishop of Coventry and Lichfield, Walter Durdent, appeared in the entourage of Ranulf, earl of Chester, the most powerful baron of his dioceses. Ranulf in turn sided with the Angevins, joined Henry upon the duke's return to England in 1149, and received the honour of Lancaster as a reward, ibid., p. li; Chibnall, *Matilda*, p. 150. It is possible that Froger's appointment to the archdeaconry was due to the newly established alliance between the earl of Chester and the Angevins.

[235] *PR* 2, H.II, pp. 40, 42; *PR* 3, H.II, p. 92; *Torigny*, p. 205.

[236] For the date of his consecration, see Delisle, *Introduction*, p. 367.

[237] *Torigny*, p. 199; Thompson, *Perche*, pp. 92–3; in 1137, King Stephen had rewarded Count Rotrou II and his nephew Richer II de Laigle for their services. They had received Moulins and Bonsmoulins respectively, K. Thompson, 'The Lords of Laigle: Ambition and Insecurity on the Borders of Normandy', in C. Harper-Bill (ed.), *Anglo-Norman Studies XVIII. Proceedings of the Battle Conference 1995* (Woodbridge, 1996), pp. 177–99, pp. 188–91. If Torigny's account is true that Rotrou III rendered to Henry the two castles which Rotrou II had seized, it seems probable that Richer II held the castle of Bonsmoulins from the counts of the Perche.

Alexander III to do so, he filled one archdeaconry with his *nepos* John.[238]
Froger's measures at the beginning of his episcopate were certainly
intended to strengthen his position in a chapter upon which he had
been imposed. But he also tried to build a good relationship with his
chapter. He granted the canons an income to assure the celebration of his
anniversary[239] and by the time of his death in 1184/5, Robert de Torigny
records that he had greatly improved the cathedral church, enlarged its
temporal possessions, and left behind an enormous treasure of gold and
silver.[240]

Froger may well have intended to prepare the way to the bishopric for
a kinsman of his, but whether he succeeded is difficult to establish, as
nothing is known about the election of Lisiard, who appears as bishop-
elect in 1187/8.[241] The political situation had changed in so far that from the
mid-1170s Henry II had been establishing a good relationship with Count
Rotrou III,[242] who was no longer a potential threat but an ally. This change
may explain why no courtier followed Froger in the bishopric of Sées.
Nonetheless, the succession was subject to protracted negotiations which
took approximately two years. The parties involved remain obscure. One
of them possibly consisted of the canons regular, wishing to elect one of
their kind, as they had done in 1156 and would do again in 1201–3.[243] If this
was the case, they failed to achieve their aim. Lisiard had been a secular
canon of the cathedral church at Le Mans. As bishop of Sées, Lisiard founded
an anniversary for William de Passavant, bishop of Le Mans, to whom he
owed his canonry at Le Mans. Perhaps Bishop William, who died in 1187,
had also played a role in Lisiard's promotion to the see of Sées.[244]

In contrast to the election of Lisiard that of his successor is extraordinarily well documented. The dispute between a part of the chapter and
King John over a suitable candidate produced material illuminating the

---

[238] *Arnulf*, ed. Barlow, nos. 33, 34, 35. In 1183, another Froger, doubtless a kinsman of the bishop and
possibly a canon of Sées, witnessed a charter of John, prior of the cathedral chapter of Sées, Caen,
AD Calvados H 6510 (cartulary, abbey of St André-en-Gouffern), fo. 43v.

[239] Sées, Bibliothèque de l'Evêché 'Livre rouge'(cartulary, cathedral chapter of Sées), fo. 83v.

[240] *Torigny*, p. 311. Torigny's statement is confirmed by S. Bidou's analysis of the churches held by the
cathedral church, S. Bidou, 'La réforme du chapitre cathédral de Sées en 1131', *Société historique et
archéologique de l'Orne*, 106 (1987), 21–32, 24–32.

[241] See infra, n. 244.   [242] Thompson, *Perche*, pp. 104–8.   [243] See supra, p. 121.

[244] Sées, Bibliothèque de l'Evêché 'Livre rouge' (cartulary, cathedral chapter of Sées), fo. 78r. Bishop
Lisiard can be identified with Lisiard, canon of Le Mans, who appeared as witness to Bishop
William's charters in the 1180s, *Cartulaire Manceau de Marmoutier*, ed. E. Laurain (2 vols., Laval,
1911–45), II, pp. 367–70, no. 9; *Liber controversarium Sancti Vincentii Cenomannensis*, ed. A.
Chédeville, no. 51. Canon Lisiard disappeared from the records of the cathedral church of Le
Mans at the time when the bishop-elect of Sées, Lisiard, appeared as witness to a charter recorded
in the chapel of Bishop William in 1187 or 1188 and as participant of the council at Le Mans in
1188, *Liber albus*, ed. Lottin, no. 468; *Gesta regis*, II, p. 30.

positions of both sides and therefore allows an insight into this election from different angles. The narrative of the election will follow the extensive account given in the papal registers, amended by the information supplied by John's administrative documents.[245]

After Lisiard's death in 1201, the regular canons were determined to prevent the election of any further candidate from outside the chapter. Arguing that Froger and Lisiard had diminished the chapter's revenues,[246] the prior made the canons swear that they would elect only a member of the chapter. Anyone who broke his promise would automatically be excommunicated. Accompanied by three members of the chapter, the prior went to King John and the archbishop of Rouen to announce the death of Bishop Lisiard and to negotiate. But John refused their wishes. After his surprising marriage with Isabella of Angoulême in late 1200, he had been able to keep his continental dominions under control. But by the time of Lisiard's death the situation had worsened drastically. The Lusignan family had appealed to Philip II, who was ready to take advantage of the situation.[247] John, therefore, was very keen to put a man in the strategically important bishopric of Sées whom he could trust to defend his interests. Probably around 17 October 1201, John himself came to Sées, proposing the election of William, dean of Lisieux, who had just proved his loyalty to the king.[248] But the chapter of Sées refused John's proposal. Having in mind that William belonged to a family that was hostile to the

---

[245] *Register Innocenz' III.*, v, no. 68 (70) [= Potthast, i, no. 1708]; cf. Packard, 'King John and the Norman Church', 20–4; Cheney, *Innocent III*, pp. 127–8.

[246] Considering the increase in wealth during Froger's time in office, the prior's accusation must be read cautiously. It may have referred to Froger's introduction of the secular archdeacon, whose income had been part of the communal revenue, *Arnulf*, ed. Barlow, no. 34. For Lisiard's time there is some evidence for the alienation of property, but by no means in the quantity scholars have suggested. He granted the church of St Martin-de-Vieux-Bellême to the priory of St Léonard-de-Bellême, which had claims towards it, Alençon, AD Orne H 2161 (charters concerning the abbey of Marmoutier). He also granted with the explicit consent of the chapter some churches to the monastery of St Evroul, Paris, BNF Lat. 11055 (cartulary, abbey of St Evroul), fos. 119r–120r. All the other cases quoted by L. Guilloreau, 'L'élection de Silvestre à l'évêché de Séez (1202)', *Revue Catholique de Normandie*, 25 (1916), 423–39, 427, refer to confirmations of donations made by a third party. Nor do Sidney Packard's additional references sufficiently substantiate the claim of Lisiard's wastefulness, Packard, 'King John and the Norman Church', 21, 36 n. 43. He spotted, however, a charter that contained the settlement of a heavy dispute between Lisiard and the chapter over the distribution of offerings, Sées, Bibliothèque de l'Evêché, 'Livre rouge' (cartulary, cathedral chapter of Sées), fos. 81v–82r (= Paris, BNF Lat. 11058, fo. 35r–v, quoted by Packard). This controversy was perhaps a major reason for the prior's reservations towards Lisiard's regime.

[247] Powicke, *Loss*, pp. 140–7.

[248] On the occasion of the election at Lisieux earlier in 1201, Dean William had accepted King John's claim to be involved in the selection process. Subsequently he had joined the king in England for negotiations and had agreed to promote the election of a candidate with strong connections to the royal court, Jordan du Hommet, supra, p. 113.

chapter,[249] they replied that they had better candidates among their own number. Royal envoys then proposed that the chapter should choose three candidates from its own members and three from outside, from which list the king then would pick the bishop. Discussing the matter, the canons named the prior himself as one candidate and authorised him to choose others from the chapter. The prior selected Sylvester, archdeacon of Sées, William, archdeacon of the Corbonnais,[250] and the canons Master Garin and Ralph de Merle. Then the prior and some of the canons, provided with letters giving the prior the power to choose their candidate, joined the king at Argentan. Again the parties could not agree, and the canons returned to Sées. Until this election, the Norman cathedral chapters had always given in to the wishes of Henry II, Richard I, and John, if there had been conflicting opinions. This time, however, it was different. The prior of Sées thought that, if possible, the king should be involved, but that the ultimate decision lay with the chapter. He appealed to the papal court to get the pope's support for his case.

Faced with this situation, John decided to break down the resistance of the chapter. Royal envoys confiscated the treasure of the cathedral and the possessions of the canons, and expelled their relatives and servants from their houses. The envoys and the mayor of the town told the canons that they would have nothing to drink or to eat until they had satisfied the king's wish (*voluntas*).[251] The prior then placed the diocese under interdict and departed with the canons for the monastery of La Trappe, leaving behind five canons as guardians of the cathedral church. The parties had reached deadlock. John therefore instructed Archbishop Walter to make the canons return to their chapter, declaring that he intended to leave the matter to them. The prior in turn lifted the interdict. Then, in January 1202, Archbishop Walter called the canons of Sées to Rouen to discuss the election. Although no solution could be found, they agreed that an election should not be held until all members of the chapter had been restored to their benefices. The archbishop pronounced excommunication on anyone who should attempt to elect without the consent of all. Whereas the prior and others were still determined to elect a canon regular, another party led by William, archdeacon of the Corbonnais, Master Garin, Presbyter Ernaud, and Martin Blandin was inclined to accept a candidate from outside the chapter. When the prior and his followers proceeded to elect Ralph de Merle on 20 January 1202, the tensions among the canons became obvious. According to the prior's

---

[249] Unfortunately there is no more information on this local conflict.
[250] One of the archdeaconries of the diocese of Sées.
[251] For John disposing over benefices in the diocese of Sées during the vacancy see *Rot. pat.*, pp. 7b, 14a.

account, Archdeacon William and his men, twelve in total, did not take part in the election, but promised that, *salva pace regis*, they would accept the election and would not appeal against it unless they were forced to. According to Presbyter Ernaud's account, Archdeacon William left with nineteen followers after having declared that they could not take part in the election because of the promise they had given to Archbishop Walter. Ernaud added that a further six canons had not participated in the election, since they had been guarding the cathedral church at Sées. Both accounts agree that the archbishop did not confirm Ralph's election. New appeals were launched.

According to Ernaud, Archdeacon William returned to Sées where he and his followers elected, with the consent of the king and 'wise men', Herbert son of Ralph L'Abbé. Ernaud also claimed that Herbert had said that he would only accept his election if the pope confirmed it. According to letters patent of King John dated 29 March, members of the chapter had approached the king at Les Andelys presenting four candidates, John de *Oilleya*,[252] Herbert son of Ralph L'Abbé, Adam, abbot of La Trappe, and Reginald, abbot of St Evroul. The canons had asked the king which one he would like to become bishop and after having taken counsel he had chosen Herbert.[253] Herbert's father, Ralph L'Abbé, was a burgess of Sées and deeply involved in the ducal administration of Normandy. Having been responsible for the ducal revenues in the diocese under Henry and Richard, he became a senior figure at the exchequer at Caen under King John, constantly active in the financial and judicial business of the duchy.[254] Ralph saw the vacancy as a convenient opportunity to promote the career of his son Herbert.[255] John in turn knew that he would be able to rely on the loyalty of Herbert as bishop of Sées. As his political situation

---

[252] Probably Master John de *Oillea* who in a charter of Bishop Froger witnessed, together with Froger's *nepos* John, archdeacon of Exmes, and others, William de St Martin's donation to St André-en-Gouffern, Caen, AD Calvados H 6550 (charters concerning the abbey of St André-en-Gouffern).

[253] *Rot. pat.*, p. 6b. On 29 February John had guaranteed safe conduct to the prior and canons of Sées so that they could elect the bishop in his presence. He had expected to meet them at Lisieux, ibid., p. 8a/b.

[254] *Rotuli Normanniae*, ed. Hardy, pp. 1, 22, 23, 31, 36, 38, 52, 55, 60, 68, 69, 71, 85, 106, 108. In 1204, he appeared as constable of Argentan, Caen, AD Calvados H 6510 (cartulary, abbey of St André-en-Gouffern), fo. 7r; *Magni rotuli*, ed. Stapleton, I, pp. 18, 214, II, p. 386; S. Perrot, 'Catalogue des plus anciens actes concernant le temporel français de Saint-Evroult' (Ecole des chartes, Paris, *thèse*, 1964), II, pièces justificatives, no. 81; cf. D. Power, 'Between the Angevin and Capetian Courts: John de Rouvray and the Knights of the Pays de Bray', in Keats-Rohan, *Family Trees*, pp. 361–84, pp. 383. I would like to thank Serge Perrot for his kind permission to consult his *thèse*.

[255] On 29 June 1202 John ordered the Norman exchequer to pay Ralph the sum of 273 *livres angevins* which Ralph had lent him at Sées, *Rotuli Normanniae*, ed. Hardy, p. 52. It is uncertain when John made this loan. It is possible that this happened during one of John's visits to Sées in October and November 1201. If this was the case then Ralph's actions may have been aimed at acquiring the

further worsened, he became all the more determined to achieve Herbert's election. According to the prior, Richard d'Argences, sent by the king, and Herbert's father, Ralph L'Abbé, intercepted the prior's party on their way to the papal court. While making many promises, they asked them to accept Herbert as bishop, boasting that Herbert would become bishop whether they agreed or not.[256] But Herbert's royal and local connections made him unacceptable to the prior's party. The prior and his men had experienced Ralph as a royal official[257] and harboured a particularly strong grudge against him, because he had not hesitated to implement John's orders to confiscate the temporalities of the cathedral church.[258] Therefore they ignored the king's wish and continued their journey. But before they arrived at the papal court, they had to overcome several obstacles. They possibly suffered from a shortage of money, for John instructed 'his' Italian merchants not to give them any credit.[259] Having crossed the Alps, they faced an even greater problem when the elect, Ralph de Merle, died. The prior, however, reacted immediately and elected Archdeacon Sylvester, allegedly a *nepos* of the former bishop Froger[260] and one of the five men who had originally been selected. Arriving at the papal court, they asked the pope to confirm Sylvester's election and to annul the election of Herbert.

There, Presbyter Ernaud argued that the prior's elections were invalid, because he had violated the agreement that had been reached as a result of the discussions with Archbishop Walter, i.e. not to carry out an election without the consent of all, and had therefore incurred excommunication. Also Canon V. des Aspres and William, archdeacon of the Corbonnais, had appealed that the election should not be held without the consent of all. In addition Herbert, archdeacon of Exmes, one of King John's messengers

---

king's favour for his son. There is a greater probability, however, that Ralph lent John this sum in June 1202, when the king was staying at Sées. If this was the case, Ralph may have hoped to keep his son in the king's favour; for John's visits to Sées, see *Rot. pat.*, p. [lxx].

[256] A short time later, a clerk and a servant of Ralph tried again to convince the prior to change his mind, Register Innocenz' III., v, no. 68 (70) [= Potthast, I, no. 1708].

[257] *Magni rotuli*, ed. Stapleton, I, p. 214, II, p. 386.

[258] *Register Innocenz' III.*, v, no. 68 (70) [= Potthast, I, no. 1708].

[259] *Rot. pat.*, p. 8a. If they did so, 'de pecunia terre nostre non reddetur'.

[260] According to GC, XI, cols. 691–2, Sylvester founded an anniversary for his *avunculus* Froger at the abbey of Tiron. I have been unable to find corroborating evidence for this. Since he held his archdeaconry at least since 1186, Sylvester probably knew Froger very well, Sées, Bibliothèque de l'Evêché, 'Livre blanc' (cartulary, abbey of St Martin of Sées), fo. 51v (Archdeacon Sylvester's attendance of the exchequer at Caen at Michaelmas 1186). If he had been a protégé of Froger and if the accusations against Froger brought forward in 1201 were based on widespread ill-feelings towards Froger within the chapter, Sylvester had apparently managed to distance himself from the memories attached to Froger's name. On the other hand, Sylvester's nomination, if indeed he was connected with Froger, could also be interpreted as a sign that Froger's reputation among the canons was not as bad as the papal letter suggests.

and almost certainly a member of Ernaud's embassy,[261] had launched an appeal that no one should disregard his, i.e. Herbert's, electoral right. Ernaud tried to convince the pope that the electoral right of some of the prior's supporters had also been ignored. Ernaud explained that even if, as was alleged by the prior, the opposing party had lost its right to take part in the election because of its excommunication, a number of canons belonging to the prior's party had not been called to Sylvester's election; their rights therefore had been violated, and, as a consequence, Sylvester's election was invalid. Ernaud's line of argument here had only very recently been developed by Pope Innocent III in the decretal *Venerabilem* issued in March 1202: the disregard of one elector could invalidate the election.[262]

The prior denied having violated the agreement to elect the bishop with the consent of all.[263] He argued that it had been agreed from the beginning that only a member of the chapter should be elected. The compromise reached at the archiepiscopal court did not mean the annulment of their original oath, because all canons could and should have participated in the election of a member of their chapter. Furthermore he stated that the chapter had already chosen five men from among whom the bishop was to be selected. Therefore one of them could and should be elected without violation of the agreement. Archdeacon Herbert's appeal was null, because he, being neither a canon nor professed, had no electoral right in the first place. On the election of Sylvester, the prior countered Ernaud's charge by stating that Sylvester was one of the five men originally chosen by the entire chapter. He then alluded to Innocent III's decretal *Cum inter*, arguing that because he was so far away from the diocese of Sées he was unable to convoke all canons.[264] Apart from that, they had promised to agree with whatever he decided. He added that, by then, the entire power of the chapter lay with him and his companions, since by electing someone from outside the chapter, the other party had automatically incurred excommunication.

Having heard the account and arguments of both parties, Innocent III confirmed the election of Sylvester in June 1202. But King John did not give in. He kept the *regalia* and admonished the clergy of the diocese of Sées not to support Sylvester.[265] In August 1202, he appealed to Archbishop Walter not to consecrate Sylvester. Sylvester had committed

---

[261] *Rot. pat.*, p. 9a.

[262] See supra, p. 36, and cf. *Register Innocenz' III.*, v, no. 68 (70) [= Potthast, I, no. 1708], p. 130 n. 38.

[263] Foreville, *Innocent III*, p. 144, states that the following arguments were brought forward by Innocent III. They were, however, brought forward by the prior, *Register Innocenz' III.*, v, no. 68 (70) [= Potthast, I, no. 1708], p. 130. I would like to thank Prof. Richard Sharpe for having discussed this passage with me.

[264] See supra, p. 37.   [265] *Rot. pat.*, pp. 14a, 16a.

adultery and therefore was an unsuitable candidate. Moreover, his election violated his dignity and contravened *ius scriptum*, because he had been elected without the king's consent.[266] This was a well-prepared attack and indicates the availability of great expertise in canon law at the royal court. Doubting the suitability of the candidate and the validity of the electoral procedure, John pursued a double interest. One aim was to prevent Sylvester from becoming bishop, but the other, much more important, aim was the recognition of his official role in the selection process of the candidates for an episcopal election. Here, his arguments are of great interest. On the one hand, he followed a very traditional line of argument when referring to his dignity. This dignity was intact, and thus his position as ruler, when his prerogatives were respected and John, like his predecessors, regarded the right to participate in the selection process as a God given prerogative, which needed to be protected at all costs.[267] On the other hand, he followed a new line of argument in referring to *ius scriptum*. While the term *ius* was frequently used in conjunction with the term *dignitas* in the traditional defence of royal rights,[268] the use of the term *ius scriptum* was something new. Considering the importance of the issue and that the addressee, Walter de Coutances, was an expert in legal matters, its deployment was certainly not accidental. Principally the term *ius scriptum* referred to the entire body of written law, thus Roman and canon law.[269] In John's case, the term might even have been applicable to royal records. In England, the recording of legal proceedings by royal judges played an important role in the genesis of the common law, because it created a body of written law. It is possible that John and his entourage perceived all royal records relating to royal rights, in particular those being recorded in the Rolls, as constituting written law. In the particular case of John's letter to Archbishop Walter, the term *ius scriptum* cannot have referred to Roman law, as this offered no support for John's claims.[270] The royal records would have been of greater use. Here, John could have referred to the letter he had sent to the chapter of Lisieux the previous year and which had been inserted in the Charter Rolls.[271] In all probability, however, John's *ius scriptum* meant canon law. The teachings of Anglo-Norman

---

[266] *Rot. pat.*, p. 16a/b.

[267] Cf. C. Cheney, *From Becket to Langton. English Church Government 1170–1213* (Manchester, 1956), p. 94.

[268] Cheney, *Innocent III*, p. 127.

[269] I would like to thank Prof. Dolezalek for his advice on *ius scriptum*.

[270] Cf. *Corpus iuris civilis Iustinianei: cum commentariis Accursii, scholiis Contii, et D. Gothofredi lucubrationibus ad Accursium*, ed. J. Fehe et al. (6 vols., Lyons, 1627), and, for example, *Placentini Summa codicis* (Turin, 1962; reprint of Mainz, 1536); *Azonis Lectura super codicem. Hugolini Apparatus in tres libros* (Corpus glossatorum juris civilis III) (Turin, 1966; reprint of Paris, 1577); *Scripta anecdota antiquissmorum glossatorum*, ed. G. B. Palmerio (Bibliotheca iuridica medii aevi I) (Bologna, 1888).

[271] Supra, pp. 113–14.

canonists were readily available to John and his advisors. For example, Honorius, who had written that the custom of some cathedral churches gave the prince the right to take part in the election, began to work for John's chancellor Hubert Walter around 1200. Equally, John of Tynemouth, who had taught that in some parts of England the king's consent to an election was required, was active for Hubert Walter at the same time.[272] Teachings like theirs, based on a thorough knowledge of canon law, offered John a platform from which he could hope to argue his case successfully. John's argument shows the high level of sophistication present at the inner circle of royal power. John and his advisors had realised that they increased their chances of winning, when, in addition to the traditional argument of the royal dignity, they placed their argumentation within a legal framework accepted and followed by the church. This was written law, more specifically canon law.

Walter's reaction to John's letter offers further instructive insight into the complex process of the application of law. A glance at Rouen's copy of the *Francofortana* would have instructed him that John's position was, to say the least, only one possible interpretation of the king's role in episcopal elections and that the opposite view was gaining strength.[273] Yet, Walter would consider such information not as an opponent of King John willing to weaken royal authority, or as a Gregorian reformer insisting on the

---

[272] Cheney, *Hubert Walter*, pp. 164–5, and supra, p. 35.

[273] It is unknown whether in 1202 Walter had already at his disposal the chapter on episcopal elections in *Rotomagensis prima*, that contained at position one the decretal *Cum terra* which declared that the ruler's consent should not be asked for during the selection process, cf. supra, p. 82. This chapter consists of five decretals, all copied by the same hand, and belongs to the later amplifications of the collection, Paris, BNF Lat. 3922A, fo. 152va–b: *1 Rot.* 3.1 = *2 Comp.* 1.3.6 = *X* 1.6.14 [= Jaffé, II, no. 17656; *WH* 319]; 3.2 (a/b) = *2 Comp.* 1.19 un(a), *2 Comp.* 1.3(b) = *X* 1.40.3 (a), 1.6.12(b) [= Jaffé, II, nos. 14310(a), 16630(b); *WH* 60]; 3.3 [= Jaffé –; *WH* 419]; 3.4 = *Register Innocenz' III.*, no. 51 [= Potthast, I, no. 53]; 3.5 = *Register Innocenz' III.*, II, no. 176 = *3 Comp.* 1.6.2 = *X* 1.6.17 [= Potthast, I, no. 836]; Cheney and Cheney, *Studies*, pp. 160–8, 176. The analysis of this chapter shows that all five decretals appear in the collection of Gilbert (1202–4), a source for the later amplifications of *1 Rot.*, *1 Rot.* 3.1 = *Gilb.* 1.3.4; *1 Rot.* 3.2 = *Gilb.* 1.20.un(a), 5.2.2(b); *1 Rot.* 3.3 = *Gilb.* 1.9.7; *1 Rot.* 3.4 = *Gilb.* 1.5.5; *1 Rot.* 3.5 = *Gilb.* 1.3.7; for Gilbert see R. von Heckel, 'Die Dekretalensammlungen des Gilbertus und Alanus nach den Weingartener Handschriften', *Savigny KA*, 29 (1940), 116–357. However, a comparison between the texts shows that Gilbert was not the source used here. *Cum terra*, for example, appears with full inscription and a reference to the papal registers, both of which are lacking in Gilbert. Another example is *Ad aures nostras* which appears in *1 Rot.* 3.2 as one decretal subdivided into two parts (*Ad aures nostras* and *Super eo*), while in Gilbert it appears as two decretals in different chapters attributing *Ad aures nostras* to Alexander III, *Gilb.* 1.20.un, and *Super eo* to Celestine III, *Gilb.* 5.2.2. Thus *1 Rot.* 3 was drawn from other sources among which was probably the extract of the papal registers which, as Walther Holtzmann has shown, was extensively used for the later additions to *1 Rot.*, Cheney and Cheney, *Studies*, pp. 166–7. The latest decretal included in this chapter dates from September 1199 (*1 Rot.* 3.5). It is, however, impossible to establish whether the chapter was compiled and inserted into the collection before or after the affair of Sées.

exclusion of laymen from ecclesiastical business, but as a prelate highly experienced in royal politics and loyal to the Angevin kings. It needed more than the presence of a decretal collection and its *Apparatus* to convince him that it would be worthwhile risking a breach with the king. Walter decided to comply with John's wishes, and withheld Sylvester's consecration. Thus the political attitude of bishops played an important part in shaping the application of canon law, and this was a major reason why loyal bishops were an important asset for the king. In the case of Sylvester's election, however, Walter was not the highest ecclesiastical authority involved. Innocent III showed an active interest in the implementation of his judgement, and he took a very clear stand on the question of the ruler's role in episcopal elections: the king was not to interfere. In fact Innocent had formulated this in September 1202, in his decretal *Quod sicut* dealing with the case of Armagh, Ireland, another see in John's realms, where he explicitly explained that the exclusion of the prince from episcopal elections did not violate the royal dignity.[274] In February 1203, he admonished John to refrain from interfering in episcopal elections, quoting the recent examples of Lincoln, Sées, and Coutances. He also demanded that John recompense any damages his actions had caused.[275] John, however, had no intention of admitting Sylvester or of returning the temporalities. In January 1203, Robert count of Alençon had handed over the city of Alençon to Philip II.[276] At around the same time, Matilda, the widowed countess of the Perche, married Enguerrand de Coucy: a marriage probably arranged by Enguerrand's cousin Philip Augustus.[277] Although Matilda continued to foster her contacts with King John,[278] the Plantagenet must have considered Matilda's marriage a further heavy blow to his interests in this sensitive border region. The temporalities of the bishopric, therefore, were the last foothold John had in this area. But in May 1203, Innocent's patience was nearly exhausted. He sent a sharp letter to Archbishop Walter ordering him to welcome Sylvester as his suffragan bishop and to persuade John to accept Sylvester and to return all possessions to the church of Sées. If the king did not do so within the next month, Walter was to place the ecclesiastical province of Normandy under interdict. He, Innocent, could in no circumstances permit the *ecclesiastica libertas* to be infringed.[279] Thus Innocent deployed the full

---

[274] See supra, p. 33.   [275] *Register Innocenz' III.*, v, no. 159 (160) [= Potthast, i, no. 1831].
[276] D. Power, 'The End of Angevin Normandy: The Revolt at Alençon (1203)', *Historical Research*, 74 (2001), 444–64.
[277] Thompson, *Perche*, pp. 147–9.   [278] Ibid., pp. 149–51.
[279] *Register Innocenz' III.*, vi, no. 73 [= Potthast, i, no. 1919].

strength of papal authority to implement his judgement and its underlying canonical principles. Receiving this letter, Walter understood that there was no other solution than to accept Innocent's conditions. John in turn realised that his precarious political situation did not allow him a breach with the pope. He granted Sylvester safe conduct to visit the arch-bishop,[280] and in October 1203 he ordered his seneschal, William Crassus, to restore the possessions to the bishop and the canons of Sées and to remedy the losses incurred. However, the king refused to accept the wider implications of Innocent's argument. In his letter to William, he made it very clear that he allowed Sylvester's admission only out of deference to the pope. Sylvester had no just claim to the see, since his election had violated John's right and dignity and the old and approved custom of the duchy. By having this letter inserted in the Liberate Rolls, John underlined that he considered Sylvester's admission as a one-off royal favour.[281]

John would not get another opportunity to press his claims at a Norman episcopal election. Shortly after Sylvester gained possession of his see, the king was driven out of Normandy, never to return. The conflict between him and the pope over royal rights in elections found its continuation in England. Here, the elections at Winchester (1204–5) and in particular at Canterbury (1205–7) were further chapters in this controversy showing how much of the royal and papal strategy had been shaped in the course of the dispute over Sées.[282] The conflict finally escalated in 1207 when John refused to accept Stephen Langton as archbishop of Canterbury. England was laid under an interdict and John was excommunicated. The situation took a dramatic turn in 1213, when John, whose political situation had drastically worsened in 1212, surrendered his crown to Innocent, becom-ing the pope's vassal for the kingdoms of England and Ireland.[283] John was absolved from excommunication, the interdict was raised, and John started to experience the advantages of full papal support. Innocent instructed his legate Nicholas, cardinal-bishop of Tusculum, to ensure that bishops elected to English sees in future were to be not only 'dis-tinguished by their lives and learning, but also loyal to the king, profitable to the kingdom and capable of giving counsel and help – the king's assent having been requested'.[284] The legate and Peter des Roches, the king's

---

[280] *Rot. pat.*, p. 33b.
[281] *Rotuli de liberate ac de misis et praestitis, regnante Johanne*, ed. T. D. Hardy (London, 1844), p. 72.
[282] For these elections, see Cheney, *Innocent III*, pp. 144–54.   [283] Ibid., pp. 298–343.
[284] *Selected Letters of Pope Innocent III concerning England*, ed. C. Cheney and W.H. Semple (London, 1953), no. 62 and n. 1; cf. no. 76.

justiciar, put this programme into practice.[285] In this period John must have realised that collaboration with the pope could be very useful in creating a loyal episcopacy. As a consequence he probably no longer saw the need categorically to insist on the recognition of his right to determine episcopal elections. John made use of this experience in the autumn of 1214, when he faced widespread baronial and clerical opposition in England after his ill-fated campaign against Philip Augustus. In a move to strengthen his relationship with the church and to weaken the ranks of his opponents he issued a charter granting free election to all cathedral and monastic churches in England and Wales. The pope confirmed this charter in March 1215 and later that year this promise was included in Magna Carta.[286] In theory, at least, the question of John's rights in episcopal elections was settled.

Returning to Sées it seems that the rift within the chapter did not heal after Sylvester's election. In 1212, Innocent III charged papal judges delegate to investigate whether the accusations against Bishop Sylvester and Prior John of 'perverse acts, which were not only useless, but also dangerous' were true. If their enquiry confirmed these rumours, they were to replace both men.[287] Sylvester and the prior were able to clear themselves, and the bishop remained in office until his death in 1220. Whether members of the chapter were behind these accusations remains unclear, but the appointment of Gervase, abbot of Prémontré, to the see of Sées after Sylvester's death points towards internal power struggles. Gervase was an Englishman by birth, who had spent his life on the continent in the French kingdom. As a boy he had joined the abbey of St Just in the diocese of Beauvais, of which he was to become abbot. Then he became abbot of Thenailles in the diocese of Laon, before being elected abbot of Prémontré and president of the whole order in 1209. During his time as abbot of Prémontré, Gervase's major occupation was to restore discipline to the order. In so doing he developed excellent connections with the papacy, in particular with Honorius III.[288] If indeed there was a longstanding dispute in the chapter of Sées, Honorius III may have thought it appropriate to promote the election of Gervase, a man of

---

[285] C. Harper-Bill, 'John and the Church of Rome', in S. Church (ed.), *King John. New Interpretations* (Woodbridge, 1999), pp. 289–315, p. 309.

[286] Cheney, *Innocent III*, pp. 168–70, 364–5, 377; N. Vincent, 'The Election of Pandulph Verraclo as Bishop of Norwich (1215)', *Historical Research*, 68 (1995), 143–63, 146–8, 160; for the charter of 1214, see *Councils and Synods with Other Documents relating to the English Church. II. A.D. 1205–1313*, ed. M. Powicke and C. Cheney (2 vols., Oxford, 1964), I, pp. 38–41.

[287] 'Innocentii Romani pontificis regestorum sive epistolarum', in *PL*, CCXVI, col. 620, no. 110 [= Potthast, I, no. 4533].

[288] There is no evidence corroborating an eighteenth-century statement that Gervase came from a noble family from Lincoln, or Lincolnshire, Cheney, 'Gervase, Abbot of Prémontré', 25–6, 30–1;

proven capability to deal with difficult situations. Besides, Gervase was not a complete stranger to north-western France. In 1220, he tried to raise money for the construction of the hospital at Argentan, situated in the diocese of Sées.[289] He also had good contacts with the seneschal of Anjou, William des Roches,[290] and these contacts may well have facilitated his election at Sées, a diocese which lay immediately to the north of William's power base at Sablé and Château-du-Loir. If his mission was to restore discipline to the regular chapter of Sées, he appears to have succeeded. No more news about scandalous behaviour reached the papacy, and, after Gervase's death in 1228, the chapter elected their prior, Hugh, whose anniversary was commemorated at St Victor, the mother house of the regular chapter of Sées. He governed the diocese until his death in 1240.[291]

The elections at Sées demonstrate very clearly that the strategic position of the diocese on the frontier between Normandy, the Chartrain, and Greater Anjou caused the dukes to watch events carefully. Their interests were particularly vulnerable at times when the locally powerful magnates circled in the orbit of the Capetians or the counts of Champagne and Blois. The dukes' efforts to secure the election of men loyal to them raised the possibility of electoral conflicts. These were further enhanced by the transformation of the chapter into one of canons regular. Tied closely together by a common rule, and part of a network spreading across political frontiers, the regular canons were less susceptible to ducal influence than a secular chapter might have been. This potential for electoral conflict was increased by problems occurring within the chapter of Sées. It appears that in 1131 the secular canons were not required to become canons regular themselves, and that just around the time when they would have died out, Bishop Froger received papal permission to install a secular archdeacon. The co-existence of regulars and seculars was a continuous source of tensions and friction within the chapter.

The electoral conflicts highlight the varying degrees of authority wielded by the Angevin dukes at the time of their attempts to intervene at Sées. In 1144, Geoffrey's position in Normandy was better than ever before, but he was still far from being able to check the local magnates or to impose his will on a hostile chapter. Thirteen years later, the Angevins had made considerable progress. Henry II was capable of removing a

Epistolae reverendissimi in Christo patris ac domini D. Gervasii Praemonstratensis abbatis postea Sagiensis episcopi ex veteri celeberrimae Viconiensis monasterii bibliothecae manu-scripto editae, ed. N. Caillieu (Valenciennes, 1663).

[289] Alençon, AD Orne H 5244 (copies of documents concerning the Hôtel-Dieu of Argentan).
[290] Cheney, 'Gervase, Abbot of Prémontré', 41, 51–2.
[291] 'Ex Uticensis monasterii annalibus et necrologio', in *RHF*, XXIII, pp. 480–91, p. 480; *GC*, XI, col. 694.

bishop-elect and of replacing him with a man of his entourage. King John's case reveals the rapid loss of his authority in Normandy. In 1200–1 he got his man elected at Lisieux and in early 1202 he was able to push through an election at Coutances,[292] but he failed in 1201–3 at Sées. Once Normandy and Greater Anjou were conquered, Sées lost its strategic importance and the Capetians developed no particular interest in its elections. It is also possible that Gervase's election in 1220 showed the first signs of papal influence on the nomination of bishops in Normandy.

BAYEUX

By the end of the eleventh century the wealth of the bishopric of Bayeux had become so notorious that the bishop of Rennes, Marbod, declared that it would support three bishops.[293] Yet, in the following years, so much of its patrimony was lost that, when Henry I's custodians took over the administration of the vacant bishopric in 1133, hardly anything was left.[294] Unhappy with this situation, Henry I ordered an inquest to be held into Bayeux's nominal possessions. The inquest brought to light that the bishop ought to have been able to command approximately 120 knights. This was substantially more than that commanded by any other church-man in Normandy. The bishop himself owed the duke the service of twenty knights. Among the Norman ecclesiastics, only the bishop of Lisieux owed as many.[295] Thus, at least in theory, the bishop of Bayeux was a very powerful man and, if he received the means to regain his temporalities, he would become an important ally. Yet, due to Henry I's death and the subsequent war between Stephen and Matilda, little had changed between 1133 and the time when the see fell vacant again in 1142.

Sarell E. Gleason has argued that the election of Philip de Harcourt as bishop of Bayeux in 1142 was King Stephen's compensation for Philip's failure to gain Salisbury in 1139.[296] In the light of more detailed research, scholars have claimed that Philip's promotion ought to be seen in the context of Count Waleran de Meulan's shift to the Angevins in

---

[292] See infra, pp. 148–9.

[293] S.E. Gleason, *An Ecclesiastical Barony of the Middle Ages. The Bishopric of Bayeux, 1066–1204* (Harvard Historical Monographs x) (Cambridge, Mass., 1936), pp. 40–1.

[294] Ibid., p. 42.

[295] There are, however, no figures available for Rouen and Evreux, *The Red Book of the Exchequer*, ed. H. Hall (Rolls Series IC) (3 vols., London, 1896), II, pp. 624–45, esp. pp. 624–5. For a discussion of this inquest and a refinement of its figures, see T.K. Keefe, *Feudal Assessments and the Political Community under Henry II and his Sons* (Berkeley, 1983), pp. 72–82 and pp. 141–53; Schriber, *The Dilemma of Arnulf of Lisieux*, p. 27.

[296] Gleason, *Bayeux*, p. 27.

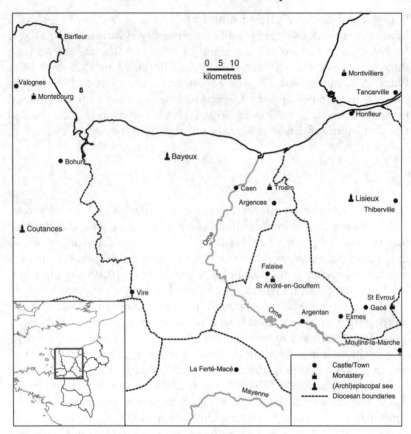

Map 6 The diocese of Bayeux

1141.[297] And, indeed, the latter position is far more plausible. Related to
the Beaumonts, the Harcourt family held land from them on both sides of
the Channel, and Philip's father, Robert fitz Anschetil, had been a friend
and advisor to Count Robert I de Meulan, Waleran's father. Waleran had
promoted Philip's career from at least the 1120s. By 1126, Philip had
become archdeacon of Evreux and, before 1131, Waleran had made him
dean of Ste Trinité, the collegiate church of Beaumont, and was probably
responsible for the grant of the deanery of Lincoln that Philip received
towards the end of Henry I's reign.[298] When the Beaumont twins were at

[297] H.A. Cronne, *The Reign of Stephen. Anarchy in England* (London, 1970), pp. 207–8; Walker,
   Episcopacy, p. 223; Crouch, *Beaumont*, p. 54.
[298] Gleason, *Bayeux*, p. 27; Crouch, *Beaumont*, pp. 45, 120–7.

the height of their influence at Stephen's court in 1139, Philip succeeded the imprisoned Roger Le Poer, bishop of Salisbury, as the king's chancellor.[299] When Roger died in December 1139, Philip resigned the chancellorship in order to obtain Roger's bishopric. But the clergy of Salisbury, supported by the papal legate for England, Henry, bishop of Winchester, resisted King Stephen's wish, and Philip's bid failed.[300] In 1141, Waleran shifted to the Angevins. This was a major boost for Geoffrey Plantagenet's campaign; a year later he had gained control of the Bessin and was aiming at extending his authority to the core of the duchy, the area around Rouen. By contrast, King Stephen's position in Normandy had become so weak that in 1142 he had hardly any influence left on political decisions in the duchy.[301] In consideration of Waleran's longstanding patronage of Philip, it is probable that it was Waleran who demanded Geoffrey's support for Philip's election at Bayeux. Through this, Waleran hoped to extend further his family's power and influence in Normandy. From Philip's point of view, Waleran's position at the ducal court allowed him to help in regaining the alienated possessions of the see of Bayeux. Relentlessly fighting for his church, Philip was able to recover most of the lost land before the end of his episcopate.[302] Thus when he died in February 1163,[303] the bishop of Bayeux's power had been transformed from potential to real.

Well aware of this situation, King Henry II was probably involved in the election of Philip's successor, Henry de Beaumont, in 1165.[304] Henry had made his career at Salisbury, where he had been archdeacon and – since at least 1155 – dean of the chapter.[305] He had been in contact with

---

[299] Crouch, *Beaumont*, p. 45.

[300] Stephen had refused Henry of Winchester's candidate, Henry de Sully, who was one of his *nepotes*, D. Knowles, *The Episcopal Colleagues of Archbishop Thomas Becket* (Cambridge, 1951), p. 7. The story of the candidates for the see of Salisbury was only one episode in the fight between Henry, bishop of Winchester, and the Beaumont twins for control at the king's court, Cronne, *Stephen*, pp. 50, 208.

[301] Chibnall, 'Normandy', pp. 102–3; For Waleran, supra, pp. 75–6, 100.

[302] Cf. *Antiquus cartularius*, ed. Bourrienne, I, nos. 43–4, 117, 139, 148; *Epistolae pontificum*, ed. Loewenfeld, no. 190 [= Jaffé, II, no. 8612; WH -]; *Papsturkunden in Frankreich. Neue Folge. II. Normandie*, ed. Ramackers, nos. 14, 19, 22–4, 30–4, 36, 41, 46, 50, 64, 67–9, 71, 89–90, 97, 101–3: [= Jaffé -; WH -]; *Regesta regum Anglo-Normannorum 1066–1154*, ed. Davis et al. (4 vols. Oxford, 1913–69), III, nos. 52–8, 60–6; *Recueil des actes de Henri II*, ed. Delisle and Berger, I, 13–14, 21–2, 38, 72, 228, 335, 366; Gleason, *Bayeux*, p. 43. However, Philip only partially regained the lands lost to Robert of Gloucester, father of Philip's predecessor on the episcopal see, *Earldom of Gloucester Charters*, ed. Patterson, no. 6.

[303] V. Bourrienne, *Un grand bâtisseur. Philippe de Harcourt, évêque de Bayeux (1142–1163)* (Paris, 1930), p. 125; *Torigny*, p. 217.

[304] *Torigny*, p. 225.

[305] D. Greenway, *John Le Neve: Fasti ecclesiae Anglicanae, 1066–1300. IV. Salisbury* (London, 1991), p. 9; *English Episcopal Acta XVIII. Salisbury 1078–1217*, ed. B.R. Kemp (Oxford, 1999), pp. lxv–lxvi.

the canons of Bayeux in the early years of Philip's episcopate, when he was among the representatives of the chapter of Salisbury who arranged an agreement about some of the treasure Philip had taken from Salisbury.[306] On this occasion, he may have made an impression on the canons from Bayeux. Furthermore there were links of kinship between the two chapters. Humphrey Bovet was arch-chaplain and chancellor at Bayeux at least from the 1140s to the 1170s. His *nepos*, Gislebert, was a canon at Bayeux in the 1150s, and Humphrey Bovet the younger was canon in 1177. Hugh Bovet was a canon from the late 1170s, and archdeacon between 1192 and 1200. Before that, Hugh Bovet can be traced as a canon of Salisbury. A member of the chapter there at least since 1161, he held as a benefice the church of Britford which he had inherited from his father. His brothers made their entire careers at Bayeux. Roger was a canon and chancellor; Alexander was a cleric. Further kinsmen appeared in the first decade of the thirteenth century: Henry Bovet as archdeacon, and William Bovet as canon.[307] It is open to speculation to what extent the cross-Channel ties of the Bovet family played a role in Henry de Beaumont's election. But it is noteworthy that Henry de Beaumont's arrival at Bayeux encouraged the prosperity of the Bovet family in the chapter.

In any case, at the time of his election Henry de Beaumont had very good connections with the Angevins, in particular with the Empress Matilda, and this may well have been the most important factor in his promotion from Salisbury to Bayeux.[308] As bishop, Henry maintained excellent relations with the royal court and Henry II proposed him to the monks of Canterbury as Thomas Becket's successor as archbishop of Canterbury in 1173–4. But the monks rejected the king's proposal,[309] so that Henry remained bishop of Bayeux until his death in late 1204.[310]

His succession was heavily disputed. A minority of the chapter led by the dean, Richard, chose Archdeacon Robert. The majority, led by the Chanter Henry, voted for Archdeacon William. Then an appeal was

---

[306] *Antiquus cartularius*, ed. Bourrienne, I, no. 61.

[307] Spear, 'Power, Patronage and Personality', p. 217; Greenway, *Fasti ecclesiae Anglicanae, Salisbury*, p. 122.

[308] *The Letters of John of Salisbury II. The Later Letters (1163–1180)*, ed. Brooke and Millor, nos. 137–8, 191. Henry, apparently, was not related to the Beaumont twins, cf. Spear, 'Power, Patronage and Personality', p. 216 n. 40; Greenway, *Fasti ecclesiae Anglicanae, 1066–1300. Salisbury*, p. 9 n. 4.

[309] *The Historical Works of Gervase of Canterbury*, ed. W. Stubbs (2 vols., Rolls Series LXXIII) (London, 1879–80), I, p. 240. The monks refused to elect him, because he was a continental bishop, *The Letters and Charters of Gilbert Foliot*, ed. A. Morey and C.N.L. Brooke (Cambridge, 1967), no. 220.

[310] Henry's obituary is celebrated at Bayeux on 19 November, at the abbey of Silli on 18 November, Caen, AD Calvados G 149 (obituary, cathedral chapter of Bayeux), fo. 53v; Alençon, AD Orne H 1069 (obituary, abbey of Silli), fo. 102v. Spear, *The Personnel*, p. 33, argues for 1205, but the evidence relating to Robert d'Ablèges election only allows for 1204.

launched to Innocent III to prevent the dean, who had the first vote in the electoral process, from completing the election without the consent of the entire chapter, or at least of its *maior et sanior pars*. The dean, however, rushed through Robert's election and appealed to the pope in order to prevent it from being annulled. He also asserted that, immediately after the election, many others had consented to it. But it was argued against the dean that something that had been wrong from the beginning could not be validated *ex post facto*; the later consent of the others, therefore, did not matter. When the dean and his followers left the chapter-house, the chanter's party abandoned their first choice, Archdeacon William, despite the fact that Archdeacon Robert's election had not been annulled and an appeal was pending. They chose Master Robert d'Ablèges, canon of Bayeux, without informing pope or archbishop, even though Robert was a subdeacon. They completed the election and enthroned him as bishop. Innocent III, to whom these events were reported when the case was brought before the papal court, annulled both elections. Then, in a letter dating from 22 April 1205, he charged John, bishop of Dol, William, abbot of Savigny, and Robert, abbot of Ardenne, to inform the chapter of Bayeux that, after the return of their members who had been at the papal court, they had two months to elect a new bishop. If they did not succeed in so doing, the papal judges delegate should nominate the bishop.[311]

Contrary to the papal instructions the papal judges delegate ordered the chapter to hold the election within five weeks and five days. The canons protested, but decided to conduct the election. This second election took a course very similar to the first. The dean, together with a minority of the chapter, elected Saxo, papal subdeacon and canon of Bayeux. Expecting such a move, the chanter and the majority of the chapter elected Robert d'Ablèges for a second time.[312] The tactics of the dean's party were obvious. Knowing that they were in the minority and so had no chance of winning by the rules, they tried to win by a coup. Certain that this would meet with fierce resistance, they chose a candidate whom they thought likely to gain the favour of the papal judges delegate and Innocent III. But their plan did not work out. The candidate favoured by the majority of the chapter, Robert d'Ablèges, was confirmed by Archbishop Walter de Coutances. The matter seemed settled, when all of a sudden the papal judges delegate intervened. Declaring both elections void, they nominated Hugh Clément, dean of the cathedral church of Notre-Dame of Paris.

---

[311] *Register Innocenz' III.*, VIII, no. 35 = *3 Comp.* 1.6.14 = *X* 1.6.29 = *3 Rot.* 91 [= Potthast, I, no. 2472].
[312] *3 Rot.* 92, Paris, BNF Lat. 3922 A, fo. 126va–b, edited by Cheney, 'Decretals of Innocent III in Paris, B. N. MS Lat. 3922A', pp. 161–2, no. 92.

The dean's party was certainly not behind this move. It is hardly conceivable that Dean Richard, son of the former seneschal of Normandy, William fitz Ralph (d. 1200) and himself a former clerk of Richard I and John,[313] could have been interested in the nomination of Hugh Clément, whose family was close to Philip Augustus. Rather, it appears that King Philip intervened. The Clément family was famous for its service to the Capetians. Hugh's father had been the marshal, Robert Clément, who had been Philip's guardian before 1181. Hugh's brother, Alberic Clément, died at Acre in 1191. Another brother, the Marshal Henry Clément, belonged to the inner council of the royal court. He played a significant role in the conquest of Normandy and was among the men awarded lands in the duchy. During the campaign of 1204, King Philip granted Henry the castle and the forest of Argentan (dioc. Sées). A third brother, Odo Clément, was a royal cleric and became dean of St Martin of Tours in 1211.[314] The see of Bayeux fell vacant at a moment when Philip had just completed the conquest of Normandy but was still fighting for Greater Anjou. With the danger of an Angevin counterattack still imminent, the Capetian court watched with particular interest the election of a prelate commanding a substantial armed force. The majority candidate, Robert d'Ablèges, had enjoyed the trust of Richard I. In the financial year 1189–90 he, together with King Richard's almoner Philip, had been put in charge of 800 marks silver from the king's treasure.[315] The news that he had been elected certainly alarmed Philip Augustus' advisors. Apparently informed about the powers of the papal judges delegate, they saw in them a convenient means to annul Robert's election and safely to place one of their own men in the disputed see.

But the royal plans were opposed by the fierce resistance of the chanter and his followers, who would not accept Hugh Clément as their bishop. Finally the case was brought again before Innocent III. At the papal court, the dean's party and the papal judges delegate were rebuked. The pope argued that, although there was nothing to be said against the suitability of their

---

[313] On 27 December 1198 Richard I granted the chapel of St Ouen-du-Château at Bayeux to his clerk Richard de St Amand, *Antiquus cartularius*, ed. Bourrienne, I, no. 271. That this Richard de St Amand became dean of Bayeux is shown by the charter of Philip Augustus granting Bishop Robert d'Ablèges the chapel of St Ouen-du-Château 'post decessam decani qui eam possidet', *Recueil des actes de Philippe Auguste*, ed. Delaborde et al., II, no. 942. Richard had become dean of Bayeux by 31 August 1199, when King John ordered the chapter of Avranches to provide his clerk R., dean of Bayeux, son of the seneschal of Normandy, with the treasury at Avranches, *Rot. chart.*, p. 15a.

[314] *GC*, VII, cols. 198–202; Baldwin, *Philip*, pp. 113, 119, 122; Q. Griffiths, 'The Capetian Kings and St Martin de Tours', *Studies in Medieval and Renaissance History*, 19 (1987), 83–133, 116; for Philip's grant to Henry, see *Recueil des actes de Philippe Auguste*, ed. Delaborde et al., II, no. 807.

[315] *PR* 2, R.I, p. 4.

candidates, the way they had elected them was unacceptable. In contrast, Robert d'Ablèges had been canonically elected by the *maior, dignior et sanior pars* of the chapter, and therefore should be consecrated. At the end of his letter instructing the archbishop of Rouen on the matter of Robert's election, the pope subtly pointed towards the Capetian role in this affair, when he asked Walter to admonish Philip Augustus to hand the *regalia* to the bishop.[316] Philip accepted the pope's decision and immediately changed his policy. He tried to win the new bishop's favour. Shortly after Robert's consecration, he issued a grant stating that 'for the love which we have towards our beloved and faithful Robert' the chapel of St Ouen-du-Château at Bayeux was to return to the bishopric after the death of its dean.[317] Philip's change of heart seems to have been effective, as there were few signs of anti-Capetian sentiment at Bayeux during Robert's long pontificate.

As to the development and application of canon law, the electoral dispute of 1205–6 highlights three points of interest. First, the lack of precisely defined electoral procedures, which could lead to great disharmony and delay in electing a bishop. Ten years later, Innocent III tried to eradicate such problems with canon twenty-four of the Fourth Lateran Council.[318] Secondly, the suitability of a subdeacon. In the first election, the fact that the chanter's party had elected a subdeacon, without prior consultation with the pope or the archbishop, contributed to Innocent's decision to quash the election. However, it cannot have been a very strong argument. In his decision on the second election, the pope stressed that Subdeacon Saxo had been a suitable candidate. Two years later, Innocent officially decreed that subdeacons counted among the clergy in higher orders and could be elected to bishoprics.[319] Thirdly, the chanter's appeal and Innocent's decision show that the *maior, dignior et sanior pars* did not have to include the most senior official of the chapter, the dean.

After Robert's death in 1231, there was another disputed election.[320] The chapter split into several parties. Twenty-four of the forty-nine canons voted for the Canon William de Tancarville, eighteen for Master John de La Cour, and seven voted for other candidates. The case was brought before Gregory IX, both parties reporting their version of events.

---

[316] *3 Rot.* 92, Paris, BNF Lat. 3922A, fo. 126va–b, edited by Cheney, 'Decretals of Innocent III in Paris, B. N. MS Lat. 3922A', pp. 161–2, no. 92. Walter consecrated Robert on 26 February 1206, 'E chronico Rotomagensi', in *RHF*, XXIII, p. 359; *GC*, XI, col. 366.

[317] *Recueil des actes de Philippe Auguste*, ed. Delaborde et al., II, no. 942; supra, n. 313.

[318] See supra, pp. 40–1.   [319] See supra, p. 51.

[320] For the following account of the dispute, see *Registres de Grégoire IX*, ed. Auvray, I, no. 741.

According to William's party, all the canons had assembled on the election day. After they had chosen scrutiny as their means of election, the *maior et sanior pars* of the chapter had decided for William. They argued that the twenty-four votes cast for William had gained him an absolute majority, because two of the forty-nine canons had no right to vote. One, Henry, did not possess a proper canonry, and the other, Guy, had been living at Belleville near Lyons and was thus too far away from Bayeux to have the right to participate in the election. William's election should therefore be confirmed by the pope.

According to John's party, the events were not so straightforward. According to their version, after the votes had been counted, long discussions had taken place to find a way in which the deadlock could be resolved. However, no solution had been found and the election had not been completed. Disregarding this situation, the dean had taken the initiative. Having neither the mandate of the chapter nor customary right, he and his allies had proceeded to the election of William de Tancarville. This, according to John's party, violated the statute of the Fourth Lateran Council that a bishop had to be elected by the *maior et sanior pars* of the chapter.[321] Like their opponents, they believed the *maior pars* to be the absolute numerical majority. They stated that, although William had received more votes than anybody else, he had not obtained the absolute majority of the chapter, since the votes of Henry and Guy were valid. They explained that, like any other canon, Henry had always participated in all activities of the chapter – including voting for dignitaries and priests. As to Guy, according to the custom of the Gallican church, absent canons must be summoned *de toto regno Francie*.[322] Stressing that an election had to be based on the participation and the consent of all, since otherwise there would be as many elections as parties, they asked Gregory IX to order the chapter to hold a new election. The pope judged in favour of John's party and demanded a new election at Bayeux. This time the canons chose unanimously Thomas de Fréauville, dean of Rouen, who was well known to the canons. Thomas, a former archdeacon of Bayeux, had

---

[321] This refers to c. 24, 'Concilii quarti Lateranensis constitutiones', in *Constitutiones concilii quarti Lateranensis*, ed. García y García, pp. 70–1.

[322] The question whether Guy had to be invited nicely reflects the situation of the archbishopric of Lyons at the time. Due to its geographical situation on the border between the empire and the French kingdom its archbishop gained a status of quasi-independence theoretically owing obedience to the emperor, but more and more drawn into the orbit of the French crown, cf. B. Galland, *Deux archevêchés entre la France et l'Empire: les archevêques de Lyon et les archevêques de Vienne du milieu du XIIe au milieu du XIVe siècle* (Bibliothèques des écoles françaises d'Athènes et de Rome CCLXXXII) (Rome, 1994), pp. 704–7.

acted together with William, bishop of Lisieux, as coadjutor of the ailing Robert d'Ablèges in 1231.[323]

Apart from canon twenty-four of the Fourth Lateran Council, there was no explicit reference in the records to the sources of canon law that influenced the arguments of both parties. On the interpretation of *maior pars* they followed the line of thought that William de *Canapello* had set out nearly a decade earlier and which had been made canon law by Honorius III. For their arguments on the absent canons their sources are more difficult to detect. William's party may have had in mind the canons *Quanto* and *Coram* when they disputed Guy's electoral right. John's party may have built their counterargument on Johannes Teutonicus' interpretation of *Cum inter*.[324] If both parties indeed used these decretals to develop their arguments, Gregory IX's judgement in favour of John's party indicates the limited practical impact of *Coram*. Regardless of the favour it enjoyed with canonists, in legal practice *Coram* was considered as only one among a number of decretals regulating the question of absent canons.

The political background of the electoral dispute between William de Tancarville and John de la Cour can only be illuminated to a limited extent. Canon William, subdean of the chapter at the time of the election,[325] was a senior figure within the chapter, who had strong local connections. His testamentary bequests[326] show him to have had deep roots in the diocese of Bayeux, and if he was related to the lords of Tancarville, he could count on the support of one of the most powerful baronial families in Normandy.[327] The other candidate, John de La Cour, was a Capetian cleric, who could count on the support of the regency.[328] If William was a member of the Tancarville family, the electoral dispute

---

[323] *Layettes*, ed. Teulet et al., II, no. 2176; supra, p. 90; Caen, AD Calvados H 164 (charters concerning the abbey of Ardenne) (William de Tancarville, subdean and Master William de Vi, official of Bayeux, authorised by William, bishop of Lisieux, and Thomas de Fréauville, dean of Rouen, coadjutors of Robert, bishop of Bayeux, receive Jocelin L'Abbé's presentation to the church of St Contest-d'Athis by the abbot and convent of Ardenne).

[324] See supra, p. 37.   [325] See supra, n. 323.

[326] *Antiquus cartularius*, ed. Bourrienne, II, nos. 369–70; cf. nos. 371, 380, 389.

[327] Powicke, *Loss*, p. 353. The Tancarville family had interests in the diocese of Bayeux, cf. *Antiquus cartularius*, ed. Bourrienne, I, nos. 84–6. In 1224, a William de Tancarville, cleric, held the church of Trungy (cant. Balleroy, Calvados), Caen, AD Calvados H 683 (cartulary, abbey of Mondaye), fos. 8r–10r, nos. 20–2 (settlement of the dispute between the abbey of Gastines and Eleanor, countess of Salisbury, and William de Tancarville concerning this church and income from the parish). In 1238, a cleric William de Tancarville witnessed a charter of Ralph de Tancarville for St Georges-de-Boscherville, Rouen, AD Seine-Maritime 13 H 15 (charters of lords of Tancarville concerning the abbey of St Georges-de-Boscherville) = Rouen, BM 1227 (Y 52) (cartulary, abbey of St Georges-de-Boscherville), fo. 159r.

[328] L. Perrichet, *La grande chancellerie de France des origines à 1328* (Paris, 1912), pp. 510–1; Pico, 'Bishops', pp. 188–9, 194, 278.

may have reflected a more general conflict between the local nobility and the Capetian regents fuelled by the activities of Henry III at this time.[329] However, the evidence does not support such an interpretation. The regency may have supported John in order to provide a loyal cleric with a bishopric, but this support was not necessarily directed against William or the chapter of Bayeux. The Tancarville family had sided with Philip Augustus in 1204.[330] The number of votes John accumulated shows that many of the chapter were in favour of the royal candidate. After the result of the first ballot became known, both candidates came together to discuss a solution to the problem that would suit everyone.[331] Furthermore the apparently smooth election of Thomas de Fréauville also suggests that John de La Cour's candidacy was not a Capetian move designed to check the Norman aristocracy. Thomas was both an aristocrat and a man with strong links to England. As surmised above, this may have been a reason for the resistance to his election to the see of Rouen in 1230.[332] Unless the regency completely lost interest in the election at Bayeux, there was no reason why they should have accepted Thomas' election, if their aim had been to limit the freedom of the Norman barons.

Each of the four elections that took place at Bayeux between 1140 and 1232 illustrates a different political phase in Normandy. First, the period of the Angevin conquest from which powerful local families like the Beaumonts could profit to promote their men to episcopal sees; then the period of Angevin rule, in which the court controlled the appointments; after that came the period of the conquest of Normandy and Greater Anjou. The election at Bayeux in 1205–6 was the only occasion on which the Capetian king attempted to place a man closely connected with him in a Norman see, presumably because King Philip needed all the support he could get. Fourthly the period of Blanche of Castille's regency showed that the regent took an interest in the elections in Normandy without forcing her candidate upon the chapter. Once again, our impression must be that by 1230 or so, the regulation of disputed elections had become a matter for the papal courts.

---

[329] Within the diocese of Bayeux, Caen may have been a centre of anti-Capetian feeling. In 1227, Henry III received an intelligence report from a burgess of Caen, *Diplomatic Documents Preserved in the Public Record Office I. 1101–1272*, ed. P. Chaplais (London, 1964), no. 206.
[330] Powicke, *Loss*, p. 353. One year later, Philip Augustus confirmed the dowry that Chamberlain William de Tancarville had given his daughter Isabel on the occasion of her marriage with Adam son of Walter the Younger, chamberlain of the king, *Recueil des actes de Philippe Auguste*, ed. Delaborde et al., II, no. 888.
[331] *Registres de Grégoire IX*, ed. Auvray, I, no. 741.   [332] For Thomas de Fréauville, see supra, pp. 87–90.

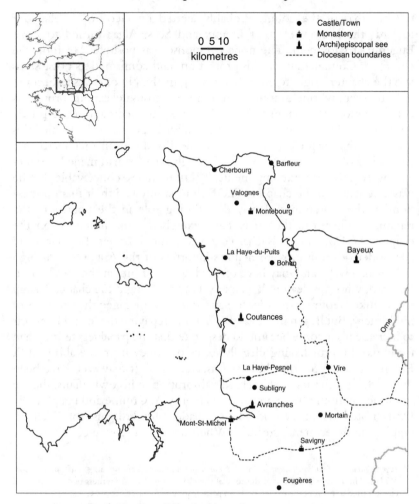

Map 7 The diocese of Coutances

COUTANCES

When Geoffrey Plantagenet set out to conquer Normandy, he encoun-
tered resistance from the bishop of Coutances, Algar. Not only did the
bishop contribute to Norman military defence,[333] he also gained an
important papal privilege to protect his church against outside force,

---

[333] 'Historia Gaufredi ducis Normannorum et comitis Andegavorum', in *Chroniques des comtes
d'Anjou et des seigneurs d'Amboise*, ed. L. Halphen and R. Poupardin (Collection des textes pour
servir à l'étude et à l'enseignement de l'histoire) (Paris, 1913), pp. 172–231, pp. 228–9.

notably that of the count. Probably alerted by Geoffrey's behaviour towards the bishops-elect of Lisieux and Sées, Algar turned to Pope Eugenius III for help. The pope's response was positive. He took the church of Coutances under his protection, and confirmed its possessions and the chapter's right to elect their bishop freely. No one was to become bishop except whom 'canonici communi consensus uel canonicorum pars consilii sanioris secundum Dei timorem et statuta sedis apostolice providerint eligendum'.[334] In 1151, five years after Eugenius III had issued this privilege, the chapter elected Richard de Bohun, dean of Bayeux and chancellor of Count Geoffrey.[335] Although Richard had made his career among Algar's erstwhile opponents, it is nonetheless conceivable that he was acceptable to the chapter. The Bohun family had their main possessions in the Cotentin and played a leading role in the politics of the region.[336] Therefore they may have exercised some influence on the chapter of Coutances. Richard's uncles, the brothers Engelger and Alexander de Bohun, were major supporters of the Angevin campaign in Normandy,[337] and may have opened doors for him at the ducal court. Richard, who was dean of Bayeux by 1137,[338] bought the chancellorship from Duke Geoffrey. In order to pay for it, he mortgaged the revenues of his deanery. But he ran into heavy difficulties repaying the loan. His efforts to increase his income became so desperate that the papal legate Imer had to rebuke him for having illegally exacted money from the abbot of St Etienne at Caen for the abbot's consecration.[339] It may well have been due to these activities, and Richard's absorption in his own affairs, that he lost touch with the Angevin court. As Henry A. Cronne and Ralph H.C. Davis noted, Geoffrey and Henry made very little use of Richard, employing other men instead.[340] When the see of Coutances fell vacant

---

[334] *Papsturkunden in Frankreich. Neue Folge. II. Normandie*, ed. Ramackers, no. 40 [= Jaffé, II, no. 8868; *WH* -]. This charter is perhaps at the root of the claim made by later writers that the cathedral chapter tried to prevent the *religiosi viri* from participating at Algar's election, C. Laplatte *Le diocèse de Coutances* (Coutances, 1942), pp. 27, 86 n. 166, refers to the eighteenth-century work of L. Rouault, *Abbrégé de la vie des evesques de Coutances* (Coutances, 1742), as the source of this story. His judgement on Rouault's work as a 'livre sans valeur critique' did not deter him from recounting this version of events as fact in his article on Coutances in the *Dictionnaire d'histoire et de géographie ecclésiastique* (28 vols., Paris, 1912–), XIII, cols. 969–90, col. 978. There is no evidence for a dispute over the electoral procedure during Algar's election.

[335] *Torigny*, p. 163; *Regesta regum Anglo-Normannorum 1066–1154*, ed. Davis et al., III, p. xxxiii.

[336] Boussard, *Henri II*, pp. 97, 238–9; Powicke, *Loss*, p. 333; 'Historia Gaufredi ducis Normannorum et comitis Andegavorum', in *Chroniques des comtes d'Anjou et des seigneurs d'Amboise*, ed. Halphen and Poupardin, p. 230.

[337] Chibnall, *Matilda*, p. 71.   [338] Spear, 'Power, Patronage and Personality', p. 214.

[339] *Antiquus cartularius*, ed. Bourrienne, I, no. 185; *GC*, XI, instrumenta, col. 80, no. 11.

[340] *Regesta regum Anglo-Normannorum 1066–1154*, ed. Davis et al., III, pp. xxxiii–xxiv. Geoffrey employed his Angevin chancellor Thomas de Loches. Henry employed Empress Matilda's chancellor William fitz Gilbert. Cronne's and Davis' argument is supported by the fact that

in 1151, the election of Richard suited all parties. The Bohun family extended their power in the Cotentin; Richard de Bohun acquired a prestigious position with sufficient income to pay his debts; and the Angevins may have ensured his support for the future by supporting his candidacy at Coutances, while taking back the chancellorship to bestow on another more suitable candidate.

Richard administered the diocese of Coutances for thirty-seven years during which he acted as patron for Bohun family members. He created a new prebend in the chapter,[341] provided his *nepos* Nicholas with a canonry, and made another kinsman, Savaric fitz Gelduin, archdeacon.[342] Richard, archdeacon of Coutances and often in the entourage of the Bohun bishops of Salisbury, was probably also a member of Bishop Richard's family.[343] Yet, the Bohuns could not place one of their own family members in the see after Richard's death in 1178.[344] Instead, after a vacancy of approximately five years, the chapter elected the dean of Bayeux, William de Tournebu. Although the election was confirmed by Archbishop Rotrou in 1183,[345] Rotrou's death in the same year prevented William's consecration. In 1184, in order to solve this deadlock, Lucius III authorised the dean of Rouen cathedral, Robert du Neubourg, to consecrate William.[346] Whether the length of this vacancy was due to an electoral dispute within the chapter, to a disagreement between chapter and king, or purely to royal financial needs, remains unclear. William de Tournebu's election appears to have been due to his own reputation as an experienced churchman and to his connections with the king. Belonging to a family that originally came from the area of Louviers,[347] he had profited from the patronage of a relative and member of a neighbouring family, Philip de Harcourt, bishop of Bayeux. During Philip's time in office William had received a benefice at Bayeux and became dean of the

---

Richard very rarely witnessed ducal or royal charters during his long episcopate. When he did so, they were usually related to his own diocese, *Recueil des actes de Henri II*, ed. Delisle and Berger, I, nos. 35*, 35 (a spurious charter whose witness list is supplied by 'Ad opera Petri Blesensis appendix', in *PL*, CCVII, cols. 1157–82, col. 1166, no. 16), 196–7, 276, 309, 406, 445, II, nos. 515, 552; Paris, BNF Lat. 10086 (cartulary, abbey of Troarn), fo. 13v.

[341] *Le cartulaire du chapitre cathédral de Coutances. Etude et édition critique*, ed. J. Fontanel (St Lô, 2003), no. 75.

[342] Spear, 'Power, Patronage and Personality', p. 214.

[343] *English Episcopal Acta X. Bath and Wells 1061–1205*, ed. F.M. Ramsey (Oxford, 1995), pp. xlix, 220; nos. 73, 92, 98, 152, 207, 237.

[344] 'Lucii III papae epistolae et privilegia', in *PL*, CCI, cols. 1248–9, no. 136 [= Jaffé, II, no. 15023; *WH*-]. Lucius III's letter is dated on 24 April 1184. The pope stated that the see of Coutances had been vacant for more than six years. Therefore 1178 as the date of Richard's death, *Torigny*, p. 280, must be preferred to 1180 given by *Gesta regis*, I, p. 269.

[345] *Papsturkunden in Frankreich. Neue Folge. II. Normandie*, ed. Ramackers, no. 235 [= Jaffé -; *WH*-].

[346] 'Lucii III papae epistolae et privilegia', in *PL*, CCI, cols. 1248–9, no. 136 [= Jaffé, II, no. 15023; *WH*-].

[347] Powicke, *Loss*, p. 355.

chapter.[348] He apparently enjoyed high esteem among ecclesiastics and acted several times as papal judge delegate.[349] But he also had contacts with Henry II. Although not an active courtier himself, his patrons, Philip and Henry of Bayeux, had excellent connections with the royal court.[350] A kinsman of his, Simon de Tournebu, nephew and seneschal of Bishop Philip de Harcourt, was involved in the ducal administration of Normandy and Thomas de Tournebu, who succeeded his brother Simon in his estates around 1180, had been a knight in Henry II's entourage at the time of Becket's murder.[351]

As in William's case, the precise circumstances of the election of his successor Vivian de L'Etang are unknown, but this time the motives for his nomination can be deduced. It was King John who provided Vivian with the bishopric of Coutances in late 1201.[352] Vivian and his brother, William de L'Etang, were among King Richard's most trusted *familiares*.[353] Richard had provided Vivian with benefices in England and France alike. In England he received the archdeaconry of Derby[354] and in France he held a canonry at St Martin of Tours.[355] He continued his royal service under King John[356] and his promotion to Coutances was certainly intended to strengthen John's position in Normandy. John may well have remembered that, a couple of years earlier, the bishop of

---

[348] *Antiquus cartularius*, ed. Bourrienne, I, no. 156. He became dean after Richard de Bohun's election to the see of Coutances in 1151, cf. ibid., no. 149.

[349] Müller, *Delegationsgerichtsbarkeit*, II, nos. 23, 32, 64; chronologische Liste, nos. 104 [= Jaffé, II, no. 14371; *WH* -], 120.

[350] See supra, pp. 137–8; Peltzer, 'Henry II and the Norman Bishops', 1215–16, 1218–19.

[351] *Antiquus cartularius*, ed. Bourrienne, no. 71; *Magni rotuli*, ed. Stapleton, I, pp. 49, 81, 93; Barlow, *Thomas Becket*, p. 229. For an early account of the family's history, see C. Fierville, 'Histoire généalogique de la maison et la baronnie de Tournebu, d'après les archives inédites de cette famille', *Mémoires de la société des antiquaires de Normandie 3rd ser.*, 6 (1869), 170–367.

[352] He had been elected shortly before 28 December 1201, *Rot. pat.*, I, p. 4a. He is traceable as bishop since 1202, Spear, *The Personnel*, p. 93. It should be noted, however, that according to Léopold Delisle's calendar of the cartularies of the chapter of Coutances Bishop William Tournebu made a donation to the chapter in 1202, Paris, N. A. Lat. 1018 (cartularies, chapter of Coutances), fo. 78r. This problem remains unresolved and thus whether it is related to King John's activities in support of Vivian.

[353] For William, see *Itinerary*, ed. Landon, passim; 'Itinerarium peregrinorum et gesta regis Ricardi', in *Chronicles and Memorials of the Reign of Richard I*, ed. W. Stubbs (Rolls Series XXXVIII, I–II) (2 vols., London, 1864–5), I, pp. 283, 415.

[354] *English Episcopal Acta XIV. Coventry and Lichfield 1072–1159*, ed. Franklin, p. lvi.

[355] *Rot. pat.*, I, p. 4a.

[356] *The Memoranda Roll for the Michaelmas Term of the First Year of the Reign of King John (1199–1200)*, ed. Richardson, p. 92. His brother William continued his service, too, *Rot. pat.*, pp. 12b, 13a, 17a; *Rotuli de oblatis et finibus in turri Londinensi asservati tempore regis Johannis*, ed. T. D. Hardy (London, 1835), p. 73; *Diceto*, II, p. 170. For William's numerous appearances as witness in the early years of John's reign, see *The Cartae antiquae Rolls 1–10*, ed. L. Landon (Pipe Roll Society N.S. XVII) (London, 1939), nos. 44, 57, 123; *Rot. chart.*, p. 12a, 24a, 30b, 33a–b, 34a–b, 59a, 110b, 138a. For a grant of John to William, see *Rot. chart.*, p. 16b.

Coutances had been heavily fined by King Richard, because his men had left the king's army without permission.[357] Although this particular obligation had been modified, and John received money instead of men from the bishop of Coutances,[358] he must have been keen on having full support from the bishop. In a letter to King John, Pope Innocent III complained about the king's intrusion into the electoral process at Coutances.[359] There is hardly any doubt that John used the same method as at Angers, Lisieux, or Sées. That is, he demanded that the chapter elect the man he had chosen. He obviously met with some resistance, but whether the majority of the chapter of Coutances opposed his conduct remains unknown.

Vivian died only four years after the Capetian conquest, and in 1208 the chapter elected Master Hugh Nereth, who was to occupy the see until 1238.[360] Hugh and his brother, Ralph, had enjoyed distinguished ecclesiastical careers. In 1184, both appeared as canons of the chapter of Dol.[361] Probably through Roland, bishop-elect of Dol, who spent much of his episcopate at the papal court,[362] Ralph came into contact with the Roman curia. Roland and Ralph apparently enjoyed high esteem there, for in February 1185 Lucius III made both of them cardinals. Roland became cardinal-deacon of S. Maria in Portico, while Ralph became cardinal-deacon of S. Giorgio in Velabro. Later, in 1188, Clement III made Ralph cardinal-priest of S. Prassede. Ralph died before August 1190, perhaps in 1189.[363]

---

[357] *Magni rotuli*, ed. Stapleton, II, p. 477.   [358] Ibid., p. 522.

[359] *Register Innocenz' III.*, V, no. 159 (160) [= Potthast, I, no. 1831].

[360] GC, XI, col. 878, states that Hugh belonged to the Morville family. Toustain de Billy also claims that Hugh was a member of this family, but his genealogy of the Morville family is not trustworthy, R. Toustain de Billy, *Histoire ecclésiastique du diocèse de Coutances* (2 vols., Rouen, 1874–80), pp. 310–11. Hugh's parents were Herbert and Emmelina, *Le cartulaire du chapitre cathédral de Coutances*, ed. Fontanel, no. 327. In 1204, appears a Herbert de Morville, who lost his lands in Portbury, Somerset, because he had chosen the French allegiance. The same Herbert owed a sixth of a knight's fee in Morville (cant. Bricquebec, Manche) between 1212 and 1220, L.C. Lloyd, *The Origins of Some Anglo-Norman Families* (The Publications of the Harleian Society CIII) (Leeds, 1951), p. 70. A Herbert de Moreville is remembered in the obituary of the abbey of Montebourg on 1 February, Paris, BNF Lat. 12885 (obituary, abbey of Montebourg), fo. 26r. But whether Hugh's father and this Herbert were identical or at least related remains an open question.

[361] Paris, BNF Lat. 5430A (charters concerning the abbey of Mont-Saint-Michel), pp. 55, 192 (both witness a charter of Bishop Roland for Mont-Saint-Michel). Hugh was active outside the diocese of Avranches. Between 1184 and 1189 Hugh witnessed, together with such prominent men as Walter, archbishop of Rouen, and William fitz Ralph, seneschal of Normandy, a charter of Henry, bishop of Bayeux, notifying an agreement between Bishop Henry and the abbey of Ste Trinité, Caen, H. Dupuy, 'Recueil des actes des évêques de Bayeux antérieures à 1205' (Ecole de Chartes, Paris, *thèse*, 2 vols., 1970), I, no. 92.

[362] See infra, pp. 178–9.

[363] Torigny, p. 310. Torigny calls Ralph *Nigellus* a dearest friend, *magnae honestatis et litteraturae et religionis virum*. He dated Lucius' creation of cardinals to 1184. However, the year must be 1185. In a charter dating from 1184 Roland and Ralph appear as bishop and canon, respectively, see supra,

Hugh's frequent commissions as papal judge delegate indicate that he was of high reputation in Normandy and the papal curia alike.[364] Archdeacon of Coutances at least since the tenure of William de Tournebu's episcopate,[365] he was familiar with the chapter and the politics of the diocese. It seems therefore that his election was the chapter's choice, influenced perhaps by Hugh's excellent connections with the papal court.

In his first year as bishop of Coutances, Hugh Nereth made the abbot of St Taurin, Evreux, a canon of the chapter of Coutances. The abbot, however, was only allowed to participate in episcopal elections if the chapter wished him to do so.[366] Over sixty years after Bishop Algar had won the papal letter granting the chapter the right to elect their bishop, the canons were still carefully protecting their electoral privileges. Yet the elections at Coutances showed that the choice of the canons was not entirely dependent on their own desires. At least before the conquest, they had had to take the ruler's interests into account.

AVRANCHES

Avranches was by far the smallest of the seven Norman dioceses. Within it, the possessions of the bishop were limited to the western parts, where the monastery of Mont-Saint-Michel also enjoyed substantial property. The eastern parts of the diocese were dominated by the collegiate church

---

n. 361. In a letter dating from 18 August 1184, Lucius III named Roland as bishop-elect of Dol, 'Lucii III papae epistolae et privilegia', in *PL*, CCI, cols. 1317–18, no. 188 [= Jaffé, II, no. 15234; *WH* -] (where the letter is dated to 18 August 1184/5). Roland and Ralph can be traced as cardinal-deacons only from April 1185, Jaffé, II, pp. 431–2. For evidence showing Hugh referring to his brother as cardinal, see Paris, BNF N. A. Lat. 1018 (cartularies, chapter of Coutances), fo. 134r, 'Cartulaire A', no. 95 (Bishop Hugh confirms and grants revenues to the chapter of Coutances); *Le cartulaire du chapitre cathédral de Coutances*, ed. Fontanel, no. 327. For Ralph's activities as cardinal, see W. Maleczek, 'Das Pieve Casorate im Streit mit der Zisterze Morimondo. Ein Beitrag zur päpstlichen delegierten Gerichtsbarkeit unter Innocenz III.', *Mitteilungen des Instituts für österreichische Geschichtsforschung*, 105 (1997), 361–92; W. Maleczek, 'Die Siegel der Kardinäle. Von den Anfängen bis zum Beginn des 13. Jahrhunderts', ibid., 112 (2004), 177–203, 197. For his death, see Jaffé, II, p. 536. I am indebted to Prof. Maleczek for his help on Ralph's career at the papal court.

[364] Prior to his election he acted as papal judge delegate in the following cases, Müller, *Delegationsgerichtsbarkeit*, II, nos. 126 [= Potthast, I, no. 1347], 135–7, 156; chronologische Liste, nos. 304–5. For the criteria according to which papal judges delegate were chosen in Normandy in the twelfth and early thirteenth centuries, see ibid., I, pp. 191–217.

[365] Paris, BNF Lat. 10087 (cartulary, abbey of Montebourg), p. 41, no. 71 (Archdeacon Hugh witnesses a charter of Bishop William).

[366] The abbot's admission as canon was part of a property exchange between the abbey of St Taurin and the church of Coutances, Evreux, AD Eure H 0793 (cartulary, abbey of St Taurin), fo. 63r–v, no. 34; Paris, BNF N. A. Lat. 1018 (cartularies, chapter of Coutances), fo. 85r, 'Cartulaire C', no. 707.

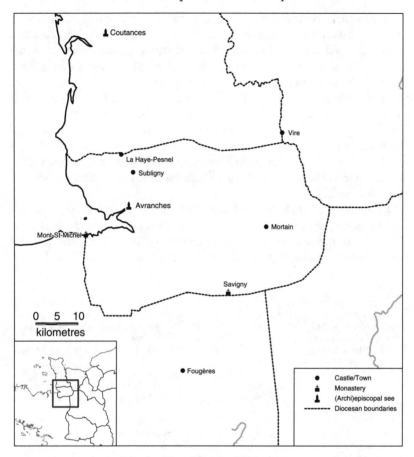

Map 8 The diocese of Avranches

of Mortain.[367] The political value of Avranches was relatively small compared with that of the other Norman dioceses. Its financial resources were limited and in strategic terms Mont–Saint–Michel was more important

---

[367] M. Lebrun, 'Le temporel des évêques d'Avranches du XIe au XIIIe siècles', *Revue de l'Avranchin et du pays de Granville*, 42 (1965), 58–80, 58, 76–80; Neveux, 'Les diocèses normands aux XIe et XIIe siècles', pp. 15–17; J. Dubois, 'Les dépendances de l'abbaye du Mont Saint-Michel et la vie monastique dans les prieurés', in *Millénaire monastique du Mont Saint-Michel. I. Histoire et vie monastique* (Paris, 1966), pp. 619–76, pp. 627–32 and map between pp. 648 and 649. For the geography and history of the diocese of Avranches, see A.-E. Pigeon, *Le diocèse d'Avranches. Sa topographie, ses origines, ses évêques, sa cathédrale, ses églises, ses comtes et ses châteaux*, 2nd edn (2 vols., Marseilles, 1981; reprint of Coutances, 1890).

at the Norman–Breton border than the bishop.[368] The dukes, therefore, who controlled the *regalia* at Avranches as in all the other Norman dioceses,[369] did not need to preoccupy themselves too much with the outcome of an election, so long as their prerogatives were maintained. The first election with which we are concerned here took place after the death of Bishop Richard de Beaufour in 1142,[370] and thus at a moment when King Stephen had effectively lost control over Normandy and Geoffrey Plantagenet had not yet firmly established his rule. This political situation, and the fact that the new bishop, Richard de Subligny, had not only been dean of the cathedral chapter, but was also brother of the locally influential lord Hasculf de Subligny,[371] point towards an election decided by local forces.[372]

During Richard de Subligny's episcopate, Geoffrey Plantagenet and his son, Henry, restored ducal authority and tried to gain control over ecclesiastical appointments in the duchy. That the Avranchin was not spared from their efforts became clear at the latest in 1152, when Henry,

---

[368] For its finances, see infra, n. 387; for Mont-Saint-Michel, see Dubois, 'Les dépendences de l'abbaye du Mont Saint-Michel', pp. 624–53; J.-F. Lemarignier, *Recherches sur l'hommage en marche et frontières féodales* (Travaux et mémoires de l'université de Lille; nouvelle série: droit et lettres xxiv) (Lille, 1945), pp. 67–9.

[369] Delisle, *Introduction*, pp. 345–7; C. Haskins, *Norman Institutions* (Harvard Historical Studies xxiv) (Cambridge, Mass., 1918), pp. 337–9.

[370] GC, xi, col. 478, quoting a Norman chronicle, placed Richard's death in 1142. If this chronicle is to be identified with Robert de Torigny's work, the year of Richard's death could also have been 1143, since Robert's chronology of these years is muddled, Torigny, p. 145; Spear, *The Personnel*, p. 4, argues for 1143.

[371] Flers, BM 22 (formerly F 9) (cartulary, abbey of Savigny), fos. 11r–15r, no. 7 (Dean Richard witnesses a charter of his brother Hasculf); for the barony of Subligny, see Pigeon, *Avranches*, II, pp. 341–3; J.A. Everard, *Brittany and the Angevins. Province and Empire 1158–1203* (Cambridge Studies in Medieval Life and Thought) (Cambridge, 2000), pp. 42, 52, 74, 83–5.

[372] The precise chronology of the events of the years 1142–3 is unknown. Robert de Torigny places the conquest of the Avranchin and the Cotentin once in 1142 and once in 1143. Because the annals of St Aubin, Angers, places the conquest in 1143, preference might be given to the latter date, Torigny, pp. 143–5; 'Annales Sancti Albini Andegavensis', in *Recueil d'annales angevines et vendômoises*, ed. L. Halphen (Paris, 1903), pp. 1–49, p. 10. According to the *Historia Gaufredi* Geoffrey Plantagenet was welcomed in Avranches by the bishop and the citizens: 'Cujus adventum tam cives quam pontifex audientes, non ut hostes hostibus, sed ut domino quidem suo laica manus, ut tutori, avo et patrono ecclesiae clerus cum presule obviam processerunt', 'Historia Gaufredi ducis Normannorum et comitis Andegavorum', in *Chroniques des comtes d'Anjou et des seigneurs d'Amboise*, ed. Halphen and Poupardin, p. 228. If this bishop was still Richard de Beaufour, then Geoffrey was already in control of Avranches by the time of Richard de Subligny's election. Since Geoffrey was in battle for Normandy virtually all the time up to 1144, he could hardly afford to upset any of the Norman barons. Thus he may have accepted Richard de Subligny's election in order to strengthen the relationship with the Subligny family. However, if the bishop receiving Geoffrey was already Richard de Subligny, his election may have been a purely local affair. In any case, the Subligny family stayed in contact with the Angevins, since a nephew of Richard, John de Subligny, became a *curialis* of Henry II, cf. Everard, *Brittany and the Angevins*, pp. 211–12.

unhappy about the procedure of the abbatial election at Mont-Saint-Michel, exercised so much pressure on the monks and the bishop that Pope Eugenius III and his successor Anastasius IV got involved, the latter even threatening Henry with excommunication and interdict. During the affair, Eugenius asked the bishop of Avranches to appear in the papal court. Richard died on this trip and, when the news of the bishop's death reached Avranches, the chapter knew what it would mean electing against the wishes of Duke Henry and his entourage.[373] The ducal court therefore decided the outcome of the election, and Herbert, chaplain of Matilda and Henry, became the new bishop of Avranches.[374] The promotion of Herbert, who had apparently played a negligible role in Angevin politics, is to be understood rather as an award by the Empress Matilda to a loyal cleric than as a political manoeuvre.

Herbert died in 1160/1 and again the see of Avranches received a ducal appointee. But this time the election of the theologian Master Achard, abbot of St Victor, Paris, was much more a consolation than an award for the elect.[375] Four years earlier, Achard had been elected bishop of Sées, but Henry II had refused to accept him, wanting a man he knew well in the important see of Sées. Despite papal confirmation Achard was forced

---

[373] *Epistolae pontificum*, ed. Loewenfeld, nos. 206, 210–11, 214–16 [= Jaffé, II, nos. 9595, 9704–5, 9737–9; *WH* -]; cf. K.S.B. Keats-Rohan, 'Bibliothèque municipale d'Avranches, 210: Cartulary of Mont-Saint-Michel', in C. Harper-Bill (ed.), *Anglo-Norman Studies. XXI. Proceedings of the Battle Conference 1998* (Woodbridge, 1999), pp. 95–112, p. 102.

[374] *Torigny*, p. 176. Herbert witnessed a number of Matilda's and Henry II's charters, *Recueil des actes de Henri II*, ed. Delisle and Berger, I, nos. 20*, 26, 78–80, 134–5; *Acta of Henry II and Richard I: Handlist of Documents Surviving in the Original in Repositories in the United Kingdom*, ed. J.C. Holt and R. Mortimer (List and Index Society/Special Series XXI) (Richmond, 1986), nos. 87, 186, 188, 217, 300; *The Cartae antiquae Rolls 11–20*, ed. Davies, no. 389; *Regesta regum Anglo–Normannorum 1066–1154*, ed. Davis et al., III, nos. 20, 372, 748, 826, 836, 839; *A Digest of the Charters Preserved in the Cartulary of the Priory of Dunstable*, ed. G.H. Fowler (Publications of the Bedfordshire Historical Record Society X) (Aspley Guise, 1926), p. 343; *Calendar of the Charter Rolls, 1226–1516* (6 vols., London, 1903–27), V, pp. 292, 328, 432, 454; *The Registrum antiquissimum of the Cathedral Church of Lincoln*, ed. C.W. Foster and K. Major (Publications of the Lincoln Record Society XXVII–XXIX, XXXII, XXXIV, XLI, XLII, XLIV, LI, LXI, LXVII, LXVIII) (12 vols., Hereford, 1931–73), I, pp. 94–6, no. 149; pp. 111–12, no. 177; London, The National Archives C 115/83/6689 (register of John Garlond), fos. 142v (117v), 210v–211r (107r–108v). No evidence supports Lecanu's claim that Herbert was a son of Henry I with a Lady Corbet of St Lô, A.-F. Lecanu, *Histoire du diocèse de Coutances et d'Avranches depuis le temps les plus reculés jusqu'à nos jours, suivie des actes des saints et d'un tableau historique des paroisses du diocèse* (2 vols., Coutances 1877–8), I, p. 249. On the identity of Henry I's illegitimate daughters, see K. Thompson, 'Affairs of State: The Illegitimate Children of Henry I', *Journal of Medieval History*, 29 (2003), 129–51.

[375] *Torigny*, pp. 207, 210; Spear, *The Personnel*, p. 5. On Achard and St Victor, see M. Lelégard, 'Le Bienheureux Achard, abbé de Saint-Victor de Paris, 1155–1161, évêque d'Avranches, 1161–1171', *Cahiers Léopold Délisle*, 35/6 (1986–7), 167–73; J. Châtillon, 'Thomas Becket et les Victorins', in R. Foreville (ed.), *Thomas Becket. Actes du Colloque international de Sédières 19–24 août 1973* (Paris, 1975), pp. 89–101; *The Later Letters of Peter of Blois*, ed. E. Revell (Auctores Britannici medii aevi XIII) (Oxford, 1993), no. 16.

to leave the see, and Henry II's almoner Froger was installed instead.[376] When the next Norman vacancy happened to be at the politically less important see of Avranches, Henry and probably the Empress Matilda, who enjoyed a good relationship with St Victor, thought it an appropriate recompense for Achard.[377]

In 1170, the archdeacon of Coutances, Master Richard L'Evêque, succeeded Achard in the see of Avranches.[378] Master Richard, who his one-time pupil John of Salisbury described as a man of great knowledge and modesty,[379] had local roots. The L'Evêque family was based in the Avranchin and Cotentin. One of its members, Geoffrey L'Evêque, abbot of Mont-Saint-Michel in 1149–50, had fought hard to defend the abbey's rights, in particular that of holding free abbatial elections.[380] The circumstances of Richard's election are unknown. But his reputation, his local connections, strengthened by his office in the neighbouring diocese, the timing of his election shortly after Becket's murder yet before the compromise of Avranches, and the fact that he seems not to have had close contacts with the royal court before his election, suggest that he was a choice of the chapter of Avranches.

After Richard's death in late 1181/early 1182, the see lay vacant until late 1183/early 1184, when the chapter of Avranches elected William Burel, dean of the royal chapel of St Pierre-de-la-Cour in Le Mans.[381] William, who may have been canon at the cathedral of Le Mans before his

---

[376] Supra, pp. 120–2.

[377] *Arnulf*, ed. Barlow, p. xviii; Chibnall, *Matilda*, p. 180. Matilda placed canons from St Victor in the abbey of Ste Marie-du-Voeu at Cherbourg. In the year of his election Achard, together with Robert de Torigny and many others, became godfather of Henry II's daughter Eleanor, *Torigny*, p. 211. King Louis VII himself tacitly referred to the good relationship between Henry II and the abbot. In a letter to the brothers of St Victor he expressed his anxiety lest Achard, the recently elected bishop of Avranches, do any business affecting the abbey's property. He reminded the brothers that St Victor is a Capetian foundation and admonished them to prevent Achard from involving it in any negotiations. They should also strive to prevent him taking part in the election of his own successor. If the brothers, not the abbot, were the ones to be roused into action, Louis VII must have regarded the abbot as lost to his rival, 'Epistolarum regis Ludovici VII et variorum ad eum volumen', in *RHF*, XVI, p. 27, no. 90; *Etudes sur les actes de Louis VII*, ed. A. Luchaire (Paris, 1885), no. 445.

[378] *Torigny*, p. 247. According to *GC*, XI, col. 481, Achard died on 29 March 1171. If the day and month are taken from an obituary, which is likely, the year must be 1170, since Bishop Richard issued a charter on 1 April 1171, *Cartulaire de la Manche*, ed. N. Dubosc (St Lô, 1878), 'Cartulaire de l'abbaye de Mont-Morel', no. 9.

[379] C. Jacquemard, 'Maître Richard l'Evêque, archidiacre de Coutances', in F. Neveux and C. Bougy (eds.), *Mélanges Pierre Bouet. Recueil d'études en hommages à Pierre Bouet* (Cahier des Annales de Normandie XXXII) (Caen, 2002), pp. 107–21, pp. 107–8.

[380] Keats-Rohan, 'Cartulary of Mont-Saint-Michel', p. 101.

[381] At Michaelmas 1183, the revenues of the Avranches manor of Swanwick were accounted for 'de ii. annis', *PR* 29, H.II, p. 146; the elect William Burel received the manor around Easter 1184, *PR* 30, H.II, p. 84. *Torigny*, p. 308, records his election in late 1183. Perhaps William's election was

promotion to the deanery in 1167, probably received this position through the influence of his father, Durand Burel, who served Henry II as cup-bearer.[382] Durand held possessions in the diocese of Le Mans[383] and also had connections with the Avranchin.[384] Given the fact that William Burel was never a courtier, it seems likely that his election was brought about by the chapter and approved by the king, rather than ordered by Henry II.

William died in 1194.[385] After his death the see lay vacant until 1196, when, according to Roger of Howden, King Richard gave William de Chemillé the episcopate of Avranches.[386] The vacancy may partially be explained by King Richard's urgent need for money in this period; his seneschal William fitz Ralph may have thought it more useful to collect at least a few rather than no revenues from Avranches at a time of great financial strains on Richard's coffers.[387] The new bishop was one of Richard's most trusted clerics, who had belonged to his household before Henry II's death.[388] Shortly after his coronation Richard appointed

---

determined at Henry II's Christmas court, which, in 1183, was held at Le Mans, ibid., p. 310. This corrects the chronology of Richard's death and William's election proposed by Peltzer, 'Henry II and the Norman Bishops', 1207.

[382] *PR* 23, H.II, p. 163; *Nécrologe-obituaire de la cathédrale du Mans*, ed. Busson and Ledru, pp. 268–9; for his parents Durand and Stephana, see S. Menjot d'Elbenne and L.-J. Denis, *Le chapitre royal de l'église collégiale de Saint-Pierre-de-la-Cour, Sainte-Chapelle du Mans* (Archives historiques du Maine x) (Le Mans, 1910), pp. cxliv, cxlvi. A canon of Le Mans named William Burel can be traced until 1167, *Cartulaire de l'évêché du Mans (936–1790)*, ed. B. de Broussillon (Archives historiques du Maine I) (Le Mans, 1900), no. 57; *Liber albus*, ed. Lottin, nos. 492, 534. But he is not necessarily identical with the dean of St Pierre-de-la-Cour, since the obituary of Le Mans records also an Archpriest William Burel, canon of Le Mans, *Nécrologe-obituaire de la cathédrale du Mans*, ed. Busson and Ledru, pp. 123–4. The biographical note on William Burel in Menjot d'Elbenne and Denis, *Le chapitre royal de l'église collégiale de Saint-Pierre-de-la-Cour*, pp. clxxvii–clxxx, is not trustworthy.

[383] *Papsturkunden in Frankreich. Neue Folge. V. Touraine, Anjou, Maine und Bretagne*, J. Ramackers, no. 164 [= Jaffé, II, no. 13057; *WH* –].

[384] He held land of Mont-Saint-Michel, *Cartulaire du prieuré de Saint-Hippolyte de Vivoin et de ses annexes*, ed. L.-J. Denis (Paris, 1894), pp. 137–8, no. 7.

[385] The chronicle of Savigny records his death between the entry for 1191 and the entry for 1194, 'Ex chronico Savigniacensis monasterii', in RHF, XVIII, pp. 350–2, p. 351. He issued a charter in 1194, Avranches, BM 210 (cartulary, abbey of Mont-Saint-Michel), fo. 120r–v; cf. *GC*, IX, col. 482.

[386] *Howden*, IV, p. 12.

[387] J. Gillingham, *Richard I* (London, 1978), pp. 269–300; N. Barratt, 'The English Revenues of Richard I', *EHR*, 116 (2001), 635–56; Moss, 'The Defence of Normandy', pp. 145–61. For William fitz Ralph as seneschal in Normandy, see Powicke, *Loss*, p. 52. At Michaelmas 1198, Richard Silvain rendered account at the Norman exchequer for '62 lib. 15 sol. de exitu episcopatu de Abroic. dum fuit in manu regis praeter statuta et neccesarias expensas et correium archiepiscopi Roth.', *Magni rotuli*, ed. Stapleton, II, p. 361. How many months the lands were in the king's hand cannot be established.

[388] He is found among the witnesses of Richard's ducal charters, L. Rédet, 'Memoires sur les halles et les foires de Poitiers', *Mémoires de la société des antiquaires de l'ouest*, 12 (1847 for 1845), 61–97, 89–90, pièces justificatives, no. 2; P. de Fleury, 'L'aumônerie de Saint-Gilles de Surgères', *Archives historiques de la Saintonge et de l'Aunis*, 6 (1879), 9–22, 11, no. 3; *The Early Charters of the Augustinian Canons of Waltham Abbey, Essex, 1062–1230*, ed. R. Ransford (Woodbridge, 1989), no. 29.

William to the archdeaconry of Richmond, Yorkshire.[389] In the follow-ing years, William was very active as justice in the royal court[390] and as an administrator. In the financial year 1195–6, for example, he acted as royal custodian of the manor of Tottenham and of the abbey St Mary, York.[391] The promotion of such a prominent royal cleric to Avranches should be seen in the context of Richard's activities towards Brittany in 1195–6. Richard felt, that, under the rule of Duchess Constance, Brittany was slipping out of Angevin control. Three years after the death of Richard's brother, Duke Geoffrey, in 1186, his widow, Constance, had married Ranulf, earl of Chester. Yet, Ranulf never exercised his right as duke *jure uxoris*. In 1195 Richard tried to change this, but his efforts came to nothing. Then, in spring 1196, Richard summoned Constance to his court in Normandy, probably to demand custody of her son and heir, Arthur, and thus to gain greater control over the duchy. As soon as Constance had entered the duchy, she was taken prisoner by her husband Ranulf. Richard tried to take advantage of the situation, but even two military campaigns into the duchy could not force the Breton magnates to hand over Arthur. In the event the Bretons managed to get Arthur into the custody of Philip Augustus.[392] Thus, in 1196, the Angevin–Breton relations were extremely tense and William's election was probably intended to strengthen Richard's position in the region.

However, William was not to stay for long at Avranches. In late 1197 or early 1198, after his confirmation but still before his consecration, he was chosen by King Richard to succeed Ralph de Beaumont as bishop of Angers.[393] But this translation caused trouble. It became a precedent-setting case; the recently elected Innocent III demonstrated that only the pope could authorise episcopal translations. This not only affected the

---

[389] Howden, III, p. 16; Greenway, *John Le Neve: Fasti ecclesiae Anglicanae, 1066–1300. York*, p. 48.

[390] *Feet of Fines of the Reign of Henry II and of the First Seven Years of the Reign of Richard I, A.D. 1182 to A.D. 1196* (Pipe Roll Society XVII) (London, 1894), nos. 21, 23, 36, 42–3, 46, 70–4, 76–9, 82–4, 88, 90, 95–6, 109.

[391] William had already been elected to the see of Avranches, when, on his behalf, his clerk Master Robert rendered account for the manor and the abbey at the exchequer at Michaelmas 1196, *The Chancellor's Roll for the Eighth Year of the Reign of King Richard the First, Michaelmas 1196*, ed. D.M. Stenton (Pipe Roll Society N.S. VII) (London, 1930), pp. 175, 208; Howden, III, p. 264, enumerates other activities. Richard I made Robert de Longchamps abbot of St Mary, York, in January 1197, *Itinerary*, ed. Landon, p. 116.

[392] For these events, see Everard, *Brittany and the Angevins*, pp. 159–65.

[393] For a discussion of possible reasons for his translation to Angers, see infra, pp. 202–3. Ralph de Beaumont, bishop of Angers, died in 1197, 'Annales Sancti Albini', in *Recueil d'annales*, ed. Halphen, p. 18. William de Chemillé can be traced as elect of Avranches at Richard's court until 16 October 1197, *Itinerary*, ed. Landon, p. 123. Howden, IV, p. 37, names William as bishop-elect of Angers, when numbering Richard I's envoys present at Otto IV's election at Cologne on 9 June 1198, B.U. Hucker, *Kaiser Otto IV*. (MGH, Schriften XXXIV) (Hanover, 1990), pp. 22–35.

election of William's successor at Avranches, but also triggered an intensive examination of canon law, in particular at Rouen. William's translation therefore provides a good opportunity to examine the introduction of a new canonical principle.

One of Innocent's chief aims in the first years of his pontificate was to establish papal authority over episcopal translations. When he heard that Walter, archbishop of Rouen, and Bartholomew, archbishop of Tours, had performed William's translation without papal authorisation, he ordered an enquiry into the case. On 27 April 1198, he instructed the archbishop of Bourges to discover whether the facts were as he had heard them and, if so, to suspend Walter and Bartholomew from their right to confirm and consecrate bishops and also to suspend William from taking up his duties as bishop of Angers.[394] After his investigation, the archbishop of Bourges suspended the three prelates. The archbishops of Rouen and Tours acted instantly. They sent messengers to the papal court excusing themselves and pleading that they had had no evil intention (*malignitas*) in translating William. They claimed that there was urgent necessity and obvious utility for the step and that they had not been aware that this was a papal prerogative.[395]

Causa 7 *quaestio* 1 of Gratian's *Decretum* provided the various texts which unambiguously stated that if there was necessity and utility bishops could be translated, but which also left much room for interpretation as to who was to determine this necessity and utility. A copy of parts of Gratian's *Decretum* in Paris, BNF Lat. 3922A suggests that Archbishop Walter had at his disposal further material supporting his defence. In the first years of the thirteenth century, thus immediately after William's translation, a scribe at Rouen copied some of the texts from C. 7 q. 1 dealing with episcopal translations.[396] C. 7 q. 1 c. 35 and c. 36 quote short passages from a letter of Pope Pelagius II to Archbishop Benignus stating that, for reasons of necessity and utility, bishops could be translated, but saying nothing about the role of the pope. The scribe copied a further passage of this letter (not taken from the *Decretum*) on the bottom margins of the manuscript, to be read after C. 7 q. 1 c. 36. In this passage, Pope Pelagius II explicitly informs Benignus that an archbishop could translate bishops for the reasons named above.[397] Clearly the Rouen scribe was copying a *Decretum* that at this particular place had been enlarged by an expert in

---

[394] *Register Innocenz' III.*, I, no. 117 [= Potthast, I, no. 108].

[395] Ibid., I, nos. 447 [= Potthast, I, no. 451], 530 (532) [= Potthast, I, no. 575].

[396] Cheney and Cheney, *Studies*, p. 141.

[397] Paris, BNF Lat. 3922A, fo. 15rb. Its standard edition is *Decretales Pseudo-Isidorianae et Capitula Angilramni*, ed. P. Hinschius (Leipzig, 1863), pp. 725–30. Compared with the usual reading of this added passage the copy at Rouen shows a slight alteration. Instead of 'Qua propter karissime his

canon law. Pope Pelagius' letter originated as one of the false decretals of the Pseudo-Isidorian forgeries in the ninth century.[398] The false decretals were copied into later decretal collections, but none of the major collections could have been the source for our expert.[399] However, there is no need to look for intermediate sources. Pseudo-Isidore had a renaissance in the late eleventh and twelfth centuries. Particularly in France, numerous copies were made and kept in the local libraries – including those of Normandy and Greater Anjou.[400] Our expert, therefore, almost certainly drew from such a copy when he added the passage of Pelagius' letter to the canons of the *Decretum*.[401] We do not know when the expert's work reached Rouen. But the fact that it was there only a few years after the process of William de Chemillé's translation suggests that it may have been available to the archbishops of Rouen and Tours in 1197–9. One can speculate that they were the driving force behind the work of the legal expert. If so, he may have worked at Rouen or Tours.

The archbishops may also have called on their practical experience, arguing that previous episcopal translations did not clearly demonstrate that the pope enjoyed sole jurisdiction. There was, of course, the case of Gilbert Foliot's translation from Hereford to London in 1163. The chapter of London, Archbishop Thomas Becket, and King Henry II had postulated Gilbert's translation from Alexander III, who had granted it.[402] Bartholomew and Walter could have been informed about this. It is questionable, however, whether they remembered it nearly forty years later. And even if they did, it is doubtful that they remembered it as constituting the only proper way to translate bishops. Walter's and

apostolicis fultus auctoritatibus muta episcopum causa necessitatis aut utilitatis super quod nos consulere voluisti et alios fratres nostros', it reads 'Qua propter karissime hiis [sic] apostolicis fultus auctoritatibus muta episcopum causa necessitatis aut utilitatis super quod nos consulere noluisti et alios fratres nostros.' Perhaps the copyist simply misread his source. But it is also possible that the scribe, well informed about the events of William's translation, altered the text on purpose dropping a hint that pointed towards Walter's behaviour. I would like to thank Prof. Sharpe for having discussed this passage with me.

[398] H. Fuhrmann, *Einfluss und Verbreitung der pseudoisidorischen Fälschungen. Von ihrem Auftauchen bis in die neuere Zeit* (MGH, Schriften XXIV, I–III) (3 vols., Stuttgart, 1972–4), I, pp. 167–96, esp. p. 189.

[399] Fuhrmann, *Einfluss*, III, pp. 842, 908, 958. Only Bonizo of Sutri's *Liber de vita christiana* contains a longer excerpt of Pelagius' letter that includes the passage added by the legal expert, *Bonizo, Liber de vita christiana*, ed. E. Perels (Texte zur Geschichte des römischen und kanonischen Rechts im Mittelalter I) (Berlin, 1930), 3.68–71. But Bonizo quotes this passage (3.70) *before* the part that was later to become C. 7 q. 1 c. 36 (3.71) and not *after* as in Paris, BNF Lat. 3922A, fo. 15rb.

[400] Williams, *Codices Pseudo-Isidoriani*, pp. 3–93, 123–32; Fuhrmann, *Einfluss*, I, pp. 168–94.

[401] The sequence of Pelagius' letter in Pseudo-Isidore entirely corresponds with the sequence in Paris, BNF Lat. 3922A, fo. 15rb. Conscious of the place of his additional text in Pelagius' letter *after* what later was to become C. 7 q. 1 c. 35 and c. 36 the legal expert placed the text after c. 36 annotating it with 'et infra'.

[402] A. Morey and C.N.L. Brooke, *Gilbert Foliot and his Letters* (Cambridge, 1965), p. 99 and n. 1; Scholz, *Transmigration*, pp. 198–201; Pennington, *Pope and Bishops*, pp. 91–3.

Bartholomew's opinion must also have been shaped by a number of other translations that had taken place in the Angevin realm in the second half of the twelfth century. The evidence is too thin to be sure of the procedures in Joscius' translation from St Brieuc to Tours in 1157 or in Rotrou's translation from Evreux to Rouen in 1164/5, but there is sufficient evidence for three other translations: Baldwin's from Worcester to Canterbury in 1184, Hubert Walter's from Salisbury to Canterbury in 1193, and most importantly Walter's own from Lincoln to Rouen, also in 1184. All three were effected through elections by the respective electoral bodies and not through postulations.[403]

Innocent III's predecessors were not concerned about establishing postulation as the only proper procedure for translation; what mattered to them was that they were asked to confirm the election of a translated bishop.[404] From this point of view, the three elections at Canterbury and Rouen can be interpreted as demonstrating the universal acceptance of the pope's exclusive right to authorise episcopal translations, since all three were brought before the pope who then confirmed them.[405] But whether Walter and Bartholomew perceived them in that way is another question. They could have interpreted them quite differently. In the second half of the twelfth century the papacy emerged as the institution that confirmed the elections of archbishops.[406] It was the pope's task to scrutinise archiepiscopal elections in the same way as the archbishops had to examine the elections of bishops. Thus when Lucius III and Celestine III confirmed the elections at Canterbury and Rouen, Walter and Bartholomew may have understood their actions as merely fulfilling their function as ecclesiastical superior.[407] From this point of view, the fact that these archiepiscopal elections were also translations added only one further point to the list the popes had to check before they could confirm the elections, but it was not the *reason* why the elections had to be confirmed by them. This interpretation may also have strengthened Bartholomew's and Walter's belief

---

[403] 'Lucii III papae epistolae et privilegia', in *PL*, CCI, cols. 1300–1, no. 173 [= Jaffé, II, no. 15117; *WH* -]; Cheney, *Innocent III*, p. 72 and n. 79; Pennington, *Pope and Bishops*, pp. 94–5.

[404] Scholz, *Transmigration*, pp. 205–6.   [405] See supra, n. 401.

[406] R. Benson, *The Bishop-Elect: A Study in Medieval Ecclesiastical Office* (Princeton, 1968), pp. 180–5.

[407] The translation of Archbishop William aux Blanchesmains from Sens to Rheims in 1176 can be interpreted on similar lines. The only source is Roger of Howden who stated that Alexander III had granted permission for William's translation. Thus it is possible that William's translation had been postulated. But since Alexander III was the ecclesiastical superior of both, the archbishop of Sens and the archbishop of Rheims, Walter and Bartholomew could have considered William's translation a papal matter which was relevant to episcopal translation only in so far as it showed that the ecclesiastical superior could translate the inferior. For William's case, see *Gesta regis*, I, p. 125; cf. L. Falkenstein, 'Alexandre III et la vacance d'un siège métropolitain: le cas de Reims', in *Sede vacante. La vacance du pouvoir dans l'église du moyen âge* (Centre de recherches en histoire du droit et des institutions; cahiers XV) (Brussels, 2001), pp. 3–37, pp. 11–12.

that they had the right to translate bishops, for as archbishops they were the bishops' superiors.

Innocent accepted Walter and Bartholomew's excuses. He considered *necessitas* and *utilitas* valid reasons for episcopal translations,[408] and he was probably aware of the inconsistencies in canon law. The pope was not interested in creating lasting conflicts. He aimed at establishing his prerogative as peacefully as possible. Thus when both archbishops accepted his point of view and Bishop-elect William came to the papal court to postulate his translation personally, Innocent had every reason to be content with the development of the case. In December 1198, he absolved the two archbishops, explaining to them again in detail why only the pope could authorise an episcopal translation.[409] Two months later, in January 1199, he sent his letter *Inter corporalia* to the chapter of Angers which, having justified once more the papal authority over episcopal translations, ordered the chapter of Angers to receive William as their new bishop.[410] In so doing, Innocent also satisfied the ambitions of the parties involved and thus assured that his relationship with them suffered no harm. King Richard I got what he wished, William received the more important see, and the two archbishops were restored to their full authority.

Innocent's firm yet careful handling of the case immediately bore fruit. After the death of Ademar, bishop of Poitiers, in 1198, the archbishops of Bourges and Bordeaux together with the chapter of Poitiers postulated the translation of Maurice de Blason, bishop of Nantes. Innocent granted the translation, on grounds of necessity and utility.[411] At Rouen itself, Innocent's decisions on episcopal translation made an impact. Perhaps on the order of Archbishop Walter, some of the pope's decretals establishing this papal prerogative were inserted into the local decretal collection. Innocent's letter *Ne si universis universa*, ordering the archbishop of Bourges to enquire into the case of William de Chemillé, was among them, but the compiler stopped short of inserting the decretal *Inter*

---

[408] He may even have defined them less vigorously than his predecessors, cf. the case of Bernard of Balbi's translation from Faenza to Pavia, *Register Innocenz' III.*, I, no. 326 [= Potthast, I, no. 342]; Pennington, *Pope and Bishops*, pp. 97–8. Canonical theory continued to consider them as necessary reasons, *Summa iuris*, ed. Rius Serra, p. 135; *S. Raimundus de Pennaforte: Summa de iure canonico*, ed. Ochoa and Diez, cols. 203–4.

[409] *Register Innocenz' III.*, I, no. 447 [= Potthast, I, no. 451].

[410] Ibid., I, no. 530 (532) = *3 Comp.* 1.5.2 = X 1.7.2 [= Potthast, I, no. 575].

[411] Innocent's letters date from 21 December 1198, ibid., I, nos. 490–2 [= Potthast, I, nos. 489–91]. At the time of Maurice's postulation William de Chemillé's case was still pending and Archbishop Bartholomew's suspension from his right to confirm and to consecrate bishops had only been lifted on 3 December, ibid., no. 447 [= Potthast, I, no. 451]. This may explain Bartholomew's passivity in this case.

corporalia which, in stressing the archbishops' faulty behaviour, may have been considered too embarrassing to include.[412]

Innocent did not reveal his source of information on the circumstances of William's translation, but it may have been Nicholas de Laigle, master of the schools at Avranches. In the months following Innocent's order to the archbishop of Bourges to enquire into the case, Nicholas took full advantage of his expertise in canon law, first to prevent an election at Avranches, then to have the election of William Tolomeus, William de Chemillé's successor at Avranches, annulled. Nicholas launched an appeal to the pope, demanding that the chapter of Avranches should only hold an election when William de Chemillé's case had been decided, since until then the church of Avranches was not without a bishop. An election therefore would contravene canon law. He was also worried that the chapter would infringe the *libertas ecclesiae* because of fear of the secular power.[413]

However, various members of the chapter ignored his appeal and, on 21 September 1198, elected William Tolomeus, a cleric of Richard I's seneschal for Normandy, William fitz Ralph. Instead of giving up, Nicholas intensified his efforts and went personally to the papal court. In a second appeal, Nicholas directed his arguments also against William Tolomeus' election. Repeating the case about William de Chemillé's translation, he added that a third of the chapter had been absent at William Tolomeus' election because they had not been invited, and that, in order to cover this up, the dean's party had put invalid subscriptions under the declaration of the election. For instance, a *nepos* of William de Chemillé was among them, who was no older than fourteen, and who was not a canon at Avranches. Furthermore Nicholas attacked the candidate, William Tolomeus. He argued that William was not yet in holy orders at the time of his election and had been ordained in a fraudulent way. He also accused William of illiteracy, of origins outside the diocese of

---

[412] Innocent's order to the archbishop of Bourges: *Register Innocenz' III.*, I, no. 117 = abbreviation of the collection of Rainier of Pomposa no. 6, Paris, BNF Lat. 3922A, fo. 237rb–vb [= Potthast, I, no. 108]. This decretal contained Innocent's earlier letters on this matter, *Cum ex illo generali*, *Register Innocenz' III.*, I, no. 50 = *3 Comp.* 1.5.1 = *X* 1.7.1 [= Potthast, I, no. 52], and *Cum ex illo*, *Register Innocenz' III.*, I, no. 51 [= Potthast, I, no. 53]. Further decretals are Innocent's annulment of William Tolomeus' election, *Register Innocenz' III.*, II, no. 18 = Paris, BNF Lat. 3922A, fo. 147ra–va [= Potthast, I, no. 630]; Innocent's *Licet in tantum*, *Register Innocenz' III.*, II, no. 266 (278) = *3 Comp.* 1.5.4 = *X* 1.7.4 = *3 Rot.* 54, Paris, BNF Lat. 3922A, fo. 124ra–b [= Potthast, I, no. 942]. *1 Rot.* 3.4 is a copy of *Cum ex illo*, Paris, BNF Lat. 3992A, fo. 152va. *Cum ex illo* as such, however, only stresses the inadmissibility to move from an archbishopric to a bishopric. At Rouen, therefore, the purpose of inserting this letter into *1 Rot.* 3 was probably other than showing the pope's right to authorise translations.

[413] *Register Innocenz' III.*, I, no. 442 [= Potthast, I, no. 457]. This letter dates from 7 December 1198.

Avranches, of close connections to the royal court, and of having children. Thus William Tolomeus was not *idoneus* for the episcopal office.[414]

It is true that we owe the information on the circumstances of William Tolomeus' election to the accusations of his opponent, but they are too detailed and precise to be dismissed as pure fiction. What seems to have happened is that the dean and a faction of the chapter of Avranches received Richard's orders to elect William Tolomeus. To secure the king's wish, they proceeded with the election as quickly as possible and were supported at least indirectly by William de Chemillé himself.

After Innocent III had enquired into the case, he ordered the chapter to hold a new election. In a letter dating from 17 March 1199, he explained that he had declared William Tolomeus' election void, not because of the unsuitability of the candidate but because the procedure had been faulty. Since none of the numerous accusations against William could be proved, the election could not be nullified on these grounds. But the fact that the chapter of Avranches had elected William Tolomeus while the case of William de Chemillé was still pending made the election unacceptable.[415] It is possible that Innocent III's decision silently signalled to the chapter and in particular to King Richard that he did not oppose his candidate.[416] In any case, the chapter had to hold a new election. In the meantime, Richard I died, but King John appears to have backed his brother's choice. In August 1199, he ordered the chapter of Avranches to provide Richard, dean of Bayeux and son of Seneschal William fitz Ralph, with the office of treasurer and a canonry at Avranches.[417] This was doubtless a move to strengthen William Tolomeus' position for the forthcoming election. However, the outcome was again disputed, since two candidates, one of them William Tolomeus, were elected. William probably could count on

---

[414] Ibid. and II, no. 18 [= Potthast, I, no. 630]. William's surname is spelt according to 'Ex chronico Savigniacensis monasterii', in *RHF*, XVIII, p. 351. For his time as cleric, see for example *Cartulaire de l'abbaye de Bonport de l'ordre de Cîteaux au diocèse d'Evreux*, ed. J. Andrieux (2 vols., Evreux, 1862), I, no. 17; *Magni rotuli*, ed. Stapleton, II, pp. ix, 295; Paris, BNF Lat. 11059 (cartulary, abbey of Silli), fo. 200r-v (William witnesses, together with William fitz Ralph and others, a charter issued by Fulk de *Clopel* in favour of the abbey of Silli); Caen, AD Calvados H suppl. 486 (cartulary, Hôtel-Dieu des Mathurins de Lisieux, II A 8), fo. 9r (William participates at an assize at Bernay in 1190).

[415] *Register Innocenz' III.*, II, no. 18 [= Potthast, I, no. 630].

[416] On 5 December 1198 Innocent sent a letter to the archbishop of Rouen ordering him neither to confirm nor to consecrate the elect of Avranches, William, until the pope had decided the validity of his election, *Register Innocenz' III.*, I, no. 443 [= Potthast, I, no. 454]. Two days later he sent the letter to the chapter of Avranches asking for an explanation for William Tolomeus' election despite the pending appeal, *Register Innocenz' III.*, I, no. 442 [= Potthast, I, no. 457]. William Tolomeus spent the whole month of December 1198 at Richard's court in Normandy, *Itinerary*, ed. Landon, p. 138. There they may have discussed the situation.

[417] *Rot. chart.*, p. 15a.

the support of more or less the same group that had voted for him on the previous occasion, while his opponent, whose identity is unknown, may have been sponsored by Nicholas. The case was brought again to the attention of Innocent III, who in spring 1200 ordered an enquiry which eventually led to the confirmation of William's election.[418] Immediately after having been enthroned as new bishop of Avranches, William started to make use of his good connections with the ruling elite to labour for the interests of his church. The bishop and the chapter of Avranches owned land at Portchester (Hampshire), which had been farmed out to William du Hommet, constable of Normandy, for an annual farm of hundred shilling. William du Hommet, however, had failed to pay this sum 'for the past twelve years'. Bishop William, anxious not to lose the property, eventually achieved its return from the constable for the prize of a palfrey, a ring, a golden buckle, and the cancellation of all debts. He then granted a tenth of its annual revenue to the chapter of Avranches.[419] Here, then, is another example of the advantages a chapter could derive from choosing a man familiar with influential figures of his time. This serves as a powerful reminder that the election of a royal cleric was not necessarily the result of the king imposing his candidate upon the chapter, but that the canons themselves may have thought such a candidate well worth considering.

The reasons for Nicholas de Laigle's actions are unclear. He may have been sincere in promoting canon law but, if he was Innocent's informant on the circumstances of William de Chemillé's translation, there is a slight and admittedly speculative possibility that he used his knowledge to advance family interests. Nicholas may have been identical with a name-sake, traceable as canon of Sées during the episcopate of Bishop Lisiard (1188–1201).[420] If this was the case, it is quite likely that Nicholas was

---

[418] This second election is only known through the fourteenth-century calendar of the lost registers of the third and fourth year of Innocent III, *Vetera monumenta Slavorum meridionalium historiam illustrantia maximam partem nondum edita ex tabulariis Vaticanis deprompta collecta ac serie chronologica disposata*, ed. A. Theiner (2 vols., Rome and Zagreb, 1863–75), I, p. 49, no. 91: 'Archiepiscopo Rothomagensi, Episcopo Sagiensi et Abbati Rectensi super confirmatione alterius electorum ad ecclesiam Abrincensem'. [= Potthast, I, no. 1058]. The see of Avranches was still vacant on 7 June 1200 when King John assigned the prebend of William Testard at Avranches to his chaplain Ralph, *Rotuli Normanniae in turri Londoniensi*, ed. Hardy, p. 25.

[419] Avranches, BM Fonds Pigeon MS 45 (Chanoine Guérin, Le diocèse d'Avranches), p. 386: charters of William du Hommet and William Tolomeus; Pigeon, *Avranches*, pp. 661–4; J. Peltzer, 'Portchester, les évêques d'Avranches et les Hommet (1100–1230)', *Annales de Normandie*, 56 (2006), 463–82. I would like to thank Prof. Nicholas Vincent for having drawn my attention to the Fonds Pigeon at Avranches.

[420] Master Nicholas de Laigle witnessed a charter of Bishop Lisiard confirming a grant in favour of St André-en-Gouffern, Caen, AD Calvados H 6551 (charters concerning the abbey of St André-en-Gouffern) = Caen, AD Calvados H 6510 (cartulary, abbey of St André-en-Gouffern), fo. 36v. If Nicholas, master of the schools at Avranches, was identical with the canonist Nicholas active at

related to the Laigle family, who had a considerable interest in the diocese of Sées.[421] The Laigle family had close links to the viscounts of Beaumont. Odeline, wife of Richer III de Laigle, was probably a daughter of Roscelin de Beaumont and thus a sister of Bishop Ralph and aunt of Ralph's protégé William de Beaumont, archdeacon at Angers.[422] At Angers, William was the candidate of the Beaumont faction after William de Chemillé's death in 1200[423] and he may have been their man as early as 1198. Were Nicholas' attempts to prevent William de Chemillé's translation intended to favour the election of William de Beaumont? The sources do not answer this question.[424]

Oxford in the early 1190s, the rare appearances of the canon Nicholas de Laigle among the canons of Sées in this period could be taken as circumstantial evidence for the identification of the master of the schools with the canon of Sées.

[421] Thompson, 'The Lords of Laigle: Ambition and Insecurity on the Borders of Normandy', pp. 196–9; Power, *The Norman Frontier*, pp. 353–5. A Master Nicholas de Laigle and his parents were commemorated in the obituary of the monastery of St Evroul, Paris, BNF Lat. 10062 (obituary, abbey of St Evroul), fo. 5v, which is partially edited in 'Ex Uticensis monasterii annalibus et necrologio', in *RHF*, XXIII, p. 485.

[422] Power, *The Norman Frontier*, pp. 482, 487. He demonstrates that older traditions claiming that Odeline was a daughter of Roscelin de Beaumont by a lady of Crépon and that Lucy, wife of Roscelin's son Richard de Beaumont, was Richer III's sister are wrong (Odeline) or unsubstantiated (Lucy). The Beaumonts had close contacts with ecclesiastical institutions of the diocese of Sées. In 1175, William, bishop of Le Mans, settled a dispute between Richard de Beaumont and the chapter of Sées over a donation made by Richard to the canons earlier that year on the occasion of the wedding between Richard's daughter Constance and the Norman baron Roger de Tosny, which had been celebrated at the cathedral of Sées. Richard confirmed that he had freed the chapter of Sées from tolls and customs on his lands in the presence of Giles, bishop of Evreux, Henry du Neubourg, and many from the *pagi* of Le Mans, Sées, and Evreux, who had been attending the ceremony. In return for Richard's recognition the chapter paid 50 s. manceaux to Richard and 20 s. manceaux to his wife Lucy and his son Roscelin, Bibliothèque de l'Evêché 'Livre rouge' (cartulary, cathedral chapter of Sées), fos. 76v (William, bishop of Le Mans, notifies the settlement), 79r (Richard confirms his grant). Some time after the death of Viscount Richard, his widow Lucy granted an annual rent to the abbey of Val-Dieu, Alençon, AD Orne H 2730 (documents concerning the abbey of St Evroul); cf. G. Cagniant, 'La chartreuse du Val-Dieu au Perche. Son chartrier et son domaine jusqu'à la fin du XIIIe siècle' (Ecole des Chartes, Paris, *thèse*, 1975), III, no. 257. In 1197, Viscount Ralph conceded and confirmed a donation made to St Martin of Sées, Sées, Bibliothèque de l'Evêché 'Livre blanc' (cartulary, abbey of St Martin of Sées), fo. 149r. Viscounts Richard and Ralph also conducted business with the abbey of Silli, Alençon, AD Orne H 1417 (charters concerning the abbey of Silli) (charters of Richard [undated] and Ralph [1211, 1235]) = Paris, BNF Lat. 11059 (cartulary, abbey of Silli), fos. 83r–84v, 86r. I would like to thank Geneviève Cagniant for her permission to consult her *thèse*.

[423] See infra, pp. 202–6.

[424] Yet, it is remarkable that in a charter of 1198 dealing with a donation made for the anniversary of Ralph de Beaumont, bishop of Angers, a canon of Angers named Ingenulf de Laigle appears among the witnesses, Angers, AD Maine-et-Loire G 562 (charters concerning the cathedral chapter of Angers), fo. 2r. Ingenulf was one of the leading names of the de Laigle family and this Ingenulf can perhaps be identified with Ingenulf, son of Richer III, cf. Thompson, 'The Lords of Laigle: Ambition and Insecurity on the Borders of Normandy', p. 183. Furthermore a royal charter suggests that Richard I tried to buy the support of the chapter of Angers. On 13 December 1198, still before Innocent III accepted William's translation, Richard confirmed to the church of Angers their English possessions, London, British Library Harleian Charters 43, c. 31.

When William Tolomeus died in 1210,[425] the Angevins no longer ruled in Normandy and its new lord, Philip Augustus, seemed little interested in what was a local affair. According to the chronicle of Savigny, William Burel junior became bishop of Avranches in the same year.[426] It is very tempting to see in him a relative of his namesake and former bishop of Avranches, William Burel senior, since they shared not only their names but also their close connections with the chapter of Le Mans.[427] In any case William Burel junior had been a local choice, whose major concerns lay not with the king but with himself and the prosperity of his diocese: in 1224 he, together with the bishops of Coutances and Lisieux, quit Louis VIII's army as it was preparing to march into Poitou. Probably fearing consequences for their English possessions, they declared that they, like all the other Norman bishops, did not owe personal military service to the king. Louis VIII accepted their retreat and ordered an inquiry into their claims, of which the outcome is unfortunately unknown.[428]

The episcopal elections at Avranches between 1142 and 1210 have features that derive from the situation of the diocese. First, since Avranches was a Norman diocese, ducal influence was present. At least four, maybe five, of the eight elections during the period considered were affected by ducal interests. In this context it is important to note that these five elections took place in the reigns of Henry II and Richard I, who oversaw a total of six elections. But nearly all of the ducal nominations were rewards for loyal service to less important figures at the ducal court,

---

[425] 'Ex chronico Savigniacensis monasterii', in *RHF*, XVIII, p. 351.   [426] Ibid.

[427] William Burel junior had been a canon at Le Mans, *Nécrologe-obituaire de la cathédrale du Mans*, ed. Busson and Ledru, p. 287; *Liber albus*, ed. Lottin, nos. 168–9. He also founded an anniversary for his mother Novella in the cathedral church of Le Mans, *Nécrologe-obituaire de la cathédrale du Mans*, ed. Busson and Ledru, p. 12. William Burel junior is also known as William de *Ostilleio*, *GC*, XI, col. 484. Considering William's connection to the Maine this surname probably relates to Outillé near Le Mans, although the exact nature of the relationship to the lords of Outillé, the family de La Jaille, remains unclear, cf. *Liber albus*, ed. Lottin, no. 58. In 1188, a William Burel, treasurer, witnessed a charter of Bishop William Burel, Flers, BM 22 (formerly F 9) (cartulary, abbey of Savigny), fos. 110r–111r, no. 75. In August 1199, King John ordered the chapter of Avranches to assign 'the vacant office of the treasurer and prebend' at Avranches to Richard, dean of Bayeux, *Rot. chart.*, p. 15a. It is not known whether this order was executed. In any case, if the copy of the charter of Bishop Richard is correct and if the office of the treasurer was vacant in 1199 due to the death of Treasurer William Burel, then a third person named William Burel existed. However, if the copy of the charter is correct and if John disposed of the office even though Treasurer William Burel was still alive, the treasurer might have been identical with the later bishop.

[428] 'Scripta de feodis ad regem spectantibus et de militibus ad exercitum vocandis, e Philippi Augusti regestis excerpta', in *RHF*, XXIII, p. 637; Petit-Dutaillis, *Louis VIII*, p. 409. The possessions of the see of Avranches were situated in Hampshire. For Henry II's reign, see *PR* 29, H.II, p. 146; *PR* 31, H.II, p. 213; for Henry III's reign, see *Rotuli litterarum clausarum in turri Londinensi asservati*, ed. T.D. Hardy (2 vols., London 1833–44), I, pp. 431a, 437b–438a.

or were a form of consolation, not decisions of great political significance. The only exception to this rule, the election of William de Chemillé in 1196, can be explained with the extremely tense Angevin–Breton relations in that year. The exceptional character of this election is underlined by the fact that, soon after his election at Avranches, William was translated to the wealthier and strategically more important see of Angers.[429] Overall, Avranches had only limited strategic value for the dukes and its relatively small revenues made the bishopric unattractive to the top-ranking courtiers at the ducal/royal court. This situation gave the families of Avranches and the neighbouring dioceses a chance to advance their interests so long as they did not run counter to ducal ones. Among these families the Burels were the most successful. Based in Maine but with connections to the Avranchin, they used their position at the ducal court to win Henry II's *placet* for William Burel senior's advancement to the see of Avranches. Twenty years later, and eight years after Philip II's conquest, they supplied the see with William Burel junior. His election demonstrates the strength and adaptability of local power structures.

CONCLUSION

The fight between King Stephen and the Empress Matilda considerably disturbed the previous routine of ducal control over episcopal elections in Normandy. Baronial families increased their influence and some cathedral chapters elected their bishops without asking for the ruler's consent. Resulting conflicts were brought before the pope, who decided in favour of the chapters. But the triumph of the Gregorian conception of a free election over ducal claims based on custom was only temporary, and did not incite the entire Norman clergy to insist on free elections. The reason why the Gregorian conception of elections became not firmly established must be seen in the rule of Henry II. Henry, aware of the prerogatives enjoyed by Henry I and William the Conqueror in ecclesiastical matters, aimed at the re-establishment of ducal authority in both the secular and the ecclesiastical sphere,[430] and, once he had gained sufficient power to back up his claims, he pursued a conscious and deliberate policy towards elections in Normandy. He insisted on being consulted in the selection process, and, in elections to sees of strategic importance such as Rouen, Sées, and Evreux, he ensured the promotion of men from his entourage.

---

[429] For Angers, see infra, pp. 202–3.

[430] Cf. his re-issue of the canons of the council of Lillebonne (1080), dealing with episcopal jurisdiction and revenues, P. Chaplais, 'Henry II's Reissue of the Canons of the Council of Lillebonne of Whitsun 1080 (?25 February 1162)', *Journal of the Society of Archivists*, 4 (1973), 627–32.

This policy revived the close links between the duke and the Norman episcopacy and revitalised the traditional right of the duke to take part in the selection process. After July 1168, an angry Becket wrote to Pope Alexander III:

Why was Abbot Achard of Saint-Victor, bishop-elect of Sées, not permitted to be consecrated? Because the supreme pontiff Adrian had confirmed his election. Why did the king later allow him to be made bishop of Avranches? Obviously because no election preceded the declaration of his will (. . . *nulla voluntatem eius precessit electio*). . .I do not doubt that the dispute between us concerning the liberties of the Church would have been extinguished if he had not found patrons for his will – not to say perversity – in the Roman Church.[431]

The archbishop's letter points towards the two key elements of episcopal elections in Normandy under Henry II: the king's will had to be considered, and churchmen considered this acceptable under canon law.

Becket's murder did little to compromise Henry's position. He had to abrogate the constitutions of Clarendon and promised free episcopal elections in England.[432] But electoral practice in Normandy was hardly affected by this. A Savigniac monk, writing between 1173 and 1186, summed up the situation: either the king or the clergy could offer a bishopric.[433] And if there was a conflict between them over the candidate, the king's wish prevailed – an appeal to the papal court was rarely if ever contemplated. Henry's increasing power also diminished the influence of the baronage on elections. He preferred men from the royal service to members of baronial families.

The common acceptance of the duke's dominant position led canonists of the emerging Anglo-Norman school to believe that to ask for the ruler's consent during the selection process was a required part of a canonical election. This situation, however, changed between *c.* 1180 and *c.* 1210. So far Norman electoral practice had influenced Norman electoral theory, but now the process was reversed. Gaining in strength, the papacy, in particular Innocent III, took a clear line against the participation of secular rulers in the selection process. Decretals were collected in Normandy and they reshaped the consciousness amongst the clergy there. King Richard who, after returning from captivity, pursued a policy towards episcopal elections similar to his father's, obtained a first taste of

---

[431] *Correspondence*, ed. Duggan, i, no. 170, pp. 782–5.
[432] *MTB*, VII, nos. 771–4, 789–90; *Gesta regis*, I, pp. 31–3.
[433] 'Vitae b. Petri Abrincensis et b. Hamonis monachorum coenobii Saviniacensis in Normannia', ed. E.P. Sauvage, *Analecta Bolandiana*, 2 (1883), 475–560, 477–8, 521. Demonstrating the humility and modesty of Hamo, a monk of Savigny, his hagiographer declared that he had stalwartly denied the frequent offers of a bishopric made to him by either the king or the clergy.

this changing climate towards the end of his reign, when William de Chemillé's translation from Avranches to Angers and the subsequent election at Avranches were brought to the papal court, the latter being the first time since 1144–7 that a Norman episcopal election was decided by the pope. King John had no intention of giving up the long-established electoral custom. In view of his difficulties first in succeeding his brother and then in defending his dominions against Philip Augustus, the defence of royal prerogatives and control over episcopal elections were very important to him. In achieving this aim John pursued a double strategy. On the one hand he used brute, political force, and on the other finely shaped legal argumentation that demonstrated close understanding of current developments in law. Aware of the growing importance of written law, John devised his counterarguments accordingly. He no longer based his claims just on the traditional arguments of royal dignity and ancient custom, but also on *ius scriptum*, which probably referred to teachings of the Anglo-Norman school of canonists supporting John's position. Aiming at the heart of the problem – the canonistic interpretation of the ruler's position in the electoral process – this was an ingenuous attempt to protect a royal prerogative. If successful, that is if John's argumentation had been accepted by the local churchmen as well as by the pope, his position concerning episcopal elections would have been secured. But John's efforts came to nothing. Not only did he lose the political power to back up his claims, but he also failed to convince the churchmen. The cathedral chapters no longer considered him as an authority on electoral matters. Now they looked to the pope and the latest canon law for guidance. Innocent III advocated an interpretation of canon law that was precisely opposite to John's position. As a consequence, John entered into an open dispute with the pope over this issue. After a first major show down over the election at Sées, the controversy was continued with much the same arguments at subsequent elections in England. In theory at least, the matter was settled in 1214, when John granted free elections to the cathedral churches and monasteries of England and Wales.

Philip Augustus and his successors pursued a different policy towards elections in Normandy. They did not openly dictate elections, but used diplomatic means to promote their interests. This meant that after the conquest the cathedral chapters usually had a free hand in choosing their bishops. Predominantly they elected men from their own ranks, who usually belonged to the local aristocracy. In the course of the twelfth century, the chapters had excluded the *religiosi viri* from the electoral body: Innocent II's decree had only occasionally been observed, and the chapters jealously guarded their exclusive electoral right. But their freedom was not to last for long. Frequent internal power struggles resulted in split elections. The weaker party saw only one way of preserving their chances of winning or at least preventing the opponent's election: an appeal to the pope. In the long run this increased the influence of the papacy on the outcome of elections, and men more familiar to the pope than to the chapter began to appear among the ranks of the Norman episcopacy.

The attractiveness of the appeal as a weapon stimulated interest in canon law. Both the appeal and the defence had to be compatible with current canon law. Norman churchmen had access to this. Gratian, the Third Lateran Council, and papal decretals were the basis for their arguments before 1215. Then the regulations of the Fourth Lateran Council provided the new rules for electoral procedure. But they failed to put an end to discord and hair-splitting. Appeals continued and, based on Lateran IV, the canons and/or their lawyers elaborated arguments that took into account the latest canonistic discussion. On a number of points such as the requirement of an absolute majority, the unsuitability of pluralists, or the need to recall canons to an election from the entire kingdom of France, the arguments brought forward by Norman parties were considered as setting new and important precedents and were incorporated into the body of canon law.

Norman electoral conflicts also give some insight into the use of the different voting procedures. In many cases the pope ordered the chapter to hold a new election. The favoured electoral procedure was usually the compromise, which was a natural choice. Once the entire chapter had engaged in a fierce dispute as result of a scrutiny, it was very difficult to ensure a peaceful election through repeating the process. The compromise, however, limited the electoral body to a few chosen men, who might more easily come to an agreement. In the words of the dean's party at Rouen in 1235, the compromise led to peace not (like the scrutiny) to discord or grief.[434] This statement also points towards the other aspect ever-present at elections: the concept of unanimity. More easily realised in a compromise than in a scrutiny, after an electoral dispute it was considered important to have a unanimous election. Discord should be remedied by a new bishop elected by divine inspiration.

---

[434] *Registres de Grégoire IX*, ed. Auvray, II, no. 2796, col. 177: 'fuit ab eisdem decano et parte sua responsum quod magis expediebat per viam compromissi, que pacis erat, procedere, quam per viam scrutinium, ex quo sepius oriuntur discordie et rancores'. See supra, p. 93.

Chapter 4

ELECTORAL PRACTICE: GREATER ANJOU

Long before Geoffrey Plantagenet set out to conquer Normandy in 1135–6, the counts of Anjou had added the counties of Touraine (in 1044) and Maine (in 1110) to their native county of Anjou.[1] These three counties formed what as a matter of convenience can be called Greater Anjou, which comprised the archbishopric of Tours and two of its suffragan bishoprics, Le Mans and Angers. The count was the most important individual baron in Greater Anjou, holding possessions in the Loire valley, western Touraine, and the towns of Le Mans, La Flèche, and Trôo in Maine. Count Geoffrey had been largely successful in his attempts to defend, strengthen, and expand comital power, but the substantial lordships of other barons in Greater Anjou posed a constant challenge to his rule. In Maine and northern Anjou, the viscounts of Beaumont and the lords of Craon, Laval, Sablé, and Mayenne were the leading families, while in southern Anjou the lords of Montreuil-Bellay were the count's greatest rivals. In northern and central Touraine the influence of the counts of Vendôme, the counts of Blois, and the lords of Amboise was particularly notable, while the lords of Ste Maure, L'Isle-Bouchard, La Haye, and Preuilly dominated the south.[2] In the absence of a dominant ruler, however, the cathedral chapters of Greater Anjou had been gaining more and more control over episcopal elections in the first half of the twelfth century.

---

[1] Boussard, *Le comté d'Anjou*, pp. 5–13; B. Lemesle, *La société aristocratique dans le Haut-Maine (XIe–XIIe siècle)* (Rennes, 1999), pp. 43–4; Chartrou, *L'Anjou*, pp. 36–41, 49–59; Guillot, *Le comte d'Anjou*, I, pp. 1–126.

[2] Boussard, *Le comté d'Anjou*, pp. 15–64; Chartrou, *L'Anjou*, pp. 26–41; D. Barthélemy, *La société dans le comté de Vendôme de l'an mil au XIVe siècle* (Paris, 1993), pp. 712–24.

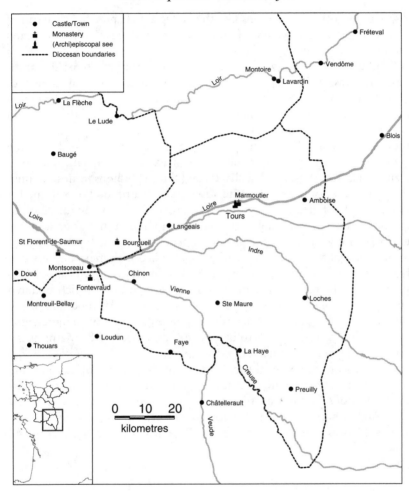

Map 9 The archdiocese of Tours

TOURS

The archbishopric of Tours was the metropolitan see for Le Mans, Angers, and the nine Breton bishoprics. Unlike its Norman equivalent, Rouen, Tours did not dominate its suffragans by the size of its archdiocese, which was roughly equal in extent to the diocese of Angers and smaller than the diocese of Le Mans. Within the archdiocese, the archbishop was rather *primus inter pares* than the leading ecclesiastical figure. He and the cathedral chapter of St Maurice of Tours had considerable *temporalia* at their disposal, but other institutions like the collegiate chapter of St Martin of Tours or the monastery of St Martin of Marmoutier near Tours competed with them for influence and patronage.[3]

Traditionally the king of France acted as patron at Tours; the archbishopric was in the Capetian king's gift and he held the lay abbacy of St Martin.[4] But in the mid-twelfth century, the Capetians had only limited political influence in the Touraine, where, since the eleventh century, the houses of Anjou and Blois had fiercely competed for rule, preventing each other from dominating the region.[5] Pushed into the background, the Capetians, as will be shown, exercised very little influence, if any at all, with the cathedral chapter and the archbishops from 1140 until the completion of the conquest in 1206. At St Martin of Tours, Capetian influence was of greater significance. Having reached a low in the eleventh century Capetian royal authority regained momentum throughout the twelfth century.[6] However, while prominent positions such as the deanery or the office of treasurer became increasingly filled with men supportive of the Capetians,[7] holding a canonry at St Martin was by no means synonymous with being a Capetian placeman. The chapter, which counted among its honorary canons the count of Anjou, had a membership of 150 canons,[8] and consequently practically all political factions were represented therein. This diversity needs to be kept in mind, because St Martin was a potential supplier of candidates for bishoprics.

As a consequence of the rivalry between the houses of Anjou, Blois, and Capet in the Touraine, no secular ruler enjoyed control of the archiepiscopal elections by the mid-twelfth century. The election of Engelbald, after Archbishop Hugh's abdication in 1147, demonstrates this state of affairs.[9] He was probably a local choice. Engelbald belonged to a powerful

---

[3] For the temporalities of the archbishopric, see *Cartulaire de l'archevêché de Tours (Liber bonarum gentium)*, ed. L. de Grandmaison (Mémoires de la société archéologique de Touraine XXXVII–XXXVIII) (2 vols., Tours 1892–4), II, pp. 290–321. For St Martin and Marmoutier, S. Farmer, *Communities of Saint-Martin: Legend and Ritual in Medieval Tours* (Ithaca, 1991), pp. 65–298; E. Vaucelle, *La collégiale de Saint-Martin de Tours. Des origines à l'avènement des Valois (397–1328)* (Mémoires de la société archéologique de Touraine XLVI) (Tours, 1907); J. Boussard, 'Le trésorier de Saint-Martin de Tours', *Revue d'histoire de l'église de France*, 47 (1961), 67–88; J. Boussard, 'L'enclave royale de Saint-Martin de Tours', *Bulletin de la société des antiquaires de France*, (1958), 157–79. For other ecclesiastical rivalries in Touraine and particularly in the Vendômois, see P. Johnson, *Prayer, Patronage, and Power. The Abbey of la Trinité, Vendôme, 1032–1187* (New York, 1981), pp. 103–14.

[4] Pacaut, *Elections*, pp. 64–5; Vaucelle, *St Martin*, pp. 80–1, 198–9.

[5] Pacaut, *Elections*, pp. 64–5; Boussard, *Le comté d'Anjou*, pp. 19–21, 40–55, 70–6.

[6] Boussard, 'L'enclave royale de Saint-Martin de Tours', 158, 166–8, 172–4.

[7] Griffiths, 'St Martin', 100–7, 115–32.   [8] Vaucelle, *Saint-Martin*, pp. 170–80, 183, 218.

[9] Pacaut, *Elections*, p. 46.

baronial family in Touraine, the descendants of Engelbald Le Breton,[10] and had made his career within the cathedral chapter, where he held the office of treasurer.[11]

Of Engelbald's successor, Joscius, little is known. When he was translated to the see of Tours in 1157, he had been bishop of St Brieuc in Brittany since before 1150.[12] François Dumas has suggested that he was perhaps identical with Joscius, cellarer of the cathedral chapter at Tours, who disappears from the witness lists of archiepiscopal charters in the 1140s.[13] That he may originally have come from Tours is perhaps implied by his presence in 1151, when Archbishop Engelbald celebrated the marriage between the Breton Count Henry de Penthièvre and Matilda, daughter of Count John de Vendôme.[14] Did Joscius' presence on the occasion mean that he had played a role in arranging the marriage? If so, he must have had some sort of contact with the family of Vendôme. Furthermore, the electoral body of Tours would not normally seek someone who was bishop at St Brieuc unless they already knew him. Joscius' candidature may even have been supported by the Capetian king, Louis VII. According to the *Gallia christiana*, Joscius had an amicable relationship with Odo, duke of Brittany.[15] When Odo was deprived of his duchy by Conan IV in 1156, he fled to Louis VII, in whose service he made his name as a successful warrior.[16] Did he work for Joscius' election? In this context it is worth noting that when Odo rebelled against Henry II in Brittany, Joscius nearly provoked a war between Henry II and Louis VII by stating that, since the kings of France were the patrons of the church of Tours, they had the right to collect the aid for the Holy Land there. Only when the rebels were subdued by Henry II did Joscius make peace with Henry.[17] On the other hand, Louis VII was not in a position in the Touraine to dictate the election of the archbishop against the wishes of the electoral body. The most he could do was to suggest Joscius or, if the

---

[10] Barthélemy, *La société*, pp. 771–2, corrects Engelbald's genealogy. He was not the son of Count Geoffrey de Preuilly as so far believed; cf. Table 2, p. 175. For the lordship of Engelbald Le Breton, see ibid., p. 588.

[11] For appearances as treasurer witnessing Archbishop Hugh's charters, see Paris, BNF Collection Housseau, IV, nos. 1542, 1553, 1605, 1611, V, no. 1650.

[12] *GC*, XIV, col. 1088.   [13] F. Dumas, *De Joscii Turonensis archiepiscopi vita (1157–73)* (Paris, 1894), p. 2.

[14] *Mémoires pour servir de preuves à l'histoire ecclésiastique et civile de Bretagne*, ed. H. Morice (2 vols., Paris, 1742–4), col. 610; *Cartulaire de l'abbaye de la Trinité de Vendôme*, ed. Métais, II, no. 545.

[15] *GC*, XIV, col. 89: 'Odoni duci placuerat Joscius'. J. Gaudemet, 'Recherches sur l'épiscopat médiéval en France', in S. Kuttner and J.J. Ryan (eds.), *Proceedings of the Second International Congress of Medieval Canon Law. Boston College, 12–16 August 1963* (MIC series C: subsidia I) (Vatican City, 1965), pp. 139–54, p. 146, interprets this as Joscius being an advisor to Duke Odo.

[16] *Œuvres de Rigord et de Guillaume le Breton*, ed. Delaborde, I, p. 177.

[17] *Torigny*, pp. 232–3. In his account of the year 1167, Torigny records Henry II's victory in Brittany before Joscius' peace with the king.

electoral body had already considered him, to support his candidature. Whatever the king's role, only one year later Joscius was brought to realise that Louis VII would not support him unconditionally. When the king saw an opportunity to stabilise his relationship with Henry II, he showed little interest in Joscius' wishes. The archbishop had asked Louis VII to support his claims to appoint the new abbot of St Julien of Tours. But part of Louis VII's agreement with Henry II was that Henry would receive guardianship over the abbey, and thus Joscius' plea remained unheard.[18]

If the reasons for Joscius' election must remain conjectural, the case of his successor Bartholomew is more clear-cut. Through his mother, Marie,[19] Bartholomew was related to a group of leading families of the Touraine and the Vendômois. Marie belonged to the family of Engelbald Le Breton and was a sister of Archbishop Engelbald,[20] to whom Bartholomew referred as his *avunculus*.[21] Bartholomew himself was an *avunculus* of John de Faye, archbishop of Tours from 1208 to 1228 and *consanguineus* of Queen Eleanor.[22] Bartholomew and John were probably related through the daughter of Marie and her first husband, Amaury Gaimard de Lavardin. This daughter, possibly called Agatha, had married Nivelon III de Fréteval, brother or perhaps more likely father of Ursio, who in turn was the husband of Griscia, daughter and heiress of Ralph de Faye, Queen Eleanor's uncle.[23] The exact degree of kinship between Bartholomew and Eleanor remains obscure, but both were aware of their connection, as is indicated by Eleanor's demand to Lawrence, abbot of Westminster (1158–73), to invest Bartholomew, then dean of the cathedral chapter of Tours, with the church of Ockendon (Essex).[24] Bartholomew's father was almost certainly Marie's second husband,

---

[18] Warren, *Henry II*, pp. 76–7.

[19] Paris, BNF Lat. 1096 (obituary, cathedral chapter of Tours), fo. 9v: 'Idus Octobris. Obiit Bartholomeus archiepiscopus Turonensis et Maria mater ejus'; cf. the entry on Bartholomew in the principal obituary of Tours, *Martyrologe-obituaire de l'église métropolitaine de Tours*, ed. J.-J. Bourasse (Mémoires de la société archéologique de Touraine XVII) (Tours, 1865), p. 61. Thus *GC*, XIV, col. 92, stating that Bartholomew was the son of Geoffrey Grisegonelle and Matilda de Châteaudun is incorrect.

[20] Barthélemy, *Société*, p. 772.

[21] Paris, BNF Collection Housseau, v, nos. 1945, 1982 (charters of Archbishop Bartholomew).

[22] *Cartulaire de l'abbaye cistercienne de Fontaine-Daniel*, ed. A. Grosse-Duperon and E. Gouvrion (Mayenne, 1896), no. 48; 'Narratio', in *Recueil de chroniques de Touraine*, ed. A. Salmon (Collection de documents sur l'histoire de Touraine I) (Tours, 1854), pp. 292–317, p. 298; 'Chronicon Gastinensis coenobii', in ibid., pp. 374–5, p. 374; Paris, BNF Collection Housseau, XVIII, fo. 304v (excerpt from the obituary of the abbey of Fontevraud): 'Johannes archiepiscopus Turonensis consanguineus dominae Alienoris reginae'; cf. Table 4, p. 181.

[23] On the relationship between Nivelon III and Ursio, see infra, Table 4, p. 181.

[24] *Westminster Abbey Charters 1066–1214*, ed. E. Mason (London Record Society Publications XXV) (London, 1988), no. 463.

Table 2 *Archbishop Bartholomew of Tours and the family of Engelbald Le Breton (a)*

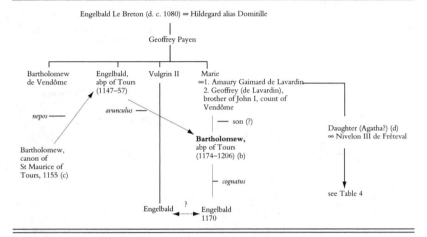

(a) In general, see Barthélemy, *Société*, pp. 568, 771–2, 798–800.

(b) Bartholomew's mother was Marie. His father was probably Marie's second husband Geoffrey (de Lavardin), see p. 175, n. 25. For Engelbald, *cognatus* of Bartholomew, see *Chartes vendômoises*, ed. Métais, no. 99.

(c) Paris, BNF Collection Housseau, V, no. 1777; infra, p. 177, n. 31.

(d) See Table 4 note (b).

Geoffrey (de Lavardin), brother of John, count of Vendôme.[25] Bartholomew referred to Lancelin, son of Count John and brother of Bourchard IV, John's successor as count of Vendôme, as his *consanguineus*.[26] In another charter, Bouchard IV's grandson, John de Montoire, was named Bartholomew's *nepos*.[27] By the time of his election to Tours in 1174, Bartholomew was dean of the chapter.[28] The evidence is too thin to

[25] 'Gaufridus pater domini archiepiscopi' reads the entry of 12 April in an obituary of the cathedral chapter of Tours. Written in the second half of the twelfth century or in the early years of the thirteenth century this entry probably refers to Bartholomew's father, Paris, BNF Lat. 1096 (obituary, cathedral chapter of Tours); cf. J.-L. Lemaître, *Répertoire des documents nécrologiques français* (Recueil des historiens de la France. Obituaires VII) (3 vols., Paris, 1980–7), III (supplément), p. 24, no. 571a.

[26] *Chartes vendômoises*, ed. C. Métais (Société archéologique scientifique et littéraire du Vendômois) (Vendôme, 1905), no. 129.

[27] Ibid., no. 155; cf. Table 3, p. 176.

[28] Ibid., no. 99. Griffith, 'St Martin', 116, states that Archbishop Bartholomew was identical with the dean of the St Martin of Tours. For evidence that this was not the case, see *Cartulaire de l'archevêché*, ed. de Grandmaison, I, no. 37, where Archbishop Bartholomew and Bartholomew, dean of

Table 3 *Archbishop Bartholomew of Tours and the family of the counts of Vendôme (a)*

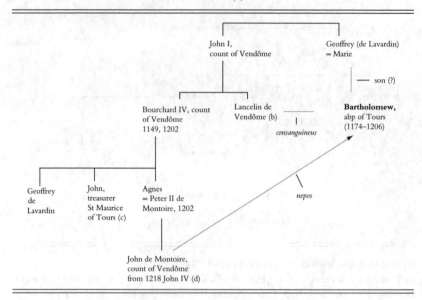

(a) In general, see Barthélemy, *Société*, pp. 798–800.
(b) *Chartes vendômoises*, ed. Métais, no. 129.
(c) Ibid., no. 111.
(d) Ibid., no. 155.

establish a full list of canons of the cathedral chapter for the third quarter of the twelfth century, but the information available suggests that a number of relatives of Bartholomew were members of the chapter at the time of his election. His brother, Hugh, who was to succeed him as dean,[29] was almost certainly a member of the chapter by then. His relative, John, who appeared as treasurer from 1177, may already have been a member of the chapter three years earlier.[30] His namesake, Bartholomew, another *nepos*

St Martin, appear together. Archbishop Bartholomew received the deanery of St Maurice during Engelbald's episcopate, as Gano still held this office in 1150, Paris, BNF Collection Housseau, v, no. 1750 (Gano witnesses a charter of Archbishop Engelbald). Bartholomew appeared as dean of the cathedral chapter in 1155, ibid., v, no. 1777 (he witnesses a charter of Archbishop Engelbald). In 1215 Archbishop John de Faye granted the chapter the right to elect the dean, ibid., xxiii, p. 252.

[29] *Cartulaire de l'archevêché*, ed. de Grandmaison, i, no. 65; Paris, BNF Collection Housseau, v, no. 1958 (Dean Hugh, Bartholomew's brother, witnesses a charter of Archbishop Bartholomew).
[30] *Cartulaire de l'archevêché*, ed. de Grandmaison, i, no. 65; *Chartes vendômoises*, ed. Métais, no. 111.

of Archbishop Engelbald and canon in 1155, may still have been alive in 1174.[31] John de Lavardin held a canonry in 1174 and, on the grounds of his name, some sort of special connection with Bartholomew might be suspected.[32] Another canon traceable in 1174, Reginald, may have been Bartholomew's chaplain.[33]

Given Bartholomew's local connections, he must have been the chapter's choice.[34] Shortly after the election in 1174, William de Passavant, bishop of Le Mans, wrote an angry letter to Arnulf, bishop of Lisieux, complaining that the chapter of Tours had elected an archbishop without having invited the suffragan bishops to participate. Arnulf replied, quoting the chapter's excuse for the way they had proceeded. They had argued that, during the rebellion of Henry II's sons in 1173–4, there had been considerable political turmoil in the region that had forced them to press ahead with the election. Therefore they had not been able to invite the bishops.[35] Knowing Bartholomew's connections with Queen Eleanor, the Fayes, and Bourchard, son of John, count of Vendôme,[36] all of them leading figures in the revolt against Henry II,[37] the chapter of Tours may have intended to

---

[31] Dean Bartholomew also witnessed this charter of Archbishop Engelbald, Paris, BNF Collection Housseau, v, no. 1777.

[32] *Cartulaire de l'archevêché*, ed. de Grandmaison, I, no. 37.

[33] Ibid. A chaplain Reginald appears as witness to a charter of Bartholomew in 1184, Paris, BNF Collection Housseau, v, no. 1976. Canon Reginald may have been the canon *Renardus*, who witnessed a charter on behalf of Bartholomew, together with relatives of the then dean in 1170, *Chartes vendômoises*, ed. Métais, no. 99. There is already a Canon Reginald, who witnessed a charter of Archbishop Engelbald in 1155, Paris, BNF Collection Housseau, v, no. 1777. It should be noted, however, that there is also a Master Reginald, canon of Tours and chaplain of Archbishop Joscius, ibid., v, no. 1703 (he witnesses a charter of Archbishop Joscius).

[34] A decretal in the *Liber extra* is assumed to be a letter of Pope Lucius III to Archbishop Bartholomew of Tours. The letter, tentatively dated to 1181, states that on the occasion of his election, Bartholomew had given money to a friend to buy off the leader of the opposition. Now, the archbishop wanted to know whether he should remain in his office. The pope recommended him to resign, X 5.3.23 [= Jaffé, II, no. 14547; WH 645]. There is, however, no other evidence corroborating the content of this letter. On the contrary it is totally unclear why Bartholomew should have enquired about the circumstances of his election seven years after it had taken place. Nothing indicates that he was willing to resign his office at a time in which he was extremely active in defending its authority against the claims of Dol. It is therefore possible that the identification of the recipient of Lucius III's letter is mistaken. If this was not the case, and Lucius III's letter was indeed directed to Bartholomew, it is conceivable that the archbishop's opponents at the papal court stood behind its content. After all, it was not Bartholomew himself, but Cardinal Matthew, who spoke to Lucius about his election. Given the intensity of the dispute over the status of Dol during Lucius III's pontificate, Bartholomew's opponents may have invented this story in order to discredit the archbishop.

[35] *Arnulf*, ed. Barlow, no. 99.   [36] Cf. Tables 2, 4, pp. 175, 181.

[37] *Gesta regis*, I, p. 63; Barthélemy, *Société*, p. 730; Boussard, *Le comté d'Anjou*, pp. 78–81. The lords de La Haye were also among Henry II's opponents. The family held some of their lands from the archbishop. Bartholomew de La Haye, a canon at Tours at least since 1180, may have been related to them, Paris, BNF Collection Housseau, v, no. 1982 (he witnesses a charter of Archbishop Bartholomew); *Cartulaire de l'archevêché*, ed. de Grandmaison, II, p. 310. Hugh de Ste Maure was another of the rebels, *Gesta regis*, I, p. 47. After his death Archbishop Bartholomew 'rogatus ab

prevent any external influence that could disturb Bartholomew's election. In this context it is important to stress that not all of Bartholomew's relations opposed Henry II. Bourchard's father, John, remained faithful to the king.[38]

But Henry II seems to have been worried by Bartholomew's connections with some of the rebels. It is certainly no coincidence that during his episcopate the king supported a new offensive by the bishopric of Dol to gain the status of an archbishopric for Brittany. Shortly after his election in 1177,[39] the elect of Dol, the Italian Roland, went to Rome, where he is said to have spent much time and money on Dol's cause.[40] Such activities, of course, were not welcomed by the archbishop of Tours, but Bartholomew found staunch support from the Capetians, who were only too glad to revive their ancient role as patrons of the see of Tours. By defending the archbishop they must have hoped to win him over as a supporter in their conflict with the Angevins.[41] And, indeed, clever diplomacy, and the death of Alexander III, prevented a possibly unfavourable decision.[42] Alexander's successor, Lucius III, continued the investigation. When, in 1184/5, Bartholomew was summoned to appear in Rome to answer Dol's case, Philip II explained to Lucius III that he had prevented Bartholomew from travelling to Rome, because he needed the archbishop's *presentia, industria, consilium,* and *auxilium.*[43] With Lucius III's death in 1185,

amicis' assisted at the celebration of his funeral, Paris, BNF Collection Housseau, v, no. 1889. According to *Gesta regis*, I, p. 47, 'Gaufridus de Lavardin filius comitis de Vendomia' was also among the supporters of Henry the Younger. The identity of this Geoffrey is not clear. If the name is correct he could have been either the brother of John, count of Vendôme, or his grandson (by his son Bourchard), Tables 2, 3, pp. 175–6, Barthélemy, *Société*, pp. 798–800. If the former was the case Geoffrey was very advanced in age in 1173–4; if the latter was true he was very young at that time. Or did Roger of Howden mean Bourchard instead of Geoffrey?

[38] In 1147, Geoffrey Plantagenet issued a charter confirming a grant of John, count of Vendôme, *amicus et fidelis noster*, who was holding the *honor Vindocinensis* of him, Paris, BNF Collection Housseau, v, no. 1724. Four years later, Henry II supported John against Theobald, count of Blois, and around 1180 Henry II intervened to have the excommunicated John absolved, 'Annales Sancti Albini', in *Recueil d'annales*, ed. Halphen, pp. 12–13, and 'Annales Vindocinenses', in ibid., pp. 50–79, p. 72; cf. Barthélemy, *Société*, pp. 729–30; *Cartulaire de l'abbaye de la Trinité de Vendôme*, ed. Métais, II, no. 573.

[39] *Torigny*, pp. 275–6.

[40] 'Epistolae Alexandri III papae', in *RHF*, xv, pp. 969–70, no. 411 [= Jaffé, II, no. 13503; *WH* -]. Although there is no evidence stating from which source Roland paid his expenses, it is possible that Henry II helped him out. On Roland's request Henry II investigated the rights of the church of Dol in 1181 in order to restore lost possessions to the church, J. Allenou, *Histoire féodale des Marais, territoire et église de Dol. Enquête par tourbe ordonnée par Henri II, roi d'Angleterre* (La Bretagne et les pays celtiques XIII) (Paris, 1917).

[41] Cf. G. Conklin, 'Les Capétiens et l'affaire de Dol de Bretagne', *Revue d'histoire de l'église de France*, 78 (1992), 241–63.

[42] 'Epistolae Alexandri III papae', in *RHF*, xv, p. 970, no. 412, pp. 971–2, no. 414 [= Jaffé, II, no. 13660; *WH* -].

[43] *Recueil des actes de Philippe Auguste*, ed. Delaborde et al., I, no. 136; cf. ibid., nos. 148–9. For the papal commissions, see *Register Innocenz' III.*, II, no. 79 (82) [= Potthast, I, no. 726]; 'Lucii III papae epistolae et privilegia', in *PL*, CCI, cols. 1317–18, no. 188 [= Jaffé, II, no. 15234; *WH* -]; 'Epistolae Alexandri III papae', in *RHF*, xv, pp. 975–7, no. 419 [= Jaffé, II, no. 14371; *WH* -].

papal activity concerning Dol's claims seems to have ceased for the next fourteen years. Dol's best advocate at the curia, Roland, cardinal-deacon of S. Maria in Portico since 1185 died in 1187.[44]

Released from this immediate pressure, Bartholomew focused on another problem that threatened the peace of his archbishopric and his relatives. In the late 1180s, the Angevin–Capetian rivalry became more explosive than ever before, and Bartholomew, knowing that war between the two parties would cause considerable devastation for the Touraine, started to work hard for a peace. His major aim was to persuade the kings to take up the cross, which would have meant at least a temporary lull for the region.

It points strongly towards the significance of Bartholomew's southern connections with the Fayes and Queen Eleanor that he focused his activities in particular on Eleanor's son Richard. In 1187, he invested him with the cross and was regularly in Richard's entourage until the king's departure for Jerusalem in 1190.[45] In this period the archbishop and the king settled some questions concerning rights in the Touraine that had caused difficulties between the counts of Anjou and the archbishops of Tours for many years.[46] In 1196, Bartholomew stood as one of Richard's sureties in the treaty of Louviers concluded with Philip II.[47] And three years later he won his reward. Unlike his father, Richard I had not supported the claims of Dol. Without Angevin diplomatic backing Dol had little chance to win its case at the papal court. In 1199, Innocent III finally decided the case in favour of Tours.[48] In the same year, Philip II offered to give up his patronage over the see of Tours to Richard I as part of another treaty between the two rulers.[49] Due to Richard's death, the treaty was never ratified,[50] but it demonstrated that Philip saw little chance of effectively controlling the archbishopric. On the other hand, he may well have thought that Richard would gain little by becoming the official patron, since so far, despite being the overlord of the

---

[44] *Torigny*, p. 310; Jaffé, II, pp. 493, 536; supra, p. 149. Cardinal Ralph Nereth, a close associate of Roland, and a former canon at Dol, was probably Roland's most eminent supporter at the papal court. He died before August 1190, perhaps in 1189, see ibid. Roland's successor at Dol was Henry fitz Harding, a former dean of Mortain and treasurer of Henry II. Henry fitz Harding was set to continue Roland's struggle, but having arrived at Rome, where he hoped to receive consecration, he and his companions died during a local epidemic, *Howden*, II, p. 353. For Henry fitz Harding, see *Episcopal Acta XI. Exeter 1046–1184*, ed. Barlow, p. xl; B. Patterson, 'Robert Fitz Harding of Bristol: Profile of an Early Angevin Burgess-Baron Patrician and his Family's Urban Involvement', *Haskins Society Journal*, I (1989), 109–22.

[45] *Diceto*, II, p. 50; *Gesta regis*, II, pp. 30, 111; *Howden*, III, p. 36; *Itinerary*, ed. Landon, pp. 24–6, 30, 36.
[46] *Cartulaire de l'archevêché*, ed. de Grandmaison, I, no. 80.
[47] *Recueil des actes de Philippe Auguste*, ed. Delaborde et al., II, no. 517. Richard acquitted Bartholomew shortly afterwards from his obligation as surety, *Diceto*, II, p. 139.
[48] *Register Innocenz' III.*, II, no. 79 (82) [= Potthast, I, no. 726].   [49] *Howden*, IV, pp. 80–1.
[50] Gillingham, *Richard I*, p. 322.

Touraine, the Angevins had not been able to control the elections or policies of Tours' archbishops.

Bartholomew's advanced age and poor health certainly contributed to his inactivity during the last years of his pontificate, when Philip II Augustus took possession of Normandy and Greater Anjou. On the whole the archbishop pursued a policy of independence from either side. Always looking for the preservation of the prerogatives of his church and peace in the region, he used his contacts with the rival houses only when attempting to secure the prosperity of those to whom he owed his position, the cathedral chapter of Tours and the local aristocracy.

Weakened by recurrent fever attacks, Bartholomew died in late 1206. His successor was Geoffrey du Lude, archdeacon of Paris,[51] who may have owed his promotion to Philip II.[52] But Geoffrey was not a stranger to the Touraine. In his youth he had held benefices from St Martin of Tours. He also had excellent connections with Hamelin, bishop of Le Mans and former master of the schools at St Martin. Hamelin was to found an anniversary for Geoffrey in the church of Le Mans, and a former cleric of Geoffrey, Simon, became canon at Le Mans.[53] Geoffrey's closeness to Hamelin, who seems to have supported Duke Arthur's cause between 1199 and 1202, and his own appearance in Paris from around 1202,[54] which suggests some sort of connections with the Capetian backing for Arthur, make it conceivable that he had belonged to Arthur's entourage. Once Philip II had driven King John out of Greater Anjou, he and his advisors aspired to control the archiepiscopal see of Tours.[55] Thus Geoffrey seemed

---

[51] Elected in 1206, Geoffrey was consecrated on 21 January 1207, 'Chronicon Turonense magnum', in *Recueil de chroniques de Touraine*, ed. Salmon, pp. 64–161, p. 150; 'Annales Sancti Albini', in *Recueil d'annales*, ed. Halphen, p. 23.

[52] The author of the chronicle of Auxerre numbered Geoffrey among the men who owed their promotion to bishoprics to Odo, bishop of Paris. Odo probably did not intervene personally each time with the respective chapters, but used other ways to promote the interests of members of the chapter of Paris. Odo was a cousin of Philip II. Philip, it is true, fell out with Odo in 1200, because the Parisian bishop obeyed the papal interdict, but shortly afterwards they were reconciled and nearly all of the promotions supposedly due to Odo's influence took place after 1206, 'Ex chronologia Roberti Altissiodorensis', in *RHF*, XVIII, pp. 247–90, p. 275; Baldwin, *Philip*, pp. 179, 438–9.

[53] *Nécrologe-obituaire de la cathédrale du Mans*, ed. Busson and Ledru, p. 88. P. Piolin, *Histoire de l'église du Mans* (6 vols., Le Mans, 1851–63), IV, p. 230, states that Geoffrey had been canon at Le Mans, but this remains unproven.

[54] *Cartulaire de l'église Notre-Dame de Paris*, ed. M. Guérard (Collection des cartulaires de France VII) (4 vols., Paris, 1850), I, pp. 84–5, no. 83; dates from 1202, where a Geoffrey appears among the canons of Paris. In a charter dating from 1204 Geoffrey appears as archdeacon, ibid., p. 133, no. 153.

[55] Philip II's eagerness to get in control of Touraine is shown by his charter to William des Roches in 1206. He granted William Anjou and Maine, but retained Touraine, *Recueil des actes de Philippe Auguste*, ed. Delaborde et al., III, no. 963; Baldwin, *Philip*, p. 235 and n. 67.

Table 4 *Archbishop Bartholomew of Tours and the family of Fréteval-Faye (a)*

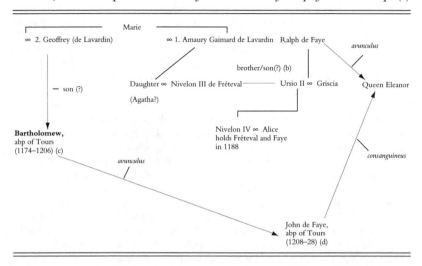

(a) In general, see Barthélemy, *Société*, pp. 568, 576, 771–2; N. Vincent, 'King Henry and the Poitevins', in Aurell (ed.), *La cour Plantagenêt (1154–1204)*, pp. 103–35, pp. 122–3 and p. 123 n. 115.

(b) According to Barthélemy, *Société*, p. 567, Ursio II was Nivelon III's brother. A. Livingstone, 'Kith and Kin: Kinship and Family Structure of the Nobility of Eleventh- and Twelfth-Century Blois-Chartres', *French Historical Studies*, 20 (1997), 419–58, 426, however, states that Ursio II was Nivelon III's son of Nivelon's second wife Alice. Barthélemy's hypothesis is possible, but it should be noted that Ursio II never figured in any charters of Nivelon III's father Ursio I. In 1139, Ursio I, his sons Nivelon (*primogenitus*), Hamelin, Philip, Reginald, and Fulcher, his daughters Beatrice and Hersendis, and Nivelon's wife Agatha made a concession to the cathedral church of Chartres, *Cartulaire de Notre-Dame de Chartres*, ed. E. de Lépinois and L. Merlet (Société archéologique d'Eure-et-Loire) (3 vols., Chartres 1862–5), I, no. 51. Since the family members made this concession at different places and times, it cannot be argued that Ursio II's name did not figure among them, because he was elsewhere at the time of the transaction. Similarly, when between 1141 and 1145, Ursio I confirmed to the abbey of Tiron its possessions in his lands, his sons Nivelon, Hamelin, Reginald, Fulcher, and Philip, and his daughter Hersendis agreed to this confirmation at different times and places, *Cartulaire de l'abbaye de la Sainte-Trinité de Tiron*, ed. L. Merlet (Société archéologique d'Eure-et-Loire) (2 vols., Chartres, 1883), no. 267. In 1146, Ursio I, gravely ill and fearing death, rendered some lands to the abbey of Tiron, and his sons Nivelon and Hamelin agreed not to make any claims to those lands in the future, ibid., II, no. 290. Ursio I died in 1149, *Cartulaire de Notre-Dame de Chartres*, ed. de Lépinois and Merlet, no. 51 n. 2. If Ursio II was Ursio I's son, his absence from these charters could be explained by either very young age or by a date of birth sometime between 1146 and 1149. In either case, both Ursio II and his son Nivelon IV became fathers at a very young age, for in 1186, Ursio, his wife Griscia, their son Nivelon and his wife Alice, and Nivelon's sons Ursiolus and Bernard appear in a charter for Marmoutier,

Note for table 4 (cont.)

Paris, BNF Lat. 5441 (cartulary, abbey of Marmoutier), part 2, p. 182. In 1188, Nivelon IV surrendered his son together with sons of other kinsmen as hostages to Henry II, *Gesta regis*, II, p. 49. Nivelon III had married a daughter (Agatha?) of Marie and Amaury Gaimard de Lavardin, 'Gesta Ambaziensium dominorum', in *Chroniques des comtes d'Anjou et des seigneurs d'Amboise*, ed. Halphen and Poupardin, pp. 74–132, p. 76. If Nivelon III and Ursio II were brothers, and if Archbishop John de Faye was a son of Ursio II and Griscia – an hypothesis for which there is no corroborative evidence – Archbishop Bartholomew was John de Faye's half-uncle. Livingstone's hypothesis is untenable. It is based on an undated charter issued by a Nivelon de Meslay in favour of the abbey of Tiron showing Nivelon's wife Alice and his sons Ursio (*primogenitus*), Hugh, and Geoffrey, and his daughters Margaret and Alice to have given their consent to the concession, *Cartulaire de l'abbaye de la Sainte-Trinité de Tiron*, ed. Merlet, no. 330. Lucien Merlet dated this charter *c.* 1183, while Livingstone attributed it to before 1177, 'Kith and Kin', 438. This Nivelon, however, is not Nivelon III de Fréteval, as assumed by Livingstone, but Nivelon IV de Fréteval, Ursio II's son, whose wife Alice and son Ursio III are attested elsewhere, e.g. *Archives de la Maison-Dieu de Châteaudun*, ed. A. de Belfort and L. Merlet (Paris, 1881), no. 121. A third hypothesis presents perhaps the most plausible solution: Ursio II was a son of Nivelon III and his wife Agatha. If so, and presuming that Agatha was Archbishop Bartholomew's half-sister, and presuming that John de Faye was Ursio II's son, Archbishop Bartholomew was John de Faye's step-granduncle.

(c) See Tables 2, 3, supra, pp. 175–6.

(d) For John and Bartholomew, see *Cartulaire de l'abbaye cistercienne de Fontaine-Daniel*, ed. A. Grosse-Duperon and E. Gouvrion (Mayenne, 1896), no. 48; 'Narratio', in *Recueil de chroniques de Touraine*, ed. Salmon, pp. 292–317, p. 298. For John and Eleanor, see Paris, BNF Collection Housseau, XVIII, fo. 304v; supra, p. 174.

an ideal choice. Familiar with the region and probably unfavourable to the Angevins, he seemed likely to be a reliable archbishop.

But Geoffrey died after only one and a half years in office[56] and the following election in 1208 witnessed the successful victory of the old local networks over a candidate with royal connections, Robert de Vitré. Robert belonged to a powerful Breton family, whose lordship was centred on the border of Brittany with Greater Anjou. The family had close contacts with the Breton ducal court, where Robert attested charters of Arthur's mother, Duchess Constance, between 1193 and 1198.[57] The Vitrés also supported Arthur's claim to Greater Anjou. In 1199, Robert and his elder brother, André de Vitré, joined Arthur's campaign. In June 1199, Arthur granted Robert the castle of Langeais about twenty kilometres west

---

[56] *Œuvres de Rigord et de Guillaume le Breton*, ed. Delaborde, I, p. 225.
[57] *The Charters of Duchess Constance of Brittany and her Family*, ed. J. Everard and M. Jones (Woodbridge, 1999), nos. C29/30, C40.

Table 5 *The archbishops of Tours: Engelbald, Bartholomew, and John de Faye*

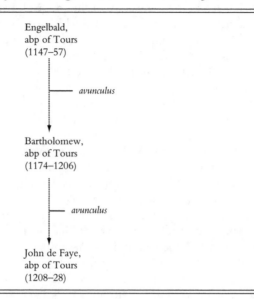

Engelbald,
abp of Tours
(1147–57)

———— *avunculus*

Bartholomew,
abp of Tours
(1174–1206)

———— *avunculus*

John de Faye,
abp of Tours
(1208–28)

of Tours. Two years later Robert acted as one of Arthur's proctors in the affair of Dol. Finally he was among the prisoners King John captured at Mirebeau. He was released from captivity in December 1202.[58] During the late 1190s, Robert became canon at Le Mans and later canon at the cathedral church of St Maurice, Tours.[59] His and his family's support of Arthur's case brought him into contact with Philip II's entourage. Doubtless due to this connection, he received the office of prechanter in the cathedral chapter of Paris around 1197/8.[60] Thus in 1208, Robert was certainly the candidate of those within the chapter and the royal entourage wishing to continue and to strengthen the links between Tours and Paris.

His opponent was the dean of the chapter, John de Faye. The fact that John was a *consanguineus* of Queen Eleanor may have rendered him suspect in the eyes of his pro-Capetian adversaries.[61] But decisive for

---

[58] For Robert's attestations of Arthur's charters, the grant of the castle of Langais, which he surrendered to Philip II in 1206, receiving lands in Normandy in recompense, and his appointment as proctor, see *Charters of Duchess Constance*, ed. Everard and Jones, nos. A9–11, A14, A16, A18. For his career in general, see ibid., pp. 199–200, and B. de Broussillon, *Robert de Vitré, chanoine de Saint-Julien du Mans et chantre de Notre-Dame de Paris (1197–1208)* (Le Mans, 1903).

[59] *Nécrologe-obituaire de la cathédrale du Mans*, ed. Busson and Ledru, p. 271; *Liber albus*, ed. Lottin, no. 9; *Martyrologe-obituaire de l'église métropolitaine de Tours*, ed. Bourasse, p. 60.

[60] De Broussillon, *Robert de Vitré*, pp. 7–8.   [61] See supra, p. 174 n. 22.

John's election was the support he received from within the chapter. John's place in the genealogy of the Fréteval–Faye family, and hence his exact degree of relationship to Archbishop Bartholomew, is not quite clear.[62] It is significant, however, that he considered Bartholomew as his *avunculus*;[63] thus he allocated himself a place very close to the archbishop.[64] When the electoral contest between Robert de Vitré and John de Faye was brought to the papal court, Innocent III decided in favour of John, reasoning that his party had by far the greater authority and number.[65] It is certainly not too far-fetched to suggest that Bartholomew's men within the chapter supported John's candidature. Who they were cannot be discovered. With the disappearance of witness lists from archiepiscopal charters after about 1206, the members of the cathedral chapter remain largely anonymous for the first decades of the thirteenth century. Nonetheless, some clues are available. Apart from John de Faye himself, who had been archdeacon before becoming dean of the chapter, Archbishop Bartholomew recruited his *consanguineus* Geoffrey de Plessis, who became chancellor and archdeacon and whose activities can still be traced after 1208.[66] Other men from the orbit of the counts of Vendôme, who joined the chapter during Bartholomew's tenure, may have been Peter de Vendôme,[67] who may still have been alive in 1208, and Archembaud de Vendôme, whose name was typical of the family of the prévôts of Vendôme, close allies of the counts.[68] In 1207 and 1211, Archembaud appeared as archpriest of Tours,[69] an office which was in

---

[62] Table 4, p. 181.   [63] See supra, p. 174 n. 22.

[64] He may have been identical with John, Bartholomew's *notarius*, who witnessed a charter of Archbishop Bartholomew in 1182, Paris, BNF Collection Housseau, v, no. 1958.

[65] 'Innocentii Romani pontificis regestorum sive epistolarum', in *PL*, ccxv, cols. 1465–6, no. 149 [= Potthast, I, no. 3505]. Innocent III's decision may also have been influenced by the fact that Robert fell ill when he was in Rome defending his case, 'Chronicon Turonense magnum', in *Recueil de chroniques de Touraine*, ed. Salmon, p. 151.

[66] In 1197, Bartholomew named him his *consanguineus* in a charter confirming a grant made by Geoffrey's parents, Gervase and Denise, to the abbey of Beaumont-les-Tours, Paris, BNF Collection Housseau, v, no. 2098. In the same year he is recorded to have been chancellor of Tours, ibid., no. 2070 bis. In 1202, he witnessed charters of Bartholomew as archdeacon of Tours, ibid., vi, no. 2164, xviii, fo. 281r. In 1211, he acted, together with Archembaud de Vendôme, archpriest of Tours, and Arnaud de *Metula* (Melle?), canon of Tours, as papal judge delegate in a case concerning the abbey of Fontevraud, Paris, BNF Lat. 5480 (cartulary, abbey of Fontevraud), part 1, p. 42. In 1192, John also held a canonry at Le Mans, *Enquête de 1245 relative aux droits du chapitre Saint Julien du Mans*, ed. Chapée et al., pp. lxix–lxx; *Cartulaire de l'évêché du Mans (965–1786)*, ed. B. de Broussillon (Archives historiques du Maine ix) (Le Mans, 1908), no. 1000.

[67] For Peter as canon, see for instance, *Cartulaire de l'abbaye de Saint-Aubin d'Angers*, ed. B. de Broussillon (Documents historiques sur l'Anjou i–iii) (3 vols., Paris, 1903), ii, no. 559. The possibility remains that Peter was related to the counts of Vendôme, even though Peter is not a typical name of the family in the twelfth century, Barthélemy, *Société*, p. 799.

[68] Barthélemy, *Société*, pp. 720–1, 775–6.

[69] For 1207, see the note in Paris, BNF Collection Housseau, xviii, fo. 281r. For 1211, see supra, n. 66.

the gift of the archdeacon of Tours,[70] then Geoffrey de Plessis. Philip, archdeacon of Outre-Loire, appears in 1205 and 1212.[71] Also canons like Master Arnaud de *Metula* (Melle?), Andrew de Chanceaux, and Master Richard, as well as the archpriest of Outre-Loire, Philip, owed their positions to Bartholomew and can be traced during John's pontificate. In several other cases it is highly probably that canons appointed under Bartholomew and appearing in his entourage until his death in late 1206 were still alive in 1208.[72] Some of these men were closer to Bartholomew than others, and not all of them necessarily favoured John. But as Innocent III's decision suggests, most of them did, and thus Bartholomew's efforts to continue and to renew the network of loyalties crucial to his own election paid off in the end.

John was in office for nearly twenty years until his death in 1228. According to the chronicler William, abbot of Andres, the canons then chose Peter de Collemezzo, later archbishop of Rouen, as John's successor. There is, however, no corroborating evidence for this, and William, who was writing at a considerable distance from Tours, might have been mistaken when mentioning in passing that Peter had refused to accept his election at Tours in the same way as he refused to accept his election at Thérouanne in 1229, the event which was the principal subject of this particular paragraph in William's chronicle.[73] In any case, John's successor in the see of Tours was Juhel de Mathefelon. Juhel was related to the lords of Mathefelon, north of Angers.[74] Before his elevation to the metropolitan see,

[70] D(om) Beaunier and J.-M. Besse, *Abbayes et prieurés de l'ancienne France. VIII. Province ecclésiastique de Tours* (Archives de France monastique xix) (Paris, 1920), p. 9.
[71] *Cartulaire de l'archevêché*, ed. de Grandmaison, II, no. 73 (1205); Paris, BNF Collection Housseau, VI, no. 2345 (he, together with Philip, archpriest of Outre-Loire, issues a charter[1212]).
[72] For Arnaud de *Metula*, see *Cartulaire de l'archevêché*, ed. de Grandmaison, II, no. 309 (1205) and supra, p. 184 n. 66 (1211); for Andrew de Chanceaux, see *Cartulaire de l'archevêché*, ed. de Grandmaison, I, no. 128 (1198), and *Chartes de Saint-Julien de Tours*, ed. Denis, I, no. 179 (1221); for biographical details on Andrew and his clan, see N. Vincent, 'Who's Who in Magna Carta Clause 50', in M. Aurell (ed.), *Le médiéviste et la monographie familiale: sources, méthodes et problématiques* (Histoires de familles. La parenté au Moyen Age) (Turnhout, 2004), pp. 235–61, pp. 240–51; for Master Richard, see *Cartulaire de l'archevêché*, ed. de Grandmaison, II, no. 309 (1205), and *Cartulaires du Bas-Poitou (département de la Vendée)*, ed. P. Marchegay (Les Roches-Baritaud, 1877), pp. 73–4, no. 5 (1220); for Archpriest Philip, see Paris, BNF Collection Housseau, XVIII, fo. 281r (he witnesses a charter of Archbishop Bartholomew [1206]) and ibid., VI, no. 2345 (he, together with Philip, archdeacon of Outre-Loire, issues a charter [1212]). In 1206, for example, Kalo, archdeacon of Outre-Vienne, appeared as witness of a charter of Archbishop Bartholomew. Other canons who regularly witnessed Archbishop Bartholomew's charters in his last years include Master Nicholas de Candé, Master William Socrates, Thomas de Sablé, Nicholas de Couléon, William Mathei, and Baldwin, Paris, BNF Collection Housseau, VI, no. 2164 (1202), XVIII, fo. 281r (1206); *Cartulaire de l'archevêché*, ed. de Grandmaison, I, nos. 72 (1202), 73 (1205), II, nos. 309 (1205), 311 (1205).
[73] 'Willelmo chronica Andrensis', in *MGH, scriptores*, XXIV, ed. Waitz et al., p. 768 and cf. supra, pp. 98–9.
[74] Boussard, *Le comté d'Anjou*, pp. 26–7; D. Pichot, *Le Bas-Maine du Xe au XIIIe siècle: étude d'une société* (La Mayenne: archéologie, histoire – supplément VII) (Laval, 1995), p. 180; A. Angot, *Généalogies*

he had been canon, master of the schools, and dean of the cathedral chapter of Le Mans,[75] but it is not known whether he belonged to the same circle as Robert de Vitré. Why he was elected cannot be determined. He remained in office until his translation to the see of Rheims in 1245.[76]

In 1174, the canons had silently disregarded the suffragans in the electoral process. In 1228, they openly denied them any right to participate in the election: the bishop-elect of St Brieuc, William, who was also a canon of the cathedral chapter of Tours, was asked to give a written and sealed declaration that he participated in the election not in his capacity as bishop-elect of St Brieuc, but as a canon of the chapter.[77] At Tours, the formation of the cathedral chapter as exclusive electoral body was completed.

The archiepiscopal elections at Tours have demonstrated first and foremost the existence of a network of canons related to local noble families. Situated between the power blocks of the counts of Anjou, the counts of Blois, and the kings of France, the archbishopric of Tours escaped the dominance of any of these houses. This situation gave the local aristocrats represented in the chapter the possibility of electing whom they wanted. A clear indication of this was the attempt of the chapter in 1174 to exclude the suffragan bishops, and thus external influence, from the elections. The archbishops also pursued a policy of strengthening these local networks and their own autonomy as players on the political stage. Both Angevin and Capetian politics affected elections, as was evident between 1174 and 1208, but, with the exception of 1206, the local network within the chapter seems to have prevailed over external influences, at least until 1228.

LE MANS

The driving forces in the election of William de Passavant as bishop of Le Mans in 1145 are unknown, but his family connections may have played a crucial role. William's father, also named William, held an important stronghold which defended Anjou's southern frontier along the road to

féodales mayennaises du XIe au XIIIe siècle (Laval, 1942), pp. 435–92, 716. It must be noted, however, that Angot's reconstruction of Juhel's place within the family of Mathfelon as son of Theobald (II) de Mathfelon is purely conjectural.

[75] *Honorii III Romani pontificis opera omnia*, ed. Horoy, II, epistolae lib. II, no. 319 [= Potthast, I, no. 5857]; *Liber albus*, ed. Lottin, nos. 69, 660, and *GC*, XIV, cols. 425–6.

[76] *Les registres d'Innocent IV*, ed. E. Berger (Bibliothèque des écoles françaises d'Athènes et de Rome 2nd sér.I) (4 vols., Paris, 1884–1911), I, nos. 1150–4.

[77] Paris, BNF Collection Housseau, XIX, fos. 73r–74r: note on the electoral procedure based *inter alia* on William's sealed letter dating from 1228 and preserved in the 'chartrier de cette Eglise [Tours]', ibid., fo. 73r.

Saintes.[78] Two of William's relatives held important ecclesiastical posts. His *avunculus*, William, had been cellarer of St Martin of Tours before becoming bishop of Saintes (*c.* 1127 – *c.* 1140). William de Passavant's *consobrinus*, Renaud de Martigné, was bishop of Angers from 1102, before becoming archbishop of Rheims in 1124.[79] William apparently belonged to Renaud's entourage. He followed him to Rheims, where he became archdeacon and acquired the reputation of being learned and wise.[80]

Over forty years later, in January 1187, towards the end of the reign of Henry II, William de Passavant died and the chapter elected one of their members, Chanter Reginald Clarel.[81] From his earliest youth, Reginald had been nourished and educated at the cathedral of St Julien of Le Mans, where he had fulfilled the offices of an archpriest and chanter.[82] By the time of his election to the see, at least three further members of the chapter belonged to his family. They were his brothers Philip, Amaury, and Peter, with the latter succeeding Reginald as chanter. All four Clarels may have belonged to William de Passavant's entourage.[83] In any case Reginald's election must be considered as the product of clever family politics within a cathedral chapter.

---

[78] *Nécrologe-obituaire de la cathédrale du Mans*, ed. Busson and Ledru, p. 22; *Actus pontificum Cenomannis in urbe degentium*, ed. G. Busson and A. Ledru (Archives historiques du Maine II) (Le Mans, 1902), p. 455 n. 2; B. Bachrach, 'King Henry II and the Angevin Claims to the Saintonge', *Medieval Prosopography*, 6 (1985), 23–45, 25.

[79] William de Passavant referred to 'Guillelmus Sanctoniensis avunculus meus olim cellerarius Beati Martini Turonensis' in a charter for St Martin in 1177, Tours, AD Indre-et-Loire G 364 (charters concerning St Martin of Tours); *GC*, XIV, col. 383; for Renaud de Martigné, see *Liber albus*, ed. Lottin, no. 123. I would like to thank the director of the Archives Départementales d'Indre-et-Loire, Luc Forlivesi, for having sent me a transcript of William de Passavant's charter preserved in G 364.

[80] *Actus*, ed. Busson and Ledru, pp. 455–71, esp. pp. 455–6; Pacaut, *Elections*, p. 125; Chartrou, *L'Anjou*, p. 181; and *GC*, XIV, col. 384.

[81] *Actus*, ed. Busson and Ledru, pp. 455 n. 2, 472 and n. 2; *Cartulaire de l'hôpital Saint-Jean d'Angers*, ed. C. Port (Angers, 1870), no. 8.

[82] *Nécrologe-obituaire de la cathédrale du Mans*, ed. Busson and Ledru, pp. 190–1.

[83] The evidence suggests that all four Clarels became members of the chapter during William de Passavant's time in office, *Cartulaire Manceau de Marmoutier*, ed. Laurain, II, no. 6, pp. 171–2; *Cartulaire des abbayes de Saint-Pierre de la Couture et de Saint-Pierre de Solesmes*, ed. by the Benedictin monks of Solesmes (Le Mans, 1881), no. 114. There is no definite proof that Peter was already canon of Le Mans at the time of the election. But the fact that he followed his brother as chanter in 1187 suggests that he had become a member of the chapter before 1187; for their relationship, see *Nécrologe-obituaire de la cathédrale du Mans*, ed. Busson and Ledru, p. 62, for his office, *Liber controversarium Sancti Vincentii Cenomannensis*, ed. Chédeville, no. 67. There were another five Clarels in the chapter of Le Mans up to the mid-thirteenth century: Matthew, John, Amaury (II), Reginald (II), and another Reginald (III). The brothers Reginald (II) and Amaury (II) were *nepotes* of Reginald (I), Peter, and Amaury (I), and became members of the chapters in the early thirteenth century at the latest, *Nécrologe-obituaire de la cathédrale du Mans*, ed. Busson and Ledru, pp. 62–3; *Cartulaire de l'évêché du Mans (965–1786)*, ed. de Broussillon, no. 1030; *Enquête de 1245 relative aux droits du chapitre Saint Julien du Mans*, ed. Chapée et al., p. 54. Reginald (II) had a *nepos*, Reginald (III), canon of Le Mans before 1266, *Nécrologe-obituaire de la cathédrale du Mans*, ed. Busson and Ledru, p. 53; *Enquête de 1245 relative aux droits du chapitre Saint Julien du Mans*, ed. Chapée

Map 10 The diocese of Le Mans

However, Reginald died fairly soon after his election. In 1190, his successor Hamelin, master of the schools at St Martin of Tours, was elected and shortly afterwards consecrated by Pope Celestine III. Hamelin was already around seventy years old, and the chapter may have regarded him

et al., p. 28 n. 1. The case of Amaury (II) demonstrates the work of a family network within a chapter. Nourished in the chapter since he had been a little boy he later received the archdeaconry of Sablé before he became chanter of Le Mans, just like his *avunculi* Reginald and Peter, *Nécrologe-obituaire de la cathédrale du Mans*, ed. Busson and Ledru, pp. 63, 137–8. John Clarel was a canon at Le Mans in 1213, but the date of his entry is unknown. He was the *avunculus* of either Reginald (II) or Reginald (III), Clarel, *Nécrologe-obituaire de la cathédrale du Mans*, ed. Busson and Ledru, p. 233; *Cartulaire de l'évêché du Mans (965–1786)*, ed. de Broussillon, no. 1030. Matthew Clarel was a canon at Le Mans, but his relationship to the other Clarels and his time in office are unknown, *Nécrologe-obituaire de la cathédrale du Mans*, ed. Busson and Ledru, p. 342.

as a stopgap.[84] Before his election, he had spent his life at St Martin, where from his boyhood onwards he had enjoyed the patronage of his *patruus* Odo, dean of St Martin from 1109/11 to 1143/4, and later of his brother Philip, dean of St Martin from 1176 to 1191.[85] Bishop William de Passavant had personal connections with St Martin, where his *avunculus* William, once cellarer of St Martin, had left him property, but whether these links had anything to do with Hamelin's election cannot be established.[86]

If the chapter of Le Mans had elected Hamelin as a temporary solution, Richard I may have had similar thoughts about the seventy-year-old candidate. But Hamelin was not to die soon. When he passed away shortly before his one hundredth birthday, in 1218, he had not only outlived Richard by nearly twenty years but also his own successor in the see of Le Mans, Nicholas, who died in 1216.[87] Hamelin had resigned his office in 1214[88] and had been succeeded by the dean of the chapter Nicholas. Before his own confirmation, Nicholas had confirmed the election of Hugh de La Ferté, canon of Le Mans, as the new dean.[89]

There is no concrete evidence on Nicholas' election. But forces within the chapter may have worked for Hamelin's abdication. After several months of preparation, King John had appeared at La Rochelle in February 1214, to open his last big offensive to win back Greater Anjou

---

[84] For his office at St Martin, see *Chartes de Saint-Julien de Tours*, ed. Denis, I, no. 120. According to the *Actus*, ed. Busson and Ledru, p. 473, Hamelin's election took place in December 1190. However, *Gesta regis*, II, p. 114, reports that while Richard I was in Italy, the king became very upset with the cardinal-bishop of Ostia, because the papal court had demanded enormous sums for certain services, among which was Hamelin's consecration. According to Richard's itinerary this must have happened in August 1190, *Itinerary*, ed. Landon, p. 39. This chronological problem remains unsolved.

[85] *Chartes de Saint-Julien de Tours*, ed. Denis, I, no. 120; *Necrologium beatissimi Martini Turonensis, 804–1495, et obituarium Majoris Monasterii*, ed. P. Nobilleau (Tours, 1875), pp. 29–30n, where Hamelin's charter concerning his foundation of anniversaries for Odo and Philip at St Martin of Tours is printed (= Paris, BNF Collection Baluze, IXXXIV, fo. 129r). For Odo and Philip, Griffiths, 'St Martin', 115–21. Neither Odo nor Philip had close links with the Capetian court. They had their power base in the Touraine and had probably been the chapter's local candidates. On the grounds that the name Hamelin occurred in the family of the lords of Langeais, Quentin Griffiths suggests that Odo and his nephews were related to that family, ibid., 119–20 n. 10, 121 n. 14. It should be noted, however, that Hamelin was rather a common name in Greater Anjou.

[86] Cellarer William granted to St Martin houses in the garden of its cloister and a vineyard on the condition that St Martin was to receive this property only after the death of his *nepotes* Boemund, William Baurraud, and William de Passavant. In 1177, Bishop William, who had outlived Boemund and William Barraud, resigned to St Martin this property and a house which Boemund had granted him for life, Tours, AD Indre-et-Loire G 364 (charters concerning St Martin of Tours).

[87] *Actus*, ed. Busson and Ledru, pp. 473, 483.

[88] Innocent III insisted on the need for papal permission to resign from the episcopal office. He did not grant such permissions easily, Cheney, *Innocent III*, pp. 78–9. Unfortunately there is no evidence on the technical circumstances of Hamelin's resignation.

[89] *Liber albus*, ed. Lottin, no. 41.

and Normandy from the French king. By 17 June, he had entered Angers, which William des Roches had abandoned because its defensive system was still suffering from damage inflicted in previous campaigns.[90] Nicholas, during his time as dean of Le Mans since 1180, had served King Richard as an envoy.[91] Nicholas' successor as dean, Hugh de La Ferté, had already played an important part in the election at Angers in 1200–2. Supported by John's money, Hugh had worked hard for John's candidate, William de Beaumont.[92] Hugh's reward was the post of treasurer at Angers.[93] In 1214, it is uncertain whether John approached them or other members of the chapter to initiate Hamelin's abdication, but it seems clear that his military activities in 1213–14 were an important, perhaps decisive, factor in securing it. Watching the king's progress, Nicholas and Hugh saw their chance of personal advancement. They had been witnesses to John's serious conflict with Hamelin in 1200, when, at the time of the king's troubled succession in Greater Anjou, John had accused the bishop as 'persone nostre et regni persecutor publicus'.[94] In his efforts to defend and to strengthen the position of the chapter, Nicholas had clashed more than once with Hamelin.[95]

---

[90] Baldwin, *Philip*, pp. 212–13.
[91] *Giraldi Cambrensis opera*, ed. Brewer, IV, p. 381. Dean Nicholas was at Richard's court in Canterbury in September 1189 and in Normandy in March 1190, *Itinerary*, ed. Landon, p. 17. He may have been identical with the royal cleric Nicholas who married Richard I and Berengaria at Limassol in May 1191, *Howden*, III, p. 110; *Gesta regis*, II, 167; cf. *Itinerary*, ed. Landon, p. 49. In 1190, Dean Nicholas witnessed a charter issued by Archbishop Bartholomew at Tours that dealt with matters concerning a crusader, *Cartulaire de Cormery précédé de l'histoire de l'abbaye et de la ville de Cormery*, ed. J.-J. Bourasse (Mémoires de la société archéologique de Touraine XII) (Tours, 1861), no. 73. Further circumstantial evidence is a charter of Bishop Hamelin issued in 1192 that records Nicholas as being absent, *Cartulaire de l'évêché du Mans (965–1786)*, ed. de Broussillon, no. 1000. *GC*, XIV, cols. 423–4, names him Nicholas Burel and it is tempting to identify the dean of Le Mans with a member of the Burel family close to Henry II's court. *GC* refers to a charter 'e Savigneii chartario' as its source. This charter must be identified with Paris, Archives Nationales L 974 (charters concerning the abbey of Savigny), no. 917, a charter in the name of William de Passavant, bishop of Le Mans, witnessed among others by Dean Nicholas Burel. This charter, however, is a forgery, to which a true seal had been attached, note by L. Delisle, Paris, BNF N. A. Lat. 1023 (charters concerning the abbey of Savigny), p. 14. Its witness list is not trustworthy. Apart from Nicholas none of the witnesses can be traced in Bishop William's charters. For example, one witness is named *Ricardus precantor*. Yet there never was a prechanter of Le Mans named Richard during Nicholas' time in office. I would like to thank Prof. Emmanuel Poulle for having discussed this charter with me.
[92] See infra, p. 204.
[93] Between 1202 and 1210 Hugh witnessed as the treasurer a charter of Bishop William of Angers, AD Maine-et-Loire H 1814 (charter concerning abbey of St Serge of Angers).
[94] *Rot. chart.*, p. 31b; cf. ibid., p. 58a; *Rotuli Normanniae*, ed. Hardy, p. 26.
[95] Cf. *Liber albus*, ed. Lottin, nos. 100–2, 212; *Cartulaire du chapitre royal de Saint-Pierre-de-la-Cour du Mans*, ed. S. Menjot d'Elbenne and L.-J. Denis (Archives historiques du Maine IV) (Le Mans, 1907), no. 32. The chapter gained such an independence from the bishop that at the beginning of the thirteenth century Guy de Laval, whose possessions had been placed under interdict by the chapter, complained to Philip Augustus that while before they had had one bishop in the diocese of Le Mans they now had forty-five, *Enquête de 1245 relative aux droits du chapitre Saint Julien du Mans*, ed.

Perhaps he and Hugh reminded their colleagues in the chapter of these events and convinced them that a bishop more congenial to the Angevins would be a better solution than the ninety-six-year-old Hamelin.[96] Whereas John was certainly not unhappy with developments at Le Mans in 1214, Philip Augustus was too busy organising the defence of his kingdom on two fronts to get involved, provided the chapter of Le Mans and its elect respected his prerogatives.

After Nicholas' election, the chapter asked the Capetian to invest him with the *regalia*. Philip reacted as he had done at Rouen in 1207. That is he ordered an enquiry into the *regalia* at Le Mans. In a writ issued at Péronne in June 1214, Philip charged William des Roches and Guy d'Athée to investigate whether Bishop Hamelin had ever sworn fealty to Henry II, Richard I, or John. If he had done so, Nicholas should do the same to William and Guy as Philip's representatives, before receiving the *regalia*. If not, the elect was to receive them on the day of his confirmation.[97] William des Roches was much better informed than the king about the political situation in Greater Anjou and the circumstances of Nicholas' election. At a time when King John's position on the continent was growing in strength, William appears to have tried to delay the investiture of this old ally of the Angevins until the general political situation became more favourable for Philip. Together with Guy, he issued a writ to Nicholas stating that Nicholas would only receive the *regalia* if he returned seventeen pounds manceaux, which were known to be part of the *regalia*, to a certain Robert de *Longa Landa*.[98] Tactical manoeuvres like this, however, were soon to be obsolete. On 2 July 1214, John, believing himself to be outnumbered, fled from Anjou. On 27 July Philip Augustus defeated Otto IV's forces at Bouvines.[99] Philip was back in control,[100] and William had no reason to withhold the *regalia* any longer.

Chapée et al., p. 50. For a summary of the relationship between Hamelin and the chapter, see N. Ogé, 'Hamelin, évêque du Mans (1190–1214). Etude d'une administration épiscopale', *La Province du Maine 5th sér.*, 96 (1994), 233–49 and 347–61, 236–41.

[96] Juror William Megret reported that, in 1200, Nicholas and other members of the chapter had approached Hamelin asking him to concede them the right to exercise canonical jurisdiction, since his repeated absence made him unable to defend the chapter, *Enquête de 1245 relative aux droits du chapitre Saint Julien du Mans*, ed. Chapée et al., p. 137. The way in which they convinced Hamelin to abdicate may have been similar.

[97] *Recueil des actes de Philippe Auguste*, ed. Delaborde et al., III, no. 1337.

[98] *Liber albus*, ed. Lottin, no. 15; *Layettes*, ed. Teulet et al., V, no. 203.

[99] Baldwin, *Philip*, pp. 214–19.

[100] It is true the treaty of Chinon concluded between John and Philip in September 1214 made clear that Philip's authority south of the Loire was weak. But the subscriptions of Amaury de Craon and Juhel de Mayenne on Philip's document as well as the support of the leading Angevin baron, William des Roches, shows that Philip's position north of the Loire was secured, *Recueil des actes de Philippe Auguste*, ed. Delaborde et al., III, no. 1340; *Layettes*, ed. Teulet et al., I, no. 1083; Baldwin, *Philip*, p. 219.

Nicholas was in office only for about twenty months. According to the *Actus pontificum Cenomannis in urbe degentium*, the principal source for the history of the bishops of Le Mans, the chapter elected his successor, Maurice, on 24 March 1216, within four weeks of Nicholas' death.[101] Thomas de Cantimpré was to cite Maurice's election as an example of the choice of an ideal bishop. According to his account, a canon went to see a famous anchoress to ask her about the forthcoming election. The anchoress answered that Maurice, once archdeacon of Troyes, would become the new bishop. But she also told the canon not to speak about this until it happened. The day of the election came, and the chapter split into two parties. One party voted for the learned and rich dean, and the other for the noble and sensible provost. Neither party withdrew until the provost proposed to the dean that they both do so and look for a worthy and humble man instead. Having made this proposal, the provost named Maurice as a suitable candidate, whom he and his friends would support. The dean accepted, on condition that he would become the new bishop if Maurice refused the offer. Thus the provost sent two canons to Maurice to offer him the see. Contrary to the dean's hopes, Maurice accepted the offer.[102]

Entertaining as the story is, it poses some difficulties. There is no other evidence for a disputed election at Le Mans in 1216. If the *Actus* are accurate, then there were only four weeks between Nicholas' death and Maurice's election. If there was indeed a disputed election, it is hard to believe that the canons could have completed the process so quickly. Furthermore, an archdeacon of Troyes named Maurice cannot be traced.[103] The dispute between the dean and the provost of the chapter was probably a *topos* in Thomas de Cantimpré's work,[104] which would

---

[101] *Actus*, ed. Busson and Ledru, pp. 483–4; *GC*, XIV, col. 394.

[102] *Thomae Cantipratani S. Theol. Doctoris, ordinis praedicatorum, et episcopi suffraganei Cameracensi, Bonum universale de apibus*, ed. G. Colveneer (Douai, 1627), lib. I, cap. I, art. 4, pp. 5–8. For Thomas de Cantimpré's life and works, in particular his *Bonum universale de apibus*, see E. Berger, *Thomae Cantipratensis Bonum universale de apibus quod illustrandis saeculi decimi tertii moribus conferat* (Paris, 1895).

[103] There is no mention of a Maurice, archdeacon of Troyes, in *Collection des principaux cartulaires du diocèse de Troyes*, ed. C. Lalore (6 vols., Paris, 1875–82). This collection includes the cartulary of the cathedral chapter of Troyes. There is the possibility that *Trecensis* is a misspelling for *Trecorensis*, thus the Breton see of Tréguier. However, there is not enough source material to identify the dignitaries of the cathedral chapter of Tréguier in the twelfth and early thirteenth centuries, so the hypothesis remains unconfirmed. In light of this Thomas de Cantimpré's other information about Maurice's life must be treated with caution. There is no evidence confirming Cantimpré's statement that Maurice was brought up by Benedictine nuns and that later, having renounced his archdeaconry, he returned to them to supervise their conduct and to preach, *Thomae Cantipratani*, ed. Colveneer, lib. I, cap. I, art. 4, p. 6. Maurice was remembered for his austere lifestyle, *Actus*, ed. Busson and Ledru, p. 484, but the sources do not refer to him as a Benedictine monk pace, Grant, *Architecture*, p. 122.

[104] In one of the examples following the account of Maurice's election, Thomas de Cantimpré again reports an electoral dispute between a dean and a provost of a chapter, *Thomae Cantipratani*, ed. Colveneer, lib I, cap. 2, art. 3, pp. 11–12.

also explain the mention of a provost of the chapter of Le Mans, since this office seems never to have existed.

Despite these doubts about the accuracy of Thomas de Cantimpré's account, there may have been an element of truth to it. According to Thomas, it was the dean who lost out; Maurice's promotion may have been achieved at the expense of Hugh de La Ferté, dean of Le Mans, in 1216. In this case his election could be interpreted as a signal to Maine that the time of Angevin domination was over. But again it must be stressed that there is no hard evidence for this, or any other explanation for Maurice's becoming bishop of Le Mans in 1216. As bishop, Maurice proved to be an energetic administrator. In 1223, he and William, bishop of Angers, agreed with King Louis VIII on what probably had been local custom: in future, as soon as the bishop-elect of Le Mans/Angers had been confirmed by the archbishop, the king was to confer the *regalia* with his letter of confirmation. The bishop in turn should swear fidelity to the king within the next forty days. If he did not do so, the king had the right to withdraw the *regalia*. Maurice and William were also absolved from personal military service, and won an assurance that the bishops of Le Mans/Angers would not owe fidelity to the counts of Maine/Anjou should the counties be separated from the Capetian kingdom.[105] This was well in line with the latest regulations provided by canon law. The ruler did not participate in the election; instead he gave his consent only after the election had been held and confirmed.[106] Maurice, who also otherwise worked very aggressively for the rights of his see,[107] reformed the administrative structure of the diocese,[108] acted as papal judge delegate,[109] and made himself a name among his colleagues and at the papal court. This may have been the principal reason why, in 1230/1, the papal judges delegate charged to decide the disputed election at Rouen nominated him as new archbishop. The case went to the papal court, where Pope Gregory IX confirmed this decision in 1231.[110]

---

[105] *Layettes*, ed. Teulet, II, no. 1617; *Liber albus*, ed. Lottin, no. 13; *Registres de Philippe Auguste*, ed. Baldwin, carte, no. 95.

[106] See supra, pp. 31–6.

[107] *Honorii III Romani pontificis opera omnia*, ed. Horoy, III, epistolae lib. V, no. 440 [= Potthast, I, no. 6694].

[108] *Liber albus*, ed. Lottin, nos. 221, 232.

[109] *Honorii III Romani pontificis opera omnia*, ed. Horoy, II, epistolae lib. II, no. 319 [= Potthast, I, no. 5857], IV, epistolae lib. IX, no. 12 [= Potthast, I, no. 7301]; *Registres de Grégoire IX*, ed. Auvray, I, nos. 374, 375 [= Potthast, I, no. 8466], 381 [= Potthast, I, no. 8467]; 'Historia Sancti Florentii Salmurensis', in *Chroniques des églises d'Anjou*, ed. P. Marchegay and E. Mabille (Société de l'histoire de France) (Paris, 1869), pp. 217–328, p. 318.

[110] See supra, pp. 87–92.

After Maurice's translation, the chapter of Le Mans elected their dean, Geoffrey de Laval,[111] probably not related to the well-known house of Laval.[112] Asking Louis IX to give Geoffrey the *regalia* of Le Mans, Juhel de Mathefelon, Geoffrey's predecessor as dean of the chapter and since 1228 archbishop of Tours, informed the court that Geoffrey's election had been canonical.[113] Geoffrey received the *regalia* and stayed in office until his death in 1234.[114]

In the six elections at Le Mans between 1145 and 1231, the absence of either comital or royal interference is apparent. It seems that the effects of Gregorian reform on the one hand and the struggles for power in Maine on the other reduced the counts' influence over episcopal elections there. Thus the chapter preserved control throughout the period studied. They elected men from Greater Anjou – Maurice was possibly an exception – if not one of their members. It has been argued here that Bishop William de Passavant's personal connections, and his activities as patron during his long pontificate, had some impact on the two elections following his death, in that his successors, Reginald and Hamelin, may have been his friends. Yet, overall there is very little information on the driving forces behind the individual elections at Le Mans.

The absence of comital or royal influence at Le Mans is striking. In purely strategic-political terms Le Mans was an important diocese, since it formed a geographical link between Normandy and Anjou as well as between Normandy and Brittany. In its symbolic significance for the counts of Anjou, Le Mans increased in importance during the second half of the twelfth century. According to Robert de Torigny, Geoffrey Plantagenet was buried in the cathedral church of St Julien and thus the first person ever to be buried within the walls of the city of Le Mans.[115] Henry II, who had been born in Le Mans, made gifts to the cathedral in memory of his father's burial.[116] Therefore it would be difficult to argue that the see of Le Mans was less important for the counts of Anjou than the see of Angers, where they showed considerable

---

[111] *Nécrologe-obituaire de la cathédrale du Mans*, ed. Busson and Ledru, pp. 203–4.

[112] A. Ledru, *La cathédrale Saint-Julien du Mans, ses évêques, son architecture, son mobilier* (Mamers, 1900), p. 232; B. de Broussillon, *La Maison de Laval 1020–1605. Etude historique accompagnée du cartulaire de Laval et de Vitré* (5 vols., Paris, 1895–1903), I, pp. 95–6.

[113] *Layettes*, ed. Teulet et al., II, no. 2147. For Geoffrey's letter asking for the return of the *regalia*, see ibid., no. 2146.

[114] *Actus*, ed. Busson and Ledru, pp. 485–6.   [115] *Torigny*, p. 163.

[116] *Actus*, ed. Busson and Ledru p. 432; *Recueil des actes de Henri II*, ed. Delisle and Berger, I, nos. 70, 354; cf. L. Grant, 'Le patronage architectural d'Henri II et de son entourage', *Cahiers de civilisation médiévale*, 37 (1994), 73–84, esp. 74. For further gifts to Le Mans cathedral by Henry II, see N. Vincent, 'The Pilgrimages of the Angevin Kings of England 1154–1272', in C. Morris and P. Roberts (eds.), *Pilgrimage. The English Experience from Becket to Bunyan* (Cambridge, 2002), pp. 12–45, pp. 20–1, n. 32.

interest in elections.[117] Le Mans' relative neglect is perhaps to be explained by chronology. Only two vacancies at Le Mans occurred in the reigns of Henry II and his sons, who generally were very active in episcopal elections. The first occasion was in 1187, at a time when Henry II was busy defending his rule against Philip II.[118] Given that the chapter's candidate showed no signs of hostility towards Henry II, and that the canons may well have sought Henry's consent, he may not have seen the need to spend more energy on this election. The second occasion was in 1190. Here, the election took place either while Richard I was securing his succession to the throne, or after his departure for the crusade,[119] thus at a moment when an election at Le Mans was unlikely to be of more than secondary importance to him. Philip II did not attempt to place men of his entourage on the episcopal throne at Le Mans.

ANGERS

At Angers the counts early lost their immediate control over episcopal elections. In the first half of the twelfth century, the cathedral chapter established itself as the principal force in choosing the bishop.[120] In 1125, the canons elected Ulger. He had been taught at the cathedral school by the reformer Marbod, before becoming master of the schools and archdeacon of the cathedral church.[121] Ulger's successor, Norman de Doué, elected in 1149, was also the chapter's choice. Norman had been archdeacon of Outre-Loire at least since 1123, and thus was thoroughly familiar with the politics of Ulger and of Ulger's predecessor Renaud.[122] The efforts of both bishops were mainly directed towards the defence and increase of the cathedral church's rights. This they undertook without pointedly opposing the counts. Indeed Ulger defended the Empress Matilda's claims to the English throne at the papal court.[123] The fact that Norman was associated with Ulger and Renaud perhaps reduced any suspicions Geoffrey Plantagenet may have harboured towards a man whose family was causing him much trouble. Through his mother Griscia, Norman de Doué was related to the lords of Montreuil-Bellay and Montsoreau. These three families belonged to a group that formed an

---

[117] See infra, pp. 195–209.   [118] Warren, *Henry II*, pp. 612–17.

[119] For Richard's activities in 1190, see Gillingham, *Richard I*, pp. 123–39.

[120] Guillot, *Le comte d'Anjou*, I, pp. 262, 278–9.   [121] Chartrou, *L'Anjou*, p. 184.

[122] *Cartulaire noir de la cathédrale d'Angers*, ed. C. Urseau (Documents historiques sur l'Anjou V) (Angers, 1908), pp. xlvi–xlvii; *L'obituaire de la cathédrale d'Angers*, ed. C. Urseau (Angers, 1930), pp. 18–19; 'Annales Sancti Albini', in *Recueil d'annales*, ed. Halphen, pp. 11–12.

[123] Chartrou, *L'Anjou*, pp. 183–90; *Historia pontificalis*, ed. Chibnall, pp. 83–4. For the discussion whether this debate took place in 1136 or on the occasion of the Second Lateran Council or whether there was a debate on both occasions, see *The Letters of Peter the Venerable*, ed. Constable, II, pp. 252–6.

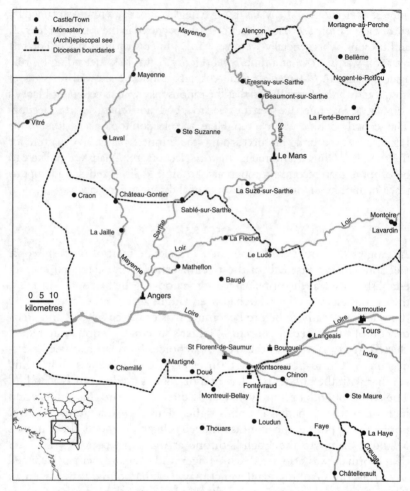

Map 11 The diocese of Angers

independent power block in southern Anjou.[124] The counts of Anjou had fought the lords of Doué several times in the first half of the twelfth century. The most recent of these campaigns was in 1147, only two years

[124] *Grand cartulaire de Fontevraud (Pancarta et cartularium abbatissae et ordinis Fontis Ebraudi)*, ed. J.-M. Bienvenu et al. (Archives historiques du Poitou LXIII–LXIV) (2 vols., Poitiers, 2000–5), I, nos. 225, 227; Chartrou, *L'Anjou*, p. 325, pièces justificatives no. 5; *Obituaire*, ed. Urseau, p. 42; *Cartulaire de l'abbaye de Saint-Laon de Thouars*, ed. H. Imbert (Niort, 1876), no. 37; Boussard, *Le comté d'Anjou*, pp. 35–6 and map between pp. 64–5.

before Norman's election, when Geoffrey had destroyed the castle of Doué.[125] One year after Norman's consecration, Geoffrey led another campaign to the south against Gerald Bellay, lord of Montreuil-Bellay, who counted Andrew de Doué among his supporters.[126]

Norman died in 1153,[127] and the subsequent election marked a clash between the cathedral chapter, unwilling to abandon recent gains, and a count determined to revive his prerogatives in episcopal elections. Familiarity with the ideas of Gregorian reform, and at least two consecutive candidates chosen by the chapter, had created confidence among the canons of the cathedral church. Having received Geoffrey Plantagenet's renunciation of the right to seize the deceased bishop's goods, the canons also considered the episcopal election to be within their sole authority.[128] This ambition, however, was unacceptable to the new count of Anjou, Geoffrey's son Henry, and a serious dispute broke out between count and chapter. As a consequence, the see of Angers was vacant from 1153 until early 1156. Although Henry II's accession to the English throne and his activities in England certainly contributed to this long delay, discord between chapter and king concerning the election was its primary cause. In late 1155, Henry II finally decided to bring the case before the pope and launched an appeal. In this, the king's messengers, the bishops of Evreux and Le Mans, the abbot of St Albans, and the dean of St Laud, claimed that the canons of Angers had violated the old Angevin custom according to which the chapter was to present three candidates to the count, who then would choose the one to be elected. The composition of this embassy shows that the king and ecclesiastics from his close entourage were not alone in considering this claim rightful. The bishop of Le Mans, William de Passavant, who was familiar with canon law and was praised by Bernard of Clairvaux for his virtues,[129] apparently shared this view. But if Henry had hoped that the recently installed Englishman on the papal see, Adrian IV, would decide in his favour, his hopes were disappointed. Adrian condemned the custom and forbade the acceptance of any bishop

---

[125] Count Fulk V had laid siege to the castle of Doué in 1109 and 1123, Chartrou, *L'Anjou*, pp. 26–7. For 1147, see C. Port, *Dictionnaire historique, géographique et biographique de Maine-et-Loire et de l'ancienne Province d'Anjou*, 2nd edn (4 vols., Angers, 1965–96), II, p. 58, col. 1.

[126] 'Annales Sancti Sergii Andegavensis', in *Recueil d'annales*, ed. Halphen, pp. 91–110, pp. 97–8, 100; cf. Chartrou, *L'Anjou*, pp. 69–76, and P. Marchegay, 'Montreuil-Bellay', *Revue de l'Anjou 3rd sér.*, 4 (October 1861 – March 1862), 129–43, 132.

[127] 'Annales Sancti Albini', in *Recueil d'annales*, ed. Halphen, p. 13.

[128] *Obituaire*, ed. Urseau, p. 33; 'Chronica domni Rainaldi archidiaconi Sancti Mauricii Andegavensis', in *Chroniques des églises*, ed. Marchegay and Mabille, pp. 3–16, p. 16.

[129] *Sancti Bernardi opera*, ed. Leclercq and Rochais, VIII, no. 294.

Table 6 Norman de Doué, bishop of Angers (1149–53), and his family

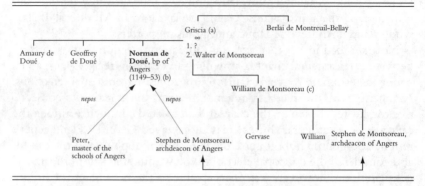

(a) For Griscia, see *Grand cartulaire de Fontevraud*, ed. Bienvenu et al., I, nos. 171 (husband Walter and son William), 225 (sons William, Amaury, and Geoffrey), 227 (brother Berlai and son William de Montsoreau); *Obituaire*, ed. Urseau, p. 42 (son Norman); Chartrou, *L'Anjou*, p. 325, pièces justificatives no. 5 (son Geoffrey).

(b) For Norman's *nepotes*, see Paris, BNF Lat. 5441 (cartulary, abbey of Marmoutier), part I, pp. 401–2.

(c) For William and his sons, *Grand cartulaire de Fontevraud*, ed. J.-M. Bienvenu et al., I, no. 479.

elected in such circumstances.[130] Other than the papal letter, there is no hard evidence on the course of the dispute. If Henry II was concerned about how episcopal elections in general ought to be conducted, then his appeal should be understood as a matter of ecclesiastical policy. But this seems unlikely. The letter refers only to elections at Angers, and Henry's actions appear to have resulted from a concrete political problem. During his short episcopate, Norman de Doué had fostered the careers of his *nepotes* Stephen de Montsoreau, who became archdeacon, and Peter, who became master of the schools.[131] Given the significance of the relationship

---

[130] *Epistolae pontificum*, ed. Loewenfeld, no. 228 [= Jaffé, II, no. 10174; *WH* -]. For a discussion of the date of this letter, see Appendix I. For the journey of Henry II's envoys, see *Gesta abbatum monasterii Sancti Albani a Thoma Walsingham, regnante Ricardo secundo, ejusdem ecclesiae praecentore, compilata*, ed. H. Riley (Rolls Series XXVIII) (3 vols., London, 1867–9), I, pp. 125–9; *Monumenta Vizeliacensia. Textes relatifs à l'histoire de l'abbaye de Vézelay*, ed. R.B.C. Huygens (Corpus christianorum. Continuatio mediaevalis XLII) (Turnhout, 1976), pp. 505–6; *Papsturkunden in England*, ed. W. Holtzmann (Abhandlungen der Akademie der Wissenschaften in Göttingen, philologisch-historische Klasse; neue Folge XXV und 3. Folge XIV, XXXIII) (3 vols., Berlin and Göttingen 1930–52), III, no. 113 [= Jaffé -; *WH* -].

[131] Bishop Norman granted the church of St Gervais of Vern-d'Anjou (cant. Lion-d'Angers, Maine-et-Loire) to Marmoutier with the consent of his *nepos* Archdeacon Stephen. Norman's other *nepos*, Peter, witnessed this charter, issued in 1152, on his behalf, Paris, BNF Lat. 5441 (cartulary, abbey of Marmoutier), part I, pp. 401–2. Archdeacon Stephen can be identified with Stephen de Montsoreau, *Cartulaire noir*, ed. Urseau, p. xlviii. In 1171, he participated at the settlement of a dispute over the revenues of this church between Marmoutier and Ralph, priest of Vern, Angers, AD Maine-et-Loire G 785 (charters concerning the Grand Séminaire of Angers), nos. 13–14 = Paris, BNF

avunculus–nepos in an ecclesiastical context, it seems possible that Norman intended to prepare one of them to become bishop.[132] If so, Henry's actions could be explained by his discontent with the candidates.

Shortly after the death of Geoffrey Plantagenet in September 1151, Henry had faced the rebellion of his younger brother Geoffrey. When Henry's counterattack made quick progress, Geoffrey fled to William de Montsoreau, father of Archdeacon Stephen. But Henry took the castle of Montsoreau and subdued Geoffrey.[133] In 1153, Geoffrey joined forces with his brother, and together they fought against Theobald, count of Blois. They were heavily defeated. Soon after Henry's accession to the throne of England, Geoffrey started claiming Anjou as his heritage, and by early 1156, based on support from southern Anjou, Geoffrey was again at war with his brother.[134] With respect to the bishopric, these political events may have made Henry resist a candidate who was connected with the southern families opposing his rule.

Although Henry II's envoys failed to gain papal support for the old Angevin custom, they seem to have been able to prevent the election of a bishop totally unacceptable to the king. The chapter's representatives were persuaded to choose a less problematic candidate. Probably while they were still at Benevento the representatives agreed on Matthew, abbot of St Florent of Saumur.[135] Matthew had close ties with the chapter

Lat. 5441 (cartulary, abbey of Marmoutier), part 1, p. 403. Stephen was a son of William de Montsoreau, *Grand cartulaire de Fontevraud*, ed. Bienvenu et al., 1, no. 479. William de Montsoreau in turn was a son from Griscia's marriage with Walter II de Montsoreau, ibid., nos. 171, 227. Norman de Doué was probably Griscia's son from a prior marriage. In another charter to Fontevraud issued between 1115 and 1124, Griscia, wife of Walter de Montsoreau, her son William, and her daughter Peregrina gave their consent to a donation made by Walter on the request of Berlai de Montreuil-Bellay, Griscia's brother. Amaury and Geoffrey de Doué, sons of Griscia, brothers of William, are then mentioned among the witnesses of this concession: 'quam videlicet partem ipse Gauterius donavit totam ecclesie Fontis Evraudi, volentibus Berlaio cum uxore sua et filio atque Rainardo, necon eciam concedentibus Griscia uxore Gauterii et Guillelmo filio et Peregrina filia. Cujus concessionis testes sunt: Aimericus atque Gaufridus de Doeo filii Griscie, fratres predicti Guillelmi, Freschet et Berniquet', ibid., no. 225. If Amaury and Geoffrey had been sons of Griscia's marriage with Walter de Montsoreau, they would have been listed together with William and Peregrina. Bishop Norman, therefore, was Archdeacon Stephen's half-uncle. For a simplified family tree of Norman de Doué see Table 6, p. 198.

[132] See infra, pp. 219–29. [133] *Torigny*, p. 170. [134] Boussard, *Le comté d'Anjou*, pp. 69–73.

[135] Ibid., p. 97, states that Matthew was elected after the papal letter concerning episcopal procedure had been issued. However, the evidence shows not only that Matthew's election took place shortly before the papal letter was issued, but also that his election was closely related to the events in Benevento in February 1156. On 29 January 1156, Adrian IV issued a charter mentioning a 'futurus episcopus Andegavensis', *Papsturkunden in Frankreich: Neue Folge. V. Touraine, Anjou, Maine und Bretagne*, ed. Ramackers, no. 90 [= Jaffé –; WH –]. Two charters issued on 20 February 1156 mention an 'electus Andegavensis', ibid., nos. 91–2 [= Jaffé –; WH –]. The information of Matthew's election cannot have been brought to Benevento by the envoys, who had left for Benevento in late 1155, since the Angevin chronicles, in particular the chronicle and the annals of St Florent of Saumur, place Matthew's election in 1156, 'Historia Sancti Florentii', in *Chroniques des églises*, ed. Marchegay and Mabille, p. 306; 'Annales Sancti Florentii Salmurensis', in *Recueil d'annales*, ed. Halphen, pp. 111–26, pp. 122–3. It seems, therefore, likely that Matthew's election was decided in Benevento.

of Angers. He was a close friend of Bishop Ulger, who once described him as 'amicus verissimus ecclesie nostre et qui multum et sepe in officiis illius et nostris sudavit et alsit'.[136] Their ties may have reached back to their youth and/or to a relationship between their families: both came from Loudun.[137] Due to his origins and his long service as abbot of the powerful Benedictine monastery of St Florent, Saumur, Matthew was also well known to the families south of the Loire, such as the Montsoreaus, the Doués, or the Montreuil-Bellays.[138] He also enjoyed good relations with the counts of Anjou. Always looking to increase the benefits of his abbey, he had maintained fruitful contacts with Geoffrey and Henry Plantagenet throughout his abbacy.[139] Therefore his election may be interpreted as a tactically clever concession by the chapter to Henry's political pressure. The king's envoys probably made clear that it would not be wise for the chapter to provoke royal anger. Matthew's election was useful for both sides, because he did not present a threat to Henry's rule, while also defending the rights and liberties of the cathedral church.

Only six years later, Matthew died, and the chapter elected their dean Geoffrey Moschet, who came from Sées and had served Henry as *clericus regis*

---

[136] Ulger gave him the church of Courcelles (Courcelles-en-Touraine?, cant. Château-la-Vallière, Indre-et-Loire) with the consent of Archdeacon Bohemund and Archpriest William de Chemillé, and the church of Chétigné (cant. Saumur-Sud, Maine-et-Loire) with the consent of Archdeacon Norman (de Doué), and Archpriest Norman, Angers, AD Maine-et-Loire H 3714 (cartulary, abbey of St Florent of Saumur, 'Livre d'argent'), fos. 77v–78r, no. 144. During his time as abbot Matthew granted some tenements to Archdeacon Ralph de Bures, Angers, AD Maine-et-Loire H 3713 (cartulary, abbey of St Florent of Saumur, 'Livre blanc'), fo. 40r–v, no. 75.

[137] For Matthew, see 'Historia Sancti Florentii', in *Chroniques des églises*, ed. Marchegay and Mabille, p. 306. For Ulger's origins, see J.-M. Bienvenu, 'Recherches sur le diocèse d'Angers au temps de la réforme grégorienne (XIᵉ siècle et première moitié du XIIᵉ)' (Paris Univ., *thèse*, 1968), p. 53.

[138] For St Florent, see J. Avril, *Le gouvernement des évêques et la vie religieuse dans le diocèse d'Angers (1148–1240)* (2 vols., Paris, 1984), I, pp. 273–6. Matthew was abbot for twenty-eight years, 'Historia Sancti Florentii', in *Chroniques des églises*, ed. Marchegay and Mabille, p. 306. In 1152, he witnessed a charter of William de Montsoreau, *Grand cartulaire de Fontevraud*, ed. Bienvenu et al., I, no. 479. It is possibly no mere coincidence that during his episcopate, William de Doué followed Peter as master of the schools, *Cartulaire noir*, ed. Urseau, p. lvii.

[139] Angers, AD Maine-et-Loire H 3714 (cartulary, abbey of St Florent of Saumur, 'Livre d'argent'), fo. 33r–v, no. 52 (against a payment of 3,000 sous Count Geoffrey renounces to 'his men of Saumur' his right to receive dues from the vineyards at Saumur, whose collection has caused much discord between the monks and comital officers; cf. Chartrou, *L'Anjou*, pp. 259–61, pièces justificatives no. 33); J. Chartrou, *L'Anjou*, pp. 377–91, pièces justificatives nos. 46, 52, 59 (57), 60 (58); Angers, AD Maine-et-Loire H 2109 (charters concerning the abbey of St Florent of Saumur) (Archbishop Engelbald reports that Duke Henry restored the revenues of the fairs of St Florent and the usage of dead wood to the abbey. Abbot Matthew had complained that Count Geoffrey's officers had appropriated those rights); *Recueil des actes de Henri II*, ed. Delisle and Berger, I, no. 124.

at least since the mid-1150s.[140] In the intervening years, Henry had greatly increased his authority in Greater Anjou[141] and Geoffrey's election symbolised this changed political situation. It secured the chapter a bishop on good terms with the king. Geoffrey was in office until his death in 1177.[142]

His successor Ralph de Beaumont, elected in 1177 and consecrated in 1178,[143] was a very well-connected man. He was the son of Roscelin II de Beaumont, who was married to Constance, one of King Henry I's numerous illegitimate children. Thus Ralph de Beaumont was a cousin of Henry II, and this fact was known to contemporaries[144] as well as to the king, who referred to him as *charissimus cognatus noster*.[145] Ralph's brother Richard, who succeeded Roscelin II, was one of the most powerful barons in Greater Anjou. His lands were situated principally in Maine, including the lordships of Beaumont, Ste Suzanne, Le Lude, and Fresnay.[146]

---

[140] Even though *Torigny*, p. 215, is clear: 'Matheo episcopo Andegavensi defuncto, successit Gaufrido Sagiensis, decanus ejusdem ecclesiae et clericus regis Anglorum', Léopold Delisle and Jacques Boussard have not identified the dean of Angers with the later bishop. Since the question of Geoffrey's background is crucial for the interpretation of his election, it is necessary to scrutinise the alternatives proposed by both scholars. The *Gauffridus capellanus regis* with whom Boussard, *Le comté d'Anjou*, p. 98, identifies Bishop Geoffrey is a different person, since the chaplain witnessed two charters issued after 1162, *Recueil des actes de Henri II*, ed. Delisle and Berger, I, no. 271, II, no. 494. Delisle *Introduction*, p. 370, follows *GC*, XIV, cols. 570–1, and states that the Dean Geoffrey of Angers was not Geoffrey Moschet, but Geoffrey Bibens Solem, since Bishop Geoffrey and Dean Geoffrey *Bibens Solem* can be found in the same charter. This charter, issued by Reginald de Château-Gontier in favour of the abbey of St Nicolas of Angers, is preserved as a copy in Paris, BNF Collection Housseau, V, no. 1883. The relevant passage reads: 'eandemque donationem in manu domini Gauffredi Andecavensis episcopi feci et posui videntibus et audientibus Michaele Abbate de Rota et Roberto abbate de Bella-Branchia et Herberto Andecavensi archidiacono, et Gaufrido Bibente Solem decano'. The attribution of the office of the dean of the cathedral chapter to Geoffrey *Bibens Solem*, however, is incorrect, since other charters show that he was dean neither during Matthew's episcopate, when he was a canon in the chapter headed by Dean Geoffrey, nor during Geoffrey's episcopate, *Cartulaire noir*, ed. Urseau, nos. 232, 235; Angers, AD Maine-et-Loire G 334 (charters concerning the cathedral chapter of Angers), fo. 11r (charter of Bishop Geoffrey issued in 1177, his last year in office, and witnessed among others by Dean Stephen and Canon Geoffrey *Bibens Solem*). Dean Geoffrey disappeared in 1162, the date from which we can trace Dean Matthew, Queen Eleanor's chancellor, *Cartulaire noir*, ed. Urseau, no. 233; H.G. Richardson, 'The Letters and Charters of Eleanor of Aquitaine', *EHR*, 43 (1959), 193–213, 193–7. This strongly supports Torigny's statement that Dean Geoffrey became bishop of Angers. The first time Geoffrey Moschet can be traced at the royal court is in 1155, *Recueil des actes de Henri II*, ed. Delisle and Berger, I, no. 70.

[141] Boussard, *Le comté d'Anjou*, pp. 73–6.

[142] 'Annales Sancti Albini', in *Recueil d'annales*, ed. Halphen, p. 16; 'Annales Sancti Sergii', in ibid., p. 105.

[143] Angers, AD Maine-et-Loire G 452 (charters concerning the cathedral chapter of Angers), fo. 11r (Ralph appears as bishop-elect in a charter issued in 1177); 'Annales Sancti Sergii', in *Recueil d'annales*, ed. Halphen, p. 105.

[144] *Torigny*, p. 280.

[145] *Recueil des actes de Henri II*, ed. Delisle and Berger, II, no. 730. For a simplified family tree of Ralph and William de Beaumont, see Table 7, p. 207.

[146] Boussard, *Le comté d'Anjou*, p. 55.

It is impossible to establish which was more important in Ralph's election: his connections with the king or the strong position of his family in north-eastern Greater Anjou. The original driving force behind his candidature may well have been his family. The election of Ralph extended the family's influence over the whole of Anjou. But the king may also have been interested in Ralph's success, because he hoped it would be easier to control Ralph's relatives, whose possessions were easily accessible from his power base in Normandy, than the troublesome barons of southern Anjou, whose interests had been a considerable factor in episcopal elections at Angers before 1156.

Ralph's successor, William de Chemillé, was the choice of King Richard I. Having promoted his election to the see of Avranches in 1196,[147] Richard initiated William's translation to the see of Angers in late 1197/early 1198.[148] Why Richard was so interested in having William as bishop of Angers is not totally clear.[149] He may have wished to reward his loyal cleric with a wealthier bishopric than Avranches; but there may have been an urgent need for a man like William in Angers. It is possible that William de Beaumont, Ralph de Beaumont's nephew and protégé,

---

[147] For William's close connections with Richard I and his election to the see of Avranches, see supra, pp. 155–6.

[148] *Register Innocenz' III.*, I, no. 117 [= Potthast, I, no. 108]. Shortly after his translation, William was active on Richard's behalf in supporting Otto IV's candidature. He went as bishop-elect of Angers to Otto's election at Cologne in June 1198 and worked at the papal court for Otto's case, *Howden*, IV, p. 37, *Rot. chart.*, p. 31a. Foreville, *Innocent III*, p. 146 n. 21, wrongly states that William's translation took place in late 1196/7. This date is probably based on her interpretation of Innocent's statement 'quia – licet inveniatur in canone "quod, si electus ultra quinque menses per suam negligentiam retinuerit viduatam ecclesiam, nec ibi nec alibi consecrationis donum percipiat" – non tamen intelligetur ecclesia viduata, quasi sponsum non habeat, sed quia, cum sponsus eius nondum sit consecratus, adhuc quoad quem quasi viri manet solatio destituta'. According to her, ibid., p. 146, this meant that the church of Angers was not yet 'widowed', but only deprived of the husband's consolation. Hence Ralph de Beaumont was not dead by the time of William's translation. However, Innocent's statement did not specifically refer to the situation at Angers; it was part of his general discourse on the marriage between the bishop and his church in the context of episcopal translations, *Register Innocenz' III.*, I, nos. 447, 502, 530 (532) = 3 *Comp.* 1.5.2 = X 1.7.2 [= Potthast, I, nos. 451, 511, 575].

[149] Avril, *Le gouvernement des évêques*, I, p. 481 n. 52, states that William was a canon of Angers and then master of the schools at Angers. He also stated that he was possibly a member of the family of the lords of Chemillé. William, however, was not a member of the cathedral chapter of Angers. An archpriest William de Chemillé who was canon at Angers at least until 1140 must not be identified with Bishop William, *Cartulaire noir*, ed. Urseau no. 192; Angers, AD Maine-et-Loire H 3714 (cartulary, abbey of St Florent of Saumur, 'Livre d'argent'), fos. 77v–78r, no. 144 (mention of Archpriest William de Chemillé in a charter of Bishop Ulger issued in 1140); *Obituaire*, ed. Urseau, pp. 20–1, 23. Nor was there a master of the schools at Angers named William de Chemillé. Avril's statement may have been due to a confusion with William de Doué, master of the schools at least until 1177, *Cartulaire noir*, ed. Urseau, p. lvii. Whether Bishop William was a member of the family of the lords of Chemillé is unclear. No direct evidence links him with that family, cf. Angers, AD Maine-et-Loire H (39) 12 (cartulary, priory of St Pierre of Chemillé); H (39) 11 (cartulary ('Censier'), priory of St Pierre of Chemillé).

was a candidate for the see after Ralph's death.[150] If this was the case, King Richard may have intended to weaken the influence of the Beaumonts in Greater Anjou. Their extensive possessions in Maine combined with the bishopric of Angers would form a power block stretching from the north to the south of Greater Anjou, which Richard I may have considered dangerous for his authority. The king found himself engaged in near constant warfare on the continent after his release from captivity. In 1197, a peace settlement had ended the war with the Bretons, but Richard's main objective, to strengthen his authority over the duchy, had not been achieved.[151] Moreover, in the same year he began a new offensive against Philip Augustus.[152] In this situation Richard may have thought a loyal cleric much more useful in the see than a member of a locally powerful family.

But Richard's plan was in danger of failing. Informed about William's translation, Innocent III suspended him from taking up his new office, because his move from Avranches to Angers had not been authorised by the pope. However, when William personally postulated his translation at the papal court, Innocent granted permission, and, in January 1199, ordered the chapter of Angers to receive William as their new bishop.[153] William's translation to Angers was of considerable significance for the development of canon law, but it had hardly any impact on the affairs of the diocese. After only one year in office, he died in 1200.[154] The election of his successor was heavily disputed.

On King Richard's death, King John was confronted with a new situation in Greater Anjou, where the majority of the barons had already accepted Arthur as their lord.[155] Knowing that Arthur's claim was supported by Philip II, John lost no time in marching into Greater Anjou to defend his own interests. When, in late September 1199, William des Roches, seneschal of Anjou, made peace with John and handed Le Mans over to him, Arthur and his mother retired to Angers,[156] hoping in vain for support from Philip II. In May 1200, Philip and John concluded the treaty of Le Goulet, and Philip received John's homage for all of Richard I's continental possessions. Arthur swore homage to John for Brittany.[157] Manifesting his victory, John entered Angers in June 1200.[158] Around this

---

[150] *Obituaire*, ed. Urseau, pp. 10, 31.   [151] Everard, *Brittany and the Angevins*, pp. 165–7.

[152] Gillingham, *Richard I*, pp. 301–20; Moss, 'The Defence of Normandy', p. 146.

[153] For a detailed examination of this case, see supra, pp. 156–60.   [154] *Obituaire*, ed. Urseau, pp. 20–1.

[155] *Howden*, IV, pp. 86–7.

[156] Ibid., pp. 96–7, states that these events took place in October. The chancery rolls show, however, that John had entered Le Mans already in late September, *Rot. chart.*, pp. 20b, 21a, 23a–b.

[157] *Recueil des actes de Philippe Auguste*, ed. Delaborde et al., II, no. 633.

[158] Boussard, *Le comté d'Anjou*, p. 93.

time, Bishop William de Chemillé must have died, and in late August/
early September John got notice of the forthcoming election. On 7
September 1200, he sent a letter to the chapter of Angers announcing
that, since he was too busy with other affairs to be present at the election,
the seneschals of Normandy and Anjou, Guarin de Glapion, and William
des Roches, or if Guarin could not be present, William alone, would
represent the king's will.[159] John was well aware that he needed a loyal
bishop to support his fragile rule in Anjou. Since William des Roches, the
leading Angevin baron, pursued his own rather than the king's policy,
Guarin's presence may have been intended to strengthen John's authority.
Despite John's efforts, the chapter did not follow his wishes unanimously
but split their votes. One party voted for the king's candidate, William,
archdeacon of Angers, the brother of the ruling Viscount Ralph de
Beaumont and *nepos* of the former bishop, Ralph de Beaumont.[160] The
other party voted for William, the chanter of St Martin of Tours.[161]

John's position in Anjou was too fragile in 1200 to force the canons to
abandon William, chanter of St Martin. He had to accept the split decision
and the consequent appeal, first to Octavian, cardinal-bishop of Ostia and
papal legate in France, and then to the papal court after Octavian had declared
both elections void. At the papal court, John supported Archdeacon William
de Beaumont by financial and diplomatic means.[162] The canons Hugh de La
Ferté, Robert de Semblançay, and Reginald asked Innocent III to make
William bishop. However, the canons Peter and Bricius representing Chanter
William, apparently fearing that Innocent III would be swayed by John's
money, begged the pope to allow the chapter to conduct a new election.
Innocent III accepted the argument of Chanter William's envoys. In his letter
of 26 April 1202, he forbade further appeals and ordered the chapter to hold
an election within the next month. If the election was conducted canonically,
the archbishop of Tours was to consecrate the elect; otherwise, the archbishops of Tours and Bourges and the bishop of Lisieux would nominate the
bishop.[163] But if Chanter William's men hoped that they could command a
majority within the chapter or that political circumstances would be in their
favour, they were proved wrong. In summer 1201, Philip Augustus had

---

[159] *Rot. chart.*, p. 98a.

[160] *Rot. pat.*, pp. 4a–b, 14a. In September 1199, John confirmed to Constance de Tosny, daughter of
Viscount Richard de Beaumont, some land that he had granted to her while being count of
Mortain, and which had been granted by Henry I to the grandmother of Constance, also named
Constance, *Rot. chart.*, pp. 20b–21a.

[161] *Register Innocenz' III.*, v, no. 27 (28) [= Potthast, I, no. 1669].

[162] *Rot. pat.*, p. 4a–b. Viscount Ralph was to pay John back the credit up to 500 marcs granted by the
king to Archdeacon William's envoys, ibid., p. 4b.

[163] *Register Innocenz' III.*, v, no. 27 (28) [= Potthast, I, no. 1669]. For the identity of the canons, see
Rot. pat., p. 4b.

invited John to Paris where they had confirmed the treaty of Le Goulet.[164] Around October 1201, the tensions between the two kings had increased markedly, and John had secured the homage both of Juhel de Mayenne, the most powerful baron in the north-east of Greater Anjou,[165] and of his mother Isabelle de Meulan. All the important barons of Maine and northern Anjou, namely William des Roches, Ralph de Beaumont, Robert III d'Alençon, Stephen du Perche, Guy VI de Laval, Hugh de Châtellerault, and Maurice III de Craon, had acted as guarantees for Juhel's and Isabelle's oaths.[166] This had been an important step in John's attempt to secure Greater Anjou.

But in Poitou, John had created bitter enemies by his treatment of the Lusignan family. Philip II used their complaints to summon John to a colloquy to discuss these matters. On 25 March 1202, the kings met and Philip asked John to surrender some of his possessions and to appear before the royal court a fortnight after Easter, where he should answer for his treatment of the Lusignans and his attacks on the possessions of St Martin of Tours. John did neither, and Philip declared his continental possessions forfeited.[167] Immediately after the conference, and again after Philip's judgement, John increased his efforts to secure the loyalties of the barons of Greater Anjou.[168] In this context he needed a friendly bishop. On 8 July 1202, the king ordered the chapter to elect Archdeacon William.[169] In view of increasing royal pressure and John's harsh treatment of the canons of Sées who had resisted the king's orders in 1201–2,[170] the canons supporting Chanter William gave in, and the chapter elected the king's nominee.

It may be that Chanter William's supporters were also Arthur's adherents. Chanter William had close connections with Hamelin, former master of the schools at St Martin and since 1190 bishop of Le Mans, and his brother Philip, dean of St Martin until 1191, to whom the chanter owed his office.[171] Hamelin had not supported John's accession to the

---

[164] A. Cartellieri, *Philip II. August, König von Frankreich* (4 vols., Leipzig, 1899–1922), IV, part 1, pp. 78–80.

[165] Boussard, *Le comté d'Anjou*, pp. 59–61.

[166] Powicke, *Loss*, p. 146; B. de Broussillon, *La Maison de Craon 1050–1480. Etude historique accompagnée du cartulaire de Craon* (2 vols., Paris, 1893), I, p. 121.

[167] Powicke, *Loss*, pp. 141–8; Baldwin, *Philip*, pp. 97–8.

[168] *Rot. pat.*, pp. 8a, 10b, 11a; cf. Cartellieri, *Philip*, IV, part 1, p. 113.

[169] *Rot. pat.*, p. 14a. Innocent III's order of April 1202 to hold the election within the next month was apparently not taken too seriously.

[170] For John at Sées, see supra, pp. 124–32.

[171] The office of the chanter was in the gift of the dean, Vaucelle, *Saint-Martin*, p. 203. According to Vaucelle, *Saint-Martin*, p. 442, a William was chanter from 1176 to 1185, a Helias in 1188, and again a William from 1191 to 1219. Vaucelle's lists of the dignitaries of St Martin are not always accurate, cf. his classification of the cellarer William in 1177, who by then had ceased to fulfil this duty for a long time, ibid., p. 444, supra, pp. 187 n. 79, 189 n. 86. Due to considerable damages

throne.[172] Arthur had been invested at St Martin with the canonry reserved for the counts of Anjou. In June 1200, John had asked the dean of St Martin to accept his overlordship, but apparently with little lasting success, as, in autumn 1201, the king devastated the church's lands.[173] At some time between 1199 and his disappearance in 1202, Arthur issued a charter in favour of the cathedral chapter of St Maurice of Angers granting *fourrage* (right to collect fodder or straw) in the lordship of Chemiré.[174] Perhaps this grant was intended to help Chanter William's candidature. It is notable that his support disintegrated around the time of Arthur's defeat and capture at Mirebeau on 1 August 1202. The letter of protection John issued in August 1202, in favour of Philip d'Yvré, canon of Le Mans and a friend of Bishop Hamelin, can perhaps be interpreted as a sign of a *rapprochement* between bishop and king.[175] More significantly, there were no protests following Archdeacon William's election, which took place at the earliest in the days immediately preceding 1 August.[176] John's letter to the chapter would have given plenty of reasons for an appeal to the pope, but the chanter's supporters remained silent and accepted Archdeacon William as bishop.

It is difficult to say whether the confrontation between John and Arthur was at the root of the electoral dispute at Angers, in the sense that each party proposed their candidate, or whether John and Arthur each used the existing split within the chapter to opt for the party that seemed more favourable to them. It can hardly be denied, however, that the election was affected by the 'high politics' of the day. John prevailed in the short term, but in the end he failed to win the very baron whom he expected to gratify.

inflicted on the evidence by World War II it is impossible to reconstruct a complete list of the chanters. However, it is noteworthy that the surviving sources do not mention a chanter named Helias. The chanter William, who held his office from at least 1191, owed his promotion to Dean Philip, active until 1191, Paris, BNF Collection Housseau, XIII, part 2, no. 8713 B (Dean Philip and Chanter William witness a charter issued in 1191). If he is the same person who can be traced as chanter between 1176 and 1185, he was related to Dean Philip and Hamelin, for in 1184, Chanter William granted a church to St Florent of Saumur with the consent of Dean Philip and Hamelin, who would have received the church after his death *de jure hereditario*, *Chartes de Saint-Julien de Tours*, ed. Denis, I, no. 120.

[172] See supra, p. 190.

[173] *Rot. chart.*, p. 97a; for the events in 1199–1200, see Powicke, *Loss*, pp. 131–2; Baldwin, *Philip*, p. 98.

[174] *Recueil des actes de Philippe Auguste*, ed. Delaborde et al., II, no. 777.

[175] *Rot. pat.*, p. 17a; Philip was Hamelin's *officialis* by 1204 at the latest, *Cartulaire de Saint-Victeur, prieuré de l'abbaye de Mont-Saint-Michel, 944–1400*, ed. B. de Broussillon (Société d'agriculture, sciences et arts de la Sarthe) (Paris, 1895), no. 45. Perhaps Philip played the role of an intermediary between the church of Le Mans and John. In 1206, John granted Philip, *clericus noster*, the possessions of the bishop and the chapter of Le Mans in Kingston Deverill, Wiltshire, *Rotuli litterarum clausarum*, ed. Hardy, I, p. 74a; cf. infra, p. 250. n. 55.

[176] King John's letter to the chapter ordering the election of Archdeacon William was issued in Normandy, at Bonport on 8 July 1202, *Rot. pat.*, p. 14a.

Table 7 *Ralph de Beaumont, bishop of Angers (1177–97), and William de Beaumont, bishop of Angers (1202–40), and their family (a)*

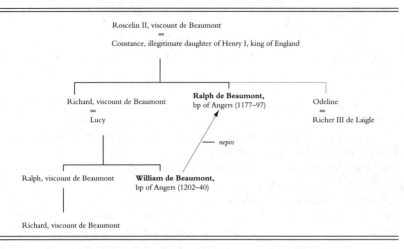

Roscelin II, viscount de Beaumont
∞
Constance, illegitimate daughter of Henry I, king of England

Richard, viscount de Beaumont
∞
Lucy

Ralph de Beaumont,
bp of Angers (1177–97)

Odeline
∞
Richer III de Laigle

— *nepos*

Ralph, viscount de Beaumont

William de Beaumont,
bp of Angers (1202–40)

Richard, viscount de Beaumont

(a) D. Power, *The Norman Frontier*, p. 487.

Despite his brother's elevation and further royal rewards,[177] Ralph de Beaumont and his baronial colleagues defected to Philip II in the early months of 1203.[178]

William's disputed election also raises the question of the chapter's attitude towards the ruler's role in the election process. Considering the chapter's staunch resistance to comital interference in 1153–6, the absence of protests against King John's actions is remarkable. It has been argued above that political circumstances prevented an appeal in 1202, but there were no political reasons to prevent Chanter William's party from complaining against John's behaviour in the appeal launched after the first election. If the canons' silence was due to their unwillingness to discuss this matter and not to the paucity of the sources,[179] this could point towards a change of their attitude towards the ruler's role in elections. It could mean that they had abandoned their Gregorian position, to embrace

---

[177] *Rotuli Normanniae*, ed. Hardy, p. 66; cf. *Rot. pat.*, p. 24a.

[178] *Rotuli Normanniae*, ed. Hardy, p. 73; *Registres de Philippe Auguste*, ed. Baldwin, carte, no. 45; Baldwin, *Philip*, pp. 192–3.

[179] There is no evidence on the nature of the arguments brought forward before the papal legate, but the fact that Innocent III made no allusions to arguments referring to John's interference strongly suggests that they had not been used. Archbishop Bartholomew's confirmation of the election indicates either that the defeated party did not inform him about John's interference or that he himself considered it tolerable.

one much more favourable to comital/royal influence. If indeed such a development had taken place, a possible explanation could be that the three bishops occupying the see between 1162 and 1200 had enjoyed very close links with the Angevin kings.

In the years following his election, William de Beaumont kept a low profile. He was recorded in the presence of King John, when John returned to Angers in June 1214,[180] but nothing is known about the bishop's politics during the Angevin–Capetian struggle in 1202–6 or during John's subsequent attempts to regain possession of Normandy and Greater Anjou. King Philip in his turn was eager to control the viscounts of Beaumont. Contracts between Philip and Bishop William's brother Ralph and Ralph's son Richard defined the viscounts' obligations towards the French king.[181] By this means, Philip may also have hoped to influence the bishop. After King John's death and Louis VIII's vain attempt to conquer England, both Beaumonts, the viscount and the bishop, went on crusade in 1218.[182] Five years later, William agreed with Louis VIII on the terms of the relationship between the bishops of Angers and the kings of France.[183] In general William seems to have dedicated himself to administering his diocese rather than to royal politics or to papal missions.[184] His long pontificate ended in 1240, when he was succeeded by Michael de Villeoiseau.

Michael's origins, education, and career are obscure. But if his good connections with the papal court imply previous contacts, Michael may have belonged to the new type of bishop, the professional cleric[185] whose career was fostered by the papacy and who did not necessarily have connections with the diocese he eventually was to govern.

The twelfth-century elections at Angers were heavily influenced by political developments in the region. When Henry came to power, the barons of Greater Anjou regarded him as no more than *primus inter pares*. The cathedral chapter considered comital interference a breach of its right to elect their bishop freely. The electoral dispute of 1153–6 clearly shows Henry's struggle to impose his authority on both the lords and the cathedral chapter. He succeeded. He subdued the barons of Greater Anjou and became an important factor in elections. Richard I maintained

---

[180] *Rot. chart.*, p. 199a.

[181] *Layettes*, ed. Teulet et al., I, nos. 932, 1197–1201, 1445; *Registres de Philippe Auguste*, ed. Baldwin, securitates, no. 18.

[182] *Honorii III Romani pontificis opera omnia*, ed. Horoy, III, epistolae lib. III, no. 6 [= Potthast, I, no. 5892]; *Layettes*, ed. Teulet et al., I, no. 1197; *The Flowers of History by Roger de Wendover*, ed. H.G. Hewlett (Rolls Series LXXXIV) (3 vols., London, 1886–9), II, p. 244; Baldwin, *Philip*, pp. 332–9.

[183] See supra, p. 193.   [184] Avril, *Le gouvernement des évêques*, II, pp. 551–3, 617–49.

[185] Pico, 'Bishops', p. 146.

a strong position towards the chapter of Angers. He was able to nominate the bishop; even a pope of the calibre of Innocent III could not prevent him from doing so. But the election that took place after Richard's death shows clear signs of the changed political situation in Greater Anjou. The chapter's split votes mirrored the opposition between Arthur and John. The canons of Angers did not act in a political vacuum. Their decisions depended very much on the leading political forces in the region.

Whereas the bishops of Angers between 1101 and 1162 came from seigniorial families based in southern Anjou, two of the four bishops in the period 1162–1240 had made their careers at the Angevin court, and the other two belonged to the Beaumont family, which were chiefly based in Maine, and were related to the Angevins. The Angevins' intentions in supporting royal clerics need no explanation. But if Henry II had thought that the Beaumonts of Maine would be more reliable supporters than the southern barons, he was only right in the short term. John, and perhaps also Richard, learned that in times of crisis there were hardly any means of controlling the baronial families of Greater Anjou, who changed their loyalties whenever they saw their interests threatened.

CONCLUSION

The elections in Greater Anjou between 1140 and 1230 clearly reflect the constant struggle of the counts to impose their authority in the region. In the Touraine, comital authority remained limited; archiepiscopal elections were firmly controlled by the chapter who, neither pro-Angevin nor pro-Capetian, played their own game. In Maine, the Angevins enjoyed stronger authority, but the longevity of Bishop William de Passavant, combined with the inconvenient timing of the deaths of William and his successor Reginald, deprived them of much opportunity to intervene in elections. As at Tours, it was the chapter that held the whip hand. Only at Angers is Angevin influence neatly discernible. Here, elections demonstrated the political tensions in Anjou in the second half of the twelfth century. The constant conflicts of the counts with the lords of southern Anjou made the political situation there very similar to conditions in the Touraine and Poitou. In 1153–6, Henry II's struggle for political survival at the beginning of his reign, then his stronger personal control of the affairs in his southern continental dominions in the 1160s, and finally the relaxation of this control towards the end of his reign become evident. After Henry's death King Richard, accustomed to governing the southern dominions and to incessant fighting against local lords, tried to regain this personal control. King John met with resistance in Greater Anjou and was determined to conquer it. It is possible that his return to the area in 1213–14 had some impact on the election at Le Mans.

The attitude of the Capetians to elections in Greater Anjou shows characteristics already familiar from the analysis of the Norman elections, although a total of seven elections is admittedly a rather narrow basis to judge from. In general, the Capetians exercised little influence over the outcome of the elections. Only the two elections at Tours, shortly after the conquest, attracted Philip's attention. It was a time when he was particularly eager to establish his rule in the Touraine. Yet Philip did not try to parachute a stranger into the archdiocese. Instead he made use of local political factions and supported men with strong antipathy to King John. Again it is striking that Philip refrained from using force to push his candidates. He deployed all diplomatic means, but when the pope decided against his man, he accepted it.

The elections in Greater Anjou offer less detail on the use of canon law and its local interpretation in the period studied than the Norman ones. Tentative conclusions can only be drawn on the formation of the electoral body. In Greater Anjou, Innocent II's decree ordering participation of the *religiosi viri* in the election had little impact. The cathedral chapters had established themselves as the exclusive electoral bodies and carefully preserved this position. The Gregorian reform had been fully embraced, and the electoral dispute at Angers in 1153–6 shows that the churchmen were ready to fight for the Gregorian idea of free elections in practice. However, the subsequent elections at Angers until 1202 suggest that Henry II's political recovery caused the chapter to adopt a view similar to that of the Norman cathedral chapters and defended by some canonists: the acceptance of the participation of the ruler in the selection process. Yet the elections after 1202 show that the new canon law was applied. The ruler had no longer a place among the electors.

Chapter 5

THE EPISCOPACY IN NORMANDY
AND GREATER ANJOU

So far the analysis has focused on the bishop as an individual. His family and his career have been considered in reconstructing possible motives for his election. However, the information on the bishop's personal background also provides a clearer view of the bishops as a group. Thus the composition of the episcopacy, the texture of this particular social group, and the nature and dynamics of ecclesiastical careers leading to an episcopal see – in other words the entry routes to the episcopacy – become visible.

THE COMPOSITION OF THE EPISCOPACY IN NORMANDY
AND GREATER ANJOU

Sixty-one elections were successfully completed in Normandy and Greater Anjou between *c.* 1140 and *c.* 1230.[1] Since Rotrou, William de Chemillé, and Maurice were chosen twice, the total of individuals elected was fifty-eight.[2] They had fifty-eight different life stories to tell, but they may also have shared common features that shaped their appearance as a group. The examination of the bishop's social origins, the location and type of their last office prior to election, and their affiliation to secular or

---

[1] This includes the elections of Rotrou at Evreux in 1139, of Maurice and Peter de Collemezzo at Rouen in 1231 and 1236, of Thomas de Fréauville at Bayeux in 1232, of Ralph II de Cierrey at Evreux in 1236, of Geoffrey de Laval at Le Mans in 1231, and of Michael de Villeoiseau at Angers in 1240.

[2] Rotrou was promoted from Evreux to Rouen, William de Chemillé was translated from Avranches to Angers and Maurice was promoted from Le Mans to Rouen. The difference between the total number of individuals elected and the total number of elections is therefore smaller when examining Normandy and Greater Anjou separately (forty-one individuals for forty-two elections in Normandy; nineteen individuals for nineteen elections in Greater Anjou). Whether Rotrou, William, and Maurice have to be counted once or twice in a quantitative analysis depends on the question being asked. If, for instance, their last office prior to election is examined, they will have to be counted twice, for their position prior to their first election was different from their position prior to their second election. If, however, their social origins are looked at, they have to be counted once, since this remained unaffected by the number of elections.

regular clergy, all help to determine characteristics of the episcopacy of Normandy and Greater Anjou during our period.

The social origins of the bishops in Normandy and Greater Anjou are difficult to establish with precision. Often they are unknown, and even if a bishop's family can be identified it is not necessarily known to which social layer a family belonged. When social origins can be identified with certainty, the result is clear: in all cases the bishops came from aristocratic families, both from comital and from knightly backgrounds. High aristocratic rank or great power on behalf of the candidate's family, therefore, were not necessary conditions for becoming a bishop. Equally, aristocratic birth was not a prerequisite for standing for election, as the case of Herbert L'Abbé, son of the influential burgess of Sées, Ralph L'Abbé, and candidate for the see of Sées in 1202, shows. Men from the urban elites, who by the end of the twelfth century can be identified among the members of the cathedral chapters, were deemed suitable candidates for a bishopric[3] and Herbert's candidacy serves as a powerful reminder that some of the bishops whose social origins cannot be established may well have come from this milieu.

Canon law prescribed that the bishop ought to be chosen from among the clergy of the diocese. Electoral practice in Normandy and Greater Anjou suggests that this was interpreted as a guideline to the ideal candidate rather than as a strict rule. The accusation that a candidate came from outside the diocese was used only once in a disputed election, and even then it appears to have carried little weight.[4] But even if the electors did not always choose men from within the diocese, they hardly appointed complete strangers to their sees. In both regions, most prelates were familiar with their dioceses prior to their election. At least eleven out of nineteen bishops in Greater Anjou, and at least fifteen out of forty-two Norman bishops, held their last office before promotion in the diocese over which they were to preside. These percentages markedly increase if the number of bishops is added who had their origins in the diocese or had once held an office there or had been active in a neighbouring diocese. Only a minority of bishops had no apparent links with the diocese. In these cases, the bishops had strong connections with the royal or papal courts. It does not follow, however, that there was a stark contrast

---

[3] For Herbert, see supra, pp. 126–7; for members of cathedral chapters coming from the urban elites, see Spear, 'Power, Patronage and Personality', p. 207. An interesting case is John fitz Luke, bishop of Evreux (1181–92), and his relative Luke, bishop of Evreux (1203–20). They probably belonged to the urban elites of Rouen, and, if *GC*, XI, col. 579, is right in stating that John was a *nobilis*, they came from an aristocratic family, cf. supra, pp. 102, 105.

[4] See supra, pp. 161–2.

between local men owing their sees to local connections and strangers owing their sees to royal or papal links. While it is true that there is no hard evidence for papal patronage fostering the career of a local candidate, there is plenty of evidence for the king's support of local men. In Angevin Normandy, in particular, royal patronage and local links interacted in so many elections that it seems unreasonable to try to distinguish a local from a royal episcopacy. This situation changed only after 1204, when bishops of local origins ceased to have royal connections; a clear indication that Normandy no longer was a royal heartland.

Turning from the geographical location of the last office held prior to election to the nature of this office, it emerges that there was something like a *cursus honorum* for men aiming for a bishopric, even though a clearly structured career ladder leading to an episcopal see did not exist. In both regions, the great majority of bishops had been in senior positions prior to their election. Four out of the six regular bishops had been abbots, the fifth had been prior, and the sixth had been an archdeacon. The positions of the secular bishops, regardless of whether they made their careers at the royal court, in cathedral chapters, or in collegiate churches, tell a similar story. The dignitaries outnumbered by far the canons or simple clerics who became bishops. Among the dignitaries, the positions of dean and arch-deacon were particularly prone to propel their holders to an episcopal see. In theory at least, this result makes perfect sense. Before becoming bishop, a cleric would have gained experience in other offices demanding either administrative, judicial, theological, or leadership skills, or a combination of those. While a locally active canon had to demonstrate these qualities to the bishop and his peers in the chapter, a royal cleric had to do so in his service at court. These men, therefore, should have been better qualified than others for the episcopal office.

Most of the bishops in Normandy and Greater Anjou belonged to the secular clergy. In Normandy thirty-six out of forty-one bishops were seculars, and in Greater Anjou eighteen out of nineteen. Regular clergy in episcopal sees, by contrast, were a rare species. Only one monk, Matthew, was elected to a see in Greater Anjou (Angers). In Normandy, too, only one monk, Richard de St Léger, was chosen, and his promotion at Evreux was a special case, for he was also a canon of the cathedral chapter. The only regular canon to become bishop at a church of secular canons was Achard at Avranches in 1161. Significantly, he had first been elected by the chapter of Sées, the only chapter of regular canons in Normandy and Greater Anjou, and after Henry II had refused to accept his election there it was probably on the king's rather than the chapter's initiative that Achard was elected at Avranches.[5] The chapter of Sées also accounts for the election of the three other regular canons who became bishops in Normandy and Greater Anjou between 1140 and 1230: Sylvester, Gervase, and Hugh. The dominance of secular clergy among bishops in Normandy and Greater Anjou was a pattern common to the Gallican church of the second half of the twelfth century. Monks and regular clergy made it only in small numbers to sees.[6] This stood in contrast with the first half of the century, when their number among the bishops was considerably higher. Scholars have advanced different explanations for this phenomenon. While Marcel Pacaut has argued that the great influence of Bernard of Clairvaux constituted a major stimulus for the recruitment of monks as bishops,[7] Constance Bouchard has attributed less weight to the saintly abbot. She has insisted that, independently from Bernard, the curve of monastic appointments reached a peak in the first half of the twelfth century before it declined again in the second half. According to her, the principal reason was the rise and fall of the prestige of monastic virtues among the electors.[8] Both Pacaut and Bouchard agree, however, that a further reason might have been the establishment of the cathedral chapter as the exclusive electoral body.[9] None of these explanations precisely fits the circumstances of Normandy and Greater Anjou. Bernard of Clairvaux was active in two elections. At Lisieux (1141–3) he successfully supported Arnulf, a secular cleric, albeit a staunch supporter of regular canons. At Sées (1144–7), he was unable to prevent the election of the secular canon Gerald, even though his protest may have been a further reason for Pope Eugenius III to demand Gerald's profession.[10] The exclusion of the *religiosi viri* from the electoral body in the course of the twelfth century deprived the regulars of their official voice in the electoral procedure, but this was not the principal reason for the low number of regular bishops. Already in the first half of the twelfth century, the regulars hardly figured among the bishops in Normandy and Greater Anjou.[11] The rise of monastic prestige did not have a notable impact on the outcome of episcopal elections in these regions except perhaps for the election of the

---

[5] See supra, pp. 153–4. [6] Pacaut, *Elections*, pp. 110–12. [7] Ibid., p. 113.
[8] Bouchard, 'The Geographical, Social and Ecclesiastical Origins of the Bishops of Auxerre and Sens', 287–90.
[9] Pacaut, *Elections*, p. 113; Bouchard, 'The Geographical, Social and Ecclesiastical Origins of the Bishops of Auxerre and Sens', 288.
[10] See supra, pp. 117–20.
[11] For Normandy, see D. Spear, 'The Norman Episcopate under Henry I, King of England and Duke of Normandy (1106–1135)' (Santa Barbara Univ. of California, Ph.D. thesis, 1982), pp. 50–1; *GC*, IX, cols. 40, 477–9, 573, 683–7, 771–4, 873–5; for Greater Anjou, see Guillot, *Le comte d'Anjou*, I, pp. 249–63; Chartrou, *L'Anjou*, pp. 173–91; *GC*, XIV, cols. 70–87, 377–83, 562–9.

Table 8: *Secular and regular clergy on episcopal sees*

	Normandy			Greater Anjou		
	1140–70	1170–1204	1204–30	1140–70	1170–1206	1206–30
Secular clergy	9 (7)	14 (13)	12 (12)	5	5	7
Regular clergy	1 (1)	1 (0)	3 (1)	1	0	0
Total	10 (8)	15 (13)	15 (13)	6	5	7

Note: Rotrou, William de Chemillé, and Maurice are counted once. Rotrou as bishop of Evreux, William as bishop of Avranches, and Maurice as bishop of Le Mans. Gerald, who needed to profess to have his election confirmed, is counted among the seculars. In brackets are given the number of secular and regular bishops in Normandy without Sées, thus for the secular cathedrals only.

Cluniac Hugh to the see of Rouen in 1130.[12] Thus there was no fluctuation to the curve of monastic appointments in Normandy and Greater Anjou. The line remained continually low.

Nonetheless, it is noteworthy that, despite failing to influence elections on a large scale, the prestige of regulars, in particular of abbots, may have played a decisive role in individual cases. In three out of the six elections of regulars, the ecclesiastical community had previously suffered serious conflicts. At Angers, in 1156, Matthew, abbot of St Florent of Saumur, became bishop after a long dispute between king and chapter. Similarly at Evreux in 1223, Richard de St Léger, abbot of Bec and canon of the cathedral chapter, was elected by a chapter that had experienced deep internal rifts under the previous bishop. At Sées, in 1220, the choice of a regular was unsurprising, but instead of a man from within the chapter the electors turned to the outsider Gervase, abbot of Premontré, to lead a church riven by substantial internal rivalries.[13]

It is necessary, then, to look for other explanations to account for the dominance of the secular bishops. The principal reason was certainly not *a priori* better qualification for the office. Abbots and priors fulfilled the canonists' requirement to be experienced in administrative and legal matters as much as any secular cleric. For example, Robert, abbot of St Etienne, Caen, who was sent to England in 1198 to reform the English exchequer,[14] belonged amongst the great administrative experts of his time. The causes for the overwhelming number of secular prelates lay elsewhere. First, there

[12] C.W. Hollister, *Henry I* (New Haven, 2001), pp. 413–41, 444–7.
[13] See supra, pp. 106–7 (Evreux), 133–4 (Sées), 199–200 (Angers).
[14] Power, 'Angevin Normandy', p. 69.

were the networks operating within the cathedral chapters which aimed at the promotion of one of their members to the see. In this case, the status of the chapter predetermined the status of the bishop. Since all but one of the chapters were secular, these internal networks produced a far greater number of secular than regular candidates.

Second, electors considered it appropriate for a candidate to share the status of the cathedral chapter of his church. If the bishop was not elected from among the clergy of the cathedral church itself, the electors turned to other institutions of comparable affiliation and organisation. At Sées, this procedure may even have been institutionalised, since the regular canons recruited from St Victor brought with them their custom of looking first among themselves for a suitable candidate, then among other institutions of regular clergy. Their supporter, Arnulf of Lisieux, bitterly complained during the electoral dispute of 1144–7 that a secular ought not to become bishop of a regular chapter. About sixty years later, in 1201, the regular canons swore to elect one of their members, because, so the prior claimed, the previous secular bishops had acted to the detriment of the church.[15]

A third, though minor, factor was the dynamics of royal patronage. A number of secular clerics enjoyed royal support at their elections, but the overall impact of royal patronage on the ratio of secular to regular bishops was very small. There is no evidence that at secular cathedrals royal candidates prevented the election of men from among the regular clergy. In fact, as has been mentioned earlier, Achard's election to Avranches – the only election of a regular to a secular cathedral church – was probably brought about by the king. At secular cathedral chapters, royal patronage was an additional, not a conditional, factor for the choice of seculars. Only at the regular chapter of Sées did royal influence make a difference as to the affiliation of the bishop. At least once the Angevins successfully insisted on the election of a secular instead of a regular cleric.[16] The royal support for secular clerics was a consequence of the affiliation of the clergy active in royal service. When concerned with elections, the Angevins tended to look for candidates from their immediate entourage who were experienced in royal administration and politics. There they found secular clerics in far greater numbers than regulars. In theory neither secular nor regular clergy should actively engage in secular business other than to remind the laymen of their worldliness.[17] In practice, however, this applied much more to the regulars than to the secular clergy who fuelled the emerging administrative machinery.

The profile of the episcopacy of Normandy and Greater Anjou has become clearer. The bishops in Normandy and Greater Anjou shared a number of

---

[15] See supra, pp. 115–32.   [16] Ibid.   [17] Aurell, *L'empire des Plantagenêt*, pp. 74–8.

features. The average bishop was probably from aristocratic stock, belonged to the secular clergy, and had held a high ecclesiastical office in his or a neighbouring diocese prior to his election, often in a cathedral chapter. Thus considering their social origins, their clerical status, and the type and location of the offices they held prior to their elections, the episcopacy appears as a fairly homogeneous group.[18] But regardless of whether two men shared all these characteristics they could have quite different career paths. It is now time to turn to the dynamics of the different types of patronage upon which clerics could build their hopes.

STRUCTURES AND DYNAMICS OF PATRONAGE

The structure of the aristocratic family of the twelfth and early thirteenth centuries was mainly shaped by inheritance patterns. These patterns were far from uniform in north-western France, but they shared an emphasis on the eldest son as successor to his father's patrimony. Younger sons were not left out in the cold, for customary law allowed and to a certain extent prescribed provisions for them, but the adequacy of their share depended very much on the extent of the family's resources.[19] As a consequence, a goodly number of the younger sons of aristocratic families may have had to be content with a relatively small inheritance or the maintenance provided by their eldest brother.[20] If they wanted to increase their wealth and to build up a proper lordship, they had to turn elsewhere. Some of them offered their military and – increasingly important – their

---

[18] Compared to England, it is worthwhile noting that, unlike their English colleagues, the bishops of Normandy and Greater Anjou counted no saints among them. This fact entirely fits the contemporary pattern on the continent and thus underlines the peculiarity of the English episcopacy in this aspect, cf. R. Brentano, *The Two Churches. England and Italy in the Thirteenth Century*, 2nd edn (Berkeley, 1988), pp. 174–237; A. Vauchez, *La sainteté en occident aux derniers siècles du moyen âge d'après les procès de canonisation et les documents hagiographiques* (Bibliothèque des écoles françaises d'Athènes et de Rome CCXLI) (Rome, 1988), pp. 334–5.

[19] J.C. Holt, 'Politics and Property in early Medieval England', *Past and Present*, 57 (1972), 3–52, 9–13, 42, 44–5, modifying L. Génestal, *Le parage normand* (Bibliothèque de l'histoire du droit normand 2e série, I, 1–2) (Caen, 1911); Everard, *Brittany and the Angevins*, pp. 194–5; Barthélemy, *Société*, pp. 530, 859–60; Lemesle, *La société aristocratique*, p. 135; J. Yver, 'Les caractères originaux du groupe de coutumes de l'Ouest de la France', *Revue historique du droit français et étranger*, 30 (1950), 18–79, esp. 41–7; H. Légoherel, 'Le parage en Touraine-Anjou au moyen âge', ibid., 43 (1965), 224–46.

[20] Geoffrey du Neubourg, younger brother of Archbishop Rotrou, is one example of a landless knight who failed or was unwilling to establish his own lordship and lived first at the expense of his eldest brother Roger of Warwick, then after Roger's death, at the expense of Roger's son and heir, Crouch, *Beaumonts*, p. 16; D. Crouch, *William Marshal. Court, Career and Chivalry in the Angevin Empire 1147–1219* (London, 1990), p. 27.

administrative services to powerful lords, hoping to make influential friends and to receive one day a fief or an heiress.[21]

An alternative route for younger sons was to join the church. The need for a living was certainly not the only motivation for such a step. Parents opting for an ecclesiastical life for one or even all of their children[22] were also guided by their spirituality and faith. But making their sons enter the church, in particular as secular clerics, also meant creating new opportunities. A cleric successfully rising within the church hierarchy, possibly to a bishopric, opened up new spheres of action not just for himself and his immediate following, but also for his family. The route to a bishopric, however, was not straightforward; there was no ticket guaranteeing an easy ride and safe arrival from the first ecclesiastical benefice to an episcopal see. Manifold paths led to the *cathedra*; the career paths of bishops could be closely intertwined with the activities of their families, but they could also take other turns leading them relatively far away from their sometimes modest knightly origins to the heights of royal or papal courts. In total four paths, which were far from equally well-trodden, can be distinguished: by way of the bishop and the cathedral chapter, the baronial family, the king, or the pope. These paths could cross or even run concurrently. The influence of a powerful family, for instance, was often a precondition for a position within a cathedral chapter or for the entry of a cleric into royal service. Yet it is equally true that each path had its own characteristic features. The mechanisms responsible for the success or failure of a royal cleric were different from those determining the career of a cleric belonging to the high aristocracy and again different from those of a cleric belonging to the *familia* of a bishop.

---

[21] In the course of the second half of the twelfth century the administrator took the place of the bachelor, i.e. the household knight active in tournament and warfare, as the typical representative of this group, Crouch, *William Marshal*, pp. 3–4 and passim; R. Turner, *Men Raised from the Dust. Administrative Service and Upward Mobility in Angevin England* (Philadelphia, 1988), pp. 12–13; G. Duby, 'Dans la France de Nord-Ouest. Au XIIᵉ siècle: les "jeunes" dans la société aristocratique', *Annales. Economie, société, civilisation*, 19 (1964), 835–46; J.C. Holt, 'Feudal Society and the Family in early Medieval England: III. Patronage and Politics', *Transactions of the Royal Historical Society*, 34 (1984), 1–25, 15–16, makes important qualifications to the general applicability of Duby's model of the *seniores* and *iuvenes*. Cadets were prominent among the royal officers in Normandy, M. Billoré, 'La noblesse normande dans l'entourage de Richard Ier', in Aurell (ed.), *La cour Plantagenêt (1154–1204)*, pp. 151–66, p. 160.

[22] C.B. Bouchard, *'Those of my Blood'. Constructing Noble Families in Medieval Francia* (Philadelphia, 2001), p. 170, quotes the case of a couple that opted for an ecclesiastical career for both of their sons.

Bishops and cathedral chapters

According to canon law, bishops were not allowed to nominate their successors.[23] Gratian explained that this was so because in the past bishops had started to appoint their successors on the basis of blood relationship rather than on the quality of their lives.[24] The implication of Gratian's argument is clear: blood relations should not matter in advancing someone's ecclesiastical career; instead the *idoneitas* of the candidate ought to be the decisive criterion. The elections in Normandy and Greater Anjou show, however, that, while there is no evidence for bishops openly designating their relatives as their successors, family relations continued to play a significant role in paving the way to a bishopric.

The bishops in Normandy and Greater Anjou had the right to fill vacant canonries and to appoint the dignitaries of their churches. The only exception was the dean, who was elected by the canons in the majority of the chapters.[25] Yet a number of restrictions limited the bishop's choice. A candidate had to be *idoneus*, and the chapter had the right and the obligation

---

[23] Cf. *Decretum Gratiani* C. 8, q. 1, c. 1–7.

[24] *Decretum Gratiani* C. 8, q. 1, p.c. 7; cf. *Summa Parisiensis*, ed. McLaughlin, p. 139.

[25] For the Norman bishops, with particular reference to the archbishop of Rouen, see *Registres de Philippe Auguste*, ed. Baldwin, inquisitiones, no. 18. For further evidence relating to individual bishoprics, see: Rouen: 'E chronico Rotomagensi', in *RHF*, XXIII, p. 334 (election of the dean by the chapter); Evreux: Evreux, AD Eure G 122 (cartulary, chapter of Evreux), fo. 10r, no. 35 (conferral of the office of the treasurer by the bishop), fo. 11v, no. 41 (election of the dean by the chapter); Lisieux: *Arnulf*, ed. Barlow, nos. 34, 134 (conferral of canonries by the bishop); Sées: the bishop elected the archdeacons, Bidou, 'La réforme du chapitre', 31-2; *Arnulf*, ed. Barlow, no. 34; there is no explicit reference to the person/group, who appointed the prior and decided on the entry of new canons. At St Victor, Paris, which possibly served as a model, the abbot and senior members of the community discussed who should be the new prior. Their candidate had then to be approved and elected by the entire community. As to men wishing to enter the community, the abbot examined their suitability before presenting them to the chapter whose approval was required, *Liber ordinis Sancti Victoris Parisiensis*, ed. Jocqué and Milis, c. 5, 22, pp. 25, 99–100; Bayeux: *Antiquus cartularius*, ed. Bourrienne, I, nos. 66, 69 (conferral of canonries by the bishop), no. 205 [= Jaffé, II, no. 15676; *WH* -] (election of the dean by the chapter); *Ordinaire et coutumier de l'église cathédrale de Bayeux*, ed. Chevalier, pp. 290, 308 (canonries and offices conferred by the bishop and the election of the dean by the chapter); the bishop ceased his right to create new prebends from his possessions in 1207, ibid., p. 418; Coutances: *Le cartulaire du chapitre cathédral de Coutances*, ed. Fontanel, no. 75; supra, p. 147 (creation and conferral of canonries by the bishop); in 1238, Gregor IX confirmed Bishop Hugh's creation of the office of the dean, who was to be elected by the chapter, *Registres de Grégoire IX*, ed. Auvray, II, no. 4181; Avranches: *Rot. chart.*, p. 15a; *Rotuli Normanniae in turri Londonensi*, ed. Hardy, p. 25 (King John conferred the office of the treasurer and a canonry during the vacancy of the see); *Pouillés de la province de Rouen*, ed. A. Longnon (Recueil des historiens de la France. Pouillés II) (Paris, 1903), p. 163, (dating from 1480: canonries and offices conferred by the bishop and the election of dean by the chapter). For Greater Anjou, see: Tours: 'Ven. Hildeberti epistolae', lib. II, no. 34 (offices conferred by the archbishop); *Cartulaire de l'archévêché*, ed. de Grandmaison, I, nos. 19, 21–4 (fourteenth century: canonries and offices conferred by the archbishop). Ibid., no. 24, also shows that, in the fourteenth century, the archbishop conferred the deanery. In 1215, however, Archbishop John had granted the chapter to right to elect their dean, Paris, BNF Collection Housseau, XXIII, fo. 252r: 'L'an 1215 il [John de

to verify the candidate's suitability.[26] In addition to this, a variety of factors could limit the bishop's freedom of choice. Some prebends belonged to the chapter, which then had the right to present a candidate to the bishop;[27] some prebends were founded for the benefit of a particular individual,[28] sometimes the king, and from the beginning of the thirteenth century increasingly the pope asked the bishop to provide at least one and sometimes several canonries for a man of his choice.[29] Finally individual canons may have tried to influence the decision as to whom their prebends would pass after their deaths.[30] Nonetheless, the nomination of canons and dignitaries was a great opportunity for the bishop to enhance his influence within the chapter and to build a network of supporters. It is, however, difficult to establish with precision the groups from which a bishop recruited canons. Information on the individual canons, such as the course of their career, their precise relationship with the bishop, or the date of their entry to the chapter, is hard to come by. The cases of Bartholomew at Tours, and Rotrou and Walter de Coutances at Rouen are enlightening. At Tours, Bartholomew tapped into different pools to fill vacant positions. His relatives constituted one of these pools. After his election in 1174, his brother Hugh succeeded him as dean of the chapter, and a couple of years later, John, son of Bartholomew's cousin Bourchard IV, count of Vendôme, appears in a charter as treasurer. Probably recruited by Bartholomew were

Faye] permit aux chanoines de sa cathédrale d'élire leur doyen. Il éteignit les offices des prévôts, et la dignité du cellarier dont il unit les revenus à celle du chancelier, et ceux des prévôts au chapitre'; Le Mans: 'Historia Gaufredi ducis Normannorum et comitis Andegavorum', in *Chroniques des comtes d'Anjou et des seigneurs d'Amboise*, ed. Halphen and Poupardin, p. 212; *Catalogue des actes des évêques du Mans jusqu'à la fin du XIII⁰ siècle avec une introduction*, ed. L. Celier (Paris, 1910), no. 599 (conferral of canonries by the bishop); *Liber albus*, ed. Lottin, nos. 41 (election of the dean by the chapter), 207 (conferral of canonries by the bishop); Angers: *Cartulaire noir*, ed. Urseau, p. xvi, nos. 122, 122bis, which imply that the bishop conferred the thirty established canonries, see infra, n. 27; *Pouillés de la province de Tours*, ed. A. Longnon (Recueil des historiens de la France. Pouillés III) (Paris, 1903), p. 242 (fifteenth century: canonries and offices conferred by the bishop; election of the dean by the chapter).

[26] See, for example, *Ordinaire et coutumier de l'église cathédrale de Bayeux*, ed. Chevalier, p. 308.

[27] At Angers, the foundation of an additional ten prebends was envisaged at the end of the eleventh century. The cathedral chapter was to have the right to present suitable candidates for these prebends to the bishop. This project, however, was never realised, *Cartulaire noir*, ed. Urseau, p. xvi, nos. 122, 122bis; for prebends to which the chapter of Evreux nominated candidates, see Müller, *Delegationsgerichtsbarkeit*, II, no. 153.

[28] At Evreux, Count Simon of Evreux founded a prebend for a cleric named Richard, *Papsturkunden in Frankreich. Neue Folge. II. Normandie*, ed. Ramackers, no. 246.

[29] Spear, 'Power, Patronage and Personality', pp. 207–9; 'Ven. Hildeberti epistolae', lib. II, no. 34; 'Historia Gaufredi ducis Normannorum et comitis Andegavorum', in *Chroniques des comtes d'Anjou et des seigneurs d'Amboise*, ed. Halphen and Poupardin, p. 212; for papal provisions, see supra, p. 66 n. 256.

[30] Spear, 'Power, Patronage and Personality', pp. 216–17; cf. also the bitter comments against canons who regarded canonries as hereditary, 'Petri Blesensi opuscula. Tractatus Quales sunt', in *PL*, CCVII, cols. 1005–52, pars II, c. 3, cols. 1015–16.

his *nepos* John de Faye, who subsequently became archdeacon, dean, and archbishop of Tours, and his *consanguineus* Geoffrey de Plessis, who became chancellor and archdeacon.[31] Another relative may have been Canon Amaury de Lavardin who seems to have joined the chapter during Bartholomew's time in office.[32] A second pool was probably the entourage of the counts of Vendôme. Archpriest Archembaud de Vendôme, who appears towards the end of Bartholomew's tenure, bore a name typical of the family of the prévôts of Vendôme.[33] Canon Peter de Vendôme, probably also recruited by Bartholomew, may also have belonged to the entourage of the counts.[34] Bartholomew de La Haye, canon at Tours at least since 1180, possibly indicates a third pool from which Bartholomew recruited canons: tenants of the archbishop. Bartholomew was perhaps related to the lords de La Haye, who held some of their lands from the archbishop.[35]

There were similar patterns at Rouen under Archbishops Rotrou and Walter. Rotrou fostered the careers of his *nepotes* Robert du Neubourg, archdeacon then dean, and Amicus, archdeacon then treasurer. Another *nepos* of his, Geoffrey, may have become a canon at Rouen. Roger of Warwick probably also owed his canonry to Rotrou; his *cognomen* – Rotrou's father had been earl of Warwick – and his activity in the royal chancery support this hypothesis. Roger's *nepos*, Elias of Warwick, probably entered the chapter in the 1170s. Waleran de Meulan, traceable as canon then archdeacon at Rouen, was probably related to Rotrou. Another Waleran, appearing as canon in the 1170s, may also have been related to the archbishop.[36] The activities of Rotrou's successor, Walter de Coutances, as patron can be traced with greater clarity. At Rouen, he fostered the careers of a considerable number of men: his *nepotes* John, succeeding Robert du Neubourg as dean *c.* 1188, William, archdeacon from about 1190, and Richard, canon from *c.* 1185, then archdeacon from about 1190. Canon Odo de Coutances (*c.* 1169?, *c.* 1188), canon Ralph of Coutances (from about 1200), and cleric Lawrence de Coutances (from about 1190) were probably also relatives profiting from Walter's promotion.[37] The case of Richard de Malpalu indicates that Walter drew from other resources besides his family. Richard was a relative of William de Malpalu, an administrator of Henry II, and a member of the Malpalu

---

[31] See supra, pp. 174–5, 183–4.
[32] In 1185, he witnessed a charter of Archbishop Bartholomew, Paris, BNF Collection Housseau, V, no. 1991. For names of the Lavardin family, see Barthélemy, *Société*, p. 568.
[33] See supra, p. 184.   [34] See supra, ibid.   [35] See supra, p. 177 n. 37.
[36] Spear, 'Power, Patronage and Personality', pp. 214–15.
[37] Ibid., p. 219; Spear, *The Personnel*, pp. 203–4, 217, 250, 253; for Lawrence, see Spear, 'Les chanoines de la cathédrale de Rouen pendant la période ducale', *Annales de Normandie*, 41 (1991), 135–76, 167. It is unclear whether Odo de Coutances was already a canon in 1169, see supra, p. 79 n. 26.

family of Rouen. He appears to have come into contact with Walter through the royal chancery. At Rouen, Richard became canon in the 1190s, then dean (*c.* 1200/1–6/7) and helped three of his *nepotes* Philip, Richard (II), and Roger to canonries.[38] Other men, who moved with Walter to Rouen, receiving prebends there, were Roger de Foucarmont, Ralph de Richespald, Drogo de Trubleville, Richard Grim, John de Sées, William de La Bruyère, William de Verdun, and probably Nicholas the Chaplain.[39] Recommendations of relatives played a significant role in distributing prebends and offices. After John de Coutances' election to the see of Worcester in 1196, William de Verdun and John of Cornwall, a former chaplain of Walter at Lincoln who had remained there, became archdeacons at Worcester. John's election also had an impact on the composition of the chapter at Rouen. While William apparently kept his canonry at Rouen, John of Cornwall, together with three others of Bishop John's clerics, Robert de St Nicolas, Gilbert fitz William, and Eustace, received canonries at Rouen.[40]

These glimpses of Bartholomew's, Rotrou's, and Walter's recruitment policies suggest that they drafted canons from at least four pools: their family, their family's entourage, the churches' feudal tenants, and from personal acquaintances made in the course of their careers. For one of these groups the evidence is sufficiently detailed to take a closer look at the underlying principles of recruitment: the bishop's relatives. Blood relationship with the bishop did not automatically qualify a cleric for a canonry, but it did not harm either. Indeed, in the third quarter of the thirteenth century, Thomas Aquinas explained that when a bishop was choosing between two suitable candidates, one of whom was a relative, he was absolutely justified in choosing his relation, for relatives were more likely to work together for the church.[41] Ecclesiastics in prominent positions were expected to help their kinsmen. When in 1182, Samson returned from his consecration as abbot of Bury St Edmunds, his kinsmen sought his patronage. Samson, however, who 'loved his kin in moderation', took only one knight into his service, whom he found useful. He adroitly outmanoeuvred the others by replying that he had to consult the

---

[38] Spear, *The Personnel*, pp. 204, 252, 257, 261; Delisle, *Introduction*, pp. 490–1.

[39] Spear, 'Power, Patronage and Personality', p. 219; Spear, *The Personnel*, pp. 237–8, 248, 250, 253, 256, 260, 265–6, 268.

[40] Spear, 'Power, Patronage and Personality', p. 220; Greenway, *Fasti ecclesiae Anglicanae, Lincoln*, pp. 130, 162.

[41] *Sancti Thomae Aquinatis doctoris angelici opera omnia iussi impensaque Leonis XIII P. M. edita* (50 vols., Rome 1882–), IX, 2, 2, q. 63 a.2; W. Reinhard, 'Nepotismus. Der Funktionswandel einer papstgeschichtlichen Konstanten', *Zeitschrift für Kirchengeschichte*, 86 (1975), 145–85, 161.

convent first before being able to provide them with anything.[42] That the author of this story, Jocelin of Brakelond, considered this a notable exception from the rule becomes apparent later in the text, when Jocelin stated that Samson 'desired to treat those as being of his blood, who had helped him as their kinsman, when he was a poor cloister monk'. Then Jocelin went on to describe the promotions these men received from the abbot.[43] Walter Map, royal clerk and archdeacon of Oxford from 1197, was even more explicit about the expectations of relatives; he complained that his *nepotes* considered him to be 'born for their benefit not [his] own'.[44] In antiquity, this obligation of higher ranked men to provide for their relatives was described by the Roman term *pietas*. Towards the end of the thirteenth century, Thomas Aquinas referred again to this definition when he declared that the principal meaning of *pietas* was the care for *patria et parentes*; piety was only its secondary meaning.[45] *Pietas* as a criterion for the recruitment of canons did not contradict the principle of *idoneitas*; a suitable relative of the bishop could meet all requirements. But there was potential for conflict if, for instance, a bishop either chose relatives incapable of fulfilling their spiritual and/or administrative duties, or completely ignored the needs of his relatives. The bishop, therefore, had a great responsibility to make the right choices, not just for sake of his church, but also for his own political survival.

What happened if he failed to get the balance right is graphically illustrated in the case of Arnulf of Lisieux. Bishop John of Lisieux fostered the careers of two of his *nepotes*, the brothers John and Arnulf. John became bishop of Sées, leaving his post as archdeacon of Sées to his younger brother Arnulf.[46] John, bishop of Lisieux, also appointed a *nepos* of Arnulf, Sylvester, as treasurer of the chapter of Lisieux. After Bishop John's death, Arnulf followed him in the see of Lisieux. This ecclesiastical network evidently operated efficiently under its first head. Under Arnulf, however, it fell apart. At the beginning of his episcopate, Arnulf made another *nepos* of his, Hugh de Nonant, archdeacon.[47] According to Arnulf's own words, he had educated and schooled Sylvester and Hugh from their earliest childhood onwards, and had

---

[42] *Cronica Jocelini de Brakelonda*, ed. Butler, p. 24.   [43] Ibid., p. 43.

[44] *Walter Map. De nugis curialium. Courtiers Trifles*, ed. M.R. James revised by C.N.L. Brooke and R.A.B. Mynors (Oxford Medieval Texts) (Oxford, 1983), d. 1, c. 10, pp. 22–5. Walter's anger was not directed against the expectations as such. He did not consider them to be improper. What disappointed him was the failure of his *nepotes* to acknowledge their obligation towards him as their benefactor, thus to live up to the reciprocity of their relationship: 'anything I spend on them they reckon as a due, and neither feel nor pay me any thanks for it', he bemoaned, ibid.

[45] *Sancti Thomae Aquinatis*, IX, 2, 2, q. 101 a.1; Reinhard, 'Nepotismus', 162.

[46] *Arnulf*, ed. Barlow, no. 34.   [47] Ibid., pp. xii–xiii; no. 133 n. c.

provided them richly with benefices.[48] So far, he had fulfilled all expectations. But their relationship turned sour, and, instead of collaborating with
his *nepotes*, Arnulf found himself in a continuous struggle with them.
Again according to Arnulf, the turning point came when he refused to
provide their *nepotuli* with vacant benefices in his church, giving such
benefices instead to literate and honest men.[49] Suitability or *idoneitas*,
Arnulf wanted to make his reader believe, was the proper criterion for
recruitment. His *nepotes*, Sylvester and Hugh, however, saw matters
differently. According to Arnulf, they argued that he should have given
preference to their *nepotuli*, because of their blood relationship.[50] If this
was indeed their argument, they appealed to Arnulf's position as their
most senior and most influential relative and thus to his responsibility to
provide for younger members of the family. Arnulf's refusal to accept this
obligation was certainly not founded on a general indifference or opposition towards such expectations. His own career and his behaviour towards
Sylvester and Hugh make clear that he was aware of the responsibility
senior family members held. In the case of his *nepotuli*, however, other
candidates were closer to his heart and, considering his past efforts for
family members, he may have felt no need to give priority to his kinsmen.
But Arnulf underestimated the consequences of his decision. His relatives
and protégés took offence at his refusal to grant their requests. From their
point of view, he had failed to perform his basic responsibilities as patron
and thus failed in his obligation of mutual support. Hugh de Nonant's
relationship with Arnulf may have been further soured by Arnulf's fall
from royal favour after 1173–4.[51] Hugh, who appears not to have worked
against Arnulf until then, may have hoped that Arnulf would use his good
connections with the royal court to provide him with a bishopric. After
1173–4, however, Arnulf could not provide this help anymore; indeed to
be associated with him was dangerous. Arnulf had become useless as a
patron, and Hugh had no reason to support him any longer. In sum, a
bishop was expected to provide for relatives; in return he could expect
their loyalty. But if he failed to fulfil these expectations – and this holds
also true for unrelated protégés – he ran the considerable risk of losing
their support, or even encountering their hostility, which would mean at
least the partial breakdown of his network.

The bishop created and held together his network of canons. It is true,
some of them may have shared blood or feudal ties, or may have known

---

[48] In a letter to Pope Alexander III, written around 1179, Arnulf used a modified quotation from
Isaiah to describe his relationship with his *nepotes* at the time: 'filios entriui et exaltaui; ipsi autem *non
tantum* spreuerunt, *sed etiam oderunt* me', *Arnulf*, ed. Barlow, no. 133; Bible, Isaiah, 1 verse 2.
[49] *Arnulf*, ed. Barlow, no. 133.   [50] Ibid.   [51] See supra, p. 110.

each other through many years of service in the episcopal or royal household. But such bonds did not guarantee that they would function together as a network in support of the bishop's policies; some may have been colleagues, but others bitter rivals, and blood relationship did not necessarily mean a common political line. What made them a functioning group – a network – was the importance of the bishop for their lives and careers. Joining his entourage and becoming canons due to his influence meant to some extent leaving their families and entering a new one, the bishop's *familia*. The bishop, instead of the parents, became the canons' principal hope for advancement in their careers, in particular if they had entered the church at a very young age.[52] Within this new family, rivalry for the bishop's patronage was certainly part of everyday business. But when in the case of an episcopal election other groups within or outside the chapter threatened their position, the best chance to assure the survival of their influence was to stick together and to focus their efforts on the election of a member of their network.

Within the episcopal *familia*, the relationship between the bishop and his *nepotes* appears to have been of particular significance. 'When God deprived bishops of sons, the devil gave them nephews' were the words Gerald de Barri put into the mouth of Pope Alexander III, when he criticised nepotism among bishops.[53] The *avunculus–nepos* relationship formed perhaps the closest link within the episcopal network, and the evidence suggests that bishops built up possible successors from among their *nepotes*. Arnulf, for example, followed John at Lisieux, while at Rouen Robert du Neubourg was originally chosen to succeed Rotrou. At Tours, the succession of Bartholomew to his *avunculus* Engelbald was only delayed by Joscius' tenure in between; similarly John de Faye became archbishop after the successor of his *avunculus* Bartholomew, Geoffrey du Lude, had died. At Angers, the short episcopate of William de Chemillé separated the episcopates of Ralph and William de Beaumont. Writers like Gerald de Barri, or the author (William, prior of Grandmont?) of the treatise *Quales sunt*, railed against the patron–protégé relationship between *avunculus* and *nepos*,[54] but other voices described it in more favourable terms. Arnulf's account of his

---

[52] Cf. the young William Marshal, whose focus shifted from his family to William de Tancarville, when he entered the latter's household, Crouch, *William Marshal*, p. 24.

[53] *Giraldi Cambrensis opera*, ed. Brewer et al., II, p. 304. Nothing can be said on the extent to which bishops in Normandy and Greater Anjou fathered sons and subsequently supported their careers. For England, see N. Vincent, 'New Light on Master Alexander of Swerford (d. 1246): The Career and Connections of an Oxfordshire Civil Servant', *Oxoniensia*, 61 (1996), 297–309, 303–6; Barrow, 'Origins and Careers', 35–6.

[54] 'Petri Blesensi opuscula. Tracatus Quales sunt', in *PL*, CCVII, cols. 1005–52, deals with this matter at great length. Particularly illustrative are the following quotations from pars II, c. I, col. 1015: 'Nepotes autem dico quoslibet illorum carne, moribus, et vita cognatos; quibus applaudunt, quibus

care for the upbringing, education, and provision of benefices of his *nepotes* Sylvester and Hugh has already been quoted.[55] Hamelin, bishop of Le Mans, expressed his gratitude for similar treatment by founding anniversaries for his *patruus* Odo, dean of St Martin de Tours, and his brother Philip, also dean of St Martin, who had fostered him at St Martin *a puerili aetate*.[56] Perhaps the most impressive evidence for the foster-father relationship between *avunculus* and *nepos* exists for Ralph and William de Beaumont. An entry on William in an obituary equated the relationship between Ralph and William with the biblical relationship between Eli and Samuel.[57] Just like Samuel, whom his mother Hanna had entrusted to the priest Eli for his upbringing, William had been in Ralph's care. This image was probably also the theme of a window at the cathedral church of Angers made in the time of Bishop William and showing the Virgin and Child and two bishops. The heraldic arms once displayed in the window and identifying the bishops have disappeared, but one of the surviving figures is likely to represent William himself, the other one possibly Ralph.[58] If so, the window impressively captured the close relationship between Ralph and William, visualising the foster-father

---

thesaurizant, quos sibi praeparant successores antistes nostri'; and c. 2, col. 1015: 'His patres acquirunt, servant, rapiunt, custodiunt. Acquirunt sollicite, servant sollicitius, rapiunt moleste, custodiunt molestius. Discurrunt, torquentur et gemunt, augere desiderantes quod adfiliatis relinquant haeredibus.' 'Dona narrantur, sed nulla donorum causae tractantur. Promotiones audiuntur, sed promotionum negotia non audiuntur.' P. Glorieux, *Pour revaloriser Migne*. *Tables rectificatives* (Mélanges science religieuse IX) (Lille, 1952), p. 76, assigns the authorship of *Quales sunt* to William, prior of Grandmont.

[55] See supra, pp. 223–4.

[56] *Necrologium beatissimi Martini Turonensis, 804–1495, et obituarium Majoris Monasterii*, ed. Nobilleau, pp. 29–30. Hamelin in turn fostered his *nepos* Odo, ibid.; *Cartulaire du chapitre royal de Saint-Pierre-de-la-Cour du Mans*, ed. Menjot d'Elbenne and Denis, no. 32; *Liber albus*, ed. Lottin, nos. 100–2.

[57] Paris, BNF Collection Baluze, XXXIX, fo. 33v: 'utpote qui [i.e. William] in ea [i.e. church] velut alter Samuel a primis cunabulis nutritus fuerat sub venerando antiste Radulfo suo Heli tanquam ibidem divina providentia dispensavit sicuti generis sic sacerdotii futurus successor et haeres et dominico sacrificio pre aliis praecipue praeferandus'; Bible, I Samuel, 1–3. Urseau reconstructed the obituary of the cathedral church from excerpts taken by seventeenth- and early eighteenth-century scholars. He also used the Baluze transcripts but omitted this particular entry. Perhaps he was concerned by the length of the obit, which runs in the Baluze transcripts from 33v to 34v. Instead, he printed a much shorter entry on William, which is equally preserved in the Baluze transcripts. Stating that 'hic, a puero in hac ecclesia educatus sub Radulfo episcopo' this entry also conveys the close relationship between Ralph and William, *Obituaire*, ed. Urseau, p. 31. It is impossible to give a precise date for the composition of the more extensive obituary. But similar obituaries were composed in Paris in the second half of the thirteenth century, which raises the possibility that William's obituary was composed at about the same time. If so, it reflects almost contemporary views on the relationship between Ralph and William. I am grateful to Professor Jean-Loup Lemaître for his advice on French medieval obituaries.

[58] K. Boulanger, 'Les vitraux du chœur de la cathédrale d'Angers: commandataires et iconographie', in J. McNeill and D. Prigent (eds.), *Anjou. Medieval Art, Architecture and Archaeology* (The British Archaeological Association Conference Transactions XXVI) (Leeds, 2003), pp. 196–209, pp. 199, 206.

relationship between *avunculus* and *nepos* to succeeding generations of bishops and canons at Angers.

In recent years, the structure and consciousness of the aristocratic family in the early and high middle ages has come under fresh scrutiny by historians.[59] The traditional claim has been that family structure and consciousness underwent a radical change around the year 1000. The argument ran that the large, horizontally organised family of Carolingian times, the *Sippe*, where connections on the father's side (agnatic) mattered as much as those on the mother's (cognatic) side, transmuted into a strictly patrilinear, vertically organised family, the *Geschlecht*, that favoured agnatic connections. The symbol of this newly gained family consciousness was the adopted *cognomen*, generally the name of the castle the family's possessions were centred upon.[60] New research, however, has cast serious doubt on the validity of some aspects of this hypothesis. Patrilinear tendencies were already visible in the early middle ages and, from the ninth century onwards, the patrilinear, vertically organised family became the dominant structure.[61] But this development did not lead to a strictly patrilinear, vertically organised family, in which agnatic connections mattered most. Emphasising the prominent role of women as regents and as transmitters of property, scholars have pointed to the considerable cognatic attributes of twelfth-century families.[62] In the context of family structure and family consciousness, episcopal patronage

---

[59] See in particular R. Le Jan, *Famille et pouvoir dans le monde franc (VIIᵉ – Xᵉ siècle). Essai d'anthropologie sociale* (Histoire ancienne et médiévale XXXIII) (Paris, 1995); Bouchard, *'Those of my Blood'*; Livingstone, 'Kith and Kin', 419–58; B. Newman, *The Anglo-Norman Nobility in the Reign of Henry I. The Second Generation* (Philadelphia, 1988), pp. 35–67; Lemesle, *La société aristocratique*, pp. 111–35; Barthélemy, *Société*, pp. 507–651.

[60] Georges Duby was most influential in arguing this thesis for high medieval France, see, for example, 'Structures de parenté et noblesse. France du nord XIᵉ–XIIᵉ siècles', in *Miscellanea medievalia in memoriam Jan Frederik Niermeyer* (Groningen, 1967), pp. 149–65. He was heavily influenced by the work of Karl Schmid on German aristocratic families, see, for example, 'Zur Problematik von Familie, Sippe und Geschlecht, Haus und Dynastie beim mittelalterlichen Adel. Vorfragen zum Thema:, Adel und Herrschaft im Mittelalter', *Zeitschrift für die Geschichte des Oberrheins*, 105 (1957), 1–62. For a more extensive discussion of the historiography on this subject, see Bouchard, *'Those of my Blood'*, pp. 59–60, 162.

[61] Bouchard, *'Those of my Blood'*, pp. 178–9; Le Jan, *Famille et pouvoir*, pp. 429–34.

[62] Newman, *Anglo-Norman Nobility*, pp. 35–67; Bouchard, *'Those of my Blood'*, pp. 120–34, 155–74. The cognatic character of families throughout the middle ages is emphasised by A. Gestrich et al., *Geschichte der Familie* (Europäische Kulturgeschichte I) (Stuttgart, 2003), p. 355, and by A. Guerreau-Jalabert et al., 'De l'histoire de la famille à l'anthropologie de la parenté', in J.-C. Schmitt and O.G. Oexle (eds.), *Les tendances actuelles de l'histoire du moyen âge en France et en Allemagne. Actes des colloques de Sèvres (1997) et Göttingen (1998) organisés par le C. N. R. S. et le Max-Planck-Institut für Geschichte* (Histoire ancienne et médiévale LXVI) (Paris, 2002), pp. 433–46, pp. 436–40; see also the pertinent remarks by B. Jussen, 'Famille et parenté. Comparaison des recherches françaises et allemandes', in ibid., pp. 447–60.

of relatives has not yet been extensively explored.[63] As will be seen, it throws some interesting light on the organisation of the family and the radius of family consciousness in the twelfth and early thirteenth centuries.

Many episcopal *avunculi* were indeed the uncles of their *nepotes*, as were Rotrou of Robert, Ralph of William de Beaumont, Engelbald of Bartholomew, and perhaps Bartholomew was a step-granduncle of John de Faye.[64] But an *avunculus* may not have had to be a biological uncle in the modern sense. In the second half of the twelfth century, a canon of St Aubert in Cambrai, Lambert de Wattrelos, wrote a genealogy of his family. He stated that his *avunculus* made him canon at St Aubert; Lambert's genealogy shows that this *avunculus* was in fact Lambert's much older cousin.[65] The usage of the terms *avunculus–nepos* to describe older and younger cousins is well known.[66] What is less well known, however, is whether they were interchangeable with the other term employed to describe cousins, *consanguineus*,[67] or whether they had a more specific meaning. At present this question cannot be answered conclusively. But the fact that in Lambert's case a patron–protégé relationship existed between *avunculus* and *nepos* raises the possibility that these terms could be employed to describe such a relationship.[68] If this was the case, then its usage could be interpreted as indicating the strong influence of a vertical and hierarchical family structure on the perception of relationships; in other words the terminology of a family structure, in which the elder generation procured for the younger, served as model to

---

[63] A notable exception is Bouchard, 'Those of my Blood', pp. 168–74; see also W.M. Newman, *Les seigneurs de Nesle en Picardie, XIIe–XIIIe siècle. Leur chartes et leur histoire. Etude sur la noblesse régionale ecclésiastique et laïque* (Memoirs of the American Philosophical Society XIC) (2 vols., Philadelphia 1971), I, pp. 100–24.

[64] See supra, pp. 77, 175, 181, 207.

[65] 'Annales Cameracenses', in *MGH, scriptores*, XVI, ed. G. H. Pertz, 2nd edn (Leipzig, 1925), pp. 509–54, pp. 511–12.

[66] Bouchard, 'Those of my Blood', p. 5; for Normandy in the eleventh century, see P. Bauduin, 'Designer les parents: le champ de la parenté dans l'œuvre des premiers chroniqueurs normands', in Gillingham (ed.), *Anglo-Norman Studies XXIV. Proceedings of the Battle Conference 2001*, pp. 71–84, pp. 81–2; for the early middle ages, see Le Jan, *Famille et pouvoir*, pp. 174–5.

[67] For example, Archbishop Bartholomew of Tours used this term to describe his relationship with Archdeacon Geoffrey de Plessis in a charter dating from 1197, Paris, BNF Collection Housseau, V, no. 2098.

[68] Cf. the definition of *nepos* in *Quales sunt*, supra, pp. 225–6 n. 54. Studies focusing in particular on the early middle ages have shown that social practice could prescribe the terms used to indicate a relationship, B. Jussen, *Patenschaft und Adoption im frühen Mittelalter. Künstliche Verwandtschaft als soziale Praxis* (Veröffentlichungen des Max-Planck-Instituts für Geschichte XCVIII) (Göttingen, 1991), pp. 9–22 and passim; Le Jan, *Famille et pouvoir*, pp. 159–77; A. Guerreau-Jalabert, 'La désignation des relations et des groupes de parenté en latin médiéval', *Archivum latinitatis medii aevi (Bulletin du Cange)*, 46/7 (1988), 65–108; K. Hauck, 'Formes de parenté artificielle dans le haut moyen âge', in G. Duby and J. Le Goff (eds.), *Famille et parenté dans l'occident médiéval. Actes du colloque de Paris (6–8 Juin 1974)* (Collection de l'école française de Rome XXX) (Rome, 1977), pp. 43–7.

denominate a patron–protégé relationship. Yet, family consciousness was neither strictly agnatic nor exclusively vertical. First, paternal *as well as* maternal uncles, thus agnatic as well as cognatic relatives, acted as patrons.[69] Second, even though the fact that 'true' nephews regularly profited from a bishop's patronage indicates a close degree of relationship was particularly helpful, the evidence from Tours and Rouen suggests that more distant kin could also count on episcopal support.[70] The patrilinear, vertical family structure, therefore, was not a rigid, exclusive principle. As much as inheritance patterns determined the position of fathers and sons in society, the need of younger sons for support activated far-reaching kinship bonds and thus determined a broader horizon of family consciousness.

The bishop as patron could shape family consciousness not only in terms of its membership, but also in terms of its political, spiritual, and even physical home, in other words in terms of its identity. If the bishop came from a knightly family there was a reasonable chance that he would become the focal point not only of his clerical *familia* but also of his biological family. At Evreux, for example, the Cierrey family founded a prebend, enrooted themselves in the chapter, and provided three generations of bishops.[71] While the secular branch continued to exist, the family probably increasingly came to identify itself with the bishopric of Evreux rather than with the family's tiny lordship outside the episcopal city.

What little we know about the precise blood relationship between the bishops of Normandy and Greater Anjou and their protégés produces an image of the local aristocratic family which is entirely consistent with the results of scholars examining in detail early twelfth-century Anglo-Norman families or twelfth-century south-eastern France.[72] The patrilinear, vertically organised family was the dominating structure of the time, but rather than excluding cognatic and horizontal connections, it absorbed them for the benefit of its members. Family consciousness was defined by the family's needs as a group or of the needs of individual members. In terms of who belonged to the family, the nucleus consisting of parents, children, and uncles was at the centre of this consciousness, but in some circumstances more distant relatives could become the focal point. In terms of family identity, the centre of the consciousness shifted with the family's political fortunes and aspirations.

---

[69] Examples for maternal uncles are Engelbald, uncle of Bartholomew (Tours), and Norman de Doué, uncle of Archdeacon Stephen de Montsoreau (Angers), see supra, Table 2, p. 175, and Table 6, p. 207.

[70] See supra, pp. 220–2.   [71] See supra, pp. 103–8.   [72] See supra, p. 227.

The baronial family

Being related to an important baronial family could occasionally be as helpful in becoming bishop as being related to a prelate. Magnates considered that having a relative in an episcopal see was a useful tool in strengthening and extending their political influence as well as in making accessible new resources of patronage. But the magnates' scope of action in elections varied substantially. In areas where the king held the *regalia* and was consulted during the electoral process, closeness to him was an essential key for magnates to succeed in advancing their own candidates. A magnate active at the royal court could, depending on the political circumstances, press or ask the monarch to promote his candidate. But in areas where the king had very little influence, for instance in western Brittany,[73] closeness to the king hardly mattered. There the local magnates were the most powerful political forces. Two examples, one from Normandy, one from Greater Anjou, shed some light on how baronial networks operated, and upon how the conditions for their efficiency could vary from region to region and over time.

The most prominent baronial network in Normandy was created by the Beaumont family. David Crouch has observed that, in the late 1130s, Waleran, count of Meulan, was the most powerful man in lower Normandy, if not in the entire duchy.[74] Waleran used his position to give family members ecclesiastical posts. He operated in two ways. At Evreux, his local power almost certainly played the crucial role in the promotion of his cousin Rotrou to the see in 1139. At Salisbury in the same year he used his closeness to King Stephen to have another relative, Philip de Harcourt, nominated as bishop. In the end Philip did not succeed to Salisbury, but after Waleran had changed sides to the Angevins, Philip received the bishopric of Bayeux, which may well have been a prize Waleran demanded of Count Geoffrey. In the following years, the Beaumonts continued to be effective as patrons. Rotrou was promoted to Rouen in 1164/5, and Giles du Perche to Evreux in 1170.

But the heyday of the Beaumonts was coming to an end. When, after Rotrou's death, the chapter intended to elect his *nepos* Robert du Neubourg, Henry II denied their wish, pushing through the election of Walter de Coutances instead.[75] Robert's candidature failed because in 1184 the political situation was different from that of the late 1130s or even the 1160s. Henry II had established himself as the undisputed ruler on both

---

[73] Everard, *Brittany and the Angevins*, pp. 67–9, 121. At Léon, for example, the local counts held the right to invest the bishop with the *regalia* still in 1235, Imbart de la Tour, *Elections*, p. 459.

[74] Crouch, *Beaumont*, p. 36. [75] See supra, pp. 78–83.

sides of the Channel. Having a particularly strong interest in the arch-bishopric of Rouen, he was the major player in the electoral process; the Beaumonts were no longer in a position to demand that he fulfil their ambitions. Moreover Waleran's son, Robert de Meulan, never enjoyed intimacy with the king and, with the death of Rotrou, the Beaumonts had lost their last family member with substantial influence at the royal court. As a consequence, they could neither forcefully demand nor even request, but only beg Henry to accept their candidate. If he refused, they had no means of changing his mind.

The increase in royal power in Normandy in the second half of the twelfth century reduced the magnates' scope of action. While the chances of royal clerics became greater, clerics from great baronial families faced increasing difficulties in advancing to important bishoprics.[76] In Greater Anjou the development was slightly different. The region was far from being outside the sphere of influence and interest of the Angevin kings, who were recognised as overlords and keepers of the *regalia*. But Henry II's success in increasing his power in the second half of the twelfth century was not as far-reaching as in Normandy. As a consequence, regional magnates maintained a higher degree of political autonomy and thus a greater influence on elections. The case of another Beaumont family, the viscounts of Beaumont, offers some insight into the strategies pursued by these families. Richly landed in Maine and northern Anjou, they belonged to the handful of leading barons dictating the political landscape of the area. Related to the Angevins, they were also well connected with the royal court, although they did not play an active role in shaping royal politics.[77] Their strategy in supporting the candidatures of their close relatives Ralph and William to the see of Angers was therefore twofold. On the one hand, viscount and candidate called upon their local connec-tions, in particular within the cathedral chapter. On the other hand, the family used its political weight and probably its blood relationship with the king to obtain his approval and further support. From a cleric's point of view, these were rather good conditions in which to strive for a bishopric.

The king

Royal patronage could propel a great variety of men into bishoprics. Clerics belonging to important baronial families could benefit from it under the conditions that have just been described. Holy men could also receive it, as in the case of Hugh of Avalon, whom Henry II made bishop

---

[76] For a more detailed analysis of this phenomenon, see infra, pp. 234–5.   [77] See supra, pp. 201–7.

of Lincoln because of his sanctity.[78] But the most usual recipients were clerics from the royal service. From the king's point of view, bishoprics served as a reward for loyal service, but also provided an occasionally very powerful platform from which royal clerics were supposed to continue that service.

Many clerics were attracted to the Angevin and Capetian courts because they hoped to receive rich rewards. But the conditions were tough. Many more ambitious and talented men came to the royal court than there were rich prebends to be won. The result was a fierce and reckless competition for the king's favour which created the poisoned atmosphere so vividly described by contemporaries at the Angevin court.[79] In such an environment, support was essential for survival; a cleric needed an already established person/group to gain an entrée into royal service and the more influential circles of the court. Froger, bishop of Sées, for example, started his career in the household of Arnulf, bishop of Lisieux, when Arnulf was at the height of his influence at the Angevin court. His patron's great standing with Henry II was almost certainly Froger's springboard into royal service.[80] Another better documented example is the career of Walter de Coutances. Walter belonged to a knightly family and probably came in contact with the royal court through his brother Roger fitz Reinfrey, who was a member of the household of Richard de Lucy, co-justiciar of England, in the late 1160s.[81] Walter must have made a name for himself at court very quickly. By the end of the 1160s, he held a canonry at Rouen, a position he owed to Archbishop Rotrou. It is not clear who recommended Walter to Rotrou. It could have been Richard de Lucy, or Richard's colleague as co-justiciar, Robert, earl of Leicester, a cousin of Rotrou, or Henry II himself. In any case, Walter kept his contacts with the royal court despite serving briefly under Giles du Perche, bishop of Evreux, another relative of Archbishop Rotrou.[82] By the early 1170s, he was fully employed in the king's service and thence rose steeply in the king's favour.[83]

Similar mechanisms operated at the Capetian court. There Marshal Robert Clément paved the way for his sons Alberic, Henry, and the cleric Odo into the inner circles. Whether the fourth brother, Hugh, candidate

---

[78] Warren, *Henry II*, p. 554.
[79] *Arnulf*, ed. Barlow, no. 10; cf. J. Lally, 'Secular Patronage at the Court of King Henry II', *Bulletin of the Institute of Historical Research*, 49 (1976), 159–84, 168–84; Türk, *Nugae curialium*, pp. 53–201.
[80] See supra, pp. 121–2.
[81] Poggioli, 'Walter of Coutances', p. 19; West, *Justiciarship in England*, pp. 37–45.
[82] Poggioli, 'Walter of Coutances', p. 20; Spear, *The Personnel*, p. 264; Türk, *Nugae curialium*, p. 41.
[83] See supra, pp. 79–80.

at Bayeux in 1205–6, was also a royal clerk is unknown, but he could undoubtedly count on the support of his brothers.[84]

These careers demonstrate the crucial significance of belonging to the retinue of a man with access to and influence at the court. But once the first step was taken, that is the cleric had some sort of occupation at the royal court, those with greater ambitions needed to make themselves indispensable by demonstrating skills in administration or diplomacy. In addition, they needed to be absolutely loyal to the king. Froger and Walter remained with Henry II at very difficult times of his reign – even when they had the opportunity to opt for his opponents. During the Becket crisis, Froger was active on behalf of the king to such an extent that Pope Alexander III asked Archbishop Rotrou to investigate whether Froger was neglecting his episcopal office, and, if this proved true, to demand that he renounce either his office as bishop, or his standing as royal servant.[85] When Henry's sons rebelled, Froger and Walter both sided with the king.[86] How difficult it was to gain the king's trust and how easy to lose it is illustrated by three examples. Gerald de Barri blamed his failure to obtain the bishopric of St David's on his association with the Welsh, which made him an unreliable candidate in the eyes of the Angevins. He also complained that the Angevins did not adequately reward literate men like himself,[87] implying that if only he had offered the 'right' services, his chances would have been better. The need for royal patronage in general, rather than a specific wish for a bishopric, was the driving force behind the letters John of Salisbury wrote to Pope Adrian IV in 1157. He lamented that the machinations of Arnulf of Lisieux had cost him (John) the trust of Henry II and begged Adrian to intervene on his behalf.[88] The mistrust of a ruler could even lead to the resignation of a bishop, as is demonstrated in the case of Arnulf of Lisieux. When, after the rebellion of 1173–4, rumours were spread that Arnulf had sided with Henry the Younger, Henry II put him under so much pressure that finally he stepped down from his office.[89]

---

[84] Comparable is the career of Walter Cornut, whose mother was a sister of the four Clément brothers. Probably through them he entered the royal service. Eventually he became archbishop of Sens; Baldwin, *Philip*, pp. 106–22.

[85] *MTB*, vii, no. 698 [= Jaffé, ii, no. 11837; *WH* -].

[86] This is based on the assumption that Walter can be identified with Walter *capellanus*, a member of Henry the Younger's entourage, who opted for the elder Henry in 1173–4, *Gesta regis*, i, p. 43; *GC*, xi, col. 51; Peltzer, 'Henry II and the Norman Bishops', 1218.

[87] Bartlett, *Gerald of Wales*, pp. 17, 48.

[88] *The Letters of John of Salisbury I. The Early Letters (1153–1161)*, ed. W.J. Millor and H.E. Butler revised by C.N.L. Brooke (Oxford Medieval Texts) (Oxford, 1986), nos. 18, 30.

[89] See supra, pp. 110–11.

Connections, skills, and loyalty were the three essential conditions for a successful career at the royal court. In light of this, a clearer view emerges of the extent of social mobility at court, in particular at the Angevin court.[90] The need for skilled and loyal men created the potential for social mobility. Indeed it was almost a commonplace among twelfth-century writers to complain that the kings raised men from humble origins to great powers. Peter of Blois bemoaned the low birth of Henry II's justices,[91] while Gerald de Barri asked Henry II reproachfully, if rhetorically, 'who raised the lowly higher or depressed the high so low?'[92] These critics expressed their concern that, in relying increasingly on men from lesser origins, the kings deprived the barons of their proper functions and, as a consequence, shook up the existing social order. The background of the royal clerics promoted to bishoprics shows that they did not stem from the higher aristocracy. Yet they were no 'serfs' or 'villeins' either.[93] The 'dust from which they were raised'[94] was of a different quality.[95] They came from knightly or bourgeois families of sufficient influence at the royal court to gain them access to the royal service; the career path of a royal cleric did not bypass the established social elite. Nonetheless the royal cleric and the cleric stemming from a baronial family were not equal in royal preferment when it came to episcopal appointments. The present analysis of episcopal elections has shown that only when the Angevin kings were in need of support from magnates did they offer their patronage to 'baronial' clerics. Otherwise, they preferred royal clerics. Familiarity, and an expectation of greater reliability, were probably the overriding motives for such decisions. Perhaps even more importantly, kings hoped that because royal clerics owed to them at least the last major step of their careers, they would show a greater loyalty to them[96] than

---

[90] On social mobility in the Angevin realm, see Turner, *Men Raised from the Dust*, pp. 1–2; R. Turner, 'Changing Perceptions of the New Administrative Class in Anglo-Norman and Angevin England: The *Curiales* and their Conservative Critics', *Journal of British Studies*, 29 (1990), 93–117.

[91] 'Petri Blesensis epistolae', in *PL*, CCVII, cols. 1–560, no. 95, col. 300; Turner, 'Changing Perceptions', 94; Türk, *Nugae curialium*, p. 150.

[92] *Giraldi Cambrensis opera*, ed. Brewer et al., V, p. 199; Turner, 'Changing Perceptions', 94; Türk, *Nugae curialium*, pp. 112–14; cf. Aurell, *L'empire des Plantagenêts*, pp. 71–94.

[93] For serfs, see *Radulphi Nigri chronica. The Chronicles of Ralph Niger*, ed. R. Anstruther (Publications of the Caxton Society) (London, 1851), p. 167; for villeins, see *Walter Map*, ed. James revised by Brooke and Mynors, d. 1, c. 10, pp. 12–5; Turner, 'Changing Perceptions', 94.

[94] *Orderic*, ed. Chibnall, VI, book XI, p. 16.

[95] N. Vincent, 'Warin and Henry Fitz Gerald, the King's Chamberlains: The Origins of the Fitzgeralds revisited', in Harper-Bill (ed.), *Anglo-Norman Studies. XXI. Proceedings of the Battle Conference 1998*, pp. 232–60, p. 252, makes much the same point.

[96] When commenting on the royal clerk Adam who disclosed to Henry II what had been discussed in Henry the Younger's household, Roger of Howden reasoned: 'Et sicut decebat, et sicut debitor erat domino regi qui eum cum filio suo posuerat', *Gesta regis*, I, p. 122.

baronial candidates whose primary concerns might lie with their families and not with their overlord. The rise of the royal clerics increased the already stiff competition for royal favour at the king's court, and their preferment was certainly not welcomed by magnates who hoped to gain bishoprics for their relatives. But there was no Angevin master-plan to deprive magnates first of their influence and second of their position in society. Instead, an almost natural result of the emerging proto-bureaucratic government was that skilled clerics from lesser origins acquired the opportunity to make their living doing work hardly appealing to men born into baronial families.[97] The more ambitious among these clerics may have aimed to reach equality with clerics from baronial families. A few fortunate ones achieved that aim by becoming bishops. This upward social mobility regenerated the social elite, but since the route was accessible only to a relatively small group of people, it was not the vehicle for a radical change of the social order.

The pope

Gregory IX's order to translate Maurice, bishop of Le Mans, to the archbishopric of Rouen in 1231 was the only known papal provision of a bishop made in Normandy and Greater Anjou during the period studied.[98] But Gregory's decision was not a direct papal provision such as would become so common under his successors. In 1230–1, the electoral body at Rouen was heavily riven and, when Gregory opted for Maurice, the case had come before him for the second time. Furthermore, Gregory did not actively engage in the search for a candidate, but followed the choice of the papal judges delegate who had elected Maurice, but whose decision had been quashed by Gregory for faulty procedure.[99] Thus Gregory's support for Maurice was accidental rather than the result of a longstanding patron–protégé relationship.

Rouen also provides the only known case of the promotion of a papal cleric. In 1236, Peter de Collemezzo was advanced to the archbishopric.[100] One case is inadequate to shed much light on the mechanisms of

---

[97] Cf. Turner, *Men Raised from the Dust*, pp. 4–12; Turner, 'Changing Perceptions', 110–17.

[98] If Matthew's election to the see of Angers had been decided during the stay of the contesting parties at the papal court in 1156, Adrian IV may have been involved in the decision making, supra, pp. 197–200. It is possible that the pope played a role in the elections of Gervase to the see of Sées in 1220, and of Michael de Villeoiseau to Angers in 1240, but positive proof is wanting. Papal judges delegate may have been responsible for the choice of Robert Poulain at Rouen in 1208, supra, pp. 83, 133–4, 208.

[99] See supra, pp. 87–92.

[100] Michael de Villeoiseau was perhaps another successful papal cleric, see supra, p. 208.

papal patronage in the early thirteenth century. But Peter's career suggests that papal service was on the verge of becoming a major path to advancement in the ecclesiastical hierarchy.

The late eleventh and twelfth centuries witnessed the emergence of the papal court, the so-called *curia Romana*. Dealing with an ever-growing amount of judicial and administrative business, it developed an increasingly complex administrative machinery. This created a situation comparable with the Angevin court.[101] The running of papal government needed skilled, loyal, and ambitious men; in return papal service offered them opportunities to make a living, and possibly to raise their social rank. The men entering papal service in the twelfth and early thirteenth centuries were predominantly from Latium, the area in which the papacy was establishing and intensifying its lordship. In particular men from the poorer zones of this area, Sabina and Campagna, were attracted by the papal court.[102] Peter de Collemezzo was such a man.[103] Coming from the small town of Collemezzo, situated in the diocese of Segni in Campagna, he may have joined the papal service under Innocent III, a member of the family of the counts of Segni. Having served as an auditor at the court from the early years of Honorius III's pontificate, his next step was a stint in the service of the papal legate to England, Pandulph. So far, his career had followed a well-trodden path. His subsequent long stay in Paris as papal representative was something new, for, until then, papal chaplains had only served for shorter periods away from the papal court.[104] In Paris, Peter made the contacts that probably played an important role in his promotion to the see of Rouen. His success set an example others were soon to follow. Continuous papal service abroad became a new element in the career prospects of clerics.

CONCLUSION

The episcopacy in Normandy and Greater Anjou was a small elite group exhibiting a number of common features. By and large they were secular clerics who came from an aristocratic milieu – at least this was the case for

---

[101] P. Toubert, *Les structures du Latium médiéval. Le Latium méridional et la Sabine du XIᵉ siècle à la fin du XIIᵉ siècle* (Bibliothèque des écoles françaises d'Athènes et de Rome CCXXI) (2 vols., Rome, 1973), II, pp. 1039–51; R. Elze, 'Die päpstliche Kapelle im 12. und 13. Jahrhundert', *Savigny KA*, 36 (1950), 145–205; B. Rusch, *Die Behörden und Hofbeamten der päpstlichen Kurie des 13. Jahrhunderts* (Schriften der Albertus-Universität. Geisteswissenschaftliche Reihe III) (Königsberg, 1936).

[102] Toubert, *Les structures du Latium médiéval*, I, p. 72, II, pp. 1039–81.

[103] For his career, see Paravicini Bagliani, *Cardinali di curia*, pp. 169–76.

[104] Elze, 'Die päpstliche Kapelle im 12. und 13. Jahrhundert', 183–4, 189; Rusch, *Die Behörden und Hofbeamten der päpstlichen Kurie des 13. Jahrhunderts*, p. 82.

those whose social origins can be established. Furthermore bishops were generally familiar with their dioceses prior to their election. But these common features made the episcopacy neither uniform nor parochial in outlook. Different power structures in Normandy and Greater Anjou, and the Capetian conquest, caused differences in the social origins and careers of bishops from region to region and over time. In Greater Anjou, men from the higher aristocracy were well represented throughout the period studied, while in Normandy, as a result of the notably increasing Angevin power, they became fewer in the second half of the twelfth century. Instead, royal clerics stemming from lesser aristocratic families appeared in greater numbers in Norman sees. Such men continued to be elevated after 1204, but royal clerics became rare. The Capetian conquest, it seems, changed the framework of episcopal elections.

As a consequence of the rise of administrative kingship, royal service became a vehicle for social elevation from the second half of the eleventh century onwards. Values, however, changed only very slowly. A royal cleric from a lesser family was not aiming to eradicate the social layer formed by the magnates and bishops, but wished to become part of it, thus to continue its function. The twelfth century witnessed distinctive changes in many aspects of society, but it did not witness a social revolution.

The strength and adaptability of existing structures is perhaps most clearly demonstrated by the organisation of the family. The role of the bishop as patron to his kin strongly suggests that family structures, and the principles according to which family consciousness developed, hardly changed from the ninth to the beginning of the thirteenth centuries.[105]

---

[105] Le Jan, *Famille et pouvoir*, pp. 429–34; Bouchard, *'Those of my Blood'*, passim, esp. 175–80; for central and northern Italy, see C. Violante, 'Quelques caractéristiques des structures familiales en Lombardie, Emilie et Toscane au XIe et XIIe siècles', in Duby and Le Goff (eds.), *Famille et parenté*, pp. 87–151.

Chapter 6

THE IMPACT OF THE CAPETIAN CONQUEST OF 1204/6

The preceding chapters have shown that in Normandy considerably fewer men with close connections to the royal court became bishops after the Capetian conquest than before. In Greater Anjou, by contrast, the personal background of the men elected changed very little after the conquest. This chapter examines in detail the nature of the conquest's impact on the framework of elections in both regions.

The topic can be approached from two perspectives: first, the approach from the 'top', that is looking at the actions of the victorious and defeated kings. Philip Augustus dispossessed John and became his successor to the prerogatives enjoyed by the Norman dukes and Angevin counts. As a result, the Angevins no longer took part in the electoral process. They also lost any informal role in elections (except perhaps for the election of Nicholas at Le Mans in 1214, when the presence of John and his army may have worked in Nicholas' favour).[1] Only the fear of Angevin counterattack, which possibly caused suspicion and resentments at the Capetian court against candidates with English connections, preserved any role for the Angevins.[2]

The second approach looks at the consequences of the actions of the conquering king on the conquered localities.[3] This requires, first, an analysis of the Capetians' policy towards elections before and after 1204/6 and of their methods of dealing with the conquered provinces. Then it is necessary to examine the policies pursued by the cathedral chapters.

When Philip succeeded to the Capetian throne in 1180, he inherited a royal domain which hardly exceeded the Ile-de-France; Orléans, Paris, and Compiègne were the centres of scattered royal possessions in this region.[4] These were by no means meagre holdings, and his predecessors

---

[1] See supra, pp. 190–1. [2] See supra, pp. 87–99.
[3] Cf. Given, *State and Society in Medieval Europe*, pp. 8–11.
[4] Pacaut, *Louis VII*, p. 119–60; Baldwin, *Philip*, p. 13.

had agglomerated their lands and intensified their lordship, yet the king's direct activity was restricted to a relatively small area. Philip, however, also inherited a means of exercising political influence in areas beyond the Ile-de-France: royal patronage of ecclesiastical institutions. There were episcopal churches and monasteries in about a third of the kingdom that recognised the Capetian king as their lord. For generations the Capetians had profited from this in promoting members of their family and entourage to episcopal sees. In particular, Philip's father, Louis VII, had successfully deployed his rights to issue the *licentia eligendi* and to confer temporalities, to establish a network of loyal bishops which operated mainly in the provinces of Sens and Rheims.[5] These bishops supported Capetian rule, but how many of them were actively engaged in making Capetian politics and policies is difficult to establish. Looking at the three prelates known to have been prominent at Louis VII's court, it becomes obvious that they all had close ties to the king before their respective elections. Hugh de Champfleury, bishop of Soissons (1159–75), had been royal chancellor since 1150, Henry, archbishop of Rheims (1162–75), was Louis' brother, and William aux Blanchesmains, bishop of Chartres (1165–68), then archbishop of Sens (1168/9–76), then Henry's successor at Rheims (1176–1202), was Louis' brother-in-law.[6] If these three cases are representative of Louis' policy towards bishops and bishoprics, two important conclusions can be drawn. The closeness of the bishop to the king depended on personal connections rather than on the significance of the bishop's diocese. The episcopal office did not automatically propel its holder to the centre of the royal government and, depending on the political circumstances, the king had some leeway to decide whether he would co-operate with bishops or keep them at arm's length. Yet, bishoprics were by no means valueless for royal politics, and consequently Louis VII was eager to see loyal men in the most important sees of his kingdom, the archbishoprics of Rheims and Sens. In comparing Louis VII's policy towards bishops and elections with that of his archrival Henry II, similarities become obvious. Both rulers were interested in co-operation with the episcopacy and, if the opportunity arose, both

---

[5] Louis VII held the *regalia* of almost all the episcopal churches in the provinces of Rheims and Sens and the *regalia* of others in the provinces of Lyons and Bourges, Pacaut, *Elections*, pp. 63–72. The French king was also the patron of the archbishopric of Tours. However, there is no evidence for the Capetian kings actually holding the *regalia* and granting the *licentia eligendi* in the archbishopric of Tours in the second half of the twelfth century. Whenever they became active in affairs of the see it was due to the initiative of the archbishops, supra, pp. 171–9.

[6] Pacaut, *Louis VII*, p. 38; for William aux Blanchesmains, see also L. Falkenstein, 'Wilhelm von Champagne, Elekt von Chartres (1164–1168), Erzbischof von Sens (1168/9–1176), Erzbischof von Reims (1176–1202), Legat des apostolischen Stuhles, im Spiegel päpstlicher Schreiben und Privilegien', *Savigny KA*, 89 (2003), 107–284.

promoted trusted men to bishoprics, especially in the heartlands of their dominions. Yet, while both kings needed good working relationships with powerful prelates, they could if they chose exclude such men from their inner circle of advisors. Here, the personal relationship between ruler and bishop was once again more important than the significance of the episcopal see the bishop held.

In the first decade of his reign, Philip and his advisors, whom he had inherited from his father, continued Louis' policies. In the 1190s, however, Philip initiated fundamental changes. One was the formation of a new inner circle of royal advisors. Many of the barons who had counselled Philip during his first decade, lost their lives on the third crusade, and after his return to Paris in late 1191, Philip made no effort to replace them with their peers. Instead, a small group, Bartholomew de Roye, Henry Clément, Guérin (since 1213/14 bishop of Senlis), and the chamberlain Walter the Younger, all of whom had made their careers in royal service, rose to great prominence. These men shaped Capetian policies in the following years, in the case of Bartholomew and Guérin even beyond Philip's death.[7] While the king and his new advisors reformed many aspects of Capetian government,[8] they continued the long-established policy towards bishops and episcopal elections. The king would guarantee cathedral chapters free elections as long as they elected a bishop 'qui deo placet et utilis sit regno'.[9] This policy was successful. Aware of the king's watchful eyes, cathedral chapters, which themselves had an interest in men with access to the royal court, tended to choose men with good connections with the king, or at least men not hostile to him. Bishops occasionally completed governmental tasks for Philip in the 1190s; two prelates in particular, Philip's uncle, William aux Blanchesmains (until 1200), and Philip's cousin, Philip de Dreux, bishop of Beauvais, were important players.[10] William eventually lost his influential position, partly because of his age, and partly because of his failure to arrange for the smooth divorce of the king from his wife Ingeborg.

Throughout the divorce dispute, Philip experienced the active support of the vast majority of the bishops, even when the pope threatened their suspension from office. In fact, Philip did expect his bishops to support him. He severely punished those prelates who obeyed the interdict pronounced by Innocent III in January 1200. His wrath was directed in particular against his cousin Odo, bishop of Paris, who was the only prelate with links to the royal court who obeyed the pope. Philip was no saint; he

---

[7] Baldwin, *Philip*, pp. 104–25.   [8] Ibid., pp. 125–75.
[9] *Recueil des actes de Philippe Auguste*, ed. Delaborde et al., I, no. 345; Baldwin, *Philip*, p. 176.
[10] Baldwin, *Philip*, pp. 105–6, 176–8.

was a shrewd politician.[11] But despite the support of his prelates, and despite his bullying of those who obeyed the papal order, Philip did not win the battle. Innocent III remained intransigent. He insisted that it was within the church's, not the king's, authority to decide upon a divorce. Finally, Philip gave in, and the interdict was lifted at the end of September 1200.[12]

Innocent's victory sent an important message to the Capetian court. Here was a pope who would not yield ground on matters he regarded as essential to the liberty and integrity of the church. This message was understood by Philip and his advisors. When it came to disputed episcopal elections at Sens in 1199–1200 and at Rheims in 1202, arguably the two most important sees in Philip's realm, the king accepted papal decisions in both cases.[13] He and his entourage were almost certainly aware of the current developments in canon law eliminating any lawful claim by a ruler to be involved in the selection process; more significantly they had realised there was nothing to gain and much to lose from a dispute with Innocent over such matters. Collaboration was Philip's key strategy in elections, not only with cathedral chapters, but also with the pope. This strategy bore fruit, as illustrated by the election of Alberic to the see of Rheims in 1207, when Innocent sided with the chapter and king against the protest of the local archdeacon.[14] Furthermore, Philip knew that friendly and very useful relationships with bishops could be established, even if such bishops had originally been promoted against a royal candidate. Peter de Corbeil, for example, whom Innocent made archbishop of Sens instead of a royal candidate, later negotiated on Philip's behalf matters concerning the king's marriage with Ingeborg.[15] Another means of advancing royal interests was the renunciation of royal prerogatives in return for material and political advantages. In 1202, after a dispute with the chapter of Mâcon in which Philip had successfully defended his rights to the *regalia*, he granted the chapter that they would always receive the licence to elect from him.[16] One year later, he granted the chapter of Langres, 'quia etiam predicta ecclesia a nobis remota est et in confinio regni et imperii sita', the right to keep the *regalia* during a vacancy and to elect a bishop without

---

[11] For a similar view, see B. Guillemain, 'Philippe Auguste et l'épiscopat', in Bautier (ed.), *La France de Philippe Auguste*, pp. 365–84.

[12] For a detailed account of the affair, see Baldwin, *Philip*, pp. 82–7, 178–9.

[13] Ibid., p. 181. Peter de Corbeil became archbishop of Sens in late 1200, thus after the interdict had been lifted, Potthast, I, nos. 1144, 1196.

[14] Baldwin, *Philip*, p. 182.   [15] Ibid., p. 181.

[16] *Recueil des actes de Philippe Auguste*, ed. Delaborde et al., II, no. 708. In 1209, Philip granted the chapter the right to enjoy the *regalia* during a vacancy, ibid., III, no. 1066.

seeking the licence to elect.[17] In the same year Philip made a similar grant to the bishop and chapter of Arras, another border diocese.[18] In all three dioceses Philip appears not to have exercised any significant influence on the choice of previous bishops.[19] Thus the king gave away little while gaining loyalties and bolstering his finances at a time when he needed money for war against John.[20]

When Evreux came under Philip's control after the conclusion of the treaty of Le Goulet in May 1200,[21] he faced a new challenge in what had become his traditional way. He permitted the canons 'to elect their bishop freely just as the other canons of French churches have the power to choose their bishops'.[22] He may have used this charter to promote his image as a just ruler to the Norman clergy, but he certainly did not intend to treat elections at Evreux differently from other elections in his realm. Free elections to the episcopal churches under his control involved royal approval of the candidate, and Philip expected this to be the case at Evreux regardless of what hopes the chapter may have built upon his charter. The choice of Robert de Roye, a *nepos* of Bartholomew de Roye, in 1201, suggests that his strategy worked successfully.[23] But the election of a loyal bishop was only an additional means to integrate the new acquisition into the Capetian realm. Much more important were other aspects of royal lordship: the issue of grants to assure loyalties, and the deployment of agents of the royal administration to collect revenues, to render justice, and to execute royal orders.[24]

Philip's attitude towards bishops and episcopal elections on the eve of the conquest, therefore, can be summed up as follows: he was interested in the choice of loyal bishops who potentially formed a network of men supporting his policies and thus contributed to a strong rule. But Philip did not consider it a political imperative to have absolute control over all elections in his realm. Having taken note of the developments in canon

---

[17] Ibid., no. 772. Philip did not renounce his rights altogether, however. After the election the chapter was required to present the elect as soon as possible to the king in order for the elected bishop to swear fealty and to receive the *regalia* from him.

[18] Ibid., no. 774. Philip granted the temporal and spiritual *regalia* to the bishop and exempted him from military service; the king retained his right to receive the *gistum* and the bishop's fealty.

[19] Baldwin, *Philip*, pp. 436–41.

[20] The chapter and the elect of Arras paid 1,000 *livres parisiens* for their privilege and Langres may have done likewise, *Recueil des actes de Philippe Auguste*, ed. Delaborde et al., II, no. 835.

[21] Ibid., II, no. 633.   [22] Ibid., II, no. 637.   [23] See supra, pp. 104–5.

[24] Baldwin, *Philip*, pp. 152–76. Philip granted Ivry and Avrilly to Robert d'Ivry probably shortly before July 1200, when Robert nominated sureties guaranteeing that he would return the castles to Philip when required to do so, *Layettes*, ed. Teulet et al., I, no. 594; D. Power, 'L'aristocratie Plantagenêt face au conflits capétiens-angevins: l'exemple du traité de Louviers', in Aurell (ed.), *Noblesses de l'espace Plantagenêt (1154–1224)*, pp. 121–37, p. 132 n. 69. Smaller grants were made to lesser men in 1203, *Recueil des actes de Philippe Auguste*, ed. Delaborde et al., II, nos. 754–7.

law, and knowing that Innocent would not tolerate any royal claims in ecclesiastical matters, Philip preferred collaboration to confrontation.

NORMANDY

The king

Philip's strategy in incorporating Normandy was directed towards gaining direct control of the two essential aspects of lordship: men and administration. His priorities were the establishment of close ties with the Norman aristocracy, and the appointment of trusted men to key positions in the administration.[25] But bishops with close ties to the Capetian court were welcome, too.

Twice candidates with close connections to the Capetian court stood for elections to Norman sees shortly after the conquest. At Evreux in 1201, Robert de Roye succeeded, while at Bayeux in 1205–6 the candidacy of Hugh Clément failed. Significantly, Philip appears not openly to have advocated Hugh after Innocent III had decided the case, nor are there any other known instances where Philip attempted to force a candidate upon a Norman chapter. In Normandy Philip showed the same attitude towards elections as elsewhere after 1200: a bishop from the royal court was an additional bonus, but not worth risking a dispute. The policy of avoiding disputes had particular priority in Norman elections, for Philip may also have feared to provoke the resistance of the cathedral churches and the families represented in the chapters. As long as the chapters respected royal rights during the procedure and chose men not suspected of disloyalty, Philip and his successors gave them their blessing. Furthermore, royal clerics coming from the old domain, may well have preferred a bishopric in familiar surroundings, the heartlands of Capetian rule, to a see in a potentially hostile environment like Normandy. It is well worth noting that both Robert de Roye and Hugh Clément belonged to families which had holdings in or near to the dioceses in which they stood for election.[26] Philip was also eager to establish good relationships with existing bishops. In late 1204, he confirmed to the bishop of Lisieux his extensive

---

[25] Baldwin, *Philip*, pp. 221–30; Power, 'Between the Angevin and Capetian Courts', pp. 361–84; D. Power, 'The French Interests of the Marshal Earls of Striguil and Pembroke, 1189–1234', in J. Gillingham (ed.), *Anglo-Norman Studies XXV. Proceedings of the Battle Conference 2002* (Woodbridge, 2003), pp. 199–225; Powicke, *Loss*, pp. 330–58; Musset, 'Quelques problèmes', pp. 294–8; D. Crouch, 'Normans and Anglo-Normans: A Divided Aristocracy?', in Bates and Curry (eds.), *England and Normandy*, pp. 51–67; K. Thompson, 'L'aristocratie anglo-normande et 1204', in P. Bouet and V. Gazeau (eds.) *La Normandie et l'Angleterre au Moyen Age. Actes du colloque de Cerisy-La-Salle (4–7 octobre 2001)* (Caen, 2003), pp. 179–87.
[26] See supra, pp. 105, 140.

jurisdictional rights in the episcopal city and its surroundings.[27] In April 1206, shortly after the accession of Robert d'Ablèges to the see of Bayeux, the king issued a grant to his 'beloved and faithful Robert'[28] and a couple of years later, in 1209, he granted Hugh, bishop of Coutances, the prebends of the collegiate church of Notre-Dame at Cherbourg, founded by William the Conqueror, as a recompense for the losses his church had incurred during the war.[29]

The cathedral chapters

Looking at the Norman cathedral chapters around 1200, three features become apparent which were of great importance for the outcome of elections after 1204. First, cathedral chapters were establishing themselves as the exclusive electoral body. Having excluded the *religiosi viri* in the course of the twelfth century, they also started to internalise the recent developments in canon law which forbade the ruler to participate in the selection process. As a consequence, the significance of internal networks in the electoral process increased, and thus the probability of bishops emerging from within the chapter. Second, bishops and canons had vested interests in the political fortunes of the duchy. They had strong personal and institutional links with England. Episcopal churches held lands across the Channel, and bishops as well as canons had sometimes very strong personal cross-Channel ties.[30] Third, for the Angevin kings, Normandy was a central region of their dominions, even though, as a result of their widespread holdings, the relationship between duke and duchy may have been less intensive than at the time of William the Conqueror.[31] As an important part of this relationship the Angevins maintained the traditionally close ties between duke and church. Norman bishops were staunch supporters of Henry II right from his accession to the duchy in 1149/50.[32]

---

[27] *Layettes*, ed. Teulet et al., I, no. 731; cf. *Registres de Philippe Auguste*, ed. Baldwin, carte, no. 36.

[28] See supra, p. 141.

[29] *Recueil des actes de Philippe Auguste*, ed. Delaborde et al., III, no. 1098; *Recueil des actes des ducs de Normandie de 911 à 1066*, ed. M. Fauroux (Mémoires de la société des antiquaires de Normandie XXXVI) (Caen, 1961), no. 224.

[30] For these possessions, see W.B. Stevenson, 'England and Normandy, 1204–1259' (2 vols., Leeds Univ, Ph.D. thesis, 1974), II, pp. 33, 340, 343, 345, 350. Walter de Coutances and his entourage provide one compelling example of the operation of cross-Channel connections, supra, pp. 221–2.

[31] Bates, 'The Rise and Fall of Normandy', pp. 19, 35. Bates points out the differences between the reigns of the early dukes and the Angevins, but concedes that Normandy played an important role within the Angevin dominions. Power, 'Angevin Normandy', p. 63, emphasises the importance of Normandy under the Angevins.

[32] The witness lists of Angevin charters provide ample proof for the presence of Norman bishops at the royal court, cf. *Recueil des actes de Henri II*, ed. Delisle and Berger; *Acta of Henry II and Richard I: Hand-list of Documents Surviving in the Original in Repositories in the United Kingdom*, ed. Holt and

Their presence in the royal entourage, and the relatively long stays of the Angevin kings in Normandy,[33] created favourable conditions for the access of Norman clerics to the royal court. They had, sometimes literally, a short journey to the centre of power. The close relationship between ruler and church also meant that Norman prebends were a natural resource with which to reward royal clerics, whether or not they were Norman by birth. Some of these men advanced to Norman bishoprics and thus perpetuated the close connection between the Norman clergy and the Angevin court. In 1203–4, therefore, the political focus of almost all Norman bishops and many of the cathedral canons was mainly directed towards the Angevin king.[34]

The conquest therefore created a great dilemma for the Norman bishops and their chapters. First of all, it was entirely unclear whether it meant a fundamental long-term change of the political landscape or just a short-lived state of military occupation to be reversed at the next opportunity. Second, it posed a threat to their ties to England, and hence to their English revenues. In late 1204, John confiscated the English property of those Normans who opted for Philip, which included the episcopal churches.[35] In late 1204/early 1205, the Norman bishops turned to Innocent III asking him whether they should accept Philip as their new ruler. Innocent III, who was himself unclear how to gauge the situation, left the decision to the bishops.[36] They decided to follow the flow of the events and accepted the Capetian king as their new overlord. If the confiscation of their English lands by John had been final, the attention of the Norman cathedral

Mortimer; *Acta of Henry II and Richard I: Hand-list of Documents Surviving in the Original in Repositories in the United Kingdom, Part II*, ed. N. Vincent (List and Index Society/Special Series XXVII) (Chippenham, 1996); *Itinerary*, ed. Landon; *Rot. chart.* For royal deployment of Norman bishops, see Peltzer, 'Henry II and the Norman Bishops', 1210–25; Power, 'The Norman Church and the Angevin and Capetian Kings', 211.

[33] Henry II spent more time in Normandy than anywhere else in his dominions, Eyton, *Court, Household and Itinerary of Henry II*; J. Le Patourel, 'The Plantagenêt Dominions', in J. Le Patourel, *Feudal Empires. Norman and Plantagenêt* (History Series XVIII) (London, 1984), no. VIII, pp. 289–308, p. 295 n. 14. The forthcoming revised itinerary of Henry II will provide more precise data for such calculations. Richard showed a greater interest and presence in the southern dominions than his father. But in the later years of his reign, when the defence of Normandy against Philip's attack required his presence there, he spent significantly more time in the duchy than anywhere else, *Itinerary*, ed. Landon. John spent more time in England between 1199 and December 1203 than Richard in his entire reign, but he, too, spent a considerable proportion of his reign in Normandy before the conquest, *Rot. pat.*

[34] Sylvester, bishop of Sées, was a notable, yet unsurprising, exception. Having obtained his see against heavy royal opposition he felt no sympathy for John. In 1203, he styled John in one of his charters as 'once king of England' ('J. quondam regis Anglie'), Alençon, AD Orne H 1335 (charters concerning the abbey of Silli).

[35] Powicke, *Loss*, p. 288; the confiscation of the property of Rouen, Lisieux, Sées, and Coutances can be deduced from *Rotuli litterarum clausarum*, ed. Hardy, I, p. 23a (Sées), 47b (Coutances), 62b (Lisieux), 68a (Rouen); *PR 8*, John, p. 208 (Rouen).

[36] *Register Innocenz' III.*, VIII, no. 7 [= Potthast, I, no. 2434].

churches would have been fully directed to Philip. But John soon reversed his decision. The opportunity of quickly raising urgently needed cash by fining the chapters for the return of their lands was too attractive to be ignored. It is unclear how much money John was able to extract from the cathedral churches, but all chapters regained their possessions relatively quickly and thus re-established their cross-Channel interests.[37]

Thus, after the conquest, Norman cathedral chapters continued to show their pre-conquest characteristics except for their political allegiance.[38] Instead of the previous, well-established Angevin allegiance, there was a deep sense of insecurity about long-term political developments. Such a political climate reinforced the tendency of the cathedral chapters to look to their own members for possible candidates for the episcopacy. The locally well-connected candidate of low political profile was therefore a much more popular choice than a cleric from the Capetian court. But some of these conditions changed in the course of the decades following the conquest. First of all, there was a generational change of personnel. Many of the incoming canons considered Capetian rule as much more natural than their predecessors had. This was not only because they had not experienced Angevin rule themselves, but also because it became clear that Capetian rule in Normandy was not to be short term. The first clear signal was Philip's victory at Bouvines in 1214, the second and decisive one came in 1230, when Henry III's attempt to regain the duchy failed miserably.[39] The Norman chapters began to adapt to these developments. Avranches, for example, withdrew from England by selling its possessions at Swanwick and Portchester.[40] Others were to follow suit.[41] The clearest indication for the slowly, but steadily changing outlook of the Norman cathedral chapters was the electoral dispute at Bayeux in 1231. Seventeen of the canons voted for

---

[37] J. Peltzer, 'The Slow Death of the Angevin Empire', *Historical Research* (in press); cf. D. Matthews, *The Norman Monasteries and the English Possessions* (Oxford, 1962), pp. 72–107.

[38] The case of Drogo de Trubleville the Younger, canon of Rouen, shows how family ties and cross-Channel holdings of cathedral churches continued to connect Norman churchmen with the English realm. In 1227, Drogo's brother Henry, recently nominated Henry III's seneschal in Gascony, granted him the custody of all his lands and property in England, *Patent Rolls of the Reign of Henry III* (6 vols., London, 1901–13), I (1225–32), pp. 122–3, 129; cf. *Close Rolls of the Reign of Henry III*, I (1227–31), p. 217; Power, 'French Interests', p. 218. During the vacancy of the archbishopric of Rouen in 1229–31, Drogo administered its English property on behalf of Henry III, *Close Rolls of the Reign of Henry III*, I (1227–31), p. 340.

[39] Henry III had some strategic interest in the dioceses of Coutances and Avranches. In a proposal to Louis VIII for a peace settlement, probably to be dated to 1229, he asked for the return of these bishoprics in order to keep open his communications with the lands further south, *Diplomatic Documents Preserved in the Public Record Office I. 1101–1272*, ed. P. Chaplais, no. 215; Vincent, *Peter des Roches*, p. 262 n. 9.

[40] *Calendar of the Charter Rolls*, I (1227–57), p. 140; cf. Vincent, *Peter des Roches*, p. 162; *English Episcopal Acta IX. Winchester 1205–1238*, ed. N. Vincent (Oxford, 1994), no. 67a and pp. 166–8.

[41] Peltzer, 'The Slow Death of the Angevin Empire'.

the royal cleric John de La Cour.[42] There was no doubt in the mind of these electors that the future was Capetian and that therefore a bishop with good connections with the royal court could only be profitable for their own interests. The consequences of this development were to be seen in the reign of Louis IX, when men with strong royal connections started to appear in Norman sees.[43]

GREATER ANJOU

The king

When, after King Richard's death in 1199, the barons of Greater Anjou received Arthur, the adolescent heir of Henry II's third son Geoffrey, the late duke of Brittany, as their new overlord instead of John, the Angevin–Capetian conflict in the Loire region entered a new phase. The subsequent struggle between Arthur and John for control of Greater Anjou gave Philip a welcome opportunity to strengthen his own position. He opted for Arthur, hoping to break up the Angevin dominions on the continent. A first attempt in 1199–1200 failed, but Philip consoled himself with substantial concessions from John in return for his recognition of John's claims in the treaty of Le Goulet in May 1200. Two years later, however, Philip declared John's continental possessions forfeit and agreed with Arthur that, if they were to be victorious against John, Arthur would rule over Brittany, Greater Anjou, and Poitou.[44] Thus Philip was not preparing for direct rule of Greater Anjou at the beginning of the campaign. However, before the plan could be put to the test Arthur died as John's captive in 1202 and Philip replaced him as the potential successor to the Angevins in Greater Anjou.

Philip knew that in order to conquer Greater Anjou he needed the support of the leading barons of the area. The strong man at the time was William des Roches, who had been acting as a power broker between leading Angevin barons and the Capetian court. The prize Philip paid in August 1204 for William's support was the confirmation of the hereditary seneschalship of Anjou, which Arthur had granted to William in 1199. In 1206 and 1207, Philip redefined the extent of William's authority, essentially withdrawing the Touraine from the area under William's control.[45] Thus the conquest split Greater Anjou into two administrative zones. One

---

[42] See supra, pp. 141–4.   [43] Pico, 'Bishops', pp. 194–6, 269.

[44] *Recueil des actes de Philippe Auguste*, ed. Delaborde et al., II, nos. 633, 723; Baldwin, *Philip*, pp. 94–8, 191.

[45] *Recueil des actes de Philippe Auguste*, ed. Delaborde et al., II, nos. 829, 831, 838, 948, 963; Baldwin, *Philip*, pp. 234–7.

zone, the Touraine, came under the immediate control of the king, administered by royal agents. The other zone, Anjou and Maine, remained under the control of William des Roches, who exercised his authority semi-independently. This decision had long-term effects. Philip's successor, Louis VIII, considered Anjou and Maine as annexed provinces, not as part of the royal domain like the Touraine[46] and despite the takeover of the administration in Anjou and Maine by royal *baillis* in 1226,[47] this remained the Capetian attitude towards the two counties. A major factor in this was probably the conflict between Peter Mauclerc, duke of Brittany, and Queen Blanche and her son Louis IX in the late 1220s to early 1230s, which turned Anjou and Maine into a war zone. In 1231, the treaty between Louis IX and Peter highlighted the separation of this area from the core of the French kingdom and underscored the different consequences of the conquest for Angevin dominions. Peter was allowed to sojourn in Maine and Anjou, but he was not allowed to cross a line running from the south-west border of Normandy in the north-east, over the western border of the Vendômois in the east, to the north-western border of the Biterrois in the south-east and the northern border of Poitou in the south.[48] Thus while Normandy, the Vendômois, and Touraine were more and more integrated into the heart of the French realm, Anjou and Maine remained on its fringes.

Philip and his successors' policy towards episcopal elections in Greater Anjou remained very like that pursued in Normandy. They carefully watched over their royal prerogatives. In 1214, when Nicholas succeeded Hamelin at Le Mans, Philip ordered an investigation into the relationship between king and bishop.[49] In 1231, the chapter of Le Mans asked Louis IX for the conferral of the *regalia*. After the approval of their request, the letter was handed over to the royal archives for preservation.[50] The Capetians welcomed the election of a bishop with close connections with the court, provided elections avoided disputes with the local elites and the papacy. Philip respected papal authority in Greater Anjou as

---

[46] In 1225, the king assigned Anjou and Maine as appanage to his by then six-year-old son Jean, Petit-Dutaillis, *Louis VIII*, pp. 361–2, 369.

[47] [L. Delisle], 'Chronologie des baillis et des sénéchaux royaux depuis les origines jusqu'à l'avènement de Philippe de Valois', in *RHF*, XXIV/I, pp. 15*–385*, pp. 157*–9*.

[48] *Layettes*, ed. Teulet et al., II, no. 2144; Berger, *Histoire de Blanche de Castille*, p. 199; cf. the terms of the truce negotiated between Queen Blanche and Peter in 1227. They agreed on the marriage between Blanche's grandson Jean and Peter's daughter Yolanda. Until they came of age, Peter was to hold Angers, Baugé, and Beaufort and, if King Richard's widow Berengaria were to die in the meantime, Le Mans, too, *Layettes*, ed. Teulet et al., II, no. 1922; Berger, *Histoire de Blanche de Castille*, pp. 84–5.

[49] *Recueil des actes de Philippe Auguste*, ed. Delaborde et al., III, no. 1337.

[50] *Layettes*, ed. Teulet et al., II, no. 2146.

elsewhere, and did not attempt to impose strangers on the cathedral chapters. In the only two cases when candidates with royal connections stood for election, these men also had links with the dioceses concerned. Furthermore it is notable that both men were candidates at Tours, part of the area of Greater Anjou which the Capetians directly controlled and where they were long standing ecclesiastical patrons. The division of Greater Anjou into two zones of Capetian lordship was thus reflected in Capetian influence over elections. In Greater Anjou, as in Normandy, Capetian engagement in elections followed the acquisition of direct territorial control: it did not prepare the ground for such control.

The cathedral chapters

The cathedral chapters in Greater Anjou around 1200 showed similar but not identical features to their Norman counterparts. They were establishing themselves as exclusive electoral bodies, dominated by strong internal networks, and had ties with England and the Angevin kings. But these ties differed in extent and quality. Le Mans and Angers had considerably closer institutional links with England and the Angevins than Tours. Both had the Angevin count as their patron, Tours traditionally the Capetian king. Angers and Le Mans held possessions in England,[51] while the archiepiscopal see did not. In these aspects, therefore, Le Mans and Angers were much closer to the Norman bishoprics than was Tours. All three sees, however, had two aspects in common that distinguished them from Norman chapters. Even though a fair number of their prelates had personal connections with the Angevin court, and some even shared ties of kinship with the ruling Angevin dynasty, there were very few royal clerics in episcopal sees. At the time of the completion of the Capetian conquest in 1206, none of the incumbents had made their careers at the Angevin royal court. Unlike their Norman counterparts, Angevin cathedral chapters less frequently elected men from the court; the almost symbiotic relationship between duke and chapters in Normandy was less intensive in Greater Anjou.

The chapters reacted differently to the conquest. At Tours, the chapter was directly confronted with Capetian lordship. The return of their traditional patron to exercise real power shaped a new framework for archiepiscopal elections. It presented the canons, who had enjoyed a large degree of autonomy, with new constraints, but also new options. The

---

[51] Le Mans held land at Kingston Deverill (Wiltshire), *PR* 6, H.II, p. 20; Angers held Henset and Totteridge (Wiltshire), *Regesta regum Anglo-Normannorum 1066–1154*, ed. Davis et al., II, no. 1204a; *PR* 16 H.II, p. 64; C.A.F. Meekings, 'The Early Years of Netley Abbey', in C.A.F. Meekings, *Studies in 13th Century Justice and Administration* (London, 1981), no. XVII, pp. 1–37, pp. 5–6.

canons quickly adapted to both. In 1206, they appear to have gone along with Philip's wish and elected Geoffrey du Lude. Some of the canons may well have appreciated such a candidate. Two years later a group of canons voted for a candidate known to Philip, and against a prominent member of Archbishop Bartholomew's network. These cases suggest that there were men who were discontented with Bartholomew and his supporters, and who hoped for a regime change. Others may have been convinced that the Capetian conquest would last, and that therefore an archbishop connected with Philip was the choice to be preferred. Significantly, however, they remained the minority, at least for one more generation. Old networks remained in place and continued to exercise substantial influence. They may not necessarily have been opposed to the new regime, but simply preferred one of their own as archbishop.[52]

The cathedral chapter at Le Mans and perhaps also at Angers[53] saw little reason fundamentally to alter their electoral policy after 1206. At Le Mans, the chapter continued to elect local men; it did not seek suitable candidates at the Capetian court. Both churches accepted Philip's succession as their secular overlord, but, unlike Tours, they were not subjected to direct Capetian lordship in their day-to-day affairs. The Capetian remained a distant king, while the return of the Angevins to power was a realistic prospect, at least until 1235. Moreover the chapters had an interest in regaining their English possessions, which John had confiscated.[54] These were sufficiently strong incentives for them to maintain their contacts with England and to keep open their political options in the years following the conquest. Still in 1206, John ordered the release of the English possessions of the church of Le Mans to Philip d'Yvré, a canon of the same church.[55] Eight years later, in 1214, when John was successfully campaigning in Anjou and Maine, Hamelin, bishop of Le Mans, and an old adversary of John, abdicated and was replaced by Nicholas, who had been a companion of King Richard on the third crusade.[56] During the

---

[52] See supra, pp. 180–5.

[53] At Angers, the first election after the conquest took place in 1240, which makes it difficult to establish the immediate impact of the regime change on the electoral behaviour of the canons.

[54] *Rotuli litterarum clausarum*, ed. Hardy, I, pp. 62b–63a (Le Mans); in 1210–12, during the interdict, William May and Thomas Lande answered the inquest for the possessions of the see of Angers, *Red Book*, II, pp. 484, 489.

[55] John granted Philip d'Yvré, canon of Le Mans and *clericus noster*, the lands of Le Mans in Wiltshire as long as it pleased him, *Rotuli litterarum clausarum*, ed. Hardy, I, p. 74a. However, it is doubtful whether Philip ever took possession of the property, cf. ibid., pp. 62b, 63a; PR 6, John, p. 247; PR 7, John, p. 160; PR 8, John, p. 181; PR 9, John, p. 201; PR 10, John, p. 192; PR 11, John, pp. 81–2; PR 12, John, pp. 66–7; PR 13, John, p. 163; PR 14, John, p. 147; PR 16, John, p. 39; *Red Book*, II, p. 489; Peltzer, 'The Slow Death of the Angevin Empire'.

[56] See supra, pp. 190–1.

same campaign, William, bishop of Angers, witnessed a charter of John and regained the English possessions of his see.[57] John's final defeat sent a strong signal to the bishops and canons of Le Mans and Angers, but they were still uncertain about their political future. The churches tried to make the best of their situation. In 1223 they drew up an agreement with Louis VIII regulating the relationship between bishop and ruler and free-ing both bishops from fealty to the counts of Main/Anjou, if the counties were to be separated from the French realm.[58] In the following decade the conflict between the Capetians and Peter Mauclerc perpetuated the political insecurity of the region. Only when Peter was finally subdued in 1234, and in 1236, when a truce between Henry III and Louis IX was concluded, did the churches of Le Mans and Angers know there was to be no Angevin comeback. It was probably at that time that they sold off their English possessions to the Tourangeau Peter des Roches, bishop of Winchester, and thus adapted to this new situation.[59]

CONCLUSION

The Capetian conquest affected episcopal elections in Normandy and Greater Anjou. The major consequence was the sharp drop of men elected who had close connections with the royal court. A number of factors were responsible for this development. Philip's role in elections was different from John's. Like his Angevin predecessors, Philip consid-ered loyal bishops an important asset for royal government, but unlike John and his entourage, Philip and his inner circle accepted the develop-ments in canon law that redefined the ruler's position in the electoral process. They quickly understood that Innocent III was unwilling to compromise on this or other matters concerning fundamental principles of the church. As a consequence, Philip refrained from violently imposing his own candidates against selections made by chapters. This increased the control of cathedral chapters over elections, and thus bettered the oppor-tunities for internal networks to succeed. This development occurred throughout churches of Philip's realm from about 1200; the conquest facilitated its transmission to Normandy and Greater Anjou.

The conquest altered the geopolitical situation of Normandy. Prior to 1204, Normandy was a royal heartland. Men well connected with the

---

[57] *Rot. chart.*, p. 199a; *Rotuli litterarum clausarum*, ed. Hardy, I, p. 167b.   [58] See supra, p. 193.
[59] Le Mans sold its possessions between *c.* July 1233 and 1236, probably not earlier than 1234, *Registres de Grégoire IX*, ed. Auvray, II, nos. 3109–11; *English Episcopal Acta IX. Winchester*, ed. Vincent, no. *25; when precisely Angers sold its possessions to Peter is unknown, *Calendar of the Charter Rolls*, I (1227–57), p. 251; Meekings, 'The Early Years of Netley Abbey', pp. 5–6.

duchy and the royal court were regularly elected to bishoprics. But the conquest changed the significance of Normandy for its ruler. The duchy was a very important acquisition for Philip. But the Capetian heartland remained the Ile-de-France. It was from the Ile-de-France that the Capetian kings drew their main support and it was also the principal area for recruiting and rewarding clerics working in the royal government. After the conquest it became much harder for Norman clerics to gain access to the court of their ruler and to make a career there. The once short way to the inner circles of royal power had become considerably longer and stonier.[60]

Greater Anjou also experienced a shift in its geopolitical situation. The consequences for elections, however, were different from those that affected Normandy and also differed within Greater Anjou itself. In general they were less dramatic. The background of the men elected changed little with the conquest. Yet nuances are detectable. The Touraine experienced the full return of Capetian lordship and as a result Capetian interests started to play a role in archiepiscopal elections. Anjou and Maine, however, remained at a certain distance. These regions continued to be dominated by a group of barons. Instead of being integrated into the inner core of the realm Anjou and Maine formed an appanage for the Capetians' younger sons. This treatment strengthened the canons' tendency to look for candidates among their own number rather than at the king's court.

Philip's conquest did not make a *tabula rasa* in Normandy and Greater Anjou. The exodus of a good number of leading men in Normandy gave Philip substantial leeway in implementing his lordship, but it did not extinguish Norman custom nor long-established structures of decision-making. In Greater Anjou, even the great local barons remained in place. The consequences of the conquest, therefore, were shaped in a dialogue between the new men brought in by the conquerors and the local barons.

---

[60] Cf. Strayer, 'Normandy and Languedoc', 11.

Chapter 7

CONCLUSION

Each election had its own characteristics, its own specific circumstances, in short its own story. For many elections this story can only be reconstructed in part. The parties involved and their motives cannot always be clearly identified; conclusions, therefore, are to a certain extent conjectural. In particular the decisions of individual members of the cathedral chapters and their motives, their alliances, their rivalries, can only be traced in a few cases. In many more, a split election shows that there were rivalries and alliances within the chapter, but we can only guess their origins and their connections with local power structures. In some cases micro-history may provide certain answers, but in others we may never know what actually caused the canons' decisions.

While it is important to emphasise the uniqueness of each decision-making process, it is equally important to recognise that the elections took place within a normative and political framework which provided rules for the electoral procedure and determined the range of groups that could have exercised influence. The development of this framework between 1140 and 1230 can be traced with relative clarity. In Normandy, at the time of Henry I's death in 1135, the commonly accepted legal tradition allowed the clergy of the diocese, in particular the cathedral chapters, and the duke to participate in episcopal elections. The turmoil after Henry's death caused a short-term change. Great barons took the opportunity to influence elections, and some churchmen advocated the Gregorian ideal of elections without any lay interference. That neither phenomenon became a permanent feature of Norman elections in the second half of the twelfth century was due to Henry II's re-establishment of ducal authority, which revived the local custom permitting the ruler to participate in the election and limited the lee-way of the great aristocratic families in elections. Royal patronage became again a major route to an episcopal see. It benefited in particular men from the growing royal administration, whose representatives, mostly from a knightly background, played an increasingly prominent role at the royal court.

A good number of the candidates who enjoyed royal support also had very good local connections. This correlation was due to Normandy's position as a central area of royal lordship under the Angevins. The distance between locality and royal court was short and, as a consequence, the links between the local cathedral chapters and the royal court were so intense that a distinction between a local and a royal bishop can often not be drawn.

Henry II's success in imposing his authority also showed in Greater Anjou. Royal authority in Greater Anjou was always less pronounced than in Normandy, and local barons continued to exercise considerable political influence, Henry managed to overcome the serious challenges to his position at the beginning of his reign, and established his rule. This also affected the ruler's role in elections. While at the time of his accession to power, comital participation in elections was successfully challenged by some local churchmen, the growing strength of Henry's position became so attractive as well as threatening that he and his sons were accepted among the participants in the electoral processes, at least at Angers. Elections at Tours, by contrast, were always beyond direct Angevin influence and became an exclusive affair of the cathedral chapter.

For the history of episcopal elections, arguably the most important development of the second half of the twelfth century was the establishment of the cathedral chapters as exclusive electoral bodies. First the *religiosi viri* were excluded from the electoral process, despite Innocent II's attempt of 1139 to stop this. The slow but steady process of exclusion also concerned the suffragan bishops, who disappear from among the electors of the archbishops of Tours and Rouen between *c.* 1180 and *c.* 1230.[1] Second, the timing of the ruler's participation in the electoral process was redefined. Instead of consulting the ruler during the selection process, the chapters only asked for the ruler's consent after the election had been completed, and even this was optional. As part of this process, the meaning of the ruler's right to issue the licence to elect was clarified. From now on, it was clear that the right to confer the *licentia eligendi* meant merely the authorisation to hold an election, not to nominate a candidate; a principle very clearly formulated by Innocent III in a letter to Stephen Langton in 1209.[2] Strongly promoted by the papal court, the new doctrine on the role of the prince in episcopal elections became accepted

---

[1] Outside Normandy and Greater Anjou, the heavily disputed elections at Canterbury in 1184 and in 1205–7 bear witness to this development, Foreville, *L'église et la royauté*, p. 480; Cheney, *Innocent III*, pp. 147–54.

[2] 'Innocentii Romani pontificis regestorum sive epistolarum', in *PL*, CCXVI, cols. 62–4, no. 56 [= Potthast, I, no. 3751]; cf. Cheney, *Innocent III*, p. 157.

Conclusion

among canonists and, from the end of the twelfth century, adopted by churchmen in Normandy and Greater Anjou. The reaction at the Angevin court under King John against this development was both determined and sophisticated, but John's efforts to preserve royal prerogatives were in vain.

Philip Augustus had learnt his lesson in dealing with Innocent III during the dispute over his marriage with Ingeborg. He and his advisors understood that there was nothing to gain from engaging in a dispute with the pope over what Innocent regarded as principles of the *libertas ecclesiae*. They accepted the exclusion of the ruler from the official electors. Nurturing their relations with the papacy, making efficient use of informal ways to influence elections, and taking advantage of the chapters' interest in reasonable connections with the royal court,[3] the Capetian kings made sure that no potential enemies were elected. Towards the end of Philip's reign his historiographer William Le Breton claimed that unlike the English king who had usurped the electoral right to make (*creare*) the bishops himself, Philip granted the monks and the clergy the right to elect their leaders according to canon law.[4] By contrast, the English chronicler, William of Newburgh, related that John aux Bellesmains, bishop of Poitiers (1162–82) and archbishop of Lyons (1182–93), reprimanded some English ecclesiastics who had complained about the harshness of Richard I's exactions: 'You ought not to speak in such a manner. I tell you that in comparison with the French king [Philip] your king is a hermit.'[5] Respecting the new official doctrine on elections while yet demanding absolute loyalty and the collaboration of the chapters and bishops was no contradiction in terms, but sound political practice.

Philip's conquest fundamentally changed the political framework of elections in Normandy and Greater Anjou. In general his attitude towards elections strengthened the position of the cathedral chapter and thus the chances of internal networks to succeed in promoting their choices. Such a policy fostered local continuities, which, even though permitting potential Angevin loyalties to survive, avoided confrontation. The impact of the conquest was particularly significant in Normandy. Under the Capetians Normandy was no longer royal heartland; the correlation between strong royal lordship, the area of recruitment of personnel, and the area of royal

[3] If it served their purpose, as, for example, during the negotiations with papal representatives at the council of Bourges in 1225, cathedral chapters were ready to point out the need for their bishops to be useful for the king and kingdom, Kay, *The Council of Bourges*, Document 1, pp. 286–7.
[4] *Œuvres de Rigord et de Guillaume le Breton*, ed. Delaborde, II, pp. 219–20.
[5] 'Historia rerum anglicarum of William of Newburgh', in *Chronicles of the Reigns of Stephen, Henry II, and Richard I*, ed. R. Howlett (Rolls Series LXXXII) (4 vols., London, 1884–9), I, II [–p. 500], II, pp. 421–2.

255

bishops ceased to exist. Valuable as Normandy was, the Capetian heart-land remained the Ile-de-France. In Greater Anjou the effects of the conquest were less dramatic. At Tours, Capetian influence was tangible, but overall episcopal elections at Tours and Le Mans demonstrate the durability of local networks. In Normandy and Greater Anjou, the cathedral chapters only very slowly accepted that the Capetian conquest was permanent. The decisive period came in the 1230s, when after Henry III's débâcle of 1230 and Peter Mauclerc's submission in 1235–6, the cathedral chapters, realising that there was to be no Angevin comeback, began to cut their (institutional) ties with England. This adds further weight to the argument that the 1230s were a crucial period in the long end of the Angevin empire.

The establishment of the cathedral chapter as the exclusive electoral body increased disputed elections. The newly gained leeway in making their decision gave the chapters room for the expression of individual ambitions. If a party was unhappy with the electoral procedure or its outcome, its only chance to overturn the result was to appeal to the pope, the supreme authority accepted by all parties. The number of these appeals rose significantly from around 1200, and it should be emphasised that this cannot be solely explained by the survival of the papal registers from 1198 onwards. For the period between *c.* 1140 and *c.* 1155 there is evidence that three elections from Normandy and Greater Anjou provoked a papal appeal. If there is no such evidence for the next four decades[6] (for which there exists a substantially greater amount of papal and royal documentation and very well-informed chronicles),[7] then the appearance of appeals concerning elections in the thirteenth century cannot be explained solely by the growth of documentation. Instead the lack of appeals 1155–97 must be explained by the strong position of the Angevin kings. Appeals became attractive around 1200, when the cathedral chapters began to gain exclusive control over the elections.

Some of these appeals were certainly launched out of a sincere desire to ensure canonical elections, but many were stimulated by the ambition to overcome a stronger opposition. For example, the accusation of the candidate's unsuitability which carried great weight at the papal court was often used as a last resort, when complaints about procedural faults had already failed to overturn an election. The appeal, and thus canon law, was a tactical means deployed to win elections. For that reason, Johannes Teutonicus' hope that the regulations of the Fourth Lateran Council

---

[6] According to Thomas Becket, Achard's election to the see of Sées in 1157 was confirmed by Adrian IV. It is not known, however, whether appeals were launched, see supra, p. 121.

[7] Clanchy, *Memory*, pp. 57–62; Gransden, *Historical Writing*, I, pp. 186–335.

would reduce electoral conflicts proved vain. A more precise definition of electoral procedure could not eradicate the desire and ambition to win.

The frequent use of appeals had two major consequences for the history of episcopal elections. First, it presented the papacy with the opportunity to increase its influence over the outcome of elections. Men connected with the papal court joined the ranks of potential candidates. Pope Gregory IX's appointment of Maurice, bishop of Le Mans, to the see of Rouen in 1231 was not yet a direct papal provision of the kind that would be established under his successors later in the thirteenth century; but it provided a foretaste of a period when the pope would be a regular participant in episcopal elections. The cathedral chapters noticed the growing papal influence on elections very early. At the council of Bourges in 1225, they argued against Honorius III's proposal to set aside the income of one canonry in every cathedral church to finance papal government, claiming that the pope would perhaps order someone to be present on his behalf at elections who might disrupt the electors. The election, therefore, might not be concluded within the prescribed six months and devolve to the curia, 'which would place Romans, or those most devoted to them, in all or most of the churches'. In the end Honorius' proposal was not accepted.[8] But this was a fruitless victory. The root of the problem was not so much papal appointees disrupting elections, but local conflicts. These did not disappear and appeals continued to flow. Growing papal authority over elections was a phenomenon to which the chapters greatly contributed.

The second major consequence of appeals was the spread, harmonisation, and refinement of canon law. Confronted with frequent appeals, the papal court developed a more coherent and better defined law. On the local level, churchmen knew about the dangers of being drawn by an appeal into long and costly litigation of uncertain outcome. Therefore, they had a strong incentive to follow the regulations provided by the latest canon law. In this atmosphere, there was little chance for long-term survival of local customs, which had hitherto played a considerable role in defining local procedures, alongside canon law. Local electoral customs, however, did not disappear altogether when the new law was fully applied in the early decades of the thirteenth century. Some of them survived, but they changed their appearance. Once accepted by popes, they became part of canon law.

At the close of this study it is appropriate to take a brief look at the broader impact of the development of electoral procedures in the twelfth

---

[8] Kay, *The Council of Bourges*, pp. 175–231, and Document 1, pp. 270–89, quote at pp. 286–7.

and early thirteenth centuries. The overriding principle of medieval elections was that the bishop was elected through God's will, and any regulation of electoral procedure was ultimately aimed at ensuring that the right candidate, God's candidate, should triumph. The twelfth and thirteenth centuries constituted a decisive period in the elaboration of electoral rules. These slowly impacted on the form of secular elections, most notably the election of the king of the Romans.[9] The extent to which they were precursors of modern democratic elections, however, is difficult to assess. Medieval and modern elections differ fundamentally in their definition of the electors' role. The focus of the modern election is on the representation of the will of the individual elector, not on his position as a mediator of God's will. In other words, while the medieval concept discouraged the idea of expressing personal interests in a vote, the modern concept encourages precisely the opposite. Thus medieval elections – ecclesiastical or secular – were certainly not the 'direct ancestors' of modern elections. Léo Moulin's thesis that most modern electoral procedures have their origins in the medieval church[10] has therefore been rejected in recent times.[11] Indeed, Moulin's thesis possibly claims too much. But the idea of continuity of electoral techniques should not be totally dismissed. Some of the electoral rules shaped in the twelfth and thirteenth centuries may well have influenced modern procedures. There is, for example, the protection of the electoral right of the elector: if the elector was able and willing to participate, he should under no circumstances be prevented from so doing. This rule is common both to early thirteenth-century episcopal elections and to modern democratic elections. Again, the motive was originally very different from what it is now: the electoral right of a canon was emphasised to ensure the participation of the entire community in the election, since only then could the chapter be sure of divine blessing. Yet once the rule was formulated, spread, and accepted, it continued to exist even when its original purpose had disappeared. Twelfth- and early thirteenth-century episcopal elections, then, had a long-term impact that contemporaries would hardly have envisaged.

---

[9] R. Schneider, 'Wechselwirkungen von kanonischer und weltlicher Wahl', in Schneider and Zimmermann (eds.), *Wahlen und Wählen*, pp. 135–71; U. Reuling, 'Zur Entwicklung der Wahlformen bei den hochmittelalterlichen Königserhebungen im Reich', in ibid., pp. 227–70.
[10] Moulin, 'Sanior et maior pars', 368 n. 1.
[11] H. Keller, 'Wahlformen und Gemeinschaftsverständnis in den italienischen Stadtkommunen (12./14. Jahrhundert)', in Schneider and Zimmermann (eds.), *Wahlen und Wählen*, pp. 345–74, pp. 373–4.

APPENDICES

THE EPISCOPACY OF NORMANDY AND GREATER
ANJOU, C. 1140–C. 1230

Key:

Name:	The names of the known alternative candidates are given in brackets
Time in office:	The dates refer to the election and the translation, resignation, or death of the bishop
Social origins:	A (a): Greater aristocratic families A (b): Lesser aristocratic families B: Burgess
Secular/regular clergy:	S: Secular R: Regular
Position prior to election:	CoC: Collegiate chapter Cleric: Person not known to have held a canonry or any other higher ecclesiastical office
Connection with diocese:	1: Candidate held an office in the diocese or otherwise had close connections with it. (C) indicates that the candidate held at some time during his career a position in the cathedral chapter of his church 2: Candidate held an office in a neighbouring diocese or otherwise had connections in the area 3: Candidate had no apparent connection with the diocese
Type(s) of patronage:	BC: Bishop and/or cathedral chapter FI: Influence of family or institution in the area P: Pope PJD: Papal judges delegate K: King Order indicates the significance of connections. For example, FI, K means that local connections were probably more important for the promotion of the candidate than his royal connections.

259

Name	Time in office	Social origins	Secular/ regular clergy	Position prior to election	Connection with diocese	Type(s) of patronage
NORMANDY						
ROUEN						
Rotrou	late 1164/ early 1165 –83	A (a)	S	bishop	1	FI, K
Walter de Coutances	1184–1207	A (b)	S	bishop	1	K
(Robert de Neubourg)		A (a)	S	dean	1 (C)	BC, FI
Robert Poulain	1208–21	?	S	canon	1 (C)	BC, PJD?
Theobald d'Amiens	1222¹–9	?	S	treasurer	1 (C)	BC
(William de *Canapello*)		?	S	chancellor	1 (C)	BC
Maurice	1231²–5	?	S	bishop	3	PJD, P
(Thomas de Fréauville)		A (b)	S	dean	1 (C)	BC
Peter de Collemezzo	1236–44	?	S	papal subdeacon³	3	P, K?
(William of Durham)		?	S	archdeacon	1	BC
EVREUX						
Rotrou	1139–64/5	A (a)	S	archdeacon	1	FI
Giles du Perche	1170–9	A (a)	S	archdeacon	2	FI, K
John fitz Luke	1181–92	A (b)/ B?	S	canon	2	K
Guarin de Cierrey	1193–1201	A (b)	S	canon?	1 (C?)	BC, FI, K
Robert de Roye	1201–2/3	A (b)	S	?	1	K, FI
Luke	1203–20	A (b)/ B?	S	dean	1 (C)	BC
Ralph I de Cierrey	1220–3	A (b)	S	dean	1 (C)	BC
Richard de St Léger	1223–36	?	R	abbot/canon	1	BC, FI
Richard II de Cierrey	1236–43	A (b)	S	archdeacon	1	BC
LISIEUX						
Arnulf	1141–81	A (b)	S	archdeacon	2	BC
Ralph de Warneville	1182–91/2	A (b)	S	treasurer	2	K
(Walter de Coutances)		A (b)	S	treasurer/ archdeacon	2	K
William de Rupierre	1191/2–1200	A (b)	S	archdeacon	1 (C)	BC, FI

Name	Time in office	Social origins	Secular/ regular clergy	Position prior to election	Connection with diocese	Type(s) of patronage
Jordan du Hommet	1201–18	A (a)	S	archdeacon	1 (C)	K, BC
William de Pont de L'Arche	1218–50	?	S	canon ?/ proctor of the chapter	1 (C)	BC
SÉES						
Gerald	1144–57	?	S/R[4]	canon	1 (C)	BC
Froger	1159–84/5	?	S	archdeacon	2	K
(Achard)		?	R	abbot	1	BC
Lisiard	1187/8(?)–1201	?	S	canon	2	FI?
Sylvester	1202–20	?	R	archdeacon	1 (C)	BC
(Ralph de Merle)		?	R	canon	1 (C)	BC
(Prior of Sées) (William/John II?)		?	R	prior	1 (C)	BC
(Garin)		?	R	canon	1 (C)	BC
(William)		?	R	archdeacon	1 (C)	BC
(Herbert L'Abbé)		B	S	cleric	1	K
(William)		?	S	dean	2	K
(John de *Oilleya*)		?	R?	canon?	1?	BC
(Adam)		A (a/ b?)[5]	R	abbot	1	BC
(Reginald)		?	R	abbot	2	BC
Gervase	1220–8	?	R	abbot	2	BC, P?
Hugh	1228–40	?	R	prior	1 (C)	BC
BAYEUX						
Philip de Harcourt	1142–63	A (a)	S	archdeacon	2	FI, K
Henry de Beaumont	1165–1204	A (b?)	S	dean	1	K
Robert d'Ablèges	1205[6]–31	A (b)	S	canon	1 (C)	BC
(Robert)		?	S	archdeacon	1 (C)	BC
(William)		?	S	archdeacon	1 (C)	BC
(Saxo)		?	S	papal subdeacon/ canon	1 (C)	BC
(Hugh Clément)		A (b)	S	dean	2	K, FI
Thomas de Fréauville	1232–8	A (b)	S	dean	1 (C)	FI, BC
(William de Tancarville)		A (a) (?)	S	subdean	1 (C)	BC
(John de La Cour)		?	S	cleric	3	BC, K

Name	Time in office	Social origins	Secular/ regular clergy	Position prior to election	Connection with diocese	Type(s) of patronage
COUTANCES						
Richard de Bohun	1151–78	A (a)	S	dean	1	FI, K
William de Tournebu	1183–1201/2	A (a)	S	dean	2	FI, K
Vivian de L'Etang	1201–8	A (b)	S	archdeacon	3	K
Hugh Nereth	1208–38	A (a)?	S	archdeacon	1 (C)	BC
AVRANCHES						
Richard de Subligny	1142/3–53	A (a)	S	dean	1 (C)	BC
Herbert	1153–60/1	?	S	cleric	3	K
Achard	1161–70	?	R	abbot	3	K
Richard L'Evêque	1170–late 1181/early 1182	A (b)	S	archdeacon	2	FI
William Burel	late 1183/ early 1184 –94	A (b)/ B?	S	dean (CoC)	2	FI, K
William de Chemillé	1196–97/9	A (a)?	S	archdeacon	3	K
William Tolomeus	late 1199/ early 1200[7]–10	?	S	cleric	3	K
William Burel jr	1210–36	A (b)/ B?	S	canon/ treasurer?	1 (C?)	FI, BC
GREATER ANJOU						
TOURS						
Engelbald	1147–56/7	A (a)	S	treasurer	1 (C)	BC
Joscius	1157–73/4	?	S	bishop	3/1?	BC?
Bartholomew	1174–1206	A (a)	S	dean	1 (C)	BC
Geoffrey du Lude	1206–8	?	S	archdeacon	1	K, FI
John de Faye	1208–28	A (a)	S	dean	1 (C)	BC
(Robert de Vitré)		A (a)	S	chanter	1 (C)	K, FI, BC
Juhel de Mathefelon	1228–45	A (a)	S	dean	2	FI?
(Peter de Collemezzo?)		?	S	papal subdeacon	3	?
LE MANS						
William de Passavant	1145–87	A (a)	S	archdeacon	2	FI
Reginald Clarel	1187–90	?	S	chanter	1 (C)	BC
Hamelin	1190–1214	A (b)?	S	chanter (CoC)	2	FI
Nicholas	1214–16	?	S	dean	1 (C)	BC

Name	Time in office	Social origins	Secular/ regular clergy	Position prior to election	Connection with diocese	Type(s) of patronage
Maurice	1216–31	?	S	?	?	?
Geoffrey de Laval	1231–4	?	S	dean	1 (C)	BC
ANGERS						
Norman de Doué	1149–53	A (a)	S	archdeacon	1 (C)	BC
Matthew	1156–62	A (a/ b?)	R	abbot	1	FI
Geoffrey Moschet	1162–77	?	S	dean	1 (C)	K, BC
Ralph de Beaumont	1177–97	A (a)	S	?	1	FI, K
William de Chemillé	1199[8]–1200	A (a)?	S	bishop	1?	K
William de Beaumont	1202[9]–40	A (a)	S	archdeacon	1 (C)	BC, K
(William)		?	S	chanter (CoC)	2	BC, FI, K
Michael de Villeoiseau	1240–60	?	S	papal cleric?	?	P?

[1] Theobald's first election in 1221 was declared void by Honorius III, see supra, pp. 84–5.

[2] Gregory IX ordered his translation in May 1231. Maurice had already been the choice of the papal judges delegate dealing with the case at some time between May 1230 and May 1231, see supra, pp. 87–9.

[3] At the time of his election, Peter held canonries at Amiens, Thérouanne, and probably Chartres. He was also provost of St Omer, see supra, p. 98.

[4] Gerald needed to profess to have his election confirmed, see supra, pp. 116–20.

[5] *GC*, XI, col. 748.

[6] Robert was elected twice in 1205. His first election was declared void by Innocent III, see supra, pp. 138–41.

[7] William was elected for the first time in 1198. This election was declared void by Innocent III in 1199, see supra, pp. 161–3.

[8] William's initial translation from Avranches to Angers in 1197/8, authorised by the archbishops of Rouen and Tours, was declared void by Innocent III, see supra, pp. 156–60.

[9] William was elected for the first time in 1200. This election was declared void by the papal legate Octavian, cardinal-bishop of Ostia, see supra, pp. 204–5.

Appendices

APPENDIX II   THE DATE OF *CAUSA SUPER CONTROVERSIA*[10]

Samuel Loewenfeld copied *Causa super controversia* from volume CCLXXIX of the Collection Baluze, Bibliothèque Nationale de France, Paris.[11] Another copy of this letter can be found in a seventeenth-century history of the bishops of Angers attributed to Guy Arthaud, archdeacon of Angers, which is preserved at the Bibliothèque Municipale, Angers.[12] This second copy was taken from the original found at Angers in November 1664.[13] Unfortunately the original disappeared some time thereafter. Whether both copies were transcribed independently from each other or whether the Angers copy or its author served as source for the Baluze transcript cannot be established with certainty.[14] According to both copies the bull was issued on the VII *kalendae maii*, thus 25 April 1156. However, there are reasons to believe that the letter dated from the VII *kalendae martii*, thus 23 February.

The abbot of St Albans, Roger, and his colleagues left for the papal court at the beginning of October 1155 to undertake 'ardua negotia regalia' for Henry II.[15] They arrived at Benevento, presumably around Christmas, and their business had been dealt with by the end of February 1156.[16] A short time later, the king's envoys must have left Benevento. According to the chronicle of Vézelay, the abbot of St Albans, the bishop of Le Mans and the bishop of Evreux spent Easter, that is 15 April 1156, at the monastery.[17] It is true that it could take some weeks between a decision in the papal court and the issue of the papal letter, but it is hardly conceivable that it could have taken nearly two months to put the decision on the procedure of episcopal elections at Angers into writing. Another papal letter issued to the chapter of Angers offers a possible solution. This letter was issued on the VII *kalendae martii* 1156[18] and contains the same final clause as *Causa super controversia*, which points to both letters being issued on the same occasion.[19] *Maii*, therefore, is possibly a scribal slip for *martii* - an easy mistake to make. If this interpretation is correct, *Causa super controversia* was issued on 23 February 1156, not on 25 April 1156.

---

[10] *Epistolae pontificum*, ed. Loewenfeld, no. 228 [= Jaffé, II, no. 10174; *WH* -].

[11] Paris, BNF Collection Baluze, CCLXXIX, fo. 227r.

[12] Angers, BM 691 (history of the bishops of Angers), fos. 554v–555r.

[13] Ibid., fo. 554r.

[14] The text of both copies is practically identical. The only differences are an abbreviated 'ben.' in the Angers copy, which is extended to 'benedictionem' in the Baluze copy, and the description of the seal which is given in French in the Angers manuscript and in Latin in the Baluze manuscript. For Baluze's connections to Greater Anjou, see *Obituaire*, ed. Urseau, pp. ix–x.

[15] *Gesta abbatum monasterii Sancti Albani*, ed. Riley, I, pp. 125–9, quote at p. 126.

[16] For the length of a journey from St Albans to Rome, see R.L. Poole, *Studies in Chronology and History* (Oxford, 1934), p. 264; cf. L. Falkenstein, 'Decretalia Remensia. Zu Datum und Inhalt einiger Dekretalen Alexanders III. für Empfänger in der Kirchenprovinz Reims', in F. Liotta (ed.), *Miscellanea Rolando Bandinelli Papa Alessandro III* (Academia Senesi degli intronati) (Siena, 1986), pp. 153–216, p. 195 n. 109. The latest of the papal letters which Roger, abbot of St Albans, obtained during this journey dates from 26 February 1156, *Papsturkunden in England*, ed. Holtzmann, III, no. 112 [= Jaffé, II, no. 10117; *WH* -].

[17] *Monumenta Vizeliacensia*, ed. Huygens, pp. 505–6.

[18] *Papsturkunden in Frankreich. Neue Folge. V. Touraine, Anjou, Maine und Bretagne*, ed. Ramackers, no. 94 [= Jaffé -; *WH* -].

[19] 'Statuentes, ut nulli hominum liceat hanc paginam nostrae confirmationis infringere uel aliquate-nus contraire. Si quis autem hoc attentare praesumpserit, indignationem omnipotentis Dei et beatorum Petri et Pauli apostolorum eius se nouerit incursum. Dat. Beneventi VII. kal. Martii.'

BIBLIOGRAPHY

MANUSCRIPT SOURCES

ALENÇON, ARCHIVES DÉPARTEMENTALES ORNE

H 544 (charters concerning the abbey of Perseigne)
H 1069 (obituary, abbey of Silli)
H 1335 (charters concerning the abbey of Silli)
H 1417 (charters concerning the abbey of Silli)
H 1956 (charters concerning the abbey of Troarn)
H 2161 (charters concerning the abbey of Marmoutier)
H 2730 (documents concerning the abbey of St Evroult)
H 5244 (copies of documents concerning the Hôtel-Dieu of Argentan)

ANGERS, ARCHIVES DÉPARTEMENTALES MAINE-ET-LOIRE

G 334 (charters concerning the cathedral chapter of Angers)
G 452 (charters concerning the cathedral chapter of Angers)
G 562 (charters concerning the cathedral chapter of Angers)
G 785 (charters concerning the Grand Séminaire of Angers)
H (39) 11 (cartulary ('Censier'), priory of St Pierre of Chemillé)
H (39) 12 (cartulary, priory of St Pierre of Chemillé)
H 1814 (charter concerning the abbey of St Serge of Angers)
H 2109 (charters concerning the abbey of St Florent of Saumur)
H 3713 (cartulary, abbey of St Florent of Saumur, 'Livre blanc')
H 3714 (cartulary, abbey of St Florent of Saumur, 'Livre d'argent')

ANGERS, BIBLIOTHÈQUE MUNICIPALE

691 (history of the bishops of Angers)

AVRANCHES, BIBLIOTHÈQUE MUNICIPALE

149, fos. 7r–77v (Richard de Mores, *Apparatus* to *Compilatio I*); fos. 79r–109r (collection *Abrincensis I*); fos. 139r–147v (Richard de Mores, *Generalia*); fos. 119r–126v (collection *Abrincensis II*)

265

210 (cartulary, abbey of Mont-Saint-Michel)
Fonds Pigeon MS 45 (Chanoine Guérin, Le diocèse d'Avranches)

BAMBERG, STAATSBIBLIOTHEK

Can.13 (Johannes Teutonicus, *Glossa ordinaria*)
Can.42 (*Apparatus Animal est substantia*)

CAEN, ARCHIVES DÉPARTEMENTALES CALVADOS

2 D 51 (charters concerning the priory of Ste Barbe-en-Auge)
G 149 (obituary, cathedral chapter of Bayeux)
H 164 (charters concerning the abbey of Ardenne)
H 1217 (charters concerning the abbey of Aunay)
H 6510 (cartulary, abbey of St André-en-Gouffern)
H 6550 (charters concerning the abbey of St André-en-Gouffern)
H 6551 (charters concerning the abbey of St-André-en-Gouffern)
H suppl. 486 (cartulary, Hôtel-Dieu des Mathurins of Lisieux, II A 8)

CAMBRIDGE, GONVILLE AND CAIUS COLLEGE

283/676 (glosses on the *Decretum*, John of Tynemouth)

EVREUX, ARCHIVES DÉPARTEMENTALES EURE

G 122 (cartulary, cathedral chapter of Evreux)
H 438 (charter concerning the abbey of Lyre)
H 490 (charters concerning the abbey of Lyre)
H 793 (cartulary, abbey of St Taurin)
H-dépôt Evreux, G 0007 (cartulary, hospital of St Nicolas of Evreux)

FLERS, BIBLIOTHÈQUE MUNICIPALE

22 (formerly F 9) (cartulary, abbey of Savigny)
23 (formerly F 10) (cartulary, abbey of Savigny)

KARLSRUHE, BADISCHE LANDESBIBLIOTHEK

Aug. per. 40 (formerly Aug. XL), fos. 83r–120r (Albertus, *Apparatus* to *Compilatio II*);
    fos. 231r–290v (Vincentius Hispanus, *Apparatus* to *Compilatio III*)

LONDON, BRITISH LIBRARY

Harleian charters 43, c. 31 (charter, Richard I for the cathedral chapter of Angers)
Egerton 2901 (collection *Francofortana*)

Bibliography

LONDON, THE NATIONAL ARCHIVES

C 115/83/6689 (register of John Garlond)

OXFORD, BODLEIAN LIBRARY

Canonici Miscellanea 429 (Johannes Faventinus, *Summa decretorum*)

PARIS, ARCHIVES NATIONALES

AB XIX 3128 (collection Lenoir)
L 974 (charters concerning the abbey of Savigny)

PARIS, BIBLIOTHÈQUE MAZARINE

1318 (Alanus Anglicus 2nd rec. *Ius naturale*)

PARIS, BIBLIOTHÈQUE NATIONALE DE FRANCE

Collection Baluze, vols. XXXIX, LXXXIV, CCLXXIX
Collection Housseau, vols. IV–VI, XIII (part 2), XVIII, XIX, XXIII
Lat. 1096 (obituary, cathedral chapter of Tours)
Lat. 3858B (collection *Tripartita*)
Lat. 3892 (Huguccio, *Summa decretorum*)
Lat. 3909 (Alanus Anglicus 1st rec. *Ius naturale*)
Lat. 3922A, fos. 2r–40r (abbreviated *Decretum Gratiani*); fos. 118v–126v (collection *Rotomagensis III*); fos. 148r–167v (collection *Rotomagensis I*); fos. 173r–209r (collection *Francofortana* [Frcf. R])); fos. 210v–227v (collection *Rotomagensis II*)
Lat. 5430A (charters concerning the abbey of Mont-Saint-Michel)
Lat. 5441 (cartulary, abbey of Marmoutier)
Lat. 5480 (cartulary, abbey of Fontevraud)
Lat. 9212 (cartulary, priory of Bourg-Achard)
Lat. 10062 (obituary, abbey of St Evroult)
Lat. 10086 (cartulary, abbey of Troarn)
Lat. 10087 (cartulary, abbey of Montebourg)
Lat. 11055 (cartulary, abbey of St Evroult)
Lat. 11058 (cartulary, chapter of Sées: copy of Sées, Bibliothèque de l'Evêché, 'Livre rouge')
Lat. 11059 (cartulary, abbey of Silli)
Lat. 12459 (collection *Sangermanensis*)
Lat. 12884 (*Chronicon Beccensi* and charters concerning the abbey of Bec)
Lat. 12885 (obituary, abbey of Montebourg)
Lat. 17137 (cartulary, abbey of St Sauveur-le-Vicomte)
N. A. Lat. 1018 (cartularies, chapter of Coutances)
N. A. Lat. 1023 (charters concerning the abbey of Savigny)
N. A. Lat. 1576 (*Apparatus Ecce vicit leo*)
N. A. Lat. 1774 (obituary, abbey of Lyre)

Bibliography

ROUEN, ARCHIVES DÉPARTEMENTALES SEINE-MARITIME

D 20 (cartulary, priory of St Martin-du-Bosc)
G 856 (papal letters concerning the archbishopric of Rouen)
G 1121 (letters of Honorius III concerning the archbishopric of Rouen)
G 2094 (obituary, cathedral chapter of Rouen)
G 3835 (charters concerning the cathedral chapter of Rouen)
G 4493 (charter concerning the archbishopric of Rouen)
G 4494 (charter concerning the election of Ralph II de Cierrey as bishop of Evreux)
13 H 15 (charters of lords of Tancarville concerning the abbey of St Georges-de
    -Boscherville)
55 HP 15 (cartulary, St Amand of Rouen)

ROUEN, BIBLIOTHÈQUE MUNICIPALE

743 (E 74), fos. 1r–142r (*Summa Omnis qui iuste iudicat*)
1193 (Y 044) (cartulary, cathedral chapter of Rouen)
1224 (Y 013) (cartulary, abbey of Foucarmont)
1227 (Y 52) (cartulary, abbey of St Georges-de-Boscherville)

SÉES, BIBLIOTHÈQUE DE L'EVÊCHÉ

'Livre blanc' (cartulary, abbey of St Martin of Sées)
'Livre rouge' (cartulary, cathedral chapter of Sées)

TOURS, ARCHIVES DÉPARTEMENTALES INDRE-ET-LOIRE

G 364 (charters concerning St Martin of Tours)

VATICAN CITY, BIBLIOTECA APOSTOLICA VATICANA

Vat. Lat. 1377, fos. 2r–98v (Tancred, *Glossa ordinaria* on *Compilatio I*); fos. 101r–145v
    (Tancred, *Glossa ordinaria* on *Compilatio II*); fos. 148r–279r (Tancred, *Glossa
    ordinaria* on *Compilatio III*).
Vat. Pal. Lat. 587, fos. 1r–105r (Ivo of Charters, *Decretum*)
Vat. Reg. Lat. 977, fos. 1r–296r (Laurentius Hispanus, *Glossa Palatina*)

ZWETTL, STIFTSBIBLIOTHEK

162, fos. 145r–173r (Richard de Mores, *Summa quaestionum*); fos. 179r–213r
    (Honorius, *Summa decretalium quaestionum*)

PRINTED PRIMARY SOURCES

*Acta of Henry II and Richard I: Hand-list of Documents Surviving in the Original in
    Repositories in the United Kingdom*, ed. J.C. Holt and R. Mortimer (List and
    Index Society/Special Series XXI) (Richmond, 1986).

Bibliography

Acta of Henry II and Richard I: Hand-list of Documents Surviving in the Original in Repositories in the United Kingdom, Part II, ed. N. Vincent (List and Index Society/Special Series XXVII) (Chippenham, 1996).

Acta Stephani Langton Cantuariensis archiepiscopi A.D. *1207–1228*, ed. K. Major (The Canterbury and York Society l) (Oxford, 1950).

Actus pontificum Cenomannis in urbe degentium, ed. G. Busson and A. Ledru (Archives historiques du Maine II) (Le Mans, 1902).

The Anglo-Latin Satirical Poets and Epigrammatists of the Twelfth Century, ed. T. Wright (Rolls Series LIX a–b) (2 vols., London, 1872).

'Annales Cameracenses', in *MGH, scriptores*, XVI, ed. G.H. Pertz, 2nd edn (Leipzig, 1925), pp. 509–54.

'Annales Sancti Albini Andegavensis', in *Recueil d'annales angevines et vendômoises*, ed. L. Halphen (Paris, 1903), pp. 1–49.

'Annales Sancti Florentii Salmurensis', in *Recueil d'annales angevines et vendômoises*, ed. L. Halphen (Paris, 1903), pp. 111–26.

'Annales Sancti Sergii Andegavensis', in *Recueil d'annales angevines et vendômoises*, ed. L. Halphen (Paris, 1903), pp. 91–110.

'Annales Vindocinenses', in *Recueil d'annales angevines et vendômoises*, ed. L. Halphen (Paris, 1903), pp. 50–79.

'Antiquarum collectionum decretalium. Liber primus. Brevarium extra Bernardi praepositi Papiensis', in *Antiquae collectiones decretalium*, ed. A. Agustin (Paris, 1609), pp. 1–149.

Antiquus cartularius ecclesiae Baiocensis, livre noir, ed. V. Bourrienne (Société de l'histoire de Normandie) (2 vols., Rouen 1902–3).

'Apparatus glossarum in Compilationem quartam', in *Antiquae collectiones decretalium*, ed. A. Agustin (Paris, 1609), pp. 797–843 (Johannes Teutonicus).

Archives de la Maison-Dieu de Châteaudun, ed. A. de Belfort and L. Merlet (Paris, 1881).

'Arnulfi Sagiensis archidiaconi postea episcopi Lexoviensis invectiva in Girardum Engolismensem episcopum', ed. J. Dieterich, in *Libelli de lite imperatorum et pontificum saeculis XI. et XII. conscripti*, ed. E. Dümmler (MGH) (3 vols., Hanover, 1887–91), III, pp. 81–108.

Azonis Lectura super codicem. Hugolini Apparatus in tres libros (Corpus glossatorum juris civilis III) (Turin, 1966; reprint of Paris, 1577).

Benedicti regula, ed. R. Hanslik (Corpus scriptorum ecclesiasticorum latinorum LXXV) (Vienna, 1970).

Bernardi Papiensis (Faventini episcopi) Summa decretalium, ed. E. Laspeyres (Regensburg, 1860), pp. 1–283.

'Bernardi Summa de electione', in *Bernardi Papiensis (Faventini episcopi) Summa decretalium*, ed. E. Laspeyres (Regensburg, 1860), pp. 307–23.

Bonizo, Liber de vita christiana, ed. E. Perels (Texte zur Geschichte des römischen und kanonischen Rechts im Mittelalter I) (Berlin, 1930).

Calendar of the Charter Rolls, 1226–1516 (6 vols., London, 1903–27).

Calendar of Documents Preserved in France, Illustrative of the History of Great Britain and Ireland, ed. J. Round (London, 1899).

The Cartae antiquae Rolls 1–10, ed. L. Landon (Pipe Roll Society N.S. XVII) (London, 1939).

Bibliography

The Cartae antiquae Rolls 11–20, ed. J.C. Davies (Pipe Roll Society N.S. XXXIII) (London, 1960).

Cartulaire de l'abbaye de Bonport de l'ordre de Citeaux au diocèse d'Evreux, ed. J. Andrieux (2 vols., Evreux, 1862).

Cartulaire de l'abbaye cistercienne de Fontaine-Daniel, ed. A. Grosse-Duperon and E. Gouvrion (Mayenne, 1896).

Cartulaire de l'abbaye de Notre-Dame de La Trappe, ed. M. Le Comte de Charency (Société historique et archéologique de l'Orne) (Alençon, 1889).

Cartulaire de l'abbaye de Saint-Aubin d'Angers, ed. B. de Broussillon (Documents historiques sur l'Anjou I–III) (3 vols., Paris, 1903).

Cartulaire de l'abbaye de Saint-Laon de Thouars, ed. H. Imbert (Niort, 1876).

Cartulaire de l'abbaye de Saint-Michel du Tréport (Ordre de saint Benoît), ed. P. Laffleur de Kermaingant (Paris, 1880).

Cartulaire de l'abbaye de la Sainte-Trinité de Tiron, ed. L. Merlet (Société archéologique d'Eure-et-Loire) (2 vols., Chartres, 1883).

Cartulaire de l'abbaye de la Trinité de Vendôme, ed. C. Métais (5 vols., Paris 1893 – 1904).

Cartulaire des abbayes de Saint-Pierre de la Couture et de Saint-Pierre de Solesmes, ed. by the Benedictin monks of Solesmes (Le Mans, 1881).

Cartulaire de l'archevêché de Tours (Liber bonarum gentium), ed. L. de Grandmaison (Mémoires de la société archéologique de Touraine XXXVII–XXXVIII) (2 vols., Tours 1892–4).

Cartulaires du Bas-Poitou (département de la Vendée), ed. P. Marchegay (Les Roches-Baritaud, 1877).

Le cartulaire du chapitre cathédral de Coutances. Etude et édition critique, ed. J. Fontanel (St Lô, 2003).

Cartulaire du chapitre royal de Saint-Pierre-de-la-Cour du Mans, ed. S. Menjot d'Elbenne and L.-J. Denis (Archives historiques du Maine IV) (Le Mans, 1907).

Cartulaire de Cormery précédé de l'histoire de l'abbaye et de la ville de Cormery, ed. J.-J. Bourasse (Mémoires de la société archéologique de Touraine XII) (Tours, 1861).

Cartulaire de l'église Notre-Dame de Paris, ed. M. Guérard (Collection des cartulaires de France VII) (4 vols., Paris, 1850).

Cartulaire de l'église de la Sainte-Trinité de Beaumont-le-Roger, ed. E. Deville (Paris, 1912).

Cartulaire de l'évêché du Mans (936–1790), ed. B. de Broussillon (Archives historiques du Maine I) (Le Mans, 1900).

Cartulaire de l'évêché du Mans (965–1786), ed. B. de Broussillon (Archives historiques du Maine IX) (Le Mans, 1908).

Cartulaire de l'hôpital Saint-Jean d'Angers, ed. C. Port (Angers, 1870).

Le cartulaire de Louviers. Documents historique originaux du Xe au XVIIIe siècle, ed. T. Bonnin (5 vols., Evreux, 1870–85).

Cartulaire Manceau de Marmoutier, ed. E. Laurain (2 vols., Laval, 1911–45).

Cartulaire de la Manche, ed. N. Dubosc (St Lô, 1878).

Cartulaire de Marmoutier pour le Perche. N.-D. du Vieux-Château, Collégiale de Saint-Léonard de Bellême, Prieuré de St-Martin-du-Vieux-Bellême, ed. R. Barret (Documents sur la province du Perche 3e sér. II) (Mortagne, 1905).

Cartulaire noir de la cathédrale d'Angers, ed. C. Urseau (Documents historiques sur l'Anjou V) (Angers, 1908).

Bibliography

Cartulaire de Notre-Dame de Chartres, ed. E. de Lépinois and L. Merlet (Société archéologique d'Eure-et-Loire) (3 vols., Chartres 1862–5).

Cartulaire du prieuré de Saint-Hippolyte de Vivoin et de ses annexes, ed. L.-J. Denis (Paris, 1894).

Cartulaire de Saint-Victeur, prieuré de l'abbaye de Mont-Saint-Michel, 944–1400, ed. B. de Broussillon (Société d'agriculture, sciences et arts de la Sarthe) (Paris, 1895).

Catalogue des actes des évêques du Mans jusqu'à la fin du XIIIe siècle avec une introduction, ed. L. Celier (Paris, 1910).

The Chancellor's Roll for the Eighth Year of the Reign of King Richard the First, Michaelmas 1196, ed. D.M. Stenton (Pipe Roll Society N.S. VII) (London, 1930).

The Charters of Duchess Constance of Brittany and her Family, ed. J. Everard and M. Jones (Woodbridge, 1999).

Chartes de Saint-Julien de Tours (1002–1300), ed. L.-J. Denis (Archives historiques du Maine XII, I–II) (Le Mans, 1912–13).

Chartes vendômoises, ed. C. Métais (Société archéologique scientifique et littéraire du Vendômois) (Vendôme, 1905).

Chartularium insignis ecclesiae Cenomanensis quod dicitur Liber albus capituli, ed. R.-J.-F. Lottin (Institut des provinces de France 2e sér. II) (Le Mans, 1869).

Chartularium universitatis Parisiensis, ed. H. Denifle and E. Chatelain (4 vols., Paris, 1889–97).

'Chronica Albrici monachi Trium Fontium', in *MGH, scriptores*, XXIII, ed. G.H. Pertz (Hanover, 1874), pp. 631–950.

'Chronica domni Rainaldi archidiaconi Sancti Mauricii Andegavensis', in *Chroniques des églises d'Anjou*, ed. P. Marchegay and E. Mabille (Société de l'histoire de France) (Paris, 1869), pp. 3–16.

'Chronica Roberti de Torigneio, abbatis monasterii Sancti Michaelis in Pericolo Maris', in *Chronicles of the Reigns of Stephen, Henry II and Richard I*, ed. R. Howlett (Rolls Series LXXXII) (4 vols., London, 1884–9), IV.

Chronica Rogeri de Hovedene, ed. W. Stubbs (Rolls Series LI) (4 vols., London, 1868–71).

The Chronicle of the Election of Hugh Abbot of Bury St. Edmunds and Later Bishop of Ely, ed. R.M. Thomson (Oxford Medieval Texts) (Oxford, 1974).

'E chronico monasterii Beccensis', in *RHF*, XXIII, pp. 453–60.

'Ex chronico monasterii Sancti Taurini Ebroicensis', in *RHF*, XXIII, pp. 465–7.

'E chronico Rotomagensi', in *RHF*, XVIII, pp. 357–62, XXIII, pp. 331–43.

'Ex chronico Savigniacensis monasterii', in *RHF*, XVIII, pp. 350–2.

'Chronicon Gastinensis coenobii', in *Recueil de chroniques de Touraine*, ed. A. Salmon (Collection de documents sur l'histoire de Touraine I) (Tours, 1854), pp. 374–5.

'Chronicon Turonense magnum', in *Recueil de chroniques de Touraine*, ed. A. Salmon (Collection de documents sur l'histoire de Touraine I) (Tours, 1854), pp. 64–161.

'Ex chronologia Roberti Altissiodorensis', in *RHF*, XVIII, pp. 247–90.

Close Rolls of the Reign of Henry III (14 vols., London, 1902–38).

Collection des principaux cartulaires du diocèse de Troyes, ed. C. Lalore (6 vols., Paris, 1875–82).

Concilia Rotomagensis provinciae, ed. G. Bessin (two parts in one, Rouen, 1717).

Conciliae Africae A.345–A.525, ed. C. Munier (Corpus christianorum Series latina CCLIX) (Turnhout, 1974).

Les conciles de la province de Tours (XIIIe–XVe siècles), ed. J. Avril (Paris, 1987).

Bibliography

'Concilii quarti Lateranensis constitutiones', in *Constitutiones concilii quarti Lateranensis una cum commentariis glossatorum*, ed. A. García y García (MIC series A: corpus glossatorum II) (Vatican City, 1981), pp. 1–118.

Conciliorum oecumenicorum decreta, ed. G. Alberigo et al., 3rd edn (Bologna, 1973).

'Continuatio altera appendices Roberti de Monte ad Sigebertum', in *RHF*, XVIII, pp. 345–8.

Corpus iuris canonici, ed. E. Friedberg (2 vols., Leipzig, 1879–81).

Corpus iuris civilis Iustinianei: cum commentariis Accursii, scholiis Contii, et D. Gothofredi lucubrationibus ad Accursium, ed. J. Fehe et al. (6 vols., Lyons, 1627).

The Correspondence of Thomas Becket, Archbishop of Canterbury, 1162–70, ed. A. Duggan (Oxford Medieval Texts) (2 vols., Oxford, 2001).

Councils and Synods with Other Documents relating to the English Church. I. A.D. 871–1204, ed. D. Whitelock et al. (2 vols., Oxford, 1981).

Councils and Synods with Other Documents relating to the English Church. II. A.D. 1205–1313, ed. M. Powicke and C. Cheney (2 vols., Oxford, 1964).

Cronica Jocelini de Brakelonda de rebus gestis Samsonis abbatis monasterii Sancti Edmundi, ed. H.E. Butler (London, 1949).

'Damasi Apparatus in concilium quartum Lateranense', in *Constitutiones concilii quarti Lateranensis una cum commentariis glossatorum*, ed. A. García y García (MIC series A: corpus glossatorum II) (Vatican City, 1981), pp. 388–460.

Decretales Pseudo-Isidorianae et Capitula Angilramni, ed. P. Hinschius (Leipzig, 1863).

'Decretum', in *PL*, CLXI, cols. 47–1022 (Ivo of Chartres).

A Digest of the Charters Preserved in the Cartulary of the Priory of Dunstable, ed. G.H. Fowler (Publications of the Bedfordshire Historical Record Society X) (Aspley Guise, 1926).

Diplomatic Documents Preserved in the Public Record Office I. 1101–1272, ed. P. Chaplais (London, 1964).

Diversorum patrum sententie sive collectio in LXXIV titulos digesta, ed. J. Gilchrist (MIC series B: corpus collectionum I) (Vatican City, 1973).

Earldom of Gloucester Charters. The Charters and Scribes of the Earls and Countesses of Gloucester to A.D. 1217, ed. R.B. Patterson (Oxford, 1973).

The Early Charters of the Augustinian Canons of Waltham Abbey, Essex, 1062–1230, ed. R. Ransford (Woodbridge, 1989).

The Ecclesiastical History of Orderic Vitalis, ed. M. Chibnall (Oxford Medieval Texts) (6 vols., Oxford, 1969–80).

English Episcopal Acta I. Lincoln 1087–1185, ed. D. Smith (London, 1980).

English Episcopal Acta IX. Winchester 1205–1238, ed. N. Vincent (Oxford, 1994).

English Episcopal Acta X. Bath and Wells 1061–1205, ed. F.M. Ramsey (Oxford, 1995).

English Episcopal Acta XI. Exeter 1046–1184, ed. F. Barlow (Oxford, 1996).

English Episcopal Acta XIV. Coventry and Lichfield 1072–1159, ed. M.J. Franklin (Oxford, 1997).

English Episcopal Acta XVIII. Salisbury 1078–1217, ed. B.R. Kemp (Oxford, 1999).

Enquête de 1245 relative aux droits du chapitre Saint Julien du Mans, ed. J. Chapée et al. (Société des archives historiques du Conger) (Paris, 1922).

'Epistolae Alexandri III papae', in *RHF*, XV, pp. 744–977.

'Epistolae Hugonis Rothomagensis archiepiscopi', in *RHF*, XV, pp. 693–703.

'Epistolae Ivonis Carnotensis episcopi', in *RHF*, XV, pp. 69–177.

Bibliography

Epistolae pontificum Romanorum ineditae, ed. S. Loewenfeld (Leipzig, 1885).

Epistolae reverendissimi in Christo patris ac domini D. Gervasii Praemonstratensis abbatis postea Sagiensis episcopi ex veteri celeberrimae Viconiensis monasterii bibliothecae manuscripto editae, ed. N. Caillieu (Valenciennes, 1663).

'Epistolae Stephani Tornacensis episcopi', in *RHF*, XIX, pp. 282–306.

'Epistolarum regis Ludovici VII et variorum ad eum volumen', in *RHF*, XVI, pp. 1–170.

Etudes sur les actes de Louis VII, ed. A. Luchaire (Paris, 1885).

Feet of Fines of the Reign of Henry II and of the First Seven Years of the Reign of Richard I, A.D. 1182 to A.D. 1196 (Pipe Roll Society XVII) (London, 1894).

Feudal Documents from the Abbey of Bury St. Edmunds, ed. D. Douglas (Records of the Social and Economic History of England and Wales VIII) (London, 1932).

The Flowers of History by Roger de Wendover, ed. H.G. Hewlett (Rolls Series LXXXIV) (3 vols., London, 1886–9).

'Fragments d'un cartulaire de Saint-Pierre-de-Lisieux', ed. R.N. Sauvage, *Etudes Lexoviennes*, 3 (1928), 325–57.

Gesta abbatum monasterii Sancti Albani a Thoma Walsingham, regnante Ricardo secundo, ejusdem ecclesiae praecentore, compilata, ed. H. Riley (Rolls Series XXVIII) (3 vols., London, 1867–9).

'Gesta Ambaziensium dominorum', in *Chroniques des comtes d'Anjou et des seigneurs d'Amboise*, ed. L. Halphen and R. Poupardin (Collection des textes pour servir à l'étude et à l'enseignement de l'histoire) (Paris, 1913), pp. 74–132.

Gesta regis Henrici secundi Benedicti abbatis: The Chronicle of the Reigns of Henry I and Richard I, A.D. 1169–1192, Known Commonly under the Name of Benedict of Peterborough, ed. W. Stubbs (Rolls Series IL) (2 vols., London, 1867).

Giraldi Cambrensis opera, ed. J. Brewer et al. (Rolls Series XXI) (8 vols., London, 1861–91).

Grand cartulaire de Fontevraud (Pancarta et cartularium abbatissae et ordinis Fontis Ebraudi), ed. J.-M. Bienvenu et al. (Archives historiques du Poitou LXIII–LXIV) (2 vols., Poitiers, 2000–5).

The Great Roll of the Pipe for the Second, Third and Fourth Years of the Reign of King Henry the Second, A.D. 1155, 1156, 1157, 1158, ed. J. Hunter (London, 1844).

The Great Roll Roll of the Pipe for the Fifth (to Thirty-fourth) Year of the Reign of King Henry the Second, A.D. 1158 (to 1188) (Pipe Roll Society I–II, IV–IX, XI–XIII, XV–XVI, XVIII–XIX, XXI–XXII, XXV–XXXIV, XXXVI, XXXVIII) (30 vols., London, 1884–1925).

The Great Roll of the Pipe for the First Year of the Reign of King Richard the First, A.D. 1189–1190, ed. J. Hunter (London, 1844).

The Great Roll of the Pipe for the Second (to Tenth [eighth missing]) Year of the Reign of King Richard the First, ed. D. Stenton (Pipe Roll Society N.S. I–III, V–VI, VIII–IX) (London, 1925–32).

The Great Roll of the Pipe for the First (to Sixteenth [fifteenth missing]) Year of the Reign of King John, ed. D. Stenton et al. (Pipe Roll Society N.S. X, XII, XIV–XVI, XVIII–XX, XXII–XXIV, XXVI, XXVIII, XXX, XXXV) (London, 1933–59).

The Great Roll of the Pipe for the Second (to Sixth) Year of the Reign of King Henry the Third, ed. E. Ebden et al. (Pipe Roll Society N.S. XXXIX, XLII, XLVII–XLVIII, LI) (London, 1964–99).

The Great Roll of the Pipe for the Fourteenth Year of King Henry the Third, ed. C. Robinson (Pipe Roll Society N.S. IV) (Princeton, 1927).

Bibliography

'Historia Gaufredi ducis Normannorum et comitis Andegavorum', in *Chroniques des comtes d'Anjou et des seigneurs d'Amboise*, ed. L. Halphen and R. Poupardin (Collection des textes pur servir à l'étude et à l'enseignement de l'histoire) (Paris, 1913), pp. 172–231.

The Historia pontificalis of John of Salisbury, ed. M. Chibnall (Oxford, 1986).

'Historia rerum anglicarum of William of Newburgh', in *Chronicles of the Reigns of Stephen, Henry II, and Richard I*, ed. R. Howlett (Rolls Series LXXXII) (4 vols., London, 1884–9), I, II [–p. 500].

'Historia Sancti Florentii Salmurensis', in *Chroniques des églises d'Anjou*, ed. P. Marchegay and E. Mabille (Société de l'histoire de France) (Paris, 1869), pp. 217–328.

The Historical Works of Gervase of Canterbury, ed. W. Stubbs (2 vols., Rolls Series LXXIII) (London, 1879–80).

The Historical Works of Master Ralph de Diceto, Dean of London, ed. W. Stubbs (Rolls Series LXVIII) (2 vols., London, 1876).

Honorii III Romani pontificis opera omnia, ed. C. Horoy (Medii aevi bibliotheca patristica seu ejusdem temporis patrologia ab anno MCCXVI usque ad concilii Tridentini tempora IV) (4 vols., Paris, 1879–80).

'Innocentii Romani pontificis regestorum sive epistolarum', in *PL*, CCXIV–CCXVI [–col. 992].

'Itinerarium peregrinorum et gesta regis Ricardi', in *Chronicles and Memorials of the Reign of Richard I*, ed. W. Stubbs (Rolls Series XXXVIII, I–II), (2 vols., London, 1864–5).

The Itinerary of King Richard I, ed. L. Landon (Pipe Roll Society N.S. XIII) (London, 1935).

'Joannis Teutonici Apparatus in concilium quartum Lateranense', in *Constitutiones concilii quarti Lateranensis una cum commentariis glossatorum*, ed. A. García y García (MIC series A: corpus glossatorum II) (Vatican City, 1981), pp. 175–272.

Johannis Teutonici Apparatus glossarum in Compilationem tertiam, ed. K. Pennington (MIC series A: corpus glossatorum III) (Vatican City, 1981).

The Later Letters of Peter of Blois, ed. E. Revell (Auctores Britannici medii aevi XIII) (Oxford, 1993).

Layettes du trésor des chartes, ed. A. Teulet et al. (5 vols., Paris, 1863–1910).

Liber controversarium Sancti Vincentii Cenomannensis ou second cartulaire de l'abbaye de St-Vincent du Mans, ed. A. Chédeville (Paris, 1969).

Liber ordinis Sancti Victoris Parisiensis, ed. L. Jocqué and L. Milis (Corpus Christianorum. Continuatio medievalis LXI) (Turnhout, 1984).

The Letters and Charters of Cardinal Guala Bicchieri, Papal Legate in England, 1216–1218, ed. N. Vincent (The Canterbury and York Society LXXXVIII) (Woodbridge, 1996).

The Letters and Charters of Gilbert Foliot, ed. A. Morey and C.N.L. Brooke (Cambridge, 1967).

The Letters of Arnulf of Lisieux, ed. F. Barlow (Camden Society 3rd ser. LXI) (London, 1939).

The Letters of John of Salisbury I. The Early Letters (1153–1161), ed. W.J. Millor and H.E. Butler, revised by C.N.L. Brooke (Oxford Medieval Texts) (Oxford, 1986).

The Letters of John of Salisbury II. The Later Letters (1163–1180), ed. C.N.L. Brooke and W.J. Millor (Oxford Medieval Texts) (Oxford, 1974).

The Letters of Peter the Venerable, ed. G. Constable (2 vols., Cambridge, Mass., 1967).

'Lucii III papae epistolae et privilegia', in *PL*, CCI, cols. 1071–376.

Bibliography

Magistri Honorii Summa 'De iure canonico tractaturus'. I, ed. R. Weigand et al. (MIC series A: corpus glossatorum V/I) (Vatican City, 2004).

Magni rotuli scaccarii Normanniae sub regibus Angliae, ed. T. Stapleton (2 vols., London, 1840–4).

Martyrologe-obituaire de l'église métropolitaine de Tours, ed. J.-J. Bourasse (Mémoires de la société archéologique de Touraine XVII) (Tours, 1865).

The Materials of the History of Thomas Becket, ed. J.C. Robertson and J.B. Sheppard (Rolls Series LXVII) (7 vols., London 1875–85).

Mémoires pour servir de preuves à l'histoire ecclésiastique et civile de Bretagne, ed. H. Morice (2 vols., Paris, 1742–4).

The Memoranda Roll for the Michaelmas Term of the First Year of the Reign of King John (1199–1200), ed. H.G. Richardson (Pipe Roll Society N. S. XXI) (London, 1943).

Monasticon Anglicanum: A History of the Abbeys and Other Monasteries, Hospitals, Frieries, and Cathedral and Collegiate Churches with their Dependencies in England and Wales, ed. W. Dugdale, revised by J. Caley et al. (6 vols., London, 1817–30).

Monumenta Vizeliacensia. Textes relatifs à l'histoire de l'abbaye de Vézelay, ed. R.B.C. Huygens (Corpus christianorum. Continuatio mediaevalis XLII) (Turnhout, 1976).

'Narratio', in *Recueil de chroniques de Touraine*, ed. A. Salmon (Collection de documents sur l'histoire de Touraine I) (Tours, 1854), pp. 292–317.

Nécrologe-obituaire de la cathédrale du Mans, ed. G. Busson and A. Ledru (Archives historiques du Maine VII) (Le Mans, 1906).

Necrologium beatissimi Martini Turonensis, 804–1495, et obituarium Majoris Monasterii, ed. P. Nobilleau (Tours, 1875).

L'obituaire de la cathédrale d'Angers, ed. C. Urseau (Angers, 1930).

Obituaires de la province de Sens. T. I (Diocèses de Sens et de Paris), ed. A. Molinier (Recueil des historiens de la France. Obituaires I), (2 vols., Paris 1902).

'Ex obituario ecclesiae Ebroicensis', in *RHF*, XXIII, pp. 460–5.

Œuvres de Rigord et de Guillaume le Breton, ed. H.F. Delaborde (Société de l'histoire de France) (2 vols., Paris, 1882–5).

'Ad opera Petri Blesensis appendix', in *PL*, CCVII, cols. 1157–82.

Ordinaire et Coutumier de l'église cathédrale de Bayeux (XIIIᵉ siècle), ed. U. Chevalier (Bibliothèque liturgique VIII) (Paris, 1902).

'Panormia', in *PL*, CLXI, cols. 1045–343 (Ivo of Chartres).

Papal Decretals relating to the Diocese of Lincoln in the Twelfth Century, ed. W. Holtzmann and E. Kemp (Lincoln Record Society XLVII) (Hereford, 1954).

Papsturkunden in England, ed. W. Holtzmann (Abhandlungen der Akademie der Wissenschaften in Göttingen, philologisch-historische Klasse; neue Folge XXV und 3. Folge XIV, XXXIII) (3 vols., Berlin and Göttingen 1930–52).

Papsturkunden in Frankreich. Neue Folge. II. Normandie, ed. J. Ramackers (Abhandlungen der Gesellschaft der Wissenschaften zu Göttingen; philologisch-historische Klasse; 3. Folge XXI) (Göttingen, 1937).

Papsturkunden in Frankreich. Neue Folge. V. Touraine, Anjou, Maine und Bretagne, ed. J. Ramackers (Abhandlungen der Gesellschaft der Wissenschaften zu Göttingen; philologisch-historische Klasse; 3. Folge XXVII) (Göttingen, 1956).

Patent Rolls of the Reign of Henry III (6 vols., London, 1901–13).

'Petri Blesensis epistolae', in *PL*, CCVII, cols. 1–560.

'Petri Blesensi opuscula. Tracatus Quales sunt', in *PL*, CCVII, cols. 1005–52.

Petri Blesensis opusculum de distinctionibus in canonum interpretatione adhibendis, sive ut auctor voluit Speculum iuris canonici, ed. T. Reimarus (Berlin, 1837).

Placentini Summa codicis (Turin, 1962; reprint of Mainz, 1536).

Pouillés de la province de Rouen, ed. A. Longnon (Recueil des historiens de la France. Pouillés II) (Paris, 1903).

Pouillés de la province de Tours, ed. A. Longnon (Recueil des historiens de la France. Pouillés III) (Paris, 1903).

'Prima collectio decretalium Innocentii III', in *PL*, CCXVI, cols. 1173–272 (Rainier of Pomposa).

Quinque compilationes antiquae nec non collectio canonum Lipsiensis, ed. E. Friedberg (Leipzig, 1882).

Radulphi Nigri chronica. The Chronicles of Ralph Niger, ed. R. Anstruther (Publications of the Caxton Society) (London, 1851).

Recueil des actes des ducs de Normandie de 911 à 1066, ed. M. Fauroux (Mémoires de la société des antiquaires de Normandie XXXVI) (Caen, 1961).

Recueil des actes de Henri II, roi d'Angleterre et duc de Normandie, concernant les provinces françaises et les affaires de France, ed. L. Delisle and E. Berger (Chartes et diplômes relatifs à l'histoire de France) (3 vols., Paris, 1916–27).

Recueil des actes de Philippe Auguste, roi de France, ed. H.F. Delaborde et al. (Chartes et diplômes relatifs à l'histoire de France) (6 vols., Paris, 1916–).

The Red Book of the Exchequer, ed. H. Hall (Rolls Series IC) (3 vols., London, 1896).

Regesta pontificum Romanorum inde ab anno post Christum natum MCXCVIII ad annum MCCCIV, ed. A. Potthast (2 vols., Berlin, 1874–5).

Regesta pontificum Romanorum ab condita ecclesia ad annum post Christum natum MCXCVIII, ed. P. Jaffé revised by W. Wattenbach et al. (2 vols., Leipzig, 1885–8).

Regesta regum Anglo-Normannorum 1066–1154, ed. H.W.C. Davis et al. (4 vols., Oxford, 1913–69).

Die Register Innocenz' III., ed. O. Hageneder et al. (Publikationen der Abteilung für historische Studien des österreichischen Kulturinstituts in Rom I–IV; Publikationen des historischen Instituts beim österreichischen Kulturinstitut in Rom V–) (9 vols., Rome, 1968–).

Les registres d'Innocent IV, ed. E. Berger (Bibliothèque des écoles françaises d'Athènes et de Rome, 2nd sér., I) (4 vols., Paris, 1884–1911).

Les registres de Grégoire IX. Recueil des bulles de ce pape, ed. L. Auvray (Bibliothèques des écoles françaises d'Athènes et de Rome, 2nd sér., IX) (4 vols., Paris, 1890–1955).

Les registres de Philippe Auguste, I. texte, ed. J.W. Baldwin (Recueil des historiens de la France. Documents financiers et administratifs VII) (Paris, 1992).

The Registrum antiquissimum of the Cathedral Church of Lincoln, ed. C.W. Foster and K. Major (Publications of the Lincoln Record Society XXVII–XXIX, XXXII, XXXIV, XLI, XLII, XLIV, LI, LXI, LXVII, LXVIII) (12 vols., Hereford, 1931–73).

Roffredi Beneventani libelli iuris civilis, libelli iuris canonici, quaestiones sabbatinae (Corpus glossatorum juris civilis VI) (Turin, 1968; reprint of Avignon, 1500).

Rotuli chartarum in turri Londonensi asservati, ed. T.D. Hardy. (London, 1837).

Rotuli de liberate ac de misis et praestitis, regnante Johanne, ed. T.D. Hardy (London, 1844).

Bibliography

Rotuli litterarum clausarum in turri Londinensi asservati, ed. T.D. Hardy (2 vols., London 1833–44).

Rotuli litterarum patentium in turri Londonensi asservati, ed. T.D. Hardy (London, 1835).

Rotuli Normanniae in turri Londonensi asservati, Johanne et Henrico quinto, Angliae regibus, ed. T.D. Hardy (London, 1835).

Rotuli de oblatis et finibus in turri Londinensi asservati tempore regis Johannis, ed. T.D. Hardy (London, 1835).

Sancti Bernardi opera, ed. J. Leclercq and H. Rochais (8 vols., Rome, 1957–77).

Sancti Thomae Aquinatis doctoris angelici opera omnia iussi impensaque Leonis XIII P.M. edita (50 vols., Rome 1882–).

San Raimundo de Penyafort. Summa iuris, ed. J. Rius Serra (Barcelona, 1945).

Scripta anecdota antiquissimorum glossatorum, ed. G.B. Palmerio (Bibliotheca iuridica medii aevi I) (Bologna, 1888).

'Scripta de feodis ad regem spectantibus et de militibus ad exercitum vocandis, e Philippi Augusti regestis excerpta', in *RHF*, XXIII, pp. 605–723.

Selected Letters of Pope Innocent III concerning England, ed. C. Cheney and W.H. Semple (London, 1953).

S. Raimundus de Pennaforte: Summa de iure canonico, ed. X. Ochoa and A. Diez (Universa bibliotheca iuris I) (Rome, 1975).

Les statuts synodaux français du XIIIe siècle. I. Les statuts de Paris et le synodal de l'Ouest (XIIIe siècle), ed. O. Pontal (Collection de documents inédits sur l'histoire de France IX) (Paris, 1971).

Les statuts synodaux français du XIIIe siècle. II. Les statuts de 1230 à 1260, ed. O. Pontal (Collection de documents inédits sur l'histoire de France XV) (Paris, 1983).

Les statuts synodaux français du XIIIe siècle V. Les statuts synodaux des anciennes provinces de Bordeaux, Auch, Sens et Rouen (fin XIIIe siècle), ed. J. Avril (Collection de documents inédits sur l'histoire de France XXVIII) (Paris, 2001).

Die Summa decretorum des Magister Rufinus, ed. H. Singer (Paderborn, 1902).

Summa 'Elegantius in iure divino' seu Coloniensis, ed. G. Fransen and S. Kuttner (MIC series A: corpus glossatorum I) (4 vols., New York, 1969–90).

The Summa Parisiensis on the Decretum Gratiani, ed. T. McLaughlin (Toronto, 1952).

Die Summa des Paucapalea über das Decretum Gratiani, ed. J.F. von Schulte (Giessen, 1890).

Die Summa des Stephanus Tornacensis über das Decretum Gratiani, ed. J.F. von Schulte (Giessen, 1891).

'Supplementum ad Regesta Innocentii III Romani pontificis', in *PL*, CCXXVII, cols. 9–282.

Die Texte des Normannischen Anonymus, ed. K. Pellens (Veröffentlichungen des Instituts für europäische Geschichte Mainz XLII. Abteilung für abendländische Religionsgeschichte) (Wiesbaden, 1966).

Thomae Cantipratani s. theol. doctoris, ordinis praedicatorum, et episcopi suffraganei Cameracensis, Bonum universale de apibus, ed. G. Colveneer (Douai, 1627).

'Ex Uticensis monasterii annalibus et necrologio', in *RHF*, XXIII, pp. 480–91.

'Ven. Hildeberti epistolae', in *PL*, CLXXI, cols. 141–312.

Vetera monumenta Slavorum meridionalum historiam illustrantia maximam partem nondum edita ex tabulariis Vaticanis deprompta collecta ac serie chronologica disposata, ed. A. Theiner (2 vols., Rome and Zagreb, 1863–75).

Bibliography

'Vincentii Hispani Apparatus in concilium quartum Lateranense', in *Constitutiones concilii quarti Lateranensis una cum commentariis glossatorum*, ed. A. García y García (MIC series A: corpus glossatorum II) (Vatican City, 1981), pp. 271–383.

'Vitae b. Petri Abrincensis et b. Hamonis monachorum coenobii Saviniacensis in Normannia', ed. E.P. Sauvage, *Analecta Bolandiana*, 2 (1883), pp. 475–560.

'Vita sancti Thomae Cantuariensis archiepiscopi et martyris, auctore Willelmo Filio Stephani', in *MTB*, III, pp. 1–154.

Walter Map. De nugis curialium. Courtiers Trifles, ed. M.R. James revised by C.N.L. Brooke and R.A.B. Mynors (Oxford Medieval Texts) (Oxford, 1983).

Westminster Abbey Charters 1066–1214, ed. E. Mason (London Record Society Publications XXV) (London, 1988).

'Willelmo chronica Andrensis', in *MGH, scriptores*, XXIV, ed. G. Waitz et al. (Hanover, 1879), pp. 684–773.

PRINTED SECONDARY WORKS

Aimone-Braida, P., 'Il principio maggioritario nel pensiero di glossatori e decretisti', *Apollinaris*, 58 (1985), 209–85.

Allenou, J., *Histoire féodale des Marais, territoire et église de Dol. Enquête par tourbe ordonnée par Henri II, roi d'Angleterre* (La Bretagne et les pays celtiques XIII) (Paris, 1917).

Angot, A., *Généalogies féodales mayennaises du XIe au XIIIe siècle* (Laval, 1942).

Aurell, M., *L'empire des Plantagenêt 1154–1224* (Paris, 2003).

Avril, J., *Le gouvernement des évêques et la vie religieuse dans le diocèse d'Angers (1148–1240)* (2 vols., Paris, 1984).

'Naissance et évolution des législation synodales dans les diocèses du nord et de l'ouest de la France (1200–1250)', *Savigny KA*, 72 (1986), 152–249.

'Sur l'emploi de jurisdictio au moyen âge (XIIe–XIIIes.)', *Savigny KA*, 83 (1997), 272–82.

Bachrach, B., 'King Henry II and the Angevin Claims to the Saintonge', *Medieval Prosopography*, 6 (1985), 23–45.

Baldwin, J.W., 'A Debate at Paris over Thomas Becket between Master Roger and Master Peter the Chanter', *Studia Gratiana*, 11 (1967), 119–32.

'Philip Augustus and the Norman Church', *French Historical Studies*, 6 (1969), 1–30.

Masters, Princes and Merchants. The Social Views of Peter the Chanter and his Circle (2 vols., Princeton, 1970).

'Studium et Regnum: The Penetration of University Personnel into French and English Administration at the Turn of the Twelfth and Thirteenth Centuries', *Revue des études islamiques*, 44 (1976), 199–215.

The Government of Philip Augustus: Foundations of French Royal Power in the Middle Ages (Berkeley, 1986).

Barker, L., 'Ivo of Chartres and the Anglo-Norman Cultural Tradition', in M. Chibnall (ed.), *Anglo-Norman Studies XIII. Proceedings of the Battle Conference 1990* (Woodbridge, 1991), pp. 15–33.

Barlow, F., 'The English, Norman and French Councils Called to Deal with the Papal Schism of 1159, *EHR*, 51 (1936), 264–8.

Thomas Becket, 3rd edn (London, 1997).

Bibliography

Barraclough, G., 'The Making of a Bishop in the Middle Ages', *Catholic Historical Review*, 19 (1933), 275–319.

Papal Provisions. Aspects of Church History Constitutional, Legal and Administrative in the Later Middle Ages (Oxford, 1935).

Barratt, N., 'The English Revenues of Richard I', *EHR*, 116 (2001), 635–56.

Barrow, J., 'Education and the Recruitment of Cathedral Canons in England and Germany 1100–1225', *Viator*, 20 (1989), 117–38.

'Origins and Careers of Cathedral Canons in Twelfth-Century England', *Medieval Prosopography*, 21 (2000), 23–40.

Barth, F.X., *Hildebert von Lavardin (1056–1133) und das kirchliche Stellenbesetzungsrecht* (Kirchenrechtliche Abhandlungen XXXIV–XXXVI) (Stuttgart, 1906).

Barthélemy, D., *La société dans le comté de Vendôme de l'an mil au XIVe siècle* (Paris, 1993).

Bartlett, R., *Gerald of Wales 1146–1223* (Oxford, 1982).

Bates, D., *Normandy before 1066* (London, 1982).

'Normandy and England after 1066', *EHR*, 104 (1989), 851–80.

'Rouen from 900 to 1204: From Scandinavian Settlement to Angevin "Capital"', in J. Stratford, *Medieval Art, Architecture and Archaeology at Rouen* (The British Archaeological Association Conference. Transactions for the Year 1986, XII) (Leeds, 1993), pp. 1–11.

'The Rise and Fall of Normandy, c. 911–1204', in D. Bates and A. Curry (eds.), *Normandy and England in the Middle Ages* (London, 1994), pp. 19–35.

'The Prosopographical Study of Anglo-Norman Royal Charters', in K.S.B. Keats-Rohan (ed.), *Family Trees and the Roots of Politics. The Prosopography of Britain and France from the Tenth to the Twelfth Century* (Woodbridge, 1997), pp. 89–102.

Bauduin, P., 'Designer les parents: le champ de la parenté dans l'œuvre des premiers chroniqueurs normands', in J. Gillingham (ed.), *Anglo-Norman Studies XXIV. Proceedings of the Battle Conference 2001* (Woodbridge, 2002), pp. 71–84.

Baumgärtner, I., 'Was muss ein Legist vom Kirchenrecht wissen? Roffredus Beneventanus und seine Libelli de iure canonico', in P. Linehan (ed.), *Proceedings of the Seventh International Congress of Medieval Canon Law, Cambridge, 23–27 July 1984* (MIC series C: subsidia VIII) (Vatican City, 1988), pp. 223–45.

Bautier, R.-H., 'Conclusions. « Empire Plantagenêt » ou « espace Plantagenêt ». Y eut-il une civilisation du monde Plantagenêt?', *Cahiers de civilisation médiévale*, 29 (1986), 139–47.

'Cartulaires de chancellerie et recueils d'actes des autorités laïques et ecclésiastiques', in O. Guyotjeannin et al. (eds.), *Les cartulaires. Actes de la table ronde organisée par l'école nationale des chartes et le G.D.R. 121 du C.N.R.S. (Paris, 5–7 décembre 1991)* (Mémoires et documents de l'école des chartes XXXIX) (Paris, 1993) pp. 363–77.

Beaunier, D(om) and Besse, J.-M., *Abbayes et prieurés de l'ancienne France. VIII. Province ecclésiastique de Tours* (Archives de France monastique XIX) (Paris, 1920).

Becker, A., *Studien zum Investiturproblem in Frankreich. Papsttum, Königtum und Episkopat im Zeitalter der gregorianischen Kirchenreform 1049–1119* (Schriften der Universität des Saarlandes) (Saarbrücken, 1955).

Beier, H., *Päpstliche Provisionen für niedere Pfründen bis zum Jahre 1304* (Vorreformationsgeschichtliche Forschungen VII) (Münster, 1911).

Bibliography

Below, G. von, *Die Entstehung des ausschließlichen Wahlrechts der Domkapitel. Mit besonderer Rücksicht auf Deutschland* (Leipzig, 1883).

Benson, R., *The Bishop-Elect: A Study in Medieval Ecclesiastical Office* (Princeton, 1968).

Berger, E., *Thomae Cantipratensis Bonum universale de apibus quod illustrandis saeculi decimi tertii moribus conferat* (Paris, 1895).

Histoire de Blanche de Castille, reine de France (Bibliothèque des écoles françaises d'Athènes et de Rome LXX) (Paris, 1895).

Bertram, M., 'Die Dekretalen Gregors IX.: Kompilation oder Kodifikation?', in C. Longo (ed.), *Magister Raimundus. Atti del convegno per il IV centenario della canonizzazione di San Raimondo de Penyafort (1901–2001)* (Institutum historicum Fratrum Praedicatorum. Dissertationes historicae XXVIII) (Rome, 2002), pp. 61–86.

'Die Konstitutionen Alexanders IV. (1255/56) und Clemens' IV. (1265/1267). Eine neue Form päpstlicher Gesetzgebung', *Savigny KA*, 88 (2002), 70–109.

'Vorbonifazische Extravagantensammlungen', *Savigny KA*, 89 (2003), 285–322.

Beulertz, S., *Das Verbot der Laieninvestitur im Investiturstreit* (MGH, Studien und Texte II) (Hanover, 1991).

Bidou, S., 'La réforme du chapitre cathédral de Sées en 1131', *Société historique et archéologique de l'Orne*, 106 (1987), 21–32.

Bienvenu, J.-M., 'La réforme grégorienne dans l'archidiocèse de Tours', in G.-M. Oury (ed.), *Histoire religieuse de la Touraine* (Tours, 1975), pp. 75–91.

Billoré, M., 'La noblesse normande dans l'entourage de Richard Ier', in M. Aurell (ed.), *La cour Plantagenêt (1154–1204). Actes du colloque tenu à Thouars du 30 avril au 2 mai 1999* (Civilisation médiévale VIII) (Poitiers, 2000), pp. 151–66.

Böhmer, H., *Kirche und Staat in der Normandie im XI. und XII. Jahrhundert. Eine historische Studie* (Leipzig, 1899).

Bouard, M. de, 'Le duché de Normandie', in F. Lot and R. Fawtier (eds.), *Institutions seigneuriales (Les droits exercés par les grands vassaux)* (Histoire des institutions françaises au moyen âge I) (Paris, 1957), pp. 1–33.

Bouchard, C.B., 'The Geographical, Social and Ecclesiastical Origins of the Bishops of Auxerre and Sens in the Central Middle Ages', *Church History*, 46 (1977), 277–95.

'Those of My Blood'. Constructing Noble Families in Medieval Francia (Philadelphia, 2001).

Boulanger, K., 'Les vitraux du chœur de la cathédrale d'Angers: commanditaires et iconographie', in J. McNeill and D. Prigent (eds.), *Anjou. Medieval Art, Architecture and Archaeology* (The British Archaeological Association Conference Transactions XXVI) (Leeds, 2003), pp. 196–209.

Bourlet, C., et al., *Répertoire des microfilms de cartulaires français consultables à l'I.R.H.T.* (Orleans, 1999).

Bourrienne, V., *Un grand bâtisseur. Philippe de Harcourt, évêque de Bayeux (1142–1163)* (Paris, 1930).

Boussard, J., *Le comté d'Anjou sous Henri Plantagenêt et ses fils (1151–1204)* (Bibliothèque de l'école des hautes études; IVᵉ section, sciences historiques et philologiques CCLXXI) (Paris, 1938).

Le gouvernement d'Henri II Plantagenêt (Paris, 1956).

Bibliography

'L'enclave royale de Saint-Martin de Tours', *Bulletin de la société des antiquaires de France* (1958), 157–79.

'Le trésorier de Saint-Martin de Tours', *Revue d'histoire de l'église de France*, 47 (1961), 67–88.

Boyle, L., *A Survey of the Vatican Archive and its Medieval Holdings* (Pontifical Institute of Medieval Studies. Subsidia mediaevalia I) (Toronto, 1972).

Branch, B., 'Willermus Peccator et les manuscrits de Fécamp 1100–1150, *Cahiers de civilisation médiévale*, 26 (1983), 195–207.

Bras, G. Le, et al., *L'âge classique 1140–1378. Sources et théorie du droit* (Histoire du droit et des institutions de l'église en occident VII) (Paris, 1965).

Brett, M., 'Urban II and the Collections Attributed to Ivo of Chartres', in S. Chodorow (ed.), *Proceedings of the Eighth International Congress of Medieval Canon Law. San Diego, University of California at La Jolla, 21–27 August 1988* (MIC series C: subsidia IX) (Vatican City, 1992), pp. 27–46.

'Canon Law and Litigation: The Century before Gratian', in M. Franklin and C. Harper-Bill (eds.), *Medieval Ecclesiastical Studies in Honour of Dorothy M. Owen* (Studies in the History of Medieval Religion VII) (Woodbridge, 1995), pp. 21–40.

'Creeping up on the Panormia', in R. Helmholz et al. (eds.), *Grundlagen des Rechts. Festschrift für Peter Landau zum 65. Geburtstag* (Rechts- und staatswissenschaftliche Veröffentlichungen der Görres-Gesellschaft N.F. XCI) (Paderborn, 2000), pp. 205–70.

Broussillon, B. de, *La Maison de Craon 1050–1480. Etude historique accompagnée du cartulaire de Craon* (2 vols., Paris, 1893).

La Maison de Laval 1020–1605. Etude historique accompagnée du cartulaire de Laval et de Vitré (5 vols., Paris, 1895–1903).

Robert de Vitré, chanoine de Saint-Julien du Mans et chantre de Notre-Dame de Paris (1197–1208) (Le Mans, 1903).

Brundage, J., 'The Crusade of Richard I: Two Canonical Quaestiones', *Speculum*, 38 (1963), 443–52.

'The Rise of Professional Canonists and Development of the Ius Commune', *Savigny KA*, 81 (1995), 26–63.

'From Classroom to Courtroom: Parisian Canonists and their Careers', *Savigny KA*, 83 (1997), 342–61.

Bulst, N., 'Zum Gegenstand und zur Methode von Prosopographie', in N. Bulst and J.-P. Genet (eds.), *Medieval Lives and the Historian: Studies in Medieval Prosopography. Proceedings of the First International Interdisciplinary Conference on Medieval Prosopography, University of Bielefeld 3–5 December 1982* (Medieval Institute Publications, Western Michigan University) (Kalamazoo, 1986), pp. 1–16.

Camargo, M., 'The English Manuscripts of Bernard of Meung's "Flores Dictaminum"', *Viator*, 12 (1981), 197–219.

Cantor, N., *Church, Kingship, and Lay Investiture in England 1089–1135* (Princeton Studies in History X) (Princeton, 1958).

Carboni, A., '"Sanior pars" ed elezioni episcopali fino alla lotta per le investiture', *Archivio guiridico 'Filippo Serafini' 6th ser.*, 27 (1960), 76–127.

Carpenter, D. *The Minority of Henry III* (London, 1990).

Bibliography

Cartellieri, A., *Philip II. August, König von Frankreich* (4 vols., Leipzig, 1899–1922).

Chaplais, P., 'Henry II's Reissue of the Canons of the Council of Lillebonne of Whitsun 1080 (?25 February 1162)', *Journal of the Society of Archivists*, 4 (1973), 627–32.

Chartrou, J., *L'Anjou de 1109 à 1151. Foulques de Jérusalem et Geoffroi Plantagenêt* (Paris, 1928).

Châtillon, J., 'Thomas Becket et les Victorins', in R. Foreville (ed.), *Thomas Becket. Actes du Colloque international de Sédières 19–24 août 1973* (Paris, 1975).

Cheney, C., 'Gervase, Abbot of Prémontré, a Medieval Writer', *Bulletin of the John Rylands Library*, 33 (1950), 25–56.

From Becket to Langton. English Church Government 1170–1213 (Manchester, 1956).

Hubert Walter (London, 1967).

Pope Innocent III and England (Päpste und Papsttum IX) (Stuttgart, 1976).

'Decretals of Innocent III in Paris, B.N. MS LAT. 3922A', in C. Cheney, *The Papacy and England. 12th–14th centuries* (London, 1982), no. IV, pp. 149–63.

'Three Decretal Collections before Compilatio IV: Pragensis, Palatina I, and Abrincensis II', in C. Cheney, *The Papacy and England. 12th–14th Centuries* (London, 1982), no. V, pp. 464–83.

Cheney, C. and Cheney, M., *Studies in the Collections of Twelfth-Century Decretals. From the Papers of the Late Walther Holtzmann* (MIC series B: corpus collectionum III) (Vatican City, 1979).

Cheney, M., *Roger, Bishop of Worcester, 1164–1179* (Oxford, 1980).

Chibnall, M., *The Empress Matilda: Queen Consort, Queen Mother and Lady of the English* (Oxford, 1991).

'Normandy', in E. King (ed.), *The Anarchy of King Stephen's Reign* (Oxford, 1994), pp. 93–115.

Chodorow, S., 'An Appendix to Rainier de Pomposa's Collection', *Bulletin of Medieval Canon Law New Series*, 3 (1973), pp. 55–61.

Clanchy, M. 'England in the Thirteenth Century: Power and Knowledge', in W.M. Ormrod (ed.), *England in the Thirteenth Century: Proceedings of the 1984 Harlaxton Symposium* (Woodbridge, 1986), pp. 1–14.

From Memory to Written Record, England 1066–1307, 2nd edn (Oxford, 1993).

Clarke, P.D., 'The Collection of Gilbertus and the French Glosses in Brussels. Bibliothèque royale, MS 1407–09, and an Early Recension of Compilatio secunda', *Savigny KA*, 86 (2000), 132–84.

Classen, P., 'Das Wormser Konkordat in der deutschen Verfassungsgeschichte', in J. Fleckenstein (ed.), *Investiturstreit und Reichsverfassung* (Vorträge und Forschungen XVII) (Sigmaringen, 1973), pp. 411–60.

Claude, D., 'Die Bestellung der Bischöfe im merowingischen Reiche', *Savigny KA*, 49 (1963), 1–75.

Clay, C.T., 'The Early Treasurers of York', *Yorkshire Archaeological Journal*, 35 (1943), 7–34.

Cloché, P., 'Les élections épiscopales sous les Mérovingiens', *Moyen Age*, 25 (1925), 203–54.

Congar, Y., 'Quod omnes tangit ab omnibus tractari et approbari debet', *Revue historique du droit français et étranger*, 37 (1958), 210–51.

Bibliography

Conklin, G., 'Les Capétiens et l'affaire de Dol de Bretagne', *Revue d'histoire de l'église de France*, 78 (1992), 241–63.

Corner, D., 'The Gesta Regis Henrici Secundi and Chronica of Roger, Parson of Howden', *Bulletin of the Institute of Historical Research*, 56 (1983), 126–44.

Cronne, H.A., *The Reign of Stephen. Anarchy in England* (London, 1970).

Crouch, D., *The Beaumont Twins: The Roots and Branches of Power in the Twelfth Century* (Cambridge Studies in Medieval Life and Thought) (Cambridge, 1986).

William Marshal. Court, Career and Chivalry in the Angevin Empire 1147–1219 (London, 1990).

'A Norman "conventio" and Bonds of Lordship in the Middle Ages', in G. Garnett and J. Hudson, *Law and Government in Medieval England and Normandy. Essays in Honour of Sir James Holt* (Cambridge, 1994), pp. 299–324.

'Normans and Anglo-Normans: A Divided Aristocracy?', in D. Bates and A. Curry (eds.), *Normandy and England in the Middle Ages* (London, 1994), pp. 51–67.

The Reign of King Stephen, 1135–1154 (Harlow, 2000).

David, C.W., *Robert Curthose, Duke of Normandy* (Harvard Historical Studies xxv) (Cambridge, Mass., 1920).

Davis, R.H.C., *King Stephen, 1135–1154* (London, 1967).

Deeters, W., *Die Bambergensisgruppe der Dekretalensammlungen des 12. Jhdts.* (Bonn, 1956).

Delisle, L., *Le cabinet des manuscrits de la Bibliothèque Nationale* (3 vols., Paris, 1868–81).

Recueil des actes de Henri II, roi d'Angleterre et duc de Normandie, concernant les provinces françaises et les affaires de France. Introduction (Chartes et diplômes relatifs à l'histoire de France) (Paris, 1909).

[Delisle, L.], 'Chronologie des baillis et des sénéchaux royaux depuis les origines jusqu'à l'avènement de Philippe de Valois', in *RHF*, xxiv/1, pp. 15*–385*.

Desportes, P., *Diocèse de Reims* (Fasti ecclesiae Gallicanae iii) (Turnhout, 1998).

Desportes, P., et al., *Diocèse de Sées* (Fasti ecclesiae Gallicanae ix) (Turnout, 2005).

Desportes, P. and Millet, H., *Diocèse d'Amiens* (Fasti ecclesiae Gallicanae i) (Turnhout, 1996).

Dondorp, H., 'Die Zweidrittelmehrheit als Konstitutivum der Papstwahl in der Lehre der Kanonisten des dreizehnten Jahrhunderts', *Archiv für katholisches Kirchenrecht*, 161 (1992), 396–425.

Douglas, D., *William the Conqueror*, 2nd edn (Yale, 1999).

Dubois, J., 'Les dépendances de l'abbaye du Mont Saint-Michel et la vie monastique dans les prieurés', in *Millénaire monastique du Mont Saint-Michel. I. Histoire et vie monastique* (Paris, 1966), pp. 619–76.

Duby, G., 'Dans la France de Nord-Ouest. Au XIIe siècle: les "jeunes" dans la société aristocratique', *Annales. Economie, société, civilisation*, 19 (1964), 835–46.

'Structures de parenté et noblesse. France du nord XIe–XIIe siècles', in *Miscellanea medievalia in memoriam Jan Frederik Niermeyer* (Groningen, 1967), pp. 149–65.

Duggan, C., 'The Becket Dispute and the Criminous Clerks', *Bulletin of the Institute of Historical Research*, 35 (1962), 1–28.

Twelfth-Century Decretal Collections and their Importance in English History (University of London Historical Studies xii) (London, 1963).

Bibliography

'The Reception of Canon Law in England in the Later-Twelfth Century', in S. Kuttner and J. J. Ryan (eds.), *Proceedings of the Second International Congress of Medieval Canon Law, Boston College, 12–16 August 1963* (MIC series C: subsidia I) (Vatican City, 1965).

Duggan, C. and Duggan, A., 'Ralph de Diceto, Henry II and Becket, with an Appendix on Decretal Letters', in B. Tierney and P. Linehan (eds.), *Authority and Power: Studies on Medieval Law and Government in Honour of Walter Ullmann* (Cambridge, 1980), pp. 59–81.

Dumas, F., *De Joscii Turonensis archiepiscopi vita (1157–73)* (Paris, 1894).

Ehlers, J., *Hugo von St Viktor. Studien zum Geschichtsdenken und zur Geschichtsschreibung des 12. Jahrhunderts* (Frankfurter historische Abhandlungen VII) (Frankfurt, 1973).

Eickels, K. van, 'Domestizierte Maskulinität. Die Integration der Normannen in das westfränkische Reich in der Sicht des Dudos von St-Quentin', in I. Bennewitz and I. Kasten (eds.), *Genderdiskurse und Körperbilder im Mittelalter. Eine Bilanzierung nach Butler und Laqueur* (Bamberger Studien zum Mittelalter I) (Münster, 2002), pp. 97–134.

Elze, R., 'Die päpstliche Kapelle im 12. und 13. Jahrhundert', *Savigny KA*, 36 (1950), 145–205.

Emden, A.B., *A Biographical Register of the University of Oxford to A.D. 1500*, 2nd edn (3 vols., Oxford, 1989).

Englberger, J., 'Gregor VII. und die Bischofserhebungen in Frankreich. Zur Entstehung des ersten römischen Investiturdekrets vom Herbst 1078', in F.-R. Erkens (ed.), *Die früh- und hochmittelalterliche Bischofserhebung im europäischen Vergleich* (Beihefte zum Archiv für Kulturgeschichte XLVIII) (Cologne, 1998), pp. 193–258.

Erkens, F.-R., 'Die Bischofswahl im Spannungsfeld zwischen weltlicher und geistlicher Gewalt. Ein tour d'horizon', in F.-R. Erkens (ed.), *Die früh- und hochmittelalterliche Bischofserhebung im europäischen Vergleich* (Beihefte zum Archiv für Kulturgeschichte XLVIII) (Cologne, 1998), pp. 1–32.

Esmein, A., 'L'unanimité et la majorité', in *Mélanges Fitting* (2 vols., Montpellier, 1907-8), I, pp. 357–82.

Everard, J.A., *Brittany and the Angevins. Province and Empire 1158–1203* (Cambridge Studies in Medieval Life and Thought) (Cambridge, 2000).

Eyton, R.W., *Court, Household, and Itinerary of Henry II* (London, 1878).

Falkenstein, L., 'Decretalia Remensia. Zu Datum und Inhalt einiger Dekretalen Alexanders III. für Empfänger in der Kirchenprovinz Reims', in F. Liotta (ed.), *Miscellanea Rolando Bandinelli Papa Alessandro III* (Academia Senesi degli intronati) (Siena, 1986), pp. 153–216.

'Zu Entstehungsort und Redaktor der Collectio Brugensis', in S. Chodorow (ed.), *Proceedings of the Eighth International Congress of Medieval Canon Law. San Diego, University of California at La Jolla, 21–27 August 1988* (MIC series C: subsidia IX) (Vatican City, 1992), pp. 117–60.

'Alexandre III et la vacance d'un siège métropolitain: le cas de Reims', in *Sede vacante. La vacance du pouvoir dans l'église du moyen âge* (Centre de recherches en histoire du droit et des institutions; cahiers XV) (Brussels, 2001), pp. 3–37.

Bibliography

'Wilhelm von Champagne, Elekt von Chartres (1164–1168), Erzbischof von Sens (1168/9–1176), Erzbischof von Reims (1176–1202), Legat des apostolischen Stuhles, im Spiegel päpstlicher Schreiben und Privilegien', *Savigny KA*, 89 (2003), 107–284.

Farmer, S., *Communities of Saint-Martin: Legend and Ritual in Medieval Tours* (Ithaca, 1991).

Ferretti, G., 'Roffredo Epifanio da Benevento', *Studi Medievali*, 3 (1908–11), 230–87.

Fierville, C., 'Histoire généalogique de la maison et la baronnie de Tournebu, d'après les archives inédites de cette famille', *Mémoires de la société des antiquaires de Normandie 3rd ser.*, 6 (1869), 170–367.

Fleury, P. de, 'L'aumônerie de Saint-Gilles de Surgères', *Archives historiques de la Saintonge et de l'Aunis*, 6 (1879), 9–22.

Fliche, A., *La réforme grégorienne* (Spicilegium sacrum Lovaniense; études et documents VI, IX, XVI) (3 vols., Louvain, 1924–37).

Fournier, P. and Bras, G. Le, *Histoire des collections canonique en occident depuis les fausses décrétales jusqu'au décret de Gratien* (Bibliothèque d'histoire du droit) (2 vols., Paris, 1931-2).

Foreville, R., *L'église et la royauté en Angleterre sous Henri II Plantagenêt (1154–1189)* (Paris, 1943).

Latran I, II, III et Latran IV (Histoire de conciles œcuméniques VI) (Paris, 1965).

'La réception des conciles généraux dans l'église et la province de Rouen au XIIIe siècle', in *Droit privé et institutions régionales: études historiques offertes à Jean Yver* (Paris, 1976), pp. 243–53.

'The Synod of the Province of Rouen in the Eleventh and Twelfth Centuries', in C.N.L. Brooke et al. (eds.), *Church and Government in the Middle Ages* (Cambridge, 1976), pp. 19–39.

'L'église anglo-normande au temps du bienheureux Achard de Saint-Victor, évêque d'Avranches (1161–1171)', in R. Foreville, *Thomas Becket dans la tradition historique et hagiographique* (London, 1981), no. I, pp. 163–76.

'Innocent III et les élections épiscopales dans l'espace Plantagenêt de 1198 à 1205', in *Recueil d'études en hommage à Lucien Musset* (Cahier des annales de Normandie XXIII) (Caen, 1990), pp. 293–9.

Le pape Innocent III et la France (Päpste und Papsttum XXVI) (Stuttgart, 1992).

Fried, J., 'Die Rezeption Bologneser Wissenschaft in Deutschland während des 12. Jahrhunderts', *Viator*, 21 (1990), 103–45.

Friedberg, E., *Die Canones-Sammlungen zwischen Gratian und Bernhard von Pavia* (Leipzig, 1897).

Fuhrmann, H., *Einfluss und Verbreitung der pseudoisidorischen Fälschungen. Von ihrem Auftauchen bis in die neuere Zeit* (MGH, Schriften XXIV, I–III) (3 vols., Stuttgart, 1972–4).

Funk, F.X., 'Die Bischofswahl im christlichen Altertum und im Anfang des Mittelalters', in F.X. Funk, *Kirchengeschichtliche Abhandlungen und Untersuchungen* (Paderborn, 1897), pp. 23–39.

Galland, B., *Deux archevêchés entre la France et l'Empire: les archevêques de Lyon et les archevêques de Vienne du milieu du XIIe au milieu du XIVe siècle* (Bibliothèques des écoles françaises d'Athènes et de Rome CCLXXXII) (Rome, 1994).

Gallia christiana (16 vols., Paris, 1744–1887).

Bibliography

Ganzer, K., 'Das Mehrheitsprinzip bei den kirchlichen Wahlen des Mittelalters', *Theologische Quartalschrift*, 147 (1967), 60–87.

Papsttum und Bistumsbesetzungen in der Zeit von Gregor IX. bis Bonifaz VIII. Ein Beitrag zur Geschichte der päpstlichen Reservationen (Forschungen zur kirchlichen Rechtsgeschichte und zum Kirchenrecht IX) (Cologne, 1968).

'Zur Beschränkung der Bischofswahl auf die Domkapitel in Theorie und Praxis des 12. und 13. Jahrhunderts', *Savigny KA*, 57 (1971), 22–82, 58 (1972), 166–97.

Unanimitas, maioritas, pars sanior. Zur repräsentativen Willensbildung von Gemeinschaften in der kirchlichen Rechtsgeschichte (Akademie der Wissenschaften und der Literatur. Abhandlungen der geistes- und sozialwissenschaftlichen Klasse, Jahrgang 2000, IX) (Stuttgart, 2000).

Gaudemet, J., 'Unanimité et majorité (observations sur quelques études récents)', in *Etudes historiques à la mémoire de Noël Didier* (Paris, 1960), pp. 149–62.

'Recherches sur l'épiscopat médiéval en France', in S. Kuttner and J. J. Ryan (eds.), *Proceedings of the Second International Congress of Medieval Canon Law. Boston College, 12–16 August 1963* (MIC series C: subsidia I) (Vatican City, 1965), pp. 139–54.

Le gouvernement de l'église a l'époque classique. II. Le gouvernement local (Histoire du droit et des institutions de l'église en occident VIII, II) (Paris, 1979).

Gauthiez, B., 'Paris, un Rouen capétien? (Développement comparées de Rouen et Paris sous les règnes de Henri II et Philippe-Auguste)', in M. Chibnall (ed.), *Anglo-Norman Studies XVI. Proceedings of the Battle Conference 1993* (Woodbridge, 1994), pp. 117–36.

Génestal, L., *Le parage normand* (Bibliothèque de l'histoire du droit normand 2ᵉsérie, I, 1-2) (Caen, 1911).

Gestrich, A., et al., *Geschichte der Familie* (Europäische Kulturgeschichte I) (Stuttgart, 2003).

Gibbs, M. and Lang, J., *Bishops and Reform, 1215–1272, with Special Reference to the Lateran Council of 1215* (Oxford, 1934).

Gilchrist, J., 'The Manuscripts of the Canonical Collection in Four Books', *Savigny KA*, 69 (1983), 64–120.

Gillingham, J., *Richard I* (Yale, 1999).

'Royal Newsletters, Forgeries and English Historians: Some Links between Court and History in the Reign of Richard I', in M. Aurell (ed.), *La cour Plantagenêt (1154–1204). Actes du colloque tenu à Thouars du 30 avril au 2 mai 1999* (Civilisation médiévale VIII) (Poitiers, 2000), pp. 171–86.

The Angevin Empire, 2nd edn (London, 2001).

Given, J., *State and Society in Medieval Europe. Gwynedd and Languedoc under Outside Rule* (Ithaca, 1990).

Gleason, S.E., *An Ecclesiastical Barony of the Middle Ages. The Bishopric of Bayeux, 1066–1204* (Harvard Historical Monographs X) (Cambridge, Mass., 1936).

Glorieux, P., *Pour revaloriser Migne. Tables rectificatives* (Mélanges science religieuse IX) (Lille, 1952).

Gransden, A., *Historical Writing in England* (2 vols., London, 1974–82).

Grant, L., 'Le patronage architectural d'Henri II et de son entourage', *Cahiers de civilisation médiévale*, 37 (1994), 73–84.

Bibliography

Architecture and Society in Normandy 1120–1270 (New Haven, 2005).

Greenway, D., *John Le Neve: Fasti ecclesiae Anglicanae, 1066–1300. III. Lincoln* (London, 1977).

John Le Neve: Fasti ecclesiae Anglicanae, 1066–1300. IV. Salisbury (London, 1991).

John Le Neve: Fasti ecclesiae Anglicanae, 1066–1300. V. Chichester (London, 1996).

John Le Neve: Fasti ecclesiae Anglicanae, 1066–1300. VI. York (London, 1999).

Griffiths, Q., 'The Capetian Kings and St Martin de Tours', *Studies in Medieval and Renaissance History*, 19 (1987), 83–133.

Grossi, P., 'Unanimitas. Alle origine del concetto di persona giuridica nel diritto canonico', *Annali di storia del diritto*, 2 (1958), 229–331.

Gryson, R., 'Les élections ecclésiastiques au IIIe siècle', *Revue d'histoire ecclésiastique*, 68 (1973), 353–404.

'Les élections épiscopales en occident au IVe siècle', *Revue d'histoire ecclésiastique*, 75 (1980), 257–83.

Guerreau-Jalabert, A., 'La désignation des relations et des groupes de parenté en latin médiéval', *Archivum latinitatis medii aevi (Bulletin du Cange)*, 46-47 (1988), 65–108.

Guerreau-Jalabert, A., et al, 'De l'histoire de la famille à l'anthropologie de la parenté', in J.-C. Schmitt and O.G. Oexle (eds.), *Les tendances actuelles de l'histoire du moyen âge en France et en Allemagne. Actes des colloques de Sèvres (1997) et Göttingen (1998) organisés par le C.N.R.S. et le Max-Planck-Institut für Geschichte* (Histoire ancienne et médiévale LXVI) (Paris, 2002), pp. 433–46.

Guillemain, B., 'Philippe Auguste et l'épiscopat', in R.-H. Bautier (ed.), *La France de Philippe Auguste. Le temps de mutation. Actes du colloque international organisé par le C.N.R.S. (Paris, 29.9.–4.10.1980)* (Colloques internationaux du centre national de la recherche scientifique DCII) (Paris, 1982), pp. 365–84.

Guilloreau, L., 'L'élection de Silvestre à l'évêché de Séez (1202)', *Revue Catholique de Normandie*, 25 (1916), 423–39.

Guillot, O., *Le comte d'Anjou et son entourage au XIe siècle* (2 vols., Paris, 1972).

Hageneder, O., 'Die Register Innozenz III.', in T. Frenz (ed.), *Papst Innozenz III. Weichensteller der Geschichte Europas* (Stuttgart, 2000), pp. 91–101.

Hanenburg, J., 'Decretals and Decretal Collections in the Second Half of the Twelfth Century', *Tijdschrift voor Rechtsgeschiedenis*, 34 (1966), 552–99.

Harper-Bill, C., 'John and the Church of Rome', in S. Church (ed.), *King John. New Interpretations* (Woodbridge, 1999).

Hartmann, W., 'Beziehungen des Normannischen Anonymus zu frühscholastischen Bildungszentren', *Deutsches Archiv für Erforschung des Mittelalters*, 31 (1975), 108–43.

Der Investiturstreit (Enzyklopädie deutscher Geschichte XXI) (Munich, 1993).

Haskins, C., *Norman Institutions* (Harvard Historical Studies XXIV) (Cambridge, Mass., 1918).

Hauck, A., *Die Bischofswahlen unter den Merovingern* (Erlangen, 1883).

Hauck, K., 'Formes de parenté artificielle dans le haut moyen âge', in G. Duby and J. Le Goff (eds.), *Famille et parenté dans l'occident médiéval. Actes du colloque de Paris (6–8 Juin 1974)* (Collection de l'école française de Rome XXX) (Rome, 1977), pp. 43–7.

Bibliography

Heckel, R. v., 'Die Dekretalensammlungen des Gilbertus und Alanus nach den Weingartener Handschriften', *Savigny KA*, 29 (1940), 116–357.

Helmholz, R., *The Spirit of Classical Canon Law* (The Spirit of the Laws) (Athens, Ga, 1996).

Hollister, C.W., *Henry I* (New Haven, 2001).

Holt, J.C., 'Politics and Property in Early Medieval England', *Past and Present*, 57 (1972), 3–52.

'Feudal Society and the Family in Early Medieval England: III. Patronage and Politics', *Transactions of the Royal Historical Society*, 34 (1984), 1–25.

Magna Carta, 2nd edn (Cambridge, 1992).

Holtzmann, W., 'Die Dekretalensammlungen des 12.Jahrhunderts. 1. Die Sammlung Tanner', in *Festschrift zur Feier des zweihundertjährigen Bestehens der Akademie der Wissenschaften in Göttingen. II. Philologisch-historische Klasse* (Berlin, 1951), pp. 83–145.

'Kanonistische Ergänzungen zur Italia pontificia', *Quellen und Forschungen aus italienischen Archiven und Bibliotheken*, 37 (1957), 55–102, 38 (1958), 67–175.

Hucker, B.U., *Kaiser Otto IV.* (MGH, Schriften XXXIV) (Hanover, 1990).

Imbart de la Tour, P., *Les élections dans l'église de France du IXe au XIIe siècle. Etude sur la décadence du principe électif (814–1150)* (Paris, 1890).

Jacquemard, C., 'Maître Richard l'Evêque, archidiacre de Coutances', in F. Neveux and C. Bougy (eds.), *Mélanges Pierre Bouet. Recueil d'études en hommages à Pierre Bouet* (Cahier des Annales de Normandie XXXII) (Caen, 2002), pp. 107–21.

Jaeger, C.S., 'The Courtier Bishop in *Vitae* from the Tenth to the Twelfth Century', *Speculum*, 58 (1983), 292–325.

Jan, R. Le, *Famille et pouvoir dans le monde franc (VIIe–Xe siècle). Essai d'anthropologie sociale* (Histoire ancienne et médiévale XXXIII) (Paris, 1995).

Jasper, D., *Das Papstwahldekret von 1059. Überlieferung und Textgestalt* (Beiträge zur Geschichte und Quellenkunde des Mittelalters XII) (Sigmaringen, 1986).

Johnson, P., *Prayer, Patronage, and Power. The Abbey of la Trinité, Vendôme, 1032–1187* (New York, 1981).

Jolliffe, J.E.A., *Angevin Kingship*, 2nd edn (London, 1963).

Jones, L.W., 'The Library of St Aubin's at Angers in the Twelfth Century', in L.W. Jones (ed.), *Classical and Mediaeval Studies in Honor of Edward Kennard Rand* (New York, 1938), pp. 143–61.

Jussen, B., *Patenschaft und Adoption im frühen Mittelalter. Künstliche Verwandtschaft als soziale Praxis* (Veröffentlichungen des Max-Planck-Instituts für Geschichte XCVIII) (Göttingen, 1991).

Jussen, B., 'Famille et parenté. Comparaison des recherches françaises et allemandes', in J.-C. Schmitt and O.G. Oexle (eds.), *Les tendances actuelles de l'histoire du moyen âge en France et en Allemagne. Actes des colloques de Sèvres (1997) et Göttingen (1998) organisés par le C.N.R.S. et le Max-Planck-Institut für Geschichte* (Histoire ancienne et médiévale LXVI) (Paris, 2002), pp. 447–60.

Kalb, H., *Studien zur Summa Stephans von Tournai* (Innsbruck, 1983).

Kantorowicz, E., *The King's Two Bodies. A Study in Medieval Political Theology*, 7th edn (Princeton, 1997).

Kay, R., *The Council of Bourges, 1225. A Documentary History* (Church, Faith and Culture in the Medieval West) (Aldershot, 2002).

Bibliography

Keats-Rohan, K.S.B., 'Bibliothèque municipale d'Avranches, 210: Cartulary of Mont-Saint-Michel', in C. Harper-Bill (ed.), *Anglo-Norman Studies. XXI. Proceedings of the Battle Conference 1998* (Woodbridge, 1999).

Keefe, T.K., *Feudal Assessments and the Political Community under Henry II and his Sons* (Berkeley, 1983).

Keller, H., 'Wahlformen und Gemeinschaftsverständnis in den italienischen Stadtkommunen (12./14.Jahrhundert)', in R. Schneider and H. Zimmermann (eds.), *Wahlen und Wählen im Mittelalter* (Vorträge und Forschungen XXXVII) (Sigmaringen, 1990), pp. 345–74.

Kéry, L., *Canonical Collections of the Early Middle Ages (ca. 400–1140). A Bibliographical Guide to the Manuscripts and Literature* (History of Medieval Canon Law) (Washington, 1999).

King, E. (ed.), *The Anarchy of King Stephen's Reign* (Oxford, 1994).

Knowles, D., *The Episcopal Colleagues of Archbishop Thomas Becket* (Cambridge, 1951).

Kuttner, S., *Repertorium der Kanonistik (1140–1234). Prodromus corporis glossarum* (Studi e testi LXXI) (Vatican City, 1937).

'Les débuts de l'école canoniste française', in S. Kuttner, *Gratian and the Schools of Law 1140–1234* (London, 1983), no. VI, pp. 193–204.

'Papst Honorius III. und das Studium des Zivilrechts', in S. Kuttner, *Gratian and the Schools of Law 1140–1234* (London, 1983), no. X, pp. 79–101.

Kuttner, S. and Rathbone, E., 'Anglo-Norman Canonists of the Twelfth Century', *Traditio*, 7 (1949–51), 279–358.

Kuttner, S. and Somerville, R., 'The So-called Canons of Nîmes', *Tijdschrift voor Rechtsgeschiedenis*, 38 (1970), 175–89.

Lally, J., 'Secular Patronage at the Court of King Henry II', *Bulletin of the Institute of Historical Research*, 49 (1976), 159–84.

Landau, P., 'Die Entstehung der systematischen Dekretalensammlungen in der europäischen Kanonistik des 12.Jahrhunderts', *Savigny KA*, 65 (1979), 120–48.

'Die Anfänge der Verbreitung des klassischen kanonischen Rechts in Deutschland im 12. Jahrhundert und im ersten Drittel des 13. Jahrhunderts', in *Chiesa diritto e ordinamento della 'societas christiana' nei secoli XI e XII* (Miscellanea del centro di studi medioevali XI) (Milan, 1986), pp. 272–97.

'Vorgratianische Kanonessammlungen bei den Dekretisten und in den frühen Dekretalensammlungen', in S. Chodorow (ed.), *Proceedings of the Eighth International Congress of Medieval Canon Law. San Diego, University of California at La Jolla, 21–27 August 1988* (MIC series C: subsidia IX) (Vatican City, 1992), pp. 93–116.

'Die Durchsetzung neuen Rechts im Zeitalter des klassischen kanonischen Rechts', in G. Melville (ed.), *Institutionen und Geschichte. Theoretische Aspekte und mittelalterliche Befunde* (Norm und Struktur. Studien zum sozialen Wandel in Mittelalter und früher Neuzeit I) (Cologne, 1992), pp. 137–55.

'Collections françaises du XIIe siècle', paper delivered at 'La Curie romaine et la France. 3ème rencontre de la Gallia Pontificia', German Historical Institute, Paris, 10 September 2003.

'Walter von Coutances und die Anfänge der anglo-normannischen Rechtswissenschaft', in O. Condorelli (ed.), *'Panta rei'. Studi dedicate a Manlio Bellomo* (5 vols., Rome 2004), III, pp. 183–204.

Bibliography

Langlois, P., *Recherches sur les bibliothèques des archevêques et du chapitre de Rouen* (Rouen, 1853).

Laplatte, C., Art. Coutances, in *Dictionnaire d'histoire et de géographie ecclésiastique* (28 vols., Paris, 1912–), XIII, cols. 969–90.

Le diocese de Coutances (Coutances, 1942).

Larrainzar, C., 'La ricerca attuale sul "Decretum Gratiani"', in E. de León and N. Álvarez de las Asturias (eds.), *La cultura giuridico-canonica medioevale. Premesse per un dialogo ecumenico* (Pontificia università della Santa Croce. Monografie giuridiche XXII) (Rome, 2003), pp. 45–88.

Lauer, P., *Collections manuscrites sur l'histoire des provinces de France. Inventaire* (2 vols., Paris, 1905–11).

Lebrun, M., 'Le temporel des évêques d'Avranches du XIe au XIIIe siècles', *Revue de l'Avranchin et du pays de Granville*, 42 (1965), 58–80.

Lecanu, A.-F., *Histoire du diocèse de Coutances et d'Avranches depuis le temps les plus reculés jusqu'à nos jours, suivie des actes des saints et d'un tableau historique des paroisses du diocèse* (2 vols., Coutances 1877–8).

Ledru, A., *La cathédrale Saint-Julien du Mans, ses évêques, son architecture, son mobilier* (Mamers, 1900).

Légoherel, H., 'Le parage en Touraine-Anjou au moyen âge', *Revue historique du droit français et étranger*, 43 (1965), 224–46.

Lelégard, M., 'Le Bienheureux Achard, abbé de Saint-Victor de Paris, 1155–1161, évêque d'Avranches, 1161–1171', *Cahiers Léopold Délisle*, 35-6 (1986–7), 167–73.

Lenherr, T., 'Die vier Fassungen von C.3 q.1 d. p. c. im Decretum Gratiani. Zugleich ein Einblick in die neueste Diskussion um das Werden von Gratian's Dekret', *Archiv für katholisches Kirchenrecht*, 169 (2000), 353–81.

Lemarignier, J.-F., *Recherches sur l'hommage en marche et frontières féodales* (Travaux et mémoires de l'université de Lille; nouvelle série: droit et lettres XXIV) (Lille, 1945).

Lemaître, J.-L., *Répertoire des documents nécrologiques français* (Recueil des historiens de la France. Obituaires VII) (3 vols., Paris, 1980–7).

Lemesle, B., *La société aristocratique dans le Haut-Maine (XIe–XIIe siècles)* (Rennes, 1999).

Livingstone, A., 'Kith and Kin: Kinship and Family Structure of the Nobility of Eleventh- and Twelfth-Century Blois-Chartres', *French Historical Studies*, 20 (1997), 419–58.

Lloyd, L.C., *The Origins of Some Anglo-Norman Families* (The Publications of the Harleian Society CIII) (Leeds, 1951).

Lohrmann, D., *Kirchengut im nördlichen Frankreich. Besitz, Verfassung und Wirtschaft im Spiegel der Papstprivilegien des 11.–12.Jahrhunderts* (Pariser historische Studien XX) (Bonn, 1983).

Lotter, F., 'Designation und angebliches Kooperationsrecht bei Bischofserhebungen. Zu Ausbildung und Anwendung des Prinzips der kanonischen Wahl bis zu den Anfängen der fränkischen Zeit', *Savigny KA*, 59 (1973), 112–50.

Madertoner, W., *Die zwiespältige Papstwahl von 1159* (Dissertationen der Universität Wien CXXXVI) (Vienna, 1978).

Maleczek, W., 'Abstimmungsarten. Wie kommt man zu einem vernünftigen Wahlergebnis?', in R. Schneider and H. Zimmermann (eds.), *Wahlen und*

Bibliography

Wählen im Mittelalter (Vorträge und Forschungen XXXVII) (Sigmaringen, 1990), pp. 79–134.

'Das Pieve Casorate im Streit mit der Zisterze Morimondo. Ein Beitrag zur päpstlichen delegierten Gerichtsbarkeit unter Innocenz III.', *Mitteilungen des Instituts für österreichische Geschichtsforschung*, 105 (1997), 361–92.

'Die Siegel der Kardinäle. Von den Anfängen bis zum Beginn des 13. Jahrhunderts', *Mitteilungen des Instituts für österreichische Geschichtsforschung*, 112 (2004), 177–203.

Marchegay, P., 'Montreuil-Bellay', *Revue de l'Anjou 3rd sér.*, 4 (October 1861–March 1862), 129–43.

Marrit, S., 'King Stephen and the Bishops', in J. Gillingham (ed.), *Anglo-Norman Studies XXIV. Proceedings of the Battle Conference 2001* (Woodbridge, 2002), pp. 129–44.

Matthews, D., *The Norman Monasteries and the English Possessions* (Oxford, 1962).

Matz, J.-M. and Comte, F., *Diocèse d'Angers* (Fasti ecclesiae Gallicanae VII) (Turnhout, 2003).

Meekings, C.A.F., 'The Early Years of Netley Abbey', in C.A.F. Meekings, *Studies in 13th Century Justice and Administration* (London, 1981), no. XVII, pp. 1–37.

Menjot d'Elbenne S. and Denis, L.-J., *Le chapitre royal de l'église collégiale de Saint- Pierre-de-la-Cour, Sainte-Chapelle du Mans* (Archives historiques du Maine X) (Le Mans, 1910).

Merzbacher, F., 'Die Parömie "legista sine canonibus parum valet, canonista sine legibus nihil"', *Studia Gratiana*, 13 (1967), 273–82.

Montaubin, P., 'Les collations pontificales dans le chapitre cathédral de Chartres au XIIIᵉ siècle', in J.-R. Armogathe (ed.), *Monde médiéval et société chartraine. Actes du colloques international organisé par la ville et le diocèse de Chartres à l'occasion du 8ᵉ centenaire de la cathédrale de Chartres 8–10 septembre 1994* (Paris, 1997), pp. 285–99.

Mooers Christelow, S., 'Chancellors and Curial Bishops', in C. Harper-Bill (ed.), *Anglo-Norman Studies XXII. Proceedings of the Battle Conference 1999* (Woodbridge, 2000), pp. 49–69.

Morey, A. and Brooke, C.N.L., *Gilbert Foliot and his Letters* (Cambridge, 1965).

Moss, V., 'The Defence of Normandy 1193–8', in J. Gillingham (ed.), *Anglo-Norman Studies XXIV. Proceedings of the Battle Conference 2001* (Woodbridge, 2002), pp. 145–61.

Moulin, L., 'Sanior et maior pars. Note sur l'évolution des techniques électorales dans les ordres religieux du VIᵉ au XIIIᵉ siècle', *Revue historique de droit français et étranger 4th sér.*, 36 (1958), 368–97 and 491–529.

Müller, H(arald), *Päpstliche Delegationsgerichtbarkeit in der Normandie (12. und frühes 13. Jahrhundert)* (Studien und Dokumente zur Gallia pontificia IV, I-II) (2 vols., Bonn, 1997).

Müller, H(ubert), *Der Anteil der Laien an der Bischofswahl. Ein Beitrag zur Geschichte der Kanonistik von Gratian bis Gregor IX.* (Kanonistische Studien und Texte XXIX) (Amsterdam, 1977).

Munier, C., *Les sources patristiques du droit de l'église du VIIIᵉ au XIIIᵉ siècle* (Mulhouse, 1957).

'Droit canonique et droit romain d'après Gratien et les décrétistes', in *Etudes d'histoire du droit canonique dédiées à Gabriel Le Bras* (2 vols., Paris, 1965), II, pp. 943–54.

Bibliography

Munk Olsen, B., 'Les bibliothèques bénédictines et les bibliothèques de cathédrales: les mutations des XIᵉ et XIIᵉ siècles', in A. Vernet (ed.), *Histoire des bibliothèques françaises* (3 vols., Paris, 1989), I, pp. 31–44.

Musset, L., 'Quelques problèmes posés par l'annexion de la Normandie au domaine royal français', in R.-H. Bautier (ed.), *La France de Philippe Auguste. Le temps de mutation. Actes du colloque international organisé par le C.N.R.S. (Paris, 29.9.–4.10.1980)* (Colloques internationaux du centre national de la recherche scientifique DCII) (Paris, 1982), pp. 291–309.

Nineham, R., 'The So-called Anonymous of York', *Journal of Ecclesiastical History*, 14 (1963), 31–45.

Neveux, F., 'La ville de Sées du haut moyen âge à l'époque ducale', in C. Harper-Bill (ed.), *Anglo-Norman Studies XVII. Proceedings of the Battle Conference 1994* (Woodbridge, 1995), pp. 145–63.

'Les diocèses normands aux XIᵉ et XIIᵉ siècles', in P. Bouet and F. Neveux (eds.), *Les évêques normands du XIᵉ siècle. Colloque de Cerisy-la-Salle (30 septembre–3 octobre 1993)* (Caen, 1995), pp. 13–18.

Newman, B., *The Anglo-Norman Nobility in the Reign of Henry I. The Second Generation* (Philadelphia, 1988).

Newman, W.M., *Les seigneurs de Nesle en Picardie, XIIᵉ–XIIIᵉ siècle. Leur chartes et leur histoire. Etude sur la noblesse régionale ecclésiastique et laïque* (Memoirs of the American Philosophical Society XIC) (2 vols., Philadelphia 1971).

Nonn, U., 'Zwischen König, Hausmeier und Aristokratie – Die Bischofserhebung im spätmerowingisch-frühkarolingischen Frankenreich', in F.-R. Erkens (ed.), *Die früh- und hochmittelalterliche Bischofserhebung im europäischen Vergleich* (Beihefte zum Archiv für Kulturgeschichte XLVIII) (Cologne, 1998), pp. 33–58.

Nortier, G., *Les bibliothèques médiévales des abbayes bénédictines de Normandie. Fécamp, Le Bec, Le Mont Saint-Michel, Saint-Evroul, Lyre, Jumièges, Fécamp, Saint-Wandrille, Saint-Ouen* (Caen, 1966).

Nortier, M., 'Les actes de Philippe Auguste: notes critiques sur les sources diplomatiques du règne', in R.-H. Bautier (ed.), *La France de Philippe Auguste. Le temps de mutation. Actes du colloque international organisé par le C.N.R.S. (Paris, 29.9.–4.10.1980)* (Colloques internationaux du centre national de la recherche scientifique DCII) (Paris, 1982), pp. 429–51.

Ogé, N., 'Hamelin, évêque du Mans (1190–1214). Etude d'une administration épiscopale', *La Province du Maine 5th sér.*, 96 (1994), 233–49 and 347–61.

Omont, H., *Catalogue général des manuscrits des bibliothèques publiques de France* (64 vols., Paris, 1886–1989).

Pacaut, M., *Alexandre III. Etude sur la conception du pouvoir pontifical dans sa pensée et dans son œuvre* (L'église et l'état au moyen âge XI) (Paris, 1956).

Louis VII et les élections épiscopales (Bibliothèque de la société d'histoire ecclésiastique de la France) (Paris, 1957).

Louis VII et son royaume (Bibliothèque générale de l'école des hautes études; VIᵉ section) (Paris, 1964).

Packard, S., 'King John and the Norman Church', *Harvard Theological Review*, 15 (1922), 15–40.

Paravicini Bagliani, A., *Cardinali di curia e 'familiae' cardinalizie dal 1227 al 1254* (Italia sacra. Studi e documenti di storia ecclesiastica XVIII–XIX) (2 vols., Padua, 1972).

Bibliography

Parisse, M., 'La recherche française sur les actes des évêques. Les travaux d'un groupe de recherche', in C. Haidacher and W. Köfler (eds.), *Die Diplomatik der Bischofsurkunde vor 1250. La diplomatique épiscopale avant 1250. Referate zum VIII. Internationalen Kongreß für Diplomatik, Innsbruck, 27.September–3.Oktober 1993* (Innsbruck, 1995), pp. 203–7.

Passy, L., 'Notice sur le cartulaire du prieuré de Bourg-Achard', *Bibliothèque de l'Ecole des Chartes*, 22 (1861), 324–67, 23 (1862), 514–36.

Patourel, J. Le, *The Norman Empire* (Oxford, 1976).

'Norman Barons', in J. Le Patourel, *Feudal Empires. Norman and Plantagenêt* (History Series XVIII) (London, 1984), no. VI, pp. 3–32.

'The Plantagenêt Dominions', in J. Le Patourel, *Feudal Empires. Norman and Plantagenêt* (History Series XVIII) (London, 1984), no. VIII, pp. 289–308.

Patterson, B., 'Robert Fitz Harding of Bristol: Profile of an Early Angevin Burgess-Baron Patrician and his Family's Urban Involvement', *Haskins Society Journal*, I (1989), 109–22.

Pellens, K., *Das Kirchendenken des Normannischen Anonymus* (Veröffentlichungen des Instituts für europäische Geschichte Mainz LXIX. Abteilung für abendländische Religionsgeschichte) (Wiesbaden, 1973).

Peltzer, J., 'Henry II and the Norman Bishops', *EHR*, 119 (2004), 1202–29.

'Portchester, les évêques d'Avranches et les Hommet (1100–1230)', *Annales de Normandie*, 56 (2006), 463–82.

'The Slow Death of the Angevin Empire', *Historical Research* (in press).

Pennington, K., 'The French Recension of Compilatio tertia', *Bulletin of Medieval Canon Law New Series*, 5 (1975), 53–71.

'The Canonists and Pluralism in the Thirteenth Century', *Speculum*, 51 (1976), 35–48.

Pope and Bishops: The Papal Monarchy in the Twelfth and Thirteenth Centuries (Philadelphia, 1984).

'Review of Wilhelm Imkamp, *Das Kirchenbild Innocenz' III. (1198–1216)* (Päpste und Papsttum XXII) (Stuttgart, 1983)', *Savigny KA*, 72 (1986), 417–28.

'Bishops and their Dioceses', in P. Erdö and P. Szabón (eds.), *Territorialità e personalità nel diritto canonico ed ecclesiastico: Il diritto canonico di fronte al terzo millennio: Atti dell' XI congresso internazionale di diritto canonico e del XV congresso internazionale della società per il diritto delle chiese orientali* (Budapest, 2002), pp. 123–35. (Online: http://faculty.cua.edu/pennington/BishopsDioceses. htm) (last visit: 12 Mar. 2003.)

Perrichet, L., *La grande chancellerie de France des origines à 1328* (Paris, 1912).

Petit-Dutaillis, C., *Etude sur la vie et le règne de Louis VIII (1187–1226)* (Bibliothèque de l'école des hautes études; IVe section, sciences historiques et philologiques CI) (Paris, 1894).

Peyrafort-Huin, M., *La bibliothèque médiévale de l'abbaye de Pontigny (XIIe–XIXe siècles). Histoire, inventaires anciens, manuscrits* (Documents, études et répertoires LX) (Paris, 2001).

Pichot, D., *Le Bas-Maine du Xe au XIIIe siècle: étude d'une société* (La Mayenne: archéologie, histoire – supplément VII) (Laval, 1995).

Pigeon, A.-E., *Le diocèse d'Avranches. Sa topographie, ses origines, ses évêques, sa cathédrale, ses églises, ses comtes et ses châteaux*, 2nd edn (2 vols., Marseilles, 1981; reprint of Coutances, 1890).

Piolin, P., *Histoire de l'église du Mans* (6 vols., Le Mans, 1851–63).

Plassmann, A., *Die Struktur des Hofes unter Friedrich Barbarossa nach den deutschen Zeugen seiner Urkunden* (MGH, Studien und Texte xx) (Hanover, 1998).

Pontal, O., 'Les plus anciens statuts synodaux d'Angers et leur expansion dans les diocèses de l'ouest de la France', *Revue d'histoire de l'église de France*, 46 (1960), 54–67.

'Les évêques dans le monde Plantagenêt', *Cahiers de civilisation médiévale*, 29 (1986), 129–37.

Poole, R.L., *Studies in Chronology and History* (Oxford, 1934).

Port, C., *Dictionnaire historique, géographique et biographique de Maine-et-Loire et de l'ancienne Province d'Anjou*, 2nd edn (4 vols., Angers, 1965–96).

Post, G., 'A romano-canonical maxim – quod omnes tangit – in Bracton', *Traditio*, 4 (1946), 197–251.

Power, D., 'What Did the Frontier of Angevin Normandy Comprise?', in C. Harper-Bill (ed.), *Anglo-Norman Studies XVII. Proceedings of the Battle Conference 1994* (Woodbridge, 1995), pp. 181–202.

'Between the Angevin and Capetian Courts: John de Rouvray and the Knights of the Pays de Bray', in K.S.B. Keats-Rohan (ed.), *Family Trees and the Roots of Politics. The Prosopography of Britain and France from the Tenth to the Twelfth Century* (Woodbridge, 1997), pp. 361–84.

'L'aristocratie Plantagenêt face aux conflits capétiens-angevins: l'exemple du traité de Louviers', in M. Aurell (ed.), *Noblesses de l'espace Plantagenêt (1154–1224). Table ronde tenue à Poitiers le 13 mai 2000* (Civilisation médiévale xi) (Poitiers, 2001), pp. 121–37.

'The End of Angevin Normandy: The Revolt at Alençon (1203)', *Historical Research*, 74 (2001), 444–64.

'Angevin Normandy', in C. Harper-Bill and E. van Houts (eds.), *Companion to the Anglo-Norman World* (Woodbridge, 2003), pp. 63–85.

'The French Interests of the Marshal Earls of Striguil and Pembroke, 1189–1234, in J. Gillingham (ed.), *Anglo-Norman Studies XXV. Proceedings of the Battle Conference 2002* (Woodbridge, 2003), pp. 199–225.

The Norman Frontier in the Twelfth and Early Thirteenth Centuries (Cambridge Studies in Medieval Life and Thought) (Cambridge, 2004).

'The Norman Church and the Angevin and Capetian Kings', *Journal of Ecclesiastical History*, 56 (2005), 205–34.

Powicke, M., *The Loss of Normandy 1189–1204. Studies in the History of the Angevin Empire*, 3rd edn (Manchester, 1999).

Rambaud-Buhot, J., 'Un corpus inédit de droit canonique de la réforme carolingienne à la réforme grégorienne', in *Humanisme actif. Mélanges d'art et de littérature offerts à Julien Cain* (2 vols., Paris 1968), ii, pp. 271–81.

Rashdall, H., *The Universities of Europe in the Middle Ages*, revised by M. Powicke and A.B. Emden (3 vols., London, 1936).

Rédet, L., 'Mémoires sur les halles et les foires de Poitiers', *Mémoires de la société des antiquaires de l'ouest*, 12 (1847 for 1845), 61–97.

Reinhard, W., 'Nepotismus. Der Funktionswandel einer papstgeschichtlichen Konstanten', *Zeitschrift für Kirchengeschichte*, 86 (1975), 145–85.

Reuling, U., 'Zur Entwicklung der Wahlformen bei den hochmittelalterlichen Königserhebungen im Reich', in R. Schneider and H. Zimmermann (eds.),

Bibliography

Wahlen und Wählen im Mittelalter (Vorträge und Forschungen XXXVII) (Sigmaringen, 1990), pp. 227–70.

Reynolds, R., 'The Subdiaconate as Sacred and Superior Order', in R. Reynolds, *Clerics in the Early Middle Ages. Hierarchy and Image* (Aldershot, 1999), no. IV, pp. 1–39.

Richard, J., *Saint Louis. Crusader King of France* (Cambridge, 1992).

Richardson, H.G., 'The Letters and Charters of Eleanor of Aquitaine', *English Historical Review*, 43 (1959), 193–213.

Roland, E., *Les chanoines et les élections épiscopales du XIᵉ au XIVᵉ siècle (Etude sur la restauration, l'évolution, la décadence du pouvoir capitulaire) 1080–1350* (Aurillac, 1909).

Rusch, B., *Die Behörden und Hofbeamten der päpstlichen Kurie des 13. Jahrhunderts* (Schriften der Albertus-Universität. Geisteswissenschaftliche Reihe III) (Königsberg, 1936).

Sägmüller, J., *Die Bischofswahl bei Gratian* (Görres-Gesellschaft. Sektion für Sozial-und Rechtswissenschaften I) (Cologne, 1908).

Sassier, Y., *Royauté et idéologie au Moyen Age. Bas-Empire, monde franc, France (IVᵉ–XIIᵉ siècle)* (Paris, 2002).

Sayers, J., *Papal Government and England during the Pontificate of Honorius III (1216 – 1227)* (Cambridge, 1984).

Scheibelreiter, G., *Der Bischof in merowingischer Zeit* (Veröffentlichungen des Instituts für österreichische Geschichtsforschung XXVII) (Vienna, 1983).

Schieffer, R., *Die Entstehung des päpstlichen Investiturverbots für den deutschen König* (MGH, Schriften XXVIII) (Stuttgart, 1981).

'Bischofserhebungen im westfränkisch-französischen Bereich im späten 9. und im 10. Jahrhundert', in F.-R. Erkens (ed.), *Die früh- und hochmittelalterliche Bischofserhebung im europäischen Vergleich* (Beihefte zum Archiv für Kulturgeschichte XLVIII) (Cologne, 1998), pp. 59–82.

Schimmelpfennig, B., 'Papst- und Bischofswahlen seit dem 12. Jahrhundert', in R. Schneider and H. Zimmermann (eds.), *Wahlen und Wählen im Mittelalter* (Vorträge und Forschungen XXXVII) (Sigmaringen, 1990), pp. 174–95.

Schmale, F.-J., *Studien zum Schisma des Jahres 1130* (Forschungen zur kirchlichen Rechtsgeschichte und zum Kirchenrecht III) (Cologne, 1961).

Schmid, K., 'Zur Problematik von Familie, Sippe und Geschlecht, Haus und Dynastie beim mittelalterlichen Adel. Vorfragen zum Thema: Adel und Herrschaft im Mittelalter', *Zeitschrift für die Geschichte des Oberrheins*, 105 (1957), 1–62.

Schneider, R., 'Wechselwirkungen von kanonischer und weltlicher Wahl', in R. Schneider and H. Zimmermann (eds.), *Wahlen und Wählen im Mittelalter* (Vorträge und Forschungen XXXVII) (Sigmaringen, 1990), pp. 135–71.

Scholz, S., *Transmigration und Translation. Studien zum Bistumswechsel der Bischöfe von der Spätantike bis zum Hohen Mittelalter* (Kölner historische Abhandlungen XXXVII) (Cologne, 1992).

Schreiner, K., 'Versippung als soziale Kategorie mittelalterlicher Kirchen- und Klostergeschichte', in N. Bulst and J.-P. Genet (eds.), *Medieval Lives and the Historian: Studies in Medieval Prosopography. Proceedings of the First International Interdisciplinary Conference on Medieval Prosopography, University of Bielefeld 3–5 December 1982* (Medieval Institute Publications, Western Michigan University) (Kalamazoo, 1986), pp. 163–80.

Bibliography

Schriber, C.P., *The Dilemma of Arnulf of Lisieux. New Ideas versus Old Ideals* (Indianapolis, 1990).

Shaw, I., 'The Ecclesiastical Policy of Henry II on the Continent', *Church Quarterly Review*, 151 (1951), 137–55.

Singer, H., *Neue Beiträge über die Dekretalensammlungen vor und nach Bernhard von Pavia* (Sitzungsberichte der kaiserlichen Akademie der Wissenschaften in Wien. Philosophisch-historische Klasse CLXXI, I) (Vienna, 1913).

Smalley, B., *The Becket Conflict and the Schools. A Study of Intellectuals in Politics* (Oxford, 1973).

Somerville, R., *The Councils of Urban II. Decreta Claromontensia* (Annuarium historiae conciliorum supplementum I) (Amsterdam, 1972).

Pope Alexander III and the Council of Tours (Center for Medieval and Renaissance Studies) (Berkeley, 1977).

'The Councils of Pope Calixtus II: Reims 1119', in S. Kuttner and K. Pennington (eds.), *Proceedings of the Fifth International Congress of Medieval Canon Law, Salamanca, 21–25 September 1976* (MIC series C: subsidia VI) (Vatican City, 1980).

Pope Urban II, the Collectio Britannica, and the Council of Melfi (1089) (Oxford, 1996).

Southern, R.W., 'The Necessity of Two Peter of Blois', in L. Smith and B. Ward (eds.), *Intellectual Life in the Middle Ages. Essays Presented to Margaret Gibson* (London, 1992).

Scholastic Humanism and the Unification of Europe. II. The Heroic Age (Oxford, 2001).

Spear, D., 'Les dignitaires de la cathédrale de Rouen pendant la période ducale', *Annales de Normandie*, 37 (1987), 121–47.

'Les chanoines de la cathédrale de Rouen pendant la période ducale', *Annales de Normandie*, 41 (1991), 135–76.

Research Facilities in Normandy and Paris. A Guide for Students of Medieval Norman History. Including a Checklist of Norman Cartularies (Greenville, 1993).

'Power, Patronage and Personality in the Norman Cathedral Chapters, 911–1204', in C. Harper-Bill (ed.), *Anglo-Norman Studies XX. Proceedings of the Battle Conference 1997* (Woodbridge, 1998), pp. 205–22.

The Personnel of the Norman Cathedrals during the Ducal Period, 911–1204 (Fasti ecclesiae Anglicanae) (London, 2006).

Stacey, R., *Politics, Policy, and Finance under Henry III, 1216–1245* (Oxford, 1987).

Stelzer, W., *Gelehrtes Recht in Österreich. Von den Anfängen bis zum frühen 14. Jahrhundert* (Mitteilungen des Instituts für österreichische Geschichtsforschung. Ergänzungsband XXVI) (Vienna, 1982).

Strayer, J., 'Normandy and Languedoc', *Speculum*, 44 (1969), 1–12.

Tabbagh, V., *Diocèse de Rouen* (Fasti ecclesiae Gallicanae II) (Turnhout, 1998).

Tellenbach, G., *Libertas. Kirche und Weltordnung im Zeitalter des Investiturstreits* (Forschungen zur Kirchen- und Geistesgeschichte VII) (Stuttgart, 1936).

'"Gregorianische Reform". Kritische Besinnungen', in K. Schmid (ed.), *Reich und Kirche vor dem Investiturstreit. Vorträge beim wissenschaftlichen Kolloquium aus Anlaß des achtzigsten Geburtstags von Gerd Tellenbach* (Sigmaringen, 1985), pp. 99–113.

Bibliography

Teske, G., 'Ein unerkanntes Zeugnis zum Sturz des Bischofs Arnulf von Lisieux. Ein Vorschlag zur Diskussion (mit Edition)', *Francia*, 16/1 (1989), 185–206.

Thompson, K., 'The Lords of Laigle: Ambition and Insecurity on the Borders of Normandy', in C. Harper-Bill (ed.), *Anglo-Norman Studies XVIII. Proceedings of the Battle Conference 1995* (Woodbridge, 1996), pp. 177–99.

Power and Border Lordship in Medieval France. The County of the Perche, 1000–1226 (Royal Historical Society, Studies in History, N.S.) (Woodbridge, 2002).

'Affairs of State: The Illegitimate Children of Henry I', *Journal of Medieval History*, 29 (2003), 129–51.

'L'aristocratie anglo-normande et 1204', in P. Bouet and V. Gazeau (eds.) *La Normandie et l'Angleterre au Moyen Age. Actes du colloque de Cerisy-La-Salle (4–7 octobre 2001)* (Caen, 2003), pp. 179–87.

Toubert, P., *Les structures du Latium médiéval. Le Latium méridional et la Sabine du XIe siècle à la fin du XIIe siècle* (Bibliothèque des écoles françaises d'Athènes et de Rome CCXXI) (2 vols., Rome, 1973).

Türk, E., *Nugae curialium. Le règne d'Henri II Plantagenêt (1145–89) et l'éthique politique* (Centre des recherches d'histoire et de philologie de la IVe section de l'école pratique des hautes études; v, hautes études médiévales et modernes XXVIII) (Geneva, 1977).

Turner, R., *Men Raised from the Dust. Administrative Service and Upward Mobility in Angevin England* (Philadelphia, 1988).

'Changing Perceptions of the New Administrative Class in Anglo-Norman and Angevin England: The *Curiales* and their Conservative Critics', *Journal of British Studies*, 29 (1990), 93–117.

King John (London, 1994).

'Richard Lionheart and English Episcopal Elections', *Albion*, 29 (1997), 1–15.

'Richard Lionheart and the Episcopate in his French Domains', *French Historical Studies*, 21 (1998), 517–42.

Vacandard, E., 'Les élections épiscopales sous les Mérovingiens', in E. Vacandard, *Etudes de critique et d'histoire religieuse* (3 vols., Paris, 1905–12), I, pp. 123–87.

Vaucelle, E., *La collégiale de Saint-Martin de Tours. Des origines à l'avènement des Valois (397–1328)* (Mémoires de la société archéologique de Touraine XLVI) (Tours, 1907).

Vauchez, A., *La sainteté en occident aux derniers siècles du moyen âge d'après les procès de canonisation et les documents hagiographiques* (Bibliothèque des écoles françaises d'Athènes et de Rome CCXLI) (Rome, 1988).

Vaughn, S., *Anselm of Bec and Robert of Meulan. The Innocence of the Dove and the Wisdom of the Serpent* (Berkeley, 1987).

Vezin, J., *Les Scriptoria d'Angers au XIe siècle* (Bibliothèque des hautes études. IVe section, sciences historiques et philologiques CCCXXII) (Paris, 1974).

Vincent, N., 'The Election of Pandulph Verraclo as Bishop of Norwich (1215)', *Historical Research*, 68 (1995), 143–63.

'New Light on Master Alexander of Swerford (d. 1246): The Career and Connections of an Oxfordshire Civil Servant', *Oxoniensia*, 61 (1996), 297–309.

Peter des Roches: An Alien in English Politics, 1205–1238 (Cambridge Studies in Medieval Life and Thought) (Cambridge, 1996).

Bibliography

'Warin and Henry Fitz Gerald, the King's Chamberlains: The Origins of the Fitzgeralds Revisited', in C. Harper-Bill (ed.), *Anglo-Norman Studies. XXI. Proceedings of the Battle Conference 1998* (Woodbridge, 1999), pp. 232–60.

'King Henry and the Poitevins', in M. Aurell (ed.), *La cour Plantagenêt (1154–1204). Actes du colloque tenu à Thouars du 30 avril au 2 mai 1999* (Civilisation médiévale VIII) (Poitiers, 2000), pp. 103–35.

'The Pilgrimages of the Angevin Kings of England 1154–1272', in C. Morris and P. Roberts (eds.), *Pilgrimage. The English Experience from Becket to Bunyan* (Cambridge, 2002), pp. 12–45.

'Who's Who in Magna Carta Clause 50', in M. Aurell (ed.), *Le médiéviste et la monographie familiale: sources, méthodes et problématiques* (Histoires de familles. La parenté au Moyen Age) (Turnhout, 2004), pp. 235–61.

'Why 1199? Bureaucracy and Enrolment under John and his Contemporaries', in A. Jobson (ed.), *English Government in the Thirteenth Century* (Woodbridge, 2004), pp. 17–48.

Violante, C., 'Quelques caractéristiques des structures familiales en Lombardie, Emilie et Toscane au XIe et XIIe siècles', in G. Duby and J. Le Goff (eds.), *Famille et parenté dans l'occident médiéval. Actes du colloque de Paris (6–8 Juin 1974)* (Collection de l'école française de Rome XXX) (Rome, 1977), pp. 87–151.

Vulliez, C., 'L'évêque au miroir de l'*ars dictaminis*. L'exemple de la *maior compilatio* de Bernard de Meung', *Revue d'histoire de l'église de France*, 70 (1984), pp. 278–304.

Walker, D., 'Crown and Episcopacy under the Normans and the Angevins', in R. Brown (ed.), *Anglo-Norman Studies V. Proceedings of the Battle Conference 1982* (Woodbridge, 1983), pp. 220–33.

Warren, W.L., *Henry II*, 4th edn (Yale, 2000).

Weigand, R., 'Studien zum kanonistischen Werk Stephans von Tournai', *Savigny KA*, 72 (1986), 349–61.

'Die anglo-normannische Kanonistik in den letzten Jahrzehnten des 12. Jahrhunderts', in P. Linehan (ed.), *Proceedings of the Seventh International Congress of Medieval Canon Law, Cambridge, 23–27 July 1984* (MIC series C: subsidia VIII) (Vatican City, 1988), pp. 249–63.

'Frühe Kanonisten und ihre Karrieren in der Kirche', *Savigny KA*, 76 (1990), 135–55.

Die Glossen zum Dekret Gratians. Studien zu den frühen Glossen und Glossenkompositionen (Studia Gratiana XXV–XXVI) (Rome, 1991).

Art. 'Kanonistik', in W. Kasper et al. (eds.), *Lexikon für Theologie und Kirche*, 3rd edn (11 vols., Freiburg, 1993–2001), v, cols. 1188–97.

Weinfurter, S., '"Series episcoporum" – Probleme und Möglichkeiten einer Prosopographie des früh- und hochmittelalterlichen Episkopats', in N. Bulst and J.-P. Genet (eds.), *Medieval Lives and the Historian: Studies in Medieval Prosopography. Proceedings of the First International Interdisciplinary Conference on Medieval Prosopography, University of Bielefeld 3–5 December 1982* (Medieval Institute Publications, Western Michigan University) (Kalamazoo, 1986), pp. 97–112.

Weise, G., *Königtum und Bischofswahl im fränkischen und deutschen Reich vor dem Investiturstreit* (Berlin, 1912).

West, F., *The Justiciarship in England* (Cambridge, 1966).

Bibliography

Williams, G., *The Norman Anonymous of 1100 A.D.* (Harvard Theological Studies XVIII) (Cambridge, Mass., 1951)

Williams, S., *Codices Pseudo-Isidoriani. A Palaeographical-Historical Study* (MIC series C: subsidia III) (New York, 1971).

Winroth, A., *The Making of Gratian's Decretum* (Cambridge Studies in Medieval Life and Thought) (Cambridge, 2000).

Wretschko, A. v., 'Die Electio communis bei den kirchlichen Wahlen im Mittelalter', *Zeitschrift für Kirchenrecht*, 11 (1901), 321–92.

Yver, J., 'Les caractères originaux du groupe de coutumes de l'Ouest de la France', *Revue historique du droit français et étranger*, 30 (1950), 18–79.

Zechiel-Eckes, K., 'Ein Blick in Pseudoisidors Werkstatt. Studien zum Entstehungsprozess der Falschen Dekretalen', *Francia*, 28/1 (2001), 37–90.

Zielinski, H., 'Zu den Hintergründen der Bischofswahl Pibos von Toul 1069', in N. Bulst and J.-P. Genet (eds.), *Medieval Lives and the Historian: Studies in Medieval Prosopography. Proceedings of the First International Interdisciplinary Conference on Medieval Prosopography, University of Bielefeld 3–5 December 1982* (Medieval Institute Publications, Western Michigan University) (Kalamazoo, 1986), pp. 91–6.

UNPUBLISHED THESES

Bienvenu, J.-M., 'Recherches sur le diocèse d'Angers au temps de la réforme grégorienne (XIe siècle et première moitié du XIIe)' (Paris Univ., *thèse*, 1968).

Cagniant, G., 'La chartreuse du Val-Dieu au Perche. Son chartrier et son domaine jusqu'à la fin du XIIIe siècle' (Ecole de Chartes, Paris, *thèse*, 1975).

Dupuy, H., 'Recueil des actes des évêques de Bayeux antérieures à 1205' (Ecole de Chartes, Paris, *thèse*, 2 vols., 1970).

McManus, B., 'The Ecclesiology of Laurentius Hispanus (c. 1180–1248) and his Contribution to the Romanization of Canon Law Jurisprudence, with an Edition of Laurentius' Apparatus glossarum in Compilationem tertiam' (2 vols., Syracuse Univ., Ph.D. thesis, 1991).

Perrot, S., 'Catalogue des plus anciens actes concernant le temporel français de Saint-Evroult' (Ecole des chartes, Paris, *thèse*, 1964).

Poggioli, P., 'From Politician to Prelate: The Career of Walter of Coutances, Archbishop of Rouen, 1184–1207' (Johns Hopkins Univ., Baltimore, Ph.D. thesis, 1984).

Pico, F., 'The Bishops of France in the Reign of Louis IX (1226–70)' (Johns Hopkins Univ., Baltimore, Ph.D. thesis, 1970).

Silano, G., 'The Distinctiones Decretorum of Ricardus Anglicus: An Edition' (Toronto Univ., Ph. D. thesis, 1981).

Spear, D., 'The Norman Episcopate under Henry I, King of England and Duke of Normandy (1106–1135)' (Santa Barbara Univ. of California, Ph.D. thesis, 1982).

Stevenson, W.B., 'England and Normandy, 1204–1259' (2 vols., Leeds Univ., Ph.D. thesis, 1974).

Thier, A., 'Hierarchie und Autonomie. Regelungstraditionen der Bischofsbestellung in der Geschichte des kirchlichen Wahlrechts bis 1140' (Ludwig-Maximilians-Universität, Munich, Habilitationsschrift, 2001).

Waldman, T., 'Hugh "of Amiens", Archbishop of Rouen (1130–64)' (Oxford Univ., D.Phil. thesis, 1970).

ELECTRONIC SOURCES

http://faculty.cua.edu/pennington/biobibl.htm (K. Pennington, *Bio-bibliographical guide of canonists 1140–1500*) (last visit: 12 Mar. 2003).

http://wtfaculty.wtamu.edu/~bbrasington/panormia.html (*Panormia*, Ivo of Chartres) (last visit: 12 Mar. 2003).

http://unicaen.fr/mrsh/crahm/revue/tabularia/peltzer.pdf (Peltzer, J., 'Conflits électoraux et droit canonique. Le problème de la valeur des votes lors des élections épiscopales en Normandie au Moyen Age central', *Tabularia « Études »*, 6 (2006), 91–107) (last visit 31 Oct. 2006).

http://www.oxforddnb.com/view/article22012 (R.W. Southern, 'Blois, Peter of (1125x30–1212)', in *Oxford Dictionary of National Biography*) (last visit: 23 Mar. 2005)

http://www.kuttner-institute.jura.uni-muenchen.de (Walther-Holtzmann-Kartei: *Regesta decretalium saeculi XII*) (last visit: 17 Aug. 2004).

INDEX

Abbeville (dép. Somme)
  Jacob d', archdeacon of Rouen 86 n. 71
  John d', dean of Amiens 85, 86 n. 71
Ablèges (Ableiges, dép. Val-d'Oise), Robert d',
  bishop of Bayeux 40, 143 and n. 323,
    244, 261
  career of 139–40
  election of 139–40, 141 and n. 316, 263 n. 6
  his familiarity with canon law 65 and n. 250
Abrincensis prima 62–5, 67
Abrincensis secunda 63 and n. 239
Achard, bishop of Avranches 154 n. 378,
  261–2
  candidacy (Sées) of 121–2, 153–4, 167, 213,
    256 n. 1
  election of 121, 153, 154 and n. 377, 167,
    213–14
Acre (Israel) 140
Actus pontificum Cenomannis in urbe degentium 192
Adam, abbot of La Trappe 261
  candidacy (Sées) of 126
Adam, royal clerk 234 n. 96
Adam, son of Walter the Younger, chamberlain
  of Philip II 144 n. 330
Ademar, bishop of Poitiers 160
Adrian IV, pope 233
  and episcopal elections
    Angers 197–8, 199 n. 135; his letter *Causa*
      super controversia 264, 235 n. 98
    Sées 121, 153–4, 167, 256 n. 1
Agatha (?), daughter of Amaury Gaimar
  de Lavardin and Marie 174–5,
    181–2
Agnes, daughter of Bourchard IV, count of
  Vendôme 176
Agnes, lady of Braine, wife of Robert, count of
  Dreux 121
Agustin, Antonio, archbishop of Tarragona
  33 n. 68

Albano (Italy), cardinal-bishop of, *see* Peter de
  Collemezzo
Alberic, archbishop of Rheims 241
Alberic, papal legate 116
Albertus, *Apparatus* to *Compilatio secunda*
  51 n. 162
Alençon (dép. Orne) 131
  counts of *see* Robert III
Alexander III, pope 50–2, 59–60, 68 and n. 270,
  69, 101, 111, 130 n. 273, 158, 159 n. 407,
    167, 178, 225, 233
  decretals of
    Ad aures nostras 130 n. 273
    Consideravimus 40 n. 112
    Qua fronte 81–2
    Quia requisistis 33 and nn. 68–9, 81–2
  on electoral body 33, 81–2
Algar, bishop of Coutances 146 n. 334, 150
  resistance against Geoffrey Plantagenet
    145–6
Alice, countess of Eu 91, 98
Alice, daughter of Louis VII 110
Alice, wife of Nivelon IV de Fréteval 181–2
Alps 127
Amaury, archdeacon of Sées 117
Amaury I, count of Evreux 100
Amaury III, count of Evreux 103 n. 136
Amboise (dép. Indre-et-Loire)
  castle of 122
  lords of 170
Amicia, wife of Simon IV de Montfort 105
  their daughter *see* Petronilla
Amicus, treasurer of Rouen 221
Amiens (dép. Somme) 86
  Hugh d', archbishop of Rouen 73, 75, 77,
    101–2, 116–18, 120, 215
  see of 98
  archdeaconry of 87, 89–90
  bishops of *see* Arnulf de la Pierre

Index

Index

Index

Duggan, Charles, historian 14
Dumas, François, historian 173
Durdent, Walter, bishop of Coventry and
    Lichfield 122 n. 234
Durham (Durham), William of, archdeacon of
    Caux (Rouen) 260
    candidacy (Rouen) of 90 n. 93, 92–8
    career of 97–8

elections, medieval and modern 258
Eleonor, countess of Salisbury 143 n. 327
Eleonor, daughter of Henry II 154 n. 377
Eli, priest, foster-father of Prophet
    Samuel 226
Elizabeth, wife of Robert de Fréauville
    90 n. 90
Emmelina, mother of Hugh Nereth, bishop of
    Coutances 149 n. 360
Emperor 142 n. 322; *and see* Otto IV
Empire 5
Engelbald, archbishop of Tours 173 and n. 10,
    174, 175 and n. 28, 177 nn. 31, 33, 183,
    200 n. 139, 225, 228, 229 n. 69, 262
    career of 173 and n. 11
    election of 172–3
    his father *see* Geoffrey Payen
Engelbald, *cognatus* of Bartholomew, archbishop
    of Tours 175
Engelbald, son of Vulgrin II (the same?) 175
England 2, 11, 61, 63, 65, 67, 76, 82, 91, 98,
    102 n. 132, 111, 122 n. 234, 124 n. 248,
    130, 132, 144, 148, 197, 199, 217 n. 18,
    225 n. 53, 249
    episcopal elections
      133, 168; *and see* Canterbury, Lincoln,
      Winchester
    papal interdict 132
Epiphanio, Roffredus de, *see* Roffredus
    Beneventanus
episcopal elections 2, 253–8; *and see* Angers,
    Avranches, Bayeux, Canterbury,
    Coutances, England, Evreux, Greater
    Anjou, Le Mans, Lincoln, Lisieux,
    Normandy, Rouen, Sées, Tours,
    Winchester
    area of study 1–5, 7–8
    electoral body 9, 21–2, 26–38, 166–8, 254
      absent canons 9, 36–8, 92–6, 125–8,
      142–3, 169
      cathedral chapter 9, 26–38, 186, 214, 254
      clerus and *populus* 20–1, 108
      religiosi viri 26–31, 78, 117, 118 and n. 213,
      146 n. 334, 168, 210, 214, 241, 254
      role of the prince 9, 21, 23–6, 31–6, 42, 79,
      81–2, 104–5, 108–10, 113–14, 119–20,

      125, 129, 130 and n. 273, 131–3, 166–8,
      193, 197–8, 207 and n. 179, 208, 210,
      241, 244, 254–5
      suffragan bishops 28, 177, 186
    groups interested in 3–4
    methodology 8–19
    sanior et maior pars 9, 22, 39, 41–8, 68, 107,
      139–41, 142–3, 184
      authority/dignity/merits/knowledge
      41–8
      intentions 42–8
      number 41–8; *and see* unanimity; absolute
      numerical majority 48, 84–5, 92–3, 96,
      142–3, 169; two-third majority 22,
      44, 48
    sources 10–19
    suitability 9, 21, 23, 24 and n. 19, 25, 48–53,
      85–6, 117, 118 and n. 212, 120, 128–9,
      161–2, 219, 256
      subdeacon, eligibility of 21 and n. 7, 49,
      50–1, 139–41
      unlicensed pluralism 51–3, 60, 69, 87
      and n. 80, 87–91, 94–5, 96
      and n. 107, 169
    translation 9, 54–5, 156–61
    voting procedures 9, 22, 38–41, 92–7, 106–7,
      118 and n. 212, 120, 138–41, 161–2, 169,
      257–8
      compromise 9, 39–40, 78, 79 and n. 25, 85,
      93–5, 169
      electio communis 39, 107
      scrutiny 9, 39–40, 92–6, 142, 169
      unanimity 9, 22, 38 and n. 103, 39, 42,
      44–5, 106, 169
Epte, river 75
Erkens, Franz-Reiner, historian 1
Ernaud, canon of Sées 125–8
Eu (dép. Seine-Maritime) 75, 90 n. 90
    countess of *see* Alice
Eugenius III, pope 153
    and elections at Sées (1144–7), 117–9, 120
      and n. 229, 214
    and see of Coutances 146
Europe 4, 61, 69
Eustace, canon of Rouen 222
Evrecin 104–5
Evreux (dép. Eure) 100, 103–4
    castle of 100
    counts of *see* Amaury I, Amaury III, Simon
    county of 104
    see of 100–8, 135 n. 295, 166, 229–30
      archdeacons of *see* Giles de Cierrey, Giles
      du Perche, Luke (bishop of Evreux),
      Philip de Harcourt, Ralph II de Cierrey,
      Ralph Louvel

Index

310

Index

Greater Anjou (cont.)
  government of by Capetians 247–9
    reflected in post-conquest episcopal
      elections 248–9
    two administrative zones (Touraine and
      Anjou/Maine) 247–9
  library holdings of 14, 25, 158
  spread of canon law 9, 12, 14, 67–72
  spread of Gregorian reform ideas 25–6, 197, 210
Gregorian reform movement 2, 20–6, 42, 50, 54,
    108, 166, 194
Gregory, archdeacon of Bayeux 60
Gregory I, pope
  decretal of
    Quanto 37
Gregory VII, pope 25
  on episcopal elections 21
Gregory IX, pope 11, 91–2, 219 n. 25, 235 n. 98
  and (archi)episcopal elections
    Bayeux 141–3
    Rouen 87–90, 92–5, 99, 193, 235, 257,
      263 n. 2
  decretals of
    Dudum ecclesia Rothomagensi 51–3, 90
    Ecclesia vestra 48
    In Genesi legitur 37–8
    Massana ecclesia 36
  on electoral body 36–8
  on suitability 51–2
  on weighing up of votes 48
Griffiths, Quentin, historian 189 n. 85
Grim, Richard, canon of Rouen 222
Griscia, mother of Norman de Doué, bishop of
    Angers 195, 198 and n. 131
Griscia, wife of Ursio II de Fréteval 174, 181–2
Grisegonelle, Geoffrey 174 n. 19
Guérin, bishop of Senlis 240
Guy, canon of Bayeux 142 and n. 322

Hamelin, bishop of Le Mans 69, 180, 189 n. 85
    190 and n. 91, 191, 194, 205 n. 171, 226,
    248, 262
  and Arthur, duke of Brittany 205–6
  career of 189
  election of 188, 189 and n. 84
  patronage of 226 n. 56
  relationship with King John 190, 205, 206
    and n. 175
  resignation of 189 and n. 88, 191 and n. 191, 250
Hamo, monk of Savigny 167 n. 433
Hanna, mother of Prophet Samuel 226
Harcourt (dép. Eure)
  family 136; *and see* Robert fitz Anschetil
    Philip de, bishop of Bayeux 138,
      147–8, 261; career of 136–7, 230;

election of 135–7, 230; government of
    137 and n. 302; library of 56, 57
Hauteville, John de
  Architrenius 58–9
Hawisa, wife of (1) Rotrou II, count of the
    Perche, (2) Robert, count of Dreux 119
Helias (?), chanter of St Martin, Tours 205 n. 171
Henry, archbishop of Rheims 239
Henry, archdeacon of Sées 117
Henry, bishop of Winchester, papal legate 137
    and n. 300
Henry, canon of Bayeux 142
Henry, canon of Sées 117 n. 209
Henry, chanter of Bayeux 138–41
Henry, count of Penthièvre 173
Henry I, count of Champagne 121
Henry I, king of England 5, 108, 135–6,
    153 n. 374, 253, 204 n. 160
  and episcopal elections 24, 73, 166
Henry II, king of England 5, 66 n. 258, 78
    and n. 20, 112 n. 185, 126, 146 and n. 340,
    152 and n. 372, 153, 155, 158, 178 n. 40,
    179 n. 44, 182, 190 n. 91, 200 n. 139, 221,
    231–3, 234 and n. 96, 244, 264
  and (archi)episcopal elections 33, 166–7, 239–40
    Angers 197–202, 208–9
    attitude towards 166–7, 198
    Avranches 153 and n. 374, 154 and n. 377,
      381, 155, 165–6, 213–4
    Bayeux 137–8
    Coutances 147–8
    Evreux 102 and nn. 128, 132, 103 n. 134, 104
    Le Mans 191, 194 and n. 116, 195
    Lisieux 110–12, 115
    Rouen 75–6, 78–83, 99, 230
    Sées 121, 122 and nn. 234, 237, 123, 213
    Tours 173 and n. 17, 177 and n. 37, 178
  and Greater Anjou
    difficulties with barons from southern
      Anjou 199, 208–9
    establishment of authority 201,
      208–10, 254
    extent of authority 231, 254
    itinerary 245 n. 33
  and Louis VII, king of France 173–4
  and Normandy
    establishment of authority 134–5, 152,
      230–1, 253
    extent of authority 231; in south-west
      Normandy 121–3, 134–5
    presence in 245 n. 33
  promise of free elections in England 167
  rebellion of 1173–4 81, 177 and n. 37, 178
    and n. 38, 233
  rebellion of 1183 81, 110

Index

315

Index

Le Mans (dép. Sarthe) (cont.)
  archdeacons of *see* Amaury (II) Clarel (Sablé)
  bishops of *see* Geoffrey de Loudun, Hamelin, Hildebert de Lavardin, Maurice, Nicholas, Philip Clarel, Reginald (I) Clarel, William de Passavant; military service 193; right to fill canonries and to appoint dignitaries 219 and n. 25
  canons of *see* Amaury (I) Clarel, Amaury (II) Clarel, John Clarel, John de Faye, Juhel de Mathefelon, Lisiard, Matthew Clarel, Philip d'Yvré, Reginald (I) Clarel, Reginald (II) Clarel, Reginald (III) Clarel, Robert de Domfront, Robert de Vitré, Simon, William Burel (archpriest), William Burel (?) (bishop of Avranches), William Burel junior (bishop of Avranches), William de Rennes
  cathedral of 80, 194
  cathedral chapter of 68–70, 165, 187 and n. 83, 188–9, 190 and n. 95, 191 and n. 96, 192–5, 209, 248, 250
  chanters of *see* Amaury (II) Clarel, Geoffrey de Loudun, Peter Clarel, Reginald (I) Clarel
  deans of *see* Geoffrey de Laval, Hugh de La Ferté, Juhel de Mathefelon, Nicholas (Bishop of Le Mans), Robert de Domfront; election of by the chapter 219 n. 25
  diocese of 69, 115, 155, 171, 190 n. 95, 194
  English possessions of 249; *and see* Kingston Deverill; confiscation of 250; restoration of 250; sale of 251 and n. 59
  episcopal elections of; 1145 186–7; 1187 187; 1190 188–9; 1214 189–91, 238; 1216 192–3; 1231 193; electoral custom at 193
  masters of the schools *see* Juhel de Mathefelon
  provost (alleged), office of, 191, 192, 194 and n. 113
  regalia of; inquest into (1214) 191, 248
Le Neubourg (dép. Eure) *see* Beaumont(-le-Roger) (family), Meulan (counts of), Robert III, earl of Leicester
  family 77
  Geoffrey du 217 n. 20
  Henry du 77, 81, 84 n. 60, 164 n. 422; his wife *see* Margaret
  Ralph du 77
  Robert du, dean of Rouen 77, 84 n. 60, 147, 228, 260; candidacy (Rouen) of;

78, 80–1, 99, 225, 230; career of 78, 221
  Robert du, seneschal of Normandy 76–7; his wife *see* Godehelda
  Robert II du 77
Leo I, pope
  on episcopal elections 20
  on weighing up of votes 41
Léon (dép. Côtes-d'Armor)
  counts of 230 n. 73
  see of 230 n. 73
  regalia of 230 n. 73
Le Poer, Roger of, bishop of Salisbury 137
Les Andelys (dép. Eure), manor of 75 n. 6, 79
Leseia, benefice of 94
L'Etang, family
  Vivian de, bishop of Coutances 83, 262
    career of 148
    election of 148 and n. 352, 149
  William de, knight 148 and n. 356
L'Evêque, family 154
  Geoffrey, abbot of Mont-St-Michel 154
  Richard, bishop of Avranches, 262
    election of 154 and n. 378
Liberate Rolls 132
liberty of the church/*libertas ecclesiae* 2, 21, 110, 120, 131, 161, 167, 241, 255
licence to elect/*licentia eligendi* 106, 108, 119, 120 and n. 227, 121, 239 and n. 5, 241–2, 254
Lieuvin 83
Lillebonne (dép. Seine-Maritime), council of (1080) 166 n. 430
Limassol (Cyprus) 190 n. 91
Lincoln (Lincs.) 133 n. 288
  see of 64, 80
    archdeacons of *see* John de Coutances (Oxford) [bishop of Worcester]
    bishops(-elect) of *see* Hugh of Avalon, Walter de Coutances
    canons of *see* Drogo (I) de Trubleville (?), Ralph de Richespald, Richard Grim, William de Coutances
    deans of *see* Philip de Harcourt
Lincolnshire 133 n. 288
Lisiard, bishop of Sées 124, 163 and n. 420, 261
  alleged wastefulness of 124 and n. 246
  career of 123 and n. 244
  election of 123
Lisieux (dép. Calvados) 126 n. 253
  see of 108–15
    archdeacons of *see* Hugh de Nonant, Hugh de Rupierre, Jordan du Hommet, William de Rupierre
    bishops of; *and* 23 n. 12, 112 n. 185 *see* Arnulf, John, Jordan du Hommet, Ralph de Warneville, William

316

Index

Index

Index

St Martin, Tours (dép. Indre-et-Loire), collegiate
church of 172, 180, 189 n. 86 205, 226
canons of *see* Vivien de L'Etang
honorary canons of 172, 206
Capetian influence at 172
cellarers of *see* William (bishop of Saintes)
chanters of *see* Helias (?), William, William
(the same?)
chapter of 172
deans of *see* Odo, Odo Clément, Philip
influence of 172
lay abbacy of 172
masters of the schools of *see* Hamelin
St Martin, William de 126 n. 252
St Martin-de-Vieux-Bellême (dép. Orne),
church of 124 n. 246
St Martin-du-Bosc (dép. Seine-Maritime),
priory of 90 n. 90
Ste Marie-du-Voeu, Cherbourg (dép. Manche),
abbey of 154 n. 377
St Mary, Hastings (E. Sussex), canonry of
Howe 98
St Mary, York (Yorks.), abbey of 156 and n. 391
abbot of, *see* Robert de Longchamps
Ste Maure(-de-Touraine) (dép. Indre-et-Loire)
lords of 170
Hugh de 177 n. 37
St Nicolas, Angers (dép. Maine-et-Loire), abbey
of 201 n. 140
St Nicolas, Evreux (dép. Eure), hospital of
105 n. 144, 106 n. 149
St Nicolas, Robert de, canon of Rouen 222
St Omer (dép. Pas-de-Calais), provost
of, *see* Peter de Collemezzo
St Ouen-du-Château, Bayeux (dép. Calvados),
chapel of 140 n. 313, 141
St Pierre-de-la-Cour, Le Mans (dép. Sarthe),
collegiate church of, dean of, *see* William
Burel (bishop of Avranches)
St Sauveur-le-Vicomte (dép. Manche), abbey of
113 n. 189
Ste Suzanne (dép. Mayenne), lordship of 201
St Taurin, Evreux (dép. Eure), abbot of
his canonry at Coutances 150 and n. 366
Ste Trinité, Beaumont-le-Roger (dép. Eure),
collegiate church of, dean of, *see* Philip
de Harcourt
Ste Trinité, Caen (dép. Manche), abbey of
149 n. 361
Ste Trinité, Vendôme (dép. Loir-et-Cher),
abbot of, *see* Geoffrey
St Victor, Paris, abbey of 91 n. 93, 111, 115, 121,
134, 154 and n. 377, 216
abbots of *see* Achard, bishop of Avranches
admission of canons 219 n. 25

appointment of prior 219 n. 25
electoral procedure at 115–6
Salerno (Italy) 70
Salisbury (Wilts.)
countesses of *see* Eleanor
John of, bishop of Chartres 108, 233
see of 135, 137–8, 230
archdeacons of *see* Henry de Beaumont
bishops of 147; *and see* Hubert Walter,
Roger Le Poer
canons of *see* Hugh Bovet
cathedral chapter of 137–8
deans of *see* Henry de Beaumont
Saloel, Gerald de, canon of Rouen 93–4, 97
and n. 109
Salomonisvilla, G. (William?) de, canon of
Rouen 66
Samson, abbot of St Bury Edmunds, patronage
of 222–3
Samuel, prophet 226
Sangermanensis 62, 63 and n. 235
compiler of 63–5
Sardica (now Sofia, Bulgaria), council of (343)
54 n. 182
Saumur (dép. Maine-et-Loire) 200 n. 139
Savigny (dép. Mayenne), abbey of
chronicle of 165
Saxo, papal subdeacon and canon at Bayeux
66 n. 256, 261
candidacy (Bayeux) 139–41
Schimmelpfennig, Bernhard, Historian 3
Schmid, Karl, Historian 227 n. 60
schools 3, 11–12, 72
Anglo-Norman school 11–13, 28, 35–6, 45,
54, 129–30, 167–8; *and see* Oxford
Bolognese school 11–12, 26–34, 35 n. 86, 36,
42–4, 54, 56, 69; *and see* Bologna
French school (Paris) 11 and n. 23, 12–13, 27,
34–5, 36, 43–4, 56 n. 194, 57 n. 198;
and see Paris
Rhenanian school (Cologne) 11 n. 23
Sées (dép. Orne)
John de, canon of Rouen 222
mayor of 125
pagus of 164 n. 422
see of 115–35, 166, 216
archdeacons of 117; *and see* Amaury, Arnulf
(bishop of Lisieux), Henry, Herbert
(archdeacon of Exmes), John, Roger,
Sylvester, William, William (archdeacon
of the Corbonnais)
bishops of 22; *and see* Froger, Gerald,
Gervase, Hugh, John, Lisiard, Sylvester;
right to fill canonries and to appoint
dignitaries 219 and n. 25

Index

Index

Index

329

Cambridge Studies in Medieval Life and Thought
Fourth Series

TITLES IN SERIES

*Also published as paperback